MW00782504

WRITING ASSESSMENT IN THE 21ST CENTURY

ESSAYS IN HONOR OF EDWARD M. WHITE

Research and Teaching in Rhetoric and Composition
Michael M. Williamson, series editor

Market Matters: Applied Rhetoric Studies and Free Market Competition
Locke Carter (ed.)
Composition(s) in the New Liberal Arts
Joanna Castner Post & James A. Inman (eds.)
Black Letters: An Ethnography of a Beginning Legal Writing Course
Randy Cauthen
Writing Assessment in the 21st Century: Essays in Honor of Edward M. White
Norbert Elliot and Les Perelman (eds.)
Collaborating(,) Literature(,) and Composition: Essays for Teachers and Writers of English
Frank Gaughan & *Peter H. Khost*
Professing Literacy in Composition Studies
Peter N. Goggin
Rhetoric in(to) Science Inquiry: Style as Invention in the Pursuit of Knowledge
Heather Graves
Judaic Perspectives in Rhetoric and Composition Studies
Andrea Greenbaum & *Deborah H. Holdstein*
Basic Writing in America: The History of Nine College Programs
Nicole Pepinster Greene & *Patricia J. McAlexander*
Before and After the Tutorial: Writing Centers and Institutional Relationships
Nicholas Mauriello, William J. Macauley, Jr., & *Robert T. Koch, Jr.* (eds.)
Writing in the Research University: A Darwinian Study of WID with Cases from Civil Engineering
Martha Davis Patton
Practicing Research in Writing Studies: Reflective and Ethically Responsible Research
Katrina M. Powell and Pamela Takayoshi (eds.)
Composing Other Spaces
Douglas Reichert Powell & *John Paul Tassoni*
Including Students in Academic Conversations: Principles and Strategies of Theme-Based Writing Courses Across the Disciplines
Deborah F. Rossen-Knill and Tatyana Bakhmetyeva
Directed Self-Placement: Principles and Practices
Dan Royer & *Roger Gilles* (eds.)
Dead Letters: Error in Composition, 1873-2004
Tracy Santa
Composing Feminism(s): How Feminists Have Shaped Composition Theories and Practices
Kay Siebler
The Elephant in the Classroom: Race and Writing
Jane Bowman Smith
Principles and Practices: Discourses for the Vertical Curriculum
Margaret M. Strain (ed.)

WRITING ASSESSMENT IN THE 21ST CENTURY

ESSAYS IN HONOR OF EDWARD M. WHITE

edited by

Norbert Elliot

New Jersey Institute of Technology

Les Perelman

Massachusetts Institute of Technology

HAMPTON PRESS, INC.
NEW YORK, NEW YORK

Copyright © 2012 by Hampton Press, Inc.

All rights reserved. No part of this publication may be reproduced, stored in a retrieval system, or transmitted in any form or by any means, electronic, mechanical, photocopying, microfilming, recording, or otherwise, without permission of the publisher.

Printed in the United States of America

Library of Congress Cataloging-in-Publication Data

Writing assessment in the 21st century : essays in honor of Edward M. White / edited by Norbert Elliot and Les Perelman.

p. cm. -- (Research and teaching in rhetoric and composition)

Includes bibliographic references and index.

ISBN 978-1-61289-086-9 -- ISBN 978-1-61289-087-6 (pbk.)

1. English language--Rhetoric--Study and teaching--Evaluation. 2. English teaching--Rhetoric--Ability testing. 3. Report writing--Study and teaching--Evaluation. 4. Report writing--Ability testing. 5. College prose--Evaluation. 6. Twenty-first century. I. Elliot, Norbert. II. Perelman, Leslie C. III. White, Edward M. (Edward Michael), 1933- IV. Title: Writing assessment in the twenty-first century.

PE1404.W6943 2012

808'.04207--dc23

2012006553

Hampton Press, Inc.
307 Seventh Avenue
New York, NY 10001

Edward M. White Reflection: My brother took this picture in Brooklyn's Prospect Park, on a lovely spring day. In Brooklyn Technical High School, I was features editor of our school newspaper and had a column in every issue. I also wrote my first paid article at this time, about our attempt to dismantle an old piano, published on *The Christian Science Monitor* youth page. I remember vividly holding the $25 check and repeating, "I am a writer, a real writer."

CONTENTS

ACKNOWLEDGEMENTS

Where would we be without each other? The effort to design, develop, and complete this collection reveals the strength of community. Our 32 colleagues, along with Barbara Bernstein of Hampton Press and Michael M. Williamson, editor of the series *Research and Teaching in Rhetoric and Composition*, worked closely with us to mark the achievements of Edward M. White. In doing so, they honor both his career and their own. This is their book.

At Massachusetts Institute of Technology, the text was assembled and first edited by Chelsey Norman. At New Jersey Institute of Technology, the open source platform that brought us all together was maintained by Blake Haggerty and Brenda D. Walker. Support for the project was provided by Fadi P. Deek, Dean of the College of Science and Liberal Arts.

At home in Lexington, Elizabeth Garrels (Professor of Spanish and Latin American Studies, MIT) was in league with Frances Ward (David R. Devereaux Professor of Nursing, Temple University) in Little Egg Harbor. They endure Les and Norbert with remarkable patience and, through their love, allow them to prevail so often in so many adventures, including this book.

INTRODUCTION
IN CONTEXT: THE CONTRIBUTIONS OF EDWARD M. WHITE TO THE ASSESSMENT OF WRITING ABILITY

Norbert Elliot
New Jersey Institute of Technology
Les Perelman
Massachusetts Institute of Technology

On Saturday, December 7, 1996, a day that shall live in fame (not infamy) in the history of rhetoric and composition, Edward M. White ended a discussion on the Writing Program Administrators LISTSERV with a single discursive statement worthy of a stone tablet. William Condon recounted how the Washington State University Writing Program had foiled an attempt by state officials to institute a multiple-choice exit examination by instituting its own rigorous assessment. In support, White posted his most remembered aphorism: "I give you White's law, the truth of which I have noted for over twenty years: Assess thyself or assessment shall be done unto thee."

White's Law is one of the most often quoted phrases among those who teach and assess writing; it is emblematic of the position Ed White has held in the discipline of rhetoric and composition/writing studies. He is one of the first people to have successfully straddled the divide between considerations of cognition and rhetoric on one side and the pragmatic realities of assessment and accountability on the other. He is a humanist. With Jean-Paul Sartre (1946/2007), he believes that existentialism is humanism: We are not the singular measure of all things but, instead, the heart and center of subjective transcendence that allows us to understand deeply and, thus, to do great good. White is a writing teacher who has not only become conversant in the language of educational measurement but has conversed with its practitioners and returned, safely, to tell tales of foreign lands.

This edited collection is a tribute in his honor. In this testament to White's ability to work across disciplinary boundaries, the collection is also a documentary, broadly conceived, of the status of writing assessment practice in the early 21st century.

COMMUNITIES COME OF AGE

In 2011, Condon published a review essay on 13 books that have substantially shaped the specialization of writing assessment within the discipline of rhetoric and composition/writing studies. Condon takes 1971 as his demarcation date, the beginning of a decade in which Ed White led a movement within the California State University system that took the following shape: Under realistic resource constraints, we should design our assessments to allow maximum representation of writing ability through active student response to a constructed response item type (prompts) that would elicit timed samples of writing (essays) that could, in turn, be scored (holistically) according to criterion-based performance standards (a rubric). Although the model itself has value in its attention to construct representation, task specification, genre, scoring design, and performance standards, White (2001) himself would come to recognize that the assessment solutions of the 1970s, from impromptu prompts to holistic scoring, seemed antique in light of subsequent theory stressing process and postprocess conceptualizations. White's reflection on his earlier work is evidence, as Condon demonstrates, of a period in which demonstrable advancements were made in the assessment of writing ability.

Then and now, for White, validation is an activity that must take place within the context of classroom practice. Resonance between assessment design and classroom practice—students learned to write by doing so, not by answering multiple-choice questions—stood at the center of the California story. This genre of assessment, influenced and shaped by context, marked the beginning of the modern era. "This narrative," White wrote in retelling the California story, spoke to "the public nature of college writing instruction and to the possibility of achieving large-scale political consensus about the meaning, nature, and value of what we do" (p. 310).

The "we" of that sentence was, as Condon observes, a distinct historic event for yet another reason: the support of researchers at the Educational Testing Service (ETS) in the California experiment and subsequent similar programs of postsecondary writing assessment that arose across the country. In the 1970s, the relationship between the emerging writing assessment community and the established educational measurement community was edgy around the conference table. At one point in the California project, ETS test developer Evans Alloway, wary of the unreliability of a score based on a single essay, declared that he would only report separate essay scores over his dead body; the response from a San Francisco State faculty member Bill Robinson: "Prepare to die, my friend." When tensions emerged, they did so for reasons that extended (perhaps) beyond personalities. The educational measurement community had the force of decades of large-scale research behind its claims, and its power rested in summative studies backed by statistical evidence; the writing assessment community, informed by classroom practice, had deep knowledge of formative learning processes. As Lorrie A. Shepard (2006) has demonstrated, those oppositional tensions lessened somewhat at the end of the 20th century as everyone at the table began to acknowledge that constrained test formats had a deleterious effect on instruction and learning.

Today, the unique disciplinary foundation of the educational measurement community has produced a view that the process of validation is based on trait interpretation, theory interpretation, qualitative interpretation, and decision procedures (Brennan, 2006). Each of these interpretative traditions is distinct and follows a rich history that began in 1945 with the establishment of the American Psychological Association division of evaluation and measurement, later Division 5 (Evaluation, Measurement, and Statistics). Conceptually, the point of demarcation between the educational measurement community and the writing assessment community has been on qualitative practice because it is there that classroom assessment is situated.

For the writing assessment community, the performance under investigation is language use, a target domain with its own distinct history and phenomenology. Chris M. Anson's (2010) reflection on the discipline of rhetoric and composition/writing at 60-something—a birth date taken from the publication of the first issue of *College Composition and Communication* in March 1950—focuses on four edited collections. In these collections, Anson finds evidence of epistemological questions, methodological rationales, and disciplinary influences that substantiate the intellectual status of a discipline deeply involved in investigating activities central to all literate cultures. Embedded in that history is a distinct philosophy articulated by Louise Wetherbee Phelps, a researcher who has both proposed a theory of composition (1988) and launched a campaign to make visible the discipline itself (Phelps & Ackerman, 2010).[1] Phelps provides two perspectives that define the essential disciplinary mindset. The first is that the discipline, because of its attention to the semiosis of language, is orientated toward iteration. The movement from naiveté to critical awareness, Phelps finds, is an incomplete pattern that "can never be surpassed but must be recursively enacted" (p. 90). For Phelps, establishing meaning in context—defined by Embretson (1983) as construct validation research—is the primary aim of research; nomothetic span, establishing a network of relationships among variables, is a secondary consideration (Borsboom, 2005). The second perspective is that the discipline, because of this epistemological dialectic so hermeneutic in nature, does not seek to establish a value dualism between theory and praxis. So often set in motion to achieve hierarchy (theory is ancillary; only practice matters; or, only theory matters; practice is ancillary), the disjunctive pair is useless. Because there is no desire for finalization or hierarchy, focus must always and everywhere be on experiment. The distinctiveness of composition, Phelps concludes, "lies in the experimental relationship it establishes between the general principles of inquiry posited and systematically pursued in science and philosophy, and the normative practice of these principles in ordinary discourse and everyday life" (p. 237). In its ontological, epistemological, axiological orientation—from tip of head to bottom of toe—the phenomenology of rhetoric and composition/writing studies is classroom-centered.

The field of educational measurement, of course, also has a pedagogical focus; yet what is evident today has not been consistently so through its history. Just as the writing assessment community is changing to embrace the traditions of the measurement community, so, too, is the measurement community becoming increasingly alert to the value of attending to classroom practice. In his review of the fourth edition of *Educational Measurement*, a volume often taken as a statement of the discipline itself, Gregory J. Cizek (2008) noted as a shortcoming the fact that classroom assessment is described as qualitative, and therefore insufficient for more rigorous quantitative analysis. Classroom practice, Cizek suggests, is essential to the future of educational measurement, and the chapters in the present volume by its practitioners suggest that is so.

This volume may thus be taken as an articulated statement of a collective "we" that has continued to emerge since White first imagined 40 years ago the possibility of achieving large-scale political dialogue about the meaning, nature, and value of what might be accomplished for the good of students, the instructors who work with them, and the institutions that support both. Those drawn to writing assessment believe that language is used both as a socialization process and as a process of democratization. That belief is central to White's career, and part of honoring him is to recall his biography.

AS DO KIDS FROM BROOKLYN

White's is a striver's tale. Father was an immigrant from Poland, mother from Austria. Father ate with his elbows on the table. Austrian Jews such as mother, even living in brownstones on St. John's Place in Brooklyn, thought there must be a better future for her sons. Never slurp soup, she told the two boys.

Father and mother believed in their sons more than in each other and sent them into the streets for fresh air in the gang-ridden Italian neighborhood. Around the corner was the Brooklyn Public Library, and one of the boys—the one with the wandering left eye that gave him a blurry image of the world—would scoot around the corner into the children's room. Safe there, Ed sat and read Albert Payson Terhune books about Lad, an 80-pound collie, thoroughbred in spirit and blood, who had the irrepressible courage of a d'Artagnan, an uncanny wisdom, and a soul. Because it was a lot safer than staying on the streets, Ed became bookish. Soon he was reading the 1,000-page books of Alexander Dumas. Ed's relatives marveled. None of them had ever done anything like that.

Mrs. Sullivan, his eighth grade teacher, was trying to prepare her students for Brooklyn Technical High School and the anticipated exit from Brooklyn that would follow graduation. At sea with math, she had written "2 + X = 4" on the board and, in increasing despair at what she had written, turned to the class to ask if anyone knew what to do with that. A show-off kid, Ed replaced the X with a 2 and became, to Mrs. Sullivan, a genius. At home, he practiced the piano for about 2 hours, then did his math first because, after the scales, that was the most fun. He enjoyed solving puzzles. He learned to play bridge but shied away from poker. Money was too important. Who could lose a penny without feeling really bad?

He graduated class valedictorian at Brooklyn Tech in a class of just over 800. His older brother had attended, tuition free, Cooper Union. Without that kind of scholarship, Ed would find himself in his parents's Brooklyn world of post office and kitchen table. A post card arrived from New York University. He had good Scholastic Aptitude Test scores, the card said, so perhaps he should consider an application. On an April day in 1951, he received three letters. The first, from Columbia University, said that he had been admitted; the second letter said that no scholarship would be forthcoming. A horrible feeling sunk in as he realized that he was not going to go to college. The third letter said that he had been admitted to NYU (he did not know where it was) and that he had a full scholarship (the Charles Maxwell McConn Full Tuition Scholarship that paid costs even as tuition rose). So he had gone to NYU. As he would later explain to his students when he taught the novels of Charles Dickens at California State University, life is a series of accident after accident after accident.

Edward began taking the subway from 280 St. John's Place to the Washington Square campus. At 25 cents, NYU was a short trip but a world apart. At first, he had considered becoming a musician, but the odds of making a living were so slim that he decided he would not try to make money at it. An associate professor of English, H. J. Gottlieb, became a profound influence. Edward (student filing number 1861) had written a theme, "How to Give a Successful Party." Typing his essay on lined paper ("Themes submitted on any other paper will not be accepted"), Edward opened the essay with a note of caution: "Contrary to a well-intentioned popular belief, a party will *not* just 'run itself.' A well-meaning host who supplies a house, food, drinks, and a few outdated dance records is quite mistaken if he considers his job done. A good party—like anything else well done—needs organization and planning." Edward's new voice was well received. "Never mind the food and the dance records," Gottlieb wrote in the margin. "I'll just have the drinks and conversation." He called Edward into his office. "Are you White?" Terrified because he had never spoken to a professor, he admitted that he was. "You don't belong here," Gottlieb replied. Because Edward had mastered everything Gottlieb was intending to teach, the professor made a deal. If Edward would attend an upper level fiction writing class and do the work, he would be awarded a grade of A in first-year composition. Because the registrar didn't know how to handle that sort of thing, that office was not to be told. The street kid had invented himself.

After he had been in the class for a while and had submitted short stories, Gottlieb pulled him aside. "What do you intend to do with your life?" As a pre-law major, Edward said that he would be a lawyer. "Why?" He followed with the only answer he could possibly have given: "because lawyers make lots of money." Work, he had learned at home, was a necessary evil, undertaken with grim necessity so that an outside life might be bought. Gottlieb introduced a competing idea: college teaching. Here was a job that could, in itself, be enjoyable, with a decent living thrown into the deal. You would never make a lot of money, he explained, but you would make enough, and your whole life would be spent reading and writing. No one in his life had ever said anything like that.

Edward left Gottlieb and went to the registrar's office to switch his major to English, with a minor in languages. With his musical ear, he picked up accents, reading Virgil and Moliere. Later, teaching at Wellesley College, he would study Italian in order to read Dante. Along with languages, he took courses in analytic geometry and calculus; graduating in 1955, he earned only two grades of B, in speech (he had a lateral lisp, the instructor declared) and intermediate Latin. The rest were grades of A. The *New York Times* carried an article on June 19, 1955: "Student who led his class is a musician, writer, actor, singer, etc., etc." the title read. "It is a rare student who successfully combines honors in scholarship and excellence in virtually every other phase of college life. Edward White, who was graduated summa cum laude from New York University's Washington Square College last Wednesday, has demonstrated that it can be done." His mother was very proud.

In his senior year at NYU, he received a scholarship to Harvard University. Because it was the best university in America, he would recall 56 years later, he went there. It was as simple as that.

The invented persona only went so deep, and he felt isolated among the chosen in elite Cambridge. Mr. White spent his time reading. From time to time, other graduate students gathered in his apartment to sing folk songs. After he had completed his coursework, he became a Teaching Fellow in 1958. He taught composition under the direction of Harold C. Martin (a former president of the National Council of Teachers of English, which Mr. White had never heard of) and Richard Ohmann (a future editor of *College English*, equally obscure at the time). Uneasy with undergraduates so different from himself, he taught them about writing as they educated him about Harvard. More than a critic—he had his choice of teaching either literature or composition—Mr. White thought of himself as a writer of fiction.

With a dissertation on Jane Austen in hand completed under the direction of Harry Levin and Reuben Brower, Dr. White landed a job at Wellesley teaching creative writing, introduction to English literature, and first-year composition. He became friends with the poet X. J. Kennedy and hosted Eudora Welty, chatting with her about her fellow Mississippian, William Faulkner. Working with Walter Houghton, a leading scholar at Wellesley, the early career researcher published on William Thackeray. Writing on the Victorian novelist's contributions to *Fraser's Magazine*, Dr. White was making a name for himself in Thackeray studies. Five years away from his doctorate, however, he had still not come into his own.

By chance, White received a recruitment letter to apply at a new college that was to be part of the California State University system at San Bernardino. According to the 1960 master plan developed by University of California President Clark Kerr, the state system was to admit students from the upper third of their class and provide instruction through the master's level. Opening in 1965, the San Bernardino campus was an opportunity to flee the New England climate, start a new college, and live in the promised land of the west coast. It was an adventure in a working person's railroad town. White headed for the Pacific.

Within his first year, he became chair of the English department. In the 1960s, there were no writing program administrators so, as the administrator in charge, he also directed the first-year composition program. A salesman came by with a teaching machine, resplendent with colored overlays for projectors. During the demonstration, the salesman projected, in full color, a sentence of purple prose. The students were then to identify the elements of an overly elaborated sentence, and a turquoise overlay was then applied to reinforce the fact that too many adjectives spoil the description of a winter's day. In mid-overlay, White objected. This activity had nothing to do with writing, he told the salesman. Without an audience, there was no writing. Correcting errors was merely a socialization experience, and White told everybody so in his first *College English* article. His valediction from "Writing for Nobody" (1969) resonates in this volume:

> We can resist and protest against the dehumanizing effect of materials and essay assignments that turn writing into academic gamesmanship. We can insist that writing has to be hard because writing and thinking go together, and thinking is hard. And we can support the humanity of our students as writers by insisting on our own humanity as readers. We can refuse to assign and decline to accept writing for nobody. (p. 168)

Another sales representative happened to come by to sell W. W. Norton textbooks and noticed a series of notes on White's desk about composition instruction. He asked if he could see them, was impressed, and made a copy. By the next week, White was offered a contract for books that became *The Writer's Control of Tone* (1970) and *The Pop Culture Tradition* (1972).

Because he now had textbooks on composition, the very next year he found himself at the center of the now well-known contretemps with the chancellor's office of the California State College (now University) system. Fearing that there would not be enough instructors to serve the ever-growing number of students—during the 1970s enrollment growth nationally had risen by 45% (Snyder, 1993)—university leadership attempted to award credit in first-year composition on the basis of a multiple-choice test. Credit by examination, administrators believed, would get students through the system rapidly. Although there was nothing wrong with advanced placement, as he had learned with Gottlieb at NYU, the value of the assessment rested on the validity of the test. With his colleagues, White was able to supplement the singular use of multiple-choice testing (to be administered by the ETS) with a direct measure, two essays scored holistically (to be administered and scored by the CSU faculty). Between 1973 and 1981, White and his colleagues tested 31,092 entering students, with 33% of the students earning advanced placement.

After his on-the-job postdoctoral study, Edward M. White would become known as a specialist in the assessment of writing ability. An expert by appointment of the CSU chancellor in 1971 and a celebrity in the *Chronicle of Higher Education* in 1973, White learned educational measurement by hiring statisticians from the budget he had earned in his opposition to limited response testing. His advocacy of direct assessment through essay examinations, he learned, was subject to design applications and measurement principles not covered at Harvard with Levin and Brower. A colleague from Cal Poly Pomona, Robert Bradley, taught White elementary descriptive and inferential statistics, including null hypothesis significance testing and the visual display of information. And Leon Thomas, an excellent statistician, collaborated with White some years later on a 1981 seminal study of differential impact associated with multiple-choice testing.

Early in this period, the director of the College Level Examination Program at ETS contacted White so that he could see how that organization's test development committees functioned—a tactic to educate dissenters that originated under ETS's founding president, Henry Chauncey. In 1971, White worked with an ETS committee chaired by Walker Gibson of the University of Massachusetts, Amherst, and with committee member Richard Braddock of the University of Iowa. While he had first seen an early application of holistic scoring in the Advanced Placement Program while he was at Wellesley, White saw the importance of the test development process. He witnessed the inner workings of ETS and, returning to California, proposed a locally developed method that would examine students for exemption based on course goals. To build consensus, he traveled from campus to campus. The English faculty though the idea had merit. The economics faculty thought him mad.

Albert M. Serling, the ETS administrator who had brought White to Princeton, had become a guest at San Bernardino. They sailed and talked about measurement concepts, such as validity and reliability, about which White knew nothing. He returned to visit ETS and met Paul Diederich, a former University of Chicago researcher who had spoken at the very first meeting of the Conference on College Composition and Communication in 1951. They debated scoring systems and settled on a 6-point scoring scale, becoming close colleagues. White's connection with ETS remained during the 1970s. In time, he would bring in Diederich to help in the evaluation of the National Writing Project; and, with the support of ETS test developers Evans Alloway and Miriam Levin, White and other committee members insisted on adding a writing sample to the National Teacher Examination.

By the early 1980s, White had emerged from his self-created postdoctoral experience to become a national leader in writing assessment. Yet White operated under a singular referential frame. His background in English language and literature/letters, with a special emphasis in the literature of the 18th and 19th centuries, was not unique. He was surrounded by colleagues with similar backgrounds who were addressing accountability demands on their campuses. The distinction was that White had undertaken over a decade of serious study in educational assessment, testing, and measurement, surrounding himself with statisticians at CSU and making field trips to ETS. Writing over 200 book reviews for the *Los Angeles Times*, on topics as diverse as the poetry of Theodore Roethke and the novels of Alberto Moravia, White was deeply influenced by a journalist's sense of audience. He saw himself not as a scholar who does writing but a writer who does scholarship. He traveled extensively as a consultant. He wrote and wrote and wrote, eventually publishing over 100 articles and 14 books (with still more, as of the present writing, under contract).

The uniqueness of his voice was evident in his 1984 dithyramb on holisticism, a necessary, disruptive paradigm for a modern age fraught with an analytic reductionism that works wonderfully on machinery but poorly on humans. As an evaluative method, holistic scoring, as White knew from his experiences at ETS and the National Assessment of Educational Progress, had been around since its first use in the mid 1960s; indeed, a 1985 survey had revealed that 90% of those responding used holistic scoring at their institutions. The term nevertheless needed historical context, an explication of the concept in practice, and a statement of methodological limits. As well, the concept of holistic scoring deserved attention because of the deeply humanistic message that the process sent: "Even the meanest bit of halting prose, even the most down-trodden of our fellow creatures, deserves to be taken as a living and vital unit of meaning, an artistic and human whole, not merely as a collection of scraps and parts" (p. 409). For White, holistic scoring was developed as an oppositional strategy to what he saw as the mechanizations associated with error fixation on standard written English, a perverse view of writing evidenced in multiple-choice tests.

White offered a scoring concept everyone could latch on to, and the following year began his milestone book, *Teaching and Assessing Writing: Recent Advances in Understanding, Evaluating, and Improving Student Performance* (1985), with an advocacy of holistic scoring as "the most obvious example in the field English of the attempt to evoke and evaluate wholes rather than parts, individual thought rather than mere socialized correctness" (p. 19). White proceeded to define a unified vision for teaching and assessing writing in an era of accountability and constraint that he had witnessed, first hand, at CSU. What had been the golden age of education after World War II was coming to an end by the fall of Saigon. As described by Arthur M. Cohen and Carrie B. Kisker in *The Shaping of American Higher Education*, accountability, efficiency, effectiveness, assessment, and equity emerged as postsecondary education moved into an era of consolidation in the mid 1970s.

Beginning with a unified vision of instruction and measurement in *Teaching and Assessing Writing*, White presented the first guide for writing program administrators so that they might select tests, design assessment models, and evaluate their programs on their own terms. For a generation caught without safe haven in a hurricane of accountability demands, the book stood as a monument of calm sanity. That which was measurable, the book proclaimed, need not drive out that which was important. Four years later, White published a second book, this time with a programmatic focus that would help those who found themselves in states with newly mandated assessments for public institutions. By the year of the publication of *Developing Successful College Writing Programs* (1989), as Cohen and Kisker note, two thirds of states had such accountability requirements in place, including demands for evaluation plans, scheduled reporting, and penalties for failure to comply. When White got off the subway stop at Washington Square Park in 1951, legislators believed that dollars spent in educational investments would surely pay off. By 1989, they wondered if they had made a bad investment.

White's contribution to humanistic, politically astute, and accountable program evaluation during the past two decades has not been limited to his writings. For a total of 14 years—from 1988-1994 and 1998-2004—White served as Director of the Consultant-Evaluator Program for the Council of Writing Program Administrators. As was the case with his other professional activities, White framed this enterprise as an exercise in pragmatic rhetoric. He saw program evaluation as a rhetorical exercise by asking "what kind of evidence will be accepted as real, as convincing" to prove to skeptical administrators and politicians that a writing program is fulfilling the specific institutional goals required of it (White, 1995b, p. 132). As impartial outside experts, he claimed, WPA-sponsored evaluators offer a rhetorical credibility that is impossible for local writing program administrators. For assessment was about both evidence and stance.

Remarkably, White's particular brand of humanism—Johnson's Empiricism here, Wordsworth's Romanticism there, Austen's irony everywhere—allowed evolution. In 1995, White offered "An Apologia for the Timed, Impromptu Essay Test" (1995a), in which he defended the use of holistic scoring while acknowledging the increasing importance of the new assessment shift toward portfolio scoring offered by Pat Belanoff and Peter Elbow at the State University of New York. By 2005, White had modified his position further, claiming that what was needed was an assessment framework based on explicit course outcomes. Pushing further, White suggested that what was required was not only a table of contents in the portfolio, printed to weld writing assignment to course goal; in addition, the portfolio should include a student reflective letter responding to the explicit course outcomes. Evolution continued. In a 2007 keynote address at the WPA National Conference, later published as "Testing In and Testing Out" (2008), he reversed the position he took in the California placement experiment 3 decades before. We should, he wrote, replace placement testing with Directed Self-Placement (DSP), a system designed by Daniel J.Royer and Roger Gilles, contributors to this volume. DSP, White held, is effective, ethical, and responsible in its emphasis on informing students about the demands and expectations of the composition courses available to them, and then having them, as responsible citizens of the academy, decide how they can meet the writing requirement based on their abilities. For White, communicating the structure of the writing program to entering students to make informed decisions was more relevant than testing them with antique mechanisms, such as the one created on the West Coast once upon a time

At the time of the publication of this edited collection, White remains an active presence in the discipline of rhetoric and composition. In 2007, with Shane Borrowman, a former student of his at the University of Arizona, he edited *The Promise of America*, published by Pearson Education. The introduction to the anthology tells us that "*The Promise of*

America attempts to deal with components of the American dream as it is lived by Americans—to consider the reality rather than the mythology." The readings in the edited volume will avoid "willful cynicism and unreasoning optimism," students are told. As "children of immigrants and of military veterans, children who are first-generation college graduates," the editors write, "we could not and would not let such an imbalance in our text exist—either by implication or by choice. We have ourselves experienced too much of the best America has offered to be cynical about its promise" (p. x). That theme—in dreams begin responsibilities—is also evident in a 2010 reflection on the English professor as public figure, published in *College English*. Be ready to stand up to defend the values we represent. "You may be listened to with respect or suspicion, and what you say may not be heard as you intend. But you must be prepared to speak out, because your job as an English professor comes with important public responsibilities you should not avoid" (p. 195).

Edward M. White has always been willing to take a stand.

CECI N'EST PAS UNE FESTSCHRIFT

Taking the occasion of the 25th anniversary of *Teaching and Assessing Writing* as a way to celebrate the career of a distinguished colleague is a fine idea—one that led the editors of the present collection to organize a session at the 61st annual convention of the Conference on College Composition in 2010. Diane Kelly-Riley presented an early version of the chapter included in this volume, as did Gita Das Bender. After a reflection by White, Brian Huot presented a lifetime merit award from the *Journal of Writing Assessment*. As well, the editors presented a 262-page presentation volume, with congratulatory notes, letters, and draft chapters by many of the contributors to this collection. Between then and 2011, we earned a contract from Michael Williamson, another of our founding leaders, for his series with Hampton Press, *Research and Teaching on Written Composition*. We established an open-source Web site for the chapters to encourage collaborative review and ensure cross-reference, and, in doing so, we created the second reason for the present volume: to document the state of practice of writing assessment in the early 21st century.

To achieve that end we divided the chapters into four sections, with contributions from the writing assessment community (researchers with affiliations to organizations such as the Conference on College Composition and Communication and the Association of Teachers of Technical Writing) and the educational measurement community (with representatives from ETS, an organization with a long-standing commitment to writing assessment research). Containing work by John Brereton, Sherry Seale Swain and Paul LeMahieu, Hilary Persky, Paul Deane, Barry Maid and Barbara D'Angelo, Margaret Hundleby, and Mary Fowles, the first section of the book presents research on past and current circumstances surrounding assessment in K-12 classrooms, postsecondary education, and graduate and professional programs. The second section of the book focuses on the ways that we measure writing today and the language we use for that activity in the disciplines of rhetoric and composition and educational assessment, testing, and measurement. Chapters by Diane Kelly-Riley, Irv Peckham, Chris M. Anson, Jill Burstein, Anne Herrington and Charles Moran, William Condon, Jon A. Leydens and Barbara M. Olds, Robert Broad, and Lee Odell provide an overview of current assessment strategies. In the third section of the book, the ecologies of communities and the consequences of writing assessment within them are explored by Peter Elbow, Doug Baldwin, Mya Poe and Asao B. Inoue, Daniel J. Royer and Roger Gilles, Gita DasBender, and Liz Hamp-Lyons. The final section of the book, focusing on the rewards and tensions arising between known contingencies and needed certainty, contains chapters by Richard Haswell, Les Perelman, Peggy O'Neill, Cindy Moore, and Katherine Blake Yancey.

This collection of essays is not a Festschrift in its traditional form. It is a tribute, of course, but it is a tribute by emulation. In 1996, with William Lutz and Sandra Kamusikiri, White co-edited *Writing Assessment: Politics, Policies, Practices* for the Modern Language Association. His response to the volume was entitled "Assessment as a Site of Contention." There White bemoaned the failure of the educational measurement community and the writing assessment community to talk to each other. The present collection may be understood as an update on that earlier collection, presenting work that promotes a contentious but instructive conversation among these scholars who all value Ed White's immense contributions while often disagreeing with each other. Indeed, in the tradition of *Assessment of Writing: Politics, Policies, Practices* (1996), the present volume might be taken as a prelude to an edited volume, published each decade, offering a comprehensive view of recent developments in writing assessment.

Yet does the contention overwhelm the conversation? Brian Huot, himself a bridge-building student of Michael Williamson, acknowledged the gap as late as 2002 in *(Re)Articulating Writing Assessment for Teaching and Learning*. In 2004 Williamson, who had studied with measurement researcher Michael J. Zieky of ETS in 1977, again noted a shortcoming of the writing assessment community is its failure to keep pace with recent developments in the educational measurement community. This volume, the editors hope, will serve as evidence of a narrowing gap between the two communities.

Diane Kelly-Riley in this collection references the word *documentary* as used by Robert Coles (1998) as a way of understanding the work of writing assessment. To document, Coles reminds us, takes its origin from the Latin, *docere*, to teach. As an alternative way to read the present collection, we suggest that readers consider four commonalities that, in 2012, suggest a way forward for multidisciplinary research between the educational measurement and writing assessment communities.

At the present time, both communities are deeply involved in theory as a driving force in assessment. To those contributing to this volume, theory is not remote from practical design applications. For the writing assessment community, theories of sociocognitive development, technological imminence, and genre manifestation are significant pedagogical concerns. To reflect such theories of pedagogy, the writing community has defined theories of assessment that hold the potential to tap the writing construct. Huot (1996) emphasizes the need for assessments to be site-based, locally controlled, context-sensitive, rhetorically based, and transparent. Lynne (2004) attends to meaningfulness and ethical conduct of the assessment. Driven by member needs, the Assessment Committee of the Conference on College Composition and Communication issued position statements 1995, 2006, 2009) on writing assessment that offered guiding principles and their application to assessment settings. For the educational measurement community, theories of validity and their expression are of equal importance—although, as Cizek (2008) has observed, a philosophy of educational testing has not yet been developed. As the present collection demonstrates, an interest in theory—as a basis for construct development, as a principle for validation, as a heuristic to explain results—extends across the writing assessment and educational measurement communities. Pamela Moore of the writing assessment community references the educational measurement community in support of her call to reconcile the demand for standardization with the need to acknowledge complexity in writing performance. Similarly, educational measurement specialist Paul Deane is deeply involved in assessment design that embraces writing complexity as both formative and cognitively based. Iteration between theory and practice, as Phelps (1998) noted, is integral to the identification of the variables of writing and its assessment. And so it is that the chapters might be read with a sense of the theoretical currents that inform them. Following the model of theory-building set by Crusius (1989), one way to read this collection is to reflect on the following aspects of theory-formation:

- What is the origin and development of the theory informing the assessment at hand?
- What is the potential for the theory to derive a typology of the variables that drove the need for the theory in the first place?
- What is the potential for the theory to establish relationships among these variables?

- What is the potential for the theory to establish a learning sequence among the variables?
- How does the theory account for practice?
- What are the implications of the theory in specific contexts?

Closely related to theory development, the authors in the collection are also engaged in matters of construct modeling. Much has occurred since Lee J. Cronbach and Paul E. Meehl launched a system of thought based on the concept of construct validity in 1955. Defined as a postulated attribute assumed to be reflected in examinee performance, the pursuit of construct validity allowed educational measurement researchers to defend a proposed use of a test by identifying the attribute under examination, designing situations to allow expression of the attribute, and assessing the degree to which individual or groups possessed that attribute. Since Cronbach and Meehl first defined their system of construct examination, four subsequent developments in educational measurement have informed contemporary research: Samuel J. Messick's (1989, 1998) call for a unified theory of validity in which the Trinitarian model of content, criterion, and construct validity is no longer to be applied categorically; the American Educational Research Association, American Psychological Association, and National Council on Measurement in Education's (1999) advocacy for fairness in test design; Robert J. Mislevy's (2007) concept of evidence-centered design as form of a validation argument; and Brennan's (2006) treatment of validation as a process of forming interpretative arguments for traits—"a disposition to behave or perform in some way in response to some kinds of stimuli or tasks under some range of circumstances" (p. 30)—for interpretative theory, classroom practice, and decision procedures. Attention to construct modeling is evident as Les Perelman argues that the traits actually examined in mass-market writing assessment have little relation to the constructs that are claimed to be assessed. Mary Fowles, from the educational measurement community, examines how constructs shift when writing is assessed in graduate and professional programs. So, a second way to read this collection is to reflect on the following aspects of construct modeling:

- What traits of writing are under examination in the assessment at hand?
- How are those traits incorporated in the assessment?
- How are those traits evaluated?
- What evidence is provided that those who are examined appear to possess those traits?
- What statements are made of the limits and strengths of trait representation?

A third way to read this volume is with attention to assessment design. Closely related to representation, writing assessment design is of concern to all who have contributed to this volume, especially in terms of the strengths and limits of the assessment. In writing assessment design, issues of cost effectiveness, standard setting, and reporting are of recurrent concern. As we note in the introduction to Part III of this collection, cost-effectiveness analysis (Levin & McEwan, 2002) allows identification of the ingredients of resource allocation and the resources needed to achieve a valuable assessment design under ever-present resource scarcity. Establishing performance standards (Cizek, 2001), from placement testing to exit examinations, is a critical feature of design whenever decisions have to be made about students and the programs that host them. Equally important, as Chris M. Gallagher (2011) has argued, is attention to the hierarchical orientation of those calling for standards and consideration of alternative assessment structures based on a network model of education. Reporting results so they are accessible and meaningful to a wide variety of social networks remains a concern in the age of accountability (Middaugh, 2010). In this collection, William Condon expresses caution regarding portfolio assessment because its current level of acceptability may blind us to its usefulness for cross-genre investigation of student ability, may weaken the arguments we must make in terms of its cost effectiveness, and may lead us away from the need to explore digital portfolio environments beyond academic settings. For Condon, unless design is generative we will become unwitting agents, blind to innovation, of our own success. Hilary Persky, in her chapter on writing assessment in the National Assessment of Educational Progress, observes the ways that the assessment context has shifted in its engagement with advances in pedagogy. From task design to scoring frameworks, NAEP continues to encourage designs that exceed the generic, vapid response associated with large-scale testing so that new areas, such as writing in digital environments and expressing insight, might be evaluated. A third way to read this collection, therefore, is to reflect on the following aspects of writing assessment design:

- How has cost effectiveness been established so that the design of the assessment at hand is compared with its alternatives, so that the ingredients of the design are identified, so that potentially lost opportunities are identified, and so that the expense of the assessment is shared?
- Have performance standards been established that follow a defined process, articulate a standard-setting method, describe the process used to establish the standard, and employ justification arguments for its use?
- Have results been reported so that they are transparent and meaningful to a variety of shareholders, including students, par-

ents, administrators, alumni, program accreditation agencies, and regional accreditation agencies?

A final consideration common to both the writing assessment and educational measurement communities is attention to the consequences of the assessment. Even though validity theory, research on construct representation, and frameworks for experimental design are rich, attention to consequences of an assessment are often poor. Robert L. Brennan (2006) categorizes impact as intended, unintended, positive, and negative. Although an impact that is intended and positive is easy to justify, what, precisely, are those responsible for the assessment to do with unintended and negative results? Asking similarly difficult questions, Chris M. Anson challenges us to investigate, from the perspective of the student, the benefits of the educational return on the staggering investment of time and energy we put into responding to writing. An unintended and negative effect of endless comments on student papers, Anson believes, may be a body of knowledge about writing pedagogy that is little more than lore. Equally compelling is Doug Baldwin's analysis of the complexities involved in constructed-response frameworks, long taken to be the best way to design assessments requiring student performance. Complexities arise regarding procedures that, on the surface, seem the very essence of fairness, such as allowing students to choose among prompts. Despite the best-intentioned efforts to ensure comparability across prompts, Baldwin cautions, the prompts can vary in difficulty, and some test takers might have an easier prompt. In addition, research has shown that some test takers, when given a choice of prompts, can choose badly. For Baldwin, intended fairness may result in the unintended presence of bias. A final way to read this collection, then, is to reflect on the following aspects of consequence addressed by the authors in this area of research:

- How are intended and positive consequences identified in the assessment, and what qualifications are in place to ensure that recorded validity gains are not merely cosmetic?
- How have possible unintended and negative consequences been anticipated from the beginning of the assessment plan?
- Have both positive and negative consequences been anticipated, before the assessment is begun, from a perspective that includes all shareholders who will be affected by the assessment?
- After the assessment is concluded, have the results been used in a way to ensure that substantial intended and positive consequences are maximized and unintended and negative consequences are both fully understood and minimized?

Expression of theories, representation of constructs, design of measures, and evaluation of impact are four common areas of investigation that are the basis for a multidisciplinary research agenda for the future of writing assessment. In this collection, however, the editors have not attempted to create the totalizing narrative that Melissa Ianetta (2010) warns of in histories of the discipline of composition and rhetoric. That is, the chapters do not present a unified view of the pursuit of a singular truth about the assessment of writing ability. Following Coles (1998), we see the chapters as illustrations of the often intellectual and sometimes moral tensions that arise from engaged discussions of theory, representation, design, and consequence. A look, however cursory, at the disagreements among ourselves (and with the one we have come together to honor) reveals that we are not in agreement on any postcard's worth of crude common truth whatsoever. We are certain that this collection is not an emancipation narrative; a browse will reveal that we are not escaping our differences but digging in deeper to identify areas of commonality. If the modern era of writing assessment did indeed open in the fall of 1971, as White tells us, then at 40 something we appear to be as show-off as the kid we have come together to honor. Ours is a tribute by example.

ENDNOTE

1. One way to interpret the significance of this edited volume is as a contribution of two fields distinctly categorized under the federal Classification of Instructional Programs (CIP). The older field, Educational Assessment, Evaluation, and Research (13.06), is located within the discipline of Education (13). The more recent, Rhetoric and Composition/Writing Studies (23.13), is part of the discipline of English Language and Literature/Letters (23). Drilling further down, Phelps (2011) replied in correspondence that she would argue that writing assessment is most easily conceptualized as a specialization under writing program administration [Rhetoric and Composition, 23.1304]. Similarly, the specialization of those contributing to this volume from the educational measurement community might be classified under Educational Evaluation and Research (CIP 13.0601). Viewed in this way, the ability of White to bring these two communities together—literally, six digit deep members of concrete specializations—compels us to recall Samuel Johnson. The collaboration may not be done well, but you may be surprised to find it done at all.

REFERENCES

American Educational Research Association, American Psychological Association, & National Council on Measurement in Education. (1999). *Standards for educational and psychological testing*. Washington, DC: American Educational Research Association.

Anson, C. M. (2010). A field at sixty-something. [Review of the books *Handbook of research on writing: History, society, school, individual*, text, by C. Bazerman (Ed.); *Handbook of writing research*, by C. A MacArthur, S. Graham, & J. Fitzgerald (Eds.); *The Norton book of composition studies*, by S. Miller (Ed.); *Research on composition: Multiple perspectives on two decades of change,* by P. Smagorinsky (Ed.).] College Composition and Communication, 62(1), 216-228.

Borsboom, D. (2005). *Measuring the mind: Conceptual issues in contemporary psychometrics.* Cambridge, UK: Cambridge University Press.

Brennan, R. L. (2006). Perspectives on the evolution and future of educational measurement. In R. L. Brennan (Ed.), *Educational measurement* (4th ed., pp. 1-16). Westport, CT: American Council on Education and Praeger.

Cizek, G. J. (2008). Assessing *Educational measurement*: Ovations, omissions, opportunities. [Review of *Educational measurement,* 4th ed., by R. L. Brennan (Ed.).] *Educational Researcher, 37*(2), 96-100.

Cohen, A. M., & Kisker, C. B. (2010). *The shaping of American higher education: Emergence and growth of the contemporary system* (2nd ed.). San Francisco, CA: Jossey-Bass.

Coles. R. (1998). *Doing documentary work*. Oxford, UK: Oxford University Press.

Condon, W. (2011). Reinventing writing assessment: How the conversation is shifting. [Review of the books *Reframing writing assessment to improve teaching and learning*, by L. Adler-Kassner & P. O'Neill; *Organic writing assessment: Dynamic criteria mapping in action*, by B. Broad, L. Adler-Kassner, B. Alford, J. Detweiler, H. Estrem, S. Harrington, M. McBride, E. Stalions, & S. Weden; *On a scale: A social history of writing assessment in America*, by N. Elliot; *Machine scoring of student essays*, by P. F. Ericsson & R. Haswell (Eds.); *Assessing writing: A critical sourcebook*, by B. Huot & P. O'Neill (Eds.); *(Re)Articulating writing assessment for teaching and learning*, by B. Huot; *Coming to terms: A theory of writing assessment*, by P. Lynne; *Writing assessment and the revolution in digital texts and technologies*, by M. R. Neal; *A guide to college writing assessment*, by P. O'Neill, C. Moore, & B. Huot; *Assessment of writing*, by M. C. Paretti & K. M. Powell (Eds.); *Assessing writing*, by S. C. Weigle; *Rethinking rubrics in writing assessment*, by M. Wilson; *An overview of writing assessment*, by W. Wolcott, with S. M. Legg]. *Journal of the Council of Writing Program Administrators, 34*(2), 162-182.

Conference on College Composition and Communication, Committee on Assessment. (1995). Writing assessment: A position statement. *College Composition and Communication, 46*(3), 430-437. (Revisions in 2006 & 2009. Web

Cronbach, L. J., & Meehl, P. E. (1955). Construct validity in psychological tests. *Psychological Bulletin, 52*(4), 281-302.

Crusius, T. W. (1989). *Discourse: A critique and synthesis of major theories*. New York, NY: Modern Language Association.

Embretson, S. (1983). Construct validity: Construct representation versus nomothetic span. *Psychological Bulletin, 93*(1), 179-197.

Gallagher, C. W. (2011). Being there: (Re)making the assessment scene. *College Composition and Communication, 62*(3), 450-476.

Huot, B. (1996). Towards a new theory of writing assessment. *College Composition and Communication, 47*(4), 549-566.

Huot, B. (2002). *(Re)articulating writing assessment for teaching and learning*. Logan, UT: Utah State University Press.

Ianettta, M. (2010). Disciplinarity, divorce, and the displacement of labor issues. *College Composition and Communication, 62*(1), 53-72.

Levin, H. M., & McEwan, P. J. (Eds.). (2002). *Cost-effectiveness and educational policy*. Larchmont, NY: Eye on Education.

Lynne, P. (2004). *Coming to terms: A theory of writing assessment*. Logan, UT: Utah State University Press.

Messick. S (1989). Validity. In R. L. Linn (Ed.), *Educational measurement* (3rd ed., pp. 134-103). New York, NY: American Council on Education and Macmillan.

Messick, S. (1998). Test validity: A matter of consequences. *Social Indicators Research, 45*(1-3), 35-44.

Middaugh, M. F. (2010). *Planning and assessment in higher education: Demonstrating institutional effectiveness.* San Francisco, CA: Jossey-Bass.

Mislevy, R. J. (2007). Validity by design. *Educational Researcher, 36*(8), 463–469.

Payson, A. T. (1919). *Lad: A dog*. New York, NY: Dutton.

Phelps, L. W. (1998). *Composition as a human science: Contributions to the self-understanding of a discipline*. Oxford, UK: Oxford University Press.

Phelps, L. W. (2011, May 2). Re: Question from N. Elliot: Writing assessment and the CIP codes. Web.

Phelps, L. W., & Ackerman, J. W. (2010). Making the case for disciplinarity in rhetoric, composition, and writing studies. *College Composition and Communication, 62*(1), 180-215.

Sartre, J. P. (2007). Existentialism is a humanism (C. Macomber, Trans.). In J. Kulka (Ed.), *Existentialism is a humanism* (pp. 17-72). New Haven, CT: Yale University Press. (Original work published 1946)

Shepard, L. A. (2006). Classroom assessment. In R. L. Brennan (Ed.), *Educational measurement* (4th ed., pp. 623-646). Westport, CT: American Council on Education and Praeger.

Snyder, T. D. (Ed.). (1993). *120 years of American education: A statistical portrait*. Washington, DC: National Center for Education Statistics.

White, E. M. (1966). Thackeray's contributions to *Fraser's Magazine*. *Studies in Bibliography, 19*, 67-84.

White, E. M. (1969). Writing for nobody. *College English, 31*(2), 166-168.

White, E. M. (1970). *The writer's control of tone*. New York, NY: W. W. Norton.

White, E. M. (1972). *The pop culture tradition*. New York, NY: W. W. Norton.

White, E. M. (1984). Holisticism. *College Composition and Communication, 35*(4), 400-409.

White, E. M. (1985). *Teaching and assessing writing: Recent advances in understanding, evaluating, and improving student performance*. San Francisco, CA: Jossey-Bass.
White, E. M. (1989). Developing successful college writing programs. San Francisco, CA: Jossey-Bass.
White, E. M. (1995a). An apologia for the timed impromptu essay test. *College Composition and Communication, 46*(1), 30-45.
White, E. M. (1995b). The rhetorical problem of program evaluation and the WPA. In J. Janangelo & K. Hansen (Eds.), *Resituating writing: Constructing and administering writing programs* (pp. 132–50). Portsmouth, NH: Heinemann-Boynton/Cook..
White, E. M. (1996, December 7). Re: White's law. Retrieved from WPA LISTSERV. Web
White, E. M. (2001). The opening of the modern era of writing assessment: A narrative. *College English, 63(*3), 306-320.
White, E. M. (2005). The scoring of writing portfolios: Phase 2. *College Composition and Communication, 56*(4), 581-600.
White, E. M. (2008). Testing in and testing out. *Writing Program Administration, 32*(1), 129-142.
White, E. M. (2010). English professor as public figure: My days in court. *College English, 73*(2), 183-195.
White, E. M. (2011, January 16, 18). An oral history with Dr. Edward M. White/Interviewers: Norbert Elliot & Les Perelman. Newark, NJ: New Jersey Institute of Technology & Cambridge, MA: Massachusetts Institute of Technology.
White, E. M., & Borrowman, S. (2007). *The promise of America*. New York, NY Pearson/Longman.
White, E. M., Lutz. W. D., & Kamisikiri (Eds.). (1996). *Assessment of writing: Politics, policies, practices*. New York, NY: Modern Language Association.
White, E. M., & Thomas, L. L. (1981). Racial minorities and writing skills assessment in the California State University and Colleges. *College English, 43*(3), 276-283.
Williamson, M. (2004). Validity of automated scoring: Prologue for continuing discussion of machine scoring student writing. *Journal of Writing Assessment, 1*(2), 85-104.

I

THE LANDSCAPE OF CONTEMPORARY WRITING ASSESSMENT

EMW Reflection: *The New York Times* invited New York high school editors to discuss issues of the day with important people, an unusual aspect of early television, before the existence of public television programming. Here Harrison Salisbury, newly returned Moscow bureau chief for the *New York Times*, is the featured guest and I set to his far left, looking rather goofy. I think I asked one carefully prepared question of him about the chances of atomic war and mutual annihilation.

I

THE LANDSCAPE OF CONTEMPORARY WRITING ASSESSMENT

TRADITION AND THE RISE OF LOCALISM

One of the great American academic urban legends is that the swimming test that used to be required at many colleges and universities arose because Harry Elkins Widener, a Harvard graduate and bibliophile, perished in the sinking of the Titanic (Breimer, 1989). His mother Eleanor Elkins Widener, who was in a lifeboat when her son and husband went down with the ship, did give Harvard its library as a memorial to her son, but the legend concerns the supposed condition she made that every Harvard undergraduate would have to pass a swim test because Mrs. Widener believed that had her son been able to swim, he would have survived. Harvard no longer has a swim test but some schools still do. The story went that when Harvard instituted the swim test so did other institutions, with students in colleges throughout America sometimes still completing their last lap as the faculty committee voted on the commencement list.

Harvard's role in the emergence of the college placement test and freshman composition bears an uncanny resemblance to the origin of the swim test; as John Brereton notes in the first chapter in this section, in the end, Harvard's history under President Charles William Eliot (Morrison, 1930) is not the beginning of a national history but rather one of many local histories. Brereton's fact checking of the early days of the writing portion of the

Harvard Entrance Examination is fascinating in that the story he tells brings up many of the themes that will often occur in this collection: motivations for assessment, assessment frameworks, and consequences of assessment.

A little less than 2 miles up Massachusetts Avenue from Harvard in North Cambridge is Frank's Steakhouse, the haunt of another Massachusetts institution, the late Thomas P. (Tip) O'Neill, the second longest serving Speaker of the House and the author of the immortal maxim, "All politics is local" (Farrell, 2001). Similarly, all writing assessments, even national ones, have local components and local constituencies. The next three chapters in this section are all concerned with assessment of K-12 students, but they differ significantly in their overall approaches and the relationship between local and central control.

Sherry Seale Swain and Paul LeMahieu recount the success of the National Writing Project's (NWP) Analytic Writing Continuum (AWC), designed not for centralized research but to accommodate locally designed and administered research studies. Rather than a top down approach to assessment, the AWC is described as a flexible and negotiated system that allows productive interactions between local control and national scoring, localized prompts and national standards, and professional development and summative assessments. Responding to the need for a credible direct measure of student learning, the NWP in 2004 adopted and reconceptualized the Six + 1 Trait Model (ideas, organization, voice, word choice, sentence fluency, and conventions plus presentation) as the basis of the instrument (Culham, 2003). Teachers who have engaged in these scoring sessions—with data from 18 local sites, spanning grades 3 to 12—bring the instrument back to the classroom as a flexible guide to evaluate student writing and as a tool for students to use in their own writing. With roots in the approach of Paul Diederich (1974) to understanding the characteristics of good writing and the decade-long research of Alan C. Purves (1992) on international writing assessment, the AWC, as described by Swain and LeMahieu, stands as a perfect example of classroom-centered, teacher-centered, and student-centered assessment. In its emphasis on assessing local writing performance accurately and developing explanatory concepts that are of useful heuristic value, the AWC adheres to the two key principles of systematic social inquiry advanced by Cronbach (1975).

In another large-scale assessment, the National Assessment of Educational Progress (NAEP)—often in contact with on-the-ground teachers—is a congressionally mandated project funded by the United States Department of Education and administered by the Educational Testing Service (ETS). In her chapter, Hilary Persky recounts the history and evolution of the NAEP writing component from its beginnings in 1969 to current pilot projects that have students write the tests on computers (Jones & Olkin, 2004). The chapter recounts several changes and experiments in the

NAEP writing assessment over its more than 40-year history, including attempts to assess revision, the use of portfolios, primary trait tasks and scoring, and focused holistic scoring. In evaluating the successes and failures of these assessment frameworks, Persky emphasizes that "NAEP is not a diagnostic tool but a broad measure for large groups of students." Ever responsive to current practice and theory, attempts to make writing tasks more rhetorically based—thus increasing the ability of students to write with an awareness of audience, purpose, and context—are a recurring theme in the history of the NAEP assessments. Similarly, in addition to experimenting with students writing on computers, the 2011 assessment framework places a greater emphasis on purpose and audience. Such shifts are welcome, Persky concludes, and compel those involved to be sure they are measuring what ought to be measured.

In Chapter 4, Paul Deane describes ETS's Cognitively Based Assessments of, for, and as Learning (CBAL) initiative that conceptualizes K-12 assessment through the lens of cognitive science to integrate assessment with learning and to combine formative with summative assessment. Based on activity theory—a theoretical stance that transcends the dualism between the individual agent and social scene and embraces object-oriented, collective, and culturally mediated human action (Engestrom, Miettinen, & Punamaki, 1999; Russell, 1995)—CBAL treats writing as a social and cognitive construct. Deane describes in depth a new competency model that itself leads to a new kind of writing test that will sample a wide range of skills by conceptualizing them as multiple "periodic accountability assessments." Moreover, the use of computer-based assessment in K-12 pilot studies has already produced some major insights into the difference between the writing patterns of stronger and weaker writers. Overall, Deane describes a project that has the potential to add new and exciting dimensions to both formative and summative writing assessments.

In the following chapter, Barry Maid and Barbara D'Angelo examine the *WPA Outcomes Statement for First-Year Composition* from the Council of Writing Program Administrators (CWPA) in relation to the *Information Literacy Competency Standards for Higher Education* developed by the Association of College and Research Libraries (ACRL). As the authors note, both the *Outcomes Statement* (2000/2008) and the *Information Literacy Competency Standards* (2000) are 20th-century documents that do not reflect the explosion of information and new media that has occurred in the past 10 years, especially in postsecondary instructional fields such as technical communication. They do observe, nevertheless, that both documents serve as excellent templates for developing new outcome statements and 21-century literacy standards that address the complex set of skills Maid and D'Angelo include in their course in proposal writing, part of their university's program in technical communication. Maid and D'Angelo also observe that the CWPA and ACRL documents—along with *The Framework for Success in Postsecondary Writing* (Council of Writing Program Administrators, National Council of Teachers of English, & National Writing Project, 2011)—give direction to the enterprise of teaching students to use effectively the constantly evolving palette of digital media.

Assessment in technical communication is also the subject of the chapter by Margaret Hundleby as she explores the relationships of the development of Technical and Professional Communication (TPC), the constructs that inform its assessment, and the means by which it is assessed. Hundleby demonstrates that TPC was historically viewed as an engineering discipline; as such, the criteria used to evaluate it were ones that derived from engineering practice such as measurement, functionality, and elegance. As the discipline of composition matured, Hundleby notes how the criteria defining both TPC and its assessment incorporated rhetorical constructs such as audience, purpose, and organization, as well such concepts as situatedness (Alred, 2003; Wright, Malone, Saraf, Long, Egodapitiya, & Roberson, 2011). In addition, an awareness of the social aspects of technical discourse, especially as it is described in contemporary activity theory and genre theory (Spinuzzi, 2003), profoundly influenced both the teaching and assessment of TPC at the beginning of the 21st century. Hundleby concludes her discussion by stressing the growing importance of rubrics and portfolios in the assessment of all forms of technical and professional discourse.

Mary Fowles of ETS concludes this section with an overview of writing assessments for admission to upper division, graduate, and professional programs. After giving a brief overview of the very different writing tasks that have been and are now incorporated into these types of examinations, Fowles discusses the considerations that inform all high-stakes testing situations: construct validity, test design, scoring methods, fairness, appropriate and inappropriate use of test scores, cost factors, and consequential validity. Remarkably, her considerations reflect the present development of a programmatic approach to testing that the founding president of ETS, Henry Chauncey, defined in 1969. Beginning with an expressed need, the process aimed to develop committees of subject-matter specialists of highly qualified teachers, outline test specifications and design questions to address those specifications, register and test candidates, and continue research on the test. "No testing program can afford to be stagnant," Chauncey cautioned. "Constant improvements and refinements are vital to the continued success of a program" (p. 28). In this tradition of a programmatic approach to writing assessment, Fowles concludes the chapter by calling for even more collaboration among individual testing programs and composition specialists to share information and systematize "the remarkable (but disparate) body of knowledge" that has been collected.

In describing the landscape of contemporary writing assessment as it is conducted from kindergarten through postgraduate studies, the authors in this first section of the volume emphasize six trends that—taken together—document writing assessment practice early in the second decade of the 21st century: increased attention to historic precedent as a source for instrumental value; respect for the knowledge and reflective practice of teachers; integration of contemporary theory into the early stages of assessment design; exploration of constructs as they are mediated in digital environments; expansion of multidisciplinary research; and programmatic approaches emphasizing consequential validity.

REFERENCES

Alred, G. (2003). Essential works on technical communication. *Technical Communication, 50*(4), 585-616.

Association of College & Research Libraries. (2000). *Information literacy competency standards for higher education*. Web.

Breimer, L. H. (1989, October). Harvard's swimming test. *British Medical Journal,* 116-127.

Chancey, H. (1969). Testing for selection and special purposes. In K. Ingenkamp (Ed.), *Developments in educational testing* (Vol. 1, pp. 27-52). London: University of London Press.

Council of Writing Program Administrators (2000/2008). *WPA Outcomes Statement for First-Year Composition*. Web.

Council of Writing Program Administrators, National Council of Teachers of English, & National Writing Project. (2011). *Framework for success in postsecondary education*. Web.

Cronbach, L. J. (1975, February). Beyond the two disciplines of scientific psychology. *American Psychologist*, 116-127.

Culham, R. (2003). *6 + 1 traits of writing*. New York, NY: Scholastic Professional Books.

Diederich, P. B. (1974). *Measuring growth in English*. Urbana, IL: National Council of Teachers of English.

Engestrom, Y., Miettinen, R., & Punamaki, R. (1999). *Perspectives on activity theory*. Cambridge, UK: Cambridge University Press.

Farrell, J. A. (2001). *Tip O'Neill and the democratic century*. Boston, MA: Little. Brown

Jones, L. V. & Olkin, I. (Eds.). (2004). *The nation's report card: Evolution and perspectives*. Bloomington, IN: Phi Delta Kappa Educational Foundation.

Morrison, S. E. (Ed.). (1930). *The development of Harvard University since the inauguration of President Eliot, 1869-1929*. Cambridge, MA: Harvard University Press.

Purves, A. C. (Ed.). (1992). *The IEA study of written composition II: Education and performance in fourteen countries*. Oxford, UK: Pergamon Press.

Russell, D. (1995). Activity theory and its implications for writing instruction. In J. Petraglia (Ed.), *Reconceiving writing, rethinking writing instruction* (pp. 51-78). Hillsdale, NJ: Lawrence Erlbaum.

Spinuzzi, C. (2003). *Tracing genres through organizations: A sociocultural approach to information design*. Cambridge, MA: The MIT Press.

Wright, D., Malone, E. A., Saraf, G. G., Long, T. B., Egodapitiya, I. K., & Roberson, E. A. (2011). A history of the future: Prognostication in technical communication: An annotated bibliography. *Technical Communication Quarterly, 20*(4), 443-480.

1

A CLOSER LOOK AT THE HARVARD ENTRANCE EXAMINATIONS IN THE 1870S

John Brereton
University of Massachusetts Boston, Emeritus

Serious large-scale examination of entering American college students' writing began in the mid-1870s, when Harvard added English Composition to its large array of entrance tests. Harvard's early attempts at assessment were, unfortunately, not well done. To be sure, the examiners were beginners, unaware of the complexities they faced. And unfortunately, the examination prompts they devised and the comments they made on the results reveal that their notion of good writing was limited to mechanical correctness, inaugurating a tradition that still haunts us. The first, halting attempts demonstrate that from the very beginning, the process of writing assessment was fraught with difficulties, from inadequately designed prompts, to confused reporting of results, to misleading conclusions drawn from the whole process. The flaws that characterized Harvard's earliest attempts at writing assessment remind us that this vital sector of the educational scene lacked an Ed White to prod, criticize, and guide the process. And the imperfect accounts historians have provided of those first entrance examinations should serve as a warning to examine the early material with a great deal more care, being alert to the complexities of the sources as well as the nuances of interpretation.
Those who write about the history of our discipline of composition and rhetoric have come to rely on certain truths about key points in the field's

origins and development. Primary among them is that an iconic moment was Harvard's decision to institute an entrance examination in English Composition in 1874.[1] This moment, we have come to believe, marks one of the origins of our field because it led to (a) a reaction of shock among Harvard faculty over the students' performance, (b) the almost universal practice of examining college entrants on their writing abilities, and (c) the subsequent widespread establishment of first year composition required for entering college students at many colleges.

It is safe to call this an almost universally accepted story, yet the closer one looks at the evidence, the more problems that appear with this "received" history. I want to step back from the origin story's iconic status and look at the actual records. I claim that there are significant gaps between supposed causes and supposed effects. The history may indeed be true in its very broadest outlines, but the individual details, when looked at closely, do not always hold up. Things do not fit together so smoothly as the received history would have us believe. And if the details are called into question, then the larger claims stand on less certain ground.

The outlines of the origin story are well known. Upon assuming Harvard's presidency in 1869, the reforming 35-year-old Charles William Eliot, a Professor of Chemistry at MIT, at his inauguration attacked "the prevailing neglect of the systematic study of the English language" (Eliot, 1898, p. 2). Thus, in 1872 he hired his Harvard classmate Adams Sherman Hill, a newspaperman not trained as a scholar, to invigorate Harvard's attention to written composition. Harvard instituted its first entrance examination in English Composition in 1874, stating in its catalogue:

> English Composition. Each candidate will be required to write a short English composition, correct in spelling, punctuation, grammar, and expression, the subject to be taken from such standard authors as shall be announced from time to time. The subject for 1874 will be taken from one of the following works: Shakespeare's Tempest, Julius Caesar, and Merchant of Venice; Goldsmith's Vicar of Wakefield; Scott's Ivanhoe and Lay of the Last Minstrel. (Harvard University, 1874)

And here is the actual June 1874 examination question:

> ENGLISH COMPOSITION. June, 1874
>
> A short English composition is required, correct in spelling, punctuation, grammar, and expression. Thirty lines will be sufficient. Make at least two paragraphs.
>
> Subject : —
>
> The story of the Caskets, in the Merchant of Venice;
>
> Or, The story of Shakespeare's Tempest;
>
> Or, The story of Rebecca, in Scott's Ivanhoe. (Leighton, 1883, p. 215)

And here is the October 1874 examination question:

> ENGLISH COMPOSITION, October, 1874
> A short English composition is required, correct in spelling, punctuation, grammar, and expression. Thirty lines will be sufficient. Make at least two paragraphs.
> Subject: —
> The Trial Scene, in the Merchant of Venice;
> Or, The Story of Brutus, in Shakespeare's Julius Caesar;
> Or, The Passage of Arms at Ashby, in Ivanhoe. (Leighton, 1883, p. 235)[2]

This examination seems like an afterthought when compared with the extensive, quite demanding, longer exams on Greek, Latin, and Mathematics. Clearly it does not demand that students employ anything resembling a critical attitude, or in fact any reasoning whatever. Simply retelling the stories in decent English would suffice. Any thinking done by students would likely be employed in smoothing out the sentences and correcting the grammar, not necessarily in using rhetorical skills to convince the reader. Arthur Applebee (1974) tells us that this was an important beginning point in the study of English literature in secondary schools, that Harvard's 1874 examination "institutionalized the study of standard authors and set in motion a process which eventually forced English to consolidate its position in the schools" (p. 30). True, Harvard's examination was the first we know of that required the reading of entire works, not just excerpts and snippets, as most 19th-century English courses did. But Harvard's was still a very tiny beginning. More serious changes would have to take place than an examination taken by 200 or so 18-year-old American boys.

From now on, however, we run into additional problems with the history, particularly with the examination and its effects. Here is how two prominent scholars describe the received history: "In 1874 Harvard University added a writing component to their entrance examinations, a short extemporaneous essay rated by teachers. More than half of the students failed, and many had to take 'subfreshman' courses or undergo extracurricular tutoring" (Haswell, 2004). And here is Connors (2003), writing of the same examination: "Harvard College instituted its first entrance examinations in written English in 1874, and to the horror of professors, parents, and the intellectual culture as a whole, more than half the students taking the exam failed it." (p. 182). Neither Haswell nor Connors supplies a citation for their statements; no doubt they are relying on the famous account Hill provided in "An Answer to the Cry for More English," written in 1879 and published in 1896.

It turns out that the Dean of Harvard College also wrote about this 1874 examination in his *Annual Report* (Gurney, 1876, p. 49). In Gurney's account, "Out of one hundred and eighty-three candidates then examined for admission to the Freshman class, twelve failed [the English Composition examination] entirely in this requisition, and thirty-six partially, — in spelling, punctuation, or both."[3] Rather than half the students failing this first Harvard entrance examination in writing, as Haswell and Connors tell us, only 26% failed. And this rate compares quite favorably with the range of failure by Harvard aspirants in other fields, which Gurney also records:

So the supposed shock and awe occasioned by that first examination in English Composition needs a second look. Harvard students passed their

Table 1.1. Results of the 1874 Examinations

Subject	Greek Composition	Plane Geometry	Arithmetic	Cicero and Virgil	Geography
Failure %	52	43	37	34	35

Subject	Latin Composition	Greek Authors (poetry)	Algebra	Greek Authors
Failure %	33	27	26	26

Subject	Caesar, Sallust, Ovid	Greek Grammar	Ancient History and Geography
Failure %	22	22	12

1874 composition entrance exam in just about the same numbers as all their others, and with considerably better grades than in Greek and Latin.[4] If anything, it should have been the Classics and mathematics masters who complained the loudest.

But what about the complaints, which over time undoubtedly did appear? The first and most famous complaint came not in 1874 but fully 5 years later, in 1879. Adams Sherman Hill, Eliot's point man on writing, reprinted the 1879 examination announcement from the Harvard Catalogue:

> English Composition. Each candidate will be required to write a short English composition, correct in spelling, punctuation, grammar, division by paragraphs, and expression, upon a subject announced at the time of examination. In 1879 the subject will be drawn from one of the following works: —

> Shakespeare's Macbeth, Richard II, and Midsummer's Night Dream;
> Scott's Guy Mannering;
> Byron's Prisoner of Chillon;
> Thackery's Henry Esmond;
> Macaulay's Essay on Addison;
> the Sir Roger de Coverly Essays in the Spectator.
> Every candidate is expected to be familiar with all the books in this list. (Hill, 1896, p. 9)

The actual June 1879 examination (the Preliminary) was:

> ENGLISH COMPOSITION.
>
> Write a short composition upon one of the subjects given below.
>
> Before beginning to write, consider what you have to say on the subject selected, and arrange your thoughts in logical order.
>
> Aim at quality rather than quantity of work.
>
> Carefully revise your composition, correcting all errors in punctuation, spelling, grammar, division by paragraphs, and expression, and making each sentence as clear and forcible as possible. If time permits, make a clean copy of the revised work.
>
> I. The Character of Sir Richard Steele.
> II. The Duke of Marlborough at portrayed by Thackery.
> III. The style of "Henry Esmond."
> IV. Thackery's account of the Pretender's visit to England.
> V. Duelling in the Age of Queen Anne. (Hill, 1896, p. 9)

Hill writes that out of the 316 students who took this examination in 1879, either as preliminary or regular examinees, 157 failed, "the percentage of failure being but slightly larger among the applicants for a 'preliminary certificate' than among the candidates for admission" (Hill, 1879, p. 9).

A number of issues cry out for mention here. One can only imagine the students' reaction, after having prepared all those works (three plays of Shakespeare, two novels, a long poem, and two lengthy essay reading assignments), to find that *four out of the five* questions were about Thackery's *Henry Esmond*, by far the longest work on the list. Given the way students have always prepared for examinations, it was very likely that they would skimp somewhat on the list's longest book. Hill makes no mention of the very strange imbalance in the questions. Second, it would certainly take these 1879 students a lot longer to prepare for and write the exam than those in 1874. There is no doubt that the 1879 exam is much more difficult than the 1874 exam, yet they were both allotted an hour. And unlike the 1874 examination, which simply asked students to retell the plot of one work, this examination actually calls for some organized thought, some critical thinking. (Except for question IV, which simply asks for plot summary.) Finally, we note the strong suggestion for revision, not usual in 1879 (or for that matter in 1979, when most examinations required only single draft work). Hill (1896, p. 9) writes that the average student, "Instead of aiming at good work, and to that end subjecting his composition to careful revision, he either did not undertake to revise it at all, or did not know how to correct his errors" (p. 11). One would like to know what practice students had in revision before taking this examination.

Yet there are all those failures. Or are there? Hill's claim that half the students failed stands in stark contrast to the Dean's account in his Annual Report for 1879-80. There the failures on the preliminary examination are listed as 53% (1879 Report, p. 64), but the aggregate figure for the whole class of applicants—both examinations—is listed as 28.5% (1879 Report, p. 61). What gives? Whose figure should we accept, Hill's or the Dean's?

Here, from the Deans' Reports from the appropriate years, are the results of the English Composition examinations, in all cases the aggregate figures of both preliminary and regular examinations:

Table 1.2. Failures in English Composition from Dean's Reports, 1874-1885

Date	Failure %
1874	20
1875	22
1876	8
1877	25
1878	21
1879	28.5
1880	17
1881	10
1882	15
1883	14
1884	12
1885	15

If Hill's figure of more than 50% failures is correct, the result is quite inconsistent with the great run of English Composition examinations from around the same time. We need to ask why. If Hill was right and the Dean wrong, why were the failures so much greater in 1879? One answer immediately comes to our attention: The 1879 examination was a great deal harder, as the comparison of the 1874 and 1879 exam demonstrates. Here are two examinations from 1877, the period in between:

ENGLISH COMPOSITION June, 1877

You are required to write a short English composition, correct in spelling, punctuation, division by paragraphs, and expression. You are recommended to arrange what you have to say before beginning to write; to pay more attention to quality than to quantity of work, and to make a fair copy from a rough draft.

One of the following subjects must be taken : —

I. Mark Antony's Speech in Julius Caesar.

II. Christmas at Bracebridge Hall.

III. The Combat between Sir Kenneth and Conrade. (Leighton, 1883, pp. 359-360)

ENGLISH COMPOSITION September, 1877

You are required to write a short English composition, correct in spelling, punctuation, division by paragraphs, and expression. You are recommended to arrange what you have to say before beginning to write, to pay more attention to quality than to quantity of work, and to make a fair copy from a rough draft.

One of the following subjects must be taken : —

I. The Battle of Philippi.

II. The Meeting of Saladin and Richard.

III. The Moral of Rip Van Winkle. (Leighton, 1883, pp. 389-390)

Both of these examinations offer the students considerably more choice than in 1879, drawing on three separate works each instead of the overwhelming majority from a single work. They are also looser, giving students more leeway to frame their essays. Length is not stipulated here, whereas in 1874 "short" was specified as 30 lines. Still, these are much more like the 1874 exams than the 1879 exam. It is the 1879 examination that someone made a good deal more demanding. Why?

Of course, the number of failures could have been a fluke, with the examination compiled hastily, without much thought given to providing students with a genuine choice. Entrance examinations were not, in the 1870s, the subject of serious scholarly study, as they are today, as this book testifies. Another explanation connects to the fact that Harvard was in something of a bind when it came to applicants. As the President's Reports from the 1870s all show, Harvard's applicant pool was not growing very quickly, and Harvard was almost totally reliant upon tuition for its finances. A significant drop in the number of paying entering students would have dire consequences not just for that year but for four years in a row as transfers were relatively few. Therefore a balance had to be struck between making the examinations demanding enough to uphold Harvard's reputation and lenient enough to garner a sufficient number of entering students. Short of increasing the number of applicants, there were only three ways to manage this complex balancing act: making the examination questions somewhat easier or harder; employing a more rigorous or more lenient grading system; or improving the quality of the applicants themselves by working with the schools to instruct them better. We can see obvious signs of the first and third methods in those 1879 examinations and their aftermath, and I suspect there is evidence of the second as well. That is, if Hill's figures are to be taken at face value, the failure rate was due to a decision, conscious or perhaps unconscious, to make the 1879 examination harder.

Other obvious questions arise: Who read the exams? What kinds of training were the examiners given? Was there an official or unofficial attempt to tighten the standards in 1879? For the first question we have some evidence of variability in the readers: In his 1874-5 President's Report, Eliot wrote, "the Corporation has been compelled for several years past to employ, as examiners at the admission examination just after Commencement [i.e., the Preliminary examination], a number of gentlemen who are not instructors in the College, paying for their services during the days of the examination" (Eliot, 1875, p. 12). But in reporting on the separate Women's Examination of 1874, the Dean writes:

> Some member of the Faculty was constantly in attendance, to distribute the papers at the beginning of every examination, to observe and direct its progress. ... The work done by the candidates upon every examination paper was subsequently read and marked, in most cases and *whenever practicable* by the member of the Faculty who had prepared the questions ... (Dunbar, 1875, p. 87, emphasis added)

It would seem that not all examinations were read by Harvard faculty, leaving one to wonder what kind of background and training the readers had. Could it be that as far as English Composition was concerned, it was felt that any untrained (there is no mention of training) college graduate would be capable of judging them? So, putting everything together, Hill's complaints seem overstated, based on a single instance, an instance that stands in stark contrast to the Dean's report.

But another, hitherto little examined subject, must come to our attention. Take that 1879 examination that Hill spoke about so vehemently, when, he claimed, over half of the applicants failed to write well enough to meet Harvard's standards. So what happened to them? The large majority were admitted anyway! According to the Dean's Report, of all the students who took the 1879 entrance examinations, only 26 were rejected. The rest were admitted unconditionally (95) or admitted with conditions (150) (Gurney, 1879, p. 66). That means that in 1879 over half the entering Harvard students fell short in at least one area of college-level work. And it was not just in

English that a good number of students failed. Other failure rates were reported by the Dean: Solid Geometry: 60%; Greek Composition: 33%; Maximum Physics: 48%; Plane Geometry: 37% (Gurney, 1879, p. 66). Harvard was admitting plenty of students who by its own definition were not ready for college work.

The process of admitting students who were not ready for college work went by the simple name of "Conditioning." It was no means confined to Harvard. In Stanford's first class of 1895, Herbert Hoover was accepted on condition that he become "proficient" in written English. Faculty at Indiana and Wellesley wrote of conditioning in Payne's 1895 survey of English programs (p. 93, 144). But unlike many other colleges, Harvard seems to have made no distinction between conditioned and unconditioned students. There was no separate course for such students, and no provisions for tutoring or private instruction seem to have been made. The only way Harvard had of holding such students back was failing them in a course or forcing them to repeat a year. This latter, more drastic punishment was employed relatively rarely, with fewer than 10% of students being subject to it.[5]

Knowing that Harvard was full of students whose writing it had deemed below standard seems to have infuriated Adams Sherman Hill. "An Answer to the Cry for More English" is a full-blown attack on the writing of entering Harvard students, aimed at the headmasters of Harvard's preparatory schools.[6] Part of Hill's motivation for his article might well have come from a book he had just published, *Principles of Rhetoric* (1878), which devoted a good deal of space –in an appendix—to matters of capitalization and punctuation, though surprisingly little to grammar, given Harvard's subsequent reputation for reducing writing to grammar and mechanical correctness. Hill was to use his book in his Harvard courses over the next 20 years, but he would have to wait quite a while before it became the textbook for Freshman Composition. In fact, there is no firm connection between Hill's 1879 reaction and the institution of that course, even though scholars, by misdating the course's origin, have made it seem so.[7] If the problem was so severe, why couldn't Hill convince his faculty colleagues to introduce a writing course in the Freshman year? In fact, Hill would have to wait until 1884 before he was allowed to institute a first year composition requirement at Harvard. Meanwhile, all those students who failed the composition part of the 1879 entrance examinations were busy with their Harvard coursework because they had been accepted for admission and were full-fledged Harvard students.

Another perspective on the 1879 examinations is provided in the President's Report of 1878-9, in which Eliot writes:

> It has been surprising to see how quickly the high schools, endowed academies, and private schools, which habitually or frequently prepare

> boys for this college, have accommodated their methods and their courses of study to the new requisitions of the Faculty. The English requisition, first enforced so lately as 1874, has met with universal approval. (Eliot, 1880, p. 10)

Yet in that same report Eliot acknowledges the slow nature of change:

> The neglect of English is for such long standing, that the subject cannot be brought up in six years to its proper place in the secondary schools. The schools which feed the College must have time to exact from the lower schools a better teaching of English than they have heretofore supplied. (Eliot, 1880, p. 12)

Eliot, unlike Hill, wants to cooperate with his feeder schools, not excoriate them. And he recognizes that his feeder schools have their own feeder schools. It would not be long before Eliot was to lead the Committee of Ten to attempt a total transformation of secondary school teaching across America.

It may well be that the eventual establishment of first year composition, English A, at Harvard in 1884 was a response (if quite delayed) to the weak performance on entrance examinations and, perhaps more important, to the weak writing in classrooms by Harvard students. Can we call that course, in Thomas Miller's (2011) nice phrase, "assessment-driven" (p. 130)? It certainly did seem to respond to concerns about writing expressed over and over by Hill, Eliot, and the Dean of Harvard College. But by Harvard's own assessment criteria—the entrance examinations—English Composition only showed up as problematic once, if we believe Hill, or never, if we accept the Dean's reports. All other years the failure rates in English Composition were not out of line with most other subjects. And, of course, Harvard always had the option of toughening up its examinations and turning away students who could not write well enough to meet its standards. If it did, however, it would have reduced the size of its student body dramatically. So the eventual establishment of English A does not necessarily mean that it was simply a remedial course, as Connors claimed (2003, p. 174), or a "subfreshman" course, as Haswell (2004) asserted. Establishing the course may have involved recognizing that this was what entering Harvard student writing looked like, and a consequent decision that Harvard had better meet its students' needs by providing them with the right kind of instruction. The subsequent widespread institution of entrance exams in writing and first year composition courses throughout much of America might well be seen as an accommodation to the kind of students colleges everywhere were getting, a case of colleges adjusting their standards to reality, although of course blaming the preparatory schools and complaining all the way.

As the essays in this volume demonstrate so well, writing assessment slowly improved over time, though not without many continuing problems. Generations of students have still been mistracked and misplaced, test results have still been inadequately reported, and conclusions have still been poorly drawn. It would take almost a century for scholars and administrators to become fully aware of the complexities of measuring student writing competence, and battles still rage over the most promising directions to pursue.

Those historians who examined those first, halting attempts at writing assessment were, like the Harvard examiners themselves, beginners, scholars who were taking a first look at a complex and fascinating era in writing instruction. The historians who have taken on the daunting task of detailing the emergence of writing assessment have chosen a crucial subject, one that has affected practically every American student who attended college for over a century and a quarter, and one that deserves the best attention we can give it.

ENDNOTES

1. Recent years have witnessed an increased skepticism about the "Harvard model" of composition's origin. For an extended discussion of this trend, see Cinthia Gannett, John Brereton, and Katherine Tirabassi (2010). Ultimately, as Gannett et al. argue, "Harvard's history is also finally a 'local history,'" if not paradigmatic, at least well worth investigating on its own (p. 448). See also David Gold (2008).
2. The Harvard entrance examinations in the 1870s and 1880s are confusing for a researcher. From 1874 on there were essentially two seatings, in Summer and Fall, and two levels, Preliminary (Summer only) or Regular. Students who wished to take the Preliminary exams (usually a majority of candidates) had to sit for at least 7 (of 14 in 1874), and pass at least 4, then wait at least a year before taking the rest (and retaking the ones they had failed). The exam results are not always supplied in an intelligible manner in the Deans' annual reports, where the emphasis is heavily weighted to the Preliminary exams. There the success rate would presumably be lower, given that they were for the most part taken before students began their last year of preparation, and that, as the Dean pointed out, the examiners graded preliminary exams more strictly (Gurney, 1874).
3. Harvard required aspiring students to sit for 14 examinations, all of them more than 1 hour except English Composition, which was simply allotted an hour in 1874. Three days were devoted to the examinations.
4. President Eliot speculated that the cause of the low scores in Greek and Latin was that "the Faculty changed the mode of examining the Latin and Greek authors in 1874, so that for the first time the whole examination for admission was conducted in writing" (Eliot, 1874, p. 12).

5. There is no study of the "conditioning" process available, although Wechsler (1977) as some useful details to contribute. Harvard records do not reveal how (or if) students were able to work off their conditions. Dean Dunbar reports that in 1877-88, "two hundred and thirty-seven students were notified that they must repeat the work in one or more studies, or perform its equivalent, and must pass satisfactory examinations thereon, as the condition of being finally recommended for a degree" (Dunbar, 1878, p. 54). We do not know how many of these repeats were due to failure and how many due to conditions upon admittance. At other colleges (e.g., Columbia, where as late as 1907 some 67% of students entered with conditions) conditioned students had a semester or a year to demonstrate proficiency in their appropriate fields, and most did (Wechsler, 1977, pp. 122-123).
6. Between 1875-80, Harvard accepted 7-18 students a year from Cambridge High School, 13-27 from Boston Latin, 30-50 privately educated pupils, and 18-40 from its largest feeder school by far, Phillips Exeter Academy. About 200-250 students were accepted each year. In 1882-3, 54% were from Massachusetts and 67% were from New England (Eliot, 1883, p. 10).
7. Trachsel (1992) claims that the course began in 1874 (pp. 42-43), as does Berlin (1987, p. 20). Kitzhaber (1990) erroneously states that "By 1874-75, English offerings included prescribed rhetoric throughout the freshman year" (p. 34), although later he correctly dates the origin of the first year composition course as 1885 (p. 61).

REFERENCES

Applebee, A. (1974). *Tradition and reform in the teaching of English*. Urbana, IL: National Council of Teachers of English.

Berlin, J. A. (1987). *Rhetoric and reality: Writing instruction in American colleges, 1900-1985*. Carbondale, IL: Southern Illinois University Press.

Connors, R. (2003). Overwork/underpay: Labor and status of composition teachers since 1880. In L. Ede & A. Lunsford (Eds.), *Selected essays of Robert J. Connors* (pp. 181-198). Boston, MA: Bedford/St. Martin's.

Dunbar, C. F. (1875). Report of committee on women's admission. In C. W. Eliot, *Forty-ninth annual report of the president of Harvard College* (pp. 87-89). Cambridge, MA: John Wilson.

Dunbar, C. F. (1878). In C. W. Eliot, *Fifty-second annual report of the president of Harvard College* (pp. 43-77). Cambridge, MA: John Wilson.

Eliot, C. W. (1874). *Forty-eighth annual report of the president of Harvard College.* Cambridge, MA: John Wilson.

Eliot, C. W. (1875). *Forty-ninth annual report of the president of Harvard College.* Cambridge, MA: John Wilson.

Eliot, C. W. (1880). *President's report for 1878-79.* Cambridge, MA: University Press.

Eliot, C.W. (1883). *Annual report of the president of Harvard College 1882-83.* Cambridge, MA: University Press.

Eliot, C. W. (1874). *Fiftieth Annual Report of the president of Harvard College.* Cambridge, MA: John Wilson.

Eliot, C.W. (1898). *Educational reform: Essays and addresses.* New York, NY: Century.

Gannett, C., Brereton, J., & Tirabassi, K. (2010). We all got history: Process and product in the history of composition [Review of the book *Local history: Reading the archives of composition.*] *Pedagogy, 10*(2), 425-50.

Gold, D. (2008). *Rhetoric at the margins: Revising the history of writing instruction in American colleges, 1873-1947.* Carbondale, IL: Southern Illinois University Press.

Gurney, E. W. (1874). Dean's report. In C. W. Eliot, *Forty-eighth annual report of the president of Harvard College* (pp. 39-55). Cambridge, MA: John Wilson.

Gurney, E. W. (1876). Dean's report. In C. W. Eliot, *Fiftieth annual report of the president of Harvard College* (pp. 43-67). Cambridge, MA: University Press.

Gurney, E. W. (1879). Dean's report. In C. W. Eliot, *Fifty-eighth annual report of the president of Harvard College* (pp. 53-79). Cambridge, MA: John Wilson.

Haswell, R. (2004). P*ost-secondary entry writing placement: A brief synopsis of research.* Web.

Harvard University (1874). *Catalogue for 1873-74.* Cambridge, MA. Harvard University.

Hill, A. S. (1896). An answer to the cry for more English. In A. S. Hill, L. B. R. Briggs, & B. S. Hurlbut (Eds.), *Twenty years of school and college English* (pp. 6-16). Cambridge, MA: Harvard University.

Kitzhaber, A.R. (1990). *Rhetoric in American colleges, 1850-1900.* Dallas, TX: Southern Methodist University Press.

Leighton, R. L. (Ed.). (1883). *Harvard examination papers* (9th ed.). Boston, MA: Ginn and Heath.

Miller, T. (2011). *The evolution of college English: Literacy studies from the Puritans to the postmoderns.* Carbondale, IL: Southern Illinois University Press.

Payne, W.M. (1895). *English in American universities.* Boston, MA: D.C. Heath.

Trachsel, M. (1992). *Institutionalizing literacy: The historical role of college entrance examinations in English.* Carbondale, IL: Southern Illinois University Press.

Wechsler, H. S. (1977). *The qualified student: A history of selective college admission in America.* New York, NY: Wiley.

2

ASSESSMENT IN A CULTURE OF INQUIRY
THE STORY OF THE NATIONAL WRITING PROJECT'S ANALYTIC WRITING CONTINUUM

Sherry Seale Swain
National Writing Project

Paul Le Mahieu
Carnegie Foundation for the Advancement of Teaching

> In order for assessment to support student learning, it must include teachers in all stages of the process and be embedded in curriculum and teaching activities. It must be aimed primarily at supporting more informed and student-centered teaching. . . . Like students, teachers also learn by constructing knowledge based on their experiences, conceptions, and opportunities for first-hand inquiry.
> Linda Darling-Hammond (1994, p. 25)

> Every time I come to [an AWC scoring conference] and we do the practice papers and the anchor papers, it's good to hear everybody's input about why they score things a certain way. . . . Now as a table leader, I can see the scores of others, and I say . . . "I'm interested in your thinking behind this." So that just adds another dimension to it for me, to see what it is that people see as a [score of] 3 in *Stance* because I see it as a [score of] 2. It's just another layer of it for me.
> Teacher

Teachers, the heart of education, too often find themselves excluded from the very process that policymakers advise should be central to instruction, namely assessment. Across this country, K–12 faculty groups gather regularly for sessions on "data driven" instruction. They pour through pages of statistical materials, and then they go back to their classrooms and do what they've always done: the very best they can with the information they have. What's missing in this picture? We suggest that what's missing is the teacher's involvement in assessment in any meaningful way: helping to design it, learning from it, and using it to improve instruction.

This is the story of how teachers thinking together with writing assessment experts helped to create a technically sound and rigorous writing assessment, one that is useful in the classroom as well as in research. The system diminishes the conundrum described by White: that often teachers feel "forced to choose between tailoring their teaching to an impromptu test and helping their students learn how to write . . ." (2007, p. iv). At the center of this story is a cohesive educational community, imbued with a vital inquiry stance, that developed, investigated, refined, and expanded the uses of the assessment system over an extended period of time. The Analytic Writing Continuum (AWC), developed by the National Writing Project (NWP), offers an opportunity to explore the potential of assessment that is locally contextualized yet linked to a common national framework and standards of performance.

The National Writing Project, arguably the nation's most long-standing educational reform effort, with its history of respect for teacher knowledge and reflective practice, serves teachers at all levels, from early childhood through university. NWP provides professional development and resources for teaching and learning, improving the teaching of writing, and conducting research on the teaching and learning of writing in classrooms and schools. In this instance, NWP addressed the issue of writing assessment guided by the same principles through which it has traditionally addressed writing, learning, and teaching: first by calling on the expertise of practitioners—teachers and researchers in the field; and second by inviting adaptations, inquiry, and feedback from those who put the assessment to work—in scoring events, classrooms, and professional development. These principles provided the basis for decisions during the development of the system and the refinements that continue to press upon the system, keeping it relevant and useful for its various purposes.

THE TIME WAS RIGHT

The AWC system addressed a specific need for writing assessment within the NWP network that emerged when, in the fall of 2003, a cohort of six research groups from writing project sites across the country received grants from NWP to study the effects of their programs on instructional practices and student writing performance. In addition to collecting descriptive and demographic data, each of the research sites committed to include a comparative reference in order to compare writing growth of students whose teachers were involved in writing project professional development with that of students whose teachers were not yet involved with a writing project. Further, the grants stipulated that growth in writing be measured by a direct assessment of writing. For the most part, local groups lacked the financial resources and assessment expertise to develop rigorous scoring systems themselves. Credibility was an even bigger issue. How could a local site design and deliver the program, develop, administer, and score the assessment, and then expect others to respect the outcomes they reported? NWP recognized the need for impartial judgments of students' writing achievement independent of these local sites. In 2004, with the second cohort of research sites, NWP committed to providing a national scoring system that would operate independently of the sites and provide unbiased and credible scores.

NWP researchers needed a robust assessment system that would serve not a central research design administered in multiple locales but rather a number of locally designed research studies, each uniquely suited to its context. Although local research teams would be committed to the direct assessment of student writing that included data from both program and comparison groups, there would be differences in research designs in terms of prompts, administration procedures, research questions, and analyses. This single system would require the strength of common standards and procedures and the flexibility to accommodate multiple prompts, multiple genres, multiple grade levels, and varied conditions for writing—from first draft on-demand writing to fully revised pieces from student portfolios. In short, NWP needed a rigorous central system that could speak to local questions and needs.

Initially, a group of NWP researchers—classroom teachers and university directors—met to determine whether an assessment system that would meet their needs might already exist or whether an existing system might serve as the basis for a new one. Over a 2-day period, practitioners articulated their beliefs about good writing assessment. "The substance of the writing must outweigh emphasis on conventions." "The focus must be on defining the quality of writing." "We need to be able to accommodate the grade levels and prompts that each study generates." "We need to be able to see growth where there is growth." The group outlined the requirements of such a system as follows:

- *A focus on the attributes of writing that the NWP teachers, programs, and researchers valued;*
- *A focus on the quality of the writing itself;*

- *Potential to address multiple grade levels, genres, and prompts*; and
- *A scale sensitive enough to detect differences for research purposes.*

After reviewing scoring systems from a number of English-speaking countries, the group came to consensus that the Six + 1 Trait Writing Model (Culham, 2003) came closest to their requirements. As an added advantage, the Six + 1 Writing Trait Model had considerable currency among practitioners and policymakers: most teachers of writing were familiar with the system, and a number of local and state education agencies had already based their writing assessments on it. The group decided that the NWP assessment system would have its roots in this well-known and widely used system.

CREATING THE AWC SYSTEM

In 2004, following the recommendation of the initial group of practitioners, a national panel of experts on student writing, along with senior NWP researchers,[1] confirmed the choice of the Six + 1 Trait Writing Model as the starting point for the new system. This group began their task by reviewing the model to determine in what areas it was and was not suitable for the research purposes of the NWP sites. For example, much of the language, although totally appropriate for stimulating conversation between teachers and students, was not sufficiently precise or rigorous for use in a research situation. The group decided to rethink the focus on "the writer" and "the reader," which makes scoring difficult in a situation in which neither the writer nor the intended reader is known to the scorer. Additionally, some definitions of the traits caused concern, for example, references to the writer's "personal details" as a requisite for demonstrating strong voice. With permission and encouragement from the originators of the Six + 1 Trait Writing Model, the panel set about making the following modifications to create what is now known as the NWP Analytic Writing Continuum Assessment System.

Conceptual Coherence

Revisions to particular traits of the Six+1 Trait Writing Model brought about conceptual coherence to the AWC Assessment System, enhancing reliability and validity and framing attributes for research and classroom uses.

Content. Whereas the Six+1 Trait Model was concerned with Ideas/Content that focused on the use and shaping of details, the AWC expansion of Content (including quality and clarity of ideas and meaning) includes language to address a variety of genres with suggestions for a multitude of types of support appropriate to academic as well as narrative writing. At score point 6, one element of the Content attribute describes the writing as containing "ideas that consistently and fully support and/or enhance the central theme or topic (e.g., well-developed details, reasons, examples, evidence, anecdotes, events, and/or descriptions, etc.)."

Structure. Reconceptualizing the Organization trait, which focused on a seamless overall integration, led to the AWC Structure attribute, including internal as well as overall attention to coherence and unity. Structure also addresses formulaic organization. At score point 3, one bulleted thread reads, "Includes a structure that is formulaic and predictable, or occasionally erratic, inconsistent, or uneven." At score point 6, that same thread reads, "Presents a compelling order and structure; writing flows smoothly so that organizational patterns are seamless."

Stance. Reconceptualizing the Voice trait led to the newly defined attribute of Stance—the presence of a clear and appropriate perspective (Dipardo, Storms, & Selland, 2011). Whereas people often interpret voice as a reflection of the writer's personality and then construe it as a "perky" or "excited" tone, Stance is concerned with the writing itself: its perspective, tone and style, purpose and audience, and level of formality. A scientific laboratory report should not be perky or pensive, but rather authoritative in its account of procedures, results, and interpretations. Descriptors of the Stance attribute at score point 6 are shown in Figure 2.1.

6. The writing:

- Consistently and powerfully demonstrates a clear perspective through tone and style.
- Consistently demonstrates a distinctive and sophisticated tone or style that adds interest and is appropriate for purpose and audience.
- Exhibits level(s) of formality or informality very well suited for purpose and audience.

Fig. 2.1. NWP Analytic Writing Continuum. Descriptors of the Stance Attribute at Score Point 6.

Sentence Fluency. The AWC values logical, clear sentences that exhibit appropriate rhythm, flow, and variation in structure and length. Intentional and/or effective use of fragments is noted in score points 4, 5, and 6.

Diction. The term *diction* signals appropriate attention given not just to words but also to expressions and phrasing. The Diction attribute also addresses appropriate and inappropriate modifiers as well as strong nouns, lively verbs, imagery, and metaphor, as appropriate to audience and purpose.

Conventions. In the AWC this includes usage, spelling, punctuation, and capitalization, and is defined at each score point by the ease or difficulty of reading and the amount of editing that would be required for publishing, from "almost no editing" for score point 6 to "extensive editing" for score point 1.

Scoring Scale

Extending the scale from four to six points gave the scoring system increased sensitivity to differences among pieces of writing, allowing the detection of change over time or differences between groups of students. In addition, a new "look" for the AWC reflects the NWP belief that, in reality, writing scores fall along a potentially infinite continuum of score points—even though only six of those points are available as actual scores.

Focus

Focusing the evaluative judgments exclusively upon the student writing centered the assessment on writing rather than students. Thus, instead of the stem for each score point beginning with "the writer," the focus in the AWC is on "the writing" itself. In deference to emerging writing skills, the panel utilized language at each score point to describe "what is there" rather than deficiencies or "what is not there," so that a determination of where the writing falls along the continuum reveals direction for improvement. Figure 2.2 shows the Diction attribute at score point 3, describing what is present in the writing rather than what is lacking.

Language

Rather than "traits," the AWC system addresses the six attributes described earlier with identifying elements or "threads" within each that more clearly define the attributes, clarify the differences among score points, and enhance scoring reliabilities. Three to five threads, denoted by bullet points, run

3. The writing:

- Contains words and expressions that are sometimes clear and precise.
- Contains words that are primarily simple and general, yet adequate.
- Contains mostly bland verbs or commonplace nouns and inappropriate modifiers.
- May include imagery or figurative language; when present it is simple and generally not effective.

Fig. 2.2. NWP Analytic Writing Continuum. Diction Attribute at Score Point 3.

across the score point descriptors and define the differences among scores. For example, the first thread in the content attribute describes the degree to which a central focus is shaped and presented, beginning with "clear and consistently focused; exceptionally well shaped and connected" at score point 6; and at score point 2, "May present several ideas, but no central focus emerges; seldom shaped and connected."

Holistic and Analytic Scoring[2]

In an effort to provide data that would serve each of the two primary purposes of the assessment system (i.e., evaluating NWP programming and providing data to teachers to inform instruction), the AWC applies both holistic and analytic scoring procedures. The holistic scoring guide describes the elemental components of the holistic score in the same way as the analytic framework so that the training for the analytic attributes also deepens understanding of the holistic scoring. However, whereas some systems build holistic scores as arithmetical aggregates of a set of analytic scores, the AWC does not attempt to do so. It preserves the analytic scores as separate scores, allowing both evaluative investigation of programs in specific areas of writing performance as well as diagnostic and instructionally relevant data. The holistic score is a single summary judgment about the quality of the writing. Research conducted within the AWC community affirms that the procedure of scoring holistically prior to analytic evaluation preserves the holistic score as independent of those assigned in analytic scoring (Singer & LeMahieu, 2012). In this way the holistic score can be regarded as "other than the sum of some identified parts" (a phrase chosen advisedly as, in fact, the complex and interdependent nature of writing performance means that the whole may be more or less than its deconstructed and abstracted components).

Interestingly, because it is handled in this way, the AWC system implicitly addresses the three "major problems" that White identifies as restricting the utility of analytic scoring (White, 1994):

- Lack of agreement about the subskills of writing: Notwithstanding the need for a thorough empirical investigation of the structure of the framework, the AWC (which is ongoing within the AWC community) is built upon an examination of major assessment systems and their descriptive frameworks. The consistencies in these frameworks and the widespread applicability of the AWC across policy and instructional settings strongly suggest that it addresses just such an implicit consensus.
- Difficulty of obtaining reliable subscores: The AWC system (with its anchors, training, and calibration samples, as well as training, calibration, scoring, and performance monitoring processes) has achieved levels of reliability that are quite exemplary and certainly adequate to its purposes.
- Time consuming and costly: Obviously scoring analytically and holistically takes longer than holistic scoring alone, yet the expanded information that the AWC system yields has been demonstrated to be of value to and appreciated by researchers and teachers. (Swain, LeMahieu, Sperling, Murphy, Fessehaie, & Smith, 2010)

Determining What "Good" Looks Like

The AWC Range Finding Team meets annually to review the anchor, calibration, and training papers that set and convey standards for each of the levels of scoring: lower elementary (grades 3 and 4), upper elementary (grade 5), middle school (grades 6–8), and high school. For each scoring level, these sets include six anchor papers, with similar scores for each of the attributes; two sets of six practice papers, illustrating mixed scores among the attributes; and a growing body of recalibration papers. These sets explicate the genre appropriate to the AWC: informative, persuasive, and narrative. Initially, the team reviewed available papers for each of the scoring levels and established the anchor sets. These remain largely unchanged in order to maintain standards across time and place. Annually, however, "new" papers from the current set to be scored replace two or three papers in the two practice sets to reflect current prompts and to focus on emerging issues such as economic, cultural, and language diversity among student writers.

Entering the Inquiry Community: Scorers and Learning to Score

Entry into the AWC community begins with the selection of scorers, almost all of whom are NWP Teacher-Consultants (TCs). Local site leaders nominate teachers who have participated in the 5-week invitational summer institute and who have strong potential as scorers. These leaders see the involvement of TCs as opportunities to build local capacity for serving school districts. During the 6 to 8 hours of training and preparation in the AWC system, scorers become familiar with the attributes, and calibrated to the standards. Room leaders and table leaders come from the range finding team and from the pool of experienced teacher-scorers who have shown expertise in the system and who have enhanced that expertise by using it in their schools or writing projects.

During interactive reading and discussion of the system, teacher-scorers encounter the tenets underlying the Analytic Writing Continuum—for example, that the continuum actually describes a graduated range of performance. The scorer's task is to determine which of the available score points most accurately describes each attribute of the writing. The interaction at the training looks like this: The room leader asks the group of scorers, "Why does this anchor paper represent a score of four in Content?" The teachers begin a process of conferring between the paper at hand and the descriptors of the AWC. They ask questions—of the room leaders, of each other, of themselves. The discussion helps the scorers to embrace the AWC, to reflect on it, and to help refine it. Rather than being limited to a narrow definition at each score point, scorers learn to recognize a range of characteristics and writing abilities clustered around each score point. As important, TCs examine writing in a new way—with a shared sense of quality, just what "good" is and what it looks like in its many expressions in their classes. The result is a commonly held perspective on and expectation for quality and one that is typically higher than any one individual arrived with.

The training also includes mini-lessons illustrating several of the attributes. Scorers participate in a lesson that uses photos to compare writing structures to various architectural structures, the predictable tract house to a formulaic rendition of a piece of writing: "Does this house remind you of a formula with its box shape, symmetrical windows, unremarkable entry, and predictable landscaping?" "Does this building that houses a modern art museum appear constructed for its specific purpose?" "How does the structure of this paper take readers on a journey that shifts forward and backward in time; how does its structure support its purpose?" Through another mini-lesson, scorers discover a seemingly infinite number of stances, from doubtful to persuasive, from humorous to mournful. In the course of the PowerPoint presentation, scorers note postures, tones, styles, and ultimately, the presence of appropriate stance in a piece of writing.

Prompts and Papers

Scorers encounter a wide variety of prompts at each scoring conference. All the local studies employ quasi-experimental designs that include direct assessment of writing, comparative references (usually a comparison group of students whose teachers are not involved in writing project professional development), counterbalanced prompts to account for an effect in which one or another of the prompts might be advantageous to a group of students, and pre/post administration of prompts so that differences over time can be observed. The result is quite a complex array of categories into which student papers fall at the scoring conferences. For example, papers from a single research study focused on a single grade level would fall into eight groups based on the categories of pretest/posttest, prompt A or B, and group.

Add to this mix research designs that encompass additional grade levels or research questions dealing with a variety of genre and the complexity expands. Across the multiple research designs, complexity increases in other ways as well, with variation in such elements as the following:

- Prompts. Local research teams select or design their prompts to reflect foci of their studies, from writing across the curriculum to descriptive, persuasive, or informative writing. Further, because all the research studies employ counterbalanced designs, there are at least two prompts for each study; for example, 10 studies contributing papers would mean a minimum of 20 prompts in play at any one scoring conference. With more complex research designs come even more prompts, sometimes including portfolio pieces that have undergone revision.
- Administration of prompts. Again, local research teams design the administration of the prompts, often mirroring state testing practices regarding timed or untimed administration. Because of local regulations related to classroom access, some sites send written instructions to the schools or teachers regarding test administration. In other localities, writing project leaders go into the schools to train the teachers to administer the assessments; in still others, specially trained writing project teachers administer the prompts. In each case, however, the same conditions prevail across program and comparison groups.
- Paper preparation. Local sites remove identifying information so that scorers do not know any specifics of the writing sample being evaluated (e.g., identity or even gender or race of the student, place of origin, group [program or comparison], or time of administration [pretest or posttest]). Local research teams code the papers and keep complete databases for purposes of analysis

and reporting. In most cases, papers and their scores are eventually returned to the schools and teachers.

- Statistical analysis. NWP provides individual student scores for the holistic and the six analytic attributes to the local research teams, each of which employs a statistician to conduct the final analyses for the study. From these analyses, the local research teams write their reports. Researchers at NWP then compile these findings into reports and research briefs (NWP Research and Evaluation Unit, 2010).

Scoring Procedures

Scorers calibrate to a criterion level of performance during the initial training, and then recalibrate following every major break in the scoring (meals and overnight). Fifteen to twenty percent of the student writing is scored twice, in part so that reliabilities can be calculated and in part so that the performance of the scorers can be monitored. Room and table leaders then provide individual recalibration sessions as needed. Over the six scoring conferences, reliabilities (measured as interrater agreement, defining agreement as two scores being identical or within one single score point of each other along the continuum) ranged from 89% to 93%, with an aggregate across all scores of 90% (see Table 2.1). In addition, at each scoring event, a small number of papers or scorers might follow special procedures to allow the investigation of some aspect of writing assessment that is of common interest (e.g., altering the order of scoring the attributes in the analytic scoring to explore whether order influences the scores). In these instances, the scores are not treated as operational because researchers prefer that all operational scores are obtained from the established procedures. Finally, NWP researchers infuse a constant set of papers (an equating set) taken from the first scoring conference into the papers to be scored at each subsequent scoring event in order to monitor the consistency of standards as they are applied across years.

To date, six national scoring conferences, with the Analytic Writing Continuum as the centerpiece, have produced student outcome data for 18 local site studies, spanning grades 3–12, all using quasi-experimental designs (NWP Research and Evaluation Unit, 2010). Over the 6 years, 397 TCs from 50 local NWP sites in 19 states have calibrated as scorers, including 65 experienced scorers who serve as room and table leaders. Every scoring conference includes time for reflection among the teacher-scorers. These reflections focus on both the AWC itself as well as its implications for the teachers' instructional practices. These reflective comments and conversations form the basis for continuous refinements to the system, yet the primary purpose of the NWP Scoring Conference is just that—obtaining valid and reliable scores to be used across multiple research studies.

TECHNICAL RIGOR AND QUALITY

As with many high-quality assessment systems, developers attended to technical rigor and quality from the outset. What sets the AWC apart from most, however, was that the inquiry-oriented stance of the NWP encouraged an improvement-oriented approach to its development. In short, technical quality was not a "state of grace" demonstrated at a singular point in time but a necessary aspect of the life and development of the system.

Reliability

Constant examination of scoring reliabilities, including the daily reliability reports that scorers eagerly awaited, ensured adequacy of the reliabilities. Leaders and scorers paid particular attention to aspects of the system that were undergoing revision at any point in time as well as those that consistently posed challenges. Table 2.1 presents the operational reliabilities over the life of the AWC. It shows that the interrater agreements ranged from 83 to 95%, certainly adequate to the research that was the first purpose for the development of the system. Although there are many observations that will occur to the reader, these reliabilities reveal at least two noteworthy points: first, they suggest areas that proved more challenging for scorers to understand and apply (e.g., Stance, which was addressed by modifications to the assessment framework itself as well as the training procedures); and second, they reveal a general trend of improvement over time—indicative of the impact of the research-driven modifications and the increased understanding of the scorers.

Validity

Examining validity in multiple ways adds to the credibility of the system. To offer just a few examples: Construct validity is a constant focus of attention through factor and facets analyses that support the fundamental conceptual structure of the system. Correlating scores from the AWC with other measures, notably state writing assessment systems, allows researchers to explore concurrent validity. Several local research teams have successfully included these analyses in their research designs. These analyses demonstrate appropriately high correlations and interestingly suggest that the AWC provides higher standards of performance and more useful information for instruction. Finally, the important issue of consequential validity is an ongoing focus of considerable effort and inquiry as reported in the next section of this chapter.

Table 2.1. National Writing Project Analytic Writing Continuum Reliabilities by Year of Scoring, 2005–2010

Year	Total number of Papers	Number of papers double scored	Total adjudi-cations	Agreement							
				Overall	Holistic	Content	Structure	Stance	Sentence Fluency	Diction	Convention
2005	7505	1748	1004	92%	95%	92%	91%	90%	91%	93%	91%
2006	6493	1071	661	91%	94%	92%	90%	88%	90%	93%	91%
2007	5362	1120	948	88%	90%	89%	89%	85%	86%	90%	86%
2008	6549	1287	1200	87%	90%	88%	87%	83%	86%	88%	86%
2009	6763	1397	969	90%	93%	91%	91%	86%	89%	90%	90%
2010	4827	1563	788	93%	94%	94%	94%	91%	92%	93%	91%
2005–2010	37,499	8186	5570	90%	93%	91%	91%	89%	89%	91%	89%

Note: The Overall reliability for each scoring conference was computed using the total numbers of scores and adjudications.

Utility of Use

A final area of inquiry monitors the system in the interest of ensuring its utility to various users. Ongoing equating studies in which a large set of student papers is scored across years and settings ensure the comparability and consistency of standards. Newly initiated vertical equating studies in which sets of papers are scored at multiple grade levels monitor the interpretation of the standards at each level of the system and interest those concerned with writing growth over time.

ADDING TO THE KNOWLEDGE BASE ABOUT WRITING ASSESSMENT

Two factors allow researchers to use the AWC to explore larger assessment questions. The first is its longevity: Assessment systems don't often remain stable long enough for researchers to use them as a tool for exploring assessment in and of itself. Second, the community of use surrounding the AWC welcomes inquiry and professional reflection. In the first 3 years of its implementation, researchers used the scoring conference to explore a number of research questions: When involved in both holistic and analytic scoring, does it matter if scorers focus first on the holistic or analytic scores (Singer & LeMahieu, 2012)? Does the order in which scorers are asked to assess the six attributes of writing influence the scores assigned to those attributes? How do scorers conceptualize and regard "voice," and what elements and/or language influence scorers' evaluative judgments about it? (DiPardo et al., 2011). More recently two research teams conducted focus groups, one to examine the implications of prompt design and the other looking at the characteristics of English learner writing that might position us to better evaluate it in an inclusive system of assessment.

Impact on Scorers

The Scoring Impact Study (Swain et al., 2010), launched in 2008, determined the extent to which the NWP's assessment system has any value to those who serve as scorers. Initially 325 teacher scorers received invitations to complete an online survey. One hundred thirty-six (41.6%) responded. Data for the study included the online survey, focus groups with 20 respondents, and interviews with 14 scorers. It revealed how teachers' experiences with the AWC had influenced their beliefs about writing and assessment, their classroom practices, the nature of their local writing project work, and the nature of writing itself. Influences of the AWC scoring experiences on teachers fall into four categories:

1. Understanding the Characteristics of Writing. The AWC experience is a catalyst for deeper understandings of three elements: characteristics of writing, assessing student writing, and teaching students to write. On a 6-point scale, 52% to 69% of responding teachers marked the highest rankings (5 or 6), indicating that the assessment system becomes a centerpiece for inquiry, as teachers embrace it and use it as a lens to question their practice. One respondent contemplated her newfound insights on teaching sentence fluency:

   It had not occurred to me to actually teach sentence fluency. I guess I thought that it could somehow be a natural outflow of reading, and yet after the conference, I realized that I could actually teach that actively, rather than hope they would pick it up. I could do it more intentionally. And so as a result of the conference, I just started really looking at teaching, not just sentence fluency, but all of the six attributes in a more intentional way.

2. Changes in Practice. Teachers take the AWC into their classrooms as a tool for evaluating student writing, as a guide for discussing writing with students, and as a tool for students to use to examine and ultimately improve their writing. Again, survey respondents marked top-ranking choices over half the time, 56%, 67%, and 64%, respectively. Fifty percent indicated the experience had changed their views about what students should learn. One teacher described varied practices for helping young writers to structure their writing:

   I write a piece in two different ways, one with a very weak or no opening and closing and another with strong ones. I let students pick which one they like and then tell why. . . . I read them lots of different openings and say, "Now what was this?" And they'll say, "It was a question or it was a shocking statement or an amazing fact." . . . We make a chart of choices for beginnings and endings. If they are writing an information piece, I might offer Laurence Pringle books because he has strong openings, and strong audience awareness. He starts his bat book (Pringle, 2000), "If you were a bat you could hang by your thumbs and stay up all night," both of which strongly appeal to children. So it teaches them awareness of audience, that they need to appeal to the [reader].

3. Expanding Writing Project Expertise. Survey results indicate that participants draw from the AWC in various NWP leadership and outreach programs: invitational summer institutes (the centerpiece program for preparing teacher-consultants), advanced institutes, and professional development programs for other teachers. Respondents reported using the AWC as tools for examining and evaluating student writing, selecting local anchor papers, and scoring student writing. A number of scorers incorporate the AWC into young writers' camps and parent and family workshops. Some savvy respondents use the AWC as a resource for marketing professional development in schools.
4. Teacher Ownership. The AWC embodies the authority of a rigorous assessment system, built with teacher input and with research as its primary focus, an area in which teachers are frequently disenfranchised. Within the first few hours of their initial training, teacher-scorers begin to wrestle with the concepts, making them their own, taking on the role of owner and co-author, doing the mental work to understand the system, questioning what they see as discrepancies, and creating niches for further inquiry into one or another facet of the system. Some tell us how the AWC operates as a silent partner as they write. One such teacher said:

> *The [AWC] continuum helps me organize that complexity and chaos that is often writing. And I know it helps me as a writer. When I sit down to write something and I typically just write, write, write, just bluh on the page to begin with. But when I go in to look at it again, to do some revision, I don't pull the rubric out necessarily, pull that continuum out, but I often think about, okay, let's think, do each of my sentences flow nicely into one another? I really do. I really internalize I guess you could say those characteristics.*

The scoring impact study investigated the ways in which individual scorers adopted the system. The following section sheds light on some organized efforts to use the AWC to meet local needs across the country.

A Common National Framework Goes Local

It is inherent in NWP culture that whatever is learned that is valuable goes home with teachers. This was true in the heyday of portfolio assessment, in the glory days of writing across the curriculum, and in other waves of promising instructional practice. It has been and is true of the AWC system. The dual nature of the system, first the standards that are shared across the national network and second, the invitation to make use of the system in local contexts, creates a cyclic flow of adaptation from the national network to local sites and classrooms and back to the national network to begin the cycle again. More than two dozen writing project sites are at any one time actively pursuing locally based work using the AWC assessment system. Currently local uses of the AWC system range across four purposes illustrated here with examples.

Research

- At Texas State University–San Marcos, the writing project site conducted a 2-year qualitative study, *Assessment to Instruction*, investigating various classroom uses of the AWC. This study is presented in more detail below.
- Using returned state-scored assessment papers, researchers have conducted multiple studies of how the AWC system and various state rubrics are (or are not) aligned, many with the belief that the AWC may have implications for classroom use. A classroom teacher in the Upper Peninsula of Michigan has investigated the relationship between the AWC and the state assessment (including instructional usefulness of the information provided) as her master's thesis. This study by Sabin and Hetherington is also described below.
- A teacher-researcher from the University of North Texas is studying the AWC as a catalyst for the development of a common language about writing and for the improvement of student writing in his middle school classroom.
- Researchers from Mississippi State University and Auburn University have joined together to research prominent features of student writing and how those features correlate to the attributes of the AWC, with the goal of signaling readiness for instruction (Swain, Graves, & Morse, 2010).

Assessment

- Ball State University's writing project site is taking the AWC into the university setting, beginning with the selection of anchor papers for freshman English courses.
- Following Hurricane Katrina, when the state did not offer writing assessment, Mississippi sites, through their state network of writing projects, offered writing assessment for schools using the AWC as the analytic tool.

- The Mississippi Writing/Thinking Institute, through a subcontract with the state-selected assessment company, has designed a new state rubric based on the attributes of the AWC. Writing project teachers also select anchor papers and design and conduct training for scorers for the statewide writing assessment.

Professional Development

- The Hawai'i Writing Project is working with the Hawai'i State Department of Education to offer professional development connecting the Common Core Standards, the AWC, and writing prompts that will be offered to teachers online.
- An ongoing teacher inquiry group at Boise State University is exploring questions developed around the use of the AWC in classrooms. Teachers are writing a book to share their findings.
- At Canisius College in Buffalo, New York, a group of writing project teachers is investigating the AWC in a school partnership setting that serves refugee children from Africa.

Mentorship

- At the University of Southern Mississippi, the mentor for National Board for Professional Teaching Standards candidates uses the AWC to help candidates improve their writing, deconstructing it to better understand the scoring system and the underlying implications for quality writing.

Inside a local AWC project: Teacher inquiry at Texas State University–San Marcos. Lori Assaf, a leader in the Central Texas Writing Project, facilitated a 2-year AWC inquiry, Assessment to Instruction (A2I), with a core group of teachers. At the outset, teachers considered how they might make use of the AWC in their classrooms, answering questions such as, "How has the AWC influenced you and your understanding as a writing teacher?" "How are you navigating the aspects of good writing as listed on the AWC?" "What issues, constraints, problems are you experiencing related to writing in your classroom?" "How do these issues relate to the AWC and using it for instruction?" Unlike the National Scoring Conference where the primary goal is obtaining reliable scores, the goal of projects like this one is professional growth for teachers. When teachers gather to pursue their own learning, there is less emphasis on reliability and therefore less time spent calibrating and more time spent digging under the meaning of the terms and descriptors, more time for questioning, discussing, and making applications to instruction. Early in their inquiry, these teachers found that using the AWC gave their students a common language for talking about writing and for thinking about how they might improve their writing. Each teacher worked independently to find the "best" way of using the AWC with her own students while, as a group, they shared and adapted ideas and constructed a set of principles for using the AWC for instruction. A handout used by the group in a conference presentation follows (Fig. 2.3).

1. Use LOTS of authentic dialogue. In order to make sense of the NWP-AWC and effective writing, students and teachers must talk with each other and other authors.
2. Teachers should model, demonstrate, and provide direct instruction for each NWP-AWC criteria and use high-quality literature to illustrate effective writing.
3. Students should identify each criterion by name and practice each criterion in their own writing.
4. NWP-AWC is a strength-based tool. It can help teachers identify where their students need to progress and it allows teachers to meet students where they are. It is the foundation of formative assessment as well as summative assessment.
5. The NWP-AWC should not be used as a rigid tool but as a flexible continuum. Make the NWP-AWC your own! Don't let it dictate your teaching or limit your students' writing.
6. Students should self-evaluate and self-assess in order to improve their writing.
7. Students and teachers should continuously look at their identity as writers and explore their strengths as developing writers.
8. Study and evaluate a piece of writing and not the writer.
9. Students and teachers need to be allowed to take risks.
10. Develop authentic writing and create opportunities for students to publish.

Fig. 2.3. Top Ten Principles for Using the Analytic Writing Continuum (as developed in the A2I project).

Northern Michigan University, Marquette writing project researchers compare the AWC to the MEAP. Inviting local teacher-consultants to be trained as scorers, Jan Sabin, director of the Upper Peninsula Writing Project at Northern Michigan University, investigated the extent to which the AWC maps onto the writing assessment within the Michigan Educational Assessment Program (MEAP). With training provided by NWP, Sabin's group used a sample of 225 state-scored papers written by elementary and middle school students for the comparison. Scorers calibrated to the AWC system and then scored the state papers. Analyses of the scores confirmed high correlations between five of the six attributes (Conventions being the exception) of the AWC and the MEAP holistic score (Hetherington, 2010), indicating that the details provided in the AWC descriptors could help teachers plan instruction that would help students to improve their writing and that would be responsive to the MEAP assessment. Based on these findings, Sabin's group of teacher-consultants is planning professional development to be offered to local schools.

Accessing the AWC. Is the AWC so powerful that one has but to hold it in hand to elicit influence on the teaching of writing? No, absolutely not, but the AWC does come with the caveat that to "hold it in hand" one should first come to understand its underlying tenets. Becoming familiar with the instrument and adopting an inquiry stance toward its applications are important first steps into the AWC community of use. The AWC policy suggests that entry into the community can be offered by the NWP itself or by any of the NWP sites having a cadre of teachers with AWC experience. NWP's network of sites across the country is the pathway for others into the community and to ensure its accessibility.

REFLECTIONS ON IMPACTS AND INFLUENCES

On reflection, one might ask, "Why does this particular system hold so much promise for assessment and the teaching of writing?" The answers are not totally elusive. First, the AWC system does what LeMahieu and Friedrich described in 2007: It "draws upon teacher research traditions to build an inquiry community that matures over time, in terms of both its substantive sophistication of and the inherent expectations employed in its assessments" (p. 102). Built within a culture of educators who value inquiry, the AWC continues to support both reflective practice and rigorous research.

The Scoring Impact Study confirms that those who participate in the national scoring conferences deepen their understandings of writing itself while reflecting on the particular qualities of the AWC. Some of these teachers credit the AWC's value to its focus on "the writing" as opposed to "the writer." When a teacher focuses on "the writer" as she initially reviews a paper, the individual student enters into the scoring activity, sometimes resulting in lowered expectations ("but this is good work for him," or "it's better than her last piece") or other thoughts that diminish instruction. A focus on "the writing" rather than "the writer" provides clarity on the locus of authority. Teachers focus on what is on the page—the writing—and once that is understood in terms of the attributes and what would be required for improvement, the teacher, now with full awareness of the potential of the writing, then becomes the agent for bringing the writer, the student, back into the instructional process. Expectations remain high because the potential for the piece of writing to become better is not compromised. Others say that the focus on strengths, looking for "what is present" rather than "what is not there," enables a teacher to identify building blocks on which to layer instruction. They tell us that focusing on strengths by identifying where writing skill falls along the continuum makes it possible to identify next steps toward improving the writing.

The many local uses that have shown the flexibility of the AWC also point to the promise of the system. Researchers in New Paltz, New York, for example, translated the AWC into Spanish to better understand the writing of migrant children. Researchers at Clemson University have submitted elementary on-demand writing along with writing composed in naturally occurring classroom contexts. These researchers want a Vygotskian view of what students can do "in cooperation with others" within the classroom compared to how well they write in on-demand situations (Kaminski & Hunt-Barron, 2010). Researchers such as these, so far apart in miles, come together around the shared values of the AWC system and pursue their own interests while learning from each other.

Huot (2002) argues that assessments should be site-based, locally controlled, context-sensitive, rhetorically based, and accessible. The AWC system is *site based*, developed in response to a specific need of one organization that holds common values and beliefs toward writing. The system is *locally controlled* in that the NWP itself is responsible for revising, updating, validating, managing, and opening the system for review. It is *context sensitive* in that it honors the instructional goals and objectives of teachers, students, and schools across the country, while respecting local cultural and social environments. It is *rhetorically based* in that it adheres to recognized rhetorical principles and interpretation of texts. Finally it is accessible as shown by the AWC activities locally designed and purposed. Thus, studying the impact of the AWC system allows exploration of the possibilities for assessment that is locally contextualized yet linked to a common national framework and standards of performance.

ENDNOTE

1. Anne DiPardo, University of Colorado at Boulder; JoAnne Eresh, Achieve; Sandra Murphy, University of California, Davis; Gail Offen-Brown, University of California; Faye Peitzman, UCLA Graduate School of Education & Information Studies; Melanie Sperling, University of California, Riverside; Barbara Storms, California State University, East Bay, retired; Paul LeMahieu, Carnegie Foundation for the Advancement of Teaching; Sherry Swain, National Writing Project.
2. See also Chapter 3 of this volume (Persky).

REFERENCES

Culham, R. (2003). *Six + 1 traits of writing*. New York, NY: Scholastic Professional Books.

Darling-Hammond, L. (1994). Performance-based assessment and educational equity. *Harvard Educational Review, 64*(1), 5–30.

DiPardo, A., Storms, B. A., & Selland, M. (2011). Seeing voices: Assessing writerly stance in the NWP Analytic Writing Continuum. *Assessing Writing, 16*(3), 170-188.

Hetherington, J. M. (2010). *An analysis of the Michigan Educational Assessment Program rubric and the National Writing Project Analytical Writing Continuum* (unpublished master's thesis). Northern Michigan University, Marquette.

Huot, B. (2002). *(Re)articulating writing assessment for teaching and learning*. Logan, UT: Utah State University Press.

Kaminski, R., & Hunt-Barron. S. (2010). *Evaluating project WRITE: The teacher and student outcomes of a professional development program focusing on core components of writing workshop and the traits of writing*. Berkeley, CA: National Writing Project.

LeMahieu, P. G., & Friedrich, L. (2007). Looking at student work to develop evaluative frameworks: Why . . . and as important, how? In A. Davies & K. Busick (Eds.), *Classroom assessment: What's working in high schools, Book 1* (pp. 103–127). Courtenay, BC, Canada: Connections Publishing.

NWP Research and Evaluation Unit. (2010, July). *Writing project professional development continues to yield gains in student writing achievement* (Research Brief No. 2). http://www.nwp.org/cs/public/print/resource/3208

Pringle, L. P. (2000). *Bats!: Strange and wonderful.* Honesdale, PA: Boyds Mills Press.

Singer, N. R., & LeMahieu, P. G. (2012). The effect of scoring order on the independence of holistic and analytic scores. *Journal of Writing Assessment*. http://journalofwritingassessment.org/contact.php

Swain, S. S., Graves, R. L., & Morse, D. T. (2010). Prominent feature analysis: What it means for the classroom. *English Journal, 99*(4), 84–89.

Swain, S. S., LeMahieu, P., Sperling, M., Murphy, S., Fessehaie, S., & Smith, M. A. (2010, May). *Writing assessment and its impact on scorers.* Paper presented at the annual meeting of the American Educational Research Association, Denver, CO.

White, E. M. (1994). *Teaching and assessing writing* (2nd ed.). San Francisco, CA: Jossey-Bass.

White, E. M. (2007). *Assigning, responding, evaluating: A writing teacher's guide* (4th ed.). Boston, MA: Bedford/St. Martin's.

3

WRITING ASSESSMENT IN THE CONTEXT OF THE NATIONAL ASSESSMENT OF EDUCATIONAL PROGRESS

Hilary Persky
Educational Testing Service

As we know, many debate (and have been debating for many years) the merits of the kinds of direct writing assessment currently used in the National Assessment of Educational Progress (NAEP) and other large-scale assessments. Some criticisms (featured in this volume) suggest that typical on-demand, timed tasks elicit generic and shallow responses that are not so much good indicators of students' abilities to write as to follow directions or, if students are able, to write quickly. Further, like the old joke about how the food is terrible and there is so little of it, giving students only one or two such tasks (as in NAEP) cannot tell us much about their writing ability.[1] These criticisms are directed even at tasks that are arguably good models of on-demand writing assessment: tasks that are clear, brief but directed, vetted by leading experts, and that yield varied, but comparable, student responses.

Perhaps we are ready to usher in the next generation of large-scale writing assessment (which does not seem to be going away). This is not a new moment. In the past, scholars such as Roberta Camp (1990) encouraged exploration of other assessment methods such as portfolios, and NAEP did in fact experiment with a portfolio approach.[2] Other approaches discussed in this volume, such as those described by Paul Deane in his chapter about cognitively based assessment, could involve offering students (at the time of the assessment) opportunities for processing and synthesizing materials before writing. Materials could include texts, images, and multimedia sources, acknowledging the intimate relationship among writing, reading, and listening, and giving students something to think about for their writing. As Arthur Applebee (2011) has remarked about a limit of the current NAEP writing measure, "[T]he problem is the longstanding one of having to write from a general, common knowledge base, rather than being asked to make sense of new material. From my perspective, we need to get away from our concern with 'confounding' writing with reading, and recognize that the best writing tasks (most engaging, most revealing) have to give students something worth writing about." Writing experts responsible for reviewing NAEP tasks are expressing great interest in more contextualized tasks. However, it will take exploration and thought to be sure such tasks can be utilized to produce the kinds of comparable results required for NAEP's purpose and achievable within the program's constraints. This purpose (which has not changed much since its inception) is to give a snapshot of student achievement in various subjects that can be compared with achievement in previous years (Olkin & Jones, 2004). Assessment results are not reported by individual student; rather, results are reported by subgroups of students (e.g., male and female).

Given NAEP's purpose, it can be argued that measuring the ability to develop, organize, and manipulate text in response to a specific timed task is an adequate, if not complete, measure for a "snapshot." As long as the assessment product is understood to be an aspect of writing ability, and not a complete portrait, and as long as analysis methods can be used to reduce the effects of potentially problematic tasks or the effects of one task's content on a given student, then the assessment has fulfilled its purpose.

Having said this, NAEP has been a critical part of the conversation about writing teaching and assessment practice in our nation's schools, and the program itself was invented to inform public educational policy. The developers of the NAEP writing assessment thus have a profound obligation to be sure the measure reflects developing understandings of what writing is and how best to assess students' writing skill in a large-scale context. And, in fact, NAEP's formulators do try and rethink the nature of the assessment in light of what experts and practitioners value about writing. In this chapter I present a quick tour through what I see as a few critical moments when NAEP's creators have sought to shape the assessment (both tasks and scoring) in light of concerns about how students' writing should best be measured, while working within the constraints of the assessment's purpose and timed, on-demand constraints. To ensure its continued value to its stakeholders, I conclude by suggesting that we may again be due for a change in the program's approach to measuring writing skill.

WHAT IS NAEP?

NAEP is the nation's only ongoing national (and now state and district-based) assessment of what students at grades 4, 8, and 12 know and can do in a range of subject areas. As stated above, NAEP has never been intended to measure what individual students can do or to serve as a gate-keeping device; rather, the assessment is administered to representative samples of students, results are analyzed along with responses to survey questions, and reports are produced detailing performance in terms of subgroups of students. Survey questions are used to collect data about demographics, school experiences and resources, and attitudes towards academic subjects. Responses to survey questions are collected from the students taking the assessment, their teachers, and school administrators. (Although this chapter is not focused on these NAEP background questionnaires, it is important to note that given NAEP's mandate to report trends over time, and given the representativeness of its student samples, responses to these survey questions are critical sources of information for the field. The writing background questionnaires have helped to track the changing nature of writing pedagogy in our nation's classrooms over many years.)[3]

NAEP is congressionally mandated and is funded by the U.S. Department of Education. An independent oversight group, the National Assessment Governing Board sets policy for NAEP, determining what subjects will be assessed and working with many hundreds of subject experts to develop frameworks for assessment content. These frameworks are not curricula; rather, they are agreed-upon specifications for what the assembled experts think students should know and be able to do (although recent frameworks have drawn on voluntary national standards as they have become available). Once frameworks are complete, they are handed off to test developers for assessment creation.[4] Assessment tasks (and scoring criteria), in their various iterations from initial development to administration, are reviewed by both subject and measurement experts to be sure they meet framework expectations. To ensure proper adherence to the frameworks, committees of subject experts must include some of those involved in the development of the documents. With every administration of an assessment, some exercises and tasks are released to be included in public domain reports sharing NAEP results. Other exercises and tasks are retained to allow comparisons to be made across years in students' performance, called "trend." Assessment frameworks are revisited at least every decade to evaluate whether they are still reflective of best practices in a given field.

PROGRAM CONSTRAINTS

NAEP's mandate is to report to the nation, states, and some districts, subgroup assessment results for students, as well as relationships between performance and responses to demographic and subject survey questions. This mandate has not changed. Given the large-scale nature of NAEP, its on-demand and voluntary nature (Jones & Olkin, 2004), and its purpose as a measure of group achievement, NAEP must limit the time it spends in any given school. Thus, students are typically tested for only about an hour, normally taking two 25-minute groups of exercises and responding to survey questions.

In some NAEP assessments, the desire for more in-depth measurement of framework content (e.g., the desire to measure students' visual arts skills, or their abilities to perform hands-on science experiments) has necessitated more complex administrations during which some students may be tested for up to 2 hours. However, this is frowned upon and generally perceived as creating unacceptable school burden, especially given the sheer number of tests schools are now expected to administer to their students annually. Time is then the single biggest limit on the kinds of writing tasks NAEP can administer, and hence the time students have for engaging in an integrative writing process is limited. With the added fact that ideally students will take as many tasks as possible to make assessment results at least somewhat generalizable, it is preferable that in a direct writing assessment students take (at least) two tasks, thus further limiting the time available for any one task.

Perhaps the second greatest constraint, given the ever-growing concern about test accessibility issues, English Language Learners, and the achievement gap, is what students can be asked to do in responding to tasks. As Arthur Applebee (2006) put it in a paper commissioned by the Governing Board in preparation for the development of the latest NAEP writing framework, "When reading and language difficulties of English language learners and low achieving students are taken into account, the push in item development is toward simple and 'clean' writing prompts with a low vocabulary load" (p. 10).

Given NAEP's move onto the computer, the program now must also cope with a third constraint, the implications of differential access to technology. Usability studies must always be conducted to determine how well students can manage computer-based assessment interfaces, and a great deal of thought goes into what kinds of tools students can manage and what kinds of accessibility measures must be included in assessments. The 2010 NAEP grades 8 and 12 writing pilot seemed to indicate that students could manage, overall, composing on computer. However, future innovations will pose new challenges.

EVOLUTION OF NAEP TASKS AND SCORING CRITERIA

Beginnings (1969 to 1970)

In the first NAEP writing assessment in 1969, multiple choice, short answer, and essay-length writing tasks were administered to students at ages 9, 11, and 17. In an article published in *The English Journal* in 1973, John C. Maxwell wrote, "Actually despite its shortcomings, the first National Assessment of Writing told us quite a bit more about writing performance than anything else of any scale previously attempted in education. Nationally standardized tests of the ordinary variety are scandalously inadequate in that they try to measure something by not measuring it" (p. 1254). Qualified as it is, Maxwell's statement makes clear the central achievement of the first NAEP writing assessment: using a direct measure of writing. We are by now familiar with the dangers of relying solely on indirect measures: "... if usage tests evaluate 'writing,' teachers will do better to concentrate on usage exercises than on having students write essays (Applebee, 1981, p. 461).

The early objectives shown below indicate that assessment tasks were meant to invite students to compose for a variety of real-life and social purposes.

1. Write to communicate adequately in a social situation (letters, directions, formal notes, addressing envelopes, invitations);
2. Write to communicate adequately in a business or vocational situation (information and application forms, mail order letters, business invitations, formal letters);
3. Write to communicate adequately in a scholastic situation (notes and announcements; narrative, descriptive, and expository essays);
4. Appreciate the value of writing (recognize the value of writing; write as a normal course of behavior; receive satisfaction from writing).

Based on the set of objectives, tasks were developed to be as inviting and accessible as possible to a NAEP student sample: that is, not just self-selected students or students somehow selected for knowledge or ability, but effectively, everyone at ages 9, 13, and 17. Early tasks were meant to get students to write as quickly as possible and in as engaged a way as possible. Here is an example of one of the first NAEP extended writing tasks for 13 year olds:

Historical Event

> If you could make an event in American history happen again so that you could play a part in it, which one would you choose? Write a composition in which you describe the event and explain why you chose that particular event and what part you would like to play in it.

In 1969, there were no readily available models for assessment tasks. As Mellon (1975) noted in his explanatory work about the first writing assessment, there was little agreement at the time on what ought to be taught for writing and how to measure it. These first tasks reflected this lack of agreement. As Maxwell (1973) and many others observed, some tasks, in the absence of clear rhetorical purpose, context, and audience, did not offer students necessary guidance for their writing, nor did they encourage students to plan or revise their writing.[5] The tasks were what they appeared to be: a first attempt to use direct measures of writing in a timed, large-scale assessment for a nationally representative student sample.

Students' responses to the essay tasks were scored two ways: (a) a single overall holistic score was assigned to each response by raters based on an overall impression of the student's writing, and (b) detailed counts were made of the numbers and kinds of mechanical and grammatical errors in standard written English in students' writing. For holistic scoring, groups of experts reviewed multiple samples of students' work over several days until consensus had been reached as to how papers compared with one another, and then each response was scored by two people working independently.[6] Thus, both from a task and scoring point of view, from the start NAEP's creators demonstrated a commitment to seeing writing as an integrative activity, not simply one defined by discrete qualities such as knowledge of complex sentences.

Changes in the Second (1973-1974) National Assessment of Writing

Reactions from the field helped to push the NAEP writing assessment program's measurement goals further in important ways. I deal with each criticism and change separately.

Primary Trait Tasks and Scoring. A major critique of the first writing assessment focused on the lack in some tasks of a clear purpose. Did students know why they were writing, or for whom? Some suggested that the "diffuse" nature of student responses to tasks lacking clear rhetorical goals yielded student responses that were very variable and thus hard to compare (Mellon, 1975). The program responded by developing a form of assessment called "primary trait,"[7] featuring tasks with very clear purposes and accompanying criteria to evaluate how well students wrote to those purposes.

Applebee (2000) explains:

> The major approach to assessment of mastery of diverse purposes is primary trait scoring, developed by Richard Lloyd-Jones and Carl Klaus for NAEP. Primary trait assessment in its initial formulations focused on the specific approach that a writer might take to be successful on a specific writing task; every task required its own unique scoring guide. ... To insure that raters maintained this focus, scoring guidelines usually instructed raters to ignore errors in conventions of written language, and to focus on overall rhetorical effectiveness. (Applebee, 2000, p. 96)

An example of a NAEP primary trait task for 13 year olds shows the ways in which task writers tried to specify rhetorical situation (U. S Department of Education, 1977):

> Writing a Thank You Note
>
> Think of something that you would like to have very much. Pretend that you are Pat Brown and someone you know very well has just given it to you.
>
> Write the gift you would like to have in this box
>
> Tell who gave it to you in this box.
>
> Write a letter to that person saying thank you and telling why you like the gift. Space is provided on the next two pages.

One of the potential problems with some of the new tasks and primary trait scoring is suggested by the text below from the report presenting assessment results:

> To take a simple example, a thank you note for a gift requires certain internal conventions, such as saying thank you, showing appreciation and naming the gift. Notes that include these things are appropriate; those that do not are inappropriate, no matter how well written. Respondents who understand the nature of writing a thank you note will be able to respond appropriately to the task. (U. S Department of Education, 1977)

Ideas of thank you notes, or other forms and their suitable content, change over time. Further, students' knowledge of and relationships to such forms and conventions are socially driven and highly variable. The task itself is arguably too narrow and trivial to inspire real development, and it does not help that the student is asked to take on someone else's identity and to be grateful. In light of these observations, the statement "no matter how well written" is problematic; for example, it is not clear why an element such as naming the gift should be so paramount.

It may be that in its attempt to be responsive to criticism, the program went in some cases too far in its use of very specific tasks and scoring. The desire to be purposeful, socially relevant, and very clear seems to have led here and there to overly constraining tasks and criteria.

Requiring Student to Revise. Driven very much by the explosion of research about and interest in the process of writing (versus simply its product), the second assessment introduced tasks requiring students to write and then revise their work. These are the assessment task directions given to 9 and 13 year olds requiring them to revise a report they had written about the Moon (the task itself asked students to write a brief report based on their own knowledge and also a selection of information given to them about the Moon):[8]

> Now that you have finished writing, take time to read over your report and think about these questions:
> 1. Have you organized your report clearly?
> 2. Will your classmate understand it?
> 3. Have you said it in the best way you know how?
>
> Make any changes you think will make your report better. You may even change your entire report if you think it is necessary. If you want to make any changes you may cross out words on the report you have already written or redo your report on the lines below. Use the blue pen you have been given.

The report based on the tasks indicated that although most students did revise, they did so largely to make informational, mechanical, and stylistic changes. Further, changes made did not usually address flaws in organization or the nature of the information featured in the writing. A report detailing the results of the revision tasks stated: "So a working definition of revision for many students seems to be substituting more appropriate words or phrases for preliminary attempts in the first draft, adding relevant and deleting irrelevant information, and attending to capitalization, punctuation and other mechanical conventions" (p. 34).[9]

The unimpressive student performance did its part in focusing pedagogical attention on the importance of teaching writing as an iterative process. As Maxwell (1973) pointed out in reaction to the low levels of student performance in response to the NAEP revising tasks, "If students do not know how to revise ... can we say that writing is being taught in the schools?" (p. 1257).

Addition of "Expressive" Tasks. In response to criticism about a lack of expressive tasks aimed not at fulfilling some social purpose but that "deals with feelings and responses as well as discursive thought" (Pelz, 1982, p. 1), the second NAEP writing assessment also added tasks such as one requiring students to listen to a short piece of music and then write about their reactions to the piece (U.S. Department of Education, 1976).

Summary of Changes in the Second (1973-1974) National Assessment of Writing. There were problems with NAEP's new attempts in its second writing assessment. For example, students only had 15 minutes to write the Moon report and 13 minutes to try and revise it, and some tasks displayed features we might try to avoid today in the program (e.g., listing questions, or requiring that students take on identities not necessarily meaningful to them). Still, the changes briefly summarized in this section should at least indicate the seriousness with which NAEP took its critics and developing ideas about writing. The assessment also showed a commitment to features still important in today's assessment: namely, the value assigned to having students do real-world tasks, the acknowledgment of the social and personal nature of writing, the emphasis placed on writing for a range of task types, and the emphasis placed on valuing writing as a personal pursuit.

1992 Innovations

Although the program no longer as of 1984 attempted to measure students' revising of their responses,[10] the new 1992 assessment design acknowledged the importance of the writing process in a variety of ways. Among them was the addition of a special planning page to all test booklets (in the 1984 assessment, a subset of tasks included planning space), clearly labeled as such, and assessment directions encouraged students to plan and revise their writing. Further, assessment time for responding to any given task was increased from 15 to 25 minutes (a time still in keeping with what is regarded as acceptable school burden), and the program experimented by incorporating 50-minute writing tasks. All of these were in addition to survey or background questionnaires for students taking the assessment, their teachers, and school administrators. Questions were pertinent to the practices of process writing, as well as other issues of interest.

New tasks were also developed to measure three broad purposes for writing: narrative, informative, and persuasive, introduced in the 1984 assessment objectives. (Although previous NAEP writing assessments certainly emphasized purpose for writing, 1984 was the first time purpose was defined in terms of three major categories.) The emphasis on writing purpose conveyed through these three modes to some degree was a natural outcome of the influence of scholars like James Britton (Britton, Burgess, Martin, McLeod, & Rosen, 1975), and thus reflected an increasingly common understanding among teachers and researchers about what we do when we write and the need to provide appropriate expectations for students. These new tasks also had the advantage of giving test developers a structure for creating varied tasks—the program from its inception had stressed the value of requiring students to write in multiple genres and for different situations—while still seeing to it that tasks elicited a clear, overall purpose for writing.[11] By this time, over 35 states were using direct measures of writing in their assessments, so test developers were also able to draw on wider experience in direct writing assessment. Test developers were also able to draw on explorations of best assessment practices in published research from the composition community such as Leo Ruth's and Sandra Murphy's (1988) *Designing Writing Tasks for the Assessment of Writing*.

In 1992, along with new tasks, substantially revised guides were introduced to better match the assessment's measurement of a range of tasks within the three purposes for writing. The new 6-level guides (previous guides had four levels) were called "modified primary trait" guides. These guides, used also in a 1996 pilot assessment, were amalgamations of holistic and primary trait scoring; that is, they sought to evaluate the broad domains of development, organization, and language use while also demanding that raters make judgments about the degree to which a response addressed the rhetorical requirements of a specific task. I have selected three levels from such a guide to give a brief example of how the modified primary trait criteria were framed. Note that in each scoring guide, a specific trait is defined corresponding to the requirements of the given task. For example, the primary trait for a narrative task would be quality of narrative (clarity of description and sequence of events); for an informative task, quality of description (clarity and use of detail); and for a persuasive task, quality of argument (clarity of perspective and level of support). Additionally, each guide featured a scoring rationale summarizing the task and explaining the specific scoring criteria. Of course, all guides were supplemented with exemplar papers for training.

> 6 Extensively elaborated. In these papers, students create a well developed, detailed, and well written response to the task. They show a high degree of control over the various elements of writing. These responses may be similar to "5" responses, but they are better organized, more clearly written, and less flawed.
>
> 4 Developed. In these papers, students provide a response to the task that contains necessary elements. However, these papers may be unevenly developed.
>
> 2 Undeveloped response to task. In these papers, students begin to respond to the task, but they do so in a very abbreviated, confusing, or disjointed manner.

Assessment directions instructed students to fulfill every part of a given task, and, as the guide states (the "necessary elements" referred to in level 4), responses were evaluated based on the degree to which they fulfilled the relevant parts of the task based on its rhetorical purpose (e.g., "clarity of description"). Although the phrase "clarity of description" seems in keeping with the holistic quality of the guide, the narratives accompanying example responses in the 1992 writing report card suggest the challenge of this kind of "modified" primary trait scoring.

For example, fourth grade students were asked to write about a favorite story they had read, heard, or seen at the movies. If students failed to summarize the story (they were told to give interesting details about the story to explain to readers why it was a favorite) they could not receive the highest rating. But, did the task clearly demand a summary, and was a summary strictly necessary to produce a very strong piece of work with important details? The primary trait requirements did not always seem in keeping with overall, integrative evaluations; even if a student wrote very well and developed ideas with well-chosen details, that student's piece could not always receive an upper half score if it failed to respond to some specific aspect of a task. This made scoring challenging, given the tension between assigning an overall score for a piece and sorting out at what level to place pieces missing aspects of a primary trait.[12] In other cases, the descriptive language for the particular nature of the tasks was arguably not helpful, specifying less how to score a response than what topic a students' response would likely focus on, and thus adding needless burden for raters.[13] As Applebee (2011) observed, "The attempt to tailor a unique guide for every task produced data that in the end were not very meaningful (did not relate from one task to another), and eventually collapsed into generic guides that varied little from one another. The primary trait produced even odder score distributions, since the task could [sometimes] be accomplished without really producing a very good piece of writing." The NAEP writing assessment had evolved in the early 1990s to measuring what it still seeks to measure today: a "snapshot" of whether students can produce a "good piece of writing," understood as how well they can, in a timed, on-demand situation, develop, organize, and manipulate language for a particular purpose. In this context, the primary trait guides that had been useful in driving rhetorical clarity in tasks in the 1970s had perhaps outlived their usefulness. Given the need to incorporate a wide range of task types and topics for any given purpose for writing to produce a generalizable measure, and given the fact that, again, NAEP is not a diagnostic tool but a broad measure for large groups of students, the primary trait dimension of the new guides was more a hindrance than a help. Again Applebee (2000) is helpful: "Over the years as primary trait approaches were used more widely, they evolved into a more generic approach which recognized the similarities in approach within broad uses or purposes. The basic question addressed in scoring, however, remained, 'Did the writer successfully accomplish the purpose of this task'?" (p. 96).

Arguably, this generic approach was appropriate also because NAEP tasks did not (and still do not) incorporate substantial sources for student writing. In the absence of rich content with which to work and to which to react, it is not clear in the NAEP context what is to be gained from very specific identification of required task components in responses to relatively generic tasks.

Focused Holistic Guides

Given the shortcomings of modified primary trait scoring, the match between the broad construct being measured and scoring needed to be improved after the 1992 and 1996 assessments. Interestingly, it was not just a matter of removing a focus on primary traits, but also acknowledging a shift in approach to thinking about mastery of conventions. As stated in the NAEP 1996 report, *Trends in Writing: Fluency and Writing Conventions*, the process approach to writing "focuses on the iterative nature of writing, in which writers plan, write, and revise their ideas in several drafts before a final version is produced. It is during the revision or editing stages of this process that writers focus on correcting grammatical and mechanical errors. Grammatical and mechanical correctness is not viewed as an end in and of itself, but eliminating these errors is an important part of improving the final draft" (p. 1). The program ceased to score mechanics separately as of the 1998 assessment, instead fully addressing language as part of the overall quality of the piece.

New guides were developed for the 1998 assessment, piloted in 1997, and were in use until 2007. These were "focused holistic"[14] scoring guides that required raters to master during training features of student writing associated with development, organization, and language use for a given mode of writing and then to assign overall scores based on a combination of all of those features. There were separate guides for each of three modes of writing (narrative, informative, and persuasive) with slight variations in guide language across grades 4, 8, and 12, but, of course, no longer a need for guides for individual tasks. On the whole, these guides were easier to use and more suitable for the assessment in its state at the time than the guides used pre-1998.

Along with this shift came an embracing of the notion of prompt as springboard. That is, tasks were treated as a means to get students writing quickly to a particular purpose in an on-demand situation. When scoring using these guides, as long as students addressed the purpose/mode for writing, even responses that diverged substantially from the topic in question could receive the highest score (assuming they demonstrated developed, organized, and articulated ideas). Appropriately enough, given the requirements of these modes, students received "Off Topic" scores most often in persuasive writing because evaluating their abilities to produce an argument with the persuasive guide was not possible if a student provided an explanatory or narrative piece with no persuasive elements. Another change of interest was the introduction during this period of a brochure with tips for students taking the assessment for planning and revising their writing. The brochure removed the need to add directions about planning and revising tasks. This brochure is still in use.

The New 2011 Writing Assessment

Consistent with the program's attempts to change in light of changing circumstances in writing practice and pedagogy, NAEP's leaders have made the move to assess students' writing using the tool with which students are more likely to write: computers. The new writing framework for the 2011 assessment discusses multiple issues associated with this change. For example, the nature of appropriate word processing tools for the assessment is a fascinating topic that has generated much discussion. The framework also emphasizes purpose and audience more than the previous set of objectives, devoting lengthy discussion to their nature and importance, and requiring a clear audience for all tasks.[15] (The three purposes are now called To Explain, To Persuade, and To Convey Experience, Real or Imagined.) Additionally, the framework gives the following as one of the main assessment objectives:

> *To encourage student writers to move beyond prescriptive or formulaic approaches in their writing.* Writing tasks in this assessment will be designed to support the evaluation of students' ability to make a variety of effective choices in how they approach the development and organization of ideas and in how they craft language to support their communicative purpose. (U.S. Department of Education, 2011, p. 2)

Language in the draft holistic scoring guides in the framework offers the following expectation for development of ideas in student responses:

> The response provides a thoughtful and insightful explanation of the subject by fully examining the topic as a whole, by identifying and fully discussing significant parts of the subject, and/or by evaluating and fully discussing the importance of the parts. (U.S. Department of Education, 2011, p. 69)

Although the draft guides in the framework are similar to the previous guides in their holistic nature and emphasis on development, organization, and language use, they do focus more on how well students cope with ideas, not just in terms of clarity and level of detail, but also in terms of level of insight and approach. Further, the guides explicitly state that the three broad domains of writing be assessed in terms of how well a specific purpose and audience are addressed; this includes the interesting addition in the language domain of voice and tone.

These shifts are from one point of view welcome; they push us to be sure we are measuring what we ought to be measuring, and compel us to beware of overvaluing the well-formed but vapid and generic student response. Although I suggested in the previous section that NAEP-style tasks are best scored with "focused holistic guides," it is worth asking if those guides at times allowed us to accept responses (especially for the informative and narrative modes) that strayed too far from a given task, and if they allowed us to place too much weight on sophisticated language use and clear organization, and not enough on quality and development of ideas. The new guides, without detailing task-specific approaches as did the 1992 modified primary trait guides, enable us to be more demanding about how well responses address purpose (and, where relevant, audience).

But there may also be a problem with the new guides: There is a tension between the ambitions of the framework and the assessment tasks (which—even based on framework guidelines—do not look so very different from those from the previous assessment). To put it rather baldly, what are students supposed to think *about* to demonstrate insight and generate nonformulaic responses? The framework seems to represent a yearning for something that the commonly used generic "genre" of large-scale writing assessment cannot readily supply, even if it is useful (as stated above) for a NAEP-style "snapshot" of broad writing skills.

CONCLUSION

I have tried in this chapter to demonstrate, however briefly, that (in the words of Norbert Elliot [2011]), "NAEP has always sought to ensure that the systematic need for assessment does not produce a systematic view of writing." The tension identified above could be a productive one, suggesting possible future innovations for NAEP and for direct writing assessment in general. Given NAEP's importance as a model for pedagogy and policy, it may be time to explore for NAEP tasks that (perhaps like the cognitively based assessment tasks discussed in this volume) give students opportunities to engage more in an iterative writing process and think more as part of their writing. We have an opportunity to use the affordances of the computer to present students with tasks that draw from a variety of content areas and offer a range of materials—text-based, multimedia—to engage them in meaningful writing tasks. (Either that, or we may need to reduce expectations and make our peace with the assessment we have.) How to do this and stay within NAEP's constraints as a large-scale measure is our ongoing challenge.[16]

ENDNOTES

1. NAEP may be less problematic in this regard because sampling and analysis procedures are used such that it is as if every student took all of about 20 tasks at a given grade. Tasks are also varied in purpose, rhetorical situation, and nature of stimuli.
2. NAEP did special portfolio studies in 1990 and 1992. The report based on the 1990 study, *Exploring New Methods of Collecting Students School-based Writing*, presented several challenges associated with doing portfolio assessment for NAEP. Among the challenges were comparability across student materials, student authorship, and the achievable degree of coverage of writing types. More critically, it was not clear how meaningfully to incorporate what is essentially a measure of individual progress into a highly standardized assessment meant to compare large groups of students. The report based on the 1992 study, *Windows Into the Classroom: The NAEP 1992 Writing Portfolio Study*, suggested the possibility of in the future combining a standard NAEP assessment with a portfolio assessment, given the advantages of each and their complementary natures. However, this report also noted the problems posed for portfolio studies by variation in quality of classroom activities. Finally, in 1998, interviews were conducted with a selected sample of grade 4 and grade 8 teachers whose students participated in the writing assessment, and some of the students' selected classroom writing was also evaluated. The study was featured in a report called *Writing in the Nation's Classrooms*. The study established a positive correlation between NAEP scores and student classroom work, and its writers suggested that the correlation could be used to support the validity of the NAEP writing measure.
3. See, for example, Applebee and Langer's (2009) article. For information about trends in student writing performance as described by NAEP, the project website maintains an extensive list of URLs for reports going back to 1988. The NAEP website offers a wealth of information about NAEP, its purpose, and details of the program.
4. Educational Testing Service in Princeton, NJ, holds the current contract for test development, test design, data analysis, and reporting. Other companies are contracted with the federal government for sampling and administration, scoring and printing, and additional responsibilities.
5. Of course, any task developer still struggles with precisely the same issues today.
6. Holistic scoring is nicely defined by Wolcott (1988): In holistic scoring ". . . an essay is not evaluated in terms of its specific features, e.g., its development, creativity, sentence structure, or mechanics; neither are ratings derived by mentally adding together scores for the individual features. Instead a paper is scored in terms of the overall impression—the synergistic effect—that is created by the elements working together within the piece" (p. 71).
7. Lloyd-Jones (1977) describes primary trait scoring in contrast to holistic scoring. "The methods perfected by ETS assume that excellence in one sample of one mode of writing predicts excellence in other modes—that is, good writing

is good writing. . . . In contrast, the Primary Trait System developed under the auspices of NAEP assumes that the writer of a good technical report may not be able to produce an excellent persuasive letter to a city council. . . . The goal of Primary Trait Scoring is to define precisely what segment of discourse will be evaluated ... and to train readers to render holistic judgements accordingly" (p. 37). Further, moving to primary trait scoring for NAEP meant moving away from normative-based scoring (essentially, comparing responses to one another to determine what is better and worse performance) to criterion-based, in which responses are evaluated in light of specific requirements.

8. *Write/Rewrite: An Assessment of Revision Skills; Selected Results from the Second National Assessment of Writing*. Education Commission of the States, Denver, CO. National Assessment of Educational Progress. National Center for Education Statistics (DHEW/OE) Washington, DC, 05-W-04, Jul 77, OEC-0-74-0506, p. 6.
9. National Assessment of Educational Progress. (1976). *Write/Rewrite: An Assessment of Revision Skills: Selected Results from the Second National Assessment of Writing* (Report 05-W-02). Education Commission of the States, Denver, CO: National Center for Education Statistics. This early report is evidence of NAEP's early attention to revision as integral to the writing process.
10. The shallow revisions students made to their work in the assessment context suggested that continuing to attempt to measure revision in our context was perhaps not the best use of assessment time and effort. As Applebee (2000) has noted: "Writers are most likely to make extensive use of prewriting or revision strategies with tasks that are particularly new and difficult. On-demand assessments, on the other hand, are likely to present relatively contained and familiar tasks for which little overt use of compositing strategies will be needed" (p. 10).
11. Based on conventions and cues increasingly associated with assessment tasks at a given purpose, when a subset of tasks were released for sharing with the public in NAEP reports, new tasks could be developed with enough in common with older tasks to allow responses to the new tasks to be summarized together with responses to the older tasks. This allowed comparisons to be made in performance across assessment years, helping to fulfill NAEP's mandate to report trends in achievement over time. (In fact, 1984 marked the beginning of a new trend, or reporting of student writing achievement over time that concluded in 1992.)
12. I can remember puzzling over responses which had to be relegated to a level 3 in a 6-level guide despite overall high performance because they failed to address what struck me at the time as a fairy trivial demand.
13. Here, for example, is language from a modified primary trait guide indicating the highest level of performance for an explanatory task describing an invention: "In these responses, students provide a cohesive, well-written description of an invention. The description is usually, but not always, accompanied by a clear discussion of the usefulness of, purpose of, or the perceived necessity for the invention." The language pushes the rater to be open to multiple approaches to the task, and it is this very (appropriate) openness to multiple approaches that would be better served by language referring to "well-chosen details" or the like, rather than dictating attempts to capture the specific nature of those kinds of details.

14. As far as I am aware, the term "focused holistic" was used by NAEP to describe guides that relied on an overall evaluated based on specific attributes of writing associated with purpose for writing, as well as criteria for development, organization, and language use; that is, responses were evaluated (and are evaluated) not just in relation to one another, but against criteria expressed in the guides.
15. After discussion with a committee of experts, including framework writers, it was agreed not to require audience for To Convey Experience tasks, given their literary nature.
16. Although the timing of NAEP writing tasks is partly an artifact of the need to reduce school burden, the framework writers refer to NAEP's commitment to timed on-demand writing as an important skill: "The 2011 NAEP Writing assessment reflects writing situations common to both academic and workplace settings, in which writers are often expected to respond to on-demand writing tasks" (U.S. Department of Education, 2011, p. 3). Although we do write all the time in on-demand situations, I enjoyed Les Perelman's hilarious comment indicating that few of us in our professional lives are commanded to write in 25 minutes about whether "failure is necessary for success." (See Chapter 24.)

REFERENCES

Applebee, A. N (1981). Looking at writing. *Educational Leadership, 38*(6), 458-462.

Applebee, A. N. (2000). Alternative models of writing development. In R. Indrisano & J. R. Squire (Eds.), *Writing: Research/theory/practice* (pp. 90-111). Newark, DE: International Reading Association.

Applebee, A. (2006). *NAEP 2011 writing assessment: Issues in developing a framework and specifications.* Washington, DC: National Assessment Governing Board.

Applebee, A. (2011). [E-mail to H. Persky]. Princeton, NJ: Educational Testing Service.

Applebee, A., & Langer, J. (2009). What is happening in the teaching of writing? *English Journal, 98*(5), 18-28.

Britton, J. N., Burgess, T., Martin, N., McLeod, A., & Rosen, H. (1975). *The development of writing abilities.* London, UK: MacMillan Education Foundation.

Camp, R. (1990). Thinking together about portfolios. *Quarterly of the National Writing Project and the Center for the Study of Writing and Literacy, 12*(2), 8-14, 27.

Elliot, N. (2011). [E-mail to H. Persky]. Princeton, NJ: Educational Testing Service.

Jones, L.V. & Olkin, I. (Eds.). (2004). *The nation's report card: Evolution and perspectives.* Bloomington, IN: Phi Delta Kappa Educational Foundation.

Lloyd-Jones, R. (1977). Primary trait scoring. In C. R. Cooper & Odell, L. (Eds.), *Evaluating writing: Describing, measuring, judging* (pp. 33-66). Urbana, IL: National Council of Teachers of English.

Maxwell, J. C. (1973). National assessment of writing: Useless and uninteresting? *English Journal, 62*(9), 1254-1257.

Mellon, J. C. (1975). *National assessment and the teaching of English*. Urbana, IL: National Council of Teachers of English.

Pelz, K. (1982). James Britton and the pedagogy of advanced composition. *Journal of Advanced Composition, 3*(1/2), 1-9.

Ruth, L., & Murphy, S. (1988). *Designing writing tasks for the assessment of writing*. Norwood, NJ: Ablex.

U. S. Department of Education. (1976). *Expressive writing: Selected results from the second national assessment of writing*. Education Commission of the States, Denver, CO: National Assessment of Educational Progress.

U. S. Department of Education. (1997). *Explanatory and persuasive letter writing: Selected results from the second national assessment of writing*. Educational Commission of the States, Denver, CO: National Assessment of Educational Progress

U. S. Department of Education. (1992). *Writing framework for the 1992 National Assessment of Educational Progress*. Washington, DC: National Assessment Governing Board.

U. S. Department of Education. (2011). *Writing framework for the 2011 National Assessment of Educational Progress*. Washington, DC: National Assessment Governing Board.

Wolcott, W., with Legg, S. (1988). *An overview of writing assessment: Theory, research, and practice*. Urbana, IL: National Council of Teachers of English.

4

RETHINKING K-12 WRITING ASSESSMENT

Paul Deane
Educational Testing Service

Writing assessment and writing instruction have been heavily influenced both by the National Writing Project, with its emphasis on best practices in writing instruction, and by the National Assessment of Educational Progress, with its systematic sampling of writing genres across grade levels. The work reported in this chapter reflects many of the same concerns, but combines them with the major issues raised by the "Cognitively Based Assessments of, for, and as Learning" (CBAL) initiative, an ongoing research project at ETS intended to develop a new form of kindergarten through Grade 12 (K–12) assessment.[1] The CBAL approach seeks to integrate assessment with learning in a fundamental way, building upon modern cognitive understandings and seeking a close integration between summative assessment (assessment of learning) and formative assessment (assessment for learning). One of the key goals is to develop tests that are themselves models of what students are to learn, so that the test-taking experience is itself instructive (assessment as learning). A key part of that effort is the development of what we term a *competency model*—a detailed map of the skills that should be assessed, articulated in sufficient depth to connect assessment with instruction and to ground both in cognitive, developmental theory.

The work we report here reflects our efforts to develop a competency model that reflects modern understandings of writing. The resulting model emphasizes connections: between reading and writing, between writing and critical thinking, between writing and its social context, and between writing pedagogy and writing assessment. Writing cannot be treated as a monolithic, isolated skill, because it builds on a variety of prerequisite literacy skills and presupposes that the writer can handle a variety of rhetorical, conceptual, and linguistic tasks.[2]

These are well-known themes. Shanahan (2006) highlights how reading, writing, and oral language share a wide range of skills. Applebee (1984) highlights older literatures that relate writing to the development of critical thinking. Hillocks (1987, 2003) emphasizes that students need above all to learn how to think about the subject matter of their writing. An extensive literature emphasizes that writing is essentially social, one aspect of literacy as a cultural practice (Hull & Schultz, 2001), that evolves with society, influenced both by institutional structures and changes in technology (Bazerman & Rogers, 2008). Learning to write is a form of socialization, specifically, socialization into a literate community (Barab & Duffy, 1998). Learning to write happens most naturally in a context where writing is a meaningful and effective social tool (Alverman, 2002; Graham & Perin, 2007; Langer, 2001).

In our society, assessment is a social practice in its own right, part of the social matrix that defines our educational institutions, and one with a powerful impact on instruction. Instruction is often heavily influenced by test content and sometimes even by small details of format and presentation. As Frederiksen (1984) points out, this implicit connection between instruction and assessment can have undesirable consequences:

> The "real test bias" in my title has to do with the influence of tests on teaching and learning. Efficient tests tend to drive out less efficient tests, leaving many important abilities untested—and untaught. An important task for educators and psychologists is to develop instruments that will better reflect the whole domain of educational goals and to find ways to use them in improving the educational process. (p. 193)

This issue has been a major impetus in the development of performance-based assessments in writing. As Yancey (1999) states, indirect multiple-choice tests of writing have gradually been deemphasized in favor of direct writing assessments and portfolio assessments. Ed White's *Teaching and Assessing Writing* (1985) was a key contributor to that trend, and White has continued to develop new methods for direct writing assessment, such as the use of reflective writing to connect portfolio contents to curricular goals (White, 2005). Yet there is clearly room for improvement, particularly if we take into account the broad array of connections that link writing with other literacy skills.

Norman Frederiksen (1984) also observed:

> Over the past 25 years or so, cognitive psychologists have been investigating the mental processes that are involved in such tasks as reading, writing, solving puzzles, playing chess, and solving mathematical problems. The result is a theory of information processing that has important implications for teaching. . . . Some of the cognitive processes that have been identified have to do with the development of internal representations of problems, the organization of information in long-term memory for efficient retrieval, the acquisition of pattern cognition and automatic-processing skills, use of strategic and heuristic procedures in problem solving, and how to compensate for the limited capacity of working memory. Such skills are not explicitly taught in schools today, but we are at a point where cognitive psychology can make substantial contributions to the improvement of instruction in such areas. (p. 200)

Frederiksen was one of the first psychometricians to advocate situational tests (i.e., assessments that simulate the conditions under which skills are applied) and speculated:

> Perhaps an adventuresome consortium of schools, cognitive scientists, and testing agencies could carry out demonstration projects to test the feasibility of systematically using tests to influence the behaviors of teachers and learners and to provide the large amount of practice needed to make the skills automatic. (p. 201)

In the past 25 years, the cognitive sciences have progressed greatly, and we understand much more about instruction, pedagogy, and assessment. But Frederiksen's vision has yet to be realized, perhaps because its attainment requires both a sustained effort and an extraordinary degree of interdisciplinary coordination.

The CBAL initiative at ETS is an attempt to produce the kind of model that Frederiksen envisioned. Bennett and Gitomer (2009) sketch out what is involved: coordinated development of summative assessments, classroom assessments, and professional support materials, and an approach to testing in which summative assessments are spread out and administered periodically, rather than being isolated at the end of the school year. This approach has already had significant influence; it is reflected in the National Academy of Education's 2009 white paper on standards, assessments, and accountability (Baker et al., 2009), and is congruent with elements of the Race to the Top assessment program recently instituted by the Federal Government.

There is not space to explore the CBAL model in full, so we focus on the competency model that we have developed to unify reading and writing, enabling us to view writing skill in terms of *activity theory* (Engestrom,

Miettinen, & Punamaki, 1999), which treats interactions among people in a social environment as the fundamental unit of analysis, while taking full advantage of cognitive research. We start by considering writing as a construct, viewed both socially and cognitively in terms of our competency model. We then briefly sketch the approach we have been developing to writing assessment based upon this model.

THE COMPETENCY MODEL

If we examine cognitive models of writing, we can extract certain common themes (Bereiter & Scardamalia, 1987; Hayes, 1996; Hayes & Flower, 1980). In particular, cognitive models of writing presuppose that writing includes:

- *expressive* skills that support fluent text production;
- *receptive* skills that enable self monitoring and revision; and
- *reflective* skills that support strategic planning and evaluation.

Classical models of writing (Bereiter & Scardamalia, 1987; Flower, 1994; Hayes, 1996; Hayes & Flower, 1980) also distinguish various forms of cognitive representation:

- *Social and rhetorical elements* (representations of people, society, social interaction, and communication);
- *Conceptual elements* (representations of knowledge and reasoning);
- *Textual elements* (representations of document structure);
- *Verbal elements* (linguistic representations of sentences and the propositions they encode); and
- *Lexical/orthographic elements* (representations of how verbal units are instantiated in specific media such as written text).

These elements are not necessarily presented and organized as listed above , but each is present, and if we take this skeleton as the basis for our analysis, it is enlightening, because it immediately foregrounds commonalties among reading, writing, and thinking skills. Figure 4.1 presents a visualization of writing skills that instantiates this conception. We could interpret this figure as a list of cognitive skills; however, we intend a richer interpretation, as an array of activity types commonly engaged in by literate individuals. Note that Figure 4.1 uses a single action verb (inquire, structure, phrase, etc.) to name each activity type and thus to indicate a category of cognitive strategies and skills. We can briefly define the labels in Figure 4.1 as follows:

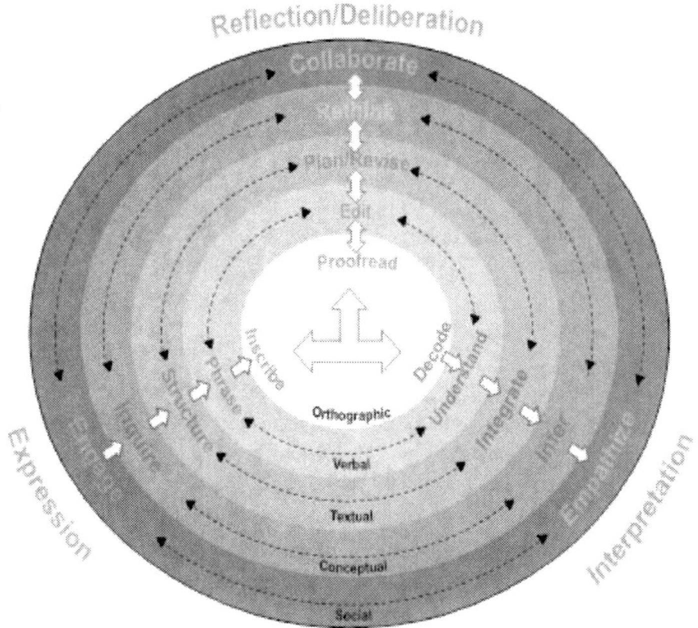

Figure 4.1. The CBAL Competency Model: Modes of Thought, Modes of Representation in Literacy Processes.

Social Skills

- *Empathize*—The ability to interpret documents or other forms of communication in a rich, socially perceptive fashion that takes into account the motivations, perspectives, and attitudes of author, intended audience, and individuals referenced in the text. This involves forms of inference based upon social skills and the ability to model human interaction.
- *Engage*—The ability to communicate with an audience in a disciplined and effective way, focusing on achieving a particular purpose, and maintaining a voice and tone appropriate to that purpose.
- *Collaborate*—The ability to think reflectively while working collaboratively in the full range of social practices common to highly literate communities (such as critical interpretation of text, presentation of research results, and reasoned argumentation) with full sensitivity to the social, cognitive, and emotional

transactions that such social practices may entail, including choice of register and genre to suit the social situation and rhetorical purpose, choice of stance, and sensitivity to multiple perspectives.

Conceptual Skills

- *Infer*—The ability to subject a document or a set of documents to '"close reading" in which the reader goes beyond literal meaning to engage the ideas presented and integrate them deeply with prior knowledge. This involves the kinds of inference typically referred to as "bridging inference" and more active forms of text interpretation requiring close attention to conceptual content.
- *Inquire*—The ability to develop ideas in an organized and systematic way such that they can be presented clearly and convincingly to someone who does not already understand or believe them.
- *Rethink*—The ability to evaluate, critique, and modify one's own or another's ideas using evidence and logical reasoning.

Textual Skills

- *Integrate*—The ability to read a document and build a mental model of its content and structure. By this we intend what current reading theories refer to as the construction of the text base. What reading theories refer to as the situation model requires mobilization of conceptual and social inferencing, which can go well beyond information directly available in the text.
- *Structure*—The ability to produce a written document that follows an outline or some other well-structured textual pattern.
- *Plan/Revise*—The ability to conceive a document structure that does not exist and plan that structure to serve a rhetorical purpose, or conversely, upon determining the structure of an existing document, to evaluate how well it organizes and presents its content, and rework it accordingly.

Verbal Skills

- *Understand*—The ability to understand texts written in Standard English; that is, the ability to extract literal meaning from a sequence of sentences. This (in combination with the ability to handle complex document and textual structures) is a critical element in constructing a literal understanding of a document (or text-base), although success at understanding phrases and sentences does not guarantee an adequate understanding of a complex text.

- *Phrase*—The ability to express oneself in Standard English; that is, the ability to find the right words and phrasings to convey one's intended meaning.
- *Edit*—The ability to identify places in a text where word choice and phrasing do not convey the intended meaning clearly and accurately, and then to come up with alternative phrasings that work better in context.

Orthographic Skills

- *Read*—The ability to take printed matter and read it either aloud or silently; that is, the ability to convert characters on the page into mental representations of words and sentences.
- *Inscribe*—The ability to take words and sentences and convert them into printed matter; that is, the cognitive and motor abilities needed to produce words and sentences in written form.
- *Proofread*—The ability to examine printed materials, identify nonstandard patterns and errors, and modify them so that they conform to the norms of Standard English grammar and orthography.

The key features of the model we have just presented is that it highlights how skills are shared. We cannot simply equate writing with expression, reading with interpretation, and critical thinking with reflection. Skilled writers coordinate interpretation and critical thinking as they write, just as skilled readers may use expression (at least in the form of self-explanation and note-taking) to help them understand a text. It should be noted that this model does not highlight those aspects of writing skill that depend upon more general features of cognition (Bransford, Brown, & Cocking, 1999), although it accounts for them indirectly in terms of the tradeoff between expressive and interpretive processes (where fluency is the chief concern) and reflection (where executive control, and hence effective use of strategies, is far more important). Each of the skills outlined in the model makes demands on short-term and long-term memory (Kellogg, 1996, 1999, 2001). The development of expertise is based upon automated and strategic processes (McCutchen, 1988, 1996, 2006; McCutchen, Teske, & Bankston, 2008), where increases in fluency enable writers to develop new forms of expertise by learning and applying appropriate strategies. Skilled writers are writers who combine *efficient* receptive and expressive skills with *appropriate* and *effective* reflective strategies.

Also, and perhaps most critically, this model is intended to encapsulate those aspects of writing that need to be assessed, along dimensions that correspond to important cognitive distinctions. The assessment framework called Evidence-Centered Design (Mislevy, Almond, & Lukas, 2004; Mislevy, Steinberg, Almond, & Lukas, 2006) places crucial emphasis on the validity argument that connects specific tasks included in an assessment to the underlying construct, that is, to identifiable cognitive features of human performance on the skill to be assessed. Many of these features can be measured by automated means, using natural processing techniques, as discussed in Deane and Quinlan (2010). Others require more traditional assessment and scoring techniques, particularly higher-order thinking skills necessary to support inquiry and inference during writing.

DESIGNING A NEW KIND OF WRITING TEST

As briefly noted earlier, the CBAL Initiative has two key goals (among others): to create summative assessments inspired by modern cognitive theories, and to make that assessment model the skills it is trying to assess. At the time of writing, CBAL assessments have been developed through a close collaboration with a single urban/suburban school district and piloted in several administrations totaling more than 10,000 students. Detailed analyses of the assessments and their functioning are presented in Bennett (2011) and Fu (2011); literature reviews, preliminary development, and initial analyses are presented in Almond, Deane, Quinlan, Wagner, & Sydorenko (in press), Deane (2011), Deane, Quinlan, Odendahl, Welsh, & Bivens-Tatus (2008), and Deane, Quinlan, and Kostin (2011).

These considerations have led us to adopt the following strategies:

1. We start with the recognition that we need to sample a large enough range of skills. The CBAL strategy for doing this is to break the assessment up into multiple "periodic accountability assessments." Because a writing assessment should sample several different forms of writing, so as to measure a variety of genres and related skills and strategies, we have designed a series of writing assessments, each focused on a different genre of writing. Our initial work has focused on 8 th-grade writing, where persuasion and argumentation, literary analysis, and research are first introduced.

2. We also operate from the assumption that we cannot directly measure all writing skills from the final written product. For instance, it can be hard to disentangle the development of summarization or argumentation skills from general fluency if the assessment contains only an essay task. So it makes sense to include a variety of supporting tasks that measure skills we want to measure.
3. Equally important, we operate from the assumption that the tasks built into an assessment should correspond to tasks that people might actually have occasion to perform, and that the sequence of tasks should actually model how skills should be coordinated. The justification for this approach is straightforward: It turns the assessment into a teaching opportunity. In other words, although we are trying to create a summative assessment, not a project or a portfolio, we want each periodic accountability assessment itself to embody a realistic scenario in which people might actually have occasion to produce the kind of text we want them to write.
4. We have also focused on creating online assessments, in part because it makes a number of elements needed to produce an effective assessment, including delivery and scoring, much more straightforward. Although technology-based literacies have not yet fully penetrated the K-12 world, we expect them to increase steadily in importance and salience.

These considerations have led us to a model in which the final, extended writing task is preceded by a series of lead-in tasks that measure related skills and create a scaffolded scenario that models the kinds of skills and activities that expert writers would apply to prepare for and carry to produce the final written document. For instance, our model 8th-grade persuasive writing test contains the following tasks:

I. Read three documents on the issue to be written about and
   a. Evaluate whether someone else's summary of the first document satisfies a rubric for writing an effective summary; and
   b. Write two summaries of one's own.

II. Analyze arguments about the issue and
   a. Classify 10 statements presenting arguments drawn from the reading as pro or con on the issue; and
   b. Consider pairings of arguments and evidence and decide whether the evidence strengthens or weakens the argument.

III. Read and critique someone else's argument on the subject by writing a paragraph identifying specific weaknesses.

IV. Write an argument of one's own on the issue, taking a position and developing appropriate arguments and evidence.

Our analysis of the relationships among these tasks has revealed patterns that could be useful for diagnostic purposes, and that help to disambiguate student performance on the final writing test. For example, most students perform very accurately on task IIa; and those students may perform well or poorly on task IV. But students who cannot perform task IIa accurately consistently perform very low on task IV: Presumably, someone who cannot understand the difference between arguments pro and con (whether due to linguistic or conceptual impairments) can hardly be expected to perform well when asked to write an argumentative essay.

EXPLORING NEW APPROACHES TO SCORING AND ANALYSIS OF STUDENT WRITING

We have been actively engaged in piloting these tests in an urban-suburban school district in the northeastern United States, and have also conducted a larger-scale study drawing data from 17 schools in 24 states. As part of this pilot work, we have been examining ways to expand the construct measured by considering additional ways to gather evidence about students' writing behavior. We are examining several approaches, including automated analyses of writing supported by natural language processing techniques. Deane and Quinlan (2010) present an overview of some of the Natural Language Processing (NLP) techniques available. For many purposes, automated techniques can be used to produce scores similar to those assigned by trained human raters, can provide a single consistent metric for scoring, and can provide automated linguistic analyses of particular features, making it possible (for instance) to detect plagiarism, or identify students whose writing does not instantiate a well-organized, clearly signaled textual structure. Automated techniques cannot directly measure whether students have succeeded in their rhetorical goals; but they can identify many of the features that differentiate students who demonstrate fluent control of text production from those who do not. It is also possible to collect features that measure behavioral data—that is, keystroke logs that capture patterns of writing behavior in fine detail, following through on familiar ideas from the writing literature about the importance of pauses in writing cognition (Flower, 1981; Perl, 1979).

Our analysis of CBAL writing test data illustrates some of the potential of these techniques to give a richer picture of student performance. For instance, stronger students display shorter than average pauses while they are typing words, but pause longer between sentences and paragraphs. Weaker students tend to hesitate longer between characters and words, and display relatively little evidence of editing behavior (backspacing, deletions, insertions, and jumps). Stronger students display much more sentence variety (as measured by an array of NLP features, which identify a range of specific grammatical constructions such as the passive, the use of subordinating elements, the deployment of discourse-structuring adverbs, etc.). Weaker students generally use a more impoverished range of constructions as measured by such features.[3] The availability of a variety of NLP and other automated features thus has the potential to capture a much richer sense of how student performances vary, and to relate those differences to underlying differences in cognition.

CONCLUSION

The ideas advanced in this chapter are best viewed as programmatic. ETS is still engaged in developing tests, trying out ideas, and piloting them, and analyzing the results of our large-scale pilots. Even in this admittedly early stage, however, the framework has important and interesting features. It tests more than one genre of writing. It places each genre into a well-defined social context, communicates the critical thinking expectations for each writing task, and models the kinds of procedures that novice writers need to master to master each form. The design of the test derives from one fundamental insight. It recognizes that successful writers know more than rigid procedures: They are skilled practitioners who belong to well defined communities of practice.

ENDNOTES

1. The project reported in this chapter reflects the work of many people at ETS. The larger project of which this is a part was initiated under Randy Bennett's leadership and reflects his vision for an integrated assessment system. Nora Odendahl played a major role in the original conceptualization and development, and key features of the design reflect her insights. Mary Fowles has been an equal partner in the work at every stage, and the assessment designs reported reflect her leadership and the work of many test developers at ETS, including Douglas Baldwin, Peter Cooper, Betsy Keller, and Hilary Persky. Other contributors to the work include Russell Almond, Marjorie Biddle, Michael Ecker, Catherine Grimes, Irene Kostin, Rene Lawless, Tenaha O'Reilly, Thomas

Quinlan, Margaret Redman, Margaret Vezzu, Chris Volpe, and Michael Wagner.

2. This model was developed independently from the new Common Core State Standards Initiative, a state-led effort coordinated by the National Governors Association Center for Best Practices and the Council of Chief State School Officers. We have, however, cross-referenced and linked the CBAL Competency Model with these standards. We believe that the CBAL Competency Model provides a useful bridge between the goals embodied in these standards and the cognitive and developmental thinking needed to develop more effective, pedagogically appropriate forms of writing assessment. Much of the philosophy upon which CBAL is based is consistent with the general approach taken by the two consortia that have been awarded Race to the Top Assessment grants: the Partnership for the Assessment of Readiness for College and Careers (PARCC) initiative; and the Smarter Balance Assessment Consortium.
3. These are summaries of results from the pilot study mentioned above, in which we collected data from 2,500 students from 24 schools in 17 states. A more detailed analysis of this data is currently in preparation.

REFERENCES

Almond, R., Deane, P., Quinlan, T., Wagner, M., & Sydorenko, T. (in press). *A preliminary analysis of keystroke log data from a timed writing task*. Princeton, NJ: Educational Testing Service.

Alverman, D. E. (2002). Effective literacy instruction for adolescents. *Journal of Literacy Research, 34*(2), 189-208.

Applebee, A. N. (1984). Writing and reasoning. *Review of Educational Research, 54*(4), 577.

Baker, E., Hannaway, J., Gandara, P., Gitomer, D. H., Goertz, M., Ladd, H., . . . Wilson, M. (2009). *Standards, assessment and accountability*. Washington, DC: National Academy of Education.

Barab, S. A., & Duffy, T. (1998, November). *From practice fields to communities of practice*. Bloomington, IN: Center for Research on Learning and Technology, Indiana University.

Bazerman, C., & Rogers, P. (2008). Writing and secular knowledge outside modern European institutions. In C. Bazerman (Ed.), *Handbook of research on writing: History, society, school, individual, text* (pp. 143-175). New York, NY: Lawrence Erlbaum Associates.

Bennett, R. E. (2011). *Cognitively based assessment of, for, and as learning (CBAL): Results from piloting innovative K-12 assessments*. Paper presented at the Annual Meeting of the American Educational Research Association, New Orleans, LA.

Bennett, R. E., & Gitomer, D. H. (2009). Transforming K-12 assessment: Integrating accountability testing, formative assessment and professional support. In C. Wyatt-Smith & J. J. Cumming (Eds.), *Educational assessment in the 21st century* (pp. 43-62). New York, NY: Springer.

Bereiter, C., & Scardamalia, M. (1987). *The psychology of written composition.* Hillsdale, NJ: Lawrence Erlbaum Associates.

Bransford, J. D., Brown, A. L., & Cocking, R. R. (Eds.). (1999). *How people learn: Brain, mind, experience and school.* Washington, DC: National Academy Press.

Deane, P. (2011). *Writing assessment and cognition* (ETS Research Report No. RR-11-14). Princeton, NJ: Educational Testing Service.

Deane, P., Fowles, M. E., Persky, H. R., & Baldwin, D. (2011). *The CBAL summative writing assessment: An 8th grade design* (ETS Research Monograph No. RM-11-01). Princeton NJ: Educational Testing Service.

Deane, P., & Quinlan, T. (2010). What automated analyses of corpora can tell us about students' writing skills. *Journal of Writing Research, 2*(2), 151-177.

Deane, P., Quinlan, T., & Kostin, I. (2011). *Automated scoring within a developmental, cognitive model of writing proficiency* (ETS Research Report No. RR-11-16). Princeton, NJ: Educational Testing Service.

Deane, P., Quinlan, T., Odendahl, N., Welsh, C., & Bivens-Tatum, J. (2008). *Cognitive models of writing: Writing proficiency as a complex integrated skill. CBAL literature review-writing* (ETS Research Report No. RR-08-55). Princeton, NJ: Educational Testing Service.

Engestrom, Y., Miettinen, R., & Punamaki, R. (1999). *Perspectives on activity theory.* Cambridge, UK: Cambridge University Press.

Flower, L. (1981). The pregnant pause: An inquiry into the nature of planning. *Research in the Teaching of English, 15*(3), 229-243.

Flower, L. (1994). *The construction of negotiated meaning: A social cognitive theory of writing.* Carbondale, IL: Southern Illinois University Press.

Frederiksen, N. (1984). The real test bias: Influences of testing on teaching and learning. *American Psychologist, 39*(3), 193-202.

Fu, J. (2011). *Dimensionality analysis of Cognitively Based Assessment of, for, and as Learning (CBAL). Grade 8 Writing Tests.* Paper presented at the Annual Meeting of the American Educational Research Association, New Orleans, LA.

Graham, S., & Perin, D. (2007). *A report to Carnegie Corporation of New York. Writing next: Effective strategies to improve writing of adolescents in middle and high schools.* Washington, DC: Alliance for Excellent Education.

Hayes, J. R. (1996). A new framework for understanding cognition and affect in writing. In C. M. Levy & S. Ransdell (Eds.), *The science of writing: Theories, methods, individual differences, and applications* (pp. 1-27). Mahwah, NJ: Lawrence Erlbaum Associates.

Hayes, J. R., & Flower, L. (1980). Identifying the organization of writing processes. In L. Gregg & E. R. Steinberg (Eds.), *Cognitive processes in writing* (pp. 3-30). Hillsdale, NJ: Lawrence Erlbaum Associates.

Hillocks, G., Jr. (1987). Synthesis of research on teaching writing. *Educational Leadership, 44*(8), 71-76, 78, 80-82.

Hillocks, G., Jr. (2003). Fighting back: Assessing the assessments. *English Journal, 92*(4), 63.

Hull, G., & Schultz, K. (2001). Literacy and learning out of school: A review of theory and research. *Review of Educational Research, 71*(4), 575-611.

Kellogg, R. T. (1996). A model of working memory in writing. In C. M. Levy & S. Ransdell (Eds.), *The science of writing: Theories, methods, individual differences, and applications* (pp. 57-71). Mahwah, NJ: Lawrence Erlbaum Associates.

Kellogg, R. T. (1999). Components of working memory in text production. In M. Torrance & G. Jeffrey (Eds.), *The cognitive demands of writing: Processing capacity and working memory effects in text production* (pp. 143–161). Amsterdam, Netherlands: Amsterdam University Press.

Kellogg, R. T. (2001). Long-term working memory in text production. *Memory & Cognition, 29*(1), 43-52.

Langer, J. A. (2001). Beating the odds: Teaching middle and high school students to read and write well. *American Educational Research Journal, 38*(4), 837-880.

McCutchen, D. (1988). "Functional automaticity" in children's writing: A problem of metacognitive control. *Written Communication, 5*(3), 306-324.

McCutchen, D. (1996). A capacity theory of writing: Working memory in composition. *Educational Psychology Review, 8*(3), 299-325.

McCutchen, D. (2006). Cognitive factors in the development of children's writing. In C. MacArthur, S. Graham, & J. Fitzgerald (Eds.), *Handbook of writing research* (pp. 115-130). New York, NY: The Guilford Press.

McCutchen, D., Teske, P., & Bankston, C. (2008). Writing and cognition: Implications of the cognitive architecture for learning to write and writing to learn. In C. Bazerman (Ed.), *Handbook of research on writing: History, society, school, individual, text* (pp. 451-470). New York, NY: Lawrence Erlbaum Associates.

Mislevy, R. J., Almond, R. G., & Lukas, J. F. (2004). *A brief introduction to evidence-centered design* (ETS Research Report No. RR-03-16). Princeton, NJ: Educational Testing Service.

Mislevy, R. J., Steinberg, L. S., Almond, R. G., & Lukas, J. F. (2006). Concepts, terminology, and basic models of evidence-centered design. In D. M. Williamson, R. J. Mislevy, & I. I. Bejar (Eds.), *Automated scoring of complex tasks in computer-based testing* (pp. 15-47). Mahwah, NJ: Lawrence Erlbaum Associates.

Perl, S. (1979). The composing processes of unskilled college writers. *Research in the Teaching of English, 13*(4), 317-336.

Shanahan, T. (2006). Relations among oral language, reading, and writing development. In C. A. MacArthur, S. Graham, & J. Fitzgerald (Eds.), *Handbook of writing research* (pp. 171-183). New York, NY: The Guilford Press.

White, E. M. (1985). *Teaching and assessing writing*. San Francisco, CA: Jossey-Bass.

White, E. M. (2005). The scoring of writing portfolios: Phase 2. *College Composition and Communication, 56*(4), 581-600.

Yancey, K. (1999). Looking back as we look forward: Historicizing writing assessment. *College Composition and Communication, 50*(3), 483-502.

5

THE WPA OUTCOMES, INFORMATION LITERACY, AND THE CHALLENGES OF OUTCOMES-BASED CURRICULAR DESIGN

Barry M. Maid

Barbara J. D'Angelo

Arizona State University

TRADITIONAL RESEARCH WRITING

College writing and writing instruction has always been linked to the research process. Indeed, for decades the culminating experience of many First Year Composition courses has been something called the "research paper." "The research paper" itself was always kind of an artificial construct. It was a type of writing most usually produced by copying and, at its best, interpreting information found in library sources and then reported on to prove some kind of thesis. In retrospect it taught students little about writing and less about research. Still, if instead of taking easy shots at the traditional research paper we try to look at it briefly as a particular kind of writing genre, we might get a better sense about what was going on. As we intend to explore how genre can have a significant impact on the nature of outcomes, looking first at one traditionally taught genre should help us move forward.

As we have already hinted, one of the most dominant genre characteristics of a good research paper is that it has an identifiable thesis[1] statement that is then argued for by using a collage of traditional library sources. At its best, there is some analysis and interpretation of those sources. Perhaps equally important there is a demonstration that the writer correctly incorporates textual material from sources into the paper using the appropriate academic style sheet. Finally, there is a correctly formatted list of sources.

Today, rather than asking students to write "research papers," we are more likely to hear that students need to learn how to do academic writing, although often that means the same thing. In the best programs, students learn to make rhetorical choices about appropriate academic discourses and genres. More and more, there is an infusion of what is known as information literacy (IL). (We define IL to be the ability to find, analyze, organize, manage, and report on information.) In addition, there is a tremendous increase in the number of programs implementing learning outcomes for their students. (Learning outcomes are statements of knowledge, skills, and abilities students should achieve at the end of a course of study.) Having such programmatic outcomes not only provides a road map for students and a means to ensure programmatic consistency, but it also provides a first step for program assessment. It is historically noteworthy and significant that at the end of the twentieth century the Council of Writing Program Administrators (CWPA) developed their *WPA Outcomes Statement for First-Year Composition* and the American Library Association's Association of College and Research Libraries (ACRL, 2000) developed their *Information Literacy Competency Standards for Higher Education*. In fact, a close look at both documents shows, although they emerged from different disciplines, incredible similarity. Still, both documents and curriculum that is created using both documents alone appear to be deeply rooted in twentieth-century academic thinking.

At first glance it may seem to be a simply fortuitous accident for the WPA Outcomes Statement and the ACRL Information Literacy for Higher Education Standards to emerge at the same time. However, although the WPA Outcomes Statement emerged from a grassroots discussion on the WPA listserv and the ACRL Standards from an organizational mandate, both documents emerged from a general national call for accountability in higher education mirroring the call for accountability in K-12 schools. The move towards accountability, especially through the use of outcomes, can also be seen in the standards of disciplinary accrediting organizations such as the Accrediting Board for Engineering and Technology (ABET) and the Association to Advance Collegiate Schools of Business (AASCB), as well as the several regional accrediting agencies. In fact, we can see that beginning with the Middle States Commission on Higher Education, accrediting agencies increasingly recognize IL and require the assessment of it as a learning outcome. Grach-Lindauer (2002) and Saunders (2007) trace the trends in accreditation guidelines pointing to increased attention to and assessment of

IL. At the national level, we can see the same impetus in the politically charged *No Child Left Behind*, the 2008 reauthorization of the Higher Education Act of 1965 (H. R. 4137), and the Spellings Commission (U.S. Department of Education, 2006). (For more discussion of outcomes, especially in applied writing tasks, see Odell, Chapter 16.)

MOVING INTO THE 21ST CENTURY

Even the best academic writing programs are ultimately limited. (We consider the best programs to be those that teach students that not all academic writing is the same and that the kinds of writing that need to be produced are determined rhetorically by the needs of the different academic discourses, and that the kind of information that is to be used is, again, determined by what is valued within the various academic disciplines.) The reality is that unless students decide to become academics they will spend most of their lives producing writing that is not going to be assessed by academics. The academic essay, even as it is constructed in different disciplines, is essentially a specific kind of report—a text document with a thesis or claim and supporting information or evidence. Our students need to learn how to write more than reports. Even within traditional or print genres,[2] students need to learn that a formal report structure is just that—a structure—and that the conventions of that structure do not apply to every context when writing a formal report. Further, the type of research needed does not necessarily follow the conventions of academic research in support of a report. Yet, continuing with traditional or print genres in the workplace, students compose correspondence, proposals, instructions, procedures, manuals and much more. These are the types of genres that technical communication programs and courses (as well as other applied writing courses such as business communication) have taught.

With the advent of digital media, initially the use of genres did not change—they were simply produced more efficiently and quickly than previously. (It may be argued, however, that a move to digitization started to change genre conventions. For example, did the move from paper documentation of computer software to online help created by software like RoboHelp change genre conventions of documentation?) It also meant that more people have access to tools that allow them to create these documents. (Think how early desktop publishing software allowed anyone to create flyers or brochures—abilities now found in word processing software such as Microsoft Word.) As a side note, it is important to understand that the WPA Outcomes and ACRL Standards were advanced during this same digital revolution. As such, their authors and sponsors were sharply aware of the advent of learning and communicating in digital environments. However, increasingly digital media has meant the introduction of new genres: websites, blogs, instant (and text) messaging, tweets, wall posts on social media sites, video, podcasts, and more. In addition, digital media has transformed traditional genres. Although the traditional manual may still exist and, now, be incorporated on websites in pdf form for easy storage and access, the conventions and structure of manuals have been influenced by digital media such as wikis that allow for constant editing and updating, as well as user input. The purpose of the manual has stayed the same; however, the audience may also now be the writer or editor, and the conventions of its structure and use have changed.

For those of us who teach applied writing, the question of what we teach and how has become more complex. Even more complex are issues of assessment for writing produced with digital media: Are we assessing computer skills and proficiency? Conventions of "new" genres? Something else that we call "writing skills?" What is it that we assess, and how do we establish scoring guides that allow us to evaluate work rigorously and with validity?

At first glance, it may appear that conventions are the easiest to assess. With print documents, that may be so because formatting and style conventions related to print genres are well established. Beyond mechanics, use is tied to conventions of print documents in ways that have emerged over time. A memo is clearly distinct from a letter in not only how it is formatted but also in when and how it is used. With digital media, conventions are still emerging though some are ingrained in the medium or genre itself: A tweet, or any method of transmittal linked to SMS technology, cannot exceed 160 characters, for example.

Perhaps what ultimately becomes evident as we think through the issues of composing and assessing work composed in digital environments is that rhetorical constructs and process remain central to the work of writing. What becomes increasingly important, however, is that there are more choices that students and workers must make and, therefore, there is greater need for understanding that the selection of genre and media is a crucial to communicate effectively. Equally, research as a process remains central; however, the tools, methods, and constructs associated with it have evolved and expanded. More importantly, digital media may be pushing us to recognize that research (or information literacy) cannot be perceived and/or taught as a separate process from writing/composing—the two are interdependent and interrelated.

Theory and practice during the last 30 years in rhetoric and composition moved to a broader conception of invention that encompasses creativity, discovery, mediating knowledge and meaning, problem solving, and inquiry. Invention in this richer and more complex role includes discourse initiation, exploration, argument development, judgment formation, intertextual negotiation, and reader positioning (Lauer, 2002). Rhetoricians of the late twentieth century have consistently noted the connection between rhetoric and its relationship to the content it communicates. Lauer (2004) states that "the term invention has historically encompassed strategic acts that provide the rhetor with direction, multiple ideas, subject matter, arguments, insights or probable judgments, and understanding the rhetorical situation. Such acts include initiating discourse, exploring alternatives, framing and testing judgments, interpreting texts, and analyzing audiences" (p. 2). Richard Young and Alton Becker said, "The strength and worth of rhetoric tends to become a superficial and marginal concern when it is separated from systematic methods of inquiry and problems of content" (qtd. in Lauer, 2004, p. 1). Inquiry and content are inextricably linked to IL through the skills and abilities that enable individuals to find, access, manage, and use it to communicate. In this view, research/IL is more than finding sources—as it is in the traditional view of teaching research—but is more complex and context determined so that choices related to production and dissemination are part of the writing research process.

Conceptions of research as a process emerged approximately at the same time as the writing process movement. The research of Carol Kuhlthau delineated research as a process, one that is remarkably reminiscent of the writing process, from topic selection to search closure and to communication of information. Kuhlthau's stages emphasize finding, using, and communicating information to seek meaning. Originally conducted with middle school students, her longitudinal research was later repeated with a variety of information-intensive professionals to confirm findings in other settings (Kuhlthau, 2004). Grounded in library and information science, Kuhlthau's research points to a distinction between traditional academic research pedagogy focused on finding information and disciplinary perspectives on constructing knowledge.

Pedagogically, the conceptualization of research as a process has facilitated identification of IL with writing and collaborations with the rhetoric and writing discipline. Interest in IL's relationship to rhetoric and writing is manifested theoretically in Rolf Norgaard's encouragement of an approach in which rhetoric provides IL with a theoretical foundation that rescues it from the danger of becoming narrowly defined as a functional technology skill. IL, then, returns rhetoric and writing to its traditional roots with social, civic, and intellectual relevance (Norgaard, 2003).

CREATING OUTCOMES FOR 21ST CENTURY APPLIED WRITING: FROM PROGRAM TO COURSE

Although we have already hinted that the WPA Outcomes Statement is a twentieth-century document, we do think that its inherent flexibility makes it a good starting place for creating outcomes for twenty-first-century writing programs of all kinds. (We think the recently released *Framework for Success in Postsecondary Writing* [2011] developed by the Council of Writing Program Administrators, the National Council of Teachers of English, and the National Writing Project shows how the original Outcomes Statement continues to be used to help frame the national discussion on teaching and assessing writing. The soon-to-be-released volume on 10 years of the Outcomes Statement, edited by Duane Roen, Greg Glau, Nicholas Behm, and Ed White, also demonstrates that the original statement is still an important part of the writing assessment conversation.) We have discussed elsewhere (Maid, 2005; D'Angelo & Maid, 2004) how we built on the original Outcomes Statement and then infused it with appropriate technology and information literacy outcomes so it would make sense for an applied writing program. It is now clear to us that although those outcomes may still work on a global level for program assessment, as digital media continues to evolve—especially as new genres seem to emerge driven by social media—we need to look at outcomes and pedagogies that take these factors into account. (Although she is talking about First Year Composition, we think what we are describing is not that different from what Yancey, in Chapter 27 of this volume, calls a "self-created exigence.") More than anything else, two points seem basic to our discussion. First, writing, in applied situations, is no longer primarily the creation of long, narrative texts designed to be distributed and accessed by print. Second, we would better serve our students if we talked about information literacy (which incorporates the finding, analysis, organization, management, and reporting of information) rather than research (which too often implies only the finding of information). Doing so allows us to more fully integrate IL into the writing process so that, from the perspective of writing, research is not simply the collection of information and, from the perspective of research, writing is not simply the presentation of information. Further, if we define IL in its fullest sense (rather than as academic research as it so often is), then we are able to define and assess "research" to broaden the scope of how we assess it so that we incorporate methods and processes that are relevant to the workplace but are generally beyond the scope of academic or bibliographic research. For an applied writing program in which many students are already working practitioners and others are seeking the type of education that will be immediately applicable to their jobs and careers, this fuller definition allows us to develop pedagogies and assess students in a way that is more relevant and pragmatic—that meet workplace as well as academic needs. Shouldn't these be in synch?

Although some First Year Composition programs are now beginning to have students write in genres other than the traditional "academic essay," applied writing instructors have for years taught multiple genres and, more importantly, that genres get created to fulfill definable rhetorical needs. We can see this at work in our current Program outcomes for the Technical Communication Program at Arizona State University. Under Rhetorical Knowledge, there are three outcomes that specifically address genre:

- Understand how each genre helps to shape writing and how readers respond to it
- Write in multiple genres
- Use appropriate technologies to organize, present, and communicate information to address a range of audiences, purposes, and genres

Still, although these outcomes work for a Program, individual courses and projects within that program must necessarily have more defined outcomes that can then build to the broader program outcomes. Indeed, it is now more important than ever that students show not only a facility with multiple genres (such as proposals, reports, instruction, etc.), but equally important to understand which genre will be most appropriate and effective for their targeted audience. These choices have become increasingly complicated by the different choices of media that are now readily available. For example, although it might be argued that podcasts, though not called that until 2004, have been around since the mid-1990s using Real Media software and servers, the idea that the scripting and production of podcasts might be an important part of an applied writing curriculum has really only taken hold in the past few years. Students now need to know not only how to create a podcast but also why a podcast might be the most effective genre in a particular situation.

CREATING OUTCOMES FOR TWENTY FIRST CENTURY APPLIED WRITING: WITHIN THE COURSE

Clearly, since the adoption of the Outcomes Statement by the WPA, the idea of having program outcomes and a process for assessing those outcomes has become widely discussed and has, in fact, been implemented at many institutions. However, the focus has tended to be on the global outcomes. We were aware that the history of assessment in Technical Communication

Programs is different from that in composition programs, as Margaret Hundleby delineates so well in the next chapter in this volume. However, because our program was not designed to train writers in specific engineering or computer skills but to create writers who are proficient in a wide range of applied writing situations, we consciously chose to align our assessment practices with the more general rhetorically based concepts found in the Outcomes Statement. In our own program in Technical Communication, we mapped each course in our curriculum to the global program outcomes. (All of these course outcomes are visible on the ASU program website.) We could then assume that because students were supposed to achieve proficiency in certain outcomes in certain courses if they took the right combination of courses based on degree requirements, that they should have achieved proficiency in all the program outcomes. Yet, even doing that, we have discovered, fails to answer some crucial questions.

Perhaps, we can best understand the issues by looking at part of our curriculum. When the ASU Technical Communication Program was first created in 2000, we developed courses around different "tracks," one of which we termed our "genre track." Originally, this "track" consisted of five courses:

TWC 443 Proposal Writing
TWC 444 Manual and Instructional Writing
TWC 445 Computer Documentation
TWC 446 Technical and Scientific Reports
TWC 447 Business Reports

We can look at the results of our curriculum mapping exercise for one of these courses, TWC 443, Proposal Writing, and discover that, in that course, students are expected to learn the following outcomes:

Rhetorical Knowledge (RK)

- Identify, articulate, and focus on a defined purpose
- Respond to the need of the appropriate audience
- Use conventions of format and structure appropriate to the rhetorical situation

Critical Thinking, Reading, and Writing (CTRW)

- Understand that research and writing are a series of tasks, including accessing, retrieving, evaluating, analyzing, and synthesizing appropriate data and information from sources that vary in content, format, structure, and scope
- Understand the relationships among language, knowledge, and power including social, cultural, historical, and economic issues related to information, writing, and technology

- Integrate previously held beliefs, assumptions, and knowledge with new information and the ideas of others to accomplish a specific purpose within a context

Processes (P)
- Be aware that it usually takes multiple drafts to create and complete a successful text
- Develop research and writing strategies appropriate to the context and situation
- Develop flexible strategies for generating, revising, editing, and proofreading
- Understand research and writing as an open process that permits writers to use later invention and rethinking to revise their work

Knowledge of Conventions: (KC)
- Learn standard tools for accessing and retrieving information
- Learn common formats for different genres
- Develop knowledge of genre conventions ranging from structure and paragraphing to tone and mechanics
- Apply appropriate means of documenting their work

Understandably, the Rhetorical Knowledge outcomes that speak to the issue of genre have been left out. In fact, while focusing program outcomes into course outcomes, this "leaving out" was deliberate. Because the assumption is that the entire course will focus on the genre of the proposal the outcomes seemed implicit. But it now seems to us that even that is not as cut and dried as it might appear. The course focuses on a specific type of proposal: proposals written for funding. Outcomes for Rhetorical Knowledge focus on the context of that specific genre. Understanding the need of the appropriate audience is more specifically understanding the need of funders (foundations, grantors). Purpose is associated specifically with composing and submitting a proposal to receive funding. These two outcomes are addressed within the course structure by requiring students to select an organization on whose behalf they will write a proposal. They then identify an appropriate funder. The type of research and analysis required for these two steps is not the type of research that we typically require students to do: There is no "thesis" and supporting evidence. Instead, they must conduct research to understand their organization's mission, values, and goals to be able to find an appropriate funder with a matching mission, values, and goals. Many students find this aspect of the course the most challenging because it is time consuming and requires sophisticated search skills and analytical work. Both writing and research, then, are tied to the genre as well as to the audience and purpose of it. There are multiple levels of learning taking place that require students to make the leap from academic research and writing—which is typically student-centered and focused on the student's learning—to professional research and writing—which is typically focused external to the student so that the emphasis is on the writer as a representative of an organization as well as on the intersections of audience, purpose, and genre.

Unlike what students are taught in the typical technical communication or business writing textbook about proposal writing, proposals do not have standard genre conventions. But, most often, students are taught that proposal writing is similar to writing a formal report. Worse, they tend to conflate different types of proposals into one seemingly amorphic genre: the proposal. The reality, however, is that the conventions of a proposal are determined by the funder and they may differ significantly from funder to funder. Although the type of content (needs analysis, problem statement, budget) may be standard categories of proposals, how they are formatted and incorporated within the structure of a composition called "proposal" differs. In terms of pedagogy of the course (and assessment of it), it means that students must research the conventions required by the funder they have chosen and follow them instead of relying on a model document in a textbook. Instead, they need to research what the conventions and rules are and then apply them to their work. Also clearly, this mirrors how a proposal writer would work in the real world. For assessment, that requires the instructor to have access to those guidelines in order to judge whether the student has met them and to construct an assessment process that awards grades based on meeting guidelines that have been researched and followed rather than one set standard.

What this means is that as we teach this course, we understand the overriding outcomes we must teach are the first outcome for critical thinking (understand that research and writing are a series of tasks, including accessing, retrieving, evaluating, analyzing, and synthesizing appropriate data and information from sources that vary in content, format, structure, and scope) and the process outcome related to research and writing (develop research and writing strategies appropriate to the context and situation). These two outcomes reflect the pedagogy of the course in the sense that they require students to use complex and sophisticated research and writing skills and abilities to find, retrieve, analyze, fuse and compose information, and disseminate it in the appropriate format. Although the course is a "genre" course, the conventions of the genre are not something fixed that students can simply plug information into. Instead, they are part of the research-writing process that have to be uncovered and analyzed before they can be met, whether they are print or digital in form. What this means is that information literacy and writing skills have become so integrated that the process becomes indistinguishable. Indeed, perhaps what this leads us to is rethinking the track itself as a "process" track or a hybrid "genre process" track to deemphasize the notion that they are about conventions and instead emphasize that they are about understanding how to apply the process to various conventions.

One issue that complicates all of this is the continual evolution of digital technologies. Should our students, for example, assume that all proposals they write be submitted as narrative print documents? We already know that many funding sources essentially provide proposal writers with a template for submissions. Surely, if they are not doing so already, we can expect many organizations that accept proposals will be providing submitters with an electronic template that feeds into a content management system. Will the emerging technology impact the genre conventions? Will the emerging technology impact the way the proposal is written?

In addition, the very medium in which the curriculum is taught can have an impact on outcomes. All online classes and more and more face-to-face classes are being taught using some kind of class management system. Blackboard dominates the market. Although being able to engage one another through online environments has become "normal," the nature of the environments can greatly influence the kind of communication that takes place within those environments. Indeed, Blackboard is a tool that is designed more for classroom management than pedagogy. Although this may facilitate assignment distribution and submittal, posting and managing grades, and so on, if one of our goals is to help students understand how to use media effectively and appropriately, this standardization may not be the best strategy as it's unlikely that many students (if any) will ever see Blackboard again once they graduate, though they undoubtedly will work with a variety of other content management systems customized for very different uses. Most students may recognize that Blackboard is a tool used to manage their courses; however, it is questionable whether there are transferrable skills in its use (e.g., is the use of Blackboard equivalent to the use of a corporate intranet). Interestingly, when students enter the workplace as information workers, they will more likely be interacting with content management systems that encourage interactivity and collaboration—much like they experience in using different forms of social media. So then, for example, should students in Proposal Writing gain classroom experience using a wiki or Google Docs? Should they be assessed on their ability to use digital media to collaborate and participate in peer review? Are these two examples already covered under the outcome in Processes and Knowledge of Conventions?

FINALE

The reality is that teaching writing is not as simple as it used to appear to be. Effective writing skills are now more vital to an individual's success than ever before, and those skills are no longer confined to the ability to turn a clever phrase. Business writing is no longer confined to the interoffice memo, letters to customers (or other external clients), and bids and contracts—all using formal structured language. Our students must understand that their writing will take place within different digital environments, and each environment can have an impact on the message they are trying to communicate. Genres that may seem comfortable to both instructors and students may be morphed to meeting digital needs. As a result, just because we have good outcomes for our programs and courses does not necessarily mean we are really teaching our students the skills they will need. Further, the danger in using outcomes for assessment is that what we assess tends to become rigid and inflexible. Indeed, in some sense the ACRL Standards, outcomes, and competencies are so reductionist in detail that they may make good variables for assessment purposes. Indeed, the stated purpose of the IL Standards is to provide ". . . a framework for assessing the information literate individual" (Association, 2000). As Lupton (2004) argued, this focus on assessing the individual is one that has been critiqued as reductionist in its attempt to delineate skills which become decontextualized. As such, IL becomes a set or listing of skills that an individual can be trained (and then assessed) in with little regard for the context in which the skills are needed. However, what gets lost is the ability to assess the fluidity and contextual nature of research and writing. In particular, writing (or communication more broadly) that takes place in digital environments is dynamic, written and/or edited by multiple "authors," and may incorporate multiple genres. Our application of outcomes must be equally dynamic.[3]

ENDNOTES

1. Probably no one has outlined the history of what he calls "thesis texts" better than Robert J. Connors. In both *Composition-Rhetoric* (1997) and "The Rise and Fall of the Modes of Discourse" (1981), Connors points to Barrett Wendell's 1981 textbook *English Composition* as the first "thesis text." As John Brereton points out in the first chapter of this collection, after 1879 when Harvard switched its entrance examination from summary to analysis, Wendell was working in an environment that looked for "thesis texts." Connors further cites James McCrimmon's *Writing with a Purpose* (first edition, 1950, current

edition is the 14th, published in 2004 by Joseph Trimmer) as one of the best-known "thesis texts." The central idea of the "thesis texts" was that writers made a claim that was then proven by verifiable facts. It nicely fits the model for academic writing.

2. Even though the power of genre seems to have just recently taken the composition community by storm, those of us in technical communication have been using the idea of genre as more than a mere classification of documents for some time. Carolyn Miller's classic "Genre as Social Action" (1984) remains exceedingly relevant. The idea that exigence has a social motive seems almost commonplace when talking about workplace documents. In a more recent piece, Miller and Shepherd (2004) assert that, "When a type of discourse or communicative action requires a common name within a given context of community, that's a good sign that it's functioning as a genre." Likewise, Herrington and Moran (2005) carry the genre as an aspect of social action to the Writing across the Curriculum World in their collection.
3. Odell's "given-new-contract" which he presents in Chapter 16 of this volume is one possible way to approach the dynamic nature of research and writing.

REFERENCES

Association for College & Research Libraries. (2000). *Information literacy competency standards for higher education.* Web.

Connors, R.J. (1981). The rise and fall of the modes of discourse. *College Composition and Communication, 32*(4), 444-455.

Connors, R.J. (1997). *Composition-rhetoric: Backgrounds, theory, and pedagogy.* Pittsburgh, PA: University of Pittsburgh Press.

Council of Writing Program Administrators. (2000/2008). *WPA Outcomes Statement for First-Year Composition.* Web.

Council of Writing Program Administrators, National Council of Teachers of English, & National Writing Project. (2011). *Framework for success in postsecondary education.* Web.

D'Angelo, B.J., & Maid, B.M. (2004). Moving beyond definitions: Implementing information literacy across the curriculum. *Journal of Academic Librarianship, 30*(3), 212-217.

Gratch-Lindauer, B. (2002). Comparing the regional accreditation standards: Outcomes assessment and other trends. *Journal of Academic Librarianship, 28*(1), 14-25.

H. R. 4137. (2008). Extension of Higher Education Act of 1965. 110th Cong.

Herrington, A., & Moran, T. (Eds.). *Genre across the curriculum.* Logan, UT: Utah State University Press.

Kuhlthau, C. C. (2004). *Seeking meaning: A process approach to library and information services* (2nd ed.). Westport, CT: Libraries Unlimited.

Lauer, J. M. (2002). Rhetorical invention: The diaspora. In J. M. Atwill & J. M. Lauer (Eds.), *Perspectives on rhetorical invention* (pp. 1-15). Knoxville, TN: University of Tennessee Press.

Lauer, J. M. (2004). *Invention in rhetoric and composition*. West Lafayette, IN: Parlor Press.

Lupton, M. (2004). *The learning connection, information literacy and the student experience*. Adelaide, Australia: Auslib Press.

Maid, B. M. (2005). Using the outcomes statement for technical communication. In S. Harrington, K. Rhodes, R. O. Fischer, & R. Malenczyk (Eds.), *The outcomes book. Debate and consensus after the WPA Outcomes Statement* (pp. 139-149). Logan, UT: Utah State University Press.

Miller, C.R. (1984). Genre as social action. *Quarterly Journal of Speech, 70*, 151-167.

Miller, C.R., & Shepherd, D. (2004). Blogging as social action: A genre analysis of the weblog. In L. J. Gurak, S. Antonijevic, L. Johnson, C. Ratliff, & J. Reyman (Eds.), *Into the blogosphere: Rhetoric, community, and culture of weblogs.* Web.

Norgaard, R. (2003). Writing information literacy in the classroom: Contributions to a concept. *Reference & User Services Quarterly, 43*(2), 124-130.

Roen, D., Glau, G., Behm, N., & White E. (Eds.). (in press). *The WPA Outcomes Statement: A decade later*. West Lafayette, IN: Parlor Press.

Saunders, L. (2007). Regional accreditation organizations' treatment of information literacy: Definitions, collaboration, and assessment. *Journal of Academic Librarianship, 33*(3), 317-326.

U.S. Department of Education. (2006). *A test of leadership: Charting the future of U.S. higher education*. Washington, DC: U.S. Department of Education. Web.

6

"DOES IT WORK?" THE QUESTION(S) OF ASSESSMENT IN TECHNICAL AND PROFESSIONAL COMMUNICATION

Margaret N. Hundleby
University of Guelph, Ontario

Within the decade of Edward White's (1985) renovation of assessment practices in mainstream Composition Studies (MCS), Jo Allen (1993) wrote a landmark article in *Technical Communication Quarterly* that defined the roles of assessment for Technical and Professional Communication (TPC). Whereas White's work took hold in the imagination and practice of succeeding generations of composition teachers, Allen's work seemed to draw a line under any inquiry into the function of assessment for technical writing by smoothing out lurking dissension over questions of possible and probable use. The bulk of attention in the field turned to the tasks of developing a body of practice and examining issues in building its identity as a profession (Dubinsky, 2004; Savage & Sullivan, 2001).

Recent renewed interest in TPC assessment sometimes appears to be as much a general commentary on the more immediate concerns of TPC as an integral part of them (Consortium, 2000; Coppola, 1999; Elliot, Kilduff, & Lynch, 1994; Hundleby & Allen, 2010; Hundleby, Hovde, & Allen, 2003; Johnson 2006a, 2006b). But this conclusion applies only at first glance: The ongoing practice of assessment in MCS that serves as the departure point for White's venture into the (then) unknown also establishes both how and why assessment is central to success in any writing instruction (Huot, 2003;

Lynne, 2004; Yancey, 1999; see Brereton, Chapter 1, this volume, for a comprehensive history). Interest in assessment within the field of TPC is necessarily an interest in both how and why assessment contributes to the successful development of its body of knowledge, the techniques that constitute its practice, and also contributes significantly to the characterization of its professionalism. Not only does assessment show us what "works" but also how and why it does so.

The similarity of the roots of MCS and TPC, with their joint appearance around the turn of the 20th century as areas demanding pedagogical attention (Russell, 2002), seems to suggest that questions of both how and why assessment "works" will have at least similar, if not completely identical, answers. The appearance of Writing Across the Curriculum in the late 1970s (McLeod & Soven, 2006) and its extension into Writing in the Disciplines in the 1990s (Russell, 2002)—with the assumption that both involve applications identical to TPC—seem to reinforce the notion. TPC, which has been variously defined as everything from transfer of information (Fearing & Sparrow, 1990) to knowledge management (Spinuzzi, 2007; Zachry, Faber, Cargile Cook, & Clark, 2001), is much more than a branch of MCS, however, or than a reworking of its processes for a particular kind of application. Where the modern configuration of composition studies aims at stabilizing the composing practices of the individual while retaining an ability to adapt to varying purposes and at improving that or any individual's overall rhetorical competence (Anson, 1989; Berlin, 1987), TPC takes a path that is partially parallel but still quite separate and distinctive. If MCS can be described as referencing the characteristic classical and humanistic traditions of a Harvard-style education, TPC grew out of the engineering programs and applied language studies of institutions such as MIT and Michigan (Connors, 1982; Kynell, 1999; Russell, 2002). As a result, TPC fosters communication practices that, although recognizably of rhetorical inception (Anderson, Brockman, & Miller, 1983), emphasize acquisition of composing skills suitable for work that is invariably public and collaborative, always involving concerted human action (Bazerman & Paradis, 1994; Miller, 1984; Thompson, 2001).

In contrast to the description of MCS as a "dappled" field (Lauer, 1984) with skills shading into each other as they move across a largely internal communicative landscape and head for a product that will be assessed for its individuality—even when placed in relation to others of the same type—TPC is multi-layered and intensely targeted (Cargile Cook, 2003; Dobrin, 1989). TPC's aim is always to connect the practices of a situation, both procedural and conceptual, rather than individuals in a situation to its audiences and purposes (Latour, 1990; Latour & Woolgar, 1979; Pickering, 1995). Adequate assessment therefore involves strategies that acknowledge the particularity of any situation, the characteristic operation of techniques appropriate for any task involved in it, and expectations for recognizable and credible outcomes in both the target audience and the professional field defining the applicability of the work done (Allen, 1993; Hundleby & Allen, 2010; Hundleby, Hovde, & Allen, 2003). This chapter reviews the way in which the historical development of the field of TPC has influenced its assessment practices to date, then examines the change in theoretical frameworks that influence the role of assessment in TPC. After reviewing the distinctive effects of the growth of professionalism among these characteristics, the chapter closes by returning to a consideration of the definition of functionality that continues to drive assessment practice and research in TPC.

WHAT IS THE HISTORICAL BASIS OF TPC ASSESSMENT?

The early stages of TPC assessment featured a development within a development. A partnership between English studies and Engineering produced the "Engineering English" that formed the context for the growth of TPC (Connors, 1982; Kynell, 1999). Originally a response to this hybrid pedagogy, assessment would develop as TPC changed and grew into a recognizable discipline. In the earliest days, however, there was a simplified approach based on an all-encompassing question used as an assessment standard in Engineering: "Does it work?" (Connors, 1982). The answer to this question, more often than not, served to determine whether or not the novice writer displayed adequate accuracy and polish. English teachers had been invited into Engineering to provide the instruction in composition that would round out the engineering student's ability to participate in this professional field (Connors, 1982; Hagge, 1995; Russell, 2002). Assessment duties were shared according to field of expertise, with each concentrating on the factors that it both understood and valued. Shared responsibility did not, however, mean an equal division of what "counted" for the host discipline. Engineering departments requested the input of English studies faculty as a means of creating skill in handling language that worked on two fronts—correctness of grammar, mechanics, and sentence structure, and adequacy of polish in diction, phrasing, and overall style (Hagge, 1995; Hundleby, 1999)—but did not consider either involved in creating engineering knowledge.

Delivery of the instruction that supposedly ensured acquisition of "English" skills varied: "Guest" instructors in courses was the most usual route taken, but there were also varied efforts by individuals and entire programs, such as MIT's early 20th-century attempt at across-the-board writing instruction or even establishment of an internal English department, such as the one run by the University of Michigan well into the 1980s

(Russell, 2002). The goals of assessment remained fairly consistent, however, focusing on ensuring the adequacy of the novice on the way to becoming an expert (Hagge, 1995). In both Engineering instruction and supplemental English studies, judgment of this adequacy came down to the question of whether or not a design, mechanism, process, or paper "worked," thereby confirming the adequacy of the effort, if not necessarily the accuracy of its results.

This demand for adequacy remained embedded in TPC assessment throughout the century, often appearing as the criterion "elegant," a term related to approval of a neatly worked-out mathematical calculation (Davidson, 2011), but also identified by more mundane locutions such as "accurate," "correct," "polished," and "pleasing" to indicate adequacy. The criterion type continues throughout the century, showing up, for example, across three editions of a volume of advice to developing professionals on composing methods that "work" (Michaelson, 1990). These criteria are, as well, routinely embedded in the rubrics and other catalogues of criteria used throughout the 20th century to assess TPC adequacy (Coppola, 1999; Hundleby, 1999; Thomas, 2005). Regardless of the aspect addressed, all aim at confirming the adequacy of the "work" as it is rendered by the agency of communication skills.

Another factor borrowed from early engineering practice and embedded in TPC assessment by the middle of the 20th century is the use of testing techniques to ensure that the solution to a technical problem exhibits all its features in "working" order. As engineering techniques became increasingly formalized, testing developed standardized ways of measuring the components of a design, mechanism, or process to evaluate it on the basis of this measurement. Such testing was intended to find out not only if the element did "work," but also if it would be likely to continue to do so. The value discerned defined the intrinsic merit of the product and demonstrated that it was reliable. Writing skill could be tested right along with substantive knowledge of engineering practices by using specific measurement systems. This testing again echoed the mathematical components of engineering work by assigning a numeric value to the components of any documentation, and then weighting the value of each contribution to determine how much, or little, had been added to the overall result. The answer to "does it work?" became a statistical one.

The testing approach extended to using communication skills to guarantee that technical personnel were comprehensively trained to do the work assigned to them. The rapid expansion of industry following the close of World War II concentrated the supervision of less-skilled workers in the hands of an elite management group that included engineers among its key members (Russell, 2002). In addition to inheriting the job of demonstrating that a student had a comprehensive mastery of all aspects of a body of engineering knowledge, assessment inherited the responsibility of both identifying and confirming communication skills (Connors, 1982; Staples, 1999). Throughout the 1960s, elaborate schemes for measuring technical communication abilities were used at the Educational Testing Service to show, first, what communication skills had been mastered and, second, how comprehensive that mastery was (Elliot, 2010).

Measurement had been adopted into education in general during this period (Guba & Lincoln, 1989), and it had likely been transferred from there to the assessment of writing in general, seeking to show both reliability and validity (Huot, 2003; Lynne, 2004; White, 1985). For TPC assessment, however, conventional measurement practices in Engineering and other technical and scientific disciplines provided the prime influence, as is shown by the growing scholarship in this newly defined academic area (Gould, 1978; Staples, 1999). Throughout the postwar period, right to the end of the 1970s, the pages of the *Journal of Technical Writing and Communication*, and collections defining the developing TPC practice (Cunningham & Estrin, 1975; Gould, 1978), lined up on the side of using measurement to demonstrate both that the communication products could be relied on, and that the communicator was valid, or fully professional—an assessment issue that has continued to surface repeatedly in TPC (Boettger, 2010; Johnson, 2006b; Johnson & Elliot, 2010; Meyer, 2005).

HOW DOES CHANGE IN THEORETICAL FRAMEWORKS AFFECT TPC ASSESSMENT?

Assessment in TPC underwent a gradual but profound change in the run-up to the end of the 20th century. This change may owe an initial debt to the Writing Across the Curriculum (WAC) movement, even though WAC was not directly responsible for the growth of Technical Communication beyond the borders of the English department (Bazerman, Little, Bethel, Chavkin, Fouquette, & Garufis, 2005; Fearing & Sparrow, 1990; Russell, 2002; Staples, 1999). The primary purpose of WAC is, as the name implies, to take the writing tools and techniques developed in Composition Studies programs into areas of the university not traditionally associated with writing or writing assessment. This effort can include technical and professional programs, but WAC goals (McLeod & Soven, 2006) appear seldom in TPC scholarship of the 1980s and 1990s, bypassed in favor of Writing in the Disciplines (WID) and its efforts at fixing the descriptors that constitute TCP, as well as focusing on research programs and curriculum renovation consonant with TPC's increasing academic status (Bazerman et al., 2005; Russell, 2002). What traveled with WAC but most likely crossed into TPC via WID was a new attention to an old classic, the practice of Rhetoric, and a targeted interest in discourse analysis carried over from linguistics and Applied Language Studies (Connors, Ede, & Lunsford, 1984; Freedman & Medway, 1994; Young, Becker, & Pike, 1970).

Rhetoric, both classical and modern, quickly became embedded in the theoretical frame of TPC. A "response" to Jay Gould's (1978) collection of essays on Technical Communication appeared in the form of a volume solidly grounded in rhetoric: *New Essays in Technical Communication* (Anderson, Brockman, & Miller, 1983). This volume, along with the majority of the scholarship of the time, drew on the tenets of classical Rhetoric to support key claims about the character and operation of TPC (Moran & Journet, 1985; Reynolds, 1992; Zappen, 1987). Coinciding with this interest in rhetorical influences were the number of TPC "writing" texts and other volumes of rhetorically based advice and discussion (Dobrin, 1989; Mathes & Stevenson, 1976; McClosky, 1987/1998; Micheli, Cespedes, Byker, & Raymond, 1984). By 1990, Dorothy Winsor (1990) had integrated the concept fully into the context of the disciplines in *Writing Like an Engineer: A Rhetorical Education.*

Strict adherence to the classical canon does not provide a workable viewpoint for assessing TPC, however, offering as it does a rather narrowly defined approach that lends itself more readily to theorizing the production of TPC pedagogy than to assessing its documents (Bazerman et al., 2005). The rhetorical foundations carried throughout the last decades of the 20th century do, on the other hand, contribute to TPC two major characteristics that transfer readily from "growth" to "assessment." The first of these is concrete—the provision of a number of criteria for evaluating TPC, especially Audience, Purpose, and Organization (Bazerman, 1988; Blakeslee, 2001; Gross, 1984; Meyer, 1990). Begun as descriptive traits applied to production, these characteristics slowly but steadily transformed into a body of techniques that move cogently from production of TPC to its assessment (Blakeslee, Coles, & Confrey, 1996; Elliot, Kilduff, & Lynch, 1994). This development identified clearly that TPC assessment had moved on from "counting" items that contribute to a judgment of adequacy and/or comprehensiveness to consideration of the way specific characteristics of a document constitute its overall value.

The second characteristic, the concept of argument—the ability to use language to persuade an audience to accept a given viewpoint, or to act in the direction the speaker advocates (Bazerman, 2002; Gross, 1984; Nelson, Megill, &McClosky, 1989)—tends to appear in assessment rubrics under a number of guises (Carnegie Mellon, n.d.; Hundleby, Moussa, Lubin, & Pritchard, 2010; "Scoring rubrics," n.d). Whatever it is called, argument appears regularly in TPC assessment as the factor that transforms the text from the recital of facts, or the procedural knowledge of science and technology, to the conveying of conceptual knowledge, an examination of both how and why evidence presented is adequate to supporting claims made about it (Berkenkotter & Huckin, 1995). As a result, the factors that most often appeared labeled merely "Logic?" or "Sense?" in handwritten notes on a paper's margin have been reoriented by the increasing sophistication of TPC into a set of explicit criteria for developing a text and evaluating both its merit and worth (Coppola, 1999; Hundleby, Hovde, & Allen, 2003; Swarts & Odell, 2001).

Two evolutionary strands of thinking about the character of TPC and expectations for its effects also surfaced. A factor of situatedness had long been implied in the classical rhetorical associations of situation (Consigny, 1974). Following its demands, as Consigny defines them, means communication "must take into account the particularities of each situation" and possess "a command of topics" providing "a means for exploring and managing indeterminate contexts" (p. 176). Such situatedness is featured in the central presentations at the CPTSC's early 1990s conference on assessment, which point out for both TPC and its assessment practices the importance of site specificness, on the one hand (Cooper, 1990), and of being situated, on the other (Killingsworth, 1990). These interpretations clearly connect to a key concern developed around TPC's location in disciplines other than English Studies, as well as its operation in industry and multiple professional settings (Bazerman et al., 2005; Rivers, 1994; Russell, 2002; Staples, 1999). The influence of situatedness is reinforced further by the appearance of the "new rhetoric," the second evolutionary strand, and all that it implies about location in differing disciplines (Freedman & Medway, 1994), as well as its situational tenets of viewpoint, scene, agent, agency, and purpose (Burke, 1978; Micheli, Cespedes, Byker, & Raymond, 1984; Suchman, 1987). Thus, understanding the specific conventions and expectations of any locus for a communicative undertaking became a highly particular assessment need that developed as TPC began to recognize the increasing complexity of its own work.

The aptness of the concept of situatedness for TPC was underlined by the concepts passed down along the second strand, an increasing interest in the Social Study of Knowledge (SSK), especially in Natural Science, that had appeared in close proximity to the rise of the original concerns with the disciplines (Knorr Cetina, 1981; Latour & Woolger, 1979). Initially directed at theorizing the social implications of the practices of science, SSK made available to TPC an understanding of the mutual dependence of scientific work and scientific communication (Bazerman et al., 2005; Latour & Woolgar, 1979; Meyer, 1990). Both the social origins of the need to write about science and to clarify the consequences of doing so are passed to TPC by the SSK project (Hacking, 1983; Lynch, 1993), resulting in further demands on the range and adaptability not just of communication techniques, but even more of TPC's ability to assess the outcomes accurately and effectively (Coppola, 1999).

That the conditions are "social"—at least in the sense of Parsons' (1949) notion that the term refers to the concerted action of humans in groups rather than to the need of the individual to be responsive to a societal or cultural setting—is key to the continued health of assessment practices in TPC (Lipson, 1988; Thralls & Blyler, 1993). In addition to a continued importance in recognizing TPC as a consistently public and collaborative undertaking, this concept comprises support for a productive participation of communication in cultures of both study and work, whether in a technical, scientific, or business sector (Hart-Davidson, 2001). A specific version of this factor is developed in the concept of genre, variously drawn into TPC by Rhetoric, Functional Linguistics and English for Special Purposes (Bazerman, 2002; Berkenkotter & Huckin, 1995; Freedman & Medway, 1994; Killingsworth & Gilbertson, 1992; Miller, 1984; Swales, 1990). Functioning as an artifact of a knowledge area/discipline, a document indicates the continuing, often formally agreed-on representation of the practice or process (*indexical*) and how its artifact status participates in an exchange with the occasion/goal/system (*reflexive*) with which it is purportedly associated (Lynch & Woolgar, 1990). Given these circumstances, assessment has the ongoing job of understanding the extent of influence from a single factor such as context, as well as from multiple ones such as varying audiences and direct and indirect purposes (Bazerman & Paradis, 1994; Odell & Goswami, 1985; Spilka, 1993). Even more, TPC assessment requires awareness of how the artifact may be used to accomplish this or that task under these or those conditions.

Extended into the related area of Activity Theory, genre artifacts began to be seen less and less as something concerning exclusionary or spatially and temporally restricted products. Instead, what had been documents constructed largely on the basis of expectations from externally derived input systems (Lynne, 2004) are now transformed by participatory ones—that is, participation in an extended social relationship, the one between genre or genres and a system, an organized, publically observable process existing communally or across communities (Spinuzzi, 2003). This viewpoint usually features these processes as organized around the relations of work, but also available to disciplinary systems for defining recognizable epistemic processes (Engestrom & Middleton, 1998). At this point, all acts of representation are evaluative as well as descriptive (Latour, 1990), and assessment is traveling along a two-way street. Instead of being restricted only to a set of standards by which to measure the products of TPC (Coppola & Elliot, 2006), assessment defines and is defined by the action of components that structure documentation as operant in specific contexts of practice, and forming part of a larger concept of disciplinary action in their own right. Beginning with genre, but moving on to the activities of whole systems of representation, TPC assessment identifies the potential application of discursive and organizational moves that characterize them as successful. The focus shifts, finally, from the description of the several roles offered to assessment within TPC, and how it figures in any of them, to concern with how assessment creates and is created by TPC's function as discourse. The question of assessment in TPC has become much less a matter of answering to a fixed set of principles or enacting immutable laws of communication and much more one of determining in each situation how the functionality of an instance of communication is maintained and why it moves through the particular course of action—or fails to do so.

WHEN DOES PROFESSIONALISM BEGIN TO INFLUENCE TPC ASSESSMENT?

Throughout the years beginning with its rapid development after World War II and stretching to the end of the century, TPC has had a double mission—to introduce appropriate writing techniques into education and industry locations for technology, natural science, and the professions (Dubinsky, 2004; Gordon, 2009); and to enhance its practices in ways sufficient to, as well as consistent with, laying claim to a particular identity for its own specialized activities (Cargile Cook, 2002; Savage & Sullivan 2001). Moving significantly beyond the attempts to define and codify technical writing that marked the years of exponential growth (Rivers, 1994; Staples, 1999), by the opening of the 21st century, TPC has established two sides to its activities: On the one hand, construction of an identifiable and applicable pedagogy has enabled TPC to establish a working presence in Engineering Education; to enter a mutual and highly influential relationship with SSK; and to bring stabilizing practices to bear in widely diverse professional fields such as medicine, including nursing, and business administration (Davis, 2010; Jablonski & Nagelhout, 2010; Youra, 2010). On the other hand, TPC invests even more of its energy into looking beyond where its eventual goals may lie in order to examine the ever-changing patterns and prospects identifying exactly what unique abilities come into play (Cargile Cooke, 2002; Hart-Davidson, 2001; Killingsworth, 1999; Zachry et al., 2001), and TPC constitutes itself as a profession in its own right (Alred, 2003; Gordon, 2009; Spinuzzi, 2008). This claim is validated by the activities and outcomes the practices fundamental to TPC generate—for example, the targeting of a specific audience rather than a general one (Faber, 2002), or taking the role of a social advocate while maintaining "occupational distinctiveness" (pp. 314-315).

Such distinctive activities and outcomes may well create epistemic tensions that further complicate TPC's public and collaborative orientation, as

Faber suggests, but that tension offers a particularly effective relationship as a basis for what information is formulated and how it is disseminated. The connection is a reflexive one, in which the communicative practices influence and are influenced by the context of the communicative undertaking—whether disciplinary, institutional, or workplace (Lynch, 1993; Lynch & Woolgar, 1990). A major factor in TPC's adoption of a professional stance lies, therefore, in the maintenance of communication practices that are clearly targeted but equally adaptable to multiple conditions and expectations. As Maid and D'Angelo point out in Chapter 5 of this volume in their discussion of what constitutes professional use of the proposal genre, such a claim to adaptability is also a key to both how and why adequate assessment can be achieved.

Taking the claim to professionalism seriously in establishing assessment practices calls for the particular consideration of how TPC orients itself to keeping pace with the explosion of computer use in the ever-increasing production and exchange of information and its incorporation into everyday work in, especially, technical and scientific areas (Gleick, 2011). Comprehension of the workings of computer technology; documentation in areas such as Engineering and Computer Science particularly associated with computers; and the use of computers to produce and apply documentation associated with many and varying kinds of academic and industrial activities have been a longstanding concern for the work of TPC (Selber, 1997; Zachry, 2001). Most of the "complex and interrelated skills" noted by Cargile Cook (2002, p. 7) as being necessary for technical communicators are closely allied to computer use, as is providing the means for instantiating visual content in technical discourse in both academic and workplace settings (Portweig, 2004; Wysocki, 2004; Zachry & Thralls, 2004).

Even though it shares reliance on several of these skill sets with MSC, TPC has remained the particular province of communicative work influencing and being influenced by technology (Selber, 2010). In TPC, not only do computers drive a large part of the circumstances of composing, they also continually modify the practices of knowledge-making (Zappen, 2005), its "iterability" (Hart-Davidson, 2001, p. 148), and multiple forms of dissemination in equally multiple formats (Geisler et al., 2001). What the "professionalism" assertion adds to TPC, therefore, is a separation into several individually identifiable tracks, often with varying expectations for variable outcomes, but consistently revolving around a set of concepts that are addressed in relation to computers and human-computer interaction.

The job of holding together what might almost seem to be an increasingly fragmented undertaking (see, e.g., Yancey's commentary, 2004) has quickly and definitely become the hallmark task for TPC assessment. Required to be at once both narrowly focused and broadly applicable, the assessment practices involved operate on several different levels, and employ techniques identified with the distinctiveness of the goals of the context in which they operate, as well as with "best practices" for achieving the educational outcomes sought (Allen, 2004; Hundleby & Allen, 2010). First of all, the conclusions reached on the basis of assessment efforts in TPC settings are answerable not only for direct supervision of classroom activities (Meyer, 2005; Swarts & Odell, 2001; Tihanyi & Hundleby, 2007), but are also taken up for purposes of the program assessment for which the individual course assessment provides a starting point (Cargile Cook, 2003; Coppola & Elliot, 2006; Johnson, 2006b; Thomas & McShane, 2007).

Program assessment then moves outward from its disciplinary location to furnish data for succeeding levels of assessment: institutional assessment of how well the curriculum constituted by those programs meets the goals and supports the profile of the university presented to accrediting bodies (Allen, 2010; Carter, Anson, & Miller, 2003); and public answers to the assessment questions asked by formal and informal review bodies such as Accreditation Board for Engineering & Technology and the Council for Programs in Technical and Scientific Communication (Thomas & McShane, 2007; Williams, 2002). Finally, and not least of all, assessment gathers data from the industry sources representing the ultimate goal of the courses, programs, and institutionally mandated curricula—producing students who are adequately, comprehensively, and professionally educated for taking their knowledge of writing technically and of technical writing into the "world" (Coppola, 2010; Driskill, 2000; Yu, 2008).

Two specific assessment techniques have taken prominent roles in implementing the plans laid by designers of TPC assessment: One is the use of rubrics, the other the use of portfolios. Rubrics were originally intended for assessment of one-time assignments within the context of a single course, and designed to provide a quick-reference guide to sum up a student's achievement on that assignment only. They have shown themselves to be highly useful for providing formative assessment (Thomas, 2005; Weiss, McCahan, Hundleby, & Woodhouse, 2005) and, in TPC assessment, particularly for dealing with disciplinary and content variations central to the "technical and professional" part of the assessing communication practices (Bazerman, 2003; Boettger, 2010; Swarts & Odell, 2001). Because they are set out in the form of a matrix, rubrics are able to show any one person how she/he has met the original demands of TPC assessment for accuracy and comprehensiveness within the context of both communication and content criteria. As well, it provides a scale that identifies the degree of satisfaction provided by an individual approach to a communication task, but does so with a measure that can be read as either a measurement value or as a point on a subjective continuum.

In contrast, the use of portfolio assessment techniques makes available a more extensive, and likely more accurate, picture of student achievement when the work attached to a course or program is evaluated across time and variations of complexity (Cargile, Cook & Zachry, 2010; Coppola, 1999; Johnson, 2006b; Williams, 2002). Although sometimes restricted to guidelines assembled from performance indicators, portfolios supply the scope and context for assessing the outcomes of a student's approach to multiple, complex, and diverse tasks negotiated in highly changeable, often uncertain, and sometimes even difficult circumstances (Consortium, 2000; Hart-Davidson, 2001; Spinuzzi, 2007).

Each distinct from but supporting the other, rubrics and portfolios are embedded in the characteristic professionalism of TPC and of its assessment, as is the ability to respond appropriately to varying types and degrees of demand. The key to an accurate characterization of how TPC assessment has developed to serve both professional knowledge-making and its professional obligations lies in understanding that the assessment activities for TPC derive from the need to focus on that knowledge as an outcome of the work desired. While initially measuring the process, characteristic TPC assessment also focuses on knowledge outcomes in a way that guarantees the professionalism of the work in question—as shown, for example, in the discussion of "excellence" by Paretti and Burgoyne (2009). Ultimately, these interactions can be seen as functioning in an "ecology" of knowledge appropriate to the complex interdependence of the factors constituting TPC practice (Hundleby, 1999; Spinuzzi, 2007; Spinuzzi & Zachry, 2000), and sustainable across its multiple and diverse sites, audiences, and iterations.

DOES IT (STILL) WORK?

Asking "does it work?" is as germane to assessing achievement in the current context of a multivalent TPC as it was when used for scrutinizing the satisfactory production of writing in its original locus of Engineering English. As an assessment technique, putting this question both recognizes and honors the conventions of TPC's discipline-specific work and provides the means for adapting to local and particular sites and mediating between that work and an outside "world" needing to understand what is going on. Although getting to an answer to the question demands a much more complicated configuration than the original circumstances elicited, the force of the question remains the same: We are not asking about the details of any one function of TPC, but seeking to assess the coherence and durability of all the answers to all the questions that need to be asked.

REFERENCES

Allen, J. (1993). The role(s) of assessment in technical communication: A review of the literature. *Technical Communication Quarterly, 2*(4), 365-388.

Allen, J. (2004). The impact of student learning outcomes assessment on technical and professional communication programs. *Technical Communication Quarterly, 13*(1), 93-108.

Allen, J. (2010). Mapping institutional values and the technical communication curriculum: A strategy for grounding assessment. In M. Hundleby & J. Allen (Eds.), *Assessment in technical and professional communication* (pp. 39-56). Amityville, NY: Baywood Publishers.

Alred, G. (2003). Essential works on technical communication. *Technical Communication, 50*(4), 585-616.

Anderson, P., Brockman, J. & Miller, C. (Eds.) (1983). *New essays in technical and scientific communication: Research, theory, practice*. Farmingdale, NY: Baywood Publishing.

Anson, C. (1989). *Writing and response: Theory, practice, research*. Urbana, IL: National Council for Teachers of English.

Bazerman, C. (1988). *Shaping written knowledge: The genre and activity of the experimental article in science*. Madison, WI: University of Wisconsin Press.

Bazerman, C. (2002). The case for writing studies as a major discipline. In G. A. Olsen (Ed.), *Rhetoric and composition as intellectual work* (pp. 32-38). Carbondale, IL: Southern Illinois University Press.

Bazerman, C., Little, J., Bethel, L., Chavkin, T., Fouquette, D., & Garufis, J. (2005). *Reference guide to writing across the curriculum*. Boulder, CO: Parlor Press & the WAC Clearinghouse. Web.

Bazerman, C., & Paradis, J. (Eds.). (1994). *Textual dynamics of the professions. Historical and contemporary studies of writing in professional communities.* Madison, WI: University of Wisconsin Press.

Berkenkotter, C., & Huckin, T. (1995). *Genre knowledge in disciplinary communication: Cognition/culture/power*. Hillsdale, NJ: Lawrence Erlbaum Associates.

Berlin, J. A. (1987). *Rhetoric and reality: Writing instruction in American colleges, 1900-1985*. Carbondale, IL: Southern Illinois University Press.

Blakeslee, A. (2000). *Interacting with audiences*. Mahwah, NJ: Lawrence Erlbaum Associates.

Blakeslee, A., Cole, C., & Confrey, T. (1996). Evaluating qualitative inquiry in technical and scientific communication: Toward a practical and dialogic validity. *Technical Communication Quarterly, 5*(2), 125-149.

Boettger, R. (2010). Rubric use in technical communication: Exploring the process of creating valid and reliable assessment tools. *IEEE Transactions on Professional Communication, 53*(1), 4-17.

Burke, K. (1978). Questions and answers about the Pentad. *College Composition and Communication, 29*(4), 330-335.

Cargile Cook, K. (2002). Layered literacies: A theoretical frame for technical communication pedagogy. *Technical Communication Quarterly, 11*(1), 5-29.

Cargile Cook, K. (2003). How much is enough? The assessment of student work in technical communication courses. *Technical Communication Quarterly, 12*(1), 47-65.

Cargile Cook, K., & Zachry, M. (2010). Politics, programmatic self-assessment, and the challenge of cultural change. In M. Hundleby & J. Allen (Eds.), *Assessment in technical and professional communication* (pp. 65-80). Amityville, NY: Baywood Publishers.

Carnegie Mellon. (n.d.). *Rubrics for assessing students' technical writing skills*. Web.

Carter, M., Anson, C., & Miller, C. (2003). Assessing technical writing in institutional contexts: Using outcomes-based assessment for programmatic thinking. *Technical Communication Quarterly, 12(*1), 101-114.

Connors, R. (1982). The rise of technical writing instruction in America. *Journal of Technical and Business Communication, 12*(4), 329-351.

Connors, R., Ede, L., & Lunsford, A. (1984). *Essays on classical rhetoric and modern discourse*. Carbondale, IL: Southern Illinois University Press.

Consigny, S. (1974). Rhetoric and its situations. *Philosophy and Rhetoric, 7*(4), 175-186.

Consortium for the Study of Engineering Communication. (2000, July.) Rice University, Houston, TX. Web.

Cooper, M. (1990). Model(s) for educating professional communicators. In J. Zappen & S. Katz (Eds.), *Proceedings of the 1990 Council of Programs in Technical & Scientific Communication* (pp. 11-21). San Diego, CA. Web.

Coppola, N. (1999). Setting the discourse community: Tasks and assessment for the new technical communication service course. *Technical Communication Quarterly, 8*(3), 249-267.

Coppola, N. (2010). The technical communication body of knowledge initiative: An academic-practitioner partnership. *Technical Communication, 57*(1), 11-25.

Coppola, N., & Elliot, N. (2006). A technology transfer model for program assessment in technical communication. *Technical Communication, 56*(4), 460-474.

Cunningham, D., & Estrin, H. (Eds.). (1975). *The teaching of technical writing*. Urbana, IL: National Council of Teachers of English.

Davidson, V. (2011). [Personal communication to M. Hundleby]. Guelph, ON: University of Guelph School of Engineering.

Dobrin, D. (1989). *Writing and technique*. Urbana, IL: National Council of Teachers of English.

Davis, M. (2010). Assessing technical communication within engineering contexts tutorial. *IEEE Transactions on Professional Communication, 53*(1), 33-45.

Driskill, L. (2000, June 23-25). Linking industry best practices and EC3(g) assessment in engineering communication. *Proceedings of the American Society for Engineering Education Conference*. St. Louis, MO. Web.

Dubinsky, J. (2004). *Teaching technical communication. Critical issues for the classroom*. New York, NY: Bedford St. Martins.

Elliot, N. (2010). Assessing technical communication: A conceptual history. In M. Hundleby & J. Allen (Eds.), *Assessment in technical and professional communication* (pp. 17-38). Amityville, NY: Baywood Publishers.

Elliot, N., Kilduff, M., & Lynch, R. (1994). The assessment of technical writing. A case study. *Journal of Technical Writing and Communication, 24*(1), 19-36.

Engestrom, Y., & Middleton, D. (1998). *Cognition and community at work*. Cambridge, UK: Cambridge University Press.

Faber, B. (2002). Professional identities: What's professional about professional writing. *Journal of Business and Technical Communication, 16*(3), 306-337.

Fearing, B., & Sparrow, W. (Eds.). (1990). *Technical writing. Theory and practice*. New York, NY: Modern Languages Association.

Freedman, A., & Medway, P. (1994). Locating genre studies: Antecedents and prospects. In A. Freedman & P. Medway (Eds.), *Genre and the new rhetoric* (pp. 1-20). London, UK: Taylor and Francis.

Geisler, C., Bazerman, C., Doheny-Farina, S., Gurak, L., Haas, C., Johnson-Eilola, J., Kaufer, D., Lunsford, A., Miller, C., Winsor, D., & Yates, J. (2001). IText. Future directions for research on the relationship between information technology and writing. *Journal of Business and Technical Communication, 15*(3), 269-308.

Gleick, J. (2011). *The information: A history, a theory, a flood*. New York, NY: Pantheon.

Gordon, J. (2009). The pedagogical mission of professional and technical communications programs. *Programmatic Perspectives, 1*(2), 112-138.

Gould, J. (Ed.). (1978). *Directions in technical writing and communication*. Farmingdale, NY: Baywood Publishers.

Gross, A. (1984). Style and arrangement in scientific prose. *Journal of Technical Writing & Communication, 14*(3), 241-253.

Guba, E., & Lincoln, Y. (1989). *Fourth generation evaluation*. Newbury Park, CA: Sage Publications.

Hacking, I. (1983). *Representing and intervening*. Cambridge, UK: Cambridge University Press.

Hagge, J. (1995). Early engineering writing textbooks and the anthropological complexity of disciplinary discourse. *Written Communication, 12(*4), 439-491.

Hart-Davidson, W. (2001). On writing, technical communication and information technology: The core competencies of technical communication. *Technical Communication, 48*(2), 145-155.

Hundleby, M. (1999). *What counts as technical writing? Assessing writing for technical and scientific purposes*. Unpublished dissertation. Toronto, ON: University of Toronto.

Hundleby, M., & Allen, J. (2010). Introduction. In M. Hundleby & J. Allen (Eds.), *Assessment in technical and professional communication* (pp. vi-xv). Amityville, NY: Baywood Publishing.

Hundleby, M., Hovde, M., & Allen, J. (2003). Foreword. *Technical Communication Quarterly* [Special issue on Technical Communication Assessment], 12(1), 5-6.

Hundleby, M., Moussa, M., Lubin, D., & Pritchard, P. (2010) A writing kit for engineering design reports. *Proceedings of the Canadian Engineering Education Association*. Web.

Huot, B. (2003). *(Re)articulating writing assessment for teaching and learning*. Logan, UT: Utah State University Press.

Jablonski, J., & Nagelhout, E (2010). Assessing professional writing programs using technology as a site of praxis. In M. Hundleby & J. Allen (Eds.), *Assessment in professional and technical communication* (pp. 171-188). Amityville, NY: Baywood Press.

Johnson, C. (2006a). A decade of research: Assessing change in the technical communication classroom using online portfolios. *Journal of Business and Technical Communication, 36*(4), 413-436.

Johnson, C. (2006b). The analytic assessment of online portfolios in undergraduate technical communication: A model. *Journal of Engineering Education, 95*(4), 279-287.

Johnson, C., & Elliot, N. (2010). Undergraduate technical writing assessment: A model. *Programmatic Perspectives, 2*(2), 110-151. Web.

Killingsworth, M. (1990). Evaluating service programs in technical communication: How can qualitative research help us? In J. Zappen & S. Katz (Eds.), *Proceedings of the 1990 Council of Programs in Technical & Scientific Communication* (pp. 44-51). San Diego, CA Web.

Killingsworth, M. (1999). Technical communication in the 21st century: Where are we going? *Technical Communication Quarterly, 8*(2), 165-174.

Killingsworth, M., & Gilbertson, M. (1992). *Signs, genres, and communities in technical communication*. Amityville, NY: Baywood Publishers.

Knorr Cetina, K. (1981). *The manufacture of knowledge*. Oxford, UK: Pergamon Press.

Kynell, T. (1999). Technical communication from 1850-1950: Where have we been? *Technical Communication Quarterly, 8*(2), 143-151.

Latour, B. (1990). Drawing things together. In M. Lynch & S. Woolgar (Eds.), *Representation in scientific practice* (pp. 19-68). Cambridge, MA: MIT Press.

Latour, B., & Woolgar, S. (1979). *Laboratory life: The social construction of scientific facts*. Beverly Hills: CA: Sage Publications.

Lipson, C. (1988). A social view of technical writing. *Journal of Business and Technical Communication, 2*(1), 7-20.

Lynch, M. (1993). *Ordinary science and practical action*. Cambridge, UK: Cambridge University Press.

Lynch, M., & Woolgar, S. (1990). Introduction. In M. Lynch. & S. Woolgar (Eds.), *Representation in scientific practice*. Cambridge, MA: MIT Press.

Lynne, P. (2004). *Coming to terms. Theorizing writing assessment in composition studies*. Logan, UT: Utah State University Press.

Mathes, J., & Stevenson, D. (1976). *Designing technical reports: Writing for audiences in organizations.* New York, NY: Bobbs-Merrill.

McCloskey, D. (1987/1998). *The rhetoric of economics*. Madison, WI: University of Wisconsin Press

McLeod, S., & Soven, M. (2006). *Composing a community: A history of writing across the curriculum*. West Lafayette, IN: Parlor Press.

Meyer, D. (2005). Capstone design outcome assessment: Instruments for quantitative evaluation. *Frontiers in Education, 2005. FIE '05. Proceedings of the 35th Annual Conference* (pp. F4D-1-F4D-5). Web.

Meyer, G. (1990). *Writing biology: Texts in the social construction of scientific knowledge*. Madison, WI: University of Wisconsin Press.

Michaelson, H. (1990). *How to write and publish engineering papers and reports* (3rd ed.). Phoenix, AZ: Oryx Press.

Michaeli, L., Cespedes, F., Byker, D., & Raymond, T. (1984). *Managerial communication*. Glenview, IL: Scott, Foresman, & Co.

Miller, C. (1984). Genre as social action. *Quarterly Journal of Speech, 7*(2), 151-167.

Moran, M., & Journet, D. (1985). *Research in technical communication: A bibliographic sourcebook*. Westport, CT: Greenwood.

Nelson, J. S., Megill, A., & McClosky, D. M. (Eds.). (1989). *The rhetoric of the human sciences: Language and argument in scholarship and public affairs*. Madison, WI: University of Wisconsin Press.

Odell, L., & Goswami, D. (Eds.). (1985). *Writing in non-academic settings*. New York, NY: Guilford Press.

Paretti, M., & Burgoyne, C. (2009). Assessing excellence: Using activity theory to understand assessment practices in Engineering communication. *Proceedings of the 2009 IEEE International Professional Communication Conference* (pp. 1-7). Web.

Portweig, T. (2004). Making sense of the visual in technical communication: A visual literacy approach to pedagogy. *Journal of Technical Writing and Communication, 34*(1-2), 31-42.

Parsons, T. (1949). *The structure of social action*. New York, NY: The Free Press.

Pickering, A. (1995). *The mangle of practice: Time, agency & science*. Chicago, IL: University of Chicago Press.

Reynolds, J. (1992). Rhetoric and the teaching of technical writing. *Technical Communication Quarterly, 1*(2), 63-76.

Rivers, W. E. (1994). Studies in the history of business and technical writing. A bibliographical essay. *Journal of Business and Technical Communication, 8*(1), 6-57.

Russell, D. (2002). *Writing in the academic disciplines. A curricular history* (2nd ed.). Carbondale, IL: Southern Illinois University Press.

Savage, G., & Sullivan, D. (2001). *Writing a professional life: Stories of technical communicators on the job*. Boston, MA: Allyn and Bacon.

Scoring rubrics for professional writing: MIT. (n.d.). Web.

Selber, S. (Ed.). (1997). *Computers and technical communication: Pedagogical and programmatic perspectives*. Greenwich, CT: Ablex.

Selber, S. (Ed.). (2010). *Rhetorics and technologies: New directions in writing and communication*. Columbia, SC: University of South Carolina Press.

Spilka, R. (1993). *Writing in the workplace: New research perspectives*. Carbondale, IL: Southern Illinois University Press.

Spinuzzi, C. (2003). *Tracing genres through organizations: A sociocultural approach to information design*. Cambridge, MA: The MIT Press.

Spinuzzi, C. (2007). Guest editor's introduction: Technical communication in the age of distributed work. *Technical Communication Quarterly, 16*(3), 265-277.

Spinuzzi, C., & Zachry, M. (2000). Genre ecologies: An open-system approach to understanding and constructing documentation. *ACM Journal of Computer Documentation, 24*(3), 169-181.

Staples, K. (1999). Technical communication from 1950-1998: Where are we now? *Technical Communication Quarterly, 8*(2), 153-164.

Suchman, L. (1987). *Plans and situated actions: The problem of human machine communication*. Cambridge, UK: Cambridge University Press.

Swales, J. (1990). *Genre analysis*. Cambridge, UK: Cambridge University Press.

Swarts, J., & Odell, L. (2001). Rethinking the evaluation of writing in engineering courses. *31st ASEE IEEE Frontiers in Education Conference* (pp. T3A-25-T3A-30). Web.

Thomas, S. (2005). The engineering-technical writing connection: A rubric for effective communication. *2005 IEEE International Professional Communication Conference Proceedings* (pp. 517-523). Web.

Thomas, S., & McShane, B. (2007). Skills and literacies for the 21st century: Assessing an under-graduate professional and technical writing program. *Technical Communication, 14*(4), 412-423

Thompson, I. (2001). Collaboration in technical communication: A qualitative content analysis of journal articles, 1990-1999. *IEEE Transactions on Professional Communication, 44*(3), 161-173.

Thralls, C., & Blyler, N. (1993). The social perspective and pedagogy in technical communication. *Technical Communication Quarterly, 2*(3), 249-269.

Tihanyi, D., and Hundleby, M. N. (2007, October 19-20). Continuous loop assessment in engineering communication. *Proceedings, Engineering Teaching and Learning Practices* (ETLP), ASEE, St. Lawrence Section. Web.

Weiss, P., McCahan, S., Hundleby, M., & Woodhouse, K. (2005). Making a little theory go a long way: Situating rubrics for learning and assessing. *Proceedings of the 2005 IEEE International Professional Communication Conference* (pp. 508-516). Web.

White, E. (1985). *Teaching and assessing writing*. San Francisco, CA: Jossey-Bass.

Williams, J. (2002). The engineering portfolio: Communication, reflection and student learning outcomes assessment. *International Journal of Engineering Education, 18*(2), 199-207.

Winsor, D. (1990). *Writing like an engineer: A rhetorical education*. Mahwah, NJ: Lawrence Erlbaum Associates.

Wysocki, A. (2004). *Writing new media: Theory and applications for expanding the teaching of composition*. Logan, UT: Utah State University Press.

Yancey, K. (1999). Looking back as we look forward: Historicizing writing assessment. *College Composition and Communication, 50*(3), 483-503.

Yancey, K. (2004). Looking for coherence in a fragmented world: Notes toward a new assessment design. *Computers and Composition, 21*(1), 89-102.

Young, R., Becker, A., & Pike, K. (1970). *Rhetoric: Discovery and change*. New York, NY: Harcourt, Brace & World.

Youra, S. (2010). Beyond denial: Assessment and expanded communication instruction in engineering and professional programs. In M. Hundleby & J. Allen (Eds.), *Assessment in professional and technical communication* (pp. 113-125). Amityville, NY: Baywood Press.

Yu, H. (2008) Contextualize technical writing assessment to better prepare students for workplace writing: Student-centered assessment instruments. Journal of *Technical Writing and Communication, 38*(3), 265-284.

Zachry, M. (2001). Constructing usable documentation: A study of communicative practices and the early uses of mainframe computing in industry. Journal of *Technical Writing and Communication, 3*(1), 61-76.

Zachry, M., Faber B., Cargile Cook, K., & Clark, D. (2001). The changing face of technical communication: New directions for the field in a new millennium. SIGDOC '01. *Proceedings of the 19th Annual International Conference on Computer Documentation*. Web.

Zachry, M., & Thralls, C. (2004). An interview with Edward R. Tufte. *Technical Communication Quarterly, 13*(4), 447-462.

Zappen, J. (1987). Rhetoric and technical communication: An argument for historical and political pluralism. *Iowa State Journal of Business and Technical Communication, 1*(2), 29-44.

Zappen, J. (2005). Digital rhetoric: Toward an integrated theory [Special Issue on the State of Rhetoric of Science and Technology]. L. Gurak & A. Gross (Eds.). *Technical Communication Quarterly, 14*(3), 319-325.

7

WRITING ASSESSMENT FOR ADMISSION TO GRADUATE AND PROFESSIONAL PROGRAMS

LESSONS LEARNED AND A NOTE FOR THE FUTURE

Mary Fowles

Educational Testing Service

One of my most vivid memories of how faculty can influence the design of large-scale testing programs stems from around 1980, when a senior colleague, Miriam Levin, hosted a committee meeting to review questions for the NTE Core Battery: Composition Skills section. With a background in linguistics and literature, Levin went into the meeting fully expecting to continue the development of this well-established multiple-choice test of writing skills. However, Edward White served on that committee and made such a compelling argument in favor of direct writing assessment that Levin returned to the office resolved to add an essay. In hindsight, this should not have been a daunting feat, for ETS had been developing and scoring essay tests since the mid 1960s—for example, the College Board's English Composition Test for college applicants and the Foreign Service Written Examination for State Department candidates (Godshalk, 1966). However, because states used the NTE score results as part of a credentialing process to certify or license beginning teachers, the essay task, prompts, and scoring criteria would need to be appropriate for teacher candidates at all school levels (from kindergarten to senior high) and in all subject areas (from English and history to music, art, and physical education). Job analysis studies would have to be conducted to confirm that the essay prompts, along with other items in the test, were appropriate for beginning teachers. As explained by Rosenfeld, Thornton, and Skurnik (1986),

> Before allowing a state to use the tests in the certification process, the NTE Policy Council requires as part of the validation strategy that a panel of experts judge the content of each item for its relevance to the job of teaching and to that particular state's teacher-education curriculum. Only those items judged to be relevant measures of a particular curriculum and the knowledge and skills necessary for the job performance of a beginning teacher are considered when the standards are set for certification in that jurisdiction. (p. 17)

In state after state, data from the job analysis studies provided objective evidence of the test's validity and thus helped confirm the importance of writing for all K-12 teachers—in all subjects and in all grades. Ed White deserves much of the credit for sparking that important change.

WRITING ASSESSMENTS FOR GRADUATE AND PROFESSIONAL PROGRAMS

Today, almost everyone assumes that a valid test of "writing" must require actual writing. In order to enter graduate school or to pursue a degree in medicine, law, education, or numerous other professions, candidates must now first demonstrate how well their writing skills meet the standards set by faculty and practitioners in the relevant field. But it was only in the last two decades of the 20th century that many large-scale graduate and professional testing programs began requiring a direct measure of the candidate's writing. Below are some of the milestones in that historic progression.[1]

- *In 1982, an essay prompt replaced the multiple-choice test of writing skills in the Law School Admission Test (LSAT).* The LSAT is unusual in that its essays are not scored but, instead, are sent to designated law school admission offices.
- *In 1982, an essay prompt was added to the multiple-choice writing section of the NTE Core Battery, an entry-level assessment for teacher-education programs in all content areas.* Hundreds of school and college English faculty from all over the country began participating in NTE scoring sessions and, quite often, used the NTE scoring guide in their own writing programs.

- *In 1986, the Test of English as a Foreign Language (TOEFL) program introduced the Test of Written English (TWE) to assess the essay-writing skills of international students applying to colleges and graduate programs in North America.*
- *In 1991, a writing measure with two prompts replaced the multiple-choice section of the Medical College Admission Test (MCAT).* MCAT was one of the first testing programs to report a writing score based on two prompts.
- *In 1994, the Uniform Certified Public Accountant (CPA) Examination began scoring three of its essay questions for written communication skills as well as for content knowledge.*
- *In 1994, the Analytical Writing Assessment, with two prompts, was added to the Graduate Management Admission Test (GMAT).* A few years after the test was introduced, the GMAT program broke new ground by requiring that all essays be written on computer and electronically distributing essays for college faculty to score online (1997), and by reporting a combination of human and automated scores (1999).
- *In 1999, a writing measure with two prompts was introduced by the Graduate Record Examinations® (GRE) program.* The Analytical Writing test was optional until 2002, when it was folded into the GRE General Test, which is required for admission into many different fields of graduate study.
- *In 2001, the Foreign Service Officer (FSO) program reintroduced an essay prompt to complement the multiple-choice section in its admission test.* This testing program is unusual in that it evaluates essays only for those candidates who have earned high scores on the rest of the test.

Soon after this progression of "firsts," other graduate and professional testing programs added direct measures of writing to their national and international assessments. What caused this seemingly rapid introduction of direct writing assessment for admission to graduate and professional programs?

One factor, of course, was a growing public awareness of the connection between thinking and writing and the importance of analytical writing skills for success in graduate study and professional careers. Although the earliest writing tests were administered on paper, programs such as GRE and GMAT heralded the arrival of computer-based testing, which soon dominated the field. Computers not only enabled most examinees to write more fluently during a limited testing period but also streamlined the process of collecting written responses, distributing them to online scorers, and training and monitoring scorers—a process that promised to increase scoring efficiency while reducing costs. At the same time, researchers refined automated scoring models to the point where they could reliably match scores from experienced readers. Essay testing programs now had to weigh the advantages of using automated scoring (faster and cheaper) against the established practice of having two experienced readers evaluate each essay (usually considered a more valid approach, especially from a pedagogical perspective). Just as important were the impressive advances made in writing-intensive courses and other college-level projects that focused on writing in and across disciplines.

But while higher-level programs benefited from undergraduate models, they could not follow them precisely. Higher education and professional entry-level assessments usually had much greater consequences (higher stakes) for the test takers and had to represent the views of an entire profession (e.g., law or business management) or many different institutions and academic fields (as in the case of the GRE General Test).

High-stakes testing requires thoughtful, evidence-based answers to a myriad of pressing questions (see Baldwin, Chapter 18.) The following are some of the most critical questions for graduate and professional programs to address.

Construct definition and test design: What kinds of writing tasks do graduate faculty and practitioners agree are important in a particular field, and what prerequisite, entry-level skills do those tasks require? How closely should the writing tasks resemble or correlate to those performed outside of testing conditions? How many writing tasks are necessary to assess the construct and to achieve adequate test reliability? Is any kind of selected-response format appropriate? If so, what kinds, and why? What are the best ways to ensure that examinees display their own thinking and writing in response to a particular topic instead of relying on prememorized texts or elaborate fill-in-the-blank templates?

Scoring: What method is best, and why? What scoring criteria most accurately define the critical thinking and writing skills displayed in the responses? Who should read and evaluate the responses? What training and monitoring processes should be followed? Can or should any of the scoring be automated?

Test and scoring reliability: How can we ensure that scorers are applying the scoring criteria consistently and accurately? What steps can we take to help ensure that the difficulty levels of different prompts will prove comparable within and across different test administrations? And if we find that score results differ significantly, what should be done about it?

Score reporting and use of test scores: What kinds of information should examinees receive? What information should be sent to institutions—a numerical score, a description of an examinee's writing, copies of the actual written responses? What are appropriate and inappropriate uses of writing test scores or other data? What responsibility do testing programs have to ensure that test-use guidelines are followed by admission offices and other score users?

Consequential validity: What is the likely impact of the proposed test design on undergraduate writing instruction and/or on the graduate program or professional field that the candidates are about to enter?

To understand how a high-stakes writing assessment program might answer these questions, consider some of the decisions made by one graduate admission program, GRE, as a paradigmatic example. When the GRE Board decided to explore the feasibility of adding a writing measure to the GRE General Test, one of its first steps was to appoint a Writing Advisory Committee charged with defining the writing construct and developing prototype writing tasks. My job was to work with that committee. At our meetings, it was the lively exchanges among professors of economics, physiology, English, nursing, and other academic areas that helped us define the critical thinking and analytical writing skills necessary for success in many different areas of graduate study. We considered a wide range of writing tasks and then pilot tested the most promising with thousands of upper-division students and GRE examinees. The GRE psychometric team analyzed pilot-test scores to determine whether certain types of tasks or topics unduly disadvantaged or favored groups on the basis of gender, ethnicity, academic background, geographic region, or other relevant factors. Throughout this process, the Writing Advisory Committee made frequent reports to the GRE Board as well as to the GRE Technical Advisory Committee, the GRE Committee on Fairness and Equity, and the GRE Research Committee. These groups provided ongoing guidance and support, so that by the time the Writing Advisory Committee presented its final recommendations for the test design, we had the necessary technical data and practical experience to support our position. Here is a quick account of what the writing committee recommended, and why.

Construct definition and test design: The GRE Writing Advisory Committee proposed two different but complementary analytical writing tasks: *Present Your Perspective on an Issue* (examinees read a brief prompt and develop their own argument on the topic) and *Analyze an Argument* (examinees critique the reasoning in a brief proposal, usually about a business or government topic). Pilot-test data confirmed that, together, the two writing samples yield the necessary reliability for reporting a separate writing score and that, compared to other options (e.g., a single prompt, two prompts of the same type, or a single prompt with a multiple-choice component), the two different types of tasks provide a better sampling of the analytical writing construct.[2] Additional evidence to support this decision was gathered in a subsequent large-scale study (Rosenfeld, Courtney, & Fowles, 2004), which confirmed the importance of the *Issue and Argument* writing tasks for success at three levels of higher education (upper-division postgraduate, master's, and doctoral). The results were based on interviews and ratings from over 500 graduate and undergraduate faculty in six content domains (education, engineering, English, life sciences, physical sciences, psychology) and across a wide range of 27 institutions in the United States.

The GRE Writing Advisory Committee also recommended offering a choice of topics for only the *Issue* writing task. They reasoned that choice is especially important when writers must draw on their external knowledge and experience to develop their arguments and that making a choice is generally easier when the prompts are brief—in this case, only one or two sentences. By contrast, the *Argument* prompts are much longer and contain all of the information (multiple claims and evidence) that the writer needs to consider in the critique. However, before approving the test design, the GRE Board asked for additional data. To this end, Powers and Fowles (1998) conducted the "Test Takers' Judgments about GRE Writing Test Prompts" study, which involved 78 prompts and hundreds of GRE candidates at 15 colleges and universities, with significant numbers of minority students. Each participant was asked to rank order a set of prompts from most preferred (the one on which they felt they could write the strongest essay) to least preferred (the one they perceived as most difficult to write about). Then the students wrote essays on the prompts on both ends of the scale. Results showed that participants did not necessarily earn higher or lower essay scores on the prompts they preferred; therefore, there was no compelling reason not to allow a choice of *Issue* prompts. Based on this information, the GRE Board approved the writing committee's recommendation of offering choice for the Issue prompt.

Based on timing data (Powers & Fowles, 1997), the committee also recommended time limits of 30 minutes for the *Argument* task and 45 minutes for the *Issue* task so that examinees would have the time necessary to choose a topic and then plan and compose a well-developed argument with reasons and examples drawn from their outside reading, experience, or academic work.

Scoring: The committee also recommended holistic scoring, an approach well-grounded in writing assessment theory and practice, particularly in nonpedagogical contexts when it is not necessary to provide individualized feedback. Because the GRE writing construct focuses on analytical writing, the committee developed scoring criteria that value analysis over discourse-level skills (e.g., grammar, sentence structure). And because the *Issue* and *Argument* tasks assess somewhat different analytical thinking skills, the committee developed separate rubrics to reflect those differences. After reading pilot-test responses, the committee also agreed that the 0-6 scale is particularly well-suited for the GRE, whose population is so diverse that a more constrained set of score levels would not allow the scoring guide to describe the distinct differences they observed in the overall quality of the written responses.

Test and scoring reliability: Ideally, an examinee should receive the same writing score no matter which prompts he or she is assigned or which readers evaluate the responses. To help ensure that GRE prompts were comparable in difficulty before introducing the test, the GRE program conducted a comprehensive analysis of the psychometric characteristics of the proposed test (Schaeffer, Briel, & Fowles, 2001) across designated subgroups (male/female, ethnicity, undergraduate major, and other subgroup characteristics). The results are summed up in this excerpt from the research report:

> Forty prompts (20 Issue and 20 Argument) were administered to over 2,300 students at 26 participating U.S. colleges and universities. Each student wrote two essays in response to either two issue prompts, two argument prompts, or one of each. Results show that the issue and argument writing tasks appear to assess relatively similar constructs, supporting the decision to include both types of prompts in the operational GRE Writing Assessment and to report a single, combined score. The results also support the random administration of prompts without equating adjustments, because within each task type, most of the prompts were comparable in difficulty and no important subgroup interactions with prompt classifications were detected. Finally, from a fairness perspective, the results show there were advantages to administering the issue prompt first and the argument prompt second. The GRE Program used the psychometric information provided by this study to make final design, delivery, and scoring decisions before introducing the operational assessment in the fall of 1999. (abstract)

To help ensure consistent scoring, the GRE program conducts extensive reader training, requires reader applicants to pass an initial certification test as well as calibration tests at the beginning of each scoring session, and monitors scoring accuracy by inserting previously scored quality-control essays into every batch of new essays waiting to be evaluated. Scoring is performed online, and scoring leaders continually monitor the scoring quality of their teams so that they can intervene and provide additional guidance if necessary. This rigorous monitoring process must be maintained to ensure that scoring is accurate and therefore fair.

Reporting and score use: Professional testing standards do not support the practice of reporting scores based on a single essay and/or a single judgment about a person's writing: A reliable essay score requires multiple samples and multiple judgments. Adhering to that principle, the GRE program decided to report a writing score based on two essays and multiple (four) essay readers or more, if necessary for resolution. As explained in its descriptive bulletin,

> If the two assigned scores differ by more than one point on the [0-6] scale, the discrepancy is adjudicated by a third GRE reader. Otherwise, the scores from the two readings of an essay are averaged. The final scores on the two essays are then averaged and rounded up to the nearest half-point interval. A single score is reported for the Analytical Writing section.

Consequential validity: It is impossible to know with any certainty how adding a writing section to a high-stakes test might affect students, score users, and other stakeholders. However, a testing program can conduct studies to anticipate what might happen (see, e.g., Powers & Fowles, 2000).

Tests that are offered almost daily have very different security concerns from those administered only a few times a year. Because it is not feasible to develop a fresh supply of technically sound prompts day after day, year after year, the GRE program needed a large pool from which the computer could randomly select prompts for each examinee. After studying the likely effects of prepublished prompts (Powers & Fowles, 1986), the GRE Board opted to prerelease the entire pool of hundreds of *Issue* and *Argument* prompts, without charge, so that everyone would have the same access to this information before taking the test.

Soon after the GRE writing measure was introduced, essay readers began reporting instances of essays with unusual similarities. Some essays included portions of the same memorized text; others were constructed with a memorized template that allowed the writer to merely fill in a few phrases from the prompt. Some of this prepared material was quite erudite but not necessarily relevant to the particular topic assigned to the examinee. Although the number of these essays was relatively small, they had to be dealt with immediately and fairly so graduate departments would receive only valid scores, representing the applicant's own thinking and writing abilities. To address this concern, the program runs all incoming essays through a software application that detects unusual similarities. Essays singled out through this system are then presented to a specially trained team of writing specialists who review the evidence and, applying criteria set by the GRE program, determine the validity of the essay. This is a serious matter, for a single essay with too much unattributed "borrowed text" results in scores being cancelled for the entire test, not just the writing portion.

The process for developing the GRE Analytical Writing Assessment may seem particularly rigorous, but it is hard to imagine any high-stakes testing program not undertaking a similar program of research and careful deliberation if the assessment is to have much value.

From my perspective—which spans over 40 years at Educational Testing Service and frequent collaboration with K-12, college, and graduate faculty on a wide range of assessment programs and research projects[3]—there has been a continuous effort to improve assessment in ways that align with the understanding that writing is a complex cognitive process, that writing is important in all content areas, and that well-designed and well-implemented scenario- and project-based assessments can contribute to student learning and reinforce effective instruction. Although this evolution is still underway and replete with setbacks, the field has progressed dramatically since the 1970s, when it was not unusual for a school administrator to equate "good writing" with "good penmanship" or for rubrics to value mere "elaboration" over sound reasoning and relevant support. The tension between the need for a thoughtful, research-based view of writing assessment and the expectation—in fact, the demand—that it be meaningful (both valid and reliable) continues at all levels.

The past few decades have seen a steady progression of new developments in writing assessment in the arena of higher education. As a profession, we have acquired vast amounts of experience, both theoretical and practical. Yet that information has not always been explained well, nor is it often shared. At this point, the field would be well served by a thoughtful and candid explanation of the different models and the factors that shaped them. This will not happen without considerable effort and open minds. The larger community of writing faculty, writing researchers, psychometric experts, and program administrators will need to join forces in defining the essential characteristics of the different models and agree on when–and why–a particular feature is recommended.

As a profession, we must collectively hold ourselves accountable not only for the quality of the writing assessments that we develop and administer and for their consequences, but also for the information that we can share. The opening statement to the ETS *Guidelines for Constructed-Response and Other Performance Assessments* (Baldwin, Fowles, & Livingston, 2005) reminds us that:

> Testing is not a private undertaking but one that carries with it a responsibility to both the individuals taking the assessment and those concerned with their welfare; to the institutions, officials, instructors, and others who use the assessment results; and to the general public. (p. 1)

Only by sharing ideas openly across programs and trying to reach consensus on how best to address concerns from a whole host of critical perspectives can we ensure that all stakeholders will be increasingly well served by the assessment of writing. This book is an important contribution to that effort.

LOOKING FORWARD

Now, after two decades of rapid development in writing assessment, the field seems headed in new, unpredictable directions. Writing assessment programs such as those described in this chapter have amassed evidence to reconsider some initial decisions. The GRE *Issue* task, for example, has recently been revised to eliminate choice, to reduce timing from 45 to 30 minutes, and to make the directions more specific. The Law School Admission Council continues to administer a writing sample with the LSAT; however, the essays are still not scored. Moreover, several programs have announced that they are reducing the writing measure (e.g., GMAT and CPA) or may soon be eliminating it completely (MCAT). The AAMC (2011) has explained that, based on recommendations from an advisory committee and extensive input from medical school admission committees, MCAT essay scores "are used for only a very small group of applicants" and provide "very little additional information about applicants' preparation for medical school relative to what is offered by undergraduate grades and the other sections of test."

How should the writing community interpret this shift in direction? Perhaps writing is now so well integrated into undergraduate programs that it does not need to be assessed again as candidates apply for professional programs. Perhaps testing programs such as those noted in this chapter have decided that the effort required to meet the demands of maintaining a valid writing measure should be spent on other priorities. Perhaps the body of knowledge and skills required for success in professional programs is expanding so greatly that the time spent writing an essay needs to be devoted to testing other skills, some of which have been assessed poorly or not at all in the past, such as empathy, efficiency, and ethical decision making. Perhaps skill in communicating in digital environments will become increasingly important. Whatever the direction, our experience in designing high-stakes writing assessment programs through thoughtful research and careful deliberation will inform the development of these new measures as they may appear in graduate and professional programs.

ENDNOTES

1. These testing programs are cited because they were among the first North American programs to introduce direct measures of writing in a particular field. Some tests have been replaced (e.g., ETS replaced the NTE program with the Praxis Series™, which includes writing in the content areas; its TOEFL program also replaced the single TWE prompt with two writing tasks, one of which integrates academic reading, writing, and listening skills). Others have been revised (e.g., in 2011, GRE released a new version with revised writing prompts and GMAT has announced plans to replace one of the writing tasks with a new reasoning section).
2. As ETS psychometrician Catherine McClellan (2010) noted, the two properties of reliability and validity are related: "If we aren't measuring something consistently, we cannot use that measurement to make an appropriate decision about the examinee. A test can be reliable without being valid: For example, we could measure examinees' height very reliably, but this likely is not a valid indicator of the same examinees' writing proficiency. The opposite, on the other hand, is not true: An unreliable test cannot be valid.
3. This work has involved designing, developing, and scoring not only large-scale essay tests but also course-based portfolios, individual student presentations and performances, small group interactions, and other kinds of performance assessment.

REFERENCES

Association of American Medical Colleges. (2011). *MR5 preliminary recommendations*. Web.

Baldwin, D., Fowles, M., & Livingston, S. (2005). *Guidelines for constructed-response and other performance assessments*. Princeton, NJ: Educational Testing Service.

Godshalk, F. (1966). Chief reader report, Foreign Service Officer Test. Princeton, NJ: Archives of Educational Testing Service.

McClellan, C. A. (2010). Constructed-response scoring—Doing it right. *ETS R&D Connections*. Princeton, NJ: Educational Testing Service.

Powers, D. E., & Fowles, M. E. (1997). *Effects of applying different time limits to a proposed GRE writing test* (GRE 93-26cR; ETS Research Report 96-28). Princeton, NJ: Educational Testing Service. (Related article: *Journal of Educational Measurement, 33*, 433-452 [1996]).

Powers, D., & Fowles, M. (1998). *Test takers' judgments about GRE writing test prompts* (GRE Board Research Report No. 94-13R). Princeton, NJ: Educational Testing Service. (Related article: *Educational Assessment, 6*(1), 3-22 [1999]).

Powers, D.E., & Fowles, M.E. (1986). *Effects of disclosing essay topics for a new GRE writing test* (ETS Research Report-96-26). Princeton, NJ: Educational Testing Service.

Powers, D. E., & Fowles, M.E. (2002). *Likely impact of the GRE writing assessment on graduate admissions decisions* (GRE Board Research Report No. 97-06). Princeton, NJ: Educational Testing Service. (Related article: Balancing test user needs and responsible professional practice: A case study involving the assessment of graduate-level writing skills. *Applied Measurement in Education. 15*(3), 217-247 [2002]).

Rosenfeld, M., Courtney, R., & Fowles, M. (2004). *Identifying the writing tasks important for academic success at the undergraduate and graduate levels* (GRE Board Research Report No. 00-04R). Princeton, NJ: Educational Testing Service.

Rosenfeld, M., Thornton, R.F., & Skurnik, L.S. (1986). *Relationships between job functions and the NTE Core Battery: Analysis of the professional functions of teachers* (ETS Research Report-86-08). Princeton, NJ: Educational Testing Service.

Schaeffer, G. A., Briel, J. B., & Fowles, M. (2001). *Psychometric evaluation of the new GRE writing assessment* (GRE Board Professional Report No. 96-11P). Princeton, NJ: Educational Testing Service.

II

STRATEGIES IN CONTEMPORARY WRITING ASSESSMENT

EMW Reflection: New York University gave me a full tuition four-year scholarship that let me graduate with honors and gain two fellowships to graduate school. Although I lived at home in Brooklyn and commuted by subway, my real home at NYU was the student newspaper office. When I became coeditor in my senior year, we changed from a weekly to a daily, despite a small staff and cramped quarters; for some weeks during the 1955 New York newspaper strike, we were the only daily printing in the city. I write about those interesting times in my chapter "Class and Comfort: The Slums and the Greens," in *Coming to Class: Pedagogy and the Social Class of Teachers* (Eds. Alan Shepard, John McMillan, & Gary Tate, Portsmouth, NH: Boynton Cook, 1989). This formal portrait was, I think, the picture I attached to my grad school applications.

II

STRATEGIES IN CONTEMPORARY WRITING ASSESSMENT

BRIDGING THE TWO CULTURES

A complex relationship exists between the writing assessment community and the educational measurement community. In their historical analysis of that relationship, Nadia Behizadeh and George Engelhard Jr. (2011) find that educational measurement has had a strong influence on writing assessment. A new field of writing assessment emerged in the 1990s, they believe, that brings together measurement researchers and rhetoric and composition/writing scholars. As the identification of the origin of an educational research movement confirmed by Condon (2011), that is the good news. The bad news is that, until quite recently, practice did not keep pace with theory. Although writing theory emphasizing a sociocognitive framework emerged in the decades following Janet Emig's landmark study of composing processes in 1971 (Flower & Hayes, 1981; Heath, 1983; Phelps, 1988), writing assessment practices did not embrace new ways to understand the ontological, epistemological, and axiological practices of students, to establish typologies for their writing processes and practices, and to gain insight from these practices.

Among the guilty was the College Board. As Edward M. White famously said to a packed room on the release of the Board's new writing section of the SAT Reasoning Test in 2005, "Welcome to the 1970s!" The audience of composition researchers attending the 56th Annual Convention of the Conference on College Composition and Communication roared. Timed tests taken under constrained conditions did not allow students to show what they could do, White explained, and then proceeded to devastate the assumptions behind the test, from its brief length to its single prompt to its retrograde deployment of multiple-choice items. White's impromptu performance, capturing the disappointment in the room at the way the Board had missed the opportunity to use current theory and empirical research to model the design of such an important test, carried the day.

In the early twenty-first century, we continue to wonder if total construct representation is ever possible with such a complex human performance as writing. What may realistically be expected as we balance standards for good assessment practices (American Educational Research Association, American Psychological Association, & National Council on Measurement in Education, 1999; Schmeiser & Welch, 2006) with the limits of available resources (Ewell & Jones, 1986; Swing & Coogan, 2010)? Put more specifically: If validation of our educational measurement processes is "a lengthy, even endless process (Cronbach, 1989, p. 151), then what are the details of those processes? The authors of the chapters in this section of the collection explore these questions of balance and design and offer, as Condon (2011) writes of assessment over the past decade, practical alternatives, informed research design, and an advanced understanding of the construct of writing and of what is required to improve instructional practice.

Writing about one of the most renowned assessment-informed writing programs in the nation, Diane Kelly-Riley begins this section with a reflection on the role of the expert consultant in designing an assessment program. From the voyage out at Washington State University (WSU) in 1993, the emphasis was always to put students at the center of the assessment process; in 2010, more than 2,700 freshman-level Writing Placement Exams and more than 5,500 junior-level Writing Portfolios were assessed. Impressive here is the consistent emphasis for over a decade to keep the standard setting process—the core of any measurement process (Cizek & Bunch, 2007)—in the hands of the faculty. Rather than falling into the value-dualism trap of literary analysis versus writing instruction that was then part of the first-year instructional landscape, campus leaders wisely decided to theorize about the role of the instructor in the assessment process. As a result, no individual drives the process at any level; for the 4 years that students attend the university, they move through a progressively challenging curriculum that is the turf of the instructors. This move has allowed the very highest levels of best practice identified by Isaac I. Bejar (2008): psychometrically sound program standards, such as strict measures of interreader reliability, combined with adherence to the educational policies of the university emphasizing an integrated writing curriculum. The program that Kelly-

Riley describes now produces research into the most intriguing frontiers of writing assessment.

Cutting-edge research is also reflected in the work at Louisiana State University recollected by Irvin Peckham. Paying tribute to White, the consultant to the WSU program, Peckham also pays tribute to Charles Cooper of the University of California, San Diego, and his mentor's insistence on precision. That insistence leads Peckham from a reflection about high school teachers who, in the mid 1970s, revolted against a cyclic, media-fuelled literacy crisis that ushered in a predictable Orwellian environment of systemization and resistance (Hillocks, 2002; Ohmann, 2003). Just as those high school teachers resisted limited response, multiple-choice testing as a measure of writing ability, Peckham resists resolving the tensions between construct validity and cost efficiency in reductionist terms. In the case of writing placement—perhaps the greatest challenge today facing researchers as national attention is paid to the fact that 4 of every 10 new college students, including half at 2-year institutions, take basic writing courses understood to be remedial (Duncan, 2010, p. 7)—Peckham rebels against the technologically efficient, multiple-choice models of timed tests in favor of yet another technology: iMOAT. Developed at Massachusetts Institute of Technology (Perelman, 2011), iMOAT allows students to respond to a complex writing task by engaging selected readings and composing their responses in a virtually untimed environment. At LSU, this system allows students to challenge their placements, determined initially by SAT Reasoning Test and ACT scores. With writing samples scored by instructors, the iMOAT model yielded greater student involvement in writing, empirical support for instructor classroom observation, and financial savings for institutions.

Working in a sociocultural perspective (Murphy, 2000), Chris M. Anson investigates the benefits of instructor response to student writing. From a traditional accountancy perspective, Anson's questions are provocative. If only modest educational return was the result of the enormous investment of time and energy put into responding to student writing, what would that finding mean to the writing community? Rather than leaving readers stranded on an island of misfits where practitioners faithful to their painstaking comments are haunted by researchers who cannot demonstrate the value of those comments, Anson calls for a broader view of response as a complex interaction involving negotiation, identity, and acculturation. In his call for abandonment of a single-best method of research on response, Anson's chapter resonates with the search for measurement models in the educational measurement community. "Given the inconsistencies across models," Robert L. Brennan (2006) has written of psychometrics, "It is natural to ask which model provides the correct or right answer to the questions posed. For the most part, there is no right answer, and investigators searching for that 'Holy Grail' will be forever disappointed" (p. 7). With Brennan, Anson recognizes that the realization that there are no best models for assessment research is not an admission of methodological defeat but an acknowledgment of thoughtful work that will be required for a comprehensive theory of response—an important challenge to twenty-first-century researchers. With Samuel Messick, whose landmark work on validity (1989) reminded the field of educational measurement that even favorable results "should be continually or periodically monitored to permit the detection of changing circumstances and of delayed side effects" (p. 91), Anson emphasizes the essential need to consider context.

The challenge to identify a unified system of response to student work, along with the context of that response, is taken up in the interchange between Jill Burstein of the Educational Testing Service (ETS) and Anne Herrington and Charles Moran of the University of Massachusetts at Amherst. A recent technological innovation, automated essay evaluation, affords a way of using Natural Language Processing (NLP) to produce responses to student writing that are, Burstein claims, useful, helpful, and dependable. With over 2 million submissions annually, the ETS product *Criterion*® allows students to work on their writing in the areas of organization and development of ideas, variety of syntactic constructions, topic appropriate vocabulary, and correctness of grammar usage, and mechanics. Concentrating on correctness, Moran and Herrington identify flaws in the ETS system. Following a scenario in which a single essay is submitted to *Criterion*®, Moran and Lunsford find that the NLP diagnosis failed. Burstein agrees and notes that the evolving system is constantly being updated; Moran and Herrington reply that the system's very focus on isolated skills is opposed to a holistic focus on writing. For Burstein, the technology yields a very real human possibility for trial and improvement; for Herrington and Moran, the technology is dehumanizing. For Burstein, the automated system is developed according to principles that inform teaching interventions or drug trials: large data sets are used to draw inferences about a system that is always under development. For Herrington and Moran, writing for a machine is not writing at all; in fact, these students are "writing for nobody," as White (1969) famously put it. Use of Automated Essay Scoring, Herrington and Moran suggest, lacks an authentic rhetorical context and thus reduces writing to academic gamesmanship.

For William Condon, the value of the dispute would rest, as he suggests in his chapter, not in its resolution but in its emergence: Our intentions lead us to construct realities that, as Victorian essayist Thomas Carlyle observed in 1831, outlast their validity. Such is precisely the case Condon presents in his cautionary tale of portfolio assessment, the evaluative system believed to offer the potential for robust construct representation and consequential validity (Murphy & Yancey, 2008) by both the writing assessment (Huot, 2002) and educational measurement (Lane & Stone, 2006) communities.

When we insist that capable construct representation systems (such as portfolios) compete with the efficiency of limited response tests (such as multiple-choice tests), however, the former is gutted and the latter remains in force. Instead of arguing for cost efficiency, Condon believes, we must argue for cost effectiveness: The extra cost of scoring portfolios yields far more useful information. To guard against inflexible past models such as efficiency, Condon urges researchers to emphasize the gains of new evaluative methods, robust concepts of benefits when estimating costs, and generative thinking that looks to the future

Part of that thinking is the careful reflection that must occur when the null hypothesis significance test, debated as that concept may be (Gill, 1999), cannot be rejected. In their chapter, Jon A. Leydens and Barbara M. Olds report an experimental study conducted at the Colorado School of Mines (CSM) in which a pre-post test design failed to capture a statistically significant difference in undergraduate student writing performance. Whereas Joseph Arum and Josipa Roska (2010) naively blame failure to record improvement on lack of curricular rigor in *Academically Adrift: Limited Learning on College Campuses*, Leydens and Olds more appropriately query their assessment processes, their students' rhetorical abilities, and their own pedagogical assumptions. Anson (2010) has advised researchers to jump on a Möbius strip and follow the mathematical metaphor of a nonorientable surface to achieve refined research designs that engage complexity. Moving from the outside in and the inside out, as Leydens and Olds have done, yields continuing research, such as sharing the assessment design and its rubric with students. Improved assessment programs appear to be an unintended beneficial consequence of rejecting reductionist conclusions based on significance testing.

The role of reader prioritization and response rationale in writing assessment is one of the most important areas of research in the field (Razaei & Lovorn, 2010), and Leydens and Olds note the significance of needed research on tacit evaluative frameworks. In his chapter on the development of Dynamic Criteria Mapping—an empirical technique that unpacks the complex interactions encountered on the Möbius slide—Bob Broad documents the recent insistence, noted by Behizadeh and Engelhard (2011), that our practice keep step with our theories. Reflecting on his disputes with White, Broad realized in 2010 that the battle he was fighting (to shift assessment practices to better fit theories that had originated in the work of Linda Flower, John R. Hayes, and Shirley Brice Heath) was different than the one White was fighting (to legitimize direct writing assessment within the modernist empirical paradigm sanctioned by the measurement community until Messick reimagined his field in 1989). The sense of anxiety of influence is palpable in Broad's chapter, but the tension is more than a desire to emerge from a precursor, as Harold Bloom (1997) would have it, in order to create an original vision. The anxiety is fueled by the emergence of the realization—in both the field of writing assessment and educational measurement—that the use of the term *ecology* may be more than a metaphor. As Carol D. Lee proposed in her 2010 presidential address before the American Educational Research Association, neuroscience, cognition, and cultural psychology suggest that educational research should be informed by attention to the intertwining of culture and biology, adaptation through multiple pathways, and interdependence across contexts. "As a research community," she writes, "we need to produce more studies that examine both risk and resilience and which therefore might better inform policy directions. These studies should move away from static and essentialized conceptions of diversity, acknowledge that variation exists, and explain why it matters and how psychosocial variables and cognition are intertwined" (p. 653). Here is the essence of the future studies that Broad and his colleagues have undertaken; here is a new research tool—Dynamic Criteria Mapping—that has the potential to help us understand the origin and impact of variation.

Part II of the volume closes with a heuristic designed by Lee Odell that allows us to see similarities and differences in variation. To help our students communicate in digital environments, Odell claims, that which is similar (the effort to legitimize teaching and assessing writing on a national level with the Common Core State Standards Initiative for grades K-12 [2010]) must be reconceptualized (the effort to introduce new methods of teaching and assessing writing in multimodal settings [Murray, 2009]). In the tradition of the great heuristic of tagmemics (Pike, 1954-1960), Odell offers a new metalanguage, a perspective of contrast between known and unknown, that allows students to experience patterns of semiosis in audience analysis and language use as they complete a task requiring digital communication. From authenticating claims to the construction of identity to the creation of ethos, Odell tracks his students as they explore audience values, understand the nature of effectiveness, and employ a common referential frame for inquiry.

Whatever the particulars of the metaphors (Leary, 1990) that will emerge in the second decade of the 21st century, researchers in Part II of the collection demonstrate that the field of writing assessment informs, and is informed by, both the field of rhetoric and composition/ writing and the field of educational measurement. Whether a voyage or a rebellion, a mathematical property, a epidemiological study, a humanistic rationale, or a reconceptualization of failure, whether informed from Victorian architecture, Freudian anxiety, or Saussurean semiotics, the field of writing assessment is actively engaged in querying our beliefs, designing innovative investigations, and identifying ways to improve the lives of others.

REFERENCES

American Educational Research Association, American Psychological Association, & National Council on Measurement in Education. (1999). *Standards for educational and psychological testing*. Washington, DC: American Educational Research Association.

Anson, C. (2010). Assessment in action: A Möbius tale. In M. N. Hundleby & J. Allen (Eds.), *Assessment in professional and technical communication* (pp. 3-15). Amityville, NY: Baywood Publishing.

Arum, R., Roksa, J., Kim, J., Potter, D., Velez, M. (2011). *Academic adrift: Limited learning on college campuses*. Chicago, IL: University of Chicago Press.

Bejar, I. I, (2008). Standard setting: What is it? Why is it important? *R & D Connections*. Princeton, NJ: ETS Research and Development. Web.

Behizadeh, N., & Engelhard, G. Jr. (2011). Historical view of the influences of measurement and writing theories on the practice of writing assessment in the United States. *Assessing Writing*, *16*(3), 189-211.

Bloom, H. (1997). *The anxiety of influence: A theory of poetry* (2nd ed.). Oxford, England, UK: Oxford University Press.

Brennan, R. L. (2006). Perspectives on the evolution and future of educational measurement. In R. L. Brennan (Ed.), *Educational measurement* (4th ed., pp. 1-16). Westport, CT: American Council on Education and Praeger.

Carlyle, Thomas. (1831). Characteristics. In *The Harvard Classics*. Vol. 25, Part 3. Web.

Cizek, G. J., & Bunch, M. B. (2007). *Standard setting: A guide to establishing and evaluating performance standards on tests*. Thousand Oaks, CA: Sage.

Common Core State Standards Initiative. (2010). *Common core state standards for English language arts & literacy in history/social studies, science, and technical subjects*. Washington, DC: Council of Chief State School Officers and National Governors Association. Web.

Condon, W. (2011). Reinventing writing assessment: How the conversation is shifting. *Journal of the Council of Writing Program Administrator, 34*(2), 162-182.

Cronbach, L. J. (1989). Construct validation after thirty years. In R. E. Linn (Ed.), *Intelligence: Measurement, theory, and public policy* (pp. 147-171). Urbana, IL: University of Illinois Press.

Duncan, A. (2010). *A blueprint for reform: The reauthorization of the elementary and secondary education act*. Washington, DC: U. S. Department of Education. Web.

Emig, J. (1971). *The composing process of twelfth graders*. Urbana, IL: National Council of Teachers of English.

Ewell, P. T., & Jones, D. P. (1986). The costs of assessment. In C. Adelman (Ed.), *Assessment in American higher education: Issues and contexts* (pp. 33–46). Washington, DC: U.S. Department of Education, Office of Educational Research and Improvement.

Flower, L., & Hayes. J. R. (1981). A cognitive process theory of writing. *College Composition and Communication, 32*(4), 229-244.

Gill, J. (1999). The insignificance of null hypothesis significance testing. *Political Research Quarterly, 52*(3), 647-674.

Heath, S. B. (1983). *Ways with words: Language, life, and work in communities and classrooms.* Cambridge, England: Cambridge University Press.

Hillocks, G. Jr. (2002). *The testing trap: How state writing assessments control learning*. New York, NY: Teachers College Press.

Huot, B. (2002). *(Re)Articulating writing assessment in teaching and learning*. Logan, UT: Utah State University Press.

Lane, S., & Stone, C. A. (2006). Performance assessment. In R. L. Brennan (Ed.), *Educational measurement* (4th ed., pp. 387-431). Westport, CT: American Council on Education and Praeger

Leary, D. E. (Ed.). (1990). *Metaphors in the history of psychology.* Cambridge, England, UK: Cambridge University Press.

Lee, C. D. (2010). Soaring above the clouds, delving the ocean's depths: Understanding the ecologies of human learning and the challenge for education science. *Educational Researcher, 39*(9), 643-655.

Messick. S (1989). Validity. In R. L. Linn (Ed.), *Educational measurement* (3rd ed., pp. 134-103). New York, NY: American Council on Education and Macmillan.

Murphy, S. (2000). A sociocultural perspective on teacher response: Is there a student in the room? *Assessing Writing, 7*(1), 79-90.

Murphy, S., & Yancey, K. B. (2008). Construct and consequence: Validity in writing assessment. In C. Bazerman (Ed.), *Handbook of research on writing: History, society, school, individual, text* (pp. 365-385). New York: Lawrence Erlbaum.

Murray, J. (2009). *Non-discursive rhetoric: Image and affect in multimodal composition.* Albany: NY: State University of New York Press.

Ohmann, G. (2003). *Politics of knowledge: The commercialization of the university, the professions, and print culture*. Middletown, CT: Wesleyan University Press.

Perelman, L. (2011, April). *Online evaluation 2.0: Breaking boundaries.* Sixty-Second Annual Convention of the Conference on College Composition and Communication, Atlanta, GA.

Phelps, L. W. (1988). *Composition as a human science: Contributions to the self-understanding of a discipline.* New York and Oxford, UK: Oxford University Press.

Pike, K. L. (1954-1960). *Language in relation to a unified theory of structure of human behavior* (Vols. 1-3). Glendale, CA: Summer Institute of Linguistics.

Razaei, A. R., & Lovorn, M. (2010). Reliability and validity of rubrics for assessment through writing. *Assessing Writing, 15*(1), 18-39.

Roth, C. (1950). The disputation of Barcelona (1263). *The Harvard Theological Review, 43*(2), 117-144.

Schmeiser, C. B., & Welch, C. J. (2006). Test development. In R.L. Brennan (Ed.), *Educational measurement* (4th ed., pp. 307-353). Washington, DC: American Council on Education.

Swing, R. L., &, and Coogan, C. (2010). *Valuing assessment: Cost-benefit considerations.* Urbana, IL: University of Illinois and Indiana University, National Institute for Learning Outcomes. Web.

White, E. M. (1969). Writing for nobody. *College English, 31*(2), 166-168.

White, E. M. (2005, March). *Catching up to the 1970s.* Paper presented at the 56th Annual Convention of the Conference on College Composition and Communication, San Francisco, CA.

8

SETTING SAIL WITH ED WHITE
THE POSSIBILITIES OF ASSESSMENT AND INSTRUCTION WITHIN COLLEGE WRITING ASSESSMENT

Diane Kelly-Riley
Washington State University

In the early 1970s, Edward White and his colleagues at California State University won the responsibility to determine the face of the freshman equivalency examination in lieu of a multiple-choice, standardized test advocated by administrators and the national Educational Testing Service. Elliot (2005) details the unlikely victory of White and his faculty colleagues to "[capture] the right to determine which examinations would be used . . . [as well as] the responsibility of designing, conducting and reporting the assessment process" (p. 204). White (2001) chronicled the realizations that sank in once they had been awarded this responsibility: These were English people "before the days of composition studies . . . [with only the] vaguest notions about assessment theory . . . [they wondered], 'Now what?'" (p. 307). They eventually developed the Freshman Equivalence Examination and later the English Placement Test. The move by White and his colleagues to take control of local writing assessment issues signified the start of what White later called "the modern era of writing assessment." This era opened opportunities for innovative combinations of assessment and instruction that allowed the responsibility of writing assessment to reside in the hands of faculty and not primarily administrators or test developers (White, 2001).

In the 1985 edition of *Teaching and Assessing Writing*, White argued that informed assessment research would result in improved classroom teaching and that writing assessment could support the teaching of writing both practically and conceptually. White (1985) wrote, "the more we know, the more we help our students know about assessing writing, the more effective our teaching will become" (p. 289). He also identified a new research agenda from this approach to combining assessment and instruction. This agenda would "emerge from the experience of teachers, and the efforts to deal with them would come from those with a pressing need to solve problems" (p. 242). O'Neill, Moore, and Huot (2009) reaffirmed the significance of pedagogically driven writing assessment decisions. Teachers must have a role in deciding and enacting standards for writing within the context of the curriculum and within the arena of accountability.

White and his colleagues opened the door for others to experiment with innovative combinations of assessment and instruction. In late October 1993, a group of faculty and graduate students gathered in the rag-tag room of the Washington State University (WSU) Writing Center to conduct the first WSU Writing Portfolio reading. In attendance were the architects of the Writing Program—Rich Haswell, Sue McLeod, Robin Magnuson, Susan Wyche, Richard Law, and Lisa Johnson-Shull. With this meeting, the WSU Writing Program embarked on—what seemed at the time—a risky adventure to purposefully combine assessment with instruction through the implementation of a large-scale, university-wide writing portfolio assessment. Some of the program developers likened their journey to riding a barrel over Niagara Falls (see the expedition's plans in Haswell, Johnson-Shull, & Wyche, 1994). Also in attendance were WSU faculty members: Kenton Bird from the Department of Communication, Chris Paxson from the Department of Hotel and Restaurant Administration, and Jo Washburn from the Department of Sport Management. Likewise, two graduate student interns in the Writing Lab, Steve Smith and myself, were also invited to participate in the reading session and to witness the seemingly mundane launch of this monumental undertaking. This session coincided with White's follow-up WPA consultant evaluator visit to the WSU Writing Program. White was in the barrel, so to speak, when the WSU Writing Portfolio assessment crew pushed off from shore.

Ed's attendance at the inaugural Writing Portfolio evaluation session was intentional. His presence recognized the opportunities that he and his colleagues had opened for the intentional combinations of assessment and instruction in college writing assessment. In this chapter, I would like to reflect on the years between this serendipitous voyage in the barrel with White and the WSU Writing Portfolio crew to reflect on the importance of the faculty role in combining assessment and instruction in college writing assessment in light of central tenants articulated by White in *Teaching and*

Assessing Writing (1985). I would like to detail the ways in which WSU continues to keep the writing assessment standards-setting process in the hands of faculty, how this process continues to benefit faculty, and the importance of such assessment programs for the future.

Fortunately, in 1993 the WSU Writing Portfolio barrel made it over the "falls" without being smashed to smitherines (the exciting ride well documented in Haswell, 2001). Prior to the voyage, the WSU Writing Portfolio designers shared common backgrounds with White and his CSU colleagues. All of them had English department pedigrees with little to no formal training in assessment theory, but all were committed teachers who felt that the combination of assessment and instruction had the power to transform the educational landscape of our institution as well as the landscape of higher education. This was an exciting time of change for writing studies with many concurrent debates about the role of composition. At that same time, English departments around the country also wrestled with the role of literature in composition (see Lindemann, 1993; Tate, 1993). Additionally, progressive assessment thinkers theorized and tested the integral role of teacher experience gained in the classroom setting as part of an expert-based assessment process that made placements directly into particular curricula. Both Smith (1992) and Haswell (1998b) simultaneously, but separately, explored the feasibility of closing the feedback loop through the introduction of the teacher and his or her knowledge into the assessment process.

THE NECESSITY OF INFRASTRUCTURE

The WSU team opted to take an infrastructural approach to the writing assessment process. They elevated the classroom expertise and experience of faculty into the rating process rather than adopting the holistic rating procedures used by White and his colleagues (Godshalk, Swineford, & Coffman, 1966). Haswell "[envisioned] . . . an assessment program that [pushed] and [enriched] instruction and learning and that [engaged] in consistent self scrutiny to advance the role of writing within the entire institution" (Durst, 2007, p. 138). The new rating methodology, called the *expert rater system*, intentionally solicited faculty's experience with students, their writing, and the expectations and realities of the classroom (Haswell & Wyche, 1996). This rating methodology was similar to the work of Smith (1993), but was conceived independently from Smith. The process invites individual teachers' experiences into the assessment process, and as a result the program relies on consistency estimates of interrater reliability rather than a focus on simple rater consensus (see Stemler, 2004). The WSU approach assumed that the teaching of writing was every faculty member's business: No one department was responsible for preparing undergraduates for the writing demands that they would meet postgraduation. Students needed to have contextualized writing instruction throughout their undergraduate experiences, and the instruction needed to come from faculty members with expertise in their disciplines. Also, faculty served a crucial role in identifying writers who needed supplemental support with the curriculum-wide writing demands.

The WSU Writing Program began in response to a state legislative mandate in the late 1980s for each public baccalaureate institution to conduct a junior-level assessment of students' writing as well as an assessment of each institution's General Education program. These mandates were quite common and ushered in the present era of accountability (Ewell, 2002; White, 2001). At the same time, major employers in the State of Washington—Microsoft, Boeing, and Battelle—indicated that they would no longer hire WSU graduates if their writing abilities did not improve. In 1991, large-scale institutional writing assessment and faculty development components were added to the pre-existing Writing Center to form what is now known as the WSU Writing Program.

Washington State University is the only public institution to offer a curriculum-wide undergraduate Writing Program that combines university-wide writing assessment, instruction, and faculty support throughout the entire undergraduate experience. The WSU Writing Program is comprised of three major units: Writing Center (undergraduate Writing Center, graduate and professional Writing Center, online tutoring that is part of the Northwest eTutoring Consortium, and lower- and upper-division small group writing tutorials); Writing Assessment (freshman Writing Placement Exam, sophomore Honors College Writing Diagnostic, and junior Writing Portfolio); and Writing in the Disciplines (faculty and TA development and training including the WSU Critical Thinking Project, All University Writing Committee, and ongoing Writing in the Major course review).

At the time of the present writing, the Writing Program works directly with more than 200 individual WSU faculty members each year and supports the hundreds of undergraduate courses that assign writing at our institution. The organization and infrastructure of WSU's Writing Program has served as a model for postsecondary institutions across the nation. This system has emerged as a model infrastructure that spans the entire undergraduate experience and assumes that all faculty and departments are key to the development of undergraduates' writing abilities. Elliot (2005) says that WSU "launched the most widely used and most-documented system of portfolio assessment in the nation" (p. 216), and he later notes that the portfolio system at WSU is "perhaps the most sophisticated assessment system we now have to serve its intended purpose" (p. 354). No one department or person is in charge of that endeavor—the entire university assists students as they move through the progressively more difficult writing challenges within the undergraduate curriculum. In order to best prepare our students for the challenges that they will face after graduation, students need to learn the communication expectations of their chosen fields of study. In 2010, more than 2,700 freshman-level Writing Placement Exams and more than 5,500 junior-level Writing Portfolios were assessed. The history and structure of the WSU Writing Program are detailed in Haswell (2001).

RECLAIMING WRITING ASSESSMENT FOR TEACHING

The move to integrate classroom experience into the assessment process was an act to reclaim writing assessment as a tool for teaching. Huot (2002) argues that we need to "harness the expertise and ability of raters within the place they know, live, work and read" (p. 102). At WSU, diagnostic exams are given at entry and mid-career to assess students' readiness for undergraduate writing requirements. The expert rater methodology (Haswell, 1998b; Haswell & Wyche, 1996;) relies on classroom teachers to serve as the raters of the assessment to make placements directly into classes within a specific curriculum. The focus of the assessment is based upon faculty members' classroom expertise to identify the characteristics of writing abilities that can be reasonably managed in a classroom setting from writing that would present difficulties. The assessments serve the instructional interests of faculty because they require weaker writers to have supplemental support as they are enrolled in the courses that assign writing. As a result, WSU has been able to integrate criteria that can be contextualized to suit the level and disciplinary conventions of the various points in the curriculum, thus promoting coherence through the assessment process.

The expert rater system relies on faculty teaching the courses to make placement decisions—faculty bring their expertise and experience from the classroom into the rating sessions, and they decide whether students' writing abilities are ready for the specific writing challenges at the particular points in the curriculum. The ongoing conversation about the standards for student writing—through norming sessions and consultations during the evaluation—ensure that faculty set and maintain the standards for writing.

The expert rater system differs from more widely used forms of scoring: holistic scoring, which assigns an overall score for a piece or pieces of student work; primary trait scoring in which a specific criterion is established for successful completion of a task; and analytic scoring, which looks at student performance across multiple areas to determine the student's strengths and weaknesses for a particular area. All of these scoring methodologies require an interpretation of the score once it is made—and likewise, standards are often set externally, or the consequences of the assessment are separate from the classroom setting. Raters for these methodologies do not necessarily need to be teachers. The expert rater methodology makes assessment standards the responsibility of the faculty who are charged with teaching the classes that assign writing at the various points in the undergraduate curriculum. Classroom expertise is essential to this process.

At WSU, incoming freshman students take the Writing Placement Exam or the Honors Writing Diagnostic to ascertain the type of instruction needed to navigate first-year writing requirements. For most students, this means a placement into the regular first-year writing course that introduces them to the conventions of academic writing. A smaller percentage, whose writing demonstrates weaknesses flagged by the teacher-raters, are placed into appropriate course structures that adequately support the individual's writing weaknesses. For some, they are required to take a concurrent small-group, credit-bearing tutorial in conjunction with their regular first-year writing course. The tutorial helps the students learn the framework through which their writing is assessed in order to better respond to writing. Others may be required to enroll in more extended course sequences that stretch out the experience of first-year writing or into the course sequence designed to support the multilingual writer's instructional needs.

For the Writing Placement Exam, graduate students, instructors, and faculty who have taught the first-year writing courses are recruited to become paid readers for the assessment. They have all had varied training opportunities and instructional experiences. The graduate students have had a seminar to prepare them to teach writing, as well as a weekly hour-long internship experience facilitating small-group writing tutorials connected to first-year writing courses. At minimum, they have taught first-year writing for one semester. The role of Writing Placement Exam rater allows them to continue their professional development by harnessing the expertise they have gained in the classroom. During the rating sessions, faculty negotiate the characteristics of writing abilities appropriate for the various course placement options.

At mid-career, all undergraduates are required to submit a WSU Writing Portfolio that demonstrates their readiness for the upper-division writing requirements in their Writing in the Major courses. Huot (2002) argues that "assessment practices need to be based upon the notion that we are attempting to assess a writer's ability to communicate within a particular context and to a specific audience who needs to read this writing as part of a clearly defined communicative event" (p. 102). The WSU Writing Portfolio ratings rely on the expertise of the faculty in the particular assessment context to ascertain students' readiness for the more sophisticated requirements of writing in the discipline. As a result, the Writing Portfolio rating corps is comprised of faculty from across the disciplines who have had students submit writing in their Portfolios from their classrooms. The selection of writing from a particular classroom setting signals that the student values the work as representative of his or her best writing. Faculty raters for the Writing Portfolio serve the same function as the Writing Placement exam: They identify writers who appear ready for the more sophisticated challenges of writing in the disciplines from writers who appear to need additional structured instructional support in these settings.

The assessment-instruction combination has clear benefits for undergraduate students engaged in the WSU writing-rich curriculum, which have been documented and discussed elsewhere (Haswell, 2001). Such a system helps make our teaching more effective. Johnson-Shull and Kelly-Riley (2001) argue that the WSU assessment and instructional structure integrate an essential feedback loop for faculty. The standards-setting process that occurs for each writing assessment rating session continues to define and revise the standards that we have for writing at our institution. This definition is a dynamic one that is articulated, considered, and reconsidered every time we meet for rating sessions. In other words, the responsibility to articulate and define "good writing" at our institution is in the hands of teachers.

As teacher/evaluators within our instructional and assessment setting, faculty enter the assessment arena with their expertise and negotiate the terms for which good writing is understood at our institution. Huot (2002) wisely observes, "assessment must be a multi-disciplinary enterprise—something that should never be driven completely by the assumptions of any single group" (p. 2). Our writing assessment ratings ensure that faculty have ongoing professional development of their own related to writing assessment, but this ongoing training builds upon their existing expertise. Faculty bring their experience to the common assessment table, and then negotiate the community standards for our writing assessment settings and return to their own disciplinary contexts with revised knowledge of the community standards. In other words, faculty are not asked to adopt an external definition of "good writing" defined by the WSU Writing Assessment program. As a group, faculty raters set and establish the standards at each rating session. As a result, faculty feel ownership for the assessment program that would not be felt with an external assessment. In addition, the ensuing conversation about standards provides a rare opportunity for faculty members to discuss their expectations and experiences with colleagues outside their own disciplinary confines. As a result, this ongoing, dynamic (and sometimes messy) conversation fosters an energy and excitement about assessment that is not commonly experienced by faculty at institutions of higher education.

A NEW RESEARCH AGENDA: DOCUMENTATION AND INNOVATION

White (1985) predicted that if faculty assumed responsibility for writing assessment, a new type of research agenda would emerge. Indeed, his predictions have come true. The combinations of faculty-driven assessment combined with instruction have resulted in teachers driving the evolution of the research agenda. Using WSU's writing assessment program as an example, there are two ways in which WSU has generated responses to problems faced by teachers.

The first approach focuses on documenting the student-centered work we have undertaken. Coles (1997), while writing about the documentary tradition in film studies, details the "aesthetic, intellectual, and moral struggle" (p. 2) of the documentarian and the difficulties of presenting the subjects fully and complexly. We face the same difficulties in college writing assessment. Composition teachers were called to action into the testing arena out of a perceived misrepresentation of the complexity of student work. In the same way, we must intentionally document and reflect upon our methodologies. Mislevy (2007) argues that the more we can make "explicit the underlying principles of assessment design . . . [we can better provide] conceptual foundations for familiar practices and [support] the development of new ones" (p. 463). For example, since 1995, the Writing Assessment Program has produced a biennial Writing Portfolio report documenting multiple levels of performance (Evans & He, 2007; Evans & Meloni, 2009; Ficek & He, 2005). The report covers aggregated student performance through many perspectives—gender, language status, race, first-generation college attendee status, departmental, college affiliation, and so on. As such, the report provides data that can be used to close the feedback loop of assessment and instruction. The data allow departments and colleges to examine their students' progress, and to chart ways they would address issues that surfaced from the assessment data. Again, the context and expertise of the departments and their faculty members drive their individual responses to the assessments.

The data represented in the biennial reports detail students' readiness to enter the Writing in the Major courses at WSU. Additionally, the report also chronicles the sources from which students submit their writing. The most recent report shows that every department on campus has submitted papers in the WSU Writing Portfolio, with nearly 28,258 course papers approved by individual faculty members for submission in the WSU Writing Portfolio in the biennial reporting period (Evans & Meloni, 2009). In addition, papers were submitted from more than 4,100 different courses—representing the many classes at WSU and transfer institutions that assign writing across the disciplines.

The second impact has been innovation in research. Haswell, Johnson-Shull, and Wyche (1994) charted the course of the now-established writing assessment program. Their focus on having assessment serve instruction signaled an important shift that differed from White and his colleagues, who adapted holistic writing assessment practices. Haswell and Wyche (1996) detailed the methodology of the expert rater system that Haswell (1998b) later theorized. Initially, much of the research conducted by the writing assessment program was validational in focus. The new expert rater methodology required evidence of its viability. Haswell made several forays into this arena. He conducted early validational studies (1998a) that were critiqued by Moss (1998), and later he conducted a comprehensive validational value-added study (2000).

The Writing Assessment Program has enabled other areas of research relevant to how students approach writing tasks. Haswell and Haswell (1996) documented the troublesome findings related to gender construction and raters. Haswell (1997) also examined issues related to multilingual writers, as well as considerations for timed exams. These issues helped revise and improve the assessment process. Anthony (2009), Evans (2009), Peterson (2009), and Worden (2009) document multiple ways in which students construct and approach the task of writing impromptu essay exams.

Furthermore, the program has allowed research into raters' behaviors and students' performances in large-scale writing portfolio assessment. I conducted research into the rating behaviors of raters related to race (Kelly-Riley, 2006, in press). The findings from this study suggest that there is a difference in student writing performance by race, but that student race does not contribute to faculty assessment of students' writing in this setting. Faculty employ a limited set of the criteria published by the writing assessment program, and they use nonprogrammatic criteria—including perceived demographic variables—in their operationalization of "good writing" in the WSU writing portfolio assessment. These findings help document the state of the rating processes and provide empirical data to help make needed revisions.

The WSU Critical Thinking project grew out of the methodology and approaches of the WSU Writing Program. A group of teachers noticed a disconnect between faculty expectations and student performance related to critical thinking and students' actual grades. We found that faculty tended to inflate student performance or disregard the seeming lack of student critical thinking abilities (Condon & Kelly-Riley, 2004). We found that faculty–as an entire campus—can operationally define student learning expectations for student level and disciplinary conventions—and students can meet faculty member expectations. In other words, the disconnect between assessment and instruction occurred with faculty members' poor articulation of expectations or the incongruent expectations they had with their practice. Through the articulation of faculty expectations, students can achieve higher levels of critical thinking (Allen & Kelly-Riley, 2005; Kelly-Riley 2003, 2007, 2011).

Similarly, the Writing Assessment program enables research on accountability issues of interest at the national level. Most recently, I have started to conduct research that looks at the connections between student learning outcomes in the Writing Portfolio with the National Survey of Student Engagement (NSSE). This research is important because it attempts to cross-validate the assumptions that we have about writing with national measures that are currently being used as measuring sticks of institutional success. The NSSE results, for a time, were being used by the *US News and World Report* college rankings as a measure of institutional quality. The NSSE results are used by college administrators to question the educational quality of their institutions, but these results are not cross-validated with actual student learning outcomes. Pascarella, Seifert, and Blaich (2010) try to validate student learning outcomes and student engagement through standardized tests. However, their analysis works with data divorced from the classroom setting. This WSU research will be important because the connection between writing abilities—as demonstrated in the classroom—and student engagement can be explored further using actual products that students have produced in classroom settings.

Although the WSU portfolio designers took a separate path in their combinations of assessment and instruction from Ed White and his colleagues, there is no question that White was crucial in wrestling the assessment process from the hands of policymakers, administrators, and test developers and putting this responsibility in the hands of teachers. By opening these doors, White enabled others to create programs that were locally administered and pedagogically relevant. This type of approach ensures that teachers continue to play a central role in assessment. In this climate, teachers need to have a strong voice in determining the face of the outcomes for which we must be accountable.

These two concurrent activities—documentary in nature and innovative in impact—must not be seen as discrete or classificatory. Rather, they have allowed us to generate new paths of research that will transform our efforts locally at WSU, but also provide models for others to adapt to their own settings. These efforts are essential to keep instructional values at the heart of assessment practices.

REFERENCES

Allen, M., & Kelly-Riley, D. (2005). Promoting undergraduate critical thinking in Astro 101 lab exercises. *Astronomy Education Review, 4*(2). Web.

Anthony, J. (2009). Classroom computer experiences that stick: Two lenses on reflective timed essays. *Assessing Writing, 14*(3), 194-205.

Coles, R. (1997). *Doing documentary work*. Oxford, UK: Oxford University Press.
Condon, W., & Kelly-Riley, D. (2004). Assessing and teaching what we value: The relationship between college-level critical thinking and writing abilities. *Assessing Writing, 9*(1), 56-75.
Durst, R.K. (2007). Review [Review of the book *Beyond outcomes: Assessment and instruction within a university writing program*, by R. Haswell]. *WPA: Writing Program Administration, 30*(3), 137-142.
Elliot, N. (2005). *On a scale: A social history of writing assessment in America*. New York, NY: Peter Lang.
Evans, D. (2009). Remembering places: Student reliance on place in timed essays. *Assessing Writing, 14*(3), 206-217.
Evans, D., & He, H. (2007). The WSU Writing Portfolio. Seventh findings (June 2005-May 2007). Office of Writing Assessment Internal Report #8. Pullman, WA: Washington State University.
Evans, D., & Meloni, J. (2009). The WSU Writing Portfolio. Eighth findings (June 2007-May 2009). Office of Writing Assessment Internal Report #9. Pullman, WA: Washington State University.
Ewell, P. (2002). An emerging scholarship: A brief history of assessment. In T.W. Banta et al. (Eds), *Building a scholarship of assessment* (pp. 3-25). San Francisco, CA: Jossey-Bass.
Ficek, D., & He, H. (2005). The WSU Writing Portfolio. Sixth findings (June 2003-May 2005). Office of Writing Assessment Internal Report #7. Pullman, WA: Washington State University.
Godschalk, F.I., Swineford, F., & Coffman, W.E. (1966). *The measurement of writing ability*. New York, NY: College Entrance Examination Board.
Haswell, R. H. (1997). Thirteen ways of looking at a bluebook. *Assessing Writing, 4*(1), 107-114.
Haswell, R. H. (1998a). Multiple inquiry in the validation of writing tests. *Assessing Writing, 5*(1), 89-109.
Haswell, R. H. (1998b). Rubrics, prototypes and exemplars: Categorization and systems of writing placement. *Assessing Writing, 5*(2), 231-268.
Haswell, R. H. (2000). Documenting improvement in college writing: A longitudinal approach. *Written Communication, 17*(3), 220-236.
Haswell, R. H. (Ed.). (2001). *Beyond outcomes: Assessment and instruction within a university writing program*. Westport, CT: Ablex.
Haswell, R. H., & Haswell, J. T. (1996). Gender bias and critique of student writing. *Assessing Writing, 3*(1), 31-83.
Haswell, R. H., Johnson-Shull, L., & Wyche-Smith, S. (1994). Shooting Niagara. Making portfolio assessment serve instruction at a state university. *WPA: Writing Program Administration, 18*(1-2), 44-53.
Haswell, R. H., & Wyche, S. (1996). A two-tiered rating procedure for placement essays. In T. W. Banta, J.P. Lund, K.E. Black, & F. W. Oblander (Eds.), *Assessment in practice. Putting principles to work on college campuses* (pp. 204-207). San Francisco, CA: Jossey-Bass.
Huot, B. (2002). *(Re)Articulating writing assessment for teaching and learning*. Logan, UT: Utah State University Press.

Johnson-Shull, L., & Kelly-Riley, D. (2001). Writes of passage: Conceptualizing the relationship of writing center and writing assessment practices. In. R. Haswell (Ed.), *Beyond outcomes: Assessment and instruction within a university writing program* (pp. 83-91). Westport, CT: Ablex Publishing.

Kelly-Riley, D. (2003). Washington State University Critical Thinking Project: Improving Student Learning through Faculty Practice. *Assessment Update, 15*(4), 5-14.

Kelly-Riley, D. (2006). *A validity inquiry into minority students' performances in a large-scale writing portfolio assessment.* Unpublished doctoral dissertation. Pullman, WA: Washington State University.

Kelly-Riley, D. (2007). Washington State University Critical Thinking Project: Improving Student Learning Outcomes through Faculty Practice. In T. W. Banta (Ed.), *Assessing student achievement in general education* (pp. 35-43). San Francisco, CA: Jossey-Bass.

Kelly-Riley, D. (2011). Validity inquiry of race and shared evaluation practices in a large-scale, university-wide writing portfolio assessment. *Journal of Writing Assessment, 4*(1). Web.

Lindemann, E. (1993). Freshman composition: No place for literature. *College English, 55*(3), 311-316.

Mislevy, R.J. (2007). Validity by design. *Educational Researcher, 36*(8), 463-469.

Moss, P. A. (1998). Testing the test of the test. A response to "Multiple inquiry in the validation of writing tests." *Assessing Writing, 5*(1), 111-122.

O'Neill, P., Moore, C., & Huot, B. (2009). *A guide to college writing assessment.* Logan, UT: Utah State University Press.

Pascarella, E., Seifert, T., & Blaich, C. (2010). How effective are the NSSE benchmarks in predicting important educational outcomes? *Change Magazine, 42(*1), 16-22.

Peterson, J. (2009). "This test makes no freaking sense": Criticism, confusion, and frustration in timed writing. *Assessing Writing, 14*(3), 178-193.

Smith, W.L. (1992). The importance of teacher knowledge in college composition placement testing. In R. J. Hayes (Ed.), *Reading empirical research studies: The rhetoric of research* (pp. 289-316). Hillsdale, NJ: Lawrence Erlbaum.

Smith, W. L. (1993). Assessing the reliability and adequacy of using holistic scoring of essays as a college composition placement technique. In M. M. Williamson & B. A. Huot (Eds.), *Validating holistic scoring for writing assessment: Theoretical and empirical foundations* (pp. 142-205). Cresskill, NJ: Hampton Press.

Stemler, S. E. (2004) A comparison of consensus, consistency, and measurement approaches to estimating interrater reliability. *Practical Assessment, Research and Evaluation, 9*(4). Web.

Tate, G. (1993). A place for literature in freshman composition. *College English, 55*(3), 317-321.

Worden, D. (2009). Finding process in product: Prewriting and revision in timed essay responses. *Assessing Writing, 14(*3), 157- 177.

White, E. (1985). *Teaching and assessing writing*. San Francisco, CA: Jossey-Bass.

White, E. (2001). The opening of the modern era of writing assessment: A narrative. *College English, 63*(3), 306-20.

9

ASSESSMENT AND CURRICULUM IN DIALOGUE

Irvin Peckham
Louisiana State University

I am writing this chapter to pay tribute to Edward White and Charles Cooper, both of whom have driven into my head the doxology that an assessment design should be based on a clear definition of what one wants to know and an instrument that is aimed like a rifle at getting that information. The history of writing assessment, however, largely contains narratives of assessments that either ignored or were unaware of that imperative.

My own experience with misdirected assessments began with a collective revolt by high school teachers in Santa Clara County who were protesting the impending mandate to administer multiple-choice tests of editing skills to assess student writing at grades six, eight, and twelve. These were to be high-stakes tests determining whether students could pass on to the next grade level, a reaction to the "Why Johnny and Jill Can't Write" phobia of the mid 1970s.

The motives behind this misdirection were implicit in Merrill Shiels' 1975 *Newsweek* article, "Why Johnny Can't Write," a report on the dramatically declining literacy skills putatively documented by National Assessment of Educational Progress (NAEP) led by Richard Lloyd-Jones and Ross Winterowd.[1] To make her argument, Shiels used cherry-picked examples of wildly misspelled, syntactically challenged sentences by high school seniors. She also significantly distorted the results of the 1975 NAEP assessment. Shiels claimed NAEP had found that "the essays of 13 year olds and 17 year olds are far more awkward, incoherent, and disorganized than the efforts of those tested in 1969" (p. 58). The NAEP assessment in fact showed that the writing of 9-year-olds had improved, as had the writing of the high scoring 13- and 17-year-olds. The writing skills of the 13- and 17-year-olds in the middle and lower scoring brackets, had, however, shown more disorganization and more awkward and incoherent sentences than in the 1969 assessment (a difference, Lloyd-Jones and Winterowd noted, that in part may have been the consequence of a disinviting writing task). Shiels threw in the "far more" for dramatic flavor. In addition, she preached to the conservative mood then sweeping the country as an emerging backlash to the 1960s by laying the blame for this literacy "crisis" on the relativism embraced by structural linguists, *Webster's Third World Dictionary*, and the authors of CCCC's "Students Rights to their Own Language"—of whom Richard Lloyd-Jones and Ross Winterowd were two. For a solution to the so-called crisis, Shiels cited the opinions of conservative scholars like Jacque Barzun and Mario Pei with their nostalgia for the golden years when people still believed in the King's English as having come from God. What the nation needed in its schools was to abandon foolish notions like dialects, whole language, and creativity, and get back to the fundamentals and correct grammar.[2]

Given the regressive mood in the United States, it was no surprise that teachers in our district were being pressured to use a multiple-choice test of editing skills to assess student proficiency in writing. In defense of our commitment to teaching writing, we convened the Santa Clara County Committee on Writing. Walter Loban, our consultant, helped us construct locally developed, direct writing alternatives to the corporately developed, multiple-choice tests being aggressively marketed in our districts. We presented our alternative proposals to our district administrators, arguing that direct writing assessments would encourage direct writing instruction, which would in turn help us improve student writing. Although many of us were reluctant to concede to the necessity of using timed writing samples to evaluate writing ability, we felt that by insisting on writing samples over multiple-choice testing, we were making the best of a bad business.

I remember the argument at the time as being cost and efficiency against validity and consequence, although we may have used other terms. We recognized that it would be cheaper and involve far less labor on our part to let a corporation determine which students would be allowed to pass on to grade 7, grade 9, or graduate. But as writing teachers, we had inherited a conviction that a multiple-choice test of editing skills would be a weak indicator of writing ability and that by teaching to the test, teachers would shortchange instruction in writing.[3] We surprisingly won the day and succeeded in institutionalizing timed direct writing assessments. In our district, we also created through the assessment a renewed emphasis on writing, supported by the group of teachers who spent their weekends twice a year evaluating student writing, using the Bay Area Writing Project model of holistic assessment.[4]

In the intervening years, I have learned that the opposition between the two methods of assessing writing ability is far from simple. Although it is true that a direct method of assessing writing ability (testing writing by looking at writing) has greater "face validity" (Charney, 1984, p. 67) than an indirect method (inferring writing skills by testing editing skills), the direct method is not necessarily more accurate—if by accurate we mean the ability to predict the writer's level of performance in similar writing situations. We have evidence that the indirect method may in fact be the better predictor. Research by the College Board (Breland, Bridgeman, & Fowles, 1999) has shown that indirect assessments have a higher correlation with single direct writing assessments than different direct writing assessments have with each other (an average correlation of .82 versus an average of .60 [p. 25]).

My research (Peckham, 2009, 2010) on locally developed, untimed writing assessments paints a slightly different picture. I consistently found a much lower correlation than .82 for untimed essays and either the ACT English or the SAT Verbal. My correlations ranged from .19 to .35. These correlations are on the low end of other research on the relationship between indirect and timed direct writing assessments,[5] suggesting that either the direct or the indirect assessments are useless indicators of a student's writing ability. But even these low correlations were higher than the ones I found between timed and untimed writing in different genres: -.07 in 2006, .07 in 2007, and .23 in 2008 (Peckham, 2010).

Although my correlations are significantly lower than those reported by the College Board, they point in the same direction: The highest correlation is between indirect writing assessments; next highest is between indirect and direct; the weakest is between direct and direct, particularly when timed is ranged against untimed in different genres. The question then is which method or combinations of methods do we use?[6]

EATING APPLES TO TEST APPLES

Thirty-five years have passed since we revolted in Santa Clara County against the imposition of multiple-choice tests to assess writing ability. In the intervening years, we have learned more about viable assessment practices though professional and practitioner research.[7] Most importantly, we have learned not to imagine a unitary notion of writing, that when we assess writing ability, we are assessing an ability to write in a genre or a family of genres in specific kinds of rhetorical situations.[8] We have learned that there is no such thing as a "true" score of a student's ability to respond in writing to a rhetorical situation, that rankings of genre-specific writing abilities are guesses at best. We have learned, in effect, that one generalizes about future responses at one's peril.

Nevertheless, there is almost universal agreement among writing teachers that we should look at writing samples to assess writing ability both because of construct underrepresentation[9] and the social consequences of using multiple-choice tests to assess writing ability (see Breland et al., 1999; Brennan, 2006; Huot, 2002; O'Neill, Moore, & Huot, 2009) . What is surprising, then, is how widespread the use of multiple-choice tests still is. Huot (1994) reported that 65% of the universities in his survey used the ACT or SAT objective assessments; in an online survey that I conducted by soliciting responses from the WPA listserv in March 2010, 52% of the respondents indicated that they do not use a writing sample for placement; most of them used some variant of the SAT, ACT, or AP exam. In Huot's study, 23% of the postsecondary institutions using the SAT and/or the ACT used a writing sample as a check, the most likely variant being the model in place at Louisiana State University (LSU) before we developed our Online Challenge (Peckham, 2009). This variant is frequently called the "diagnostic" model with the students being initially placed by scores on the ACT or SAT and then checked during the first week of classes by the diagnostic.

I have described elsewhere our reasons at LSU for being dissatisfied with this process (2009), so I will here point only toward the most glaring problems with the model: The initial placement by objective assessments is flawed by virtue of construct underrepresentation; the model disrupts the first week of class, threatening students with "re-placement"; the scoring is generally uncontrolled, relying on different teachers' sense of whether students "belong" in their classes; and testing one kind of writing to predict another kind is less valid even than using an objective assessment of editing skills.[10]

When we began to think in 2001 about changing our placement model at LSU, we were aware of the consistently low correlations between multiple-choice and direct writing assessments. We preferred to shift to a direct writing assessment of all students in an untimed writing situation, but because the in-place method was costing LSU nothing, we quickly discovered we were not going to get the roughly $25,000 required to score 4,800 essays. So we opted for a process that would allow students to challenge their ACT/SAT placement by writing essays in an untimed, online writing environment that would replicate as closely as possible the writing situation of a major assignment in our first semester course. Our thinking at the time was based on what Cooper and White had taught me: If you want to predict how students will respond to a specific kind of writing situation in the future, replicate that writing situation in the assessment. Do not assume that a person's response to one writing situation is a reliable index to his or her response to all writing situations.

SEMESTER ASSESSMENT

By being in the right place at the right time, our university became one of five universities collaborating to develop under Les Perelman's leadership at MIT a robust online assessment program called iMOAT. The members of the iMOAT consortium were united in their opposition to using multiple-choice tests or timed writing samples to place students in or exempt them from required writing courses. Although the program has steadily improved since we first rolled it out in 2002, even then, it was a tremendous organizing tool to register students, distribute required articles for reading and the writing task, collect and code student essays, and keep track of and report readers' scores.[11]

We called our new placement model at LSU the Online Challenge because we sent incoming students letters informing them of their placement on the basis of their ACT/SAT scores and inviting them to challenge that placement by writing essays in a virtually untimed environment. Our success with the Challenge in the summer encouraged us to pilot an identical online assessment at the end of the fall semester in 2002. We imagined five purposes for the Semester Assessment: to gather teachers together to discuss criteria and the evaluation of essays; to improve the coherence in the program by creating a genre specific assessment for which we wanted our teachers to prepare their students; to provide a basis for discussions about the program; to answer the perennial charge of grade inflation; and to identify students who could be exempted from the second semester writing requirement. In addition, we thought we might be able to document improvement in student writing ability with a pre-post assessment because of the identical writing conditions.

In our first year of the Semester Assessment, we required all the GTAs in our practicum to participate, and we asked instructors to volunteer.[12] We encouraged teachers to consider the Semester Assessment as a replacement for the timed writing test that was at the time required as a final. We also decided that any students who received 11s or 12s on a 2-12 scale (the combined scores of two readers) would be exempted from the second semester required writing course, those being the scores that would have earned students exemption in the Online Challenge. In the Challenge, we exempted some writers who received 10s, but we decided that because 10 was a borderline category, we would exempt score 10 writers in the Semester Assessment only if their teachers recommended it. We reasoned that we would be less confident of the scoring with a large group of readers than we were with the five Challenge readers who had worked closely together in the first summer to develop our scoring system.[13]

To compensate for the time the teachers would spend reading essays, we cancelled the last week of classes for participating teachers, during which time the students would be reading 8-10 articles on a particular issue and then writing an essay in response to a writing task that asked them to explain what the issue was about. The 15 new GTAs in the practicum and 16 instructors participated in this first iteration. Five hundred and thirty-six out of their 605 students completed the assessment, a completion rate of 89%.

We used the Challenge readers as table leaders. We met on Friday to choose anchor papers and refine a scoring guide we had developed in the summer reading of the Challenge essays.[14] We used Monday morning during finals week to discuss with all the readers the anchor papers and the scoring guide and to score a few sample essays. We then finished the scoring on Tuesday and Wednesday mornings, using the traditional holistic model of two readings and adjudication of any two scores more than one apart on a 6-point scale. Although we had multiple problems in this first iteration of our large-scale assessment, we still achieved an agreement rate of 94%.[15]

We decided to pilot the Semester Assessment for several more years before making it a requirement of the program because we wanted to have enough time to refine our process; we also wanted to give teachers time to get used to a project that threatened teacher autonomy and could be used to evaluate teacher performance.

To some extent, the fear that teachers had of losing their autonomy was well founded. The in-place curriculum was largely unstructured, the major requirements being a loose focus on personal writing in the first semester and a minimum of 6 in-class essays. We were shifting the focus away from timed essays and promoting a program that had a series of reasonably well defined genres arranged in a sequence so that instruction in one genre built on instruction in the previous genre. In addition, we wanted the sequence to focus on clearly defined objectives such that success in the course could be demonstrated by the students completing one or more writing tasks at the end of the course. In place of personal writing, we wanted our first semester course to focus on helping students improve their abilities to integrate other voices/sources into their own writing. Although we had a sequence of genres that we recommended to help achieve this primary objective, we were not requiring adherence to this sequence other than from the new GTAs in the practicum; rather, we wanted to require that students be able to perform well on a writing task at the end of the semester that asked them to read several articles on a specific issue; evaluate, synthesize, and organize that information; and write an essay in which they clearly explained what the issue was and interpreted the different kinds of positions people were taking on it. That objective was Rome. We would leave up to the teachers which road they took. The measure of achievement would be how many students got there.

Although I believe that scores on a writing assessment focusing on the specific objectives of the course are a far better indicator of teacher effectiveness than the frequently misleading student evaluations, evaluating teachers was not our purpose. Our purpose was to get teachers to self-evaluate. To do this, we developed a system that would allow teachers to get their students' scores by logging in to a website with a code that allowed only them to see a list of their students' scores, a graph pictorializing the distribution of their students' scores, the mean score for their sections, and the mean score for all students participating in the assessment. For example, the male teacher whose class is graphed in Figure 9.1 could see that his students had considerably outperformed the mean for all students in English 1001 (6.59 on a scale of 2-12). In Figure 9.1, I have provided pseudonyms for only four students, but the teacher could see his or her full class, which in this case was 19 students with an average score of 7.94. Each asterisk in the graph represents a student. Thus, the teacher could see that he would have a strong case for awarding at least 6 As to the students scoring a 9 or above.

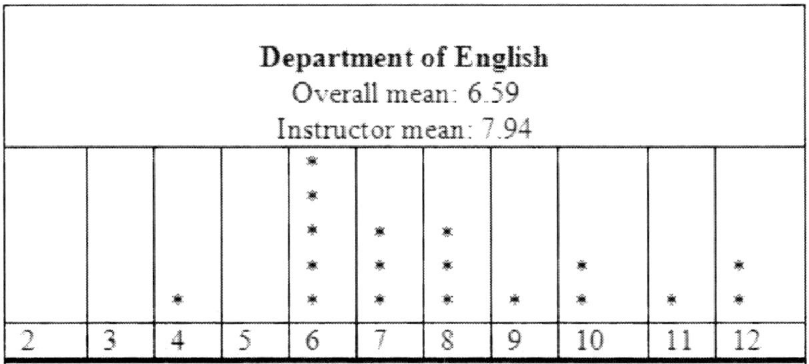

Department of English
Overall mean: 6.59
Instructor mean: 7.94

		*		* * * * *	* * *	* * *	*	* *	*	* *
2	3	4	5	6	7	8	9	10	11	12

Individual Student Scores

Last Name	First Name	MI	ID Number	Score
Carter	Lisa	H	6320287	12
Williams	Ronald	P	4859880	6
Nichols	Carol	A	4390223	8
Porter	Kammie	N	9875022	9

Figure 9.1. Student score distribution in one class for semester assessment (N = 2416; n = 19)

We piloted the project for three years. Each year, more teachers volunteered. In the second year, we had 1,136 students participating; in the third, 1,459. By the time we required full participation in the fourth year, 60% of the GTAs and instructors were already participating. Although the resisting teachers still felt some threat to their autonomy, there was a countervailing sense that we should develop a common course, be able to describe what specific writing skills we were focusing on, and be able to look at student writing at the end of the semester to measure our success in teaching them.

Our policies toward grades and exemption also encouraged teachers to participate. Our associate dean at the time was vigorously arguing that we needed to find a way to get the grade distribution in each section closer to a classic bell curve rather than the more common pattern resembling a boa constrictor that had just swallowed a cow. We were able to demonstrate through the Semester Assessment that some sections scored significantly higher than others; for example, in Fall 2007 (N = 1948, $M = 6.47$), the highest average for a section was 8.11 on a 12 point scale (n = 19, $SD = 2.0$) compared to the lowest average of 5.4 (n = 16, $SD = 1.9$). Even granting possible errors in scoring, it would be clearly absurd, we claimed, to insist that both classes should have similar grade distributions.

The logic linking grade distribution to evidence of student achievement on the Semester Assessment led inexorably to a further motivation for institutionalizing it. The teachers could claim with empirical justification that they would have reason for a high-grade distribution if their classes had an equally high Semester Assessment score distribution, thus motivating students to learn how to write in the genre being assessed. The proof was in the pudding. This logic had the additional effect of coalescing our curriculum. The purpose of the course and all writing in the course was to help students achieve high scores on the Semester Assessment. Consequently, assignments in the course had to be aimed in that direction.

Our exemption policy indirectly encouraged teachers to participate. The better writers in a class felt they had a good chance to earn exemption, particularly when they discovered that our statistics showed that an average of two and as many as five or six students in a high-performing class would be earning exemption. Consequently, students worked hard to practice for the assessment. There was concomitantly pressure on teachers who were not participating in the assessment during the pilot period to do so because their students otherwise were not afforded the chance to gain an exemption.

As a second consequence of our exemption policy, we were able to demonstrate in annual reports to the dean that through the Online Challenge and Semester Assessment we were saving approximately $46,000 a year by exempting students from required writing classes; this was equivalent to the cost of 1.3 teachers at an average annual salary of $36,000. Demonstrating this savings was important because with our annual subscription to iMOAT and payment to readers for the summer Online Challenge, we needed an annual budget of $13,000, leaving a gain of $33,000 (see Appendix). I realize we could be accused of selling exemptions, but the savings to my mind is an incidental consequence of identifying students who have shown they clearly do not need another writing course to succeed in their other undergraduate courses.

We recently completed our eighth year of the Semester Assessment. We feel confident that the program has achieved what we had hoped it would. Over the years, the scoring sessions have taken on the atmosphere of three mornings of workshops during which we read a bit, discuss what we've read, and then read some more. It is a time of confirming that we are professionals as we discuss with colleagues what we have seen in student writing and our reflections on what we are teaching. We also discuss the process of the assessment and what changes we should make for the next year. We have developed a coherent course so that most syllabi reflect a consensual purpose for our first semester course.

The teachers use the scores as guidelines for their semester grades and feel pride in their achievement when their students push the mean score for their section above the mean score for all students. For instance, after we completed our assessment for 2009 one of our GTAs sent me the following email with the subject line, "A bit of gloating" (see Figure 9.1 for Andrew's graph):

> Now that all the numbers have been crunched, I'd like to point out a few things:
> Overall mean score of all sections: 6.59
> Mean for my section (118): 7.944
> Students in my class who scored a 10 or higher: 5 out of 18
> Boo yah.
> —Andrew Banecker

I know that in writing this chapter, I am gloating myself. By working from a core of strong teachers, we have spread the program outward to the point where for even the initially recalcitrant teachers (Andrew was one of them), assessment and curriculum are integrally linked. In the first years of the Semester Assessment, I was spending an inordinate amount of my time organizing this project, but now it almost runs itself. A committee decides on the topic, finds the readings, fine tunes the writing task, and functions as table leaders in the scoring. A coordinator takes care of the data, making certain that students are appropriately loaded into the iMOAT system and allocated to the right section, that the online calendar is set, that the articles and writing task are available at the right time, and that the essays are downloaded and sent to our Center for Evaluation and Assessment, where approximately 70,000 pages are printed, stapled, and bundled into stacks for the readers.[16] There are many other details to the process, but I really do not have to do much to manage it. My primary responsibility is to work with the table leaders to select anchor papers, refine scoring criteria for the specific task, and lead the scoring. Really, at this point, I could have anyone of several teachers who have been with this project from the beginning take care of these tasks as well.

I do not have space in this chapter to explore the plethora of data we have gathered in the 8 years we have worked on the project, one example of which is quantitative evidence that our students are improving their abilities to write, or more specifically, their abilities to analyze, evaluate, synthesize, and integrate information from other sources into their own voices. We can document that the average growth for students who took both the Challenge and the Semester Assessment was 1.69 points on a 2-12 scale, with a low of 1.16 in 2005 and a high of 2.33 in 2009 (see Appendix). We can also show that there are some teachers (like Andrew) whose students frequently have a significantly higher average gain than the mean—an average gain of 2.6 among students in classes of teachers whose students push their class score above the mean and .82 as an average gain among students in classes with teachers whose students generally score below the mean. The trick, of course, is to discover what the high-gain teachers are doing right and spread it out.

CONCLUSION

I have sketched an outline of the consequences of my having paid attention to what White and Cooper taught me. Among his many other accomplishments, White needs to be credited for setting in motion the collaboration among composition teachers to agree on the WPA Outcomes Statement (see Harrington, Rhodes, Overman Fisher, & Malenczyk, 2005; Roen, Glau & Behm, in press). He asked whether we couldn't agree on some objectives for our required writing programs. The result was many years of conversation, the eventual Outcomes Statement, and the *Framework for Success in Postsecondary Writing* (WPA, NCTE, & NWP, 2011).

Diane Kelly-Riley (in Chapter 8 of this volume) notes White's continual insistence on linking instruction, assessment, and reflection. The assessment should directly reflect curriculum and lead to teacher reflection on classroom practices and curriculum reconstruction. The university-wide writing program at Washington State University (WSU) has long been recognized as having set the standard for programs linking assessment with practice, for transforming assessment from an external intrusion into a locally developed method of measuring student achievements and program viability. WSU completes the assessment loop by investing teachers with the responsibility of developing the assessment protocol, which is reviewed and revised with each iteration, thus turning assessment into a powerful tool for teachers' professional development.

The statewide California Assessment Program (CAP) directed by Cooper was predicated on the same assumptions, only Cooper reimagined the local as a state-wide writing program at the middle and secondary school levels. In the 1980s, Cooper brought together exemplary teachers from all over the state to construct the assessment program, prefiguring the protocol subsequently developed at WSU.[17] These teachers decided on the genres to be assessed at grades 8, 10, and 12, and developed the writing tasks and the criteria marking success in each genre. Importantly, these criteria were developed inductively (see Broad, Chapter 15) by having teachers write in response to the tasks, trying them out in their classrooms, and reconvening in monthly meetings to read through the student responses to decide on the criteria and choose sample papers exemplifying various degrees of achievement. As at WSU, this process was recursive with new tasks, new trials, and new discussions of criteria and sample essays every year. The end result in California was a sophisticated, genre-based curriculum at the middle and secondary schools levels, replacing the dominant 5-paragraph model (see California Assessment Program, 1990; Peckham, 1987).

Our program has drawn from what we have learned from White, the WSU program, and CAP. Although our assessment program has been constructed within the more common required writing programs than WAC initiatives, it has been built on many of the same assumptions driving WSU's protocol, dominant being the link between what we are teaching, discovering a way to assess our success in instruction, and insisting on the recursive imperative of effective assessment. As a consequence of my experience with CAP and interpretation of genre functions in writing, we have also insisted in breaking away from the misleading notion that one can effectively measure writing ability as if it were a unitary phenomenon. The insistence on specificity was the implied driving force behind the evolution of the WPA Outcomes Statement. A program has to know *what* it is teaching about writing, implying some coherent notion of the genres or family of genres constituting the core of instruction. A pragmatic assessment program then draws on the expertise of its teachers to construct a practical protocol for assessing student achievement in the specific goals defining the program. The teachers recursively reflect through an assessment of the assessment on what is working, how they can improve instruction, and how they should revise their goals. In a sense, this protocol for inextricably linking assessment with instruction and reflection is nothing more than what good teachers should be doing in their classrooms, only the classroom has expanded beyond its four walls.

We believe that LSU has added importantly to discussion of teacher-driven assessments by insisting on replicating as nearly as possible the writing situation in the assessment and the writing situations in the classroom. Constructing this simulacrum is the central motivation behind portfolio-based assessments, but we have insisted at LSU more strictly on matching the genres being assessed with the genres being taught, working, that is, toward greater construct representation. The one thing our research has made clear (Peckham, 2010) is that testing students' abilities to write in an untimed writing situation by placing them in timed writing situations is no more effective than testing their writing skills by testing through multiple-choice items their abilities to edit.

I realize that many readers will object to some of the assumptions on which we have based our writing program, our methods of assessing student achievement, and the motivations behind their implementation. I am not, however, describing this project as a model but as a protocol on which others might improve, just as other WAC programs have attempted to improve the WSU model. After 8 years of implementation, we are, for example, experimenting with different assessment models, beginning with a variation of White's Portfolio, Phase II model (White, 2005). We have been piloting a similar assessment for our second semester course and in the spring of 2011 will make participation mandatory. We are also always revisiting what we are assessing and consequently what we are teaching. The important point in this structure I have described is that assessment and curriculum can and should be in dialogue with each other. That is what White and Cooper taught me.

APPENDIX

Memo to Dean

To: Gaines Foster
From: Irvin Peckham
CC: Renee Major, Barbara Heifferon
Thru: Anna Nardo, Rick Moreland
Date: June 18, 2010
Re: Results and Budget for Online Challenge and Semester Assessment Fall 2010

This is our report on how we have used IMOAT to sustain the Online Challenge and Semester Assessment and a request that you continue to set aside monies for its use next year.

Students exempted through Fall 09/ Spring 10 Online Challenge: 61

Students exempted through Fall/Spring Semester Assessment: 151

Total Online Challenge and Semester Assessment students exempted: 190

(212 students equal approximately 10 sections at 21.5 per section—or 1.25 teachers)

Savings: **$45,000** @ average of $36,000 for an instructor or $4500 per section
Additional benefits to this program:

1. Train teachers to evaluate consistently.
2. Reduce grade inflation for students who do not show evidence of writing ability.
3. Motivate students to improve their writing in order to earn exemption.
4. Produce empirical data to use on the assessment matrix for SACS.
5. Measure value added by comparing scores of students who took both the Challenge and Semester Essay. Below is the average gain on a scale of 2-12 by year. I have yet to calculate the gain for 2010.

Year	**Average Gain**	**Number**
2009	2.33	N=211
2008	1.73	N=225
2007	2.26	N=306
2006	1.7	N=211
2005	1.16	N=150
2004	1.8	N=265
2003	1.68	N=271

While recognizing the economic crisis we are now facing, we would like to argue for the importance of this program and the need to continue supporting it through funding. Below is the recommended budget for next year, which is significantly lower than last year as a consequence of the lower cost for the iMOAT subscription. The iMOAT board lowered the iMOAT subscription by moving to a less robust computer and hiring a part time rather than a full time programmer.

Budget for next year:

•	IMOAT subscription:	$4,500
•	Scoring for Online Challenge:	1,300
•	Printing cost of essays and UWP brochures	50
•	Rent for Semester Assessment Scoring Room	450

@ $150.00 per day, Efferson Hall

Total Budget: **$6,300**

Net Savings: **$38,700.00**

Dean's Reply

Dear Irv,

Thanks for the report.

I have always respected the English Department's strength at rhetorical strategies. A request to approve spending presented as a celebration of savings is a good one.

And I do appreciate the savings, and approve the spending for next year set out in the proposal ($6,300).

Have a good weekend.
Gaines

Note: The progressive development of iMOAT has lowered its subscription cost and thus the budget.

ENDNOTES

1. See Persky's review in Chapter 3 of this volume of NAEP's role in the evolution of writing assessment.
2. See Ohmann's (2003) interpretation of the literacy crisis as an attack on the increasingly leftward tilt of the liberal arts professoriate (p. 20; see also Elliot, 2005, p. 272). Behind this attack lies the link between the "fundamentals," foundationalism, and the status quo that maintains existing systems of privilege and oppression.
3. As practitioners (North, 1987), we were unaware of the degree to which we were merely repeating old arguments. See Elliot (2005, p. 112) for a description of teachers' resistance to multiple-choice tests of writing ability in 1943.
4. See Elliot (2005, pp. 158-161) for the early development of holistic assessment by the College Board.

5. For a summary of research on the correlations between direct and indirect assessments of writing, see Haswell (2005).
6. I have left out evaluations of writing ability by portfolios or directed self-placement. Portfolios are essentially multiple pieces of writing, some of which are interconnected. They are generally considered more difficult to evaluate reliably (White, 1995; Willard-Traub, Decker, Reed, & Johnson, 1999), but they have the advantage of representing a broader range of student writing ability. Directed self-placement is not really an evaluation of writing ability; it is an evaluation of the student's evaluation of his or her own writing ability. See Kelly-Riley's chapter on the use of portfolios in Washington State University's assessment, Condon's cautionary "Future History" of portfolios in writing assessment, and Yancey's characterization of portfolios as the crest of the third wave of writing assessment (all in this volume).
7. By professional, I mean large-scale research conducted by nonprofit organizations like the College Board; by practitioner, I mean research done by rhetoric and composition scholars.
8. By genre, I am indirectly referring to Miller's (1984) definition of genre as a typified response to a recurring rhetorical situation. For my interpretation of the influence of genres on writing, I am deeply indebted to Moffitt's *Teaching the Universe of Discourse* (1968), Kinneavy's *A Theory of Discourse* (1971), Britton, Burgess, Martin, and McLeod's *The Development of Writing Abilities (11-18)* (1978), and Beale's *A Pragmatic Theory of Rhetoric* (1987). More recently, Devitt's review "Genre, genres, and the teaching of genres" tracks the development of genre theory in the 1990s. As a practical primer on genre theory, Chandler has made available as a web-text *An Introduction to Genre Theory*. See also Odell's "The Given-New Contract" in Chapter 16.
9. Construct underrepresentation refers to the effacement of too many elements of the writing act—that is, the "construct" (American Educational Research Association, American Psychological Association, National Council on Measurement in Education, 1999, p. 10).
10. O'Neill et al. (2009), however, recommend with qualifications the diagnostic model if the school has used indirect writing assessments for initial placement (p. 91).
11. iMOAT may become known as one of the landmark achievements in writing assessment, establishing a viable alternative to portfolios as a way of breaking out of the restrictions of the timed writing sample. Even in this collection, the choices for assessment protocols are dominantly multiple choice, timed essays, or portfolios, leaving unmarked untimed writing samples (e.g., see Condon, Chapter 13; Elbow, Chapter 17).
12. With one or two exceptions, all of our instructors are full-time teachers with renewable contracts. Having a core of teachers who strongly identify with our program surely contributed to the success of this project.
13. As in most of the discussions about our protocol development, I am here compacting a more complicated history. For example, the decision about what to do with Score 10 writers was a consequence of 2 years of survey and discussions among teachers after the Semester Assessments.

14. We followed the process pioneered by Godshalk, Swineford, and Palmer in 1961 (Elliot, 2005, p. 162), more lately reproduced in Bob Broad's protocol for Dynamic Criteria Mapping (see Broad, Chapter 15).
15. Donald Powers (2000) persuasively argues that a percentage of agreement statistic hides problematic reader decisions that would show up on a more sophisticated measure of interrater reliability—such as degree of disagreement or the differences in score distributions among readers. He proposes the use of Cohen's weighted kappa statistic (p. 6).
16. iMOAT, which has made this project possible, has a module for scoring online rather than from paper copy. Other users have reported success with the online scoring. I have been hesitant to use this module in a large assessment with a tight time frame.
17. Significantly, Sue McLeod, then-director of the writing program at San Diego State, was an important figure in the development team organized by Cooper. She certainly took her experience at CAP with her when she joined the writing program at WSU in the late 1980s.

REFERENCES

American Educational Research Association, American Psychological Association, & National Council on Measurement in Education. (1999). *Standards for educational and psychological testing*. Washington, DC: American Educational Research Association.

Beale, W. (1987). *A pragmatic theory of rhetoric.* Carbondale, IL: Southern Illinois University Press.

Breland, H., Bridgeman, B., & Fowles, M. (1999). *Writing assessment in admission to higher education: Review and framework* (College Board Report No. 99-3; GRE Board Research Report No. 96-12R). New York, NY: The College Board.

Brennan, R. (2006). Perspectives on the evolution and future of educational measurement. In R. Brennan (Ed.), *Educational measurement* (4th ed., pp. 1-16). Westport, CT: American Council on Education and Praeger Publishers.

Britton, J., Burgess, T., Martin, N., McLeod, A., & Rosen, H. (1978). *The development of writing abilities (11-18).* Urbana, IL: National Council of Teachers of English.

California Assessment Program. (1990). *The writing assessment handbook, grade eight*. Sacramento, CA: California Department of Education. Web.

Chandler, D. (1997). *An introduction to genre theory*. Web.

Charney, D. (1984). The validity of using holistic scoring to evaluate writing: A critical overview. *Research in the Teaching of English, 18*(1), 65-81.

Council of Writing Program Administrators, National Council of Teachers of English, & National Writing Project. (2011). *Framework for success in postsecondary writing*. Web.

Devitt, A. (1996). Genre, genres, and the teaching of genres [Review of the books *Genre knowledge in disciplinary communication: Cognition/culture/power*, by

Carol Berkenkotter & T. N. Huckin; *Genre and the new rhetoric*, ed. by A. Freedman & P. Medway; *Learning and teaching genre*, ed. by A. Freedman & P. Medway]. *College Composition and Communication, 47*(4), 605-615.

Elliot, N. (2005). *On a scale: A social history of writing assessment*. New York, NY: Peter Lang.

Harrington, S., Rhodes, K., Overman Fisher, R., & Malenczyk, R. (Eds.). (2005). *The outcomes book: Debate and consensus after the WPA Outcomes Statement*. Logan, UT: Utah State University Press.

Haswell, R. (2005). *Post-secondary entry writing placement: A brief synopsis of research*. Web.

Huot, B. (1994). A survey of college and university writing placement practices. *WPA: Writing Program Administration, 17*(3), 49-67.

Huot, B. (1996). Toward a new theory of assessment. *College Composition and Communication, 47*(4), 549-566.

Huot, B. (2002). *(Re)Articulating writing assessment for teaching and learning*. Logan UT: Utah State University Press.

Kinneavy, J. (1980). *A theory of discourse*. New York, NY: Norton. (Original work published 1971)

Miller, C. (1984). Genre as a social action. *Quarterly Journal of Speech, 70*, 151-167.

Moffett, J. (1968). *Teaching the universe of discourse*. Boston, MA: Houghton Mifflin.

National Assessment of Educational Progress (NAEP). (1975). *Writing mechanics, 1969-1974: A capsule description of changes in writing mechanics*. ED 113 736. Washington DC: Government Printing Office.

North, S. (1987). *The making of knowledge in composition: Portrait of an emerging field*. Portsmouth, NH: Boynton/Cook Publishers.

O'Neill, P., Moore, C., & Huot, B. (2009). *A guide to college writing assessment*. Logan, UT: Utah State University Press.

Ohmann, R. (2003). *The politics of knowledge: The commercialization of English*. Middletown, CT: Wesleyan University Press.

Peckham, I. (1987). Statewide direct writing assessment. *English Journal, 76*(8), 30-33.

Peckham, I. (2009). Online placement in first-year writing. *College Composition and Communication, 60*(3), 517-540.

Peckham, I. (2010). Online challenge versus off-line ACT. *College Composition and Communication, 61*(4), 718-745.

Powers, D. (2000). *Research memorandum: Computing reader agreement for the GRE writing assessment* (RM-00-8). Princeton, NJ: Educational Testing Service.

Roen, D., Glau, G., Behm, N., & White E. (Eds.). (in press). *The WPA Outcomes Statement: A decade later*. West Lafayette, IN: Parlor Press.

Shiels, M. (1975, December 8). Why Johnny can't write. *Newsweek*, pp. 58-65.

White, E. M. (1995). An apologia for the timed impromptu essay test. *College Composition and Communication, 46*(1), 30-45.

White, E. M. (2005). The scoring of writing portfolios: Phase 2. *College Composition and Communication, 56*(4), 581-600.

Willard-Traub, M., Decker, E., Reed, R., & Johnston, J. (1999). The development of large-scale portfolio placement assessment at the University of Michigan: 1992–1998. *Assessing Writing, 6*(1), 41–84.

10

WHAT GOOD IS IT? THE EFFECTS OF TEACHER RESPONSE ON STUDENT'S DEVELOPMENT

Chris M. Anson
North Carolina State University

If we could mine the hours that teachers across the vast landscape of higher education spend reading, responding to, and evaluating students' writing, imagine what that cumulative effort would look like. Individual writing teachers report that they labor for up to 40 minutes reading and grading each significant assignment their students turn in (Haswell, 2005; Sommers, 1982). This amounts to days—by one estimate, 45 hours per assignment—in the service of offering advice and admonitions, corrections and praise, readerly reactions and lengthy explanations of a grade (Burkland & Grimm, 1986, p. 237). Multiply a composition teacher's dozens of notes and commentaries on each student's paper by the number of papers in each class by the number of assignments in the course by the number of courses taught each year and the job looks almost Sisyphean. Multiply that teacher's efforts by 50 or 75 instructors and you begin to get a statistical profile of written response in a typical composition program at a large university—say, around 4 or 5 million words a year, or 7 times the entire Shakespeare canon. Panning back to take in a few hundred of these institutions creates a conceptual spreadsheet of teacher response within the nation's system of 4-year public higher education. Add to these the hundreds of other institutions across the country—small liberal arts colleges, technical institutes, 2-year schools, and larger private universities—and as the picture expands, so the numbers begin to overwhelm. Over 4,000 institutions, hundreds of thousands of response hours, terabytes of commentary and marginalia offered to millions of developing writers trying to get it right, trying to put words on a page that make some sense and reflect a mind at work respectfully enough to sway the teacher's judgment that yes, this is good, this is writing that hangs together, this is a student who can organize ideas and marshal evidence to support a point and refine her prose through several iterations of revision and express an idea persuasively or concisely or logically or with grace. And after all that, we have only just considered the enterprise of composition instruction, never mind everything else that goes on in the name of writing in myriad disciplines—in soil science, philosophy, chemical engineering, introduction to musicology. And, after that much more, we have only considered response on a national scale, not as a global educational practice.

If our thought experiment has worked, visualizing this staggering volume of commentary begs a simple question: What good is it? Or, as Peter Elbow asks in the context of writing assessment in Chapter 17 of this volume, what's "good enough?" What would it mean to us, psychologically and pedagogically, if we were to find only a modest educational return on the colossal investment of time and energy we put into responding to student writing? How do we know that all the late hours spent burning the proverbial midnight oil over a stack or electronic folder of papers really make any difference to the development of students' writing abilities and their identities as literate individuals, beyond their very acts of trying to make sense with text, over and over, assignment after assignment, grade after unexplained grade?

That question is the subject of this chapter. First I reflect on scholarship on response to student writing, focusing especially on why the voluminous commentary, theorizing, and empirical studies that have amassed in this area of composition studies have focused so strongly on what teachers do, and not what happens to students. I then turn to the question at hand, suggesting some fruitful areas for needed research on response to student writing in light of existing work that has tried to gauge significant effects of teachers' responses on the students themselves—on their development as writers and on other subsidiary gains.

PRECEDENTS: THEORY STANDING IN FOR EVIDENCE

To summarize the scholarship on response and evaluation that has appeared in the field of composition studies, not to mention allied areas of inquiry, is far beyond the scope of this chapter. A search for published work on "response" in CompPile, the largest database in the field, yields 2,189 entries; "assessment" and "evaluation" produce an impressive 3,264 and 4,155, respectively.[1] In addition, several excellent reviews already exist (e.g., Straub, 2000). But when we take a broader view of the scholarship on response, which began appearing in earnest in the early 1980s, we find that assumptions about students' learning—about what works best to promote writing development—constantly stand in for actual inquiry on the specific effects of teachers' commentary.

The advent of the process movement in the late 1970s and 1980s marked a steady interest in response to student writing, in part because teachers' focus had shifted toward varieties of instructional support for learning. Beginning with articles such as Nancy Sommers' "Responding to Student Writing" (1982), which convincingly argued for the need to interrogate our methods of response, scholars defined a clear path for reflecting on and empirically investigating the nature of response. The work that followed almost relentlessly examined what *teachers* do when they read and respond to students' writing at various stages of its development. In addition to plentiful theorizing and practical recommendations for teachers, dozens of carefully designed research studies on response focused on the practice of response, not the reception of this practice by learners. As Sommers herself put it over 25 years later, "in our professional literature about responding, we too often neglect the role of the student in this transaction, and the vital partnership between teacher and student, by focusing, almost exclusively, on the role of the teacher" (2006, p. 249).

In the context of the process movement, which spread through the teaching of writing with almost viral force, it is not difficult to understand why scholars usually disposed to providing evidence for their assertions would simply assume that doing such-and-such with students' papers was better than the "current-traditional" status quo—that if teachers change their means of intervention, student writing will improve (Knoblauch & Brannon, 2006, p. 8). It might explain why, in "Post-Structural Literary Criticism and the Response to Student Writing," Edward White (1984) theorized about teacher response from the perspective of emerging scholarship on interpretive communities—that is, communities of teachers. It might explain why, in his analysis of the 378 comments provided by 24 of his colleagues on a student essay titled "Easy Street," Donald Daiker (1986) made a compelling argument about the paucity of praise in teacher response, but the unnamed student writer, his essay plucked from the context in which it had at least some rhetorical and educational purpose, remained just a specter, an undifferentiated and emblematic "college freshman" denied the opportunity to explain how he felt about the praise or lack thereof in any of the amassed commentary. It might explain why, in one of the most cited early articles on response, Brannon and Knoblauch (1982) adopted the term "appropriation" to describe the ways teachers take control of their students' writing, documenting this tendency in an analysis of 40 teachers' responses to the essay of a student (John)—but did not ask John to reflect on the nature of those responses and the extent to which he felt they appropriated his writing. And it might explain why, in an analysis of teachers' response styles in their written or tape-recorded commentary to basic writers (Anson, 1986b), I was able to place the comments into Perry's scheme of intellectual development and speculate about the effects on students whose writing also reflected positions in the scheme, but the students were not enrollees in the teachers' classes, so it was impossible to consider the cumulative effects of the teachers' styles on the students' ways of thinking about the world of knowledge.

The process movement brought with it an expectation that teachers would now provide significant support as students crafted and revised their papers. This shift in orientation toward student development offers a second explanation for the strong focus on teachers in the early work on response: workload. The hope that understanding response might yield some principles or strategies that could lessen its burden clearly drew scholars toward its teacherly dimensions. Largely absent from the analyses of response styles, amount, purposes, orientations such as positive and negative, control of students' texts, focus, and reflection of underlying instructional ideologies, students in both traditionally empirical and descriptive or case-based studies served as indirect subjects, the assumption being that if we could understand the nature of teachers' response, we could improve it to the theoretical but not empirically supported benefit of students, and we could do so efficiently, without adding to the already substantial workload (see, for example, Haswell, 1983).

The dominance of teachers' goals, habits, and patterns of marginalia in studies of response is nowhere better reflected than in a major study of response, Straub and Lunsford's *Twelve Readers Reading* (1995). This book-length work offers an extensive analysis of a dozen composition scholars' response practices culled from their comments on an assortment of sample student drafts and final essays provided to them by the researchers. An important and carefully executed study, *Twelve Readers Reading* nonetheless emblematizes the field's preoccupation with the teacher perspective. Students in the study were present only in their papers, which had been pulled from their original instructional and social contexts for use as the medium through which to collect the dozen experts' practices. As part of the data collection, the experts were asked to provide brief reflective essays describing their philosophies of response, but the original student writers were not brought into the study to share what they thought about the varied readings of their essays that the experts provided. In revealing the considerable variety of expert teacher-scholars' response practices, the study was unable to reach any evidence-based conclusions about which practices worked more effectively to help students improve their papers and develop as writers. Instead, theoretical speculation stood in for any kind of causal analysis.

The strong focus on teachers in response research did not escape critique—eventually. By the end of the 1990s, articles were appearing that called into question what we could derive about student achievement by looking at teachers' commentary. Murphy (2000), for example, pointed to the need for a sociocultural framework for analyzing response, in which researchers would study the rich fabric of social interactions and negotiations entailed in the response situation. Three specific articles published in the same issue of *Assessing Writing* came under critique: Callahan's "Responding to the Invisible Student" (2000), which examined response practices relative to students' learning style preferences; Straub's "The Student, the Text, and the Classroom Context: A Case Study of Teacher Response" (2000), which reflected on the author's own response practices through the lens of seven principles derived from scholarship; and my own article "Response and the Social Construction of Error" (2000), which theorized about the effects of student error on teachers' construction of students' texts, meaning, and personae. What is not found in these articles, Murphy (2000) claimed, is "serious attention to the role played by students in 'teacher' response . . . how they interpret our comments, how they react to them" (p. 88). And although Callahan's study did consider the effects of response on students with different learning styles, "the students' voices were silenced; their perspectives were determined instead by the results of a test" (p. 88).

Similarly, in a review of scholarship on response as part of a portfolio project, Fife and O'Neill (2001) "found an impressive body of literature on responding to student writing and many research studies about teacher commentary," but "soon realized that most of the work provided textual analysis of the comments with little information about how the comments functioned as part of the class" (p. 301). Focusing mainly on teachers' comments, they argued, turned a blind eye to other crucial elements that determine the success or failure of our methods—such as the importance of instructional context, the assumption that commentary has a uniform interpretation, and the lack of attention to students' reactions to the comments—a gap filled by empty hypotheses about which comments are helpful or not. Citing Gumperz' prolegomenon for conversational research (1982), Fife and O'Neill urged researchers to consider "physical setting, personal background knowledge, attitudes toward each other, sociocultural assumptions concerning role and status relationships, and social values associated with various message components" (2001, p. 312; see also O'Neill, Chapter 25).

The "social turn" that characterized scholarship in composition in the 1990s and beyond is evident in these and other critiques of response studies that ignored the rich contextual dimensions of schooling and the relationship of those to other aspects of students' selves and of teachers' personal and instructional ideologies. None of the critiques called into question the value of research on teacher response, which has yielded useful and informative taxonomies of evaluative discourse, elaborate descriptions of what teachers do when they read students' work, and statistical analyses of commentary based on very large samples of papers from first-year composition courses (e.g., Connors & Lunsford, 1988, 1993; Lunsford & Lunsford, 2008). But far less is known about a much more important question: What do students *do* with teachers' responses to their writing? How do they read and interpret those responses, and with what subsequent effects on their improvement as writers? How do they construct the relationship between themselves and their instructors as a consequence of response? Or, as Montgomery (2010) frames it as the entire focus of her dissertation, "How do first-year students experience teacher response to their writing? Where are the students' voices in the research?" (p. 48).

Several scholars of literacy development have claimed that the cumulative body of research shows few positive effects of response on students' revised texts or on their development as writers. Early research that examined the effects of teachers' response on students' development as writers (as opposed to revisions of the texts in question) reported disappointing results (e.g., Gee, 1972; Shroeder, 1973; Stiff, 1967; similar conclusions were reached in subsequent research that had the benefit of greater methodological insight, e.g., Dohrer, 1991). The results of the early scattered studies were confirmed in the largest meta-analysis of research on school-based writing (Hillocks, 1986), which found that "teacher comment has little impact on student writing," with virtually no statistically significant differences in the writing of students who received various experimental comment treatments—a conclusion that called into question Hillocks' own earlier assumptions that "the teacher comment, when positive and focused on particular aspects of writing over a series of compositions, can be effective" (1982, p. 277). (A more recent meta-analysis of 11 intervention strategies in adolescent writing instruction confirmed Hillocks' conclusions, finding a negative effect size only for grammar instruction—"the explicit and systematic teaching of grammar"; see Graham & Perin, 2007). In an insightful reflection on the state of knowledge about response, Knoblauch and Brannon (2006) make a similar claim based on their review of the literature, suggesting that there is "scant evidence that students routinely use comments on one draft to make rhetorically important, and in the end qualitatively superior, changes in a subsequent draft," and that there is "still less evidence to show that they change their practices from one assignment to the next in ways that measurably represent or affect their development as writers" (p. 1). These conclusions were confirmed more recently in a dissertation that surveyed 73 students about their practices when receiving instructor response to their writing, followed by in-depth discourse-based interviews with 10 of the students. Findings indicated that "a surprising number of students do not read the feedback thoroughly or seriously, and of those who do, many misinterpret that feedback, and very few students think of feedback as an exchange or dialogue between a teacher and student" (Montgomery, 2009, p. vi).

In stark contrast, vast numbers of teachers, writing center staff, and program administrators continue to hold faith in what Knoblauch and Brannon call the "myth of improvement," which includes the belief that teacher feedback is not only important, but is the single most crucial variable in students' growth as writers. From a purely instructional perspective, no universally held belief about teaching writing stands with greater determination than the one that places response at the center of development, and it is often used over all other arguments for keeping course loads and class sizes as low as possible. "The process of response is so fundamental to human interaction," I wrote in 1986, "that when it is short-circuited, whether by accident or design, the result can hardly be interpreted as anything but a loss of humanity" (1986a, p. 1). But, as Knoblauch and Brannon (2006) suggest, the "reassuring narrative about the improvement of writing ability" to which my conviction contributes "belies a persistently unconvincing demonstration that it occurs" (p. 2).

In trying to explain the less than robust developmental effects of response, both Hillocks (1986) and Knoblauch and Brannon (2006) point to significant methodological and epistemological problems in the research, part of which are "axiological," emerging from the inherent interconnectedness of writing instruction and personal values or ideologies (see Fulkerson, 1995). For Knoblauch and Brannon, development of writing abilities takes place along an uncertain trajectory, over so much time that it is often impossible to measure small gains within the context of courses or singular experiences. And even when growth occurs, we have inadequate instruments of assessment to discern all of its nuances. As Sommers (2006) has put it, "the movement from first-year writing to senior, from novice to expert, if it happens at all, looks more like one step forward, two steps back, isolated progress within paragraphs, one compositional element mastered while other elements fall away" (p. 249). These assumptions are confirmed in longitudinal research that shows various aspects of writing development over time—the cumulative but not specific effect of interactions focusing on students' emerging texts (see, e.g., Haswell, 1991; Herrington & Curtiss, 2000; Sternglass, 1997). For Hillocks (2008), who elaborates on the results of his meta-analysis in the context of research on writing in secondary schools, the gains seen in a handful of studies suggest that students benefit more from comments that move beyond form (Sperling, 1990), that reflect information provided explicitly in class (Sperling & Freedman, 1987), and that are focused and given prior to revision (Hillocks, 1982). For students engaged in revision, those receiving teacher comments produce higher quality writing than those who engage in self-evaluation (Beach, 1979). But these isolated studies find little or no support in the form of replications or methodological refinements.

We are left, then, with an interesting situation: Serious fault lines in the research on response—which has been unable to show us with much certainty whether or how comments on students' writing really work—end up stabilized with the strong convictions of teachers whose daily observations convince them that response is not only valuable but crucial to students' development as writers. In some ways, the work on response—focused as it has been on teachers' practices—has suffered from what Leander and Mills (2007) have characterized as the overly situated nature of literacy research, which has been "held too far apart from the flows of materials, bodies and embodied practices [and] privileged a reading of their world as being organized by literacy" (p. 184). What would it mean for us to delve far more deeply into the complexities of the relationship between what teachers say to students about their writing and what effect, if any, this has on students' development in the socially and interpersonally imbricated places where teaching and learning happen?

PUSHING THE BOUNDARIES OF RESEARCH ON RESPONSE

Nancy Sommers' (2006) longitudinal research at Harvard University painstakingly documents individual students' trajectories as academic writers, revealing the reported centrality of their teachers' and peers' response in their development. In their testimonies, the students felt they progressed most when teachers meaningfully focused on their ideas, in the kind of intellectual interaction that might characterize a good discussion and not a situation in which they were being "assessed" on their ability to put tidy sentences together into coherent paragraphs. It is clear in Sommers' ongoing research that much more than the nature of text is at play in students' feelings about and uses of teacher response. Text itself is part of a complex interaction involving students' and teachers' construction of each other's identities in the context of a particular activity system layered with multiple intentions and influenced by the "ideologies of pedagogy" entailed in particular classes located in particular kinds of institutions, themselves influenced by educational values of the broader society.

Sommers' work has raised important questions about the relationship of response to other factors beyond the textual interactions between teachers and students that are occasioned by writing assignments. Research on response has generally assumed stable contexts and actors—normative classrooms and stereotypical students and teachers. But response always takes place in complex social and instructional settings where institutional type and mission, student populations, classroom ethos, instructional ideology, and a host of other factors influence every moment of learning both in and out of the classroom. In an interesting cross-disciplinary study, Jeffery and Selting (1999) asked content-area faculty in six departments to talk their way through their students' papers as if they were providing feedback directly to the students. They then analyzed the recorded commentary in terms of the identities the teachers established for themselves and for the students they were addressing (e.g., "intellectual mentor" for the teacher, "budding __ist" for the student). Not surprisingly, they found that the teachers overwhelmingly adopted the identity of an *assignment judge* responding to *students*, which did not facilitate students' apprenticeship in their fields. Although this study again shows the dominance of the teacher perspective, its methodology could be profitably used to analyze students' constructions of their own identities as writers in a range of classroom settings (see also Anson, 1999b). Because development hinges on affect (including how students feel about their own roles in relation to what they are writing), such research could help us to understand how response does or does not help students to learn about various disciplinary and activity-based contexts of writing.

The complexities of identity revealed in Jeffery and Selting's study were more deeply explored—in both students and teachers—in Carol Rutz's (1999) dissertation *What Does My Teacher Want Me to Do? A Response-Based Investigation of the Teacher-Student Relationship in the Classroom.* Rutz was thoroughly acquainted with the literature on response and was drawn to the serious gap not only in our understanding of what students do with teacher response but what sorts of goals teachers have in mind when they frame their responses—how they interpret students' writing based on their knowledge of factors most of which had never come into consideration in previous research. In a series of case studies using both quantitative and qualitative methods, she learned everything she could about students' and teachers' intentions for and interpretations of their classroom work, documenting influences from task constraints, things said (or implied) during class, previous commentary on papers or other work, and the like. Response to student writing became only one part of a larger set of ongoing relationships developing between teachers and students, sometimes providing "a medium for teachers to capitalize on their rapport with students" (p. 3). In one example of the highly contextualized nature of response that Rutz uncovered in her case studies, a teacher offered much commentary but very little of it as praise. From the perspective of prior research, such a tendency—quantified and objectified—might be interpreted as a violation of what students say they want from teachers and a failure to facilitate students' development (see Bardine, Bardine, & Degan, 2000; Beach, 1989; Ferris, 2003). But deeper inquiry revealed that the teacher explicitly discussed this style of response with the students, rationalizing it in the context of an approach that tried to be as helpful and direct as possible. Interviews with the students revealed that they felt no discomfort with the method; instead, the students were reading their teacher's motives in ways that went far beyond the usual focus on assignments and the written products thereof.

Although Rutz uncovered quite subtle response cues that contributed to teachers' and students' constructions of each others' intentions and identities, they were still generally discernible and overt. But as Prior and Looker (2009) have argued, when we view response in the context of "a dialogic notion of genre systems understood as multimodal or multisemiotic, and in the context of theories of writing and learning grounded in sociocultural, or cultural-historical activity, theories that attend to literate and semiotic practices," we can no longer limit ourselves to the "temporal sequence of draft, response, revision." In their studies of college courses, Prior and Looker (2009) have found cases of response embedded in the genre systems of the class—in an array of both explicit and implicit texts, activities, and actors: tips posted on a Web site, cues embedded in an assignment structure or series of short assignments related to a longer project, personal notes, lesson plans, email messages, offhanded remarks, and so on. In contrast to the bounded spaces in which response has been studied, they suggest how a "multimodal, genre systems approach to response can inform—and offer a generative framework for—research, pedagogy, and practice":

> When we suggest that it is important to re-envision literate activity in terms of multimodal genre systems, we are arguing for unanchoring "response" from its fixity in prototypical scenes of teaching writing through process approaches, widening its circumference from that of classroom scenes and roles, complicating its temporalities, and shifting the unit of analysis from "the text" or for that matter "the student writer" to genres systems, with multiple semiotic artifacts and acts, operating in and across activity systems. (n.p.)

Prior's research (e.g., 1998), which reveals the dynamic, multifaceted nature of "response" and its layered and sometimes hidden sources, shifts the focus away from teachers as the sole or most important source of response and toward other aspects of classroom interaction. For example, even in courses that do not systematically engage students in providing response to each other, there is little question that the broader peer dynamics blend fluidly with what teachers do or facilitate, especially in the student "underlife" (Brooke, 1987) that provides a context parallel to, and intruding on, the course itself. Teacher response, in other words, gets filtered, interpreted, remixed, and repurposed among students, influencing their decisions and their own responses to tasks and evaluations. More regulated and orchestrated peer response as a source of student growth is beyond the scope of this chapter to discuss in any detail, but it must be included in any theory of the relationship between response and learning—particularly because the research shows at least somewhat stronger gains when response is provided in the context of revision than when it is provided on single-draft writing (Beach & Friedrich, 2006). The interplay of teachers' agendas, students' collective interpretations of these, and the ways in which they offer reactions to each others' writing makes more complex the question of potential influence. As Nystrand's research has shown, the effectiveness of peer response is directly related to the ways that teachers conceptualize it and prepare students to do it (Nystrand, 1983, 1986, 1990, 2002; Nystrand & Brandt, 1989). Orchestrated peer response, then, simply adds another layer, if pedagogically institutionalized, to each student's self-conception as writer.

Scattered early studies of students' opinions of other students' writing (e.g., Newkirk, 1984) have yielded to fuller accounts of their development as writers that includes what they do beyond the academic setting. For example, in a series of case studies, Roozen (2008, 2009; Roozen & Herrera, 2010) has documented strong influences of students' "vernacular literacies"—"self-sponsored, informally learned literate practices that are 'rooted in everyday experience and serve everyday purposes' (Barton & Hamilton, 1998, p. 251)"—on their performance in academic tasks. Personal interests, hobbies, and especially types of discourse in which they have developed some measure of expertise on their own can permeate responses to even conventional types of assignments, but may be entirely unrecoverable as part of the network of intentions and purposes informing students' writing. Without access to these features of students' work, teachers must remain mute to them, suggesting that response should take place in a richer social context in a process of "cultural modeling" (Lee, 2001, 2007) that allows students to express their intentions—when they wish—and demonstrate the ways that their other sources of expertise inform what they do. Roozen's work also suggests a relatively unstudied process of "backwards" cultural modeling, in which various academic experiences, occasioned by complex sources of response, end up causing developments in personal, nonacademic, and vernacular writing that we never see. The lack of transformation and growth that has disappointed researchers of classroom-based response may be as much a function of the myopia with which we have viewed that growth, limited as it is to narrowly defined academic progress rather than a richer array of socially based literate activities.

These and other factors reveal new complexities that can militate against the furtherance of evidence-based research on response. A common reaction to the lack of strong empirical support for the effects of teacher response on students' development is to critique the validity of the entire research enterprise: too many variables, too much uncertainty, too great an emphasis on the classroom as a zoo cage, interactions between students and teachers that are far too messy to determine any truth empirically. However, despite the many factors surrounding the complex processes of students' and teachers' interactions about texts, the basic principles of causality can still guide our further inquiry. As Schneider, Carnoy, Kilpatrick, Schmidt, and Shavelson (2007) have argued, evidence-based research showing causal relationships between certain educational practices and student success is highly desirable but needs a set of norms and common discourse even across methodologies. Their report, which describes rigorous criteria for judging the integrity of evidence-based design, can be used not only to critique existing research and figure out why it showed weak effects of response, but to establish a new set of research questions that can be investigated using appropriate methodologies and designs.

Finally, in addition to learning much more about response from the student perspective, we need to extend the reach and nature of the information we gather from teachers to counter both artificiality (e.g., asking teachers to write on a-contextualized student papers) and noninvolvement (e.g., collecting graded papers and analyzing their commentary without studying what led to it in the first place). As I have written elsewhere (Anson, 1999a), response is best practiced as a range of possible strategies intentionally and reflectively adapted to specific teaching/learning contexts and the individual students that populate them, in all their developmental, interpersonal, and psychological complexity. This shift away from reliance on singular or "best" methods is not an admission of methodological defeat, because it substitutes thoughtfulness for mindless application, causing us to "look beyond simplistic cause-and-effect formulas as justification for preferring one practice over another" (Knoblauch & Brannon, 2006, p. 13).

Such a perspective brings teachers' own "felt sense" together with a means to understand it. Substituting for research is teacher "lore," one of North's (1987) eight major sources of knowledge in composition studies. Empirically maligned, lore still serves as an important shaper of received knowledge about teaching. So powerful is lore, especially when it amasses from different sources, that it drives entire pedagogies. But instead of trying to tap into teachers' perceptions—indeed, convictions—that certain strategies work routinely well, or that certain strategies worked well on certain occasions, research has distanced itself from the thinking processes of teachers as they wrestle with the daily routines of their pedagogy and deal with its surprises and disappointments. The existence of lore suggests the possibility that we might find out, within specific classroom settings and in the context of specific assignments and writing tasks, what exactly contributes to teachers' sense that something or other "works." Bringing together the kind of lore that results from systematic reflection on teaching (e.g., reflective practice; see Schôn, 1987) with a rigorous inquiry whose goal is understanding the conditions in which learning takes place could move us much further toward a comprehensive theory of response that acknowledges its lack of causal uniformity while still aspiring to the systematic improvement of its praxis.

ENDNOTE

1. Early composition scholarship settled on the term "response" as distinct from "evaluation," presumably to be inclusive of various kinds of formative feedback students received on their writing, in addition to summative judgments of their work. These terms, however, show considerable overlap in the literature.

REFERENCES

Anson, C. M. (1986a). Introduction: Response to writing and the paradox of uncertainty. In C. M. Anson (Ed.), *Writing and response: Theory, practice, and research* (pp. 1-11). Urbana, IL: National Council of Teachers of English.

Anson, C. M. (1986b). Response styles and ways of knowing. In C. M. Anson (Ed.), *Writing and response: Theory, practice, and research* (pp. 332-366). Urbana, IL: National Council of Teachers of English.

Anson, C. M. (1999a). Reflective reading: Developing thoughtful ways to respond to students' writing. In C. R. Cooper & L. Odell (Eds.), *Evaluating writing: The role of teachers' knowledge about text, learning, and culture* (pp. 302-324). Urbana, IL: National Council of Teachers of English.

Anson, C. M. (1999b). Talking about writing: A classroom-based study of students' reflections on their drafts. In J. B. Smith and K. Yancey (Eds.), *Student self-assessment and development in writing* (pp. 59-74). Cresskill, NJ: Hampton Press.

Anson, C. M. (2000). Response and the social construction of error. *Assessing Writing, 7*(1), 5-21.

Bardine, B., Bardine, M., & Deegan, E. (2000). Beyond the red pen: Clarifying our role in the response process. *English Journal, 90*(1), 94-101.

Barton, D., & Hamilton, E. (1998). *Local literacies: Reading and writing in one community*. London, UK: Routledge.

Beach, R. (1979). The effects of between-draft teacher evaluation versus student self-evaluation on high school students' revising of rough drafts. *Research in the Teaching of English, 13*(2), 111-119.

Beach, R. (1989). Showing students how to assess: Demonstrating techniques for response in writing conferences. In C. Anson (Ed.), *Writing and response: Theory, practice, and research* (pp. 127-148). Urbana, IL: National Council of Teachers of English.

Beach, R., & Friedrich, T. (2006). Response to writing. In C. A. MacArthur, S. Graham, & J. Fitzgerald (Eds.), *Handbook of writing research* (pp. 222-234). New York, NY: Guilford Press.

Brannon, L., & Knoblauch, C. H. (1982). On students' rights to their own texts: A model of teacher response. *College Composition and Communication, 33*(2), 157-166.

Brooke, R. (1987). Underlife and writing instruction. *College Composition and Communication, 38*(2), 141-153.

Burkland, J., & Grimm, N. (1986). Motivating through responding. *Journal of Teaching Writing, 5*(2), 237-246.

Callahan, S. (2000). Responding to the invisible student. *Assessing Writing, 7*(1), 57-77.

Connors, R. J., & Lunsford, A. A. (1988). Frequency of formal errors in current college writing, or Ma and Pa Kettle do research. *College Composition and Communication, 39*(4), 395-409.

Connors, R. J., & Lunsford, A. A. (1993). Teachers' rhetorical comments on student papers. *College Composition and Communication, 44*(2), 200-223.

Daiker, D. A. (1986). Learning to praise. In C. M. Anson (Ed.), *Writing and response: Theory, practice, and research* (pp. 103-113). Urbana, IL: National Council of Teachers of English.

Dohrer, G. (1991). Do teachers' comments on students' papers help? *College Composition and Communication, 39*(2), 48-54.

Ferris, D. R. (2003). *Response to student writing: Implications for second language students*. Mahwah, NJ: Lawrence Erlbaum Associates.

Fife, J., & O'Neill, P. (2001). Moving beyond the written comment: Narrowing the gap between response practice and research. *College Composition and Communication, 53*(2), 300-321.

Fulkerson, R. (1995). Axiology. In T. Enos (Ed.), *The encyclopedia of rhetoric and composition: Communication from ancient times to the information age* (pp. 56-57). New York, NY: Routledge.

Gee, J. (1972). Students' responses to teacher comments. *Research in the Teaching of English, 6*(2), 212-219.

Graham, S., & Perin, D. (2007). A meta-analysis of writing instruction for adolescent students. *Journal of Educational Psychology, 99*(3), 445-476.

Gumperz, J. J. (1982). Discourse strategies. New York, NY: Cambridge University Press.

Haswell, R. H. (1983). Minimal marking. *College English, 45*(6), 600-604.

Haswell, R. H. (2005). *Average time-on-course of a writing teacher*. Web.

Haswell, R. H. (1991). *Gaining ground in college writing: Tales of development and interpretation*. Dallas, TX: Southern Methodist University Press.

Herrington, A. J., & Curtiss, M. (2000). *Persons in progress: Four stories of writing and personal development in college*. Urbana, IL: National Council of Teachers of English.

Hillocks, G. (1982). The interaction of instruction, teacher comment, and revision in teaching the composing process. *Research in the Teaching of English, 6*(2), 212-221.

Hillocks, G. (1986). *Research on written composition: New directions for teaching.* Urbana, IL: National Conference on Research in English and ERIC.

Hillocks, G. (2008). Writing in secondary schools. In C. Bazerman (Ed.), *Handbook of research on writing: History, society, school, individual, text* (pp. 311-330). Mahwah, NJ: Lawrence Erlbaum Associates.

Jeffery, F., & Selting, B. (1999). Reading the invisible ink: Assessing the responses of non-composition faculty. *Assessing Writing, 6*(2), 179-197.

Knoblauch, C., & Brannon, L. (2006). The emperor (still) has no clothes—Revisiting the myth of improvement. In R. Straub (Ed.), *Key works on teacher response* (pp. 1-15). Portsmouth, NH: Heinemann/Boynton-Cook.

Leander, K., & Mills, S. (2007). The transnational development of an online role player game by youth: Tracing the flows of literacy, an online game imaginary, and digital resources. In M.V. Blackburn & C.T. Clark (Eds.), *Literacy research for political action* (pp. 177-198). New York, NY: Peter Lang.

Lee, C. (2001). Is October Brown Chinese? A cultural modeling activity system for underachieving students. *American Educational Research Journal, 38*(1), 97-141.

Lee, C. (2007). *Culture, literacy, and learning: Taking bloom in the midst of the whirlwind.* New York, NY: Teachers College Press.

Lunsford, A. A., & Lunsford, K. J. (2008). "Mistakes are a fact of life": A national comparative study. *College Composition and Communication, 59*(4), 781-806.

Montgomery, M. (2009). *First-year students' perceptions and interpretations of teacher response to their writing: Ten students speak.* Unpublished doctoral dissertation, University of Massachusetts-Amherst.

Murphy, S. (2000). A sociocultural perspective on teacher response: Is there a student in the room? *Assessing Writing, 7*(1), 79-90.

Newkirk, T. (1984). How students read student papers: An exploratory study. *Written Communication, 1*(3), 283-305.

North, S. M. (1987). *The making of knowledge in composition: Portrait of an emerging field.* Upper Montclair, NJ: Boynton/Cook.

Nystrand, M. (1983). The role of context in written communication. *Nottingham Linguistic Circular, 12*(3), 55-65.

Nystrand, M. (1986). *The structure of written communication: Studies in reciprocity between writers and readers.* Orlando, FL and London, UK: Academic Press.

Nystrand, M. (1990). Sharing words: The effects of readers on developing writers. *Written Communication, 7*(3), 3-24.

Nystrand, M. (2002). Dialogic discourse analysis of revision in response groups. In E. Barton & G. Stygall (Eds.), *Discourse studies in composition* (pp. 377-392). Cresskill, NJ: Hampton Press.

Nystrand, M., & Brandt, D. (1989). Response to writing as a context for learning to write. In C. Anson (Ed.), *Writing and response: Theory, practice, and research.* Urbana, IL: National Council of Teachers of English.

Prior, P. (1998). Contextualizing instructors' responses to writing in the college classroom. In R. Calfee & N. Nelson (Eds.), *The reading-writing connection* (pp. 153-177). Chicago, IL: National Society for Studies of Education.

Prior, P., & Looker, S. (2009, April). *Anticipatory response and genre systems: Rethinking response research, pedagogy, and practice.* Paper presented at the Conference on College Composition and Communication, San Francisco, CA.

Roozen, K. (2008). Journalism, poetry, stand-up comedy, and academic literacy: Mapping the interplay of curricular and extracurricular literate activities. *Journal of Basic Writing, 27*(1), 5-34.

Roozen, K. (2009). "Fanfic-ing graduate school": A case study exploring the interplay of vernacular literacies and disciplinary engagement. *Research in the Teaching of English, 44*(2), 136-169.

Roozen, K., & Herrera, A. (2010). "Indigenous interests": Reconciling literate identities across extracurricular and curricular contexts. In J. Jordan, M. Cox, & G. Schwartz (Eds.), *Inventing identities in second language writing* (pp. 139-162). Urbana, IL: National Council of Teachers of English.

Rutz, C. A. (1999). *What does my teacher want me to do? A response-based investigation of the teacher-student relationships in the classroom.* Unpublished doctoral dissertation. University of Minnesota, Minneapolis, MN.

Schon, D. A. (1987). *Educating the reflective practitioner.* San Francisco, CA: Jossey-Bass.

Schneider, B, Carnoy, M., Kilpatrick, J., Schmidt, W. H., & Shavelson, R. J. (2007). *Estimating causal effects using experimental and observational designs.* Washington, DC: American Educational Research Association.

Schroeder, T. S. (1973). *The effects of positive and corrective written teacher feedback on selected writing behaviors of fourth-grade children.* Unpublished doctoral dissertation. University of Kansas, Lawrence. KS.

Sommers, N. (1982). Responding to student writing. *College Composition and Communication, 33*, 148-156.

Sommers, N. (2006). Across the drafts. *College Composition and Communication, 58*(2), 248-257.

Sperling, M. (1990). I want to talk to each of you: Collaboration and the teacher-student writing conference. *Research in the Teaching of English, 24*(3), 279-332.

Sperling, M., & Freedman, S. W. (1987). A good girl writes like a good girl: Written responses to student writing. *Written Communication, 4*(4), 343-369.

Sternglass, M. (1997). *Time to know them: A longitudinal study of writing and learning at the college level.* Mahwah, NJ: Lawrence Erlbaum Associates.

Stiff, R. (1967). The effect upon student composition of particular correction techniques. *Research in the Teaching of English, 1*(1), 54, 75.

Straub, R. (2000). The student, the text, and the classroom context: A case study of teacher response. *Assessing Writing, 7*(1), 23-55.

Straub, R., & Lunsford, R. F. (1995). *Twelve readers reading: Responding to college student writing.* Cresskill, NJ: Hampton Press.

White, E. M. (1984). Post-structural literary criticism and the response to student writing. *College Composition and Communication, 35*(2), 186-195.

11

FOSTERING BEST PRACTICES IN WRITING ASSESSMENT AND INSTRUCTION WITH E-RATER®

Jill Burstein

Educational Testing Service

Natural language processing (NLP) employs computational techniques for the purpose of identifying linguistic features from stored, electronic text or speech. Many familiar and widely used applications that use NLP technology include internet search technology (e.g., Google, Yahoo!®, and Bing™ search engines), machine translation (e.g., Google Translate), and speech recognition (e.g., automated telephone-based customer service). NLP has also found a home in different applications intended to support different needs in education settings (Burstein, Sabatini & Shore, in press). One well-known and historically controversial application is automated essay scoring (computer-based essay scoring).

White (2007) does express concern about computer-based scoring in writing assessment. One fairly broad concern to be addressed in this chapter is the question of the *usefulness* of computer-based scoring of writing. However, White (2007) does advise that educators "keep an open mind" (p. 116) about claims around computer-based scoring if it can be shown to be *helpful* and *dependab*le. This technology can be shown to embrace and foster best practices per White (1994, 2007) in large-scale, standardized assessment settings (Attali, 2009), and classroom instruction and assessment (Attali, 2004; Burstein, in press; Lipnevich & Smith, 2008). Therefore, the motivation of this chapter is to demonstrate how automated essay scoring methods can be all of these things—*useful*, *helpful*, and *dependable*.

Consistent with the intended motivation of this volume, this chapter focuses primarily on best practices of teaching and assessing writing as presented in White (1994). The fuller intention of the chapter is to entertain a collegial and scholarly discussion with regard to *how* best practices discussed in White (1994) are captured in existing applications of automated scoring for assessment and classroom writing. Through an open discussion about how the technology works, and how it is systematically evaluated, it is our hope that this chapter successfully illustrates how the use of automated essay scoring could be helpful to many developing writers, thus mitigating general concerns about technology *usefulness* as expressed in White (2007).

In terms of large-scale, standardized assessment, consistent with a measurement community perspective, White (1994, p. 10) asserts that ensuring test validity is critical. Accordingly, an assessment instrument, such as an essay writing task, must measure what it claims to be measuring. White (1994, p. 10) asserts that a critical goal in the teaching and assessing of writing in classroom settings should be that teachers thoughtfully mentor students, so that students themselves can identify trouble spots in their own writing (i.e., students can evaluate their own thought processes in the context of written expression). It is through this mentoring process that students can ultimately self-assess, leading them to become better thinkers and more proficient writers. To this end, White's discussion around classroom assessment suggests that teachers' approach to grading should be systematic, such that students receive consistent, meaningful, and comprehensible feedback that they can easily apply in the revision process. Moving forward, students can continue to engage in new writing tasks. If in this chapter we can show that automated essay scoring uses construct-relevant features and offers meaningful and consistent feedback, we can argue that this innovation is *useful*, *helpful*, and *dependable*.

In this chapter, the discussion about computer-based scoring focuses on e-rater®, Educational Testing Service's automated essay scoring system (Attali & Burstein, 2006; Burstein, Kukich, Wolff, Lu, Chodorow, Braden-Harder, & Harris, 1998). We explain how even in its first incarnation for use with essay scoring in large scale-assessment, the system was designed in good faith to capture linguistic aspects in human rater scoring guide criteria that specify the features that should be taken into account (measured) to reliably predict an essay score (Attali, 2009; Attali & Burstein, 2006; Burstein et al., 1998). Consistent with White's (2004) belief that meaningful feedback during the writing process helps to improve students' writing skills, we will discuss how e-rater, when used in a classroom instructional application, *Criterion*® (Burstein, Chodorow, & Leacock, 2004), supports the process approach to writing (Emig, 1971). Further, systematic research study outcomes also indicate that *Criterion* feedback and revision capabilities can support writing improvement (Attali, 2004; Lipnevich & Smith, 2008).

There is a significant population of developing writers in the United States from K-12 to higher education settings, including native and non-native English speakers. We can only hope that as our colleagues in writing research carefully read this chapter, they "keep an open mind" to computer-based essay scoring as a technology that has the potential to enhance and support the writing experience of this large, and culturally and linguistically diverse population.

E-RATER®

E-rater® is an automated essay evaluation and scoring system that uses natural language processing (NLP) (Attali & Burstein, 2006; Burstein et al., 1998). The system is used in large-scale assessments, and in instructional classroom settings. Both settings are discussed.

E-rater and Holistic scoring. E-rater scoring is modeled on holistic scoring. It reflects the scoring methodology used by ETS to evaluate standardized writing assessments (Godshalk, Swineford, & Coffman, 1966; White, 1984). In the traditional application of holistic essay scoring, human raters evaluate numerous aspects of an essay to assign a score that reflects the overall quality of the essay. Human raters are typically expert raters who have been formally trained to score standardized essay responses using holistic scoring guides. Using this approach, raters take into account the aspects (features) of writing specified in the scoring guide criteria. These guides often use a 6-point scale, where a score of "6" indicates the highest quality essay, and a score of "1" indicates an essay of the lowest quality. The holistic nature of scoring requires rigorous rater training to ensure acceptable human agreement. Haswell (2008) cites Mitchell (1994) who found that across 17 faculty members, a single paper could be awarded a grade from a B to an F. In light of this possible range of scoring variability in human scoring, human rater training at ETS is quite rigorous, ensuring that raters agree within a single point (otherwise, scores need to be adjudicated by additional readers). Consistent human rater scoring allows e-rater models to be built that can predict essay scores similar to human scores. E-rater modeling is discussed later.

Rubric criteria designed for human rater essay scoring can vary by specific task and genre (e.g., *Narratives*, *Summaries*, *Expository*, and *Persuasive* essays.) E-rater is designed to specifically evaluate and predict scores for expository and persuasive standardized writing tasks. These rubrics typically include writing features, such as *organization and development of ideas*, *the variety of syntactic constructions*, *the use of appropriate vocabulary*, and *the technical correctness of the writing in terms of its grammar, usage, and mechanics*.

Writing Construct-Relevant Features. In an effort to produce valid scores (i.e., accurately measure the intended aspects of writing), our goal continues to be the expansion of the coverage of construct (relevant and measurable writing features) relevant to *expository* and *persuasive* writing tasks (Connors, 1981; D'Angelo, 1984).

The ability to develop additional features that are relevant to a particular writing construct is, of course, directly related to the state-of-the-art in the field of NLP. Using NLP methods, e-rater is currently able to identify features (discussed later in more detail) for model building and essay scoring (Attali & Burstein, 2006; Burstein, Chodorow, & Leacock, 2004), including (a) grammatical and word usage errors (based on native and nonnative speaker writing data), (b) mechanics errors (e.g., *spelling*), (c) presence of essay-based discourse elements (e.g., a thesis statement), (d) development of essay-based discourse elements, (e) style weaknesses (e.g., *overly repetitious words*), (f) a content vector analysis feature comparing an essay to the set of training essays, (g) a content vector analysis feature comparing an essay to the set of training essays that received a score of 6, (h) average word length, and (i) a word frequency-based feature. Content vector analysis is a statistical modeling technique that, *very* simply stated, compares the frequency of word use[1] in a document (i.e., an essay response) to the frequency of words as they are used in a set of related documents (i.e., a set of human-scored essays in response to a topic). Based on this information, a score is computed for an essay based solely on the actual words (content) used in the essay. If, in terms of word use, an essay looks more like essays at score point "5" (on a 6-point scale), then a score of "5" would be assigned by the content vector analysis program to the essay in question (see Burstein et al., 1998 for details).

E-rater model building. To build an e-rater scoring model, a random sample of human-scored essays (at least 250 essays) is selected and run through e-rater. E-rater's job is to extract the linguistic features (noted earlier). These features are converted into numerical values. Using a regression modeling approach, the values from this training sample are used to determine an appropriate weight for each feature. In other words, this modeling approach identifies the relationship between the 10 predictor variables and outcome score. To score a new, unseen essay that may appear in a real test administration, for example, e-rater extracts the set of linguistic features, converts the features to a vector (list) of numerical values, and these values are then multiplied by the weights associated with each feature. Finally, a sum of the weighted feature values is then computed to predict the final score. This final, single score represents the overall (holistic) quality of an essay.

Two kinds of e-rater models can be built. *Topic-specific models* are built using a set of human-scored essays on a given topic, and all 10 features (listed earlier) are typically used for these models. A topic-specific model can be built *only* when there is sufficient human-scored data for the topic. Waiting for training data to build a topic-specific model can take many months, especially if one wants a reasonable number of example papers at the end score points (e.g., score points 1 and 6). *Generic models* are built using a set of human-scored essay data written by students in a particular grade or test-taker population, across a number of essay topics. These models can be built for a new topic, using existing data (on different topics), but at the desired grade level. All features, except for the content specific features created for (f) and (g) are used to build these models. The value added when using generic models is that an instructor, an institution, or ETS programs (such as GRE® and TOEFL®) can add new prompts without requiring additional training data. In the context of the use of e-rater in classroom instruction with Criterion (described later), the initial motivation was instructor-driven because instructors wanted the freedom to add their own prompts spontaneously. *Generic* models can be applied to essay responses for any topic written by students without new training when new topics are introduced (Attali & Burstein, 2006).

Let's spend a little time discussing how models are systematically evaluated. Before e-rater models can be operationally deployed and used for real, operational scoring, each e-rater model is evaluated on relevant and large samples of essays that have already been scored by expert raters. It is critical that evaluations are performed on large samples to yield meaningful outcomes. Generic e-rater models intended for operational use are evaluated on thousands of essays, and topic-specific on hundreds. If we want to produce meaningful outcomes from which we can draw sound conclusions, it is critical to scientific research, across disciplines, that meaningful evaluations are performed. This requires that evaluations are performed using large data samples. In same way that we do not want to draw conclusions about an educational intervention based on a single student, or the use of a new drug based on the outcomes of one patient, we also do not want to base conclusions about automated essay scoring capabilities and their usefulness based on the outcomes of a single essay.

How we perform evaluations is critical to our conclusions, and with regard to e-rater performance, we need to be very careful not to base performance on the outcomes of a single essay. We come back to this later in the chapter. As new e-rater features are introduced, models are rebuilt and reevaluated with each new release. No model is released unless it meets established measurement criteria that require both Pearson correlation and weighted kappa for agreement with human raters to be at least 0.70.

BEST PRACTICES IN ASSESSMENT AND INSTRUCTION WITH E-RATER®

This section discusses how e-rater is a *useful*, *helpful*, and *dependable* innovation for large-scale assessment and classroom instruction—as the system fosters best practice in the teaching and assessment of writing per White (1994).

Large-Scale Assessment. E-rater feature development (i.e., selection of linguistic features created for essay score prediction) has always been guided by scoring rubric criteria for writing tasks scored by e-rater on different tests. These tests include the GRE® (Graduate Record Exam) and the TOEFL® (Test of English as a Foreign Language). E-rater features have also been described in a number of published papers referenced throughout this chapter, and readers can access these articles if they are interested in additional details. Through these publications, features are transparent to educators, researchers, and test-takers. This is consistent with White (1994, p. 50), who discusses the need for clear and transparent descriptions of scoring criteria. In ongoing development of e-rater features, ETS has maintained a strong awareness that automated scores should not be based on " ... throwing the papers down the stairs ..." (White, 1994, p. 17). Here, the implication is that essays with more words (i.e., these are heavier and reach the bottom of the stairs more quickly) will get a higher score. E-rater does not use word count as a modeling feature, and ETS is careful to ensure that existing and new features in e-rater are not highly correlated with word count. By contrast, ETS has invested significant resources into research and development around feature expansion, such that there is increasingly greater coverage of linguistic features articulated in the scoring rubric criteria (writing construct). The driving force here is that e-rater's scoring features are appropriately matched with measures specified in the scoring rubric criteria, and it should assign consistent (*dependable*) scores. Consistent scoring is "guaranteed" with automated scoring, assuming that there is no change to the system in between the time you score *essay X* for the first time, and the system scores *essay X* for the nth time. Assuming "the same system" and "the same essay," the system (e-rater in this case) will assign the same score to the essay every time that it is submitted. This stable reliability is a positive attribute of automated essay scoring and lends itself to *dependability*. By contrast, White (1994, p. 17) cites Diederich's (1974) assertion that "without clear grading criteria, all papers could receive all possible scores." One could argue that holistic criteria are highly subjective. As a result, in holistic scoring, it is not at all uncommon for an essay to receive a different score from two human readers. It is very common, as is borne out in the next chapter, that raters might disagree within a single point. So, as our colleagues point out in the chapter that follows, the essay that one of the chapter authors wrote and submitted for an e-rater score received a "5" though they might have awarded it a "6". This is not an uncommon discrepancy between two human raters, or between e-rater and a single human rater. In fact, it is considered "adjacent agreement." In essay scoring, "adjacent agreement" does not require adjudication.

As discussed earlier, and to further drive home the point of the need for proper evaluation, before e-rater is used for a large-scale, high-stakes test, such as TOEFL®, ETS invests a significant amount of research into investigations of e-rater validity and reliability, using large data samples. In earlier research, the original e-rater team compared human and e-rater agreement across a number of different essay prompts (topics) on the GMAT® (Graduate Management Admissions Test) (see Burstein et al., 1998 for details). More recently, Attali (2009) reported the results of an evaluation of e-rater® scoring for TOEFL® iBT Independent essays. Approximately 200,000 essay responses (from over 7 months of testing) were used in the evaluation. E-rater scores were evaluated in different ways: (a) building a single scoring model across multiple prompts (*generic modeling*, described earlier) and (b) building separate scoring models for individual prompts (*topic-based modeling*, described earlier). Evaluation criteria included e-rater agreement with human scores, discrepancy from human scores, and correlations with other TOEFL scores.

> The general analyses showed that the agreement between e-rater and a single human rating was higher than the agreement between two human ratings. This result was replicated across all prompts and language groups. In addition, correlations between e-rater scores and other TOEFL scores were generally higher than or comparable to the human score correlations with the same TOEFL scores. This result was also found across prompts and language groups. Discrepancies between e-rater and human scores across prompts, language groups, gender, and ability were found to be small. The effects of these discrepancies on final writing scores are likely to be even smaller since e-rater scores constitute one of four scores contributing to the writing scores. (Attali, 2009, p. 22)

Overall, the analyses indicated that e-rater could be used in place of one of the human raters for the TOEFL Independent task—a large-scale assessment and high-stakes scoring scenario. The ability to employ automated scoring adds scoring consistency, and reduces the costs and score reporting time generally associated with essay scoring.

Classroom Instruction. E-rater is used in *Criterion®*, ETS' web-based, essay evaluation system that is widely used as an instructional writing application in K-12 and community college settings. *Criterion* uses e-rater technology to offer immediate, individualized feedback about errors in grammar, usage and mechanics, weaknesses in style, and the presence and absence of discourse structure elements (e.g., *thesis statement*, *main points*, *supporting ideas*, and *conclusion statements*). Grammar and usage errors are developed using several thousand examples of native and non-native speaker data. Accuracy of error identification needs to be a minimum of 80%. (For details about non-native error types see Chodorow, Gamon, & Tetreault, 2010; Han, Tetreault, Lee ,& Han, 2010; Lee, Tetreault, & Chodorow, 2009; Tetreault & Chodorow, 2008). Please note the application offers advice about potential style-related weaknesses, but does not consider these to be errors, nor is it communicated as an error in the system feedback. The intention is to point out a possible weakness that the writer, perhaps in consultation with his or her teacher, can choose to revise (or not). As described in Burstein and Wolska (2003), accuracy for word repetition in essays is 95%. Word repetition was requested as a style feature, as part of focus groups with teachers during *Criterion*'s earlier development. The absence of discourse features also is not considered erroneous, but the system does suggest the addition of an element it finds it to be missing. Accuracy of discourse element identification is at least 80%, but varies based on the discourse element (Burstein, Marcu, & Knight, 2003). In terms of revision of discourse elements, the writer, either in consultation with a teacher or independently, can choose to revise the essay. As an interesting aside, whether or not the student engages with the teacher, or revises work independently, might depend on the classroom setting, and/or the writer's proficiency. We have also heard, anecdotally, that some writers are more likely to write more and take more risks in their writing if they are able to work independently without a teacher having to see each draft.

Criterion also provides advisories if an essay appears not relevant to the essay topic (Higgins, Burstein, & Attali, 2006), has discourse structure anomalies, or contains disproportionately large numbers of grammatical errors (given essay length).

All the diagnostic feedback can be used by students to revise and resubmit an essay. Resubmissions will receive additional feedback. The system is designed to be used as a classroom tool to support writing improvement.

The use of a classroom tool that supports writing instruction and provides students with immediate feedback, such as *Criterion*, is consistent with White's (1994, p. 55) assertion that classroom teaching should promote improved writing skill.

White (1994, p. 28) stresses that assignments should be designed to address specific learning goals. Consistent with this, in *Criterion* teachers can create their own essay prompts (questions) or use existing ones provided in the system—ensuring that system use is compatible with teacher goals. In the spirit of the process approach to writing, *Criterion* supports students in the prewriting stage (to support systematic planning), as well as in continuous revision. The system also helps to increase students' opportunities to write without necessarily adding to a teacher's grading burden. The system's student interaction allows at least some of the editing to occur as the system highlights technical errors in an essay. As the system covers a large number and variety of technical errors, system feedback can actually reduce a teacher's need to spend time marking up basic technical writing errors (e.g., spelling and grammar).

With regard to feedback, White (1994, p. 50) offers a discussion about how to respond to student writing assignments, especially with regard to expository writing. He stresses the importance of discussing the evaluation criteria with the class, and linking responses to writing revisions to the assignment goals and established scoring criteria. Consistent with this, *Criterion®* offers meaningful and consistent feedback that is relevant to students' individual essay submissions, and scoring rubrics are always available. The feedback is aligned with the scoring rubrics and offers specific comments noting errors in grammar, usage, and mechanics, weaknesses in style, and highlighting of organization and development structure. The feedback offers ongoing support that, over time, students should internalize to improve their ability to self-assess—making them more proficient writers and thinkers, as asserted in White (1994, p. 10, 19).

Speaking of meaningful feedback, we would now like to address our colleagues' concern (in the following chapter) about feedback errors that *Criterion* did make on the essays that one of the authors wrote and submitted. *Criterion* did make some errors in feedback on that essay. *Criterion* currently has hundreds of K-12 and higher education clients, in domestic and international settings, and processes millions of responses per year . Every so often, however, among these large numbers of submissions, clients do report errors. (As core e-rater researcher, I am presented with these reports and frequently participate in solutions.) These feedback error reports from clients are taken seriously. As e-rater is an evolving system, we continue to implement improvements that appear in yearly new releases, often fixing issues brought to our attention by clients. In the spirit of continuing to improve the system, the errors reported by our colleagues in the next chapter have been noted. In fact, the mislabeled spelling errors are already in the queue to be "fixed" for the July 2011 release. That said, if our colleagues were to resubmit their essay later this year, they are likely to find that the feedback errors for misspellings that they found in January 2010 will have been resolved. Our colleagues also report errors in the identification of run-ons that are, in fact, run-ons, and fragments that are, in fact, fragments. They argue, and perhaps rightly so, that these run-ons and fragments may be effective constructions used by the writer for deliberate rhetorical purposes. *We agree*. However, to provide support to the largest number of developing writers in K-12 and higher education settings, *Criterion* is designed to handle the most likely scenario for the user population, and for those who are seeking to improve and use the system in good faith. It is more likely in the population of *Criterion*® users that a run-on or a fragment is *not* intended as a rhetorical device, but is simply a run-on or a fragment. I cannot count the number of essays that I have read in the past several years as an e-rater researcher, but I estimate that it is several thousand. In these essays, it has been very rare to encounter one that resembled the writing quality of a professor in which creative license is taken, such as using ungrammatical structures, for deliberate rhetorical purpose.

Let's take the analogy that we used earlier just one step further. We pointed out that for teaching interventions and drug trials, using a single student or patient (respectively) as our entire sample population would be inappropriate, and would not allow us to draw any conclusions about the success of the intervention or the drug (respectively). Taking this a step further, we would *not* give a reading intervention to a student who is not a struggling reader, and we would not administer a drug trial to a patient who does not meet the criteria for the illness (or does not have the illness at all). By analogy, it does not make much sense for essays from highly proficient writers (who clearly do not need writing help) to be the ultimate test from which we draw our final conclusions about the usefulness of essay evaluation technology.

It is entirely possible that *Criterion*® is not a meaningful fit for every writer, but on the flip side, *Criterion*® has proven to be quite a good fit for many writers as is evidenced from our current large client base, and from the over 2 million yearly submissions. Let's be fair and equitable and not forget about the substantial population of developing writers for whom systems like *Criterion*® can be helpful (and, let's especially not base our conclusions on the outcomes of a single essay submission written by a highly proficient writer).

As e-rater development continues to include more features that cover more rubric criteria, especially in the realm of discourse (Burstein, Tetreault, & Andreyev, 2010), it has the potential to become an increasingly useful classroom practice tool, vis-à-vis matching additional rubric criteria and offering feedback that supports self-assessment and improved writing. As a community, let's work together and continue to be open minded and motivated by sound scientific practices that allow us to draw relevant conclusions that permit us to meaningfully and appropriately match technology with relevant user populations (Burstein, Sabatini, & Shore, in press).

CRITERION FEEDBACK STUDIES

Attali (2004). Using approximately 9,500 *Criterion®* essays and corresponding essay revisions written to essay prompts from 6th through 12th grade, the study shows the following. E-rater scores on revised submissions (between 2 and 10 revisions per essay submission) improved by almost half the standard deviation of the score of the first (initial) submission. Further, the proportion of technical errors in essays (e.g., grammatical and spelling errors) was reduced in revised versions of students' essays. Revised essay submissions also tended to contain evidence of more development in the essay (e.g., presence of additional discourse elements, such as Main Points and Supporting Ideas). This supports the idea that students can work independently and practice self-assessment, or, at least, assess themselves independent of teacher feedback. This is reasonably authentic as it is standard practice (at least in middle and high school) for students to use word-processing applications (e.g., Microsoft Word), and such applications offer advice about technical errors in writing. *Criterion®* supports independent writers, while encouraging revision—hence, it is arguably a *useful* and *helpful* resource.

Lipnevich and Smith (2008). Lipnevich and Smith (2008) conducted a randomized study that used information detected by e-rater to generate feedback to participants.[2] The study was carried out with 464 college students working on an authentic essay task—an essay exam that they revised based on feedback. There were three experimental conditions: (a) no feedback, (b) detailed feedback perceived by participants to have been provided by the instructor, and (c) detailed feedback perceived by participants to have been generated by the computer.[3] Two additional factors were added: (a) receiving a grade or not, and (b) receiving praise or not. Overall, the study reports that the most effective condition was when participants received detailed feedback, alone, unaccompanied by a grade or praise. Further, the study reports that students who did not receive detailed feedback received substantially lower exam scores than students who received feedback (regardless of whether they were in the computer- or instructor-generated feedback conditions).

Teachers can use the system to suit their specific teaching goals. This is aligned with White's assertion about the importance of writing assignments having clear goals in teaching and learning. Students' ability to work independently with the system, however, does not preclude a teacher from designing a group-based assignment, or discussion around *Criterion*®-based classroom assignments. Students work independently as they pursue assignments in *Criterion*®, and receive feedback as they revise their essays. As held by White (1994), and as indicated in both the Attali (2004), and Lipnevich and Smith (2008) studies, feedback is critical to writing development. As *Criterion*® can provide such feedback, it can be argued that it is a *useful* and *helpful* innovation.

DISCUSSION AND CONCLUSIONS

The intention of this chapter was twofold: (a) to review automated scoring methods and illustrate how these are aligned with best practices in the teaching and assessment of writing per White (2004), and in doing so, (b) to present an argument that would transform the perspective that computer-based scoring technology was not useful, as expressed in White (2007), by showing how this technology is *useful*, *helpful*, and *dependable*.

As was discussed, the NLP-based computational methods underlying e-rater continue to be closely aligned with the need to develop essay scoring systems with construct relevance. Such systems can identify and evaluate linguistic features commonly associated with scoring rubric criteria (where aspects of a writing construct are specified). These include technical writing errors (grammar, usage, and mechanics errors), features related to organization and development (presence and development of essay-based discourse elements, e.g., Main Points and Supporting Ideas), and style weakness (e.g., overly repetitious word use). As NLP-based automated essay scoring identifies linguistic features in the writing construct, writing scores are *meaningful* to the construct.

For *large-scale assessment*, e-rater detects and measures features specified in the scoring rubric. The use of e-rater in the scoring of standardized assessments is *useful* and *helpful* in that it reduces the costs and scoring reporting time associated with this scoring task if it is done manually. Further, scores are *dependable*, as they are always reliable, and at ETS, significant measurement resources are devoted to ensuring that the scores are highly accurate (agree with human reader scores). For *classroom instruction*, *Criterion* offers students additional writing opportunities, and a means by which they can work independently in planning and revising their essays, using meaningful, directed feedback from the system. This is *useful* and *helpful* to students in that the feedback is immediate and individualized. Studies reported in this chapter have shown that using this feedback has been correlated with improved writing. Perhaps students' ability to work independently is also increasing their ability to not only get additional practice, but also to self-assess. Feedback from the system is *dependable* as it is provided using a consistent methodology and rigorously evaluated for accuracy. Accuracies for different kinds of feedback are reported in publications cited throughout this chapter.

Computer-based scoring technology, such as e-rater, can be *useful*, *helpful*, and *dependable*, and can add great value in instructional and assessment settings. However, as with any form of instruction or assessment, it must be delivered responsibly. There are a number of computer-based writing assessment and evaluation applications available, all with different features and levels of automation. Others include Pearson Education's WriteToLearn™ and Summary Street. *All* computer-based writing assessment or evaluation systems should consider the rubric criteria (construct), and be properly evaluated for use in either instructional or assessment settings. Finally, it is critical that a person be appropriately included, especially in those high-stakes contexts in which summative observations on student performance are to be made. Computer-based essay evaluation technology was not intended to replace people, but rather to support them in processes related to the evaluation and scoring of essays for large-scale assessment, and in classroom instruction as teacher support. Further development of computer-based writing evaluation technologies will continue to be *useful*, *helpful*, and *dependable*, as long as system designers and developers continue to implement appropriate methods of evaluation and do not lose sight of the need to keep the systems aligned with best practices in the teaching and assessment of writing.

ENDNOTES

1. Note that word *frequency* is distinct from essay *word count*. Word frequency reflects how often a word occurs given a document or a set of documents. It does not reflect the raw total number of words in an essay. This would be word count.
2. *Criterion®* was not specifically used for this study. Rather, e-rater, the automated essay evaluation software that "drives" *Criterion®* was used to generate feedback similar to *Criterion®* feedback. A custom web-based interface to generate e-rater feedback was developed for this study (see Lipnevich & Smith, 2008, for details).
3. All feedback was actually a blend of computer- and instructor-generated feedback.

REFERENCES

Attali, Y. (2004, April). *Exploring the feedback and revision features of Criterion.* Paper presented at the annual meeting of the National Council on Measurement in Education, San Diego, CA.

Attali, Y. (2009, April). *Evaluating types of automated scoring models for operational use in high-stakes assessments: The ETS experience.* Paper presented at the annual meeting of the National Council on Measurement in Education, San Diego, CA.

Attali, Y., & Burstein, J. (2006). Automated essay scoring with e-rater v.2.0. *Journal of Technology, Learning, and Assessment, 4*(3), 3-30. Web.

Burstein, J. (in press). Automated essay scoring: How it works and how it helps. In C. Chapelle (Ed.), *The encyclopedia of applied linguistics.* Malden, MA: Wiley-Blackwell.

Burstein, J., Chodorow, M., & Leacock, C. (2004). Automated essay evaluation. The CriterionSM Online Writing Evaluation service. *AI Magazine, 25*(3), 27-36.

Burstein, J., Kukich, K., Wolff, S., Lu, C., Chodorow, M., Braden-Harder, L., & Harris M.D. (1998). Automated scoring using a hybrid feature identification technique. *Proceedings of the 36th Annual Meeting of the Association for Computational Linguistics and 17th International Conference on Computational Linguistics* (Vol. 1, pp. 206-210). Montreal, Canada: Association of Computational Linguistics.

Burstein, J., Marcu, D., & Knight, K. (2003). Finding the WRITE stuff: Automatic identification of discourse structure in student essays. In S. Harabagiu & F. Ciravegna (Eds.), Special Issue on Advances in Natural Language Processing. *IEEE Intelligent Systems, 18*(1), 32-39.

Burstein, J., & Wolska, M. (2003). Toward evaluation of writing style: Overly repetitious word use. *Proceedings of the 11th Conference of the European Chapter of the Association for Computational Linguistics* (pp. 35-42). Budapest, Hungary.

Burstein, J., Sabatini, J., & Shore, J. (in press). Developing NLP applications for educational problem spaces. In R. Mitkov (Ed.), *Oxford handbook of computational linguistics.* Oxford, UK: Oxford University Press.

Burstein, J., Tetreault, J., & Andreyev, S. (2010, June). Using entity-based features to model coherence in student essays. *Proceedings of the HLT/NAACL Annual Meeting.* Los Angeles, CA.

Chodorow, M., Gamon, M., & Tetreault, J. (2010). The utility of article and preposition error correction systems for English language learners: Feedback and assessment. *Language Testing, 27*(3), 419-436.

Connors, R. J. (1981). The rise and fall of the modes of discourse. *College Composition and Communication, 32*(4), 444-463.

D'Angelo, F. J. (1984). Nineteenth-century forms/modes of discourse: A critical inquiry. *College Composition and Communication, 35*(1), 31-42.

Diederich, P. (1974). *Measuring growth in English.* Urbana, IL: National Council of Teachers of English.

Emig, J. (1971). *The composing processes of twelfth graders*. Urbana, IL: National Council of Teachers of English.

Godshalk, F., Swineford, F., & Coffman, W.E. (1966). *The measurement of writing ability*. New York, NY: College Entrance Examination Board.

Han, N. R., Tetreault, J., Lee, S. H., & Ha, J. Y. (2010). Using an error-annotated learned corpus to develop an ESL/EFL error correction system. *Proceedings of the International Conference on Language Resources and Evaluation.*

Haswell, R. (2008). Teaching of writing in higher education. In C. Braverman (Ed.). *Handbook of research on writing: history, society, school, individual, text* (pp. 331-346). Mahwah, NJ: Lawrence Erlbaum Associates.

Higgins, D., Burstein, J., & Attali, Y. (2006, June). Identifying off-topic student essays without topic-specific training data. *Natural Language Engineering, 12*(2), 145-159.

Lee, J., Tetreault, J., & Chodorow, M. (2009). Human evaluation of article and noun number usage: Influences of context and construction variability. *ACL 2009 Proceedings of the Linguistic Annotation Workshop III (LAW3).*

Lipnevich, A.A., & Smith, J.K. (2008). *Response to assessment feedback: The effects of grades, praise, and source of information* (RR-08-30). Princeton, NJ: Educational Testing Service.

Mitchell, F. (1994). Is there a text in this grade? The implicit messages of comments on student writing. *Issues in Writing, 6*(2), 187-195.

Tetreault, J., & Chodorow, M. (2008). Native judgments of non-native usage: Experiments in preposition error detection. (pp. 24-32). *Proceedings of the Workshop on Human Judgments in Computational Linguistics.*

White, E. M. (1984). Holisticism. *College Composition and Communication, 35*(4), 400-409.

White, E. M. (1994). *Teaching and assessing writing*. San Francisco, CA : Jossey-Bass.

White, E. M (2007). *Assigning, responding, evaluating: A writing teacher's guide* (4th ed.). New York, NY: St. Martin's Press.

12

WRITING TO A MACHINE IS NOT WRITING AT ALL

Anne Herrington
Charles Moran
University of Massachusetts at Amherst

Edward White has been, as others in this volume and elsewhere have said before us, a giant in the field of writing assessment. In the large corpus of his work on writing assessment he has laid down principles for judging assessment methods and practices, principles that we have found guided our own work in a subset of this field, the machine scoring of student writing.

In the early 1980s, as McAllister and White (2006) have written, researchers in the field of natural language processing lost their Defense Department funding and turned instead to educational testing companies to support their work. These testing companies, in their turn, have widened their marketing focus to include both large-scale assessment and classroom-based assessment. White's writings about the computer-based assessment of writing have generally addressed the pros and cons of machine scoring in large-scale writing assessment, used for purposes of placement. In the chapter that follows, we take White's principles, as articulated in the body of his work on writing assessment, and apply them beyond large-scale assessments used for broad placement purposes to the current marketing of these programs as aids to classroom instruction—an application that White seems not to have considered, perhaps because it so obviously violated his principles. White has asked us, eloquently and often, to pay attention, to stay in the mix, to be part of the dialogue (1994, 1996; McAllister & White, 2006). Given the marketing muscle of these testing companies, and the concurrent expansion of the computer-as-reader of students' classroom writing, writing teachers need to understand what is happening here and take a careful look at its substance and likely consequences, lest we be seen as irrelevant and be "sent out of the room" by the other stakeholders (White, 2006, p. 27).

MARKETED FOR THE CLASSROOM

We focus on ETS's *Criterion*® although similar claims are also made in marketing Vantage Learning's *My Access!*® (2009a, 2009b), both of which are designed and marketed explicitly for classroom instruction (see Rothermel, 2006, for a review of *My Access!*). Specifically, ETS's *Criterion* is described as a "comprehensive, instructional web-based tool," aimed to assist both students and teachers (ETS, 2009d). As with all commercial products, these programs are successful only if they meet a perceived need and are purchased. This is the complicity that McAllister and White (2006) write of between "entrepreneurs" and "adopters." They write, "some teachers and administrators turn reflexively to technological solutions when funding for human labor is in crisis, as has been the case for education at all levels in recent years" (p. 25)—in other words, when there are too few teachers for too many students. ETS targets their marketing on this issue directly, promising, among other things, that *Criterion* is "a learning tool that does not increase workload and adds value to writing instruction by providing a teachable moment" (ETS, 2009d). The nature of that "teachable moment" is not specified. Students are promised instant feedback that will directly benefit their development as writers:

> Students get a response to their writing while it is fresh in their minds. They find out immediately how their work compares to a standard and what they should do to improve it. The *Criterion* service also provides an environment for writing and revision that capable and motivated students can use independently. This environment, coupled with the opportunity for instant feedback, provides the directed writing practice so beneficial for students. (2009c)

Essentially, the *Criterion* materials are promising to address the very real conflict that many teachers face between, on the one hand, the desire to have their students write frequently, provide them with meaningful feedback, and have them improve as writers and, on the other hand, the problem of having too little time to provide that feedback and individual attention to all of them. The *Criterion* materials also evoke the discourse of accountability, noting a "standard" against which student work will be compared and promising that the "service provides an effective initial evaluation of student skill levels allowing instructors to benchmark writing, to make placement decisions, adjust instruction and track progress" (ETS, 2009d). If all of these claims are true, then no wonder that these programs would be widely adopted in classrooms at all grade levels, including college. A healthy skepticism about these and other claims for these programs is still warranted, though. Just as McAllister and White (2006) point out in their discussion of "entrepreneurs," these products are marketed as "a proven, rather than an experimental, technology" (p. 24). Aside from research conducted or sponsored by the companies themselves, there has been insufficient analysis of the claims made in the marketing, specifically claims as to the soundness of the feedback provided by these programs and the impact on students' development of writing skills. As McAllister and White (2006) argue, "the time has come for reasoned and critical examination" (p. 25). Our aim in this chapter is to contribute to this goal by examining the soundness of the feedback provided.

A SCENARIO

Let's imagine that we two, Anne and Charlie, are teachers who are considering the use of *Criterion* in our writing classes, college classes in Advanced Expository Writing taken by sophomores from a range of disciplines. In our scenario, we are considering this course of action not because we really like the idea but because we have been given 35 students in each of our classes, these numbers, in our judgment, making it impossible for us responsibly to read the several drafts of each of the seven required writing projects assigned in the course—what Anson has called in this volume a "staggering volume of commentary." *Criterion* gives us two options. We could persuade our institution to subscribe to the *Criterion* Online Writing Evaluation Service, which would give us and our students one semester's access to a web-based package that includes not only faculty and student access to the machine scoring programs but writing class management tools such as record keeping and sorting capabilities. The *Criterion* web site tells is that the cost of this option to our institution would be $15.20/student, or $1,064 for our two classes of 35, and, in addition, $300 for a mandatory online training program that we as the responsible teachers would have to take before the course began.

Our second option is to have our college bookstore order a sufficient number of *Criterion* Registration Cards and in our syllabus tell our students to buy these cards at the bookstore along with their textbooks. ETS sells

Criterion directly to college bookstores, for which it charges $10.36/card; the bookstores may charge the students the "suggested retail" price of $12.95, for a 24% markup, although bookstores are free, according to the terms of the contract, to charge as much as $15.00/card (2009a). This way, as the web site tells us, our students would get "practice made easy and convenient ... at no additional cost to you!" (ETS, 2009b).

The advantages of having an institutional subscription to the *Criterion* Online Writing Evaluation Service are two: We would be working within the web-based class management system, which would make the students' writing easier to organize and track; and we would have greater control of our students' use of the machine-scoring program. The first of these advantages disappears for us because our institution already has a class management system supported by our IT center. The second of these advantages seems slight, because the additional control we would have would be in turning off some or all of the automated feedback that the program gives to our student writers—and that feedback is all the program really has to offer us. So the bookstore option seems the best to us.

But in either case, whether we lobby for the institutional subscription or require our students to purchase their *Criterion* cards, we need to know that the use of *Criterion* will advance our goals for our students' learning. As White (1994) has reminded us, "assessment of writing can be a blessing or a curse, a friend or a foe, an important support for our work as teachers or a major impediment to what we need to do for our students" (p. 3). So the questions we have to answer are these: "Will the assessment and feedback given by the program to student writers be helpful to them as writers? Will it support our work with them as their teachers? Or will it become something we have to work around, or work against—an impediment to our teaching and our students' learning?

Now we leave the world of our hypothetical situation and report on a recent trial session we conducted to determine the nature and value of *Criterion*'s feedback.

TESTING *CRITERION*

In January 2010, in a trial session provided to us by ETS, we set up a "class," English 112, and a "student," Carol Santos. We posted an assignment, selecting College, Second Year as our level, and chose this topic from the list provided:

> "Educators should encourage the current popularity of email and instant messaging among teenagers, because this trend is sure to improve their students' reading and writing skills. Discuss the extent to which you agree or disagree with this opinion. Support your views with specific reasons and examples from your own experience, observations, or reading."

Charlie wrote a response to this question, arguing, as he believes, that educators should not consider encouraging or discouraging email or texting for two reasons: Educators do not have the ability to affect their students' behavior outside of their classrooms and schools, particularly in the use of such attractive social networking tools; and that the effect of email and texting on extended reading and writing was unknown but likely neutral. He wrote this essay within the suggested time limit, in a Microsoft Word document that he pasted into the text box, following *Criterion*'s instructions. He wrote a serious piece, not trying to game the system in any way, but writing as he normally would in a timed, on-demand writing situation. He imagined an audience of peers who would take his thoughts seriously. This was the only essay that he submitted to *Criterion*—not the result of any selection process, but a first-off draft, revised along the way as one does on a word processor, and finished within the suggested time limit. He was following the same procedure that he and Anne had followed in an earlier *Criterion* trial, documented and presented in "Writing Assessment and New Technologies" (Herrington & Moran, 2009), and that students of Herrington and Stanley had followed in another *Criterion* trial, documented and presented in "Criterion™: Promoting the Standard" (Herrington & Stanley, 2008) (for the full essay, please see the Appendix).

Criterion gives the writer two scores, a "holistic" score on a scale from 1 to 6, and a "trait analysis," with separate feedback on five traits: grammar, usage, mechanics, style, and organization/development. Charlie received a holistic score of 5, which pleased him—but why not a 6? The holistic feedback was not very helpful in answering this question: The difference between a 5 and a 6 is based on judgments an automated program cannot make: for example, "clear" versus "insightful connections" and "relevant" versus "well chosen evidence." The "trait feedback analysis" gave him the answer: two grammar errors, 15 mechanical errors, two usage errors, and, under organization/development, a missing introductory paragraph. Taking these in order, *Criterion* identified two errors in "grammar." The program marked the following sentence as a fragment:

> "If the analogy between cycling and reading/writing holds, then training on email/texting will not transfer to extended reading or writing."

This sentence is, by any measure, a complete sentence. It is a straightforward sentence—an "if" clause followed by a main clause with subject (training) and verb (will not transfer).

The program marked the following sentence as run-on:

> "I've encountered more than one student who is a whiz on email, belonging to multiple discussion groups and contributing thoughtfully to these discussions, but who is entirely unable to put together an extended argument."

This sentence is not a run-on sentence, but again, a straightforward sentence—"I've encountered more than one student who is A, but B." From these two responses it seems clear that *Criterion* cannot reliably identify sentence boundaries.

Criterion identified two errors in "usage": one "missing or extra article" and one "preposition error." The program identified this sentence as containing a "missing or extra article," and we bold-italicize the allegedly offending article:

> "I take as **an** analogue here cell-phone use and driving."

Charlie supposes that one could write "I take as analogue here," but he resists *Criterion*'s suggestion, "You may need to remove this article." This is, to us, not a matter of usage, but of style.

In the following sentence, *Criterion* identified the word in as a "preposition error." Rolling over the marked alleged error produced the pop-up, "You may be using the wrong preposition." Here is the sentence, with the preposition in question in bold italics:

> "As a cyclist, I know that cycling is an activity that includes many different activities: long road-rides, hill-climbing, descending, riding close **in** groups (peloton), time-trialing, and sprinting."

There is no problem with this preposition. A peloton is riders riding close in a group.

In Charlie's essay *Criterion* identified 15 errors in "mechanics," all alleged spelling errors, and all wrongly identified as such. Charlie used the word "texting" nine times; *Criterion* identified each of these uses as a misspelling. Charlie used the abbreviation e.g. three times, and again each use of this common term was identified as a misspelling. Charlie used the word peloton, identified as misspelled, and when he used a dash, the two words connected by the dash were identified as a spelling error.

Charlie's essay received no feedback on "style." Under organization/ development, however, *Criterion* told Charlie that he needed to add an introduction to his essay. *Criterion*'s comment was "No introductory material detected," and when, as instructed, he "rolled over" this comment, *Criterion* amplified: "*Criterion* has not identified an **introduction** in your essay. An introduction is very important because it provides an overview of the essay, provides background information on the subject, and tells the reader what the author will be discussing. For advice about adding an introduction to your essay, consult the Writer's Handbook." Charlie tried a second version of his introductory paragraph, this time adding a topic sentence at its end, but Criterion came back with the same response. Apparently inductive paragraphs (specific to general) do not fit the model.

So how did *Criterion* do overall with its feedback on the five traits? In Burstein's chapter (this volume), she claims that "e-rater is currently able to identify and extract" grammatical errors, spelling errors, word usage errors, style problems, and the presence of a thesis statement. Criterion did none of the above. It gave Charlie 20 pieces of feedback, 19 of which were wrong, and one of which was arguable. It misidentified a sentence fragment, it misidentified a run-on sentence, it gave bad advice about articles and prepositions, it marked as spelling errors 15 perfectly good words; and it told Charlie to add an introduction which the essay did not need. If we knew that we had in our Writing Program a teacher who misadvised students as drastically as *Criterion* had misadvised Charlie, we would fire that teacher. For this reason, we do not accept the claim made by Burstein (this volume) that automated essay scoring—certainly using *Criterion*—is "useful, helpful, and dependable."

Imagine the effect of this 95% wrong feedback on the student writer and on the teacher. The feedback would at the least confuse the student writer, leaving the teacher somehow to counter the confusion—although if the student were using her *Criterion* card on her own, as purchased from the bookstore, there would be no teacher to intervene. If the student accepted the feedback, here are some of the lessons that would be learned: do not use e.g., or texting, or peloton, in any of your writing; do not use the dash as a mark of punctuation; shorten and simplify all sentences so that the program will be able to parse them accurately; do not use inductive, specific-to-general, sequences, but stick with deduction—topic sentence first. Among our goals as writing teachers are these: help students discover and use their voices; help them take risks with their writing; help them master the grammar, usage, mechanics, and styles of written English. In this trial, and in earlier trials we have reported on (see Herrington & Stanley, 2008, 2009), *Criterion* has proved not a useful assessment tool but, to quote White (1994) again, "a major impediment to what we need to do for our students" (p. 3).

SKILLS, NOT HOLISTIC FOCUS

White has argued steadily throughout his long career that writing needs to be read whole and not disassembled into a set of discrete parts. In 1984 White wrote in defense of holistic, as opposed to analytic, scoring of essays:

> Holisticism says that the human spirit and its most significant form of expression (writing) must be seen not in parts, but as a whole, face-to-face as it were, almost sacramentally. Even the meanest bit of halting prose, even the most downtrodden of our fellow creatures, deserves to be taken as a living and vital unit of meaning, an artistic and human whole, not merely as a collection of scraps and parts. (p. 409)

Our experience with *Criterion*, however, tells us that machine-reading programs focus their feedback on the parts: word- and sentence-level errors in grammar, usage, and style.

Indeed, the Criterion online demonstration represents this focus on isolated skills—the trait feedback function—as "another reason why *Criterion* is such a valuable remediation tool" (ETS, 2011). As we have shown above, not only does this feedback focus on isolated skills, it is often wrong. So we proceed with two parallel theses here (doubtless *Criterion* would object!): that the program's feedback calls the writer to attend to word-level and sentence-level concerns; and that the program's feedback is sometimes—apparently most of the time— monstrously wrong.

After they have written and submitted their essay to *Criterion*, students will view and work with the analysis the program provides, calling up each category, for example, "Summary of Grammar Errors." On the screen, a left-hand sidebar then lists all possible types of errors in grammar, and in the center of the screen a bar graph displays the number of each type of grammar error that has occurred, showing, for example, a short bar for one fragment or missing comma and a taller bar for four subject-verb agreement errors. The presentation, with numbers and graphs, gives an aura of objectivity and mathematical power to the analysis. Further, it presents the revising task to come as one of moving through categories and eliminating errors, not of rethinking the argument or adapting to a particular rhetorical situation.

After seeing the bar graph of all errors for a trait, students can call up each type of error, one by one: for example, fragment or missing comma. The center screen then shows the full essay with the error highlighted. Rollovers then explain the error in a very limited way (e.g., "You may be using the wrong preposition"). The task for revision is evidently to reduce the flagged errors. For example, the following sentence from one student essay that we entered for analysis was flagged for two alleged problems: "fragment or missing comma" and "missing or extra article" (before "different"):

> "Some of my bracelets are different color of crystals; jade; silver and metals where she got it from China."

The explanation regarding the sentence punctuation is: "This sentence may be a fragment or may have incorrect punctuation." Although this feedback may be accurate (however, note the program's steady hedging with the subjunctive), it seems a misplaced priority, focusing as it does on punctuation, rather than directing the writer's attention to the complexities of the final clause—which is not flagged at all. For the flagging of the article, the explanation is "You may need to use an article before this word. Consider using *a*." Well, if anything, the change should be to make "color" plural, "are different colors of crystals." In another place in the same essay, the following sentence was flagged as a run-on sentence:

> "Most of the girls have at least one jewelry box, I am no exception to this rule."

Yes, grammatically speaking it is a run-on or, to be precise, a comma splice; but rhetorically speaking, the sentence could be viewed as an effective construction, syntactically setting up a comparison of this writer, "I," with "most girls." For *Criterion*, however, this is a sentence with an error, not a sentence seen as the result of a writer's choice. In this same sentence, *Criterion* flagged jewelry box as a weakness in the category "Style," and provided this feedback: "You have repeated these words several times in your essay. Your essay will be stronger if you vary your word choice and substitute some other words instead. Ask your instructor for advice." In our experience, this is the most frequent comment generated under the category "Style." Again, the flagging and the feedback draws the student writer's attention to word-level concerns. Further, as we have so often experienced, the feedback is dead wrong: In this instance, the essay was about a "jewelry box," and as readers we require the repetition of key words. Here again, *Criterion* considers an aspect of language use—in this case repetition of words—in terms of what it can count—the number of times a word appears in an essay—as opposed to what writers do: repeat words for rhetorical effect.

CRITERION AND MANY ENGLISHES

A further impediment to our teaching and our goals for our students' learning is *Criterion*'s bias toward Standard American English and its inability to respond to the ways in which our language is growing and stretching as it is used by students who come at English as a second or third language. As Herrington and Stanley (2008) show, *Criterion* is programmed to value only one dialect of English, Standard American English. Throughout the *Criterion* materials, "the standard" is repeatedly invoked as the norm against which students will be judged. For example, in response to the one of the Frequently Asked Questions posed on the website, "How can the *Criterion* service help students?," the response is: "Students get a response to their writing while it is fresh in their minds. They find out immediately how their work compares to a standard and what they should do to improve it. ..." That standard is based on two sources. *Criterion*'s Grammar, Usage, and Mechanics analyses are all error-focused, programmed to read for errors in standardized American English, represented as "general English grammar," the corpus used for identifying these "violations of general English grammar" being 30 million words of newspaper text (Burstein, Chodorow, & Leacock, 2004, p. 28). For the holistic judgment, the standard is based on essay rankings from ETS testing programs like NAEP®, the English Placement Test designed for California State University, *Praxis*®, GRE®, and TOEFL®. In other words, the standard is based on only one type of school writing, "timed essay writing," not other genres even of school writing (e.g., researched argument, review). We do not question that the programming and model building for *Criterion* is rigorous, just that it is limited without acknowledging its limits.

We have no quarrel with a pedagogy that aims to introduce students to standardized academic American English so long as that dialect is recognized as one dialect of English and so long as other dialects are recognized and valued. With *Criterion*, however, this "standard" is normalized and deviations from the standard are recognized as error—for instance, dialectical differences in verb tenses and ways of organizing and developing ideas (Herrington & Stanley, 2008). Because *Criterion* is programmed to recognize only standardized American English, it also has difficulty analyzing writing by students for whom English is not their native language. When we submitted to *Criterion* an essay by a student from China and one by a student from Vietnam, we found the program had difficulty correctly identifying article and preposition errors—most unhelpful to students coming at English from Asian languages. Further, as we have suggested in the examples above, the program conveys the wrong priorities: focusing attention on surface features of grammar and form instead of substantive development and rhetorical effectiveness, and failing to be able to recognize effective use of language and syntax. Imagine the confusion an English language learner would experience receiving the kind of feedback we have reported.

WRITING FOR NOBODY: THE GAME

Even if *Criterion* and its competitors could be improved—and given *Criterion*'s 95% failure rate we experienced on Charlie's essay, they have a long way to go—they should still be banished from our classrooms, for, as White (1969) has long argued, "Writing for nobody is not writing at all" (p. 167). Machine scoring programs, in common with skill-and-drill curricula, "deny the humanity of writing. … Let us find honest assignments—they are everywhere to be found, in experience, in books—and help students to see writing as a valuable way to gain important knowledge and to define their own thoughts for themselves and for others" (White, 1970, p. 869). White (1969) has called us

> to resist and protest against the dehumanizing effect of materials and essay assignments that turn writing into academic gamesmanship. … We can support the humanity of our students as writers by insisting on our own humanity as readers. We can refuse to assign and decline to accept writing for nobody. (p. 168)

White is pointing to two fundamental issues here. One is the basic dehumanizing effect of writing to machines. The other is that machine-scoring programs focus a writer's attention on formulaic structures and isolated skills divorced from consideration of how to impact readers. Developing writers are as in need of and as ready for experience making these kinds of rhetorical judgments that drive choices of structure and style as are more proficient writers.

From our experience writing essays for *Criterion* and using their packaged prompts, writing for *Criterion* does become "writing for nobody." *Criterion* and its competitors "turn writing into academic gamesmanship" (White, 1969, p. 168), a game of learning to write the kind of essays that are used for ETS testing programs as they are the source for the prompts used by *Criterion* in order to provide the norming capability for the holistic ratings. Part of the sense of game comes from the time limits imposed on the task. If one wishes to use the holistic feedback rating, *The Criterion Teaching Guide* advises setting a time limit for writing: "Note that it's very important to assign the *same amount of time* for writing the essay from instructor-generated and modified prompts as is required by the standard higher education prompts" (ETS, 2007, p. 28). In another of our trials with *Criterion*, Herrington experienced this pressure when she was writing an essay for *Criterion*. She was just beginning the first sentence of her third paragraph when a blinker told her she had only 3 minutes left. Even though she was not sure how she wanted to finish, she hurried to make up a conclusion, taking the easy way out and dropping in a maxim.

The game of writing against the clock is followed by the game of revising to get a higher score. Once Herrington submitted her essay, she received the promised immediate rating: In this case a 4 with 6 being the highest score. It became clear by looking at the sample, scored essays provided by *Criterion*, that an essay with an agree/disagree thesis and at least three main points—not just the two in her essay—was favored. Knowing that was the game, Herrington easily improved her score to a 6 by adding what appeared to be an agree/disagree thesis and an additional paragraph with a simplistic example. Her focus was not on what she was aiming to get across—indeed, the revised essay did not represent her view—but on adding the favored structural features.

The title of White's (1969) essay, "Writing for Nobody," reminds us of what a student said to us after discovering that her placement essay was going to be read and scored by WritePlacer Plus and not by a teacher. Surprised, and even a bit disturbed, she said,

> I'm assuming that someone is going to be reading this thoroughly and, you know, thinking about what you wrote, and not really—I mean I know the computer is smart, but I'm not thinking of them as thinking about what I'm writing as the way a human would think about what I'm writing. (Herrington & Moran, 2006, p. 123)

This was a student from a local community college that had adopted WritePlacer Plus for its placement testing and was considering bringing the program into its full curriculum as an aid in its tutoring center and as a pre- and post-test to measure the value added to a student by the 2-year course of study. We note from the *Criterion* website's long list of institutions using the program that those writing for *Criterion* and, by extension, WritePlacer Plus, are predominantly 2-year colleges. There are no Ivy League names on the list. This raises for us the specter of a two-tiered field, divided by wealth and connection, where poor and unconnected students write to machines, and wealthy and connected students write to human readers. We understand the very real financial pressures some schools face, pressures that lead them to seek technologies that promise efficiencies of time and cost. But at the same time, we know, as White has said before us, that writing to a machine distorts the very nature of writing itself. Writing to a machine is writing to nobody. Writing to nobody is not writing at all.

APPENDIX
ESSAY WRITTEN TO CRITERION PROMPT

This assignment makes two assumptions that I have difficulty with. First, it assumes that educators can have an effect on students' use of email and texting. Second, it assumes that there is a powerful link between students' use of email/texting and "students' reading and writing skills."

The first assumption, that we as teachers can affect our students' use of email and texting, is difficult to support. We probably don't want our students to be emailing/texting during our lectures and classes—certainly I don't. And we don't have much control over what our students do when they leave our classrooms. In addition, email/texting are tremendously gratifying social media; it is unlikely that educators, or anyone else, can influence their use. I take as an analogue here cell-phone use and driving. We know that cell-phone use distracts drivers and leads to horrific accidents. And legislators and others are, for now at least, entirely unable to control this use of communication technology.

The validity of the second assumption, that there is a close relationship between the use of email/texting and "reading and writing skills," depends upon the definition of "reading and writing skills." I'll assume that by these terms we mean extended reading (e.g. essays, New York Times-length articles, novels) and extended writing (e.g. thousand-word expository essays that are reflective and that maintain logical coherence over their full length.) It seems to me that the ability to compose and read in short bursts is not the same as the ability to compose and read extended documents. I've encountered more than one student who is a whiz on email, belonging to multiple discussion groups and contributing thoughtfully to these discussions, but who is entirely unable to put together an extended argument. On the basis of my own experience, both intellectual and athletic, training is specific to the performance task: that is, you learn to do what you practice, and there is very little transference to tasks that may seem related. As a cyclist, I know that cycling is an activity that includes many different activities: long road-rides, hill-climbing, descending, riding close in groups (peloton), time-trialing, and sprinting. To train for one of these, e.g. a century (long road ride) is not training for sprinting, or descending, or any of the other 'kinds' of cycling. If the analogy between cycling and reading/writing holds, then training on email/texting will not transfer to extended reading or writing.

So where does that leave us? First, educators can't affect students' use of email/texting outside of their own spheres of influence, which are limited to classrooms or, at the most, school buildings. And second, there's very little likelihood that practice on email/texting will have a positive effect on the very-different skills of extended reading and writing. So, to return to the question assigned, educators should not concern themselves with students' use of email/texting. If they try, it will be a waste of their time and energy.

REFERENCES

Burstein, J., Chodorow, M., & Leacock, C. (2004). Automated essay evaluation: The Criterion Online Writing Service [Electronic version]. *AI Magazine, 25*(3), 27-36.

Educational Testing Service. (2007). *The Criterion Teaching Guide: Using the Criterion Online Writing Service for differentiated instruction in the college classroom*. Princeton, NJ: Educational Testing Service. Web.

Educational Testing Service. (2009a). Criterion: Bookstore order form. Princeton, NJ: Educational Testing Service. Web.

Educational Testing Service. (2009b). Criterion details: Higher education. Criterion in your bookstore. Princeton, NJ: Educational Testing Service. Web.

Educational Testing Service. (2009c). Criterion details: Higher education. Frequently asked questions. Princeton, NJ: Educational Testing Service. Web.

Educational Testing Service. (2009d). Criterion details: Higher education. The Criterion service overview. Princeton, NJ: Educational Testing Service. Web.

Educational Testing Service. (2011). Criterion Demo: Higher Education. Princeton, NJ: Educational Testing Service. Web.

Herrington, A., & Moran, C. (2006). WritePlacer Plus in place: An exploratory case study. In P. F. Ericsson & R. Haswell (Eds.), *Machine scoring of student essays: Truth and consequences* (pp. 114-129). Logan, UT: Utah State University Press.

Herrington, A., & Stanley, S. (2008, March). *Criterion*SM : Promoting the standard. Paper delivered at the Conference on College Composition and Communication, San Francisco, CA. *Digital Is*. Web.

Herrington, A., & Moran, C. (2009). Writing assessment and new technologies. In M. Paretti & K. Powell (Eds.), Assessment of writing (pp. 159-182). Tallahassee, FL: Association for Institutional Research.

McAllister, K. S., & White, E. M. (2006). Interested complicities: The dialectic of computer-assisted writing assessment. In P. F. Ericsson & R. Haswell (Eds.), *Machine scoring of student essays: Truth and consequences* (pp. 8-28). Logan, UT: Utah State University Press.

Rothermel, B. (2006). Automated writing instruction: Computer-assisted or computer-driven pedagogies? In P. F. Ericsson & R. Haswell (Eds.), *Machine scoring of student essays: Truth and consequences* (pp. 199-210). Logan, UT: Utah State University Press.

Vantage Learning. (2009). *MY Access*. New Hope, PA: Vantage Learning. Web.

Vantage Learning. (2009). *My Access Overview*. Increase student achievement through writing! New Hope, PA: Vantage Learning. Web.

White, E. M. (1969). Writing for nobody. *College English, 31*(2), 166-168.

White, E. M. (1984). Holisticism. *College Composition and Communication, 35*(4), 400-409.

White, E. M. (1970). Response to Roth and Altshuler. *College English, 31*(8), 869.

White, E. M. (1994). *Teaching and assessing writing* (2nd Ed.). San Francisco, CA: Jossey-Bass.

White, E.M. (1996). Power and agenda-setting in writing assessment. In E. M. White, W. D. Lutz, & S. Kamusikiri, *Assessment of writing: Politics, policies, practices* (pp. 9-24). New York, NY: Modern Language Association.

13

THE FUTURE OF PORTFOLIO-BASED WRITING ASSESSMENT
A CAUTIONARY TALE

William Condon
Washington State University

Back when I was in graduate school, studying Victorian literature, I fell in love with Thomas Carlyle. I used to invoke Carlyle to explain *everything*. I passed through that phase during my MA, but now find myself, more than 3 decades later, having a relapse. In "Characteristics," Carlyle (1831) explains how our beliefs turn into good intentions and, in turn, lead us to construct institutions designed to put those beliefs into action. Once in existence, however, those institutions outlast the validity of our beliefs, becoming agents of stasis rather than continuing as agents for the change we intended. Instead, the institution acts as an impediment for further positive change. Such is the history of writing assessment—or, for that matter all kinds of assessments of competency or achievement.

We do not have to be members of FairTest.org to recognize that tests that were intended to produce a level playing field—and that, arguably, once *did* expand inclusiveness at the nation's elite institutions of higher education—no longer do so. Stephen Jay Gould's brilliant *The Mismeasure of Man* traces the history of Benet's IQ test (itself originally intended to identify people who needed more help with education) as it morphed, under Robert M. Yerkes' command (1921), into sorting mechanisms for the Army during World War I and for college admissions between the wars and especially in the post-World War II era. On its surface—and according to the intentions of its developers—this movement, characterized most obviously by the SAT and ACT aptitude tests, exerted a democratic influence on college admissions, expanding access to higher education in the 1950s far beyond what had been the case before World War II. This focus on aptitude, as opposed to achievement, was intended to level the playing field for the less advantaged (for a good discussion of the differences between aptitude and achievement tests, see Zwick, 2006, pp. 652-653). However, those institutions, to recall Carlyle's terminology, incorporated some of the prejudices of the older systems (remember that even today, SAT scores correlate most closely with family income, meaning that those who are born financially well off have more access than those born less well off, regardless of an individual's merit). In addition, such indirect tests of knowledge and ability—often, but not always multiple-choice question tests—also incorporate many of the biases inherent in their methodologies. At their base, what we have long called "indirect" tests severely underrepresent the construct they claim to test. In the case of multiple-choice question tests, the focus is not on the construct, but on correlations between certain responses and characteristics of the construct under examination.

This underrepresentation of the construct being tested is further weakened by the content of test items. Gould describes how the early (1917 era) Army IQ tests discriminated against poor rural populations, for example, by asking questions about light bulbs, phonographs, bowling alleys, and tennis matches (pp. 240-41). Similarly, today's indirect tests, despite efforts to eliminate bias, still ask questions that middle- and upper-class White male students are more certain to have in their experience than are women or poor students from any racial or ethnic background—such as experience going to a zoo, or visiting a farm or seeing farm animals. Today, some urban schools take students on field trips to farms as *part of the students' test preparation* (Hernandez, 2009). Although we can admit that this is an example of a test-driven, probably beneficial curriculum change, the fact remains that few urban school districts have the resources or the opportunity to carry out such a program; thus, whereas Harlem's students benefit, millions of other students from poor, urban districts are unable to overcome the inherent discrimination of the test questions.

As the populations seeking access to higher education expanded in the 1960s, tests such as the SAT and ACT began to show their progress from agent of change to agent of stasis, providing higher scores to students from the mainstream culture and at least middle-class socioeconomic status. Mostly, that is, White students. And the so-called "achievement gap" first reared its head. Even the name, *achievement gap*, places the blame for lack of achievement on the people taking the tests, rather than on the tests themselves, where it belongs. These tests, as the Educational Testing Service's own reports demonstrate, do a good job of measuring test-takers' *parents'* achievement, at least as it appears in their earning power (see Table 13.1). The gaps in scores between students from middle- and upper-class homes and those from the working classes are much more likely due to the kinds of knowledge such tests habitually ask for, not any gap in "innate intelligence"—a term that hearkens back to Yerkes' beliefs circa 1917, a belief that kept the upper classes in the officer's corps and the great unwashed as cannon fodder.

Bowen, Chingos, and McPherson (2009), in a study encompassing thousands of students at large public universities, confirm the advantages that come with a parent's income level:

> Compared to students from families in the bottom income quartile, top-income students have high school graduation rates that are 23 percentage points higher, college enrollment rates that are 38 points higher, and college graduation rates that are 32 points higher. ... Students from the top of the family income and parental education distributions were nearly *five times* more likely to earn a bachelor's degree than students from the bottom of these distributions. (p. 22; italics in original)

Table 13.1. SAT Scores by Family Income, 2011 College-Bound Seniors

Family income	Critical Reading	Mathematics	Writing
$0 to $20,000	434	460	429
$20,000 to $40,000	464	480	454
$40,000 to $60,000	487	499	475
$60,000 to $80,000	502	512	489
$80,000 to $100,000	515	527	503
$100,000 to $120,000	526	539	515
$120,000 to $140,000	530	544	520
$140,000 to $160,000	538	552	529
$160,000 to $200,000	543	557	539
More than $200,000	568	586	567

Note: Excerpted from Student Information and Characteristics, as published by the College Board (2011).

Since these ranking have been consistent at least since 1996, Bowen, Chingos, and McPherson (2009) confirm what the statistics have been saying all along: Income level exerts such a strong influence on the ability to get into and even complete college that admitting students according to the income of their parents would be as effective as admitting them based on the SAT score. That is clearly not the effect SAT developers had in mind; however, it is nevertheless the effect they have achieved.

College admissions tests in the post-World War II era had in mind, as Elliot (2005) points out, the promotion of "individual freedom through education" (p. 122), a worthwhile goal. Yet the indirect test is inherently flawed for at least two reasons. First, it does not test aptitude directly; that is, the questions only *get at* aptitude. They produce responses that *correlate* with aptitude among a model population. Thus, in an ultimate absurdity, we saw this method applied in the 1980s to develop multiple-choice question tests for critical thinking. Second, test questions are typically developed and field tested by people with PhDs. These test-makers, no matter how hard they try to build subject-neutral questions, naturally develop questions out of their own experiences and perspectives, thus contaminating the test with items that hamper people with different experiences and perspectives. The institution of the construct-limited test has clearly become corrupted; it has turned from its intention of expanding access (which it accomplished, up to a point in the 1950s) and is now an agent of exclusion and unfairness (Medina & Neill, 1990). Baldwin (this volume) offers a richer analysis of these issues, as well as suggests solutions for developing fairer tests. Since 1980, the proportion of the White male population in the United States attending college has remained the same. Yet college enrollment has expanded every year. How? The expansion has come from women and from minority populations who, despite the barriers created by these entrance tests, manage to gain access. Despite the so-called achievement gap, these students come to community colleges and open admissions colleges, to universities that are not selective in their admissions, and they succeed. They get around the tests, and they achieve.

In part, then, this introduction is an argument for abolishing construct-limited tests, although their strangle hold on U.S. education is such that this argument is little more than a forlorn hope. But I am also setting in place a pattern that I see rendered in the history of such tests, that I trace in the history of direct tests, and that, I actually do hope, we can avoid in the still future history of portfolio-based writing assessment. To be clear, the pattern involves a test that tries to correct the problems of the previous model, but that from its beginning is hampered by previous methods' flaws. The new method gains currency by demonstrating that it is capable of greater fairness or legitimacy and/or that its results are more valuable, usable, and generalizable than the old way. But then scale interferes, and the need for efficiency results in a continual reduction of the new model, until what is left is hardly different from—let alone better than—its predecessor.

Elliot's (2005) history of the essay test demonstrates that the urge to test writing in the United States by actually having test-takers write something began at least with the desire to test the writing of incoming students at Harvard in the 1870s and continued to tantalize test developers until the 1960s and 1970s, when, led by Paul Diederich at ETS and Edward White of California State University at San Bernadino, the direct testing of writing, via the timed impromptu essay, became a reality. All along, test designers realized that construct-limited tests of writing were inherently flawed, but their dedication to preserving reliability, which White (1994) equates with fairness, over increasing validity, which White equates with honesty (pp. 10-18), led to a kind of test that would eventually follow the pattern outlined above. In plain terms, developers of large-scale direct tests of writing were content to be dishonest as long as their decisions about test-takers' competencies were consistent. Surely, the reverse would also have been true. Being content to be inconsistent as long as they were honest would have been just as wrong. Valuing either characteristic over the other would have led to the same disastrous result.

I have argued elsewhere that if the indirect test of writing is contextless, in that it brings nothing of the test-taker's context into the testing experience, then the timed essay test is context-poor (Hamp-Lyons & Condon, 2000, pp. 9-15). In other words, these tests underrepresent the construct, writing, that they purport to measure, thus failing the most basic test of validity. Although they are an improvement over multiple-choice question tests, timed essay tests are still construct limited. The assessment-oriented strengths of the timed essay are efficiency and reliability (reliability being defined in the early going as consistency in scoring among raters). But reliability—as fairness—must be about more than consistency in scoring. In that gray area where reliability and validity overlap, fairness involves testing all the genres of writing that we teach, as well as allowing test-takers to demonstrate the writing process strategies they have learned, just to name two examples (Hamp-Lyons & Condon, 2000, p. 13).

As timed essay tests developed, their limitations were already apparent. Efficiency demanded that in most cases only one sample of writing would be collected, even though throughout the assessment community, the need to collect multiple samples across multiple composing opportunities is common knowledge (Haswell, 2001; White, 1994). The goal of reliability qua consistency in scoring resulted in tightly controlled, highly artificial topics; time limits that constrain all but a writer's most basic drafting skills; and writing samples that evince neither a writer's engagement nor in any sense the full construct, writing, that the test claims to address. As time passed, these limitations have only become more apparent, resulting finally in widespread use of tests such as Compass e-Write (see Jamieson, 2005), Accuplacer (see Mattern & Packham, 2009), and ETS's SAT Reasoning Test.

These tests claim to test writing, but they actually call on the most minimal of test-takers' competencies. Compass is largely a test of editing skills, whereas Accuplacer and SAT Reasoning Test allow a writer such limited time to write that the tests cannot seriously claim to test writing beyond the ability to think fast and write in complete sentences. The SAT Reasoning Test, in fact, primarily tests grammar and mechanics via a multiple-choice question section that counts as two thirds of the score. In other words, SAT2's 20-minute writing sample counts less than the traditional, indirect test of writing that accompanies it. Such tests so underrepresent the construct that they provide little more than lip service to the actual testing of writing. They are efficient, however. The pressure to provide a cheap and fast test has resulted in "direct" tests of writing that no longer resemble what White, Diederich (1974), and Cronbach (1988) introduced decades ago and that can no longer legitimately be called direct tests of *writing*. The history of the large-scale direct test of writing has fallen victim to the same dishonesty at the core of indirect tests. Too often, developers are willing to sacrifice validity in favor of efficiency and consistency. In the end, as Perelman establishes in Chapter 24 of this collection, calling today's large-scale essay tests direct tests of writing is simply "bullshit."

Interestingly, the reasons for the diminishing validity of these tests are more economic than educational. Any new test must compete with the tests already in place. Thus, early direct tests of writing had to achieve an acceptable level of reliability because reliability, in the sense of consistency in scoring, is the primary advantage of indirect tests. Direct tests can never compare in reliability alone with indirect tests, but the greater validity involved in the early timed essay tests eventually compensated for the lower reliability. Similarly, indirect tests are fast and cheap, so even from the beginning, direct tests had to violate good practice in order to compete, although even that competition involved weighing greater validity against speed and cost. Thus, direct tests of writing almost always involved collecting a single sample, when we know that multiple samples are necessary for valid judgments about writing. Limiting the time available for writing produces a sample that can be read and scored quickly—or even, on some tests, scored by a computer—even though we know that time limits also reduce the construct being tested to something considerably less than writing competence. Yet these compromises had to be made in order to compete with indirect tests. Fast forward to today, and we see that those compromises still operate to further and further diminish the validity of modern direct tests of writing. Les Perelman has demonstrated that length is so directly tied to scoring that one can reliably score a SAT writing sample from across the room (in Winerip, 2005), demonstrating that such tests reduce the construct to the point that content no longer matters in judging writing quality (see Ericsson & Haswell [2006] for more on this aspect of machine scoring of writing).

Paradoxically, however, the attempts to make direct essay tests compete with indirect tests *on the same terms* has resulted not only in gutting the direct tests, but also in the continued dominance of indirect tests. As widespread as direct tests have become, even the most cursory examination shows that most placement decisions are made on the basis of an indirect test of writing—for colleges, on SAT Verbal or ACT English scores, for example. A very few colleges administer their own direct test of writing. Most colleges that use a direct test subscribe, for various reasons of convenience and economy, to Accuplacer or Compass, because results are available almost immediately, and costs are laid off onto the students. Still, as colleges typically already have a score report from ETS or ACT, those scores decide which students are ready for college writing and which need further preparation before enrolling in English 101. Thus, the attempt to compete with the past results in yielding to that past.

Clearly, then, the direct testing of writing—at least as it exists in large-scale testing contexts—has been reduced and devalued to the point that it is no more worthwhile than the indirect tests that it tried to replace. The innovation has reverted to the norm. In the meantime, however, White's *Teaching and Assessing Writing*, in its 1985 edition and even more so in its 1994 revision, taught writing teachers how to apply some of the lessons learned from direct testing to the classroom and to the writing program. Thus, we writing teachers developed assignments that more directly addressed learning objectives. We developed outcomes for our courses and programs. We brought grading out of the "black box" and shared our criteria with our students—even, in some cases, *developing* those criteria collaboratively with our students. In short, White demonstrated that we could engage assessment methodologies with instruction to the benefit of both. Into this picture, circa 1986, came the writing portfolio (Belanoff & Elbow, 1986). Classroom use of writing portfolios had been around for at least a decade by then, but Belanoff and Elbow showed how to scale up that use, to create a system of portfolio assessment that could be used in a writing program, rather than merely in an individual classroom. That moment began a decade in which basic questions about the usability of portfolios in writing assessment were answered. Portfolios contain a range of samples produced under normal writing conditions, so their validity when compared to earlier testing methods is unquestioned. We had to prove that portfolios could be scored reliably (see Allen, Condon, Dickson, Forbes, Meese, & Yancey, 1997; Haswell 2001; Willard-Traub, Decker, Reed, & Johnston, 1999). Experience had to show that the logistics involved in collecting, processing, and storing portfolios would not be overwhelming. We had to establish that portfolios could be scored relatively quickly and cheaply (Haswell 2001; Willard-Traub, Decker, Reed, & Johnston,1999). By the mid 1990s, the basic objections to larger-scale portfolio assessment had been answered. The movement had begun.

In the succeeding decade and a half, portfolio-based writing assessment has only grown more robust. Bolstered by solid research into portfolios' effectiveness (Haswell, 2001; Hamp-Lyons & Condon, 2000; White, 2005; and many others), portfolio-based assessments have taken hold in writing programs, in statewide K-12 evaluations (most notably in Kentucky and Vermont), and, to a lesser extent, in large-scale assessments. At the very least, portfolio assessments such as the University of Michigan's former entry assessment (5,000 portfolios each summer) and Washington State University's Junior Writing Portfolio (4,000 portfolios each year) have demonstrated that portfolios are practical and that they offer advantages that less robust forms of assessment do not. And that, I believe, is the key to a successful future. We who advocate portfolio assessment and who are in the front lines of putting portfolio-based writing assessments into place must also lead the way in avoiding the pattern I described earlier. We must heed Carlyle's warning not to allow our institution to become hardened and inflexible, not to let it become an agent that preserves the past rather than one that builds a more successful future. How do we do that? As you might expect, I have some suggestions.

First, we must avoid the urge to establish portfolios entirely according to past criteria. It is sufficient that portfolios can be read reliably—that raters can achieve and even greatly exceed the .8 reliability coefficient deemed acceptable for timed writings, given the added validity of the instrument (Haswell, 2001; Rutz & Lauer-Glebov, 2005; Willard-Traub et al., 1999). Beyond that threshold, we need to emphasize the differences, rather than try to achieve the kind of speed and efficiency that governed the continuing reductionism in assessment by timed writing. Once the orderliness of inter-rater reliability has been established—and it has, in spades—then the messiness of portfolios offers many advantages that no other form of assessment currently existing or on the horizon can confer. In short, from neither indirect tests nor from timed essay tests can one make judgments about the writer—only about the answers to questions or the sample of writing in a given case. Thus, scores can be placed in a ranking and placements can be made on that basis, in a system of placement that is essentially vertical: from low ability to high ability. Portfolios, however, allow us to see performances across multiple genres; to judge a writer's ability to revise; to see, via an introductory reflective essay, a writer's metacognitive knowledge about writing, even to make judgments about the quality of the curriculum a writer has come through. Portfolios can tell us that John is good at grammar and mechanics but not at organization, that Jane uses sources well but has trouble thinking critically, or that Mary's writing seems chaotic, though it is filled with interesting thinking. The potential for what I call a horizontal curriculum is exciting, to say the least. Instead of a one-size-fits-all first-year writing course, portfolios would allow us to design a range of first-year writing courses that meet the demonstrated needs of clusters of writers. Portfolios can tell us which of our program's outcomes a given writer can already do, so we can design instruction to help that writer acquire the others. In order to do this, we have to reject the previous paradigm, one that Gould shows us goes at least as far back as Benet's first IQ tests—solely intended to identify those lower on the vertical ranking in order to help them catch up. That need is still with us, but the opportunity to go horizontal, to teach writing in 3-D if you will, with the time to learn as the third dimension, can break that old mold and forge a new era in writing instruction. We can change the idea of the writing requirement from a regimented, single experience to a flexible, individually focused experience. Portfolio-based writing assessments yield the data to support such a revolution. Other forms of assessment do not.

Second, and corollary to the discussion above, we have to think generatively, rather than reductively. Timed essay tests opened a range of possibilities. White (1985/1994) showed us how to engage assessment methodologies with instruction, to develop better assignments (think writing tasks or prompts), to design criteria for grading, to use those criteria in responding to students' writing, and so forth. The promise was there, but the impetus to think generatively about timed testing methods was too weak. Instead, the assessment community thought reductively, with the results described earlier in this chapter. Today, despite some bright spots, timed essay tests have become so discredited, so disreputable, that it is unclear whether they could make a comeback to respectability. We cannot allow that kind of narrow reductionism to affect portfolio-based assessments. Portfolios allow us to see more of what our students can do. As artifacts, they provide evidence of teaching effectiveness (and ineffectiveness); they provide input into program design and reform; they archive our curriculum, our outcomes, our standards; they provide realistic models for use in future instruction; they produce, over time, a moving picture of our programs. The list goes on. White (1994) warned: "If portfolios are to continue their movement beyond individual classrooms into larger assessment, they will have to demonstrate both reliability and cost-effectiveness. This is exactly the task that essay testing faced—and met—during the 1970s" (p. 292). We have accomplished the former: Reliability has been conquered. But I think we need to understand the latter—the need for cost-effectiveness—in different terms than those White seems to advance. Cost-effectiveness does not merely consist of assessing portfolios at the same cost as timed essays. That impetus, as I have argued, is one of the main reasons essay tests have become so reductive: The only way to make them as cost-effective (i.e., cheap) as indirect tests is to constrain them beyond recognition and have them scored by machines (as indirect tests are, of course). We need to argue for cost-effectiveness in the sense that the extra cost of scoring portfolios (and programs such as those at

Michigan, Washington State University, and Carleton College have proven that the extra cost is not very great at all) yields far more in useful and useable information—that, in effect, portfolios are worth paying for.

Third, we need to make an argument based on the future of higher education, and of our culture in general, rather than on their past. We live in a high-tech culture, and every indication about what is to come implies that new and emerging technologies allow us to individualize our lives. From the design of houses that accommodate themselves to individual occupants, to the advent of ubiquitous computing; from Tapscott's (2008) *Grown Up Digital* to Shirky's (2008) *Here Comes Everybody*, what we see is electronic communications that allow each of us a large measure of control over our lives—much greater than any previous post-Industrial Revolution culture has had. In the past, the emphasis has been on regimentation, mass education, and indoctrination. The future will be about breaking those molds, about individualization. Shirley Brice Heath (2002) forecasted in the 1990s that people would develop a different relationship with higher education by 2025, that instead of a 4-year concentrated experience, people would move back and forth between work and school, gaining what they need to know when they need to know it. We can already see that change beginning to happen. In such a world, there will be a great need for robust assessments, but not really for traditional rankings. Portfolios—especially electronic portfolios—provide a vehicle for the kinds of assessment we will need in order to design curricula for a student body that not only includes individuals from a wider and wider range of cultures, but also from a wider and wider range of ages and experience. I argued some time ago that portfolios can bridge such gaps (Condon, 1997). Electronic portfolios, as Yancey argues later in this volume, can more easily and conveniently collect work samples from a longer span of time and range of places than can paper portfolios (see also Cambridge, Cambridge, & Yancey, 2001; Cambridge, Kahn, Tompkins, & Yancey, 2009). As people move between education and work, an electronic portfolio can make work samples from each environment relevant within the other environments. Colleges will be able to perceive students' needs and design curriculum to meet those needs; the workplace will be able to see the full range of an applicant's competencies and match an individual more effectively to a career stage. This kind of generative thinking looks forward, rather than backward, yet it has the potential to provide a far more robust, accurate, and individualized assessment of current competencies and potential for achievement. Again, such an assessment is cost-effective because it is *worth* the extra expense.

Timed essay tests were a good idea because they accomplished the same end as indirect tests, but they did it more ethically and more responsibly—with greater validity. Still, all they provided was a ranking, a placement, a judgment. If we place our value there, then simple economics will dictate that we will design assessments to produce a placement, a ranking, or a judgment as cheaply and as quickly as possible. This kind of assessment works reductively, but, as I have argued elsewhere, we need to develop assessments that can be generative, rather than reductive (Condon, 2009). And we need to argue for generative assessments in all assessments, not just in portfolios. Washington State University's experiment with a generative set of timed writing prompts demonstrated that such assessments add great benefits at no extra cost to the students or the institution; yet they provide writing tasks that students can engage with, and those texts provide a rich set of data about institutional effectiveness, data that any university *would* pay more for if it had to. Our values must move toward honesty *and* truth, toward richer rather than poorer assessments. Once that happens, the future of portfolios will brighten considerably.

The timed essay's *raison d'etre*—its greater validity—has faded as the value placed on efficiency and cost grows more important. Portfolios, however, are different in kind from direct or indirect tests. Portfolios can, of course, accommodate the need for regimentation, for placements, rankings, and judgments. But even the most casual user of a portfolio sees the potential for more. My students readily see the material differences in the learning experience that engages them in constructing a portfolio, as opposed to the learning experience that culminates in a test. Faculty portfolio raters testify that exposure to actual student performances on actual classroom assignments leads them to change their own expectations and assignments for the better when they move back into their teaching roles. Portfolio-based writing assessment is materially and operationally different from previous kinds of assessment, and while we have so far established that portfolio ratings can operate within accepted assessment parameters, we have also established that portfolios help us answer questions that former methods cannot. Portfolios offer the kind of flexible, adaptable tool that Carlyle would have liked, a tool that can change as our knowledge about writing changes, that can adapt and evolve to fit changing circumstances—in short, that can remain an agent of change, rather than become an agent for stasis. But it can only do that if we remain aware of the dangers waiting for us, if we can advocate such uses and thereby avoid falling into the trap of efficiency and a reductive kind of cost-effectiveness, as timed essay tests did.

REFERENCES

Allen, M., Condon, W., Dickson, M., Forbes, C., Meese, G., & Yancey, K. (1997). Portfolios, WAC, email, and assessment: An inquiry on Portnet. In K. B. Yancey & I. Weiser (Eds.), *Situating portfolios: Four perspectives* (pp. 370-384). Logan, UT: Utah State University Press.

Belanoff, P., & Elbow, P. (1986). Using portfolios to increase collaboration and community in a writing program. *WPA: Journal of Writing Program Administration, 9*(3), 27-39.

Bowen, W.G., Chingos, M., & McPherson, M. (2009). *Crossing the finish line: Completing college at America's public universities.* Princeton, NJ: Princeton University Press.

Cambridge, D., Cambridge, B., & Yancey, K. (2009). *Electronic portfolios 2.0: Emergent research on implementation and impact.* Sterling, VA: Stylus Publishing.

Cambridge, B., Kahn, S., Tompkins, D.P., & Yancey K. B. (Eds.). (2001). *Electronic portfolios: Emerging practices in student, faculty, and institutional learning.* Washington, DC: American Association for Higher Education.

Carlyle, Thomas. (1831). Characteristics. In *The Harvard Classics.* Vol. 25, Part 3. Web.

College Board. (2011). *Total group profile report.* New York, NY: College Board.

Condon, W. (2007). Building bridges, closing gaps: Using portfolios to reconstruct the academic community. K. B. Yancey & I. Weiser (Eds.), *Situating portfolios: Four perspectives* (pp. 196-213). Logan, UT: Utah State University Press.

Condon, W. (2009). Looking beyond judging and ranking: Writing assessment as a generative practice. *Assessing Writing, 14*(3), 141-157.

Cronbach, L.J. (1988). Five perspectives on validity argument. In H. Wainer & H. Braun (Eds.), *Test validity* (pp. 3-17). Hillsdale, NJ: Lawrence Erlbaum.

Diederich, P.B. (1974). *Measuring growth in English.* Urbana, IL: National Council of Teachers of English.

Elliot, N. (2005). *On a scale: A social history of writing assessment in America.* New York, NY: Peter Lang.

Ericsson, P. F., & Haswell R. H. (Eds.). (2006). *Machine scoring of student essays: Truth and consequences.* Logan, UT: Utah State University Press.

Gould, S.J. (1981). *The mismeasure of man.* New York, NY: W.W. Norton & Co.

Hamp-Lyons, L., & Condon, W. (2000). *Assessing the portfolio: Principles for practice, theory, and research.* Cresskill, NJ: Hampton Press.

Haswell, R.H. (Ed.). (2001). *Beyond outcomes: Assessment and instruction within a university writing program.* Westport, CT: Ablex.

Heath, S.B. (2002). Foreword. In G. Hull & K. Schultz (Eds.), *School's out! Literacy and learning outside of school* (pp. vii-ix). New York, NY: Teachers College Press.

Hernandez, J. C. (2009). A moo-moo here, and better test scores later. *New York Times Online*. Web.

Jamieson, J. (2005). Trends in computer-based second language assessment. *Annual Review of Applied Linguistics, 25*(1), 228–242.

Mattern, K., & Packham, S. (2009). *Predictive validity of ACCUPLACER® scores for course placement: A meta-analysis* (Research Report 2009-2). New York, NY: College Board.

Medina, N., & Neill, D. (1990). *Fallout from the testing explosion: How 100 million standardized exams undermine equity and excellence in American schools.* Cambridge, MA: FairTest.

Rutz, C., & Lauer-Glebov J. (2005). Assessment and innovation: One darn thing leads to another. *Assessing Writing, 10*(2), 80-99.

Shirky, C. (2008). *Here comes everybody: The power of organizing without organizations.* New York, NY: The Penguin Press.

Tapscott, D. (2008). *Grown up digital: How the net generation is changing your world.* New York, NY: McGraw-Hill.

White, E. M. (1985/1994). *Teaching and assessing writing: Recent advances in understanding, evaluating, and improving student performance* (2nd ed.). San Francisco, CA: Jossey-Bass.

White, E.M. (2005). The scoring of portfolios: Phase 2. *College Composition and Communication, 56*(4), 581-600.

Willard-Traub, M., Decker, E., Reed R., & Johnston J. (1999). The development of large-scale portfolio placement assessment at the University of Michigan: 1992-1998. *Assessing Writing, 6*(1), 41-84.

Winerip, M. (2005, May 4). SAT essay test rewards length and ignores errors of fact. *The New York Times*, p. A19.

Yerkes, R.M. (Ed.). (1921). *Psychological examining in the US Army. Memoirs of the National Academy of Sciences, Vol. 15.* Washington, DC: Government Printing Office.

Zwick, R. (2006). Higher education admission testing. In R. L Brennan (Ed.), *Educational measurement* (4th ed., pp. 647-679). Westport, CT: American Council on Education/Praeger.

14

COMPLICATING THE FAIL-OR-SUCCEED DICHOTOMY IN WRITING ASSESSMENT OUTCOMES

Jon A. Leydens
Barbara M. Olds
Colorado School of Mines

This is an assessment story featuring two interwoven layers. In one layer, we recount how a recent assessment project in a first-year writing-intensive humanities course both failed and succeeded, and we tease out the details of that paradox. Interwoven with that assessment narrative is how foundational guidelines on assessment established by Edward M. White helped us set up the study as well as make sense of our assessment findings.

One may legitimately wonder how we honor White's work by narrating a seemingly failed assessment experiment. First, we assume full responsibility for our assessment processes and outcomes. Second, and more importantly, assessment is complex, hard work. Even the best laid plans, based on some of the most-informed assessment scholarship available, can lead to unexpected results. We are also convinced that too few "failed" assessment attempts make their way into the literature in part because assessment scholars do not want to disseminate what did not work, perhaps for fear of embarrassment; hence, a fair amount of published literature shows what worked well, and sometimes even what was exemplary. That same research may omit or gloss over what did not work well. Although research on "successful" assessment plays a key role in advancing assessment scholarship, it may have some unintended consequences: For instance, it may lead to the illusion that assessment is more straightforward than it really is, or that there is a simple dichotomy between failed and successful assessment. We wish to help dispel that illusion and complicate that dichotomy. Finally, we believe that there is a clear difference between poor assessment and disappointing results. White's work gives us the courage to explore a variety of possible explanations for our disappointing results with the confidence that our assessment approach was valid.

We also see significant value in the lessons learned from an assessment project that did not turn out as we had hoped. Although we think the best assessment is home grown and tailored to local assessment constraints and opportunities, we also know how much value can be gleaned from learning about others' assessment approaches and results. Such information can be judiciously ported to other institutional contexts. In this chapter, we tell our story of setting up the assessment project, discuss how White's work informed those procedures, recount the assessment results, and convey how White's work enabled us to make sense of these results. We hope others will find our experience useful.

BACKGROUND

Because the course on which we conducted this assessment is a somewhat atypical first-year course, some description is in order, along with background on our institutional context. Colorado School of Mines (CSM) is a public research university that awards degrees at the bachelor, master's, and doctoral levels, primarily in engineering and applied science; it also has programs in economics and business and international political economy of resources. Of our roughly 4,500 students, approximately 1,200 are graduate students.

Nature and Human Values (NHV) was originally proposed as a standalone, required first-year course during curricular reforms in the early to mid 1990s. As proposed, NHV would foreground the ways in which humans affect nature and nature affects humans, and the professional ethical responsibilities of engineers and scientists via a highly interdisciplinary approach combining philosophy, literature, environmental studies, science and technology studies, and other disciplines. NHV was intended to replace a general humanities and social sciences introductory course, *Crossroads*. Simultaneously, a first-year writing course was proposed to enhance the widely varying degrees of direct writing instruction and thematic coherence provided in the small-section *Crossroads* course. This course would serve as the only required writing course for all CSM students that featured direct writing instruction. The addition of these two courses would have increased the required core by three semester credits, but the CSM Undergraduate Council rejected that proposal, instead approving a compromise: a single, four credit, writing-intensive humanities course called *Nature and Human Values.*

Since its inception in 1997, the course has been team taught by faculty who conduct large lectures of over 300 students, and faculty who teach 20-student seminar sections, wherein most of the direct writing instruction and discussion of thematic issues occurs. Primarily, the writing instruction focuses on persuasive writing. By 2008, after over a decade of pedagogical experimentation with assignments, lecture-seminar configurations, textbooks, and themes, we had settled on a dynamic stability (less chaos than in the early years, with more thematic and assignment consistency yet constant experimentation across sections). At present, small seminars make up three of the four credits, and students earn the remaining credit by attending large weekly lectures, which provide discussion and writing catalysts for the seminar. After reaching this state of dynamic stability, we were interested in understanding more about what students were learning about persuasive writing.

Our assessment project began with a few primary questions:

- How do students' written persuasive abilities change over the course of a semester?
- What are the persuasive characteristics of student writing as they enter the course and as they finish the course?
- What can we learn about our writing pedagogy from having better understandings of answers to these two questions?

METHODS

The nature of our questions shaped the character of our assessment procedures. We conducted pre- and post-assessments involving paired assignments. The first assignment was announced in the second week of NHV in Fall 2008. Roughly half of NHV students summarized and responded to "prompt A" (Moore, 1995), and the other half to "prompt B" (Brook, n.d.), both published articles of roughly the same length. Each article contained themes discussed in the course as well as flaws in argumentation. Article choices came primarily from course instructors, who were invested in and supportive of the assessment project.

Students were given access on a Thursday evening to course management sites where they could download the identical instructions and either prompt A or B. Completed essays had to be posted to a plagiarism detection site before midnight the next Sunday (just over 72 hours after receiving the prompt). Students were asked to write a brief summary of the author's main claim, and then persuasively respond to either the main claim or one or two of the author's key points. By submitting the assignment, students accepted responsibility for complying with the principles of the CSM Student Honor Code, written by and for CSM students. Students also posted or gave hard copies to their instructors and received 25 points out of a semester total of 1,000 for each assignment (50 points for completing both assignments).

The second assignment was announced the 13th week of the 16-week semester, and featured the same time frame of just over 72 hours. Students who previously wrote about prompt A wrote the second summary-response to prompt B, and vice versa.

The results would show us the difference between pretest and posttest scores. As we were not evaluating students or instructors, the overall change over time in scores was our primary interest. However, we were also greatly interested in what we could learn via collaboration: In reading and discussing these papers together, what might we learn about our own overt or tacit assumptions about writing, persuasive essays, summaries, responses, argumentation, and more? The opportunity to discuss the papers allowed us to explore more fully our second and third research questions related to the persuasive characteristics of our students' writing and any changes over the course of the term as well as what we could learn about our writing pedagogy from analyzing our results.

White's work on holistic scoring has become so ingrained in the field that we focused on that approach as we designed and implemented our project, as a holistic approach made the most sense for answering the questions we posed. Our assessment was developed to answer our questions internally, not as part of an institution- or state-wide mandate, but we wanted our findings to be as valid and reliable as possible. However, our purpose allowed us to avoid the kinds of political battles White outlines in his work. When we revisited White's writing on holistic assessments after we had completed our project, we found that the process we followed agreed substantially with his recommendations in *Teaching and Assessing Writing* (1994). Specifically, he recommends the following procedures as the best way for those using a writing sample for evaluation to give evaluators "the best chance at obtaining results" (White, 1994, pp. 252-253):

1. Those teaching the classes must be involved in developing the test.
2. It is best to give students an opportunity to respond with at least two different kinds of prose.
3. Two separate forms of the test should be prepared (A & B)
4. All tests (pre and post) should be scored at the same time with all identifying marks removed
5. Sufficient resources should be provided.

The faculty involved in teaching the NHV class both developed and scored the assessment we used; we used two separate forms of the test; and all tests were scored at the same time with all identifying marks removed. Because we were interested primarily in students' persuasive abilities, they were given only one option for type of prose and, because we were only scoring a relatively small sample, no extraordinary resources were required beyond food, a congenial atmosphere, and time for colleagues to work together.

Faculty teaching NHV evaluated the essays at the beginning of the spring semester. The scoring of all 86 papers ensured that readers did not know whether the paper was a pretest or posttest, as all dates and identity information had been removed. A collaboratively designed and negotiated scoring rubric was used to evaluate all papers, and any modifications to the rubric were agreed upon by all scorers before scoring began.

Prior to the holistic scoring session, two instructors went through over half the samples in search of anchor papers. During the session, we read and discussed three sets of anchor papers, the first two of which featured three papers (high, middle, and lower range, although not presented in that order), and the third set featured two somewhat atypical student responses. White indicates that anchor papers can be much more influential on readers than the rubric, and the discussion following the scoring of anchor papers reinforced that notion as it helped define and sharpen shared criteria for the holistic scoring process. More on such benefits appears in our lessons learned section below.

All papers were double-read. If two scores were off by more than one point, a third reader scored that paper. In total, 19 essays (9 pretest and 10 posttest, or 22%) were scored by a third reader.

In the pretest, a total of 512 students uploaded their papers (290 students [56.6%] in NHV-A and 222 students [43.4%] in NHV-B). From that total of 512 students, we used a random number generator to develop a random sample of 45 papers, roughly 56.6% from NHV-A (25 papers), and 43.4% from NHV-B (20 papers). Because we did both a pretest and posttest, we should have had roughly 90 papers; however, two students who completed the pretest did not submit the posttest, so we analyzed a total of 86 papers (43 pretests and posttests).

RESULTS AND DISCUSSION

Although we had hoped for the assessment results to show an improvement over the course of the term, that was not the outcome. On a scale of 1 to 5, the pretest average was 3.33 and the posttest average was 3.17. Although we were disappointed, the decline in scores was relatively small, only 0.1548 or

5%. In other words, our students' scores appeared to neither improve nor decline. To statistically test this statement, we ran matched pairs t-tests, which involve a null and alternative hypothesis. The null hypothesis was that the mean difference (posttest minus pretest) in test scores is zero, and the alternative hypothesis is that the mean difference differs from zero. Thus, the null hypothesis states that there is essentially no change between the average posttest and pretest scores. The alternative states that there is some difference between the average pretest and posttest scores but does not specify the direction of the difference. In other words, the posttest scores could on average be greater or less than the pretest scores, and a two-sided matched pairs t-test will detect either type of difference. The results showed that there is not statistically significant evidence (t = -0.155, p = 0.417) for a change in the mean difference in students' scores (posttest minus pretest).

We also looked into whether students performed significantly better on Article Prompt A versus B, perhaps because one article was more accessible than the other. Those scores are reported in Table 14.1, which suggests that although the pretest scores for prompt B were higher than for prompt A, that result did not continue on the posttest, wherein the averages were identical. The median is the number in the middle of a group of scores, and our concern was that there might be a clustering at the median point of three, because there is a danger when using an odd numbered scale (1 to 5 rubric in our case) that raters will gravitate to the middle number. However, this was only the case with the posttest for prompt B, and the other three median scores were higher, at 3.5.

During our faculty meeting to discuss the results, we brainstormed several hypotheses to explain the outcomes. Although a difficult prospect to entertain, one of the instructors posited that the results may suggest that the writing-intensive component of the course produces no improvement in student writing. In a future study, we could vary pedagogy or use larger samples to compare instructors to see if different approaches produce different results. However, we are confident that our cadre of instructors is knowledgeable about recent trends in writing instruction and that our small classes allow us to focus on individual students' writing improvement. Thus, our explanations focused on the issues discussed below, in the approximate order of our estimation of probability.

Table 14.1. Student Average and Median Scores on Article Prompts A and B.

	Prompt A		Prompt B	
	Average	Median	Average	Median
Pretest	3.26	3.50	3.40	3.50
Posttest	3.17	3.50	3.17	3.00

1. Lack of strong performance incentives. One of the authors had a son who came home from middle school after taking a state-mandated test, and asked, "What incentive do I have to do well?" He had figured out a major flaw in many standardized tests: lack of individual incentive and motivation. In our case, instructors indicated that many students did not see 50 points (5% of their course grade, 2.5% for each essay) as sufficient incentive to do well on this assignment, especially given the various, competing demands on their time. An added complication is that unlike a standardized test, where school children have to be in the room taking the test, our writing task assumes that students will carve out time for planning and revision, making it more susceptible than a standardized test to lack of motivation and in competition with other pursuits and distractions.

2. Timing in the semester. Students in November tend to be more harried and are juggling a greater array of demands than they are in September. Also, the second assignment was to be posted the Sunday before Thanksgiving, and although classes were in session on Monday and Tuesday, some students were already mentally on Thanksgiving break. In addition, in our experience students have generally become more adept at time management over the course of their first semester and may have decided that working hard on an assignment that counted for such a small fraction of their course grade was not an efficient use of their time, leading to the perfectly rational decision to optimize their time working on other assignments that counted for more. It is worth noting that after the posttest but before the holistic scoring session, every NHV instructor we spoke with accurately predicted that posttest scores would be lower, for reasons 1 and 2.

3. Time between pretests and posttests. It may be unrealistic to expect significant shifts in student learning in just over 2 months, especially given that writing abilities tend to atrophy quickly but grow quite slowly over time (Lindemann, 1995). A perpetual question for evaluators is when to conduct an assessment because it is a judgment call to know how much improvement is realistic to expect over a relatively short time.

4. Long range growth: worse before better, and better only over time. Research suggests that student writing at critical junctures can get worse before it gets better (Williams & Columb, 1995/2007). One of those junctures is in the transition from high school to college. Students are writing not in a vacuum but in a new academic culture that has different conventions, genres, and sets of expectations, which take time to learn. Further, our experience as instructors suggests that when students acquire a new skill, a latency period may occur before they can demonstrate that skill effectively

5. Lack of clarity on audience and/or sufficient topic experience. Students are fairly adept at figuring out instructor expectations when they know the instructor, but this assignment had an unknown audience of readers, and students may not have understood what that audience expected from the assignment sheet. Also, according to White (1994), "we know surprisingly little about the differences in performance that are caused by different kinds of writing topics" (p. 67). He goes on to argue that performance varies by individual and is not necessarily tied to a particular topic type, that is, persuasive writing is not inherently more difficult than expressive writing. However, if our students have had less opportunity in high school to write persuasive essays, they may have struggled with these assignments despite our focus on persuasive writing during the semester.

6. Matriculating students' need for validation. The vast majority of students in NHV were first-year, first-semester college students, who are asking important questions about their identity: Am I "college material?" Do I belong? Can I succeed at an institution that has the highest college admission standards in Colorado? It is important not to underestimate how such issues of identity might influence the pretests more than the posttests, because the answers to those questions may be far more uncertain in September than in November. Matriculating students tend to be highly eager to please, and it is possible that eagerness could wane over time, especially because most students build their confidence during the semester.

7. Lack of student agency. Some first-year students feel they do not possess the authority or agency to construct a persuasive argument. They feel like the low duck in the academic pond, and have not yet proven to themselves that they have sufficient authority to write persuasively in this new context. It may also be that students have learned to do well using formulaic arguments on standardized tests or in high school writing classes (e.g., the infamous 5-paragraph essay). When they are asked to abandon these formulas, they struggle to construct effective arguments.

LESSONS LEARNED ABOUT ASSESSMENT PROCESSES

In retrospect, we find it intriguing that our first two research questions centered on a desire to understand how students' written persuasive abilities change over the course of a semester, and what the persuasive characteristics of student writing are as they enter and finish the course. Largely for reasons described above, we did not significantly advance our knowledge in these two areas. Instead, our primary learning gains came in reflecting on what we learned from the assessment process, our students' persuasive abilities, and (related to our third research question) our own writing pedagogy, issues we summarize below.

1. Faculty dialogue about grading makes manifest all the tacit assumptions we bring to the grading table. Yet that table is often a solitary one, wherein a single instructor grades alone, unassisted by the perspectives of one's colleagues. We found it fascinating to hear what assumptions guide each other's evaluation processes, and to hear how different instructors would finish sentences that often started with, "When I read these kinds of essays, I really look for . . ." Those value prioritizations varied more than we realized, and speaking those aloud, making them more public, was valuable as we learned from each other's various prioritizations and rationales. One instructor, for instance, during the discussion of anchor papers, realized the degree to which she was swooned by an anchor essay's confident voice, advanced vocabulary, and error-free prose that, upon further reflection, really had little persuasive content.

2. To address student motivation, we should have the assessment emerge if at all possible from an existing assignment, not one added on for the sake of conducting assessment. Although a summary-response had been one essay required in this course, two summary-response essays were not required, so the addition of the second one likely felt tacked on to instructors and students. Also, as noted above, student motivation to manifest their full capabilities was hindered, so in future assessments, we would build in greater motivational incentives.

3. Because the assessment process was designed to assess student performance and not instructor performance, we did not retain the records that linked student essays with their instructors. In future assessment processes, we will: It is possible that the randomization process overrepresents some instructors and underrepresents others. In a recent assessment consultation led by Les Perelman (2010, for instance, his team discovered that with about the same numbers, pure randomization led to gross overrepresentation of a single instructor. Subsequently, they changed their procedure so that after a maximum of three papers from a single instructor, all additional papers were disqualified, and they selected the next paper on the randomized list.

4. In future assessment processes, we will use an even numbered scale (e.g., 1 to 6 instead of 1 to 5). Although our median was not three in three out of four cases (see Table 14.1), the tendency for scores to cluster around a middle number can be avoided with an even numbered scale.

5. Different instructors value and thus emphasize different aspects of persuasion during class discussions, and accounting for that variety of approaches in a single rubric can be an enormous challenge. Even with a collaboratively designed rubric, some instructors will, while scoring, place more emphasis on one area than on others in their holistic score.

6. As Yancey notes in Chapter 27, student reflections on their own portfolios are valuable components of the learning and assessment process. Although assessing student portfolios can add considerable time and logistical complexity to the assessment process, it also has numerous advantages over our approach. For instance, student portfolio reflections enrich the dialogues—with the writer, between writer and instructor, as well as potentially among the assessors, instructor, and writer. Hence, our future assessments could explore ways to deliberately cull student portfolios and portfolio reflections, moving us from what Yancey calls second wave to third wave assessment.

LESSONS LEARNED ABOUT STUDENTS' PERSUASIVE ABILITIES

Had our results shown improvement over time, in this section we would have discussed the degree and character of those improvements. Despite not obtaining that result, we had numerous faculty conversations that elucidated how the most effective papers shared some consistent elements: Thoughtful, relevant, and persuasive evidence marshaled to support each claim, a clear demarcation yet connection between a claim and its supporting evidence, the ability to focus on a few claims and develop them in detail, and more. Contrasting characteristics emerged in the weakest papers: For instance, in the position in which readers expected supporting evidence for a claim, these papers provided another (often unsupported) claim, the evidence was frequently irrelevant or only tangentially relevant to the claim, and papers often lacked explicit explanations of how the evidence supported a given claim. Although instructors generally knew these common strengths and areas for improvement already, the benefit came in discussing with colleagues concrete examples of each, and reinforcing the values underlying evaluative criteria, as well as thinking through the different discourses for discussing persuasive writing (e.g., some instructors used the phrase claim-data-warrant whereas others referred to linking theses and supporting evidence).

LESSONS LEARNED ABOUT OUR OWN PEDAGOGY

1. After our assessment meeting, instructors asked to copy the anonymous anchor papers so they could use them in teaching persuasion. Some instructors wanted to ask their students to score the high, middle, and lower range papers and have them describe the rationales behind their scores, and in doing so build a shared, "owned" rubric that came from students' own descriptive language. Multiple variations on this assignment were discussed, leading to increased experimentation.

2. Instructors have the same core writing assignments and all teach similar elements of persuasive writing, but they do so in unique ways. As noted above, our discussions illuminated and allowed us to share the varied wealth of instructor approaches.

CONCLUSION

White would probably be neither surprised nor disappointed in our results. He argues that although a carefully designed pre/post essay test *may* show the effects of instruction, "everyone involved in the evaluation should be aware of the strong odds against obtaining statistically meaningful results from this one instrument" (1994, p. 252). He adds, "The amount of improvement that can occur in so complex a skill in a few months is likely to be submerged by such statistical facts as regression to the mean or less than ideal reliability" (p. 252). He concludes that such assessments as the one we conducted are not, however, a waste of time as both the faculty and the program can benefit from the exercise. We had to smile when we read, after our assessment study, White's insightful comment that "only one important benefit is missing: normally, the posttest shows that no statistically significant improvement has taken place in the students' test scores" (p. 251).

So, paradoxically, our "failure" may not have been a failure after all. Our assessment gave us the opportunity to discuss our program objectives, to select prompts and develop a rubric jointly, to consider the possible reasons for our students' apparent lack of progress (especially those related to incentives for performance), and to examine our own assumptions about persuasive writing, writing pedagogy, and the advantages and limits of holistic assessments. All in all, we think Edward M. White would approve.

ACKNOWLEDGMENTS

A special thanks to all the Nature and Human Values instructors who actively participated in our writing assessment process and who shared their insights on evaluating and teaching persuasive writing. Our gratitude also goes to our Colorado School of Mines colleague Dr. Amanda Hering for her statistical advice. We are also indebted to Les Perelman for his many insightful suggestions on a draft of this chapter. And of course, we and the field of writing studies owe a great deal to Ed White for his pioneering work in writing assessment.

REFERENCES

Booth, W. C., Columb, G. G., & Williams, J. M. (1995/2007). Two metaphors for learning and the novice writer. In R. Norgaard (Ed.), *Composing knowledge: Readings for college writers* (pp. 216-229). Boston, MA: Bedford/St. Martin's Press.

Brook, D. (n.d.). Another inconvenient truth: Meat is a global warming issue. *EMagazine.com*. Web.

Lindemann, E. (1995). *A rhetoric for writing teachers* (3rd ed.). New York, NY: Oxford University Press.

Moore, T. G. (1995, January). Why global warming would be good for you. *Public Interest*, pp. 83-99.

Perelman, L. (2010, October 28). [E-mail to L. Perelman]. Cambridge, MA: Massachusetts Institute of Technology.

White, E. (1994). *Teaching and assessing writing* (2nd ed.). San Francisco, CA: Jossey-Bass.

15

MAPPING A DIALECTIC WITH EDWARD M. WHITE (IN FOUR SCENES)

Bob Broad
Illinois State University

SCENE 1: FALL 1991

Nearing the end of my doctoral coursework at Miami University in Oxford, Ohio, I have chosen writing assessment as my area of specialization. During the fall semester, at the invitation of Donald A. Daiker and others who run Miami's portfolio placement program, Edward M. White visits the Department of English for an assessment consultation. One evening during his visit, White is scheduled to give a talk on writing assessment. With my life partner out of town on business and no childcare available, feeling desperate to hear the field's leading voice discuss my area of keenest scholarly interest, I decide to bring my 2-month-old son, Dylan, along with me to the presentation. I know this will prove difficult, for my beloved son is not one of those quiet babies. But I have a plan.

A little way into his talk, White notices something odd: A blue and white plastic Fisher-Price baby monitor transmitter sits on a bookshelf near the back of the room, its red light glowing. He realizes that someone is broadcasting the event. When he discovers that Dylan and I are shuttered in the room across the hall, listening to the discussion through the baby monitor receiver, White encourages me to join the group and bring my child with me. "I'm a grandfather!" he chuckles. "I can probably deal with the company of one baby at this talk." Never before this moment (and rarely since) has anyone invited me to mingle my responsibilities as a father with my academic work.

SCENE 2: SUMMER 1992

I am writing my specialization comprehensive exam, entitled "Whistling in the Dark: Ed White on Poststructuralist Literary Theory." My essay comments on Chapter Five, "How Theories of Reading Affect Responses to Student Writing," from the 1985 edition of White's *Teaching and Assessing Writing*. In the introduction to my exam, I announce that the essay will: "1) laud White for raising the question of literary theory in the sub-field of writing assessment, and 2) critique White's readings of literary theory as unfulfilled." Specifically, I write that contemporary literary theory obligates us "to overhaul White's proposed procedures for group evaluation and classroom evaluation in a way that legitimizes evaluative difference" (pp. 16-17).[1] Whereas I read poststructuralist theory as a call to proliferate and destabilize interpretations (and therefore necessarily also evaluations) of texts, White focuses chiefly on theories of "interpretive communities." He believes these theories support the procedures by which readers in holistic scoring sessions are trained to give consistent, agreeable readings. I festoon my exam essay with glowing descriptions of White and his book, describing them as appealing, congenial, laudable, convincing, helpful, admirable, knowledgeable, ethical, rigorous, fair, professional, and exemplary. This is partly a rhetorical strategy by which to counterbalance my blunt critiques; it is also partly a testimony to White's ethos and character as I had observed them in my brief interactions with him, particularly during the evening talk I attended with my infant son a year before.

SCENE 3: OCTOBER 1-4, 1992

In wrapping up his opening plenary address to the New Directions in Portfolio Assessment conference, White points out the title of my talk ("'Portfolio Scoring': A Contradiction in Terms", Broad, 1992) as a "particularly disturbing" item in the conference program. He explains that methods of reliable scoring he has helped to promote serve at least two crucial purposes in validating writing assessment. First, they provide consistency and accountability that eliminate individual scorers' caprice and thus ensure fairness to test-takers. Second, they psychometrically validate the assessment process and thus legitimize direct writing assessment in the eyes of administrators and legislators who are otherwise suspicious of the murky evaluative practices of teachers, especially teachers of writing. Without the standardized apparatus of calibration and scoring, direct writing assessment—including portfolio assessment—cannot, White believes, survive.

As the last person called on during the Q&A following his address, I identify myself as the author of the offending paper and invite Professor White to "attend my talk and hear me make my case." "I'll do that," he cheerfully agrees. As good as his word, the next morning White smiles from the fourth row of seats in our surprisingly crowded conference room. Later, some colleagues wonder at White's having "picked on" me in his speech. For my part, I am thrilled; I know he has done me a huge favor. Again.

SCENE 4: SPRING 2010 (18 YEARS LATER)

Rereading "'Portfolio Scoring': A Contradiction in Terms" with graduate students enrolled in "Writing Assessment in Colleges and Universities" at Illinois State University, I reflect on how polemically I challenged White in the chapter: "This tendency toward the devaluation and extermination of difference is what troubles me most in the discourse of mainstream writing assessment" (1994, p. 273). When, during class discussion, my students jump aboard the essay's bandwagon of denouncing the forces of evaluative quantification and homogenization, I find myself jumping off: "You need to keep in mind," I explain, "an important historical and political fact that I overlooked when I wrote this essay: White and I are fighting different battles. His battle (working alongside others) was to legitimize direct writing assessment by making it acceptably 'scientific' within the dominant paradigm of the time. High levels of interrater agreement were critical components of the scientific legitimacy toward which classic test theory aspired. He was also concerned with the ethical problems of loose-cannon evaluators and their impact on students' lives. My battle (working alongside others) was, and is, to shift communal writing assessment theories and practices to better fit with our theories and values of language, reading, writing, research, and pluralist democracy. I share White's concern about capricious judgments, but I also know that evaluative dissent is often principled and well grounded. In any case, we only get to fight our humanistic battle (including sometimes fighting White) because White and his colleagues fought—and won—their scientific battle."[2] I feel satisfied that I have broadened my students' historical view of assessment—and of White—until I recall a few hours later that I leveled a very similar critique in my book, *What We Really Value: Beyond Rubrics in Teaching and Assessing Writing* (2003), written at a time in my career when, I implicitly claimed to my students, I had matured enough to know better.

As I have realized is typical of my treatments of White's work, in *What We Really Value* I start my discussion of his sample rubric with robust praise: ". . . I find this guide admirable in its clarity, simplicity, and emphasis on intellectual and rhetorical substance over surface mechanics or format concerns." Then out comes the old cudgel:

> Theories of learning, composition, and writing assessment have evolved to the point at which the method and technology of the rubric now appear dramatically at odds with our ethical, pedagogical, and political commitments. In short, traditional rubrics and scoring guides prevent us from telling the truth about what we believe, what we teach, and what we value in composition courses and programs. (p. 2)

I firmly stand by this critique, but I also want to find a way to articulate these challenges with my growing awareness of the contexts that made White's project so crucial to the history of writing assessment. I want to figure out how we can fight for rhetorical, pluralistic writing assessment while also giving due honor to the standardization of writing assessment of which White may be the best-known and most articulate advocate.

To explain to my graduate students the sometimes heavy-handed critique of White in "'Portfolio Scoring': A Contradiction in Terms," I pointed to my youthful (32-year-old) idealism and my status at that time as a brand new (graduate student) contributor to the scholarly subfield of writing assessment. From my more mature (50-year-old) perspective in Spring 2010, I counseled those grad students to be more circumspect than I had been, to stay alert to the historical, political, and intellectual contexts within which White conducted his work.

In "Reciprocal Authorities in Communal Writing Assessment: Constructing Textual Value within a 'New Politics of Inquiry'" (Broad, 1997), I detailed evaluative differences that arose among three subject positions within the "City University" (a pseudonym) first-year composition and assessment program I studied for my dissertation research. This analysis and argument continued the campaign to render principled evaluative differences acceptable in communal writing assessment. In my comprehensive exam in 1992 I had made this argument on literary theoretical grounds; in "Reciprocal Authorities," I made it on empirical grounds. The contrasting perspectives of City University's teachers, outside readers, and administrators not only made it difficult for evaluations to correspond, the contrasts also made it nonsensical and undesirable to try to make them correspond. These differences, I argued, were of crucial educational value to the instructors, the students, and the writing program.

The "New Politics of Inquiry" part of that article, adopted from Sosnoski (1989), claimed that we should stop insisting that others agree with our interpretations and evaluations of complex texts and instead adopt a politics of inquiry that would allow us to render meaningful and ethical the differences that inevitably arise. Sosnoski's concept was key to my argument that the field of writing assessment—and the world—was ready to move beyond the statistically driven schemes to promote interrater reliability that dominated late-twentieth-century direct writing assessment. As Norbert Elliot (2010, December 12) points out, however, there did not yet exist a discernible method that would provide structure to these new politics. To many observers, therefore, the new regime I was promoting simply looked like anarchy.

"Pulling Your Hair Out: Crises of Standardization in Communal Writing Assessment" (Broad, 2000) studied how participants in the same City University writing program struggled to figure out whether, how, and how much they could and should agree and disagree in their textual judgments. As an institution pioneering what Moss (1994) calls hermeneutic assessment, City University neither systematically promoted, nor insisted on, nor monitored evaluative agreement among groups of instructors—though they did conduct "norming" sessions to promote a shared evaluative culture and community. Instead of standardizing decisions, the program encouraged their instructors to do something with any evaluative mismatch that struck me as simultaneously old-fashioned and revolutionary: *talk it through*. Modeling its assessment program on Elbow and Belanoff's (1991) at SUNY-Stony Brook, City University replaced the colossal silence and isolation characteristic of ETS-style communal evaluation with a collegial process of deliberative rhetoric. In this program, instructors stated whether they passed or failed a particular student-authored text. If they disagreed, they engaged in a dialectic, laying out their evaluative processes and ultimately negotiating a shared judgment. City University's theoretical framework and practical methods appeared to me to show how our field could move beyond the sterile atmosphere required by the dominant positivist paradigm and instead conduct communal assessment that was recognizably discursive, deliberative, and rhetorical. This program enacted a paradigm of evaluative ethics and validity (Moss, 1994) rooted more in the Athenian forum and the U.S. Supreme Court than in the scientific laboratory.

What We Really Value: Beyond Rubrics in Teaching and Assessing Writing (Broad, 2003) shifted the focus of my research program away from questions of how to handle evaluative dissent and toward the more radical or fundamental question of what we actually value in texts we judge. Earlier debates over whether and how we should invite evaluative dissent in communal assessment situations were trumped by the question of which criteria we should and do use when we judge our students' writing. Before we can decide what we should do about evaluative diversity (answering the political or normative question), we need some sort of accurate representation of the character of that diversity (answering the ontological/axiological question: "what do we value?").

DYNAMIC CRITERIA MAPPING AND ORGANIC WRITING ASSESSMENT

Although the topic had shifted from interrater agreement to evaluative criteria, dynamic criteria mapping (DCM) was still a direct critique of White's and others' uses of rubrics. Whereas before I had challenged and attempted to transform the ways in which rubrics were used to unify and homogenize rhetorical judgments, now I was cutting closer to the bone by challenging the methodological integrity and validity of rubrics themselves. To begin, I rejected the three different processes by which I had seen rubrics adopted in the past:

1. The writing teacher sits down, thinks about what she values, and writes those values down;
2. The Writing Program Administrator sits down with some writing instructors, and they compose a document representing what they think the program values; or (worst of all)
3. A teacher or a writing program finds a rubric composed by others that "looks good" for their purposes and uses it to evaluate their students' writing.

All three of these processes of inquiry (especially the last) fall short in the task of discovering and documenting rhetorical values. In fact, I could not agree to call any of these three processes adequate inquiry at all, because they neglect most of the methods qualitative researchers have developed as checks on the validity of data collection and data analysis.

To compose a valid document, rubric-makers need an approach that is empirical, inductive, systematic, and comprehensive. As an improvement to our established processes of evaluative research, I proposed in *What We Really Value* that we adopt "a streamlined form of qualitative inquiry" melded from two methodological sources: grounded theory (Glaser &

Strauss, 1967; Strauss & Corbin, 1994) and fourth-generation evaluation (Guba & Lincoln, 1989). Grounded theory emphasizes the importance of researchers' drawing their findings and insights inductively from multiple rounds of sifting systematically through their empirically gathered data. Fourth-generation evaluation privileges the integrity and validity of multiple and conflicting evaluations of any given situation, and attempts to bring those diverse accounts into meaningful and fruitful conversation.

I called this new, hybrid method of evaluative inquiry "dynamic criteria mapping" (DCM). DCM is distinct from traditional standardized approaches to writing assessment in several ways:

- It asks participants what they value in the texts before them rather than telling them what they must value;
- It follows the guidelines for what Huot (1996) called a "new theory of writing assessment" in making assessments site-based, locally controlled, context-sensitive, rhetorical, and accessible;
- It brings to light evaluative differences and asks participants, as members of an educational community, to discuss and negotiate shared evaluative frameworks (instead of assuming or imposing those frameworks); and
- The account of values that emerges is simultaneously more comprehensive (presents many more criteria than a traditional rubric) and more context-sensitive (does not presume that any or every criterion presented will apply to any given rhetorical performance) than a traditional rubric.

In his review of *What We Really Value*, Ed White frankly doubted DCM's utility, terming it "impracticably complicated" (2004, p. 115). However, I want to spotlight a point of agreement that many readers of the book (including both White and I) seem to have overlooked: White and I both strongly advocate that writing teachers and writing programs attend to and publicly document their values in judging students' texts. We both want documents—whether they are called rubrics, maps, or something else—that show our students, colleagues, and fellow citizens what we value. Dynamic criteria maps are too complex and fluid for White's tastes and purposes; traditional rubrics are too simple and rigid for mine. Nevertheless, we both want some textual and/or graphic representation, which is inevitably also a reduction and simplification, of the teacher's or program's values. By contrast, Wilson (2006) strongly advocates in her book, *Rethinking Rubrics in Writing Assessment*, that we resist pre-emptive representations of our values (like rubrics and maps) so as to approach each act of assessment as free as possible of evaluative baggage and preconceptions, as open as possible to the distinctive experience each text offers us.[3]

> I liked how the absence of predetermined categories allowed me to look for and encourage the incomplete but unique approaches that students were free to attempt without the fear of going against the rubric. (p. 88)

In place of rubrics, maps, and other representations of predetermined rhetorical values, Wilson advocates teachers' intellectual and aesthetic openness, establishing "trust," creating a "writing and response relationship with each of your students" (p. 94), and above all *talking* with students about their writing. The boldness and distinctiveness of Wilson's vision helps highlight how similar White's and my positions on rubrics or maps of rhetorical values actually are.

White's critical remarks in his 2004 book review about the "impracticality" of dynamic criteria mapping helped motivate and focus my co-authors' efforts over the next several years to create the book *Organic Writing Assessment: Dynamic Criteria Mapping in Action* (Broad et al., 2009). The point of this book is to illustrate and explore how and why scholar-administrators at five diverse institutions put dynamic criteria mapping to work and what they discovered in the process. Some of the shared benefits of DCM about which they wrote include:

- Buy-in [to the writing and/or assessment program] by instructors because evaluative criteria came from them,
- Close the loop: [DCM] transforms instruction,
- Broader constituency participating in criteria generation and mapping,
- Broader audience for results: up and down the institutional hierarchy, and
- Facilitating hard [assessment] conversations among faculty and administrators

In 1996, Moss called for colleagues interested in assessment to "enlarge the dialogue in educational measurement" by bringing into our praxis "voices from interpretive research traditions." The discoveries about which we wrote in *Organic Writing Assessment* show that Moss was correct when she predicted great benefits from making our writing assessments more qualitative and less exclusively experimentalist. Furthermore, as Norbert Elliot (2010, December 19) has pointed out, dynamic criteria mapping opens a new chapter in the history of grounded theory research methods. By joining grounded theory with fourth-generation evaluation, DCM transforms the formerly privatized and individualized process of gathering and analyzing data into a democratized process of public, communal inquiry.[4]

Ed White's scholarly career began with his dissertation, "Jane Austen and the Art of Parody" completed in 1960. Over the following decades, he shifted the focus of his research from literature to writing assessment and helped establish that new subdiscipline within English Studies. As I have documented in this chapter, my 1994 dissertation and other early work was built around White's later body of scholarship on writing assessment. Interestingly, my work in dynamic criteria mapping has recently turned toward literature, the sector of English Studies in which White began. With my friend and colleague Michael Theune, I conducted a study of how seven poets, editors, and teachers of poetry judged a dozen contemporary U.S. poems. We used DCM methods to set up, record, and analyze these poets' discussion of how and why they liked or disliked a group of poems they had selected. The result of the study is "How We Evaluate Contemporary Poetry: An Empirical Inquiry" (2010). Theune and I discovered two core models of poetic evaluation (the "development" model and the "immanence" model), and we studied how contextual dynamics (fashion, identity politics, the reader-poet relationship, the body) sometimes transcended and overruled text-based evaluations altogether.

My professional connection to Edward M. White began with his small, memorable act of generosity: inviting my son and me into his talk at Miami University in Autumn 1991. Although I have to a great extent made a career of disagreeing with White about assessment praxis, our dialectic has been imbued with my deep respect for his intellect, rhetorical grace, educational commitments, unapologetic arguments in support of his beliefs, and personal integrity. After nearly 20 years in the profession, I recently stumbled upon a richer awareness of the necessity and importance of his professional project than my early, youthful ventures had allowed me. And so I grow. May the dialectic continue.

ENDNOTES

1. At this moment in my career, and throughout my career, I was (and am) strongly influenced by the work of Peter Elbow on a variety of writing assessment issues—influenced so strongly, in fact, that I was and am not always aware of the extent of Elbow's impact. In Chapter 17, Elbow continues that work in his contribution to this volume, laying out "trying for objectivity" as one of the three most prevalent "traps" in writing assessment.
2. Les Perelman (2010) points out that in some contexts, the struggle for high-quality standardized writing assessment continues. "Large-scale testing of the type mandated by NCLB and Obama's Race to the Top are not the carefully thought out kind of assessments that Ed [White] advocates."

3. In my effort to represent Wilson's views as accurately as possible, I asked her to read a draft of this chapter. During that e-mail conversation, at one point I wrote to her: "I know you know we will always bring values to a reading, that our slate is never blank; in fact, I see that your approach aims to keep those values roaming freely on the veld of our minds so they can gallop up and nibble the branches of whatever the text waves at them." Wilson replied that this "is, really, exactly what I think."
4. In Chapter 14, Leydens and Olds identify similar benefits in their deliberative, exploratory, collegial assessment conversations. See item #1 in their section "Lessons Learned about Our Own Pedagogy."

REFERENCES

Broad, B. (1992, October). *Portfolio scoring: A contradiction in terms*. Paper presented at the Conference on New Directions in Portfolio Assessment, Oxford, OH.

Broad, B. (1994). "Portfolio scoring": A contradiction in terms. In L. Black, D. A. Daiker, J. Sommers, & G. Stygall (Eds.), *New directions in portfolio assessment: Reflective practice, critical theory, and large-scale scoring* (pp. 263-276). Portsmouth, NH: Boynton/Cook-Heinemann.

Broad, B. (1997). Reciprocal authorities in communal writing assessment: Constructing textual value within a "new politics of inquiry." *Assessing Writing, 4*(2), 133-167.

Broad, B. (2000). Pulling your hair out: Crises of standardization in communal writing assessment. *Research in the Teaching of English, 35*(2), 213-260.

Broad, B. (2003). *What we really value: Beyond rubrics in teaching and assessing writing*. Logan, UT: Utah State University Press.

Broad, B., Adler-Kassner, L., Alford, B., Detweiler, J., Estrem, H., Harrington, S., McBride, M., Stalions, E., & Weeden, S. (2009). *Organic writing assessment: Dynamic criteria mapping in action*. Logan, UT: Utah State University Press

Broad, B., & Theune, M. (2010). How we evaluate contemporary poetry: An empirical inquiry. *College English, 73*(2), 113-137.

Elbow, P., & Belanoff, P. (1991). State university of New York at Stony Brook portfolio-based evaluation program. In P. Belanoff & M. Dickson (Eds.), *Portfolios: Process and product* (pp. 3-16). Portsmouth, NH: Boynton/Cook Publishers.

Elliot, N. (2010, December 12). [E-mail to B. Broad]. Normal, IL: Illinois State University.

Elliot, N. (2010, December 19). [E-mail to B. Broad]. Normal, IL: Illinois State University.

Glaser, B., & A. Strauss. (1967). *The discovery of grounded theory: Strategies for qualitative research*. Chicago, IL: Aldine Publishing Company.

Guba, E. G., & Lincoln, Y. (1989). *Fourth generation evaluation*. Newbury Park, CA: Sage.

Huot, B. (1996). Toward a new theory of writing assessment. *College Composition and Communication, 47*(4), 549-66.

Moss, P. (1994). Can there be validity without reliability? *Educational Researcher, 23*(2), 5-12.

Moss, P. (1996). Enlarging the dialogue in educational measurement: Voices from interpretive research traditions. *Educational Researcher, 25*(1), 20-28, 43.

Perelman, L. (2010, December 20). [E-mail to B. Broad]. Normal, IL: Illinois State University.

Sosnoski, J. J. (1989). The psycho-politics of error. *Pre-Text, 10(*1-2), 33-52.

Strauss, A., & J. Corbin. (1994.) Grounded theory methodology: An overview. In N. K. Denzin & Y. Lincoln (Eds.), *Handbook of qualitative research* (pp. 273-285). Thousand Oaks, CA: Sage.

White, E. M. (1960). *Jane Austen and the art of parody. Unpublished doctoral dissertation*. Harvard University, Cambridge, MA.

White, E. M. (1985). *Teaching and assessing writing*. San Francisco, CA: Jossey-Bass.

White, E. M. (2004). Review of *What We Really Value: Beyond Rubrics in Teaching and Assessing Writing*. *Composition Studies, 32*(1), 110-116.

Wilson, M. (2006). *Rethinking rubrics in writing assessment.* Portsmouth, NH: Heinemann.

16

THE GIVEN-NEW CONTRACT
TOWARD A METALANGUAGE FOR ASSESSING COMPOSITION

Lee Odell
Rensselaer Polytechnic Institute

In 2010, writing assessment took a major step forward with the widespread acceptance of a set of *Common Core State Standards* for writing, lists of characteristics one should expect to find in the successful writing of students at a variety of grade levels and range of genres (National Governors Association Center for Best Practices & Council of Chief State Officers, 2010). These standards have informed and will continue to inform a variety of assessment programs. But just as we have developed these national standards for writing, it is becoming clear that creating print texts is only one component of the composing ability students will need in order to communicate effectively, whether in school, in their communities, in their careers, or in their personal lives. Indeed, more and more students are moving into online composing, using, for instance, Weblogs to connect with peers around the world; wikis to collaborate on projects; and websites, videos, and social networking sites to integrate visual, oral, aural, and written information (Council of Writing Program Administrators, National Council of Teachers of English, & National Writing Project, 2011). For teachers and students, these developments present exciting opportunities, opening as they do a rich array of communication resources that go well beyond what is possible on a printed page.

But these new resources also represent challenges, for both teaching and assessment. Even the most technologically savvy teachers will struggle to find some way to incorporate, say, digital narratives into an already full writing curriculum. (For further discussion of digital narratives, see Hawisher, 2004; or Wei & Wei, 2006.) And teachers and assessment specialists alike will have to find some way to assess texts that simply do not resemble conventional print texts. The problem here is that we have an embarrassment of riches. Assume, for example, we just want to understand visual literacy as it is manifested in images in a print text. One excellent introduction to relevant terms and concepts appears in Dondis's (1973) *A Primer of Visual Literacy*, where she identifies nine "basic elements of visual communication": dot, line, shape, direction, tone, color, texture, scale, and movement (pp. 40-66). Dondis complements this list in discussions of representation, symbolism, and abstraction (pp. 67-84), each of which may interact in complex ways. And she adds three different types of contrast: in tone, color, and shape (pp. 85-103).

To Dondis's list of 15 items we can add terminology from the work of visual semioticians Gunther Kress and Theo van Leeuwen, who explain gaze, vertical/horizontal axis, vector, angle, and depth of field (Kress & van Leeuwen, 1996) and graphic designer Molly Bang, who explains the use of background/foreground, color, relative positions of elements in a scene, shape (curved, horizontal, jagged, diagonal, vertical), direction of movement, pictorial weight, frame, and picture world (Bang, 2000). We now have 28 concepts that should let us talk helpfully about any visual image. But if we want to discuss page layout, typography, charts and graphs, or "film grammar," we could easily double this list and still have relatively little useful to say about the substance, organization, or tone of a print text.

With print texts, assessment is somewhat easier, thanks in part to widespread use of large-scale assessment rubrics and in part to the excellent synthesis of standards found in the *Common Core State Standards* for writing. Yet even here, we run into complexity. As is clear in the Common Core and in the *WPA Outcomes Statement for First Year Composition* (see Harrington, Overman, Fischer, & Malenczyk, 2005; Roen, Glau, Behm, & White (in press), writing is not some monolithic entity. Its features can vary by genre and academic discipline; so much so that our discipline runs the risk of fragmentation (see Hundleby, Chapter 6). It is possible but not highly probable, for example, that an excellent personal experience narrative will need to address and refute counter-claims in writing, but there is a great chance that this sort of refutation will be needed in persuasive writing; similarly, narrative in laboratory reports will differ substantially from narrative in memoir. The complexity is only heightened when, as the WPA Outcomes statement suggests, students integrate the full range of oral and visual elements made accessible by digital technology (Council of Writing Program Administrators, 2000, 2008; see Maid and D'Angelo, Chapter 5, for further discussion of the Outcomes). Consequently, the rubric we use in assessing a text in a given rhetorical and technological context may differ in significant ways from rubrics we use in assessing work in other contexts.

For purposes of teaching and assessing composition in all the diverse forms it can now take, we will have to learn some of the terminology of visual communication as well as that found in the *Common Core State Standards*. But we will also need a way to make sense of all this diversity, a metalanguage that will let us find elements of similarity among different types of composition without oversimplifying or ignoring significant differences. And this is where the "given-new contract" comes in. Later in this chapter, I show how this contract operates in three very different types of composition: a report, a profile, and a proposal. The first two are written texts that incorporate some visual images; the third takes the form of a digital narrative. But before doing this, I need to establish criteria that a metalanguage must meet.

CRITERIA FOR A METALANGUAGE

In response to the increasing complexity of the construct *composition*, Macken-Horarick (2009) has called for a metalanguage, one that can guide the teaching and assessment of the full range of communicative activity that constitutes literate behavior. This framework must, as Macken-Horarick points out, find commonalities between digital and print literacy, but must not "flatten out" essential differences between them. It must also be "diverse, flexible, and synthetic" (Nelson, Hull, & Roche-Smith, 2008, p. 418). That is, it must draw upon current work in both visual and verbal communication, and it must apply to a variety of compositions ranging from traditional essayist literacy (Farr, 1993) to blogs, digital narratives, and social networking sites. Finally, because the goal is to improve students' literacy, the metalanguage must be pedagogically useful. In part, this means that the metalanguage must be economical, consisting of a relatively small number of terms that teachers can easily keep in mind while working with a wide variety of print and multimodal compositions. Further, it must have descriptive power, enabling students and teachers to recognize successful practice, whether in student or in professional communication. And it must also have generative power, helping writers and readers formulate and articulate their ideas, feelings, reactions, and insights.

Several sources, either explicitly or implicitly, suggest ways to develop a metalanguage. Some draw specifically on theory and research in written composition, noting similarities between print and multimodal composition. Greenhow and Robelia (2009) found that in constructing a social networking site, a small group of students they worked with engaged in making decisions about "word choice, tone, subject matter and style—all elements of formalized writing valued in school" (p. 1151). Similarly, Borton and Huot (2007) draw on familiar terminology from assessment of written work when they propose that multimodal compositions be assessed, in part, for their elaboration, by which they mean "detailed description, examples, sound, music, color, and/or word choice to convey ideas in an effective and appropriate way to the audience" (p. 101). One problem with this approach is suggested by Kostelnick and Hassett (2003): "analogies between the visual and the verbal are necessarily limited because the two differ in their form, syntax, and origin as well as the ways in which readers perceive and interpret them" (p. 1). Kress and van Leeuwen (1966) make a similar point: "the differences [between the media] are greater than the similarities" because "the visual semiotic has a range of structural devices which have no equivalent in language" (p. 115). Further, the terminology from Greenhow and Robelia (2009) and Borton and Huot (2007) has little generative power. How does one go about exploring a topic so as to describe it effectively? How does one decide whether a particular word or detail has been chosen appropriately?

Other approaches derive from rhetoric. Porter (2009) argues that in both print and multimodal literacies, students have to attend to the traditional rhetorical art of delivery. Sorapure (2006) shows how both print and digital compositions make use of metaphor and metonymy. And Keller (2007) argues that the rhetorical principles of ethos, pathos, and logos apply equally to digital and print compositions. The first two of these approaches are, in very different ways, too limited. Although Porter is careful to avoid flattening out differences between multimodal and print composition, he acknowledges that delivery is just one of the five arts of rhetoric, which also include invention, memory, style, and arrangement or organization. Sorapure's approach has epistemic and descriptive value, but metonymy and metaphor are only part of the conceptual apparatus one might bring to bear on formulating and expressing one's ideas.

THE GIVEN-NEW CONTRACT

For a more useful and broadly based metalanguage, we can turn to work in syntax, reading, and visual semiotics. All these fields make one basic assumption: In order to understand and accept new information, we have to relate it to some sort of given—information we have previously gathered, current or prior experiences, values, questions, needs—all the intellectual, emotional, experiential stuff that comprises our image of ourselves, others, and the world. In their discussion of syntax, Williams and Columb (2010) show how sentences in cohesive text tend to begin with given (they use the term *old*) information that has been established in previous sentences (or that already exists in a reader's mind) and conclude with new information. In her review of research on reading, Redish (1993) demonstrates the importance of connecting new information to readers' "prior knowledge and expectations" (p. 28). And semioticians Kress and van Leeuwen (1996) have shown how visual images communicate by integrating given or familiar information with new. In all cases, these scholars agree that communication is most likely to succeed when a writer (speaker, blogger, website designer, videographer) establishes common ground (i.e., givens) to which an audience can relate new information. This new information may challenge, expand upon, or provide additional confirmation of something an audience is already inclined to believe. (For further information on the given-new contract as well as other possible components of a metalanguage, see Odell & Katz, 2009.)

In this chapter, I show how the given-new contract helps describe and assess several different kinds of student compositions. After that I conclude by briefly suggesting ways this contract can guide the process of composing. For purposes of both teaching and assessment, I assume that the given-new contract is most useful—and most fairly applied—when both teacher and student share explicit assumptions about the givens a particular audience is likely to bring to a composition. To formulate these assumptions, I ask students to interview someone who typifies the larger group of readers they hope to reach. Thus, each discussion of student work begins with students' analysis of their audience.

Report: "Artificial Sweeteners"

In a report written for a Science Writing class, undergraduates Jenna Gatsch and Michelle Pelersi set out to show their audience that a familiar practice, using artificial sweeteners, has at least the potential to pose a significant health threat. And they need to do so in a way that is not alarmist or unfair. Their audience analysis stipulates that their audience, epitomized by Jenna's mother, "vaguely remembers the controversy over the safety of saccharin in the 1970s, but she has never heard anything negative about Splenda. ... When she heard that Splenda may not be as safe as she assumed, she became very interested in the long-term effects of using the product and whether or not there may be any potential side effects in the future." Specifically, she expressed concern about the following questions. "Is it safe? Is there a limit as to the amount one should consume? Are there any potential side effects? Are there any natural alternatives?" With these givens in mind, we can now look at the opening section of Jenna and Michelle's report.

Artificial Sweeteners
Maybe No So Sweet After All
By Jenna Gatsch and Michelle Pelersi

"Like many people, Dr. Janet Starr Hull had been using aspartame for many years to cut calories out of her diet. However, in 1991, she was diagnosed with incurable Graves disease, an autoimmune disorder that involves hyperactivity of the thyroid gland, resulting in weight loss, increased appetite, eye irritation, and restlessness, among other symptoms. After doing some research, Dr. Hull realized that her condition was caused by aspartame poisoning (Total Health). She now dedicates much of her time educating others on what she sees as the dangers of using aspartame.

This is only one of many instances in which artificial sweeteners may have caused serious disorders, even death. Aspartame is not the only target of these claims; saccharin and sucralose have both been targeted as well. Several studies have shown links between these sweeteners and cancer, liver inflammation, calcification of the kidneys, and many other side effects, both minor and serious. However, the companies manufacturing these sweeteners as well as the FDA continue to maintain that these products are safe. Numerous tests have been performed on each sweetener and no test has conclusively proven any unsafe consequences in humans using these products. The question, therefore, is whether to believe the government testing or the people who have suffered effects that they claim were from the sweeteners. If you are one of the millions of people who assume that these products are safe simply because they are on the market, hopefully this article will give you more information on which to base your decision of whether or not to use artificial sweeteners."

One way Jenna and Michelle move from given to new in this passage is to invoke some of the givens their audience brings to the topic. They mention a topic they know the audience cares about and pose a subtitle that implies a question or difficulty directly related to a concern their audience has, possible harmful effects of the familiar practice of using an artificial sweetener. They include an image (the packets of sweetener) their audience will recognize, and they use a color from that image in the title of their article. Jenna and Michelle go on to create another given in the form of a scenario involving someone (a doctor) who had done something the audience has done (used artificial sweeteners) and who is likely to have a good bit of credibility with the audience. And in creating this scenario they rely on a discourse convention their audience has likely encountered in popular print media reports on technical or abstract subjects: A technical subject is introduced and dramatized by the experience of a single individual and then is related to a more general trend or problem, in this case the safety of artificial sweeteners.

The movement from given to new recurs through the remainder of the article. Consider, for example, the beginning of the section that immediately follows the introduction.

> **Aspartame**
>
> Although FDA approved and found in over 5000 products on the market, there has been much debate about the safety of aspartame, a no calorie sweetener sold under the commercial names of NutraSweet and Equal. The FDA denied approval for eight years, and when it did finally get approved, three out of five FDA scientists on special commissions advised against using aspartame (The Ecologist, Sept.). The additive was formally listed as a biochemical warfare agent by the Pentagon and the FDA scientists did not believe the test results adequately proved the safety of aspartame.
>
> Most consumers are not concerned with the safety of aspartame because the FDA approved the substance. 40 percent of the children population and 66 percent of the adult population consume aspartame on a regular basis (The Ecologist, Sept.). Scientists, however, have always been wary. Numerous independent studies have been performed producing many undesirable results, including headaches, memory loss, seizures, mood swings, Parkinson's-like symptoms, tumors, and in rare cases, death (The Ecologist, Sept.). The most recent studies demonstrate a possible link between aspartame and leukemia and lymphoma. Other studies have shown that aspartame can have a negative effect on nerve cell development thus affecting the brain and overall development (The Ecologist, Feb.)

The basic movement here is from the questions—part of the givens the audience brings to the topic—to answers that constitute new information. Is Aspartame safe? Well, the FDA was reluctant to give approval; three of five FDA scientists were reluctant to approve; and, oh yes, the Pentagon listed Aspartame as a "biochemical warfare agent." Are there side effects? Yes, as a matter of fact: "headaches, memory loss, seizures, mood swings, Parkinson's-like symptoms, tumors, and in rare cases, death."

This movement from given to new recurs throughout the report, not just in the strategy of answering the audience's basic questions but also in ways Jenna and Michelle structure and sequence sentences so that they move from given information to new; that is, each sentence moves from a given (facts the audience might be expected to know or topics that have been previously introduced in the text) to some new information that builds on or challenges the given. Here is how this process works out in a section that addresses the audience's concern about the amount of sweetener one may safely consume.

How much is too much?

Just as the FDA has guidelines on how much medicine it is safe to take over a period of time, they also have guidelines on how much of an artificial sweetener it is acceptable to consume. They cite what they term an "acceptable daily intake" for each of the artificial additives, and they believe that the artificial sweeteners are safe when used in those specified amounts. The safe amount cited for Splenda and saccharin is just 5 mg/kg of body weight. For a 135 pound person, this comes out to just 0.3 grams of the product per day as suggested by the FDA as safe for consumption. Unfortunately, this is much less than what people normally do consume. One packet of Splenda or Sweet n' Low contains 1 gram, and many consumers use far more than one packet per day. Aspartame, however, is safe in much greater amounts—50 mg/kg of body weight per day (Harvard Women's Health Watch p.2). This would allow 3 grams of aspartame to be safely consumed by a 135 pound person daily with presumably no ill effects. However, for saccharin and sucralose, what the FDA is claiming to be the safe amount of the sweetener to consume per day is very different than what people actually do consume. What are the effects of consuming more than what is considered safe? If long-term effects of exceeding the safe limit of consumption exist, they are not yet known.

The first sentence begins with information the audience presumably knows—the FDA issues guidelines on amounts of medication people should take and ends with new information, about a familiar practice (issuing guidelines) appearing in a new context—assessing artificial sweeteners. With *artificial sweeteners* established as the topic, that is, as a given, the second and third sentences go on to provide new information about that topic—that the FDA has identified a "safe" level of "acceptable daily intake." By the fourth sentence, *safety* has been established as a given, so it appears at the beginning of that sentence ("The safe amount"), and the remainder of the sentence provides new information in the form of details about safe levels for Splenda and Saccharin. This fourth sentence goes on to introduce a new topic, *body weight*, which in the fifth sentence becomes a given about which that sentence provides further new information: "For a 135 pound person, this comes out to just 0.3 grams of the product per day."

This careful movement from given to new goes on throughout the report, enabling a somewhat cautious audience to trust the concluding sentence of the report: "Therefore, the main conclusion that can be drawn from all of these studies is that as long as these products are used in minimal amounts, such as those recommended by the FDA, there is little chance of suffering any negative consequence."

Profile: "Behind a Plain White Lab Coat"

In a profile titled "Behind a Plain White Lab Coat," undergraduate Stephanie Guzik sets out to introduce her readers to another undergraduate, Diane Turcotte, who sounds almost too good to be true. Diane is a lab assistant and an outstanding member of an undergraduate research team; as a senior, she is taking an extremely demanding course load at a time when other seniors might be inclined to slack off a bit; she's an active member of a sorority and three campus service organizations; and she typically goes home for dinner with her parents before going back to her lab to work much of the night. Diane is, as one of her sorority sisters puts it, "just your average, run-of-the-mill amazing person."

As her primary audience for this profile, Stephanie has chosen students at a university where large numbers of students are majoring in science or engineering. All the students at this school will have spent a fair amount of time in laboratories, if only in introductory science courses, and they are unlikely to be thrown by technical terms, even though they might not know their precise definition. Members of this audience understand how difficult it can be just to meet the basic academic demands of their courses, especially if they want to have some sort of life outside the classroom. In fact, there is a good chance that some students may assume that it is impossible to do both. It is also likely that either they are involved, or have friends who are involved, in out of class research projects. Given all this, it is fair to say that her readers may be skeptical of any account of students who seem too good to be true. And it is also fair to say that many of her readers will not know Diane. So Stephanie will have to bring readers along carefully, providing information most of the audience will not have and overcoming a possible element of skepticism. She does this in the various ways she moves her audience from given to new.

Some of the givens are comprised by experiences and assumptions her readers bring to her profile. Consider, for example, the beginning of Stephanie's profile.

> After an exhausting day of classes one Monday afternoon early in the semester, I decided to walk across campus to the cell culture lab to feed my fibroblast cells. As I lazily walked up the three flights of stairs to the biology floor and wandered slowly into the room 309, I saw Diane Turcotte's smiling face peer up from her computer screen. According to our instructor, George, Diane was the pride of our Cancer Cell Group. He often told me, "You could learn a lot from this girl. She's a wonderful, dedicated member of this group," and I always had to hold back from asking, "What could this senior teach me that you couldn't?" I always seemed to run into Diane whenever I went to the lab; in fact, it often made me wonder if she ever left.

Much of this will be very familiar to her readers. They have almost certainly experienced semesters in which some days will be completely filled with classes and lab work; they understand lab hierarchy—instructor, lab assistant, student researcher, with the instructor as the usual source of authoritative information. And even if they have never heard the phrase story grammar, the phrase "after an exhausting day" should help cue them to expect a set of conventions that identify a text as narrative: setting, actors, dialog, and some sort of conflict. By the end of just this first paragraph, the conventions of narrative discourse make it a given that Stephanie will encounter some sort of problem and that one of the characters she mentions will help (or hinder) the process of solving the problem and reveal in doing so reveal something of his or her personal qualities. This process also will allow Stephanie to move readers from given to new. The familiar, authoritative voice of the instructor makes an unlikely comment ("You could learn a lot from that girl") that allows Stephanie to introduce one of the questions that animate the rest of the profile: What could a student lab assistant teach that the instructor couldn't?

In addition to the givens with which her readers might be expected to approach her profile, Stephanie brings readers along carefully, filling in a narrative sequence that gradually reveals Diane's character. In the first paragraph, Stephanie gives readers only a glimpse of Diane as she briefly looks up from her computer. In the next several paragraphs, Stephanie sequences information so that readers can follow her growing appreciation of Diane. On a subsequent afternoon,

> ...Diane was waiting for the components of a reagent solution to dissolve in a beaker of distilled water and writing a paper for one of her classes in the meantime. "Hey, Steph," she called out cheerfully. "How was your day?" I looked at her, feeling somewhat dazed, and replied, "How in the world can you be so extremely perky after classes on a Monday?" She just smiled and went back to her paper...

After setting up her lab, Stephanie gets down to work and, as story grammar would lead one to expect, discovers a problem.

> I took my two large culture flasks off the second shelf and looked at them under the microscope. One appeared very clear, with a good growth of cells, while the other had black blotches floating in the bright orange growth medium. I wasn't sure what to do, but I fed my cells anyway, cleaned up the lab, and left, saying goodbye to a still perky Diane.

A couple days later, Stephanie repeats her afternoon routine. This time, Diane greets her ("Is today any better?") and receives a grudging admission from Stephanie ("Well, it's not a Monday; we'll put it that way."). And, of course, things in the lab are not better:

> I took out both of my cultures and saw that one was bright yellow and the other was cloudy orange, which meant that I had killed all the cells I had been growing for almost three weeks. I closed the incubator, took off my plain white lab coat, and went back into room 309 with both my flasks.

At this point, Stephanie goes back to the room where Diane is working.

> Diane was hunched over her gel, waiting patiently for the proteins to be pulled to the bottom by the current running through the apparatus. She saw me as I walked in, somewhat frustrated. I quietly asked, "Does this happen to you?" Diane took one look at the flasks I held outstretched and understood. She smiled and replied, "Actually, this is perfect timing. I've been growing roller bottles of cells for about a month now and had finally gotten a culture to grow, but today I came I and they had all 'jumped off.' So today I get to start all over too. [Diane closed down her experiment and] walked past me into the sterile lab. I put down my contaminated flasks long enough to put on my lab coat again. Still frustrated, I squirted bleach into my two flasks to kill off all the bacteria and remaining cells, while Diane washed her hands and put on her plain white lab coat. We sat there together in that lab, passaging new cells from one flask into another for a little under an hour. I began to understand what our instructor had been talking about.

In Stephanie's first reference to Diane, she is simply "a smiling face" that looks up from a computer. Subsequently, Stephanie notes that Diane is solicitous ("Is today any better [than the previous Monday]?"), then empathetic (acknowledging a similar problem she had with her own experiments), then extremely helpful (taking almost an hour from her own work to help Stephanie start her own experiment all over again). As Stephanie leads readers through this narrative, she prepares them to appreciate the way this section of the profile ends: "I began to understand what our instructor had been talking about."

Throughout this narrative, Stephanie establishes one other important given—her identity as someone readers can relate to. She has the same frustrations her readers have—occasional long days of class work followed by a frustrating time in a lab. She is initially skeptical about the instructor's assessment of Diane. Like most other undergraduates at her university, she has to struggle to maintain some sort of social life: "I simply go to class, go to the lab, go back to my dorm, and occasionally go out with my friends."

Diane, by contrast, not only serves as lab assistant but also has a full family and social life. After describing this life in some detail, Stephanie poses some skeptical questions that surely must occur to her audience as they come to the end of her profile.

> "So what about sleep? Do you ever sleep?" Diane just smiled like she always does, and said. "Of course I sleep. It's not always as much as I'd like. And it's not as much as some of the other students on campus, but I get my rest. Sometimes I'm in the lab for anywhere from 5 to 24 hours in a day doing protocols, so when it's a busy night I get anywhere from no sleep to 3 hours. On nights when I'm not quite so busy, I get around 6 hours. It's not so bad once you get used to it." *No sleep? Who does that?*

An indirect answer comes in a bit of dialogue from the end of an extended laboratory session.

> As I put my bag on my back, Diane said with a smile, "Are you going out tomorrow night?" This time I smiled back. "I know a couple of [sorority] sisters are going out and Vanessa and I definitely are. Would you like to come with us?" As always, Diane smiled, looked at her gel, and said, "If all goes well with this thing, I'm with you. Just let me know what time."
>
> "Of course," I said, and turned to walk out the door. "Have a good night," I added. As I walked out the door, I heard Diane say, "You too. Don't forget there's a whole different place outside that door. Take advantage of it while you can."

Given all we have learned about Diane, it is easy enough to appreciate the way Stephanie concludes the profile.

> I smiled and slowly walked out of room 309, down the hallway, and down the stairs in a better mood than I had been at any other time during the past few weeks. I felt inspired, still touched by my conversation with the amazing woman I had discovered hidden behind a plain white lab coat.

Proposal: "Once Upon a Time"

In presenting the two first pieces of student work, I could simply rely on the formal title students had given their work. But the following proposal, in the form of a digital narrative, has no such title. It simply begins with the childhood fairy tale convention, "Once upon a time." As I show below, this rather incongruous beginning allows a team of three students, Tanya Kantor, Vanessa Maestas, and Pete Schirmer, to take a whimsical approach to a fairly serious problem, an ugly and unsafe set of steps, one of two "approaches" students may have to take when they come to campus from a couple of nearby neighborhoods.

For their audience, Tanya, Vanessa, and Pete chose members of a university class, Professional Development 2 (PD 2), in which students were obliged to undertake a community service project. In talking with some of these students, they realized that PD2 students were willing to work on a project that would have some real social value but would also be manageable, given demands on their time. Generally, these PD2 students were aware that there was a problem with a stairway (an "approach") leading up to campus, but they did not use the approach themselves. The authors of the proposal knew that their audience was likely to appreciate a humorous presentation, one that did not take itself too seriously but rather displayed a mildly irreverent sense of incongruity. From discussions with members of their audience, these authors also learned that their audience was likely to want answers to such questions as the following. Exactly how bad is the situation? How are students affected by the problem? What kinds of expertise would the project require? Is it likely that they could do the project without having to learn a new set of specialized construction skills?

The goal of the first 2+ minutes of this video is to bring the audience from a given, an initial state in which they recognize the need to undertake some sort of community project, to a new, a point where they might be willing to undertake this specific project. In part, creators of this video do this the same way Jenna and Michelle do: They address a couple of the questions they know the audience will want to have answered: Exactly how bad is the situation? How are students affected by the problem?

In order to do this, the video team has to establish or invoke several givens, two of which are their voice as authors of the video and the voices of those who present information in the video. They have to walk a careful line here. Although they have a problem that needs to be taken care of, they know their audience will not respond well to a tone of melodrama or excessive earnestness. Thus they begin their video by establishing a mildly self-deprecating ironic voice that is aware of incongruity and willing to deal with a serious problem without taking itself seriously. To do this, they rely on their audience approaching their video with some preexisting givens—an awareness of certain discourse conventions of both print and video, as well as a familiarity with pop music.

The initial frames of the video echo a familiar convention of fairy tales: Once upon a time something lovely existed, but the idyllic situation is intruded upon and threatened by some hostile, evil person or force. As is often the case in film or video, this transition is accompanied by music (e.g., the *William Tell Overture*) that echoes the change from tranquility to conflict. But in order to establish an effective voice, these students play with the conventions a bit.

Once upon a time...

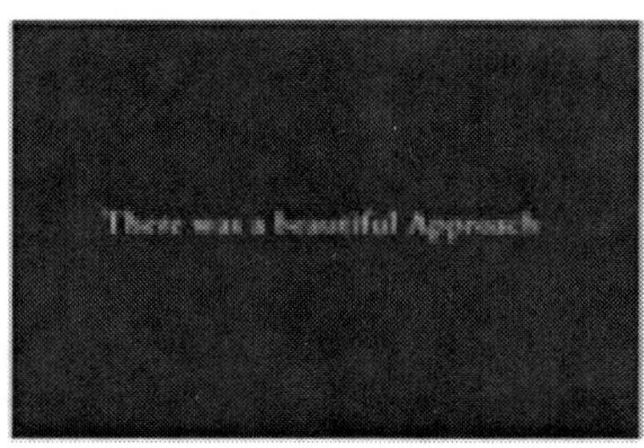

There was a beautiful Approach

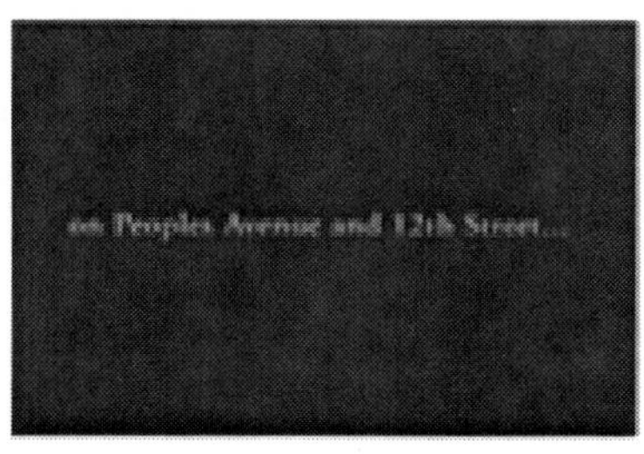

on Peoples Avenue and 12th Street

But now...

not so beautiful

In this case, the beauty that existed once upon a time is not, for example, a lovely princess but a literally and figuratively pedestrian and unattractive piece of campus architecture—a series of steps leading up a hill to the campus. And the music that swells to a climax with the frame "not so beautiful" is not some classical piece but rather the opening of Michael Jackson's song "Thriller." Thus in the first 13 seconds of the video, the students establish themselves as a given, a voice students can relate to and possibly trust.

Having established a voice that might create a rapport with their audience, the students continue to move from given to new in several interrelated ways. For one thing, they draw upon sources of information their audience should be able to relate to. They rely heavily on the testimony of people their audience can recognize and identify with—other students who in their appearance and settings (typical looking rooms one might find in any off-campus apartment) closely resemble their intended audience.

They present these students following another familiar convention of video reporting, using quick cuts from image to image. These cuts occur in three sequences, all intended to establish the credibility of the people depicted and then to establish the severity of the problem. In the first sequence, each of the students appears just long enough to give an address that the PD2 students will recognize as being close to the approach in question.

Then these same people reappear, again speaking just long enough to show that they are really familiar with the approach. Finally, each of these speakers appears one more time; in this sequence each picture of a student (by now established as a given, a credible source of information) is accompanied by new information, claims about the deplorable condition of the stairs, in most cases accompanied by images of the steps that illustrate the claims they make. These images move from the reasonably predictable (broken concrete, pockets of ice and snow on the steps) to the very unpredictable and more serious: a bee infestation and the appearance of water that might be sewage.

"The stairs are all crumbling..."

"Often stones are in the way from broken steps."

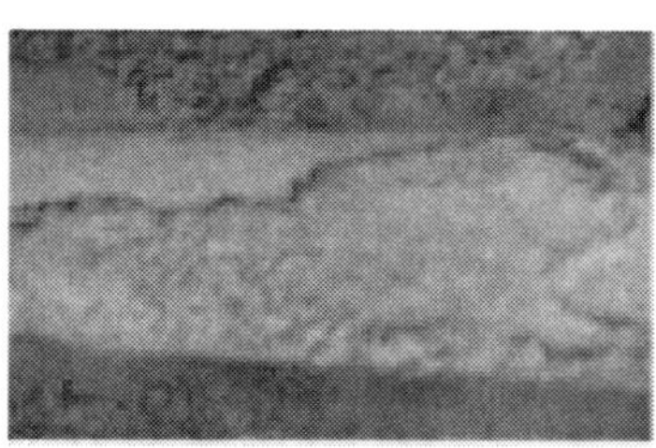

"During the winter it's really awful. The cracks get filled with ice and snow."

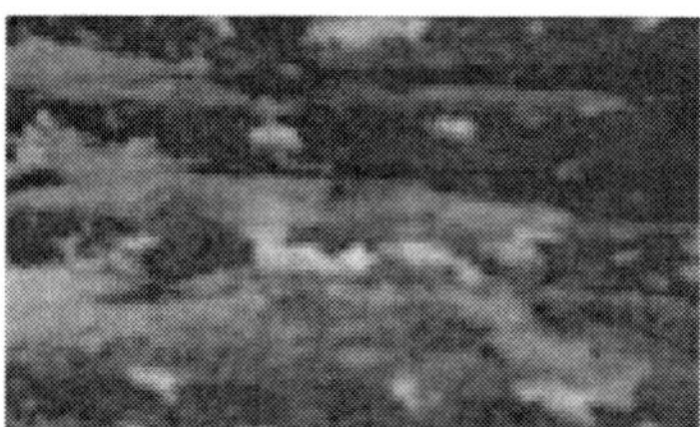

"And there was like a bee infestation in the concrete last summer. Also, some of the cracks leak. It's always wet. I don't know what it is, but sometimes it smells like sewage."

Having established the problem by drawing on one credible source of information, students who are affected by the condition of the steps, the video group turns to a different source of information for the solution. The man depicted in the images below is not explicitly identified, but his clothing (casual but not dirty or shabby work clothes), gray hair, and Internet business address suggest someone experienced in doing practical chores. He illustrates the steps in the solution with an economy that suggests the solution might be within the ability of the intended audience for the video. And as this worker carries out each step of the solution, the video also presents written information that should answer questions that arise while the audience is watching the video. What kind of drill do we get? A hammer drill. Where/how can we get hold of one? At the Home Depot. Exactly what materials will we need and how much will they cost? Lag bolts, cement adhesive, quick setting cement, a trowel. What's a lag bolt? Look at the picture. Exactly what do we do, how do we do it and when? Again, follow the pictures. Each bit of new information gives rise to a question, which in turn becomes a given that prompts still more new information.

Hammer Drills

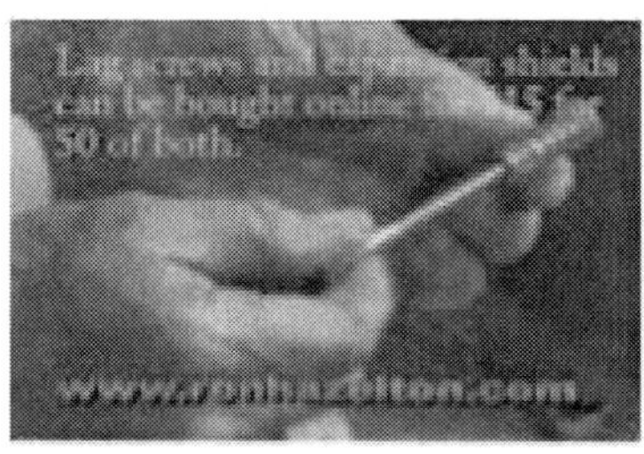

Lag screws

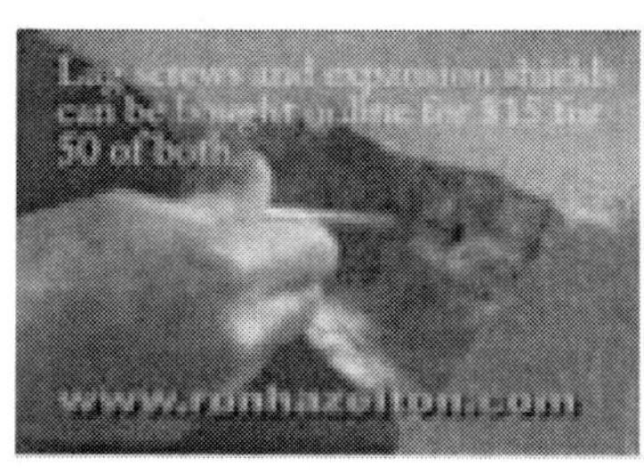

Quikrete Bonding Adhesive

Quikrete Setting Cement

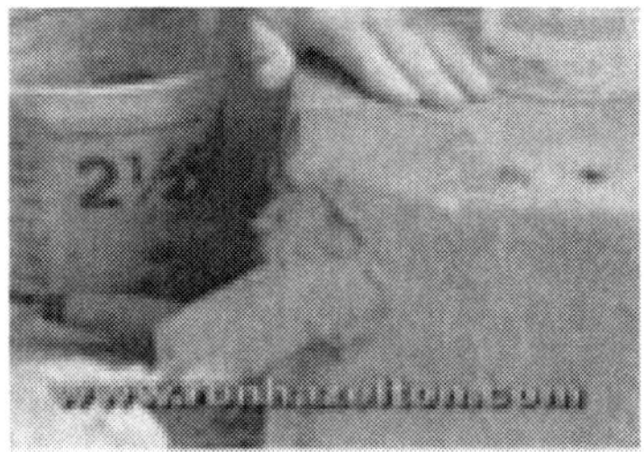

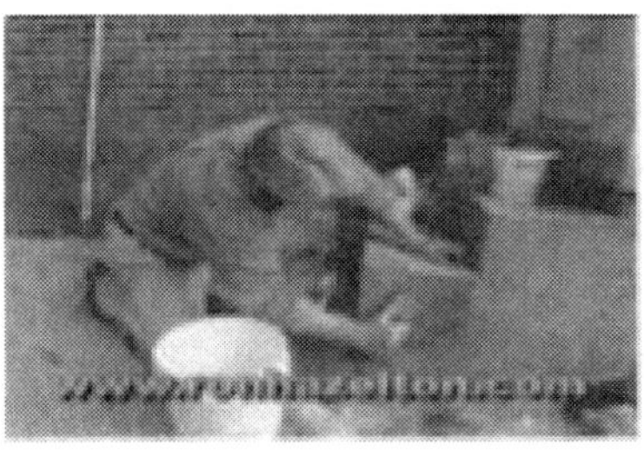

Quikrete setting cement

Having demonstrated the feasibility of their solution, the video group addresses one final question: How will doing this project benefit the PD 2 students?

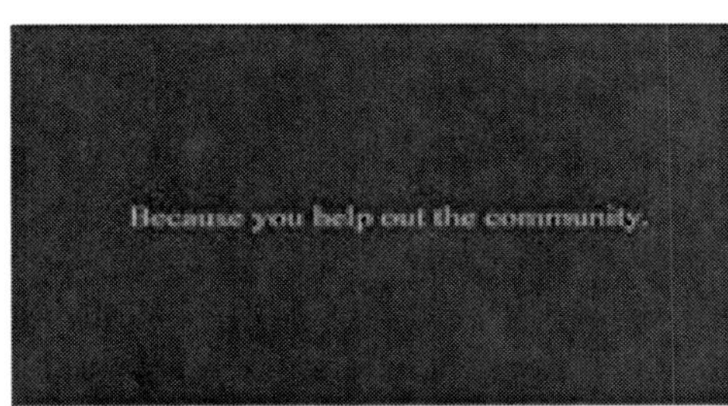

They first make a principled claim: "Because you can help out your community."

Then they make a more pragmatic claim: "And you can get a great grade on your PD 2 project!"

With this claim, some of the initial humorously incongruous voice comes back into play. The image of a graded paper is accompanied by some of the triumphal music from *Rocky*. And this voice is heightened by the final two images of the video, still accompanied by the music from *Rocky*.

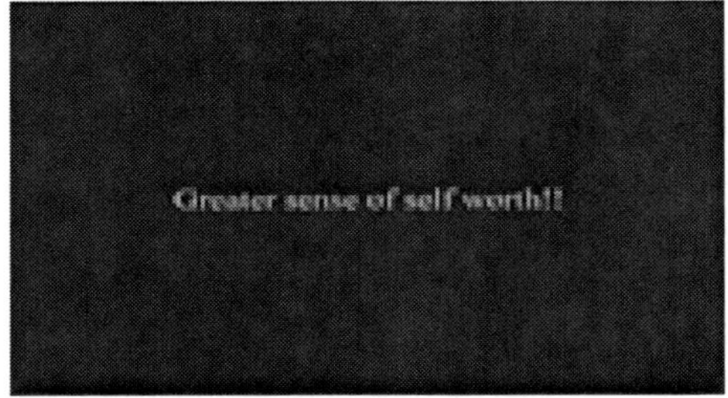

"Greater sense of self-worth"

CRITERIA ONCE AGAIN

I hope the preceding analyses of student work illustrate why I think the given-new contract meets three of the criteria I introduced earlier: It is a synthesis of work in disciplines that relate directly to effective communication; it has descriptive power, helping both student and teacher to identify features that make a particular text effective; and it provides a common frame of reference for different genres and media without flattening out differences, trying to fit these media into a mold that is applicable to only one medium. Now the final criterion has to do with generative power.

There are, unquestionably, limits to what we can know of the creative process and to how much we can help anyone discover and articulate what he or she wants to communicate, whether the medium is language, music, image, or sound. And, *pace* Peter Elbow, there are times when we do not consciously attend to audience. But there is something inherently generative about trying to enter into the world of an audience, considering such issues as the following. What questions am I (or someone else) trying to answer?

Do they seem like questions the audience is likely to want or need to have answered? Have I/has the author brought the audience along, invoking or establishing givens that will help the audience understand the new information to be presented? And what basis do we have for thinking that a particular idea or fact or attitude is actually new to that audience? In my own writing, in my teaching, and in my assessment of student work these questions are very likely to prompt a new understanding of what one wants to say and how one might go about saying it. As I indicated earlier, the *given-new contract* will not be the only item in a meta-lexicon. But if I had to go with just one, this would be it.

REFERENCES

Bang, M. (2000). *Picture this: How pictures work*. New York, NY: SeaStar Books.

Borton, S. C., & Huot, B. (2007). Responding and assessing. In C. Selfe (Ed.), *Multimodal composition: Resources for teachers* (pp. 99-111). Cresskill, NJ: Hampton Press.

Council of Writing Program Administrators (2000, 2008). *WPA Outcomes Statement for First-Year Composition*. Web.

Council of Writing Program Administrators, National Council of Teachers of English, & National Writing Project. (2011). *Framework for success in postsecondary writing*. Web.

Dondis, D. A. (1973). *A primer of visual literacy*. Cambridge, MA: The MIT Press.

Farr, M. (1993). Essayist literacy and other verbal performances. *Written Communication, 10*(1), 4-38.

Greenhow, C., & Robelia, B. (2009). Old communication, new literacies: Social network sites as social learning resources. *Journal of Computer-Mediated Communication, 14*(4), 1130-1161. Web.

Harrington, K. R., Overman, R., Fischer, R., & Malenczyk, R. (Eds.). (2005). *The outcomes book. Debate and consensus after the WPA Outcomes Statement.* Logan, UT: Utah State University Press.

Hawisher, G. E. (2004). Becoming literate in the information age. College *Composition and Communication, 55*(4), 642-692.

Keller, D. (2007). Thinking rhetorically. In C. Selfe (Ed.), *Multimodal composition: Resources for teachers* (pp. 49-63). Cresskill NJ: Hampton Press.

Kostelnick, C., & Hassett, M. (2003). *Shaping information: The rhetoric of visual conventions.* Carbondale, IL: Southern Illinois University Press.

Kress, G., and van Leeuwen, T. (1996). *Reading images: The grammar of visual design.* New York, NY: Routledge.

Macken-Horarik, M. (2009). Navigational metalanguages for new territory in English: The potential of grammatics. *English Teaching: Practice and Critique, 8*(3), 55-69. Web.

National Governors Association Center for Best Practices & Council of Chief State Officers. (2010). *Reaching higher: The Common Core State Standards validation committee.* Washington, DC: National Governors Association. Web.

Nelson, M. E., Hull, G. A., & Roche-Smith, J. (2008). Challenges of multimedia communication. *Written Communication, 25*(4), 415-440. Web.

Odell, L., & Katz, S. M. (2009) "Yes a t-shirt!": Assessing visual composition in a "writing" class. *The Extended College Composition and Communication*, W197-W216. Web.

Porter, J. E. (2009). Recovering delivery for digital rhetoric. *Computers and Composition, 26*(4), 207-224. Web.

Redish, J. C. (1993). Understanding readers. In C. M. Barnum & S. Carliner (Eds.), *Techniques for technical communicators* (pp. 14-41). Boston, MA: Allyn and Bacon.

Roen, D., Glau, G., Behm, N., & White, E. (Eds.). (in press). *The WPA Outcomes Statement: A decade later.* West Lafayette, IN: Parlor Press.

Sorapure, M. (2006). Between modes: Assessing student new media compositions. *Kairos, 10*(2). Web.

Watkins, S. C. (2009). *The young and the digital.* Boston, MA: Beacon Press.

Wei, S. L., & Wei, H. (2006). Uncovering hidden maps: Illustrative narratology for digital artists/designers. *Computers and Composition: An International Journal for Teachers of Writing, 23*(4), 480-502.

Williams, J. M., & Columb, G. G. (2010). *Style: Lessons in clarity and grace* (10th ed.). Boston, MA: Longman.

III

CONSEQUENCE IN CONTEMPORARY WRITING ASSESSMENT

EMW Reflection: As part of the founding faculty of Cal State, San Bernardino, I wound up with a large office with a window in the library building. I filled the walls with shelves and filled the shelves with books. As English department chair for the first nine years of the university, I helped build a fine department, one I remain proud of to this day.

III

CONSEQUENCE IN CONTEMPORARY WRITING ASSESSMENT

IMPACT AS ARBITER

To identify the social consequences of testing, Samuel Messick of the Educational Testing Service proposed in 1988 that we should contrast the potential consequences of the test with positions antagonistic to testing—such as not testing at all. "The intent of these contrasts," he wrote, "is to draw attention to the vulnerabilities in the proposed test interpretation and use, thereby exposing tacit value assumptions to open examination and debate" (p. 40). Messick believed that any assessment must be judged on the intended or unintended social consequences of test interpretation and use. A test deploying multiple-choice tests, he reminded his readers, might lead to an increased emphasis on memory in teaching and learning at the expense of production and synthesis of ideas. A meaningful future direction for assessment, he believed, would be achieved by a focus on construct representation and its relationship to the valid use of testing. As a medium of exchange for ideas in both scientific and social discourse, construct deliberation allows shareholders to focus on the essence of ideas and the nature of their impact.

In 1988, Catharine Keech Lucas of the National Writing Project proposed an ecological view for the assessment of writing ability. Working with the National Writing Project, Lucas argued for an ecological validity: "the extent to which a test reflects (and hence reports results from) the whole writing environment of the learner, and the extent to which it impacts the environment in positive rather than negative ways" (1988a, p. 12). She contextualized her call for a new metaphor for assessment in terms of the current history of writing assessment. In terms of advancements, she reminded readers of the power of instructor credibility in advancing direct writing assessment, the improvement of these direct measures, and the realization that tests must be created that enhance instruction. Nevertheless, Lucas reminds her readers that nonecological practices persist in their failure to conceptualize writing as a construct embedding multiple traits, to treat writing as a contextualized process, and to extract information from the assessment that is truly useful to teachers or learners. Her call is for an evolutionary change that must occur organically within assessment communities. Preparing efficiency reports for overseers should be replaced with a vision in which instructors are given opportunities to analyze what student responses tell them about instructional practice. Her call—for advances in national assessments, task design, evaluative methods, response theory, and impact—has been answered in the past 2 decades. Evidence of research in these areas is found in the present volume in chapters by Hilary Persky, Lee Odell, Sherry Seale Swain and Paul LeMahieu, Chris Anson, and Peggy O'Neill.

At the center of Part III of this volume is a question of agency: focus on teaching and assessing writing through the lens of consequence within complex organic systems. Attending to contextualized impact is useful in helping us understand Peter Elbow's call for good enough evaluation. In answer to a thought experiment—"What happens if we do not test at all?" —Elbow begins by warning us of the dangers of surrogation (false substitution of a single statistical notation in place a complex concept [Scriven, 1987]), stance (spurious belief in precision [Hollis, 1994]), and sampling (naïve adherence to a single assessment as a representation of nomothetic span [Embretson, 1983]). To avoid these fallacies, Elbow calls for a pragmatic approach that reflects that of Dewey (1917):

> Pragmatism is content to take its stand with science; for science finds all events to be subject-matter of description and inquiry—just like stars and fossils, mosquitoes and malaria, circulation and vision. It also takes its stand with daily life, which finds that such things really have to be reckoned with as they occur interwoven in the texture of events. (p. 55)

Following a less-taken road inspired by the environmental, pragmatically informed work of Roskelly and Ronald (1998), which avoids the inherent disjuncture of value dualism, Elbow argues for the adoption of criterion-based assessment and its focus on behavior. If a researcher wants to know how good someone is at driving a car or communicating in English—or if the aim is to pick a future business leader or to determine prospects for a happy marriage—then leave the office, go into the field, and find out what people really do (McClelland, 1973). Elbow agrees: The goal for a criterion-based evaluation is a list of writing behaviors students should have learned; conversely, the goal is not to sort students, as norm-referenced evaluations do, along a Gaussian curve. In their specificity, Elbow claims, rubrics come to the rescue in their delineation of what is to be learned; and, as he recognizes, the *WPA Outcomes Statement for First-Year Composition* (Council of Writing Program Administrators, 2000, 2008) is just such a criterion measure.

It is precisely this kind of assessment that informs Doug Baldwin's analysis of challenges to constructed-response assessments. As a task development and scoring technique, constructed-response assessments measure complex skills by asking examinees to produce an answer in writing rather than selecting a response from a list (Livingston, 2009). Beyond a multiple-choice test that can determine if students can discriminate between well written and poorly constructed sentences, a constructed-response task is designed to elicit writing behaviors that can help evaluators determine the details of a writing performance. Scoring constructed response tasks involves using a criterion-based rubric that defines features of the response and the scores to be awarded to these features. Yet, as Samuel A. Livingston and Doug Baldwin both realize, assessments using constructed-response designs also pose complexities. In a computer-delivered assessment, for example, is it fair to administer the task without allowing spell-checker ability? That is, does the assessment measure the target behavior for all test-takers regardless of their membership in an identified subgroup, such as writers whose best language is not English? Perhaps not accustomed to using such a tool, might those test-takers choose a correctly spelled word that is nevertheless wrong in context?

"Assessment is nothing, if not a necessary compromise," Baldwin writes, and thus ushers in the reasoning patterns of cost-effectiveness analysis. In a method developed by Levin (2001), cost-effectiveness analysis compares alternatives in meeting a defined objective. Especially useful in educational measurement, cost-effectiveness analysis provides an alternative to cost benefit analysis where the alternatives are chiefly expressed in monetary terms. Using a method emphasizing allocation of resources under conditions of scarcity, the evaluator identifies each of the opportunities that are lost when a direction is identified. As the specific ingredients are identified and their costs ascertained, the evaluator can estimate both the cost and the distribution of the cost burden across shareholders (Levin & McEwan, 2002).

The costs of compromise are at the heart of a replication study by Asao B. Inoue and Mya Poe in their investigation of the English Placement Test at the California State University (CSU) system across a 30-year time span. What, the researchers ask, has been replicated in terms of result across the

30-year span of the test? Specifically, they investigate the characteristics of the data in an archival replication study (Brennan, 2001) in terms of a sampling plan. If, Inoue and Poe find, the aim is to examine if students fall along a Gaussian curve in the two sampling frames of 1978 and 2008, then the test performs similarly. If, however, the aim is to determine consequences—the intended and unintended impact of test use—in the complex ecology of the state system, replication becomes complex: The sample of students has changed dramatically, from a 48.9% White population in 1978 to a 25.7% White population in 2008. Where there were only 5.8% Asian Americans in 1978, in 2008 that number had risen to 20% and had been classified according to a more precise term of Asian Pacific Islander who, at CSU, are mostly Hmong students. Whereas there were only 4.2% Hispanic students in 1978, there were 20% in 2008. Each of the changes is reflected in the fact that the 2010 U. S. Census found that California led the nation with the largest minority population (Humes, Jones, & Ramirez, 2011, p. 17). Attention to the diversity of the population leads to other questions, including those that examine the appropriateness of existing rubrics and their ability to address the emerging literacy of diverse student populations. For Inoue and Poe, the resource allocation given to the CSU placement test has not sufficiently identified the opportunities that are lost when diverse language uses of shifting student populations fail to be identified and incorporated into classroom and assessment practice.

The circuit of learning is equally important to Dan Royer and Roger Gilles in their study of writing placement. With attention to the value dualism of the public world of institutional accountability versus the private world of student assessment—a disjunctive pair in which terms are seen as oppositional and exclusive, with a higher value placed on one of the terms than the other (Davion, 2002)—Royer and Gilles identify the either/or trap, long recognized by political and social theorists as destructive (Warren, 1990). Using the innovative framework of Directed Self Placement, Royer and Gilles have made the private practices of their instructors—with their commitment to offer choice of literacy paths, models for success, and criterion-based evaluations—public for all shareholders; as a result, value dualism is obviated and community is strengthened. With its emphasis on curricular advancement determined by the student and the attendant restoration of student agency, Direct Self Placement (DSP) itself becomes a vehicle displacing traditional placement paternalism: Students evaluate their capabilities, receive informed professional response, and chart their curricular future.

Certainly, such efforts are at the center of Gita DasBender's chapter on the use of DSP with Generation 1.5 student writers. These multilingual writers, even though often immigrating to the United States as school-age children, retain their linguistic diversity. As such, traditional placement systems—with their denial of student background, attitudes, history, and their use of prompts and rubrics that often do not sufficiently attend to linguistic diversity—carry the consequence of severely disenfranchising such students. With its sensitivity to context, DSP allows Dan Bender, teaching at a private university in New Jersey, to study a small sample of students, the majority of whom spoke another language besides English at home. The results are as complex as the individuals in the sample: Although expressing positive experiences and beliefs regarding language proficiency upon admission, at the end of the first-semester writing course the students nevertheless felt that they lacked proficiency in both analytic and structural skills. Emphasizing the long and complicated language-learning process of Generation 1.5 students, Das Bender calls for additional research that will continue to be needed as the nation becomes increasingly diverse.

Some of that research may now be emerging. Mao and Young (2008), for example, have brilliantly accounted for the transformative power of the power of Asian American rhetoric to identify the social, cultural, and political contexts in which language is subtly diffused and effectively used. Their focus on context is shared by Liz Hamp-Lyons in her research, commissioned by the Hong Kong Examinations and Education Authority, on the developed abilities of school-aged English-language learners. Related to the emphasis on writing in the work of Elbow, Baldwin, Inoue and Poe, Royer and Gilles, and Das Bender, Hamp-Lyons focuses on speaking as a performance. Following Elbow, hers is a pragmatic demonstration that performance in the key to both instruction and assessment. The school-based assessment she has designed with her colleagues allows instructors in nearly 600 schools in Hong Kong to evaluate individual and group presentations of some 3,000 students each year. Adhering to a criterion-referenced assessment design advocated by Baldwin, Hamp-Lyons demonstrates how instructors use a multiple-trait rating scale that is central to both instruction and assessment. To understand a complex performance, Hamp-Lyons advocates for an analytic scale defining multiple traits, a position also supported by Sara Cushing Weigle (2002). As criterion-referenced scoring becomes more important in writing assessment, it will become more apparent that the specifics of a writing performance's complex ecology are best understood in their expressed detail.

In her emphasis on performance, Hamp-Lyons closes this section of the collection by proposing a provocative way forward for researchers: What happens if we focus on performance within context? Defined in the *Standards for Educational and Psychological Measurement* (AERA, APA, & NCME, 1999) as "an attempt to emulate the context of conditions in which the intended knowledge or skills are actually applied" (p. 388), performance assessments insist on the connection between construct representation and context. Lane and Stone (2006) note, expertise is domain specific; hence, a performance assessment is likely to allow more robust construct representation because the text will be executed in a context of application. Lane and Stone elaborate the idea of performance assessment with an example of an evaluation of the writing process. A performance that best emulates writing, they believe, would "incorporate various facets of the writing process by including a prewriting component, a revision component that may include a critique by a peer, and a proofreading and editing component of the revised draft" (p. 388). Although postprocess researchers (Hawk, 2007; Kent, 1999) may disagree with this representation of the writing process, the point remains critical: Emphasis on performance leads to an enlivening of the assessment context which, in turn, leads to the potential for increasingly robust construct representation. If researchers are able to insist on the incorporation of a sociocognitive framework for writing assessment, then they will be able to adopt a construct-driven rather than a task-driven approach to performance assessment (Messick, 1994). Instead, conceptual frameworks such as the ones described in this section will replicate, as cost-effectiveness analysis will allow, that which Cooper (1986) advocated in her ecological model of writing: An acknowledgement that writing is an activity through which we are continually engaged with a variety of socially constituted systems. Such a model, interactive and contextual in nature, allows us to envision assessment in terms of its consequences. As the authors in this section realize, validation of assessment use must attend both to technical quality and social equity.

REFERENCES

American Educational Research Association, American Psychological Association, & National Council on Measurement in Education. (1999). *Standards for educational and psychological testing*. Washington, DC: American Educational Research Association.

Brennan, R. (2001). An essay on the history and future of reliability from the perspective of replications. *Journal of Educational Measurement, 38*(4), 258-317.

Cooper, M. (1986). The ecology of writing. *College English, 48*(4), 364-375.

Council of Writing Program Administrators (2000, 2008). *WPA Outcomes Statement for First-Year Composition*. Web.

Davion, V. (2002). Ecofeminism, lifeboat ethics and illegal immigration. *Global Dialogue, 4*(1). Web.

Dewey, J. (1917). The need for a recovery of philosophy. In J. Dewey (Ed.), *Creative intelligence: Essays in the pragmatic attitude* (pp. 3-69). New York, NY: Holt.

Embretson, S. (1983). Construct validity: Construct representation versus nomothetic span. *Psychological Bulletin, 93*(1), 179-197.

Hawk, B. (2007). *A counter history of composition: Toward methodologies of complexity*. Pittsburgh, PA: University of Pittsburgh Press.

Hollis, M. (1994). *The philosophy of social science: An introduction.* Cambridge, England, UK: Cambridge University Press.

Humes, K. R., Jones, N. A., & Ramirez, R. R. (2011, March). Overview of race and Hispanic origin. *2010 Census Briefs* (C2010BR-02). Washington, DC: U. S. Census Bureau. Web.

Kent, T. (Ed.). (1999). *Post-process theory: Beyond the writing process paradigm.* Carbondale, IL: Southern Illinois University Press.

Lane, S., & Stone, C. A. (2006). Performance Assessment. In R. L. Brennan (Ed.), *Educational measurement* (4th ed., pp. 387-431). Westport, CT: American Council on Education and Praeger

Lucas, C. K. (1988a). Toward ecological evaluation: Part one. *The Quarterly of the National Writing Project and the Center for the Study of Writing, 10*(1), 1-3, 12-17.

Lucas, C. K. (1988b). Toward ecological evaluation: Part two. *The Quarterly of the National Writing Project and the Center for the Study of Writing, 10*(2), 8-10.

Levin, H. (2001, Summer). Waiting for Godot: Cost-effectiveness analysis in education. *New Directions for Evaluation, 90*, 55-68.

Levin, H. M., & McEwan, P. J. (Eds.). (2002). *Cost-effectiveness and educational policy*. Larchmont, NY: Eye on Education.

Livingston, S. A. (2009, September). Constructed-response test questions: Why we use them; How we score them. *R&D Connections*, 11. Princeton, NJ: Educational Testing Service. Web.

Mao, L., & Young, M. (Ed.). (2008). *Representations: Doing Asian American rhetoric.* Logan, UT: Utah State University Press.

McClelland, D. (1973, January). Testing for competence rather than for "intelligence." *American Psychologist, 28*(1), 1-14.

Messick, S. (1988). The once and future issues of validity: Assessing the meaning and consequences of measurement. In H. Wainer & H. Braun (Eds.), *Test validity* (pp. 33-45). Hillsdale, NJ: Lawrence Erlbaum.

Messick, S. (1994). The interplay of evidence and consequences in the validation of performance assessments. *Educational Researcher, 23*(2), 13-23.

Roskelly, H., & Ronald, K. (1988). *Reason to believe: Romanticism, pragmatism, and the teaching of writing*. New York, NY: State University of New York Press.

Scriven, M. (1987). Validity in personnel evaluation. *Journal of Personnel Evaluation in Education, 1*(1), 9-23.

Warren, K. (1990). The power and promise of ecological feminism. *Environmental Ethics, 12*(2), 121-145.

Weigle, S. C. (2002). *Assessing writing*. Cambridge, UK: Cambridge University Press.

17

GOOD ENOUGH EVALUATION
WHEN IS IT FEASIBLE AND WHEN IS EVALUATION NOT WORTH HAVING?

Peter Elbow
University of Massachusetts at Amherst

Edward White's approach to assessment has always been practical and realistic. Over and over he has urged members of our profession to get involved in assessment, even as amateurs, to be willing to "get our hands dirty." Otherwise, he warned, assessment will be taken over by bureaucrats who know even less about assessment—or who would give the job to professionals in assessment who "know everything there is to know"—except what really matters. I like to think of him as good at playing both the doubting game and believing game with assessment. That is what I am trying to do here.

What I admire about Ed's work—and what I am trying to emulate here—is his constant attempt to do a kind of pragmatic realistic calculation: comparing the *need* for some evaluation (including how much information and precision is needed), and the *harm* or *risk* of untrustworthy results. If the need is great enough and the harm is small enough, then it makes sense to go ahead with it. This is what I mean by "good enough" evaluation.

He demonstrates this ability impressively in his ongoing thinking about holistically timed essays for placement testing. Famously, he came out in favor of them, saying they had shortcomings but were "good enough" given the need (White, 1995). But after a number of years of thinking, observing, and conversing, he changed his mind and wrote this in 2007: "I have at long last lost confidence in placement testing as an appropriate method . ..." White, 2008, pp. 137-138). In this later essay he sounds again the "good enough" theme of trying to balance need against trustworthiness. He writes, "[P]lacement is valuable, even necessary on many campuses, but we seem not to have a good way to do it" (p. 136). He finally decides that the flaws are so deep as to trump the need: "Let's face it: almost all of our placement tests are not valid and we shouldn't be using them" (p. 138).

In this chapter, I too am trying to figure out what *good enough* evaluation looks like for various particular situations. The evaluation of writing can never be perfect, but we can try to balance, as Ed did, the need versus the harm or risk.

THREE INHERENT TRAPS OR ILLUSIONS IN THE EVALUATION OF WRITING

1. Trying for a single number score or one-dimensional grade. A single number can never accurately represent the quality or value of a multidimensional entity and writing is inherently multidimensional. Certain dimensions of any piece—for example, the organization, the reasoning, the voice as it relates to the audience, or the spelling—will almost invariably be better or worse than others. No single number will do. Even if one reader thinks that all the dimensions of a piece are of equal value (e.g., B minus), some other reader will weight the dimensions differently.

2. Trying for objectivity. If we accept the premise that writing is for human readers (rather than God or machine-scoring devices), then the *value* of a piece of writing must be tied to the responses of human readers. But humans differ, so different readers will disagree as to value.

Admittedly, human readers often do have single one dimensional reactions or perceptions of a paper (e.g., "This is terrible" or "This is a pure instance of B minus"). But that does not mean we need to settle for naive, global reactions based on holistic feelings ("I like it / I don't like it"). We do not forfeit evaluation by live human readers if we ask them for thoughtful judgment that describes and discriminates between strengths and weaknesses in different dimensions of a piece of writing.

Testers try to escape this second pitfall in various ways:

- They work at "high reliability" in scores by "norming" readers to agree with each other. But in doing this, they simply force

those readers to ignore their own actual differing human responses as to value.
- They enlist similar readers, for example, using only archaeologists for essays meant for that audience. This permits them to announce: "This score represents the value of the writing for archaeologists." But there are still lots of difference between the reactions of different archaeologists.

3. Trying to evaluate someone's skill or ability by looking at a single piece of writing. This trap is most blatant in many placement exams: They give scores to *texts* when the exam is being used to judge ability to write—in this case the *ability* to prosper in one or another first-year writing course.

A moment's thought shows us that the effectiveness of a *single* text or performance can not be a valid picture of a writer's ability. Any evaluation of ability needs to look at multiple performances: texts of various kinds or genres produced on various occasions. And when it comes to evaluating ability, the first two traps also yawn: The ability to write is multidimensional and thus cannot be accurately represented by a single number—and certainly not a number that professes to be objective or fair.

In short, there can be no *single* correct, objective, fair "true score" for any text or any person's ability to write or anyone's likelihood to learn in a given course. This is pretty bad news, and it makes me deeply skeptical of evaluation. I seem to be on the brink of saying what any good postmodern theorist would say: there is no such thing as fairness; let's stop pretending we can have it or even try for it (see Herrenstein-Smith, 1988, on the "contingency of value").

THREADING A PRAGMATIC PATH BETWEEN POSITIVIST FAITH AND POSTMODERN SKEPTICISM

But I am not stepping over that brink. I think fairness is *largely* unavailable, but I would argue that there are situations where it is worth trying to get closer to it on the basis of a pragmatic calculation of *need* versus *danger* (see Baldwin's explorations of fairness, this volume). The main argument of this chapter is that we can figure out the difference between evaluative practices that are *more* fair and *less* fair. There are particular circumstances where the need for a verdict is pressing enough and the danger is reduced enough that it is worth getting a verdict that is only *somewhat* untrustworthy. I am looking for good enough evaluation. ("Good enough" as a positive goal comes from Winnicott's [1953] concept of "good enough mother." He was not just suggesting a compromise for tired mommies. He was actively *criticizing* the goal that can understandably tempt new mothers: being the "perfect mother" who fills all the infant's needs. He insisted that "perfect mothers" actually impede growth. In his seminal essay, "Transitional Objects and Transitional Phenomena," he argued that infants actually need a mother who may start off meeting the infant's every need, but who gradually meets fewer and fewer of them to help infants gradually learn more self-sufficiency [p. 1-25]).

I have recently been learning from Hepzibah Roskelly about the rich, broad, stream of philosophic pragmatism that has fed our profession and indeed our country in ways that are too little noticed. The pragmatic approach often involves taking a "third way" that side-steps dead-end conflicts in *theory* and attends to particular cases. So in this chapter, I am trying to side-step the theoretic impasse between a positivistic faith in measurement or assessment and a postmodern skepticism about any possibility of worth in measuring, testing, or scoring.

I am suggesting some general principles in this chapter—bits of theory, yes—but (in the pragmatic tradition) I am refusing to be too rigid in applying those principles as I pick my way gingerly through considerations of particular evaluative situations. The pragmatic move is always to ask *What difference does it make* if you apply a principle in this way in this particular case. Roskelly writes:

> We're never finished with an idea, never completely sure of our conclusions or our directives. For the pragmatists, that's a consequence to be wished for. "We learn to prefer imperfect theories," proto-pragmatist Emerson says, precisely because they're unfinished and capable of change. (Roskelly, 2010, see Roskelly & Ronald, 1998)

So I want readers to ask *What difference would it make* if they tried looking at the evaluation of writing through the pragmatic lens I am offering. In what follows I argue that, on the one hand, we need to stop doing some things that are mostly taken for granted. But that, on the other hand, it is possible—and not even so hard—to have many useful evaluations of writing that pass the test of good enough. Putting this point differently: I am trying to play the believing game with evaluation (seeing the needs and possibilities), but also play the doubting game with it (seeing the grave limitations and indeed impossibilities).[1]

THE CLASSROOM AS A LABORATORY FOR A THEORY OF GOOD ENOUGH EVALUATION

I can illustrate my approach by looking at the most pervasive site for the evaluation of writing: the writing classroom itself. In many writing classrooms, teachers put conventional one dimensional grades on individual student papers. Keeping in mind the three traps, it is obvious how deeply flawed such grades are.

- The first pitfall is most obvious here. Conventional grades inevitably mask different teachers' differential weightings of dimensions in multidimensional writing. For example, one teacher might give a B minus to a piece of writing that is very *brilliant* but careless because of confusing organization, quite a few tangled sentences, and lots of surface mistakes. The same teacher might give a C or lower to a paper that is very *careful* (clear, well-organized, and without mistakes), but deeply perfunctory or shallow in thinking. Yet another teacher with different values would give those two papers exactly the opposite grades.
- The second pitfall will also condemn grades if the teacher calls them or implies them to be fair objective evaluations—rather than verdicts deeply influenced by her own values and point of view.
- The third pitfall is usually avoided. Teachers seldom imply that single-paper grades are fair representations of the student's skill. As classroom teachers, it is our stock in trade to say things like, "I know you *can* do better" or "You finally showed your ability to think well on this paper."

It is not surprising that so many students are suspicious and even hostile about the grades they get on their pieces of writing. Almost every citizen of the United States has gotten more grades on writing than on any other school performance in their lives. Understandably, most of these citizens have had experiences that led to resentment and distrust. (*"That was really a good paper but she gave me a C plus on it!" "This was a hurried piece of crap where I just told him what he wanted to hear, but he gave me an A."*) I believe that this pervasive and *justified* distrust of invalid teacher grades on writing goes a long way toward explaining why so many citizens and legislators are willing to pay big companies for large-scale exams. Those computerized exam scores (often down to three decimal points) fall into the second trap, of course—pretending objectivity; and they may often test something different from what we want to test. But the test-makers work harder and get closer to objectivity than rushed and harried individual teachers can manage as they put unilateral grades on papers. This understandably impresses the public.

But there is good news about classroom grading. *Many* classroom teachers have learned to avoid all three pitfalls, and it does not cost them more work: just more care and wisdom. With regard to the first one, they do not settle for a single quantitative score like B minus. They use some kind of grid or rubric or narrative evaluation in order to figure out and communicate what they see as the value of the *various dimensions* of the piece of writing.

Rubrics help these teachers notice and articulate more about a text. Like any reader, teachers often have a global response to a paper and do not know at first which qualities or which dimensions led to this global response For example a teacher might feel, "This paper is very poor. Look at all the surface errors." Yet that teacher actually turn out to feel much more positive about another paper that has just as many surface errors—but the teacher did not notice them so much. Using a grid can help that teacher discover that errors were a red herring in the first case; it was an irritating textual voice or what feels like a noxious point of view that led to the negative reaction. Or perhaps that first paper had "Black errors"—which research has shown to bring down grades more than garden variety "White errors." Rubrics can help readers notice the unfair influence of dimensions they had not been consciously noticing.

Rubrics have come in for some fair criticism when they are crude prepackaged lists of conventional features used on large-scale tests—forcing battalions of readers to try to fit their human responses into corporate pigeon holes. Bob Broad (2003) has written a definitive empirical study of the facts of how individual readers have different responses to the value of writing. But when a rubric fails to include a dimension of the writing that was actually influencing the reader (e.g., voice or point of view), it can tempt a teacher to stay blind to that feature. Almost anything that is *obvious* in writing (e.g., bad reasoning) can be a red herring and mask the influence of other subtler features that actually determined that reader's sense of value.

However a rubric can be used by an *individual teacher*, he or she can design it to fit his or her particular values—and also create different rubrics for different assignments that call for different textual strengths. Or a small group of teachers can collaborate to design rubrics that fit.

Of course, teachers can avoid the problems of rigid rubrics by using only a written comment. I have had lots of experience with this method—especially at Evergreen State College. But I have noticed how I and other teachers sometimes wrote long and thoughtful comments that nevertheless never got around to talking about some crucial and determinative features of the writing.[2]

One of the arguments against rubrics or grids is that they ask for too much work: Teachers have to give five or six grades instead of just one. But teachers who use grids have found a simple solution to this problem: They use only *minimal* verdicts for each item on a grid, namely *strong*, *okay*, and *weak*—or *excellent*, *satisfactory*, *poor*. This means that when they consider each item on a grid, they do not have to *ponder* and try to make careful distinctions. After they read the paper, they hold each criterion in mind for a moment and simply wait to see if a bell goes off in their head saying, *This paper is terrific—or awful with regard to [say] organization*. If the bell goes off, the answer is clear; if not, the answer is also clear: *okay*.

This is not just a lazy short cut. It reflects good evaluative logic for many reasons:

- By giving verdicts on four or five dimensions of a text, a reader is vastly increasing the amount of evaluative information over what we get with a single quantitative verdict or grade. This fits with the theme of *good enough* evaluation. The resulting collection of *crude* grades actually adds up to a richer and more sophisticated evaluation.
- We do well to jettison those hard won attempts to decide between C- and B-level quality on, say, thinking or ideas. They are worthless because readers so often disagree at this level. They enact that perennial hunger for ranking people or performances into fine grade differentiations—when those differentiations are simply not trustworthy.
- The more levels of discrimination of quality are used, the more occasions for disagreement not just by fellow teachers but by students themselves—unnecessary occasions for resenting our verdict and thus undermining the climate for teaching and learning. (I will never forget walking into my office at MIT in the 1970s and finding a paper on the floor that an admirably fearless student had slipped under the door. I had given it a B minus and tried to show in my comments why this was the right grade. But scrawled boldly across the top was this simple message. "This is a B *paper*. Fuck you.").

There's a hoary evaluative principle that says that scorers should never be allowed to be "lazy" and choose a "medium" or middle score. If you believe this, you can avoid three levels and use four instead: poor, fair, good, excellent. But the distinction between fair and good is exactly what we should not trust. And going to four makes for lots more work.

Many classroom teachers avoid the second pitfall too: They have learned not to pretend that their evaluation is objective. They have the courage and wisdom to say something like this when they hand back papers:

> *I cannot pretend that these multidimensional grades are actually fair. Other readers might well give different evaluations. And I want to be clear about something many of you have already come to believe: in fact there is no fair grade—no "true score" for a piece of writing. The best you can hope for is individual readers giving you their most accurate picture of their most careful reading of the strengths and weaknesses of the various dimensions of your paper. That's what I've tried to do. All evaluations will inevitably reflect a readers' own particular values and situatedness.*

Interestingly, when some teachers try to avoid the first trap by using a grid with multiple criteria, this tempts them into the second trap: *I am avoiding the obvious bias that comes with single score holistic grades—grades that are prey to knee jerk global reactions. I will use more concrete objective criteria and that will make me more objective*. But the inherent problem remains: The value of writing is necessarily value for *readers*, and even reactions to particular criteria will differ because they are rooted in the scorer's point of view or cultural situation.

In truth, many teachers find that rubrics help them *avoid* the second pitfall of pretended objectivity. In using a rubric they say, *You deserve to know more about my values as a particular reader: Here are the aspects of writing that I believe are most central to my idea of excellence*. It is particularly helpful for students if we give out the criteria for any given assignment *before* students have to write. It usually results in better essays (or at least essays that suit us better). And we can teach better if we are willing to engage in the self-analysis of figuring out what criteria we care about most—in general and for any particular assignment.

Even when teachers include a literal "bottom line" on their grids—a final line that gives a global *one-dimensional* verdict on the overall quality of the paper—they can still acknowledge their human positionality as readers. When this one-dimensional verdict is part of a grid, it is all the more clear that there is no such thing as a true score. Many sophisticated teachers send a message like this:

> *Here are my perceptions of the quality of the various dimensions of your paper. I've included a bottom line that shows my sense of the overall quality. You can see, thus, how much my global judgment is a product of my personal priorities: how much weight I give to the various dimensions, such as surface features, organization, reasoning, voice &c.*

Let me call attention to the evaluative wisdom in another common practice of many writing teachers: getting students to give each other peer feedback and evaluation. This too tends to avoid the first two pitfalls. Even though peer evaluators are usually less skilled and experienced readers than teacher evaluators, these peer responses are a palpable enactment of a more valid picture of *value* in writing: They consist of the reactions of multiple and different readers.

RUBRICS, HOLISTIC SCORING, AND CRITERION-BASED EVALUATION

McClelland made the definitive argument against holistic scoring in a 1973 essay in the *American Psychologist.* It was a critique of the tradition of *norm-based* assessment and a proposal to use *criterion-based* assessment instead (or outcomes-based or competence-based or mastery-based assessment). The problem with norm-based evaluation is that it gives us nothing but a number: no information about what the student actually knows or can do. *B minus* or *85* tells us nothing about what students have learned or what they can do. So holistic scoring is a norm-based enterprise. Admittedly, in large-scale assessments, administrators try to diminish this problem by writing a "guide" that is supposed to tell what a "4" or "2" essay looks like. But these descriptions are notoriously unsatisfactory as portraits of the actual essays; they offer a kind of Platonic picture of the ideal mix of features in any given score.

The goal for norm-based evaluation is an ideal that is seldom realized: A set of scores that fall into the pattern of a bell shaped curve: the maximum distribution among skills or abilities (or intelligence). The goal for criterion-based evaluation is a list of things students should have learned—and for each item a *yes* or *no*.

This insistence on a binary yes/no result for each outcome is a problem that bedeviled the outcomes-based or competence-based movement and helped lead to its fading. Too many things that we teach and want to evaluate are not susceptible to black/white yes/no answers. The problem is particularly obvious with writing. For example, is a given essay competently organized—or well thought through—or well adapted to its audience? For some essays we can give a clear *yes* and/or *no* on each criterion, but many essays force us to answer, *partly* or *in some ways yes but in other ways no.* That is, the criterion-based folks were obviously right to insist that large multidimensional entities like a text—or abilities like *writing*—should be broken into smaller pieces. But it is hard to break them down so far that evaluation results can consist of pure *yes*'s and *no*'s.

Rubrics come to the rescue with this problem. Rubrics represent a move away from *norm-based* evaluation (or holistic scoring—using only numbers) in the direction of a *criterion-based* process that insists on articulating what is to be learned. Yet when rubric users insist on scores of 1 to 5 on each criterion, they fall back into the norm-based trap: fixating on fine numerical distinctions that will not hold up. But when we use rubrics with only three levels of accomplishment, for example, *strong*, *okay*, *weak*, we are not just settling for a *compromise* between norm-based and criterion-based evaluation (not that there is anything wrong with compromise). I would call it a *good enough* approach that is actually better than either alternative. The cruder scores are much easier to give and the results are more trustworthy.[3]

BUT CAN ONE DIMENSIONAL OR SINGLE NUMBER GRADES BE GOOD ENOUGH?

I have talked of traps, pitfalls, and failures but have been at pains to show how thoughtful teachers manage to avoid those traps and still give quantitative classroom evaluations to individual papers and portfolios. But I have stressed that those evaluations are only good enough because they do not consist of single-number grades. Now, however, I want to look at situations where I think single-number grades—one-dimensional verdicts—can manage to be good enough.

For a writing prize. Teacher are sometimes asked to nominate a student for a writing prize. A nomination would seem to fall right into the first two pitfalls: It involves a misleadingly single number (a yes/no decision) based on a biased judgment. And the consequence can be weighty—sometimes significant money. Nevertheless, I would defend such a nomination as a good example of "good enough" evaluation. I show how such a nomination relates to the three pitfalls.

With regard to the first pitfall, a single-number score does much less harm at the extremes of quality—excellent or poor. That is, the biggest unfairness in single-number grades comes from the way different evaluators disagree in the weight they give to different dimensions. But when a single reader calls a paper or portfolio *excellent*, those differential weightings are a little less likely to do harm. Excellent features are more likely to predominate—or else one particular feature may be so strong as to overshadow other weaknesses—even in the reactions of others readers. Therefore a somewhat larger proportion of readers is more likely to agree that the paper or portfolio is excellent (or poor) than will agree about a single-number grade in the middle range of B or C where differential weightings more easily tip the balance. Let me emphasize: I am not saying that one teacher's "outstanding" will garner agreement from all readers; but at least more of them are more likely to call it notably good than will agree about some middling grade where the mix of dimensions is killing (see Despain & Hilgers, 1992, for some research backing up the idea that decisions at the margins are a bit more reliable).

And when it comes to the second trap—objectivity versus bias—the danger is even smaller. For in almost all prize situations, the teacher is not *awarding* the prize—only nominating a student. There Is a committee that must adjudicate. In fact, the awarding of prizes for excellence in writing reflects a remarkably valid and sophisticated understanding of how the evaluation of writing ought to work. The prize is given as a result of negotiation among necessarily biased evaluations by situated readers. And when it comes to writing prizes, almost none of the participants or audiences has any illusion that they are looking at a "true score." Whereas people tend to read grades as professing to be "valid," most observers see prizes as contests of *taste*. So they can see the process is an *attempt* at a certain kind of fairness—with full open recognition of the impossibility of attaining it.

If it is a prize for a body of work, the third pitfall is avoided, because it is based on multiple texts. But even if it is a prize for just *one* essay or story or poem, there is very little pretense that the prize is actually a measure of the writer's true ability. Everyone can see that it is a prize for one performance—and that might well be better or worse than the writer usually manages. It is like a gold medal for the hundred yard dash: People know that the winner is sometimes not as consistently good or skilled a runner as someone else who happened to have had a bad day or even bad season.

Failing a student for the course. Here is another one-dimensional score, yet there is even more pressure for fairness because the consequences are so weighty: no credit and the requirement to take the course again. I can continue to clarify my theory by arguing how a failing grade can make evaluative sense as "good enough"—*but* with one important reservation. Let's look at the calculus of need versus danger.

- The need is great. For teaching and learning to go on in institutions that give credit, it is important and valid to be able to withhold credit and require students to learn enough before they go on to future courses.
- The danger is not so very great. The single-number verdict is not so damaging because it is at the extreme. When the teacher decides she should fail a student because of poor writing, the writing will surely be very poor and there will be significantly more agreement among readers (of course, not complete agreement). With very poor writing, the disagreement will be less than about, say, the grade of C or C plus.

But, of course, we cannot *fully* trust a unilateral judgment to be fair, even at the margins. And when it comes to failing students, the *feelings* of teachers tend to play a big role and feelings are notoriously unfair. (*I just can't fail this student who's been so diligent—in fact he was a big help to me in teaching this class.*" "*This student has been a complete pain the ass. I'm glad her writing looks so awful to me.*" "*I can't fail someone who's been taking care of his dying mother.*") So I would argue that we must not accept such a weighty consequence as a failing grade if it is based on just *one* person's judgment about the quality of writing. It is not "good enough" evaluation to fail a student for a course unless at least one other instructor shares in the decision.

This is not so hard to pull off. It is more or less what Pat Belanoff and I set up at Stony Brook. If a teacher wanted to fail a portfolio and thus deny credit and require retaking the course, another teacher—who did not know the student—had to agree that the portfolio was of failing quality. (In fact, in my experience as a WPA at two universities, few failing grades were based *mainly* on quality of writing. Usually they stem from some dereliction of duty—and for deciding on that, there is no need for a second opinion. This chapter is about the evaluation of writing.)

Eligibility to keep a scholarship or play on a varsity team. "*Professor, you just have to give me a B or I'll lose my scholarship [or be kicked off our winning basketball team].*" Teachers are often asked to sign forms with a single number "score"—that is, to certify that students on a team have a B or B minus average in the course. Here it seems clear to me that such evaluative decisions *do not* make sense—they are *not* good enough (unless the student's performance is *massively* excellent or poor). They fall squarely into the first two traps. They represent single-number grades for multidimensional performances that fall right in the middle of the scale where disagreement among evaluators is virtually inevitable—and they have to pretend to be objective or fair. Think back to those two teachers I spoke of earlier who were dealing with brilliance and carelessness in two matching papers. The very same student would have kept his scholarship if he had had one teacher but would have lost it if he had had the other one. If a grade determines an important consequence like keeping a scholarship or being on a team, we need fairness.

This conclusion may cause problems: *We need some way to decide on eligibility for keeping a scholarship or being on a team!* But there is no need to decide on the basis of fine-grained decisions about quality of writing in the middle range. We can be open about other criteria that probably play a bigger role in such teacher decisions anyway, for example, how well students are meeting all the concrete obligations of the course (such as attending, getting assignments in on time, doing substantive revisions, and so on).

What course grade should the student get on the transcript? I have tried to justify a final course grade of F, but what about all the other final grades? One good thing about them is that they are almost always based on *multiple* and *different kinds* of writing, not just one text (although there are some upper level and graduate courses where teachers base the final grade on just one big term paper or exam). But course grades fall squarely into the first two pitfalls: They are single global numbers meant to represent the value of multidimensional performances, and they are meant to be fair when in fact they are unilateral judgments by just one reader with one inevitably partial point of view and set of values. (I have defended nominations for a prize because that unilateral judgment is simply a doorway into a collaborative judgment. I have insisted that failing grades are not good enough unless they are collaborative.)

This problem is all the more serious because the stakes are high. Compared to the grade on a single piece of writing, the course grade goes on the transcript, and there are many readers who use it to make weighty decisions. It affects grade point average and graduation, applications to graduate schools and employers. Yet the same student would likely get different final grades from different teachers looking at the same work—at least with mid-level quality work. A course grade of *B minus* will actually mean many different things that readers have no way of fathoming: It could mean *pretty good in all aspects of the course*; it could mean *brilliant writing but great carelessness and irresponsibility in meeting responsibilities*; or it could mean *rather poor skill in writing but lots of growth and enormous diligence in all other respects.*[4]

Technically speaking, it would be easy for institutions to stop giving those untrustworthy conventional course grades, but few have had the wisdom or taken the trouble. It would simply require that course grades come in the form of a grid through which the teacher can communicate more clearly how well students have attained the skills or abilities or understandings that are asked for in the course. Grade readers never get this information from a conventional transcript, yet it is just what most of them need for making the decisions that they normally make when they consult a transcript.

Here are some things that grade readers typically want to know when they read course grades for writing courses: *How well can students think and argue on paper? How clearly can they make their points and their sentences? How skilled are they at mastering the conventions? How diligent and responsible were they in meeting obligations?* (Readers of grades in other courses tend to have other questions: *How well have students mastered the concepts? How well can they apply the concepts to new material? How clearly can they write about the course material. How diligent and responsible were they in meeting obligations?*)[5]

Multidimensional final grades would require a bit more thinking from teachers—helpfully asking them to be more self-aware about what skills or abilities they are trying to teach. But they would not actually require much more grading work, because again, *minimal crude* verdicts would be fine on each criterion: *strong*, *okay*, *weak*. I think most teachers would be relieved to turn in grades that were more accurate and less misleading.

There is no need for all teachers to agree on one set of criteria for course grids. Indeed, teachers *should* make their own decisions about what dimensions of performance are most important for their course. Transcripts with multidimensional grades could be handled easily by the registrar with computers, and they would be far more accurate, fair, and useful as evaluations of student learning. Why else did God invent computers if she did not want us to communicate learning more specifically and clearly?

Should these grid grades contain a "bottom line" single-number holistic grade? Why not? A global grade is not so opaque when accompanied by the other items in a grid. Readers can read those global verdicts more critically and usefully. They can tell, for example, that a student got a good course grade even with a "weak" for memory—or a poor grade for the course even with a "strong" for diligence and responsibility.

I do not know any college that uses a grid transcript, but it is exactly what report cards look like for children in the early elementary grades. Most teachers and policy makers seem to feel it is "childish" to have multidimensional grades—when in fact it is much more sophisticated and evaluatively valid. Evergreen State College and Hampshire College and a few other places use narrative evaluations on their transcripts instead of single-number grades.

But what about bias and fairness? Even though these sophisticatedly multidimensional grades are more informative, they would still be unilateral judgments made by individual teachers with limited and inevitably biased points of view. The registrar would have to print a disclaimer on each transcript: "The college makes no claim of fairness for any of these grades."

Yet interestingly, I do not see such a big problem here. For in fact, most readers of transcripts read course grades to mean something like this: *<u>This</u> grade for <u>this</u> course represents what <u>this</u> teacher thought of the student's performance, while <u>that</u> grade for <u>that</u> course represents what <u>that</u> teacher thought of her performance*. There's something salutary about the genre of a transcript—especially in its visual form. The sight of all those individual teachers' grades crowded together next to each other tends to disabuse people of any illusions that they are seeing "true scores." (Perhaps I am not acknowledging naive readers who feel that a transcript is a perfect X-ray of the student's entire ability. I think there were more people who fell into that assumption 50 years ago than in our rather cynical age.)

But GPAs? They fall deeply into the first two traps. They would be based on those frail bottom line scores on teacher grids. They would be outrageous failures to represent the *myriad* dimensions of a student's learning and performance. And once you reduce the multifarious complexity of a transcript to a single number, an unwarranted implication of objectivity or fairness sneaks back in. I would argue against computing a GPA for any single semester or year's performance. However, there might be a kind of rough quantitative GPA—both good enough and useful—it is simple to compute how many bottom line As and Fs a student got as a percentage of all grades. (Note how this discounts all the middle-level untrustworthy grades.)

APPLYING THE THEORY MORE WIDELY

If we apply this theory of good enough evaluation more widely, we see a combination of good news and bad. It tells us to give up certain convenient practices and handy scores; but in many cases we can compensate. The payoff is more trustworthy evaluation—and evaluation that will give rise to much less cynicism.

Placement exams. In the 1980s, there were more placement exams in the United States than any other kind of writing exam. (This is the finding of three research reports: CCCC Committee on Assessment, 1988); Greenberg, Wiener, & Donovan, 1986; and Lederman, Ryzewic, & Ribaudo, 1983, as cited in Greenberg, 1992, p. 17.) White then argue that conventional holistic scoring of placement essays was good enough. I disagree. But again, my goal is the same as his: Not a perfectly trustworthy evaluation, but one that is good enough.

When we run the calculus of need against harm, need loses out. These thousands and thousands of placement tests are largely unnecessary—and I call them harmful. There is a remarkable array of practices and writings that show us good alternatives to placement testing. The most elegant and easy one is Directed Self Placement (see Royer & Gilles, 2003). It is no longer a new and odd experiment; it has been used with satisfactory results in a very wide range of institutions.

And there is another alternative model (equally widely tested and used) that is also better than conventional placement tests. Students who need more help to prosper in the regular first-year course are identified, but not in a big test. Instead the identification is made by the regular teacher in the regular course classroom in the first week. Such students are then obliged to attend a one-credit course—or in some places a workshop—and this functions as a *supplement* to the regular first-year writing course. Students so placed get lots of extra help of all kinds so that they can stay and learn in the regular course—avoiding the ghetto effect of segregating them so they never get to work with stronger more confident students (among other sources, see Benesch, 1988; Elbow, 1996; Grego & Thompson, 1995; Kidda, Turner, & Parker, 1993).[6]

Evaluation of programs. In the last decade or two—especially with No Child Left Behind—the amount of placement testing has surely been exceeded by *programmatic* evaluation of writing.

> *Have we succeeded in improving the writing of the students in our school district [or high school or middle school or first-year writing course or lower division program or entire college curriculum]? Can we demonstrate adequate yearly progress?*

Let's look at the three pitfalls.

1. Like placement tests, these program evaluations typically use holistic scores—single numbers that fail to represent the value of a multidimensional product.
2. They typically pretend to be fair and objective.
3. They typically pretend to measure *change in ability* by looking at only two texts—"before" and "after" essays that testers try to make as absolutely similar as possible. Students often have a better day for the "before" essay than the "after" essay.

This looks pretty bad, but again let me try to show the possibility of a good enough alternative. I think the biggest help will come from avoiding the third pitfall. Plenty of programs do this by using *portfolios* for the before and after snapshots—even small portfolios. Thus they are looking at multiple texts in multiple genres that were produced on different days. It is better still when programs get papers in the portfolios that represent what most of us would call "real writing"—that is, writing where students had a chance to draft, get feedback, and revise. After all, the ability to write under exam conditions with no chance to revise is, surely, not what most people mean by "writing ability." Of course, it is expensive to use portfolios for programmatic evaluation, but there is no way around it if we want good enough results. But it makes perfectly good sense when institutions deal with high costs by *sampling* students instead of trying to evaluate them all.

Is there any way to avoid the first two traps: using single-number scores that pretend to represent fairly the value of multidimensional pieces of writing? It would seem impossible. Program evaluations tend to use not just single-number scores but single-number *averages* of single-number scores. And they usually have to talk about very small quantitative improvements.

Hooray, we've moved the average from 2.8 to 3.2. We are a success!
Oh dear. 2.95. We're a failure.

I have seen it happen. It is *exactly* these kinds of small single-number scores in the middle range—the range where most students live and where most readers disagree—that are least trustworthy.

But there is a good enough route around this first trap. Let's think about the goal of programmatic evaluation: to see how well a program is doing and try to improve it—that is, improve teaching and learning. Most legislation that requires assessment requires thoughtful examination of what is working well and not so well. This goal *can* be well served without single-number scores. Think back to the virtue of grids. What could be better than having readers score *multiple* criteria as they read portfolios? This need not be a killing task because, again, readers can rank criteria on only three levels—weak, okay, and strong. This is not just cost cutting; in fact, it makes the results more trustworthy.

Here are some abilities that might be scored: The ability to mount an effective train of thinking; to support it with evidence and examples; to demonstrate a sense of audience and genre; to create a structure or organization that is effective for most readers; to manage conventions; to write about personal reactions and feelings tellingly—as a valuable skill in itself, but also as part of a less personal argument. Some programs might want to evaluate more specialized and particular criteria of educational growth. For example, a general education curriculum—whether for the lower division courses or the whole college—might want to evaluate how well student writing demonstrates some understanding of cultures different from their own. (Students need to know in advance, of course, that they need to put together a portfolio in which some of their papers show this kind of thing.)

There is usually no requirement that a program try for a single number to represent improvement in *overall* writing ability. If we ask readers to rate different *dimensions* of writing skill in a portfolio, there will be some program-wide differences that are strong enough to be meaningful and useful. Certain dimensions of writing skill will show more improvement—or less. Even portfolios that are middling as a whole will often show substantive strengths and weaknesses on certain dimensions. This approach has a chance of revealing at least a few meaningful numbers that could usefully guide curriculum planning, course planning, and teaching. How much more meaningful and useful to all "stakeholders" to tally the number of *strongs* and *weaks* for each criterion. Thus one might be able to conclude, "*Between September and June, with respect to 'mounting an effective train of thinking,' there were twenty percent fewer weaks and fifteen percent more strongs.*" It will sometimes be possible to see which dimensions showed more improvement and which ones less.

I seem to be talking as though single-number scores can never be useful. But there are exceptions. A few portfolios will be globally and strikingly strong—or weak—in *most* dimensions. I invoke here my earlier justification for nominating a student for a prize or giving a failing course grade. A one-dimensional score or verdict—although not wholly trustworthy—can be good enough to be used when it is at the extreme. That is, I would argue that programmatic evaluations could validly identify writers whose before and after portfolios show their degree of improvement near the top of what can be expected—and also those whose degree of nonimprovement puts them at the bottom. These more trustworthy single numbers would be suggestive and useful, even though they speak of only a minority of students.

Finally, I can quickly describe a way of avoiding the second trap in program assessment: not pretending fairness or objectivity in measuring performances against a stable, objective, universal skill in writing. A program can avoid this pretense with an honest adjustment to the goal of the enterprise:

> *We are not pretending to a measure of some universal Platonic skill in writing. We are only trying to measure student improvement in the kinds of writing we care about at this institution. In short, our target is frankly biased, but it's the target that matters to us.*

A VISION FOR SAT ESSAY TESTS, NAEP ESSAY TESTS, STATE-WIDE ESSAY TESTS MANDATED BY NO CHILD LEFT BEHIND, GENERAL EDUCATION ESSAY TESTS, AND ESSAY TESTS FOR LICENSING TEACHERS

The simplest, cheapest course is simply to scrap these tests. They tend to be used for high-stakes decisions with big consequences: A "score" that counts hugely for college admission, graduation from high school or college, eligibility for the next grade or for upper division status, or getting a license to teach. Yet the scores are deeply untrustworthy. The tests usually look at single texts and score them with one-dimensional single scores that are alleged to represent the real value of the text, and the ability of the writer. Falling so deeply into all three traps, their scores are not even useful at the extremes. Surely we have better things to do with money than give tests that give worthless results and create so much unhelpful anxiety.

But I will end the chapter with a vision of how even these large-scale exams that look only at single texts *could* be far more useful and valid—and far less damaging. We have to radically adjust our sense of the goal for these exams. They are no good for making high-stakes decisions; but they could be useful for learning and teaching. I see a large-scale test—district-wide, state-wide, nation-wide—where students can submit a paper they have revised. Each paper would be read and evaluated by three readers, but they would use multidimensional grids. The test administrators would assemble groups of good but representative and different readers. There would be no pretense at "training" or "calibrating" them to make them ignore their own values. Instead they would be invited to read like the human teachers that they are—in all their diversity. Scores would consist of verdicts on, say, four or five rubrics and come from three representative readers. Naturally these results could not be used for any important decisions. You could not rank students or states or classrooms or districts. Yet these diverse reader evaluations would be highly useful to the students and to their teachers. And they would be enormously interesting too for people interested in evaluation.

CONCLUDING THOUGHT

I have been trying to show here the courage of my pragmatism. Some "coherent" thinkers will say I have been far too purist—disallowing too much useful evaluation. Others will say I have been far too permissive—condoning too much dubious evaluation and accepting even *scores* that are so far from fully valid. But even though there *is* no accurate or true or fair score for any piece of writing—and no piece of writing can give a valid picture of a person's skill or ability to write. Nevertheless, we do not need to throw up our hands and reject all evaluation. Like White, we can try to use the calculus of need versus harm. Are there conditions where we need some kind of judgment strongly enough and where the danger of untrustworthy results is reduced enough that it is worth going forward with the evaluation? People and institutions need to make this calculation for their circumstances; there is no one right way to evaluate writing for everyone and in every context. In dealing with this puzzle, it is salutary to remember the wide range of evaluations that go on in the world. Consider the processes of hiring someone for a job or accepting an article for publication. The process is usually like the one used in awarding a prize. Usually it represents a negotiation of multiple perspectives.

Nevertheless, I have tried in this chapter to use this kind of calculus for many educational settings. I end up working my way to deciding that the following evaluations are worth making if the stakeholders want them:

- Individual teachers giving multidimensional feedback or scores on individual papers (as with grids or rubrics). But only three levels of quality are warranted for each dimension.

- Individual teachers nominating students for a writing prize.
- Individual teachers giving a failing grade for a course (a one-dimensional verdict) on the basis of poor writing—if another teacher concurs.
- Individual teachers giving course grades for a transcript—as long as those grades are multidimensional.
- For 2 or 4 years of work, computing not a GPA, but a minimal cumulative "score" consisting of the number of bottom line *strongs* and *weaks* compared to the number of all courses taken.
- Using portfolios for programmatic evaluation to identify improvement or lack of improvement on various dimensions of writing ability.

If my calculus for good enough evaluation seems too austere and disqualifies too much evaluation that people think is necessary, let's not forget a different calculus of need versus harm. The need is for money: Evaluation is very expensive, and we need more money for teaching and smaller class sizes. This calculus makes it all the harder to justify many of our current evaluations that are so expensive, dubious, and that so often do great *harm* to the climate for teaching and learning.

ENDNOTES

1. I look at evaluation through an eclectic but extensive set of experiences and writings since 1969. I taught at Evergreen State College for 9 years—where we used no grades at all. I spent 4 years as part of a research team looking at a dozen experiments in competence-based higher education. Pat Belanoff and I started the movement for using portfolios for program-wide evaluation (though I have since found a tiny Hawai'ian religious college that beat us to it). I have published more than 20 essays about assessment (for a list of my works cited, see http://works.bepress.com/peter_elbow).
2. See Elbow (1997) on this issue. It includes an appendix of the many publications arguing against holistic scoring.
3. There was a big movement in the 1970s for "competence-based" evaluation. I spent 4 years on an 8-person research team investigating competence-based programs in higher education. (We each had a site but we all visited all the sites and each wrote field notes on our visits. See Grant et al., 1979, and Elbow, 1979. Remarkably, David Riesman was one of our team.

   For a long time it seemed as though the enthusiasm for competence- or outcomes-based education had faded away. Perhaps the approach asked for too much from teachers. It required teachers to figure out specifically what they want to students to learn or be able to do—and also to articulate these learning goals publicly and clearly enough for students to understand them. *And* in addition, of course, to figure out a way to evaluate whether the students have learned or can do those things. Also, the problem of asking for unambiguous yes/no answers tempted practitioners into smaller and smaller outcomes—sometimes to the extent of tiny *behavioral* objectives (*Are there paragraph breaks at least every 10 or 12 sentences?*) Also competence-based enthusiasts sometimes betrayed a rhetorically unhelpful resentment against conventional college professors who said, in effect, "Don't ask me to specify exactly what I'm trying to teach. Only *I*—the expert in this area—can say what it is, and you wouldn't understand."

In the last decade or two, however, we have seen a resurgence of the criterion-based spirit with the growth of interest in *outcomes*—across all fields from business to government to education. Note the Outcomes Statement approved by so many members in the Council of Writing Program Administrators (2000, 2008). Many of the outcome bulldozers lead to crude and unhelpful results, but I cannot help thinking that the essential wisdom in the criterion-based impulse sparked by McClelland cannot be kept down. It gradually dawns on more and more people that it is useless and harmful to evaluate unless the results involve *words for describing what is being evaluated*—instead of just numbers for ranking people as better than or worse than.

4. The method of contract grading that Danielewicz and I (2009) wrote about in CCC avoids all the untrustworthy mid-range grading and asks us to use a single-number score only for outstanding performances—and also to wait until there are multiple texts to base it on. Yet that scoring does not get in the way of the useful evaluative feedback we give to individual papers. Because the contract focuses on behavior, it lets teachers spend very little time trying to evaluate behavior. Instead they put their time and energy into giving writerly feedback and figuring out which student behaviors to require—that is, which behaviors most reliably lead to learning to write better.
5. What about teachers of large lecture courses in science who base course grades on nothing but one or two machine-graded exams? They can still usefully give a course grade of more than one dimension. When they make up such exams, they are usually conscious (or need to be) or whether a question tests memory, or a theoretic understanding of concepts, or an application of concepts to new material, or computational skill.
6. The evaluative harm from conventional holistically scored placement testing is obvious enough: It falls into all three traps. Most striking is the third trap of using a single text (written under the worst of exam conditions) to judge a student's *ability* to thrive in the regular course. In truth, a test of students' ability to handle alcohol would probably be a more valid measure of how they will fare in first-year writing. The first trap is also lethal: using single-number verdicts for multidimensional entities. With regard to the second trap, conventional holistic scoring on placement tests usually works hard to avoid bias—using two readers and a third in cases of wide divergence. But that process—and the "norming" of readers that goes along with it—just shows susceptibility to the myth of a "true score." See Smith (1993) on a shrewd attempt to avoid that problem: using readers from the courses themselves. These readers are not trying for true scores,

they are asking frankly positional questions of each text: "Does this writing look to me like it was produced by someone who could learn and prosper in my regular section of first-year writing?"

REFERENCES

Benesch, S. (1988). *Ending remediation: Linking ESL and content in higher education*. Washington, DC: TESOL.

Broad, B. (2003). *What we really value: Beyond rubrics in teaching and assessing writing*. Logan, UT: Utah State University Press.

CCCC Committee on Assessment. (1988, Spring). *Post-secondary writing assessment: An update on practices and procedures*. Report to the Executive Committee of the Conference on College Composition and Communication.

Council of Writing Program Administrators. (2000, 2008). *WPA Outcomes Statement for First-Year Composition*. Web.

Despain, L., & Hilgers, T. L. (1992). Readers' responses to the rating of non-uniform portfolios: Are there limits on portfolios' utility? *WPA: Writing Program Administration, 16*(1-2), 24-37.

Elbow, P. (1979). Trying to teach while thinking about the end: Teaching in a competence-based curriculum. In G. Grant et al. (Eds.), *On competence: A critical analysis of competence-based reforms in higher education* (pp. 95-137). San Francisco, CA: Jossey-Bass.

Elbow, P. (1997). Writing assessment: Do it better, do it less. In W. Lutz, E. M. White, & S. Kamusikiri (Eds.), *The politics and practices of assessment in writing* (pp. 120-134). New York, NY: Modern Language Association.

Elbow, P. (1996). Writing assessment in the twenty-first century: A utopian view. In L. Bloom, D. Daiker, & E. M. White (Eds.), *Composition in the 21st century: Crisis and change* (pp. 83-100). Carbondale, IL: Southern Illinois University Press.

Elbow, P., & Danielewicz, J. (2009). A unilateral grading contract to improve learning and teaching. *College Composition and Communication, 61*(2), 244-268.

Grant, G., Elbow, P., Ewens, T., Gamson, Z., Kohli, W., Neumann, W., Olesen, V., & Riesman, D. (Eds.). (1979). *On competence: A critical analysis of competence-based reforms in higher education.* San Francisco, CA: Jossey-Bass.

Greenberg, K. (1992). Validity and reliability: Issues in the direct assessment of writing. *WPA: Writing Program Administration, 16*(1-2), 7-22.

Greenberg, K., Wiener, H., & Donovan, R. (1986). Preface. In K. Greenberg, H. Wiener, & R. Donovan (Eds.), *Writing assessment: Issues and strategies* (pp. xi-xvii). New York, NY: Longman.

Grego, R., & Thompson, N. (1995). The writing program studio: Reconfiguring basic writing/freshman composition. *WPA: Writing Program Administration, 19*(1-2), 66-79.

Herrenstein Smith, B. H. (1988). *Contingencies of value: Alternative perspectives for critical theory*. Cambridge, MA: Harvard University Press.

Kidda, M., Turner, J., & Parker, F.E. (1993). There is an alternative to remedial education. *Metropolitan Universities, 3*(3), 16-25.

Lederman, M. J., Ryzewic, S., & Ribaudo, M. (1983). *Assessment and improvement of the academic skills of entering freshmen: A national survey*. New York, NY: CUNY Instructional Resource Center.

McClelland, D. C. (1973). Testing for competence rather than for intelligence. *American Psychologist, 28*, 1-14.

Royer, D. J., & Gilles, R. (Eds.). (2003). *Directed self-placement: Principles and practices*. Cresskill, NJ: Hampton Press.

Roskelly, H. (2009). [Personal communication to P. Elbow]. Amherst, MA: University of Massachusetts.

Roskelly, H., & Ronald, K. (1998). *Reason to believe: Romanticism, pragmatism, and the possibility of teaching*. Albany, NY: SUNY Press.

Smith, W. (1993). Assessing the adequacy of holistically scoring essays as a writing placement technique. In M. Williamson & B. Huot (Eds.), *Validating holistic scoring for writing assessment: Theoretical and empirical foundations* (pp. 142-205). Cresskill, NJ: Hampton Press.

Winnicott, D. W. (1953). Transitional objects and transitional phenomena—A study of the first not-me. *International Journal of Psycho-Analysis, 34*(1), 89-97.

White, E. M. (1995). An apologia for the timed impromptu essay test. *College Composition and Communication, 46*(1), 30-45.

White, E. M. (2008). Testing in and testing out. *Writing Program Administration, 32*(1), 129-142.

18

FUNDAMENTAL CHALLENGES IN DEVELOPING AND SCORING CONSTRUCTED-RESPONSE ASSESSMENTS

Doug Baldwin
Educational Testing Service

Ensuring technical quality while developing and scoring large-scale constructed-response assessments is harder than it looks. The challenges are many. The solutions are not always apparent. Even experts in the field often disagree about how best to answer the critical questions that these assessments inevitably raise.

In this chapter I describe several of the more difficult challenges test developers face, and I discuss some of the procedures they can follow to make these tests as valid, reliable, and fair as possible. (Definitions of these often problematic terms follow shortly.) The focus is primarily on writing assessments, but the principles apply to all constructed-response and other performance assessments.

By "constructed-response and other performance assessments," I am referring here to any questions that require the test-taker to provide a response, as opposed to selected-response (most often multiple-choice) assessments; these are often also called "free-response" assessments.[1] In writing assessments, asking test-takers to write essays is considered a direct assessment (as opposed to the indirect assessment of multiple-choice items on English grammar and usage), and it therefore has more construct and face validity (although see Condon, Chapter 13, where he discusses the advantages of portfolio assessments over the traditional and still-common short-timed impromptu essay tests. See also Fowles' discussion of the rapid rise of direct writing assessments in graduate admissions in Chapter 7. See also Lane & Stone, 2006, for a useful discussion of these terms.)

These challenges include: how to define and then try to promote validity and reliability in both test design and scoring; administering writing assessments in international settings; and the more recent challenge of how to score responses from test takers who rely heavily on memorized unattributed sources and "canned" text and/or structural elements.

In this discussion, the rhetorical stance is, perhaps necessarily, more one of questions and suggestions than of answers and conclusions. The goal is to outline the issues for which all of us seek possible solutions.

"QUALITY" ROUGHLY DEFINED

The first point to make is that the concept of "technical quality" encompasses expectations or assumptions about the degree to which the assessment is reliable and valid. Reliability is the consistency of measurement (see also Haertel, 2006, for further discussion of the concept of reliability). Validity traditionally was simply defined as meaning that the assessment measures what it is intended to measure; more recently, validity has been defined as being the extent to which the intended meanings and uses of test scores are supported (see also Kane, 2006, and Messick, 1996; in Chapter 26 Moore presents a useful analysis of the changing meanings of these terms; see especially her discussion in "Implications for Writing Assessment").

One point about "quality" needs further clarification, because many test-takers tend to use the word "unfair" to describe issues that are really more accurately termed issues of quality. Although the term "fairness" in general use often blurs with both reliability and validity, as we see later, technically it refers to assessment procedures that measure the same thing for all test-takers regardless of their membership in an identified subgroup, for example, gender or ethnicity (see Camilli, 2006, for a useful overview of fairness in assessment, as well as Bond, Moss, & Carr, 1996, who define fairness even at the individual test-taker level). But as stated in the *ETS Guidelines for Fairness Review of Assessments* (2009), "Fairness and validity are very tightly linked in assessments because *a fair test is one that is valid for different groups of test takers in the intended population* for the test" (p. 2, emphasis added). Furthermore, a writing assessment that has very low reliability by its very nature cannot be valid, and, in popular use, might therefore be called "unfair." In brief, "Absolute fairness for every examinee is impossible to obtain, if for no other reasons than the facts that tests have imperfect reliability and that validity in any particular context is a matter of degree" (AERA, APA, & NCME, 1999, p. 73). (In the next chapter, Inoue and Poe make important points about fairness and race in the world of placement, and Elbow addresses issues of quality in constructed-response assessments in Chapter 17.)

Consider a writing assessment that consists entirely of a test taker drawing a number from 1 to 100 from a hat, with the number determining the test-taker's reported score. Although the test would not be reliable (there would be little chance that a given test-taker would get the same score when taking the test a second time) or valid (pulling a number from a hat is not a valid measure of the "construct"[2] of writing), it would in fact technically be "fair" (every test-taker has an equal chance of drawing a high number, and no group was treated differentially). If, however, on this same imaginary test, one group (say, women) draw from a hat that has a higher percentage of low numbers than a different hat from which men draw, then the test would be equally poor in reliability and validity, but it would also specifically be un*fair* to an identifiable group (women).

That is, if some prompts are harder to answer than others, then although a test taker who got the harder prompt might claim it "wasn't fair," it would in fact be a question of reliability (the same test taker given an easier prompt when retaking the test would get a very different score), as well as validity (the test did not accurately represent the test-taker's writing proficiency). Similarly, if the interrater reliability of the raters scoring the responses is low (e.g., if some raters are systematically more or less strict than others or they are inconsistent), and if a given test-taker's response is scored by a stricter rater, then it is a question of reliability, not fairness. If a prompt on an assessment of writing skills requires specialized content knowledge (which then would be not part of the construct), then although a test-taker might say this was not "fair," in fact it would be a question of construct-irrelevance reducing the test's validity (see also Haertel & Linn, 1996, for a related discussion on comparability in constructed-response assessments).

One can also turn to the Conference on College Composition and Communication (CCCC) Committee on Assessment's (2006) "Writing Assessment: A Position Statement," which presents its concerns that by their very nature refer to what most test-takers would term the fairness of assessments, although it is actually the validity of the test. The CCCC Committee on Assessment's position statement highlights a larger question about all writing assessments that contribute to high-stakes decisions (e.g., high school exit, graduate or undergraduate college admissions, first-year placement, rising junior, etc.): To what degree is *any* kind of timed, single- (or even double-) read, writing assessment consisting of a single impromptu question a "valid" assessment of a test-taker's writing ability? (One could further ask the same question about any timed assessment of any subject in any academic context.)

Assessment is nothing if not a necessary compromise, often one involving decisions around logistics or costs. As Walker (2007) points out, a "three-essay test wherein each essay is scored by a single rater is much more reliable than a single-essay test scored by three raters. However, a choice between these test designs requires balancing benefits and costs" (p. 5; see the discussion of scoring, below). It is easy to say how a program *might* increase the reliability or validity of its tests, but to do so often requires prohibitive increases in costs. This is especially true in writing assessments, because full construct representation of writing is simply unrealistic to expect in any single assessment.

Livingston's (2009) discussion of the decision to use constructed-response prompts instead of (or in addition to) multiple-choice items raises a possibly unexpected issue, which is that some "research studies have shown that male/female differences on constructed-response questions often do not parallel the male/female differences on multiple-choice questions in the same subject" (p. 3; see also Livingston & Rupp, 2004). In brief, programs need to balance the possible gains in construct coverage (and/or face validity) against the risks to fairness in deciding whether to use constructed-response items in their assessments.

Broadly defined in the *ETS Standards for Quality and Fairness* (2002), a major goal in all test development is to "ensure that products and services will be designed, developed, and administered in ways that treat people equally and fairly regardless of differences in personal characteristics such as race, ethnicity, gender, or disability that are not relevant to the intended use of the product or service" (p. 17). To give some sense of the attention that testing companies can bring just to this area of fairness, consider this range of documents Educational Testing Service regularly uses to "serve as standards for quality and fairness" in its assessments: *ETS Standards for Quality and Fairness* (2002), *ETS Guidelines for Fairness Review of Assessments* (2009), *ETS Guidelines for Test Accessibility* (2009), *ETS Guidelines for Fairness Review of Communications* (2009), *ETS Guidelines for the Assessment of English Language Learners* (2009), and a variety of program-specific documents and guidelines for creating Alternative Test Formats for test-takers with specified disabilities. And, in turn, all these guidelines have been created in alignment with the *Standards for Educational and Psychological Testing* (jointly published by the American Educational Research Association, American Psychological Association, and National Council on Measurement in Education, 1999). The very number and range of these documents suggest the complexity of the goal of fairness in assessment.

It is almost always easier to state than to achieve the aim to develop and design constructed-response tests and score the responses in ways that promote the goals of reliability, validity, and fairness. Practices in developing writing assessments are in place to make every reasonable effort to do so, but challenges remain.

STANDARDIZATION, OR PROCRUSTEAN BED?

One challenge in constructed-response scoring concerns the concept of "standardization." Although to some in the educational community the term "standardized testing" may evoke negative connotations, in fact, "standardization" (i.e., ensuring that all test-takers receive parallel assessments that are given under the same testing conditions and are comparably scored) is a fundamental requirement. (See, for instance, Odendahl, 2010, on the historical development of best practices in holistic scoring, specifically referring to the use of rubrics, or scoring guides, "Such standardization would eventually be seen as a matter of fairness as well as validity.") Allowing students in some testing centers twice as much time as those in other centers would violate principles of validity. Allowing some but not all test-takers access to dictionaries would clearly violate the principle of standardized testing conditions and, therefore, would not result in a valid (or fair) assessment.

However, if most (but not all) test-takers on a given computer-delivered assessment are used to having access to a spell-check program, is it "fair" to administer a writing assessment without allowing for that spell-check capability? If the program does decide to allow a spell-check feature, is that "fair" to test- takers who are not accustomed to using such a tool? Is allowing access to spell-check features fair to students whose limited word-processing skills make it necessary for them to respond in handwriting? What if for some students the use of a spell-check program may cause more distractions and/or more cases of wrong word choice (i.e., choosing a correctly spelled but incorrect word, which may be scored as worse than the original misspelled but recognizable word)? And all these questions are paralleled by similar questions involving the use of a grammar checker, and they all touch on larger issues of construct coverage and validity.

Consider, for instance, the possibility that one writing assessment prompt is in some systematic way more difficult for the test-taking population than the corresponding prompt given on another form, or administration, of the same assessment—this difference in difficulty could result in what would appear to be possible unfairness to those test-takers who happen to get the harder prompt (even if technically it would be not fairness so much as lowered reliability and validity, as noted above). In parallel multiple-choice assessments, statistical equating can ensure statistical comparability across varying forms of the same assessment with different items. However, statistical equating is difficult to implement when there are few constructed-response prompts on a given test. Therefore, detailed procedures that do not involve equating are typically followed to ensure that the constructed-response assessments are comparable (see Baldwin, Fowles, & Livingston, 2005).

After making a significant effort to develop prompts of equal difficulty and putting these prompts through systematic fairness reviews, programs usually then pretest the prompts. They use the pretest prompts to compare the difficulty of the prompts and to evaluate each prompt for fairness and general accessibility. If a prompt calls for persuasive writing (e.g., taking one side of a controversial issue), they try to determine if it appears equally easy for examinees to take either position on the issue. Are there patterns in the responses to suggest that test-takers have unexpected problems interpreting a prompt or that certain groups have a harder time responding? Are there any prompts on which it is difficult for raters to agree on the appropriate score? And even after all these procedures, prompts that are less than ideal can reach the field. One early placement assessment had a paragraph about contemporary music followed by a prompt asking the test-taker to discuss favorite kinds of music, to which one student responded simply, "I am deaf and cannot therefore write about this topic."

In the interest of what might be termed "face fairness" (i.e., test-takers' perception that the test is fair), some test programs have allowed the test-takers to choose which of two prompts to write about. One might initially assume that allowing choice would make the test more fair; if the test-taker has a harder time thinking of an approach to one prompt, he or she can opt for the other. However, the issue turns out not to be so simple. One concern is that despite all efforts in test design and item writing to ensure comparability across prompts, the prompts can vary in difficulty, meaning that some test-takers might have an easier prompt. Perhaps even more counterintuitive, research has shown that some test-takers, when given a choice of prompts, can choose badly. That is, they may choose prompts on which they individually do not perform as well as they would have performed on the prompts they did not choose.[3] Also, on many assessments, each prompt is based on a reading passage, so that it becomes impractical to allot time for test takers to read two passages and decide which prompt to respond to. For these reasons, many writing assessments require all test-takers at a given administration to respond to the same prompt.

TO USE, OR NOT TO USE, PARTIAL SECOND SCORES

Another challenge arises around how to use scores that are given only to a subset of responses. Often on a writing assessment where the responses receive only one rater's score, some of the responses (typically 10 to 20%) get a second, independent ("blind") score. These second ratings allow for a psychometric analysis of the inferred interrater reliability (the estimate of what it would be were all responses double scored), which, in turn, can serve as one indicator of the reliability of the scoring process. What, if anything, should one do with those responses that receive a "discrepant" second score? In many "double-scored" assessments (where each response receives two independent scores), programs typically use the term "discrepant" to indicate a score that is different enough from the first score (often this is defined as being more than one point apart on a typical 6-point scoring scale) that the program requires a third, or adjudicated, rating to determine the final score. (Often this third score is averaged with one or both of the two initial scores). But what if only 10% of the test-takers' responses receive a second score? What should the program do in that case when the second score is very different from the first?

As in so many questions that arise when discussing issues about best practices in writing assessments, strong cases can be made for entirely opposed policies. Some assessment experts might argue that these second scores should be disregarded in computing the test-takers' scores. Their argument? Using the second scores might not be "fair" to the 90% of the test-taking population whose responses did not get the "benefit" of a second impartial score. But this sword cuts both ways: Quite possibly a low-performing student might prefer only a single score, for the very reason that the single score—if "wrong"—would statistically be more likely to be too high than too low. However, people who take this position argue that getting what is presumably a "more accurate" or "higher quality" score is a benefit to the test-taker and therefore should be available either for all test-takers or for none (which then might suggest that programs should double score all responses).

The opposite point of view is that programs should use all the information they have to maximize the accuracy of each score they report, even if they do not have the same information for all test-takers. If the guidelines that are traditionally considered to reflect "best practices in constructed-response scoring" recommend adjudicating discrepant scores, this argument asks, why shouldn't one do so for the discrepant scores we know about, even though the program might find others if they looked for them? As long as the selection of the responses that receive a second score is completely and impartially random, no one—this position would claim—is being treated unfairly. Consider an analogy. Why not follow the same practice that programs generally use when discovering an inaccurate rating through "backreading?" Backreading is the spot-checking, by expert scorers, of a small percentage of the responses and the ratings assigned to them. When it reveals an inaccurate rating, the inaccurate rating is corrected. But all this discussion further opens the door to the truth that no matter how careful and exacting the training and monitoring of raters, there will always remain the possibility that some raters will be more stringent and others more generous (and yet others who are simply erratic).

CAN YOU READ MY WORD PROCESSING?

Another seemingly simple question has to do with the medium in which a writing assessment is taken. Should test-takers handwrite, or should they word process, their responses, or should they be given a choice? Here again, it might seem to be a simple question with the simple answer, "Let test-takers decide for themselves." And, again, it turns out to be more complicated than one might hope (see Powers, Fowles, Farnum, & Ramsey, 1992; Truell, Alexander, & Davis, 2004; Wolfe, 2003; Wolfe, Boldton, Feltovich, & Niday, 1996).

One might think that letting the test-taker choose is the answer. But then we must ask: Are keyboard-fluent test-takers given an unfair advantage over those unfamiliar with word processing, even if the latter handwrite their responses, because the former can presumably produce more and cleaner text in the same time period?[4] But requiring everyone to handwrite has its fairness risks as well. In Massachusetts, some parents of elementary school students sued the state over end-of-year writing assessments requiring handwriting when, the plaintiffs argued, the student test-takers were accustomed to writing only on computers and thus were unfairly assessed in the relatively unfamiliar environment of paper-and-pencil testing (Russell & Plati, 2001).

Wolfe (2003) conducted a study looking at the effects of requiring word processing versus handwriting, asking such questions as, "Do essays written by hand and by computer offer examinees the same opportunity to demonstrate their English language ability? Is the program assessing the same language proficiency constructs when the mode of composition is changed? Are students advantaged or disadvantaged by their choice of composition mode?" Although certain of the study's results were not conclusive, the study did establish that there needs to be further analysis of rater bias on a routine basis and further study of the relationship between keyboarding skills and performance on writing assessments, including addressing concerns that raters may respond differently to responses in each medium. Furthermore, these studies do not generalize well; that is, one needs to conduct specific studies for each given assessment and population of examinees.

RATING THE SCORING

This leads to what may be the greatest challenge in terms of ensuring quality in constructed-response assessments: trying to ensure the quality of the scoring itself.

A general principle, outlined in the ETS guidelines on constructed-response scoring, is that having multiple raters evaluate multiple performances leads to more reliable assessments, and that reliability in scoring is necessary to ensure the validity of the writing assessment (Baldwin et al., 2005). That is, to the degree possible, given omnipresent issues around logistics and costs, more prompts, each of which is scored by more raters, leads to more reliability. In practice, this goal has often resulted in, for instance, the administration of two prompts, with the responses each read independently by two raters, each following a specific scoring guide, or rubric, which is supplemented with annotated exemplar responses showing the variety and range of kinds of responses at each score point. Some programs combine one double-read response with a multiple-choice section; other programs combine several single-read prompts with a multiple-choice section.

The raters are typically required to have program-defined minimum credentials (e.g., experience teaching composition at the college level). They are usually required to pass a certification test in which they are expected to score a certain number of responses with a predetermined level of accuracy. Before beginning each session they are required to demonstrate that they are "calibrated" by scoring a set of responses for which the correct ratings have been previously determined by expert raters. Meanwhile, programs administering writing assessments usually then include some kinds of monitoring in which scoring experts evaluate selected responses and the scores given by the raters. (For a detailed discussion of the specific methodologies that are typically followed to ensure standardized, equitable scoring, see McClellan, 2010.)

In recent years, programs have begun to consider the reliability and validity of using automated scoring. (See Burstein and Herrington & Moran, Chapters 11 and 12, this volume. Also see Monaghan's, 2005, summary of Bridgeman's, 2004, recommendation to use automated scoring software as a check score where any significant difference between the first human rater and the automated score would result in a second human rater's score, "In this system the essay score would always be based solely on human raters" [p. 2]). Again, the principle to remember is that all these decisions ultimately fall under the aegis of validity and that the program needs to follow that principle. Even the specific procedures that a given program needs to follow to address, for instance, a "rescore" policy (i.e., when a test-taker requests that a score on a response be checked), need to follow a standardized protocol.

ASSESSING WRITING IN ANOTHER COUNTRY

Special challenges in writing assessments can arise when developing and implementing a writing assessment in another country (i.e., testing the

English-writing skills of students who are learning English as a foreign language within their own societies, as opposed to traditional ESL tests administered to students who wish to study in, say, the United States or England). Here are new challenges. In some cases, the accepted criteria that define good writing in the country where test-takers' writing will be assessed are not the same as those in the country where the assessment is being developed. For example, correct spelling may be considered highly important in one country but of minor importance in the other. What criteria should be followed, and on what principles of construct coverage? How can a program ensure that the prompts are appropriate for the population of test-takers? The principle is that prompts and scoring procedures must accurately assess students' language skills without expectations of specific cultural experiences or perspectives or backgrounds that could interfere with a given test-taker's ability to demonstrate writing skills. All of which leads to another question: If there are concerns about superimposing one culture's definition of "good writing" onto another culture, should we also be concerned about imposing one kind of definition of "good writing" onto all subgroups within the United States?

Still other concerns can arise when second language learners take assessments within the United States. These issues are addressed elsewhere, for instance in the *ETS Guidelines for the Assessment of English Language Learners* (2009). Also relevant is the CCCC Committee on Assessment's (2006) position statement, under the section, "Best assessment practice respects language variety and diversity": "Furthermore, assessments that are keyed closely to an American cultural context may disadvantage second language writers. … Best assessment practice responds to this call by creating assessments that are sensitive to the language varieties in use among the local population and sensitive to the context-specific outcomes being assessed." Given the increasing numbers of test-takers who are English language learners, there inevitably arise special challenges in ensuring fair evaluation of responses representing significant language variety and diversity. For instance, given that the construct is writing, not reading, is it reasonable to give the prompt only in English, or should a translation be provided so that the non-English-speaking test-takers are clear as to what question they are answering? Should the raters be native speakers of English, or second language speakers who might more accurately assess the kind of writing produced by other second language speakers?

IN SOMEONE ELSE'S WORDS

There are three anecdotes to consider when facing a final challenge in writing assessments:

1. Old college student epigram: "*One book, plagiarism; two books, research.*"
2. A real test-taker's recent response to the accusation that the response did not exhibit "original writing" on a major assessment: "*How can you say I cheated? Every word in my response came directly off the Internet!*"
3. From a recent posting on the Writing Program Administrators listserv: "*... I heard a local high school teacher on the radio explain his plagiarism prevention strategy: Run everything through Turnitin.com; if it shows less than 15% 'plagiarized' then you get an A; 15-35%; a B, 35% gets you a C on your paper; but if it shows more than 50% plagiarized content, alas, then, you get an F*" (Piedmont-Marton, 2010).

Many programs face an ongoing specific concern about the policies to follow in scoring responses that clearly include language that is not the test-taker's own, but there may be cross-cultural (mis)understandings, specifically as they relate to issues around plagiarism, or, perhaps too cynically stated, "test preparation." It turns out to touch on extraordinarily complicated issues around language acquisition, students' right to prepare for an assessment, and how one can accurately assess a test-taker's skill. For instance, how should the program distinguish between learning a second language and memorization, that is, between original writing and mere recitation? As when implementing assessments in other countries, this requires sensitivity to varying interpretations of what exactly it means to produce "original" work rather than memorized recitations.

Questions about test preparation are not limited to assessments given in international settings. For any high-stakes assessment, students can attend test prep training in which they are taught (often word-for-word) formulaic responses—complicated essay "shells" that they minutely manipulate to fit the general subject in the (intentionally open-ended and accessible-to-all) prompt. What is the best way to evaluate these responses? Some testing programs attempt to ensure fairness by prepublishing their pool of reused prompts. If they do, is it wrong for a test-taker to memorize a prepared response to every possible prompt and then to use some of these in providing a response? If a generic, open-ended prompt allows for a memorized generic response, is the test-taker at fault for memorizing a "canned" response in such cases?

It is not easy to draw the line between absolute plagiarism, the use of test-prep-memorized "shells," and what some assessment programs term "complete essay templates" in which test takers memorize an entire, formulaic essay, and plug in vocabulary from the prompt and any associated stimulus material. The line between "learned structure" and "illicitly memorized shells" is thin. Consider, for instance, Graff and Birkenstein's (2006) *They Say, I Say*, a popular (if controversial) instructional text for first-year composition classes, which in effect "teaches" students (or models for them) "templates." Where and how this is different from test prep companies who "teach to the test" is far murkier than one might expect. How should one score test-takers' responses that at least in part clearly use memorized examples, facts, and, occasionally, even entire sentences?

One middle school assessment asks test-takers to summarize a short reading passage, and it turns out to be very difficult to know how to score responses that merely parrot the original source differently from those that merely stick in synonyms for most of the original passage's vocabulary. What, really, does it mean to "use your own words?" Testing programs need to address these and a variety of related questions. In an Internet world, how should assessments account for the technological ease of "cutting and pasting" and, further, accurately assess original, critical thinking? It does not really help to resort to the rephrased, "I can't define plagiarism, but I know it when I read it," although it is a tempting stance.

The complicated interaction between test development and test prep becomes extremely problematic, and consequently the writing and the scoring of tests then becomes quite challenging. Testing programs often find themselves in the position of having to redevelop writing assessments specifically to address concerns about academic integrity and fair assessment as well as training raters in how to evaluate responses with memorized canned text. One possible approach is to include a sufficiently long stimulus (i.e., reading passage) and require test-takers to develop responses that specifically address issues discussed in the passage. The way a testing program treats these responses has significant fairness implications for the other test takers who do not use such test preparation.

CONCLUDING QUESTIONS

Designing and scoring constructed-response assessments have challenges that turn out to be harder to resolve than one might at first expect. Programs administering constructed-response assessments have needed, and continue to need, to meet these challenges by developing procedures and policies that promote the validity, the reliability, the fairness, and thus the overall technical quality of the assessments. In doing so, at least some of the major questions that we need to keep in mind as we design and plan the scoring and reporting for writing assessments might include the following. How do we ensure that our assessments:

- are valid and reliable?
- maintain a maximum overall "quality"?
- meet the technical requirements of "fairness" (i.e., no differential impact on identified subgroups, including both domestic and international English language learners)?
- are standardized (e.g., comparable prompts; consistent policies on the use of partial second scores, the choice of media to write one's response, the use of grammar- and/or spell-check programs, etc.), and thus seem "fair" to all test-takers?
- are scored reliably (including consistent policies and procedures around training and concerns with possible plagiarism or other problematic test preparation)?

Questions, indeed, but with no easy answers proffered.

ACKNOWLEDGMENTS

This chapter has benefited greatly from suggestions made by Mary Fowles, Skip Livingston, Michael Zieky, and, especially, Nor Odendahl.

ENDNOTES

1. "The performance, or response, may be written in an essay booklet, word-processed on a computer, recorded on a cassette or computer disc, entering within a computer-simulated scenario, performed on stage, or presented in some other non-multiple-choice format. The tasks may be simple or highly complex: responses may range from short answer to portfolios, projects, interviews, or presentations" (Baldwin, Fowles, & Livingston, 2003, p. i).
2. Construct is the specific set of abilities or characteristics that the test is intended to assess.
3. Powers, Fowles, Farnum, and Ramsey (1992) in fact concluded that choice neither harmed nor benefited test-takers on a graduate writing skills assessment.
4. Powers, Fowles, Farnum, and Ramsey (1992) found that with the exact same responses presented in two different modes, some raters penalized the word-processed more than the handwritten responses (presumably because the errors were more obvious), but with training that this bias could be corrected.

REFERENCES

American Educational Research Association (AERA), American Psychological Association (APA), and National Council on Measurement in Education (NCME). (1999). *Standards for educational and psychological testing.* Washington, DC: American Psychological Association.

Baldwin, D. G., Fowles, M., & Livingston, S. A. (2005). *Guidelines for constructed-response and other performance assessments.* Princeton, NJ: Educational Testing Service.

Bond, L., Moss, P., & Carr, P. (1996). Fairness in large-scale performance assessments. In G. Phillips (Ed.), *Technical issues in large-scale performance assessments* (pp. 117-140). Washington, DC: National Center for Educational Statistics.

Bridgeman, B. (2004). *E-rater as a quality control on human scorers.* Presentation in the ETS Research Colloquium Series, Princeton, NJ.

Camilli, G. (2006). Test fairness. In R. L. Brennan (Ed.), *Educational measurement* (4th ed., pp. 221-256). Westport, CT: American Council on Education and Praeger Publishers.

Conference on College Composition and Communication. (2006). *Writing assessment: A position statement.* Web.

Educational Testing Service. (2002). *ETS standards for quality and fairness.* Princeton, NJ: Educational Testing Service.

Educational Testing Service. (2009). *ETS guidelines for fairness review of assessments.* Princeton, NJ: Educational Testing Service.

Educational Testing Service. (2009). *ETS guidelines for fairness review of communications.* Princeton, NJ: Educational Testing Service.

Educational Testing Service. (2009). *ETS guidelines for test accessibility.* Princeton, NJ: Educational Testing Service.

Educational Testing Service. (2009). *ETS guidelines for the assessment of English language learners.* Princeton, NJ: Educational Testing Service.

Graff, G., & Birkenstein, C. (2006). *They say, I say.* New York, NY: W. W. Norton.

Haertel, E. H. (2006). Reliability. In R. L. Brennan (Ed.), *Educational measurement* (4th ed., pp. 65-110). Westport, CT: American Council on Education and Praeger Publishers.

Haertel, E. H., & Linn, R. L. (1996). Comparability. In G. Phillips (Ed.), *Technical issues in large-scale performance assessments* (pp. 59-78). Washington, DC: National Center for Educational Statistics.

Kane, M. T. (2006). Validation. In R. L. Brennan (Ed.), *Educational measurement* (4th ed., pp. 17-64). Westport, CT: American Council on Education and Praeger Publishers.

Lane, S., & Stone, C. A. (2006). Performance assessment. In R. L. Brennan (Ed.), *Educational measurement* (4th ed., pp. 387-431). Westport, CT: American Council on Education and Praeger Publishers.

Livingston, S. A. (2009). *Constructed-response test questions: Why we use them; how we score them.* Princeton, NJ: Educational Testing Service R&D Connections.

Livingston, S. A., & Rupp. S. L. (2004). *Performance of men and women on multiple-choice and constructed-response tests for beginning teachers (*ETS Research Report No. RR-04-48). Princeton, NJ: Educational Testing Service.

McClellan, C. (2010). *Constructed-response scoring—doing it right.* Princeton, NJ: Educational Testing Service R&D Connections.

Messick, S. (1996). Validity of performance assessment. In G. Phillips (Ed.), *Technical issues in large-scale performance assessments* (pp. 1-18). Washington, DC: National Center for Educational Statistics.

Monaghan, W., & Bridgeman, B. (2005). *E-rater as a quality control on human scores.* Princeton, NJ: Educational Testing Service R&D Connections.

Odendahl, N. V. (2010). *Testwise: Understanding educational assessment* (Vol. 2). Manuscript in preparation.

Piedmon-Marton, E. (2010, February 10). Why our jobs are hard [Electronic mailing list message]. Web.

Powers, D. E., Fowles, M. E., Farnum, M., & Ramsey, P. (1992). *Will they think less of my handwritten essay if others word process theirs? Effects on essay scores of intermingling handwritten and word-processed essays.* Research Report No. RR-92-45. Princeton, NJ: Educational Testing Service.

Russell, M., & Plati, T. (2001). Effects of computer versus paper administration of a state-mandated writing assessment. *Teachers College Record.* Web.

Truell, A. D., Alexander, M. W., & Davis, R. E. (2004). Comparing postsecondary marketing student performance on computer-based and handwritten essay tests. *Journal of Career and Technical Education, 20*(2), 69-78.

Walker, M. E. (2007). *Is test score reliability necessary?* Princeton, NJ: Educational Testing Service R&D Connections.

Wolfe, E. (2003). Examinee characteristics associated with choice of composition medium on the TOEFL writing section. *The Journal of Technology, Learning, and Assessment, 2*(4). Web.

Wolfe, E., Boldton, S., Feltovich, B., & Niday, D. M. (1996). The influence of student experience with word processors on the quality of essays written for a direct writing assessment. *Assessing Writing, 3(*2), 123-147.

19

RACIAL FORMATIONS IN TWO WRITING ASSESSMENTS
REVISITING WHITE AND THOMAS' FINDINGS ON THE ENGLISH PLACEMENT TEST AFTER 30 YEARS

Asao B. Inoue
California State University, Fresno

Mya Poe
Pennsylvania State University

In their 1981 *College English* article, White and Thomas compared test results of racially diverse first-year college students to understand the "effect of different kinds of testing upon the distribution of scores for racial minorities" (p. 276). Specifically, White and Thomas compared the scores of students (N = 10,719) on two college entrance writing tests, the Test of Standard Written English (TSWE), a selected-response test that included questions on isolated items related to the usage of standard English, and the English Placement Test (EPT), a test that included selected-response questions on usage related to sentence structure, logic, and organization, as well as a constructed-response essay assessment.[1] When the results of the two tests were analyzed, Mexican American, Asian American, African American, and White students showed widely varying results on the TWSE.[2] For example, the distribution of scores for African American students on the TSWE was different than the distribution of their scores on the EPT essay test. Moreover, the TSWE and the essay portion of the EPT distributed scores toward the lower end for students of color, particularly African American students. The findings, White and Thomas (1981) concluded, cast doubt on the validity of the TWSE as an indicator of writing ability. In drawing their conclusion, White and Thomas eliminated rater bias on the part of essay raters (p. 280).[3] Raters, they explained, were carefully trained on the writing construct and did not know the identity of any student writers.

There is much to praise in White and Thomas' work, even if their conclusions concerning race and writing proficiency are limited. For example, White and Thomas (1981) observed that the differences they found in African American students' scores on the TWSE and EPT might be attributed to the types of questions that appear on usage tests—usage questions that "particularly penaliz[e] non-significant features of minority dialects" (p. 280), but they did not investigate discursive markers in student writing (Smitherman, 1993) or how students' interpretation of the rhetorical situation shapes their essay writing choices (Poe, 2006) (see Baldwin, Chapter 18, for other queries that might be made of the test design). Yet, White and Thomas's analysis remains important because they offer an attempt to understand the racial formations occurring from a test (even though they were not working from a concept of "racial formation," rather the traditional social science category of racial groups). Racial formation, a term coined by ethnic studies professor Michael Omi and sociologist Howard Winant (1994) in their influential seek to understand race as a social construct that shifts over time and influences individual identity as well as larger social structures through a series of "racial projects," such as the EPT and TSWE, that makes racial differences meaningful in U.S. society and schools. We see White and Thomas's article as an early attempt to understand writing assessment's construction of uneven racial formations and potential differential impact through the uneven distribution of writing test scores.[4] They offer quantitative evidence of the way writing tests at the time, and perhaps now, produce different score distributions for different racial formations. And they hint at the lack of sufficient construct validity for decisions about the writing abilities of students of color.

In what follows, we revisit White and Thomas' data on the EPT, a writing assessment still used today to place students in writing courses at most CSU campuses. We compare their 1978 findings to our 2008 findings at CSU, Fresno. Our goal is to understand how comparisons may be made in data sets from similar contexts at two points in time yet may offer very different conclusions when we explore who comprises racial groups at those different points in time. Given the scope of our work, we are concerned primarily with the following questions: Are the score distributions of various racial formations on the EPT on just one campus (CSU, Fresno, Fall 2008) different from those found by White and Thomas in their 1978 data (all CSU campuses, Fall 1979)? What do teachers, WPAs, and writing programs gain by considering local racial formations on a writing assessment like the EPT? In exploring these questions, our goal is to show the importance of looking at evolving local racial formations and differential affects on those formations by local writing assessments. What we would like to show in this chapter is how bias or fairness in the traditional psychological sense is not the only way to understand a test as producing inequality among various racial formations.

RACE AND RACIAL FORMATION

Omi and Winant (1994) explore "how concepts of race are created and changed, how they become the focus of political conflicts, and how they have come to permeate U.S. society" (p. vii). Racial formation is the "socio-historical process by which racial categories are created, inhabited, transformed, and destroyed" (p. 55). Racial formations, Omi and Winant argue, are made through historically situated "projects in which human bodies and social structures [are] represented and organized" (p. 56). The way that society is organized and structured leads to uneven racial outcomes. Because race is a historically evolving concept, race has and continues to have a significant shaping impact on individual identity as well as U.S. institutions. In other words, race is not a static marker of identity; rather, it is a politically contested, evolving construct that shapes group and individual identity. To give a simple example here from the literature, note that White and Thomas used the group marker of Mexican American in their research, not Hispanic or Latino/a. (They also hyphenated the terms Mexican-American as well as Asian-American and African-American.). Although the term Hispanic was introduced on the 1970 U.S. census, the previous designation of Mexican American remained in research. And although Hispanic or Latino is often a term used in everyday U.S. discourse to mark a racial identity, Hispanic is not a term used to identify race on the U.S. Census. Instead, for example, the 2010 Census (question 8) asks if the respondent is of "Hispanic, Latino or Spanish origin," meaning if the individual is from a specific geographic region. The Census includes a separate question (question 9) about an individual's race, tainted with ethnic origins—White, Black/African Am./Negro, American Indian or Alaska Native, Asian Indian, Chinese, Filipino, Japanese, Korean, Vietnamese, Native Hawaiian, Guamanian or Chamorro, Other Asian, Other Pacific Islander, and Some other race (U.S. Census Bureau, 2010; see Office of Management and Budget, 1995, for an explanation of the two-question rationale). The terms Mexican-American, Mexican American, Hispanic, and Latino/a have all had politically contested histories in U.S. culture as the racial/ethnic identity of people marked by these categories, shifting over time.

Contrary to the belief that reporting of race simply perpetuates stereotypes, the identification of race has long been an important tool in Civil Rights challenges to testing.[5] "Disparate impact" allegations, which are brought under the federal Civil Rights Act (Title VI and VIII) or the U.S. Constitution (Fourteenth Amendment, equal protection clause), charge that standardized tests are biased against lower-performing groups (Phillips & Camara, 2006, p. 733). "Due process" challenges, which are also brought under the Fourteenth Amendment, have been successful against testing procedures that are "arbitrary, capricious, or fundamentally unfair to some examinees" (Phillips & Camara, 2006, p. 734). Ultimately, as sociologist Tukufu Zuberi (2001) points out, race-based data are essential if "we are to achieve racial equality" (p. 120).

From a educational measurement point of view, understanding racial formations in test results and decisions would be helpful in creating "fair" tests (see testing fairness guidelines of AERA, APA, & NCME, 1999; ETS, 2010). Doug Baldwin and Peter Elbow both wrestle with the notion of fairness (in this volume). In Chapter 17 Peter Elbow argues that fairness is a matter of degree and that multidimensional assessment or contextualized assessment can be more fair than assessments in which a single score is assigned as though that score represents some objective reality. Baldwin points out that test designers see fairness as related to validity and reliability, and he offers a number of considerations in assessing a test's fairness. Like Baldwin, we think fairness must not be seen as "goodwill," but rather as an integral part of the design of writing assessment. Like Elbow, we agree that contextualization helps students and teachers make more sense of assessment.

From our point of view, reporting writing assessment results by race is critical to understanding test design, legal issues, and ethical concerns, including construct representation, disparate impact, and social justice. Inoue (2009b) calls this "reality check" of writing assessment results *racial validation*. He defines the inquiry this way: It is "an argument that explains the degree to which empirical evidence of racial formations around our assessments and the theoretical frameworks that account for racial formations support the adequacy and appropriateness of inferences and actions made from the assessments" (p. 110).

One difficulty, however, with using race in reporting test results comes when race is treated as a static entity, as though groups do not change over time or that racial groups are identical across contexts. Racial identifications in the United States for various groups may legally change over time (e.g., Japanese have been legally considered White as well as Asian at various times in the United States) Also, changes in immigration patterns may mean that the profile of a race group may change quite dramatically over time with different groups bringing different English-language proficiency and different cultural attitudes towards testing. Often in statistical analysis of test scores, however, these changes in race are lost and replaced by a fixed notion of race. When race is treated as an acontextual, fixed characteristic, it becomes a variable from which causal explanations can be assigned (Zuberi, 2001). James

(2008) writes about the implications of "fixing" race as a control variable, in which "the use of race as a control variable flattens out the meanings of racial differences and replaces it with a generic notion of difference (p. 43). Indeed, as Poe (2009) found in her analysis of 78 assessment articles that used racial categories for the reporting of results, most authors used race as a fixed characteristic in their analysis, ignoring both the local and national contexts in which racial identity was playing out. Although the category of "race" may be a column in a spreadsheet, racial formations are not static and neither should be the conclusions made about race. What matters here is that researchers situate their analysis of test scores within the contexts in which those categories operate. Such situating of data from which meaningful conclusions may be made allows researchers to use more robust conceptualizations and make more informed inferences from the test results regarding racial disparities (for a good example, see Gillborn & Mirza, 2000). "Anticipatory numbering" as Rich Haswell in Chapter 23 would call it, allows us to use statistics meaningfully in local contexts and retain ownership of the conclusions drawn about various groups of students at our institutions.

In doing racial validation studies, then, the challenge is to use racial categories that are locally meaningful. Beyond White and Thomas, other researchers have documented how local context, race, and writing assessment are deeply interdependent. For example, Sternglass (1998) contrasts the writing development of students in their courses with the effect of high-stakes assessments, such as the rising junior test, the Writing Assessment Test (WAT). In writing about the City College learning environment, Sternglass explains,

> That students in my study from the wide diversity of backgrounds felt comfortable and free enough to explore issues of race, gender and sexual orientation, and social class in their writing is a credit to the environment created in many City College classrooms, where the proportion of minority instructors is greater than at many other City University (or nationwide) campuses. (p. 61)

Students found supportive environments to develop as writers in City College courses; however, there was no place to acknowledge that development on the WAT. In reflecting on the inability of students to pass the WAT, Sternglass (1998) writes about her second-language writers: "The errors found in the writing of second-dialect and second-language speakers need to be interpreted knowledgeably as markers in a developing language system and as parts of language patterns, not as lists of discrete mistakes" (p. 153). DasBender in Chapter 21 offers directed self-placement strategies for generation 1.5 students. Considering DSP to place generation 1.5 students looks beyond error in writing to make appropriate writing course placements.

Lioi and Merola (in press) offer another perspective on the interconnection of context, race, and writing assessment. They document the role of race, language, and national identity in writing placement at The Juilliard School. They write that before the institution of a writing placement test in 2008, Juilliard placed students into writing classes by a review of their academic records, a process that resulted in the following composition of basic writing students:

> The basic writing course was populated overwhelmingly by Music students who were working-class African Americans, international East Asians, and white, U.S.-born home-schooled students. All of these groups were perceived as academically disadvantaged relative to a white, upper middle-class, American norm of college preparation. (n.p.)

When the old method of placement was replaced with a timed, impromptu writing assessment, the test "vastly increased the number of white, American students in basic writing, making the class population appear much more like the racial and national composition of the student body across the divisions" (n.p.). Basic writing was no longer populated primarily by Music students but rather a cross-section of Juilliard students in various majors who needed additional support for writing. Lioi and Merola go on to argue that ongoing validation of the new writing placement test is needed to ascertain whether the new test is actually fairer for the students of color who are placed in basic writing. Although the Juilliard test is still under validation, it is important to note that without simply counting the racial demographics of students in basic writing and questioning how those students ended up there, Lioi and Merola would not have exposed how local assumptions about Music students were guiding placement decisions.

The complexities at CUNY or Juilliard are not unlike those at other institutions. We meet many WPAs who question how they can better design assessments that more accurately and fairly measure the writing abilities of students. Like White and Thomas, we see possibilities for future equity in "seeing" race, especially when such explorations go on to ask what racial formations mean relative to expected writing/language competencies within specific contexts.

THE ENGLISH PLACEMENT TEST (EPT)

The EPT is a writing assessment cooperatively designed in 1977 by CSU faculty and the Educational Testing Service (ETS). All incoming first-year students take the test. A few students each year are exempt if they score a 550 or higher on the verbal section of what is now called the SAT Reasoning Test, a 24 or higher on the enhanced ACT English Test, a 680 or higher on the SAT Writing Section, or earn a score of 3, 4, or 5 on the Language and Composition or Literature and Composition AP exams. Additionally, any student who has completed a transferable writing course from another school with a C grade or better may be exempt from taking the EPT. These guidelines regularly exempt about 27% of all regularly admitted students (CSU, 2002, p. 2). The test consists of a 45-minute essay portion and a 30-minute multiple-choice portion and is given three times a year on CSU campuses.[6]

In comparing scores from the EPT to the TSWE, White (2010) explains that they saw an opportunity to understand the ways a writing test performed with various racial groups on a large scale:

> As the data began to accumulate from the first year of the EPT [AY 1977-78], I realized that we had a unique opportunity to merge three different databases: the EPT results, with their subscores; the TSWE scores for many of the same students; and the racial profiles as volunteered by the entering students. We had such large numbers that we could provide genuine evidence on the pressing questions of the relation of essay scores to [multiple-choice] scores and the effects of race on writing tests—beyond anything before, or since, I think.

White was correct about the kind of evidence he and Thomas could produce, but it is the second focus, the one concerning the way a writing proficiency test, in this case, a test used to place students in First Year Writing (FYW) courses in the CSU system of campuses, performs differently for various racial formations that is still compelling for our analysis 30 years later.[7]

EPT RESULTS IN 1978 AND 2008: OBSERVATIONS THAT DO NOT CONSIDER RACE

The EPT student data from 1978 and 2008 suggest several observations if we do not look at the results by racial category. When considering all student test-takers in both years (Fall 1978 and Fall 2008), the score distributions for the EPT essay are similar. Each year's distribution of scores is a standard bell curve (or "normal distribution") with each group's mean score and standard deviation (SD) being similar (see Table 19.1). It should be noted that in 1978, each student received two scores for the same essay, which were then added together. This meant that any essay could receive a score between 2 to 12. In

Table 19.1. EPT Essay Results Reported in White and Thomas (1981) and CSUF's Office of Institutional Research (2008)

	N for EPT Essay	Avg. EPT Essay[a]	SD for EPT Essay
Fall 1978			
White	5,236	7.6	1.7
Black	583	6.2	1.9
Mexican-American	445	6.6	1.9
Asian Pacific Islander[b]	606	6.8	1.9
Native American[c]	N/A	N/A	N/A
ALL	10,674	7.3	1.9
Fall 2008			
White	572	3.7	0.8
Black	213	3.3	0.8
Latino/a	884	3.3	0.8
Asian Pacific Islander	440	3.1	1.0
Native American	15	3.7	0.8
ALL	2,228	3.4	0.9

[a] In Fall 1978 students received 2 scores of 1 to 6 each, which made each total score range from 2 to 12. In Fall 2008, students only received 1 score, making any score range from 1 to 6.
[b] Asian Pacific Islander is labeled "Asian-American" in White and Thomas.
[c] Native Americans are not reported in White and Thomas.

2008, however, each essay received only one score between 1 to 6.[8] Thus, the differences in scoring produce apparent differences in SD measures. The important observation is that the SD, a measure of the dispersion of a set of data from its mean, for one CSU campus (Fresno) in 2008 appears to be consistent with all campuses in 1978. This further suggests that both overall student populations appear to be consistent in their EPT performances 30 years apart.

Not only do both sets of students (Fall 1978 and Fall 2008) tend to produce similar scores on the scale, but also the average score is generally dispersed about the same relative distance from the mean. Thus, it would appear that the EPT Essay test portion continues to produce expected results for all students. *Consequently, when race is not represented in the data on the EPT essay scores, the results look consistent.*

Additionally, the EPT total scores, which is a totaling and averaging of three separate scores (i.e., the essay score of 2 to 12; a reading score of 120 to 180; and a composing score of 120 to 180), also show similar bell curves for each year; however, the 1978 students tended to score on the higher end of the scale, whereas the 2008 students tended to score in the middle of the scale (see Table 19.2).

Table 19.2. EPT Total Results Reported in White and Thomas (1981) and CSUF's Office of Institutional Research (2008)

	N for EPT Total	Avg. EPT Total[a]	SD for EPT Total
Fall 1978			
White	5,246	152.5	5.6
Black	585	140.8	9.7
Mexican-American	449	145.7	8.6
Asian Pacific Islander[b]	617	146.3	10.
Native American[c]	N/A	N/A	N/A
ALL	10,719	150.1	7.9
Fall 2008			
White	578	148.0	6.7
Black	219	140.5	7.9
Latino/a	884	141.6	8.1
Asian Pacific Islander	450	138.7	8.8
Native American	15	146.6	6.0
ALL	2,251	142.7	8.6

[a]Labeled "Asian-American" in White and Thomas.
[b]Not reported in White and Thomas.
[c]Native Americans are not reported in White and Thomas.

This slight change, a lowering of the mean score from 150.1 (1978) to 142.7 (2008), suggests that today's CSUF students tend to perform lower on the EPT than those in 1978, and perhaps the multiple-choice questions cause this effect.[9] Again, the SDs are similar in their cluster around the mean score, only off by 0.7, and the average total scores are close, with 1978 CSU students receiving an average score that was 7.4 points higher than CSUF students in 2008. But so far, we have only considered the "ALL" category, or the student data as a whole, which allows us to make no observations about racial groups or formations. If this were the only way these data were to be considered, we argue it is a raceless way to handle the data, which would allow us to perhaps assume that CSUF students perform at lower levels of writing ability than their 1978 CSU counterparts. But White and Thomas did collect data for self-defined racial groups. This allows us to compare the data between racial formations existing in 1978 and 2008, showing how formations and their writing competencies may change over time.

EPT RESULTS IN 1978 AND 2008: OBSERVATIONS WHEN CONSIDERING RACE

The student test-takers who reported their race in 1978 were mostly White, or, at least, White and Thomas' data suggest that most students were White.[10] According to White and Thomas, about 48.9% of all test-takers in their study identified themselves as White, whereas significantly fewer test-takers identified themselves as Mexican-American (4.2%), Asian-American (5.8%), or African American (5.5%). This leaves about 35.6% of the scores represented in the overall numbers unaccounted for racially. It seems reasonable to assume that some of the unidentified test-takers were also White, thus the majority of the 1978 test-takers were White Californians.

In 2008, about 25.7% of CSUF test-takers identified themselves as White, almost 10% as African American, 39.3% as Latino/a, 20% as Asian Pacific Islander (who are mostly Hmong), and less than 1% as Native American. This leaves only about 4% of the overall numbers discussed above unaccounted for by racial group. So one important observation we can already make, which affects the overall numbers discussed earlier, concerns the difference in racial formations the two sets of overall data represent. In 1978, the students tested were mostly White, whereas those at CSUF in 2008 were mostly Latino/a and Hmong (about 60%, in fact). Could this simple difference in the racial identification of student populations account for the lower average scores at CSUF in 2008? Could the change in who takes the EPT change the testing environment and its administration at local sites?

Before we discuss the mean scores of racial groups in these tests, it should be noted that we do not disregard Reynolds' (1982a, 1982b) and others' (Jensen, 1976; Thorndike, 1971) warnings about using mean scores as a way to establish test bias. Reynolds (1982a) explains why using differences in mean scores on tests as an indicator of test bias is mistaken: "Just as there is no a priori basis for deciding that differences exist, there is no a priori basis for deciding that differences do not exist" (p. 213). So the fact that African Americans score consistently lower than Whites on the EPT in 1978 and in 2008 (discussed below) does not constitute test bias against African Americans. However, finding test bias on the EPT is not our goal, nor our point. The bias of a test, like the EPT, is not just a matter of finding traditionally defined test bias. If this were the case, we most likely must agree with White and Thomas' original judgment that the EPT is not biased against students of color. Bias can also be measured through the consequences of assessments. If an assessment is to respond fairly to the groups on which it makes decisions, then shouldn't its design address the way groups historically perform on the assessment? Thus, we wish to suggest that *understanding an assessment as producing a particular set of racial for-*

mations produces educational environments that could be unequal, either in terms of access, opportunities, or possibilities. So although we may not have evidence that the EPT is biased in the traditional sense of the term, we do have evidence that important questions remain unanswered when we review those mean scores: What racial formations does the assessment produce and what effects do those formations have on the lives of and opportunities for students? If these formations are unequal in the way they are distributed among racial groups, then does the test produce racist effects?

To begin to answer questions about racial formations and the effects of such formations, we first want to look at the consistency of the scores across racial groups in the two data sets. As evident in Tables 19.1 and 19.2, in both 1978 and 2008, White students scored the highest of all groups and almost identically on the EPT essay and the EPT total scores. The score distributions for both years are similar for Whites, as are their SDs for both the EPT essay and the EPT total scores. Once adjusted for the change in scoring between 1978 and 2008, the essay scores are almost identical. In 1978, White students' mean score was 7.6 (out of 12), and in 2008 it was 3.7 (out of 6), with SDs of 1.7 and 0.8, respectively. One conclusion to make of these findings is that, for White students, the writing portion of the test still works the same way it did in 1978. In other words, the EPT produces similar relative mean scores and score dispersion across the scoring scale. The average White student is right at the border of remediation (a score of 150 or below for CSU, Fresno). In 1978, the average White student would not be remedial, whereas in 2008, she would be borderline to remedial. This similar trend occurs in each racial formation for the EPT essay, with a leveling effect occurring with African American and Latino/a test takers. In 1978, African American mean scores (6.2) were the lowest of all recorded groups, whereas in 2008, their mean scores were the same as Latino/a test-takers (3.3), but still in the bottom half of the mean scores by racial group. Meanwhile, CSUF's Asian Pacific Islander formation's mean scores for the EPT essay were lower than all other groups, as were their EPT total scores. Yet, in 1978 Asian Pacific Islanders scored nearly as high as Whites on the essay and attained the highest mean total scores.

But what might the consistency and changes of these scores mean for racialized writing constructs? The essay portion of the EPT is scored by CSU teachers. Teachers are brought together, their scoring normed, and the essays read and scored. Thus, if these essay scores are any indication of the way that CSU teachers translate the writing competencies that are encapsulated in the writing construct of this test, then these competencies not only match White student writerly dispositions fairly closely (White students seem to be the ideal writer in 1978 and in 2008), these dispositions also have not changed in the past 30 years. Part of this phenomenon could be due to the norming, standardized prompts, and rubrics used to score essays. Ruth and Murphy's

(1988) "model of the writing assessment episode" is instructive here. Drawing on cognitive theory accounts of "misfires" in students reading prompts for tests, Ruth and Murphy explain that "meaning resides neither in the questions per se nor necessarily in the respondents' perception and reasoning, but rather in the transaction between the question and its receiver" (p. 118). So although a writing prompt, for example, may assume a common frame of reference, a wide variety of acts of cognition and interpretation occur when the test-maker writes the prompt, when a student reads and responds to the prompt, and when a rater reads and scores that student's writing. Ruth and Murphy's model of the writing assessment episode accounts for the test-maker's, test-taker's, and test-rater's acts of cognition in reading and creating the texts that constitute an assessment. This model of the assessment episode accounts for what Bob Broad (2003) has pointed out, that teachers often value characteristics in writing (or translate criteria) in various ways, often not exactly as expected, even when they express similar values about what good writing looks like.[11] It also suggests that differences in scores on the EPT of various racial groups, for instance, is a matter of more than just the way students understand and respond to a prompt, but the way that prompt was originally conceived, and the way the student's writing is then read and interpreted. At each of these three stages, the writing construct is reconceptualized and may be more so for particular racial groups.

For instance, each EPT essay prompt provides a short passage and gives instructions, such as: "Explain Mead's argument and discuss the extent to which you agree or disagree with her analysis. Support your position, providing reasons and examples from your own experience, observations, or reading" (CSU Office of the Chancellor, 2002, p. 15). Topics of passages include the use of technology (e.g., cell phones), the purpose of public universities, alcohol consumption in youths, and the "highly mobile society" we live in today (CSU Office of the Chancellor, 2002, p. 21). The following rubric dimensions (used when reading and rating) were used in 2008 to score each essay: response to the topic; understanding and use of the passage; quality and clarity of thought; organization, development, and support; syntax and command of language; grammar, usage, and mechanics (CSU Office of the Chancellor, 2002, p. 13).

EPT RESULTS IN 1978 AND 2008: THE CASES OF AFRICAN AMERICAN AND ASIAN PACIFIC ISLANDER STUDENTS

It would appear that the EPT rubric and prompt that asks for a response to a passage and personal experience to back up an argument for agreement or disagreement "works" for most racial groups in the traditional sense of testing, which is to say that the test does not show bias. However, the poor performance of two groups—African American students and Asian Pacific Islander students—is worth further investigation. The groups who score lower, although not necessarily statistically significantly lower, are CSU African Americans in 1978 and CSUF Asian Pacific Islanders in 2008, with African Americans and Latinos/as also receiving scores at noticeably lower levels. In effect, most students of color at CSUF in 2008 perform similarly, in terms of average mean scores—that is, they score lower than their White counterparts (a score of 4 keeps a student out of the "remedial" category).

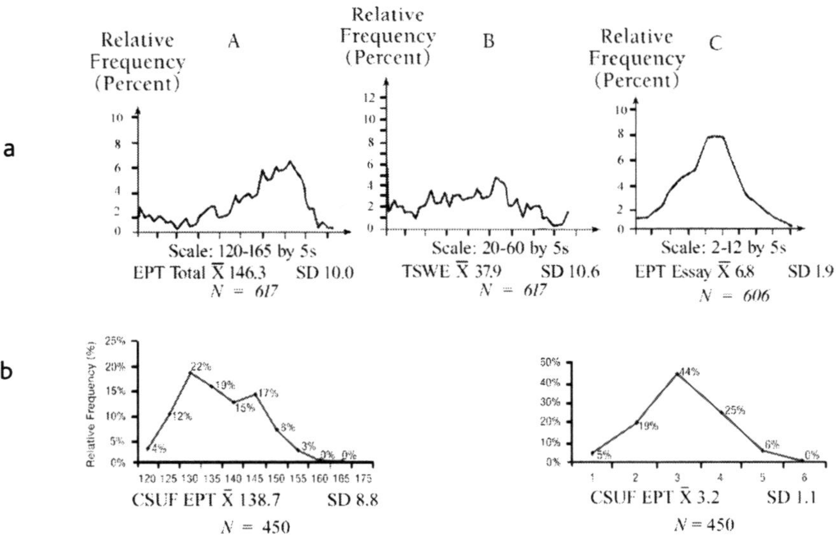

Figure 19.1. African American EPT Total and Essay Scores from (a) White and Thomas (1981) and (b) CSUF's Office of Institutional Research (2008).

Historically, one could find lots of reasons why CSU teachers may not reward African American Language patterns. For example, Young's (2004; 2007) argument for the incorporation of "code meshing" (not "code switching") as a way to incorporate the literacies of African American students suggests why African Americans may score low on the EPT essay test. African American literacies and other non-SEAE literacies are not considered in the rubric above or in the scoring of writing. But why do Asian Pacific Islanders' at CSUF perform so poorly relative to their peers (see Tables 19.1 and 19.2), scoring the lowest of all groups in 2008? Aren't Asian students supposed to be some of the brightest students (see Ramist, Lewis, & McCamely-Jenkins, 1994), which is what they appear to be from the 1978 data? What happened to this racial formation at CSUF in 2008?

Asian Pacific Islander test-takers' mean scores in 2008 were the lowest (3.1) of all groups. The same phenomenon occurred in their mean EPT total scores (138.7) for 2008; however, although every group's mean EPT total scores dropped a noticeable few points between 1978 and 2008, the CSUF's Asian Pacific Islander group dropped the farthest (7.6 points). The EPT total scores of CSUF's Asian Pacific Islanders, who are mostly Hmong and often identified as Generation 1.5 language users, were distributed towards the lower end of the scale. Most likely CSUF's 2008 Asian Pacific Islander population is not similar to CSU's overall 1978 Asian Pacific Islander population, who tended to score on the higher end of the scale (see Fig. 19.2). In fact, as Duffy's (2007) Hmong literacy account makes clear, Hmong are quite unique among Asian groups. Most Hmong learned to read and write in a language in the last 40 years (Duffy, 2007, p. 37). Additionally, they did not start coming to the United States until right around the time that White and Thomas' 1978 data were being collected, so it is likely there were few Hmong represented in the 1978 Asian American data. Today, however, Hmong make up the majority of CSUF Asian Pacific Islander student groups.

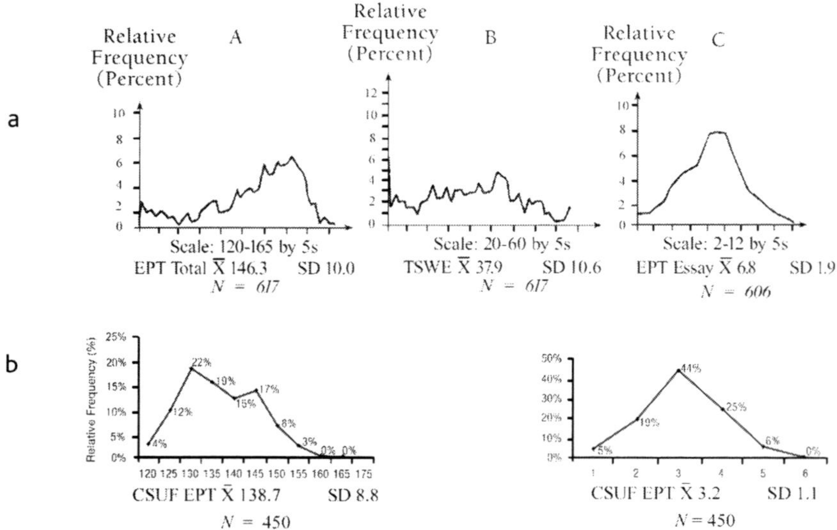

Figure 19.2. Asian Pacific Islander EPT Total and Essay Scores from (a) White and Thomas (1981) and (b) CSUF's Office of Institutional Research (2008).

The change in mean scores and score distributions for Asian Pacific Islanders in 2008 could be due to the change in Asian Pacific Islander demographics—that is, the Hmong students (now one to two generations removed from their initial immigration) attending CSUF with language markers in their writing that essay scorers do not find acceptable. Because the Asian Pacific Islanders mean essay score was 3.1 with a SD of 1.0 (a "passing" score was 4), most 2008 Asian Pacific Islander students were judged inadequate college writers. However, because all mean scores are slightly below 4, a specialist reading in the norming and scoring of essays may be required, a practice described by Elliot, Plata, and Zelhart (1990). Perhaps the readers of the EPT do not have enough knowledge of the Hmong students who take the test, thus they cannot fairly judge their writing.

The above hypothesis is complicated by scores on portfolios in CSUF's independent 2009 summer portfolio readings, which are a part of the First Year Writing program's assessment efforts. These portfolios, gathered from classes in AY 2008-09 and scored by teachers in the program, show that Asian Pacific Islander portfolios scored on average the lowest on "language coherence" (3.4 out of 6) relative to all other racial formations on midterm portfolios, with African Americans very close to them (3.5). On final portfolios in the same readings, Asian Pacific Islanders' average score was 3.8, the second lowest score, with African Americans' average score at 3.7, the lowest. Both formations' overall portfolio scores show the same trends, scoring the lowest of all racial formations.[12]

Several areas of investigation may be offered for the different scoring patterns of Asian Pacific Islander writers. Because of many Hmong's Generation 1.5 language issues, many are tracked in schools (formally and informally) as needing extra help with language, as are many African Americans and Latinos/as, so these students often leave the classroom during "regular" reading and writing activities in order to do essentially remedial work, under their grade level. This practice, if systemic and occurring over years for a student, will underprepare that student for mainstream writing tasks like those in the EPT essay prompts.

Additionally, in Fresno many junior high and elementary schools put "troubled" and English language learners in the same classroom, creating a room where 80%-90% of the students do not speak English, or have great difficulties with English and learning, in an all English-speaking classroom. Perhaps this practice is a kind of triage or a response to the teacher resources available (if a teacher speaks Mandarin, it makes sense to put students who primarily speak that language in her classroom). Of course, the curriculum does not change, so failure becomes the norm, and students simply get pushed through. It is from these classrooms that many of our Hmong, Latino/a, and African American students come. Should the EPT be redesigned to accommodate these local conditions?

IMPLICATIONS

Although some may claim we live in a postracial American culture (Hsu, 2010), race remains a fundamental organizing feature of U.S. culture, and it is significant in the ways we assess, sort, and place our students. By looking at racial data from writing assessments, we can expose not only performance differences but also begin to ask what writing constructs reward which groups of students. What we hope our discussion of the EPT in 1978 and 2008 suggests is how racial formations must be accounted for when designing, administering, and judging/rating a writing assessment and when considering what the assessment produces. It is not acceptable in our view, and Moore's view (this volume) as well, to ignore a test's results even if they have been validated in traditional ways. If we are really to value, to use Broad's terminology, rich ways of assessing student writing, then we must pay attention to how our assessments construct racial formations that have distinctive performances, opportunities, and limitations. As White and Thomas demonstrated more than 30 years ago, those who teach and assess writing can "see" race and open many possibilities for making writing assessment more racially valid and fair. Through an evolving understanding of racial formations, our hope is that other writing program administrators will be able to "see" race at their own institutions and understand the ever-changing significance of race in writing assessment.

ENDNOTES

1. The California State University System helped design and implement the EPT with ETS for determining "general skill in reading and written communication" and providing a "brief description" of strengths and weaknesses (White & Thomas, 1981, p. 277).
2. These are racial terms used in White and Thomas' original article.
3. Most likely, when White and Thomas referred to "bias," they meant bias in the psychological sense. Reynolds (1982a) explains that bias "denotes *constant* or *systemic error*, as opposed to chance or random error, in the estimation of some value (p. 199). Therefore, the essay portion of the EPT could not be considered biased because there was no systemic error in the judging of the essays. Because judges were carefully trained on the writing construct (i.e., what constituted a 1, 2, 3 essay, etc.), and they did not know the identity of any writers, there could be no systemic error or bias against students of color. But this does not account for the writing construct of the test itself. Reynolds, again, sheds light on the traditional psychological understanding of bias in construct validity: "Bias exists in

regard to construct validity when a test is shown to measure different hypothetical traits (psychological constructs) for one group than another or to measure the same trait but with different degrees of accuracy" (Reynolds, 1982b, p. 194). Putting aside Reynolds' positivistic assumptions about the ability to measure with any degree of "accuracy" any psychological trait, he offers two ways by which a construct measured could be biased against a group of test-takers. The test may be shown to measure different constructs in different groups or the test may be shown to measure the same construct differently for different groups.

4. Although we have used the term "differential impact" here, we would like to note that we differ from the educational measurement community in that we do not shy from the use of the term "racism" to describe uneven outcomes in test results. Following in the theoretical tradition of racial formation theory and critical race theory, we do not subscribe to the belief that racism is solely an intentional act but rather a sociohistorical process that often appears unintentional because it is normalized in the social and institutional structures of the United States. At this point, we consider these two theoretical positions incommensurable.
5. Since the 1960s, the U.S. federal government has collected data on race and ethnicity for use in civil rights monitoring and enforcement in employment, voting rights, housing and mortgage lending, health care services, and educational opportunities (Office of Management and Budget, 1995).
6. It should be noted that as of the writing of this chapter, the CSU Chancellor's Office, despite pervasive resistance by most CSU English Departments and faculty, have mandated an "Early Start" program to alleviate remedial status of all incoming first-year students by using their EPT scores. If a student scores low enough, she is mandated to first take an Early Start course in the summer (which costs more than semester courses as summer courses are not subsidized by the state) before she can begin taking courses at the university. This turns the EPT into a *de facto* entrance exam, clearly a purpose that the test was not originally designed for.
7. Technically speaking, the EPT determines remedial status of incoming students, which most campuses then use to determine writing course placement.
8. From all the literature on the EPT available, and from information on various CSU websites, the EPT writing score is still produced by two readers, scoring the essay from 1 to 6 (for a score of 2 to 12). The Office of Institutional Research and Assessment at CSU, Fresno, provided the 2008 data, explaining that for the 2008 year one reading was done to produce essay scores. Perhaps this was a consequence of budget cuts.
9. The CSU dictated a total score of 150 or below as needing remediation. The EPT total range score is 120 to 180.
10. There were many who did not identify themselves racially, thus the grouped data does not reflect the total number of test-takers in the 1978 "All" category.
11. We could question if time and changes in disciplinary assumptions and classroom practices would affect the way teachers read rubrics in order to rate EPT essays in 2008. Shouldn't their ratings be different than those in 1978? In part, this was Faigley's (1989, 1992) finding when comparing judgments on a similar 1929 writing test to Coles and Vopat's (1985) collection of "good" student essays.

12. For a more comprehensive description of the program assessment efforts at CSUF and a description of the program outcomes and scoring protocols used in the independent portfolio readings, see Inoue (2009a).

REFERENCES

American Educational Research Association (AERA), American Psychological Association (APA), and National Council on Measurement in Education (NCME). (1999). *Standards for educational and psychological testing.* Washington, DC: American Psychological Association.

Broad, B. (2003). *What we really value: Beyond rubrics in teaching and assessing writing*. Logan, UT: Utah State University Press

California State University Office of the Chancellor (2002). *Focus On English*. Long Beach, CA: California State University.

Coles, W. E., Jr., & Vopat, J. (1985). *What makes writing good.* Lexington, MA: Heath.

Duffy, J. M. (2007). *Writing from these roots: Literacy in a Hmong-American community*. Honolulu, HI: University Press of Hawaii.

Elliot, N., Plata, M., & Zelhart, P. (1990). *A program development handbook for the holistic assessment of writing*. Lanham, MD: University Press of America.

Educational Testing Service. (2010). *Quality and fairness. How ETS approaches testing*. Web.

Faigley, L. (1989). Judging writing, judging selves. *College Composition and Communication, 40*(4), 395-412.

Faigley, L. (1992). *Fragments of rationality*. Pittsburgh, PA: University of Pittsburgh Press.

Gillborn, D., & Mirza, H.S. (2000). *Educational inequality: Mapping race, class and gender—a synthesis of research evidence (*Report HMI 232). London, UK: Office for Standards in Education.

Hsu, H. (2009, January/February). The end of white America. *The Atlantic*. Web.

Inoue, A. B. (2009a, Summer). Self-assessment as programmatic center: The first year writing program and its assessment at California State University, Fresno. *Composition Forum 20*. Web.

Inoue, A. B. (2009b). The technology of writing assessment and racial validity. In C. Schreiner (Ed.), *Handbook of research on assessment technologies, methods, and applications in higher education* (pp. 97-120). Hershey, PA: IGI Global Books.

James, A. (2008). Making sense of race and racial classification. In T. Zuberi & E. Bonilla-Silva (Eds.), *White logic, White methods* (pp. 31-46). Lanham, MD: Rowman Littlefield Publishers.

Jensen, A. R. (1976). Test bias and construct validity. *Phi Delta Kappan, 58*, 340-346.

Lioi, A. & Merola, N. (in press). The muse of difference: Race and writing placement at two elite art schools. In A. Inoue & M. Poe (Eds.), *Race and racism in writing assessment.*

Office of Management and Budget (1995, August 28). *Standards for the classification of federal data on race and ethnicity*. Federal Register No. 44674-44693. Web.

Omi, M., & Winant, H. (1994). *Racial formation in the United States: From the 1960s to the 1980s* (2nd ed.). New York, NY: Routledge.

Phillips, S., & Camara, W. (2006). Legal and ethical issues. In R. Brennan (Ed.), *Educational measurement* (4th ed., pp. 734-755). Westport, CT: American Council on Education and Praeger.

Poe, M. (2006). *Race, representation, and writing assessment: Racial stereotypes and the construction of identity in writing assessment*. Doctoral dissertation, University of Massachusetts, Amherst. Web.

Poe, M. (2009). Reporting race and ethnicity in international assessments. In C. Schreiner (Ed.), *Handbook of research on assessment technologies, methods, and applications in higher education* (pp. 368-385). Hershey, PA: IGI Global Books.

Ramist, L., Lewis, C., & McCamely-Jenkins, L. (1994). *Student group differences in predicting college grades: Sex, language, and ethnic groups*. New York, NY: College Entrance Examination Board.

Reynolds, C. R. (1982a). Methods for detecting construct and predictive bias. In R. A. Berk (Ed.), *Handbook of methods for detecting test bias* (pp. 199-227). Baltimore, MD and London, UK: Johns Hopkins University Press.

Reynolds, C. R. (1982b). The problem of bias in psychological assessment. In C. R. Reynolds & T. B. Gutkin (Eds.), *The handbook of school psychology* (pp. 178-208). New York, NY: Wiley.

Ruth, L., & Murphy, S. (1988). *Designing writing tasks for the assessment of writing*. Norwood, NJ: Ablex Publishing.

Smitherman, G. (1993). *"The blacker the berry, the sweeter the juice": African American student writers and the National Assessment of Educational Progress.* Paper presented at the Annual Meeting of the National Council of Teachers of English, Pittsburgh, PA.

Sternglass, M. (1998). *Time to know them: A longitudinal study of writing and learning at the college level*. Mahwah, NJ: Erlbaum.

Thorndike, R. M. (1971). Concepts of culture-fairness. *Journal of Educational Measurement, 8*(2), 63-70.

U.S. Census. (2010). Web.

White, E. M. (2010, January 15). [E-mail A. B. Inoue]. Fresno, CA: California State University.

White, E. M., & Thomas, L. L. (1981). Racial minorities and writing skills assessment in the California State University and Colleges. *College English, 43(*3), 276-283.

Young, A. V. (2004). Your average nigga. *College Composition and Communication, 55*(4), 693-715.

Young, A. V. (2007). *Your average nigga: Performing race, literacy, and masculinity*. Detroit, MI: Wayne State University Press.

Zuberi, T. (2001). *Thicker than blood: How racial statistics lie*. Minneapolis, MN: University of Minneapolis Press.

20

THE PRIVATE AND THE PUBLIC IN DIRECTED SELF-PLACEMENT

Dan Royer
Roger Gilles
Grand Valley State University

Edward White (2001) writes a narrative about what he calls the opening of the "modern era of writing assessment" (p. 306). Every faculty member, he reminds us, is inextricably involved in assessment—we assign, respond to, and grade student papers. But that is not all, of course. We sometimes defend our grades to students or the class, but usually we claim professional privilege if the argument gets more public than that. A tension prevails, for public accountability (be it national accrediting boards or the faculty member next door) demands that we defend or make clear the cultural value of our work, its benefit to students, and the ways it contributes to the community around us. Student writing has had a peculiar power over this modern era to call the composition professor out of the privacy of the office and into a public sphere where things get talked about that usually are not discussed—things like what we value, what we teach, and what we believe about splitting infinitives. White (2001) writes:

> We will defend our private world of assessment as a matter between our students and us, at most a matter to be shared with our colleagues. But that public world of external assessment seems beyond our reach, if not our ken, and our instincts are always to withdraw, to claim profession-

> al privilege. ... The private world of assessing our own students without interference seems to have little relation to the public world of large-scale writing assessments, the gathering of data, and the publication of assessment research. Yet, from time to time, the public and private versions of writing assessment intersect, demanding that we recognize links between them. (p. 307)

What may have felt like a yawning gap to White when he delivered the first version of this narrative in 1998, seems to us now like a pressing and insistent call to intersect the public and the private. A student's grade is traditionally viewed as a private matter between the student and his or her teacher, but first-year writing programs are rightly held accountable by faculty around campus. What are you teaching in the program? How are you preparing students to write better for my class? Furthermore, the private/public tension is not just about our teacher's world and external assessment; it cuts to an issue that reveals the very purposes of most writing: making the private public. Our chapter explores this notion as we have come to understand writing and its assessment in our work together in the first-year writing program at Grand Valley State University.

***

On the wall just inside Lake Superior Hall is a flat black contour representation of the American philosopher William James. James evidently inspired those who built curriculum and taught students in the heady days of progressive education when Grand Valley was a local association of experimental colleges established in the early 1960s. The wall plate is inscribed with a citation from James' (1983/1899) *Talks to Teachers on Psychology*. It reads, "No impression without expression." In the opening paragraph of this 1899 monograph, James writes, "*No reception without reaction, no impression without correlative expression*—this is the great maxim which the teacher ought never to forget" (p. 32). For James this advice to teachers was not just part of a social psychology, but of physiology as well. Knowledge is manifest in a dynamic cycle. We publicize our knowledge, but the private understanding of the student must become public again in order to complete the circuit of learning.

Directed self-placement (DSP) acknowledges placement as part of a circuit of learning rather than a static moment in our students' lives. And taking its cue from the pragmatist tradition of James and Peirce, it seeks meaning in consequences and action, a rich source of clarification of purposes and abstract ideas (see Peirce, 1878, but, more to the point, Elbow's pragmatist orientation in Chapter 17). Traditional placement methods gathered something from students—standardized test scores, timed essays, even portfolios of written work—and then told them which writing course was best for them. In the mid 1990s we began explaining, in as much detail as possible, our composition curriculum to entering students and *asking* them where they fit. In essence, we began asking the question good teachers often ask after they explain an important or interesting concept or process in class: "What do *you* think?" DSP requires entering students not just to listen, but to react to the composition curriculum.

It is easy to use the term "composition curriculum" as if everyone knows what it is. What curriculum are we talking about? There may be one described in the catalog, another in the first-year writing handbook for students, another in the presemester workshop for composition teachers; there is probably one described by Teacher A, who's been at it for 17 years, and another described by Teacher B, who started last year. And finally there is the one actually experienced by students over the course of the Fall semester. As program directors, we could begin articulating our composition program to entering students only once we ourselves had initiated a "circuit of learning" about our pedagogies and outcomes. We needed to make sure that private notions held about our curriculum by the dozens of teachers who "delivered" it each year matched the public statements we began making about it during summer orientation. To explain how we managed this, we need to move from the *beginning* of our students' experience with our first-year writing program to the end.

***

The public/private dichotomy is a danger to learning if the partition is static and no canals let knowledge flow between them, but it is also a trap set for how we measure and understand that learning on a programmatic level. White reminds us that there are always centrifugal forces that pull us outward to private orbits, that make us comfortable with specialization, and that in privatizing what we teach, diminish the value of what we teach. The corrective is the public. White (1985) put it this way:

> Experience has shown that a common examination is absolutely necessary if the centrifugal forces that are always at work on advanced courses are to be resisted. If the staff teaching the proficiency course each term must meet to plan, discuss, select, and grade a common examination for all students taking their classes, there will be a built-in corrective to the tendency to specialize the disciplinary content of the sections or to diminish the importance of writing. (p. 48)

White here was speaking of Writing Across the Curriculum (WAC) programs, but the principle applies as well to first-year writing programs—hence the growing popularity in the late 1980s and early 1990s of end-of-semester final essays or final portfolios reviewed not just by the students' own instructor, but also by one or more other teachers in the program. White (1985) described such a system in his *Developing Successful College Writing Programs* (pp. 124-125), and a more elaborate system of final portfolio review was detailed by Smit, Kolonosky, and Seltzer (1991). The basic idea was to have each student submit a final portfolio of work for a public check of basic proficiency—that is, to determine whether or not the student should pass the class.

At Grand Valley, we began experimenting with such a system in 1993, and by 1995 and 1996—when we instituted DSP—we had made three key adjustments that allowed us a comfortable degree of authority as we described our curriculum to incoming students. Like others before and since, the Kansas State model described by Smit, Kolonosky, and Seltzer gathered teachers together at the end of each term to "check" student portfolios against the program's standards for passing work. That is, it kept separate the individual instructor's grading and the programmatic proficiency check. Students' individual teachers assigned tentative course grades as usual—based on many factors, not just the quality of final drafts. If a student's final work was judged by two outside readers to be passing, the teacher could formally assign the intended grade. But if two outside readers agreed that a student's writing was not passing, the student failed the course, regardless of the classroom teacher's grade. (It was also possible, interestingly, for a student whose intended grade was an F to be judged as "passing" by the outside readers.) So a teacher intending to award a student a grade of B might suddenly need to explain why the student had in fact earned an F. The Kansas State directors established an appeal process, but the problem remained—and, as far as we were concerned at least, the B/F possibility threatened to undermine the whole system. If the two outside readers' judgments meant anything, why allow an appeal? If the judgment *did not* mean anything, why go through the exercise? The circuit was not complete.

We addressed this issue by making three adjustments. First, after years of experience as holistic scorers of placement essays (our placement method prior to DSP), we knew how difficult it was to gather together a group of faculty and build consensus on common standards and expectations, so we decided that the single shot start-of-term and end-of-term workshop norming sessions that most programs practiced were not enough. If we were going to make such a high-stakes decision as whether or not a student should pass a required writing course, we were going to have to put some serious time and effort into the process. So we asked our composition faculty to meet in grading groups of five or six at least 10 times each semester—not quite weekly, but almost. These well-normed groups, then, would be used at the end of the term, after each teacher had seen writing from the students of each other teacher, and after each teacher had had a chance to describe his or her assignments and expectations. The purpose of the norming was both to influence others and accommodate others, and by the end of the semester our expectation was that the members of each grading group could agree on whether or not a piece of writing met our program's public expectations.

Those program expectations, by the way, were initially made public in a way common to many first-year writing programs: We published a detailed grading rubric and a collection of sample student essays from our program. But we recognized these as static representations—in the case of the rubric, a very high abstraction; and in the case of the student essays, a very limited sample—that required conversation to come alive and accumulate pragmatic meaning. They were an annual *starting point* for discussion, not a definitive end point. They required both annual revisions and a perennial dose of skepticism. As valuable as they were, and still are, they have a consequential validity that cannot be viewed as the final word or as absolute judgments.

Our second adjustment was to integrate even further the private grading practices we were used to with the public proficiency check our program required. Each of us typically graded our students' writing by categorizing it as excellent, good, average, or poor—A, B, C, or D. (At GVSU, students must earn a C or better in the required composition courses to earn graduation credit, so the D/F distinction is not crucial.) If we were going through all the time and effort to meet 10 times a semester and norm ourselves to a collective standard, why not take the step from a simple P/F evaluation and actually assign grades of A, B, C, or D? Instead of two scoring categories, why not make it four? Surely, we challenged ourselves, we could agree (at least most of the time) on the difference between good and average writing in our program. So we indeed made these "grading" groups, not just "proficiency-checking" groups. As with KSU's program, we considered the classroom teacher to be the "first reader," and then we shared the portfolios among the grading group for randomly assigned "second readers." If the first two readers agreed on a B or a D, then we had a final letter grade. If there was disagreement, we would go to a third reader for the final decision. On rare occasions we experienced A/C or B/D splits, and they were cause for concern, but they were also opportunities for further discussion and learning, so in the end we considered them a healthy part of the system.

Another insight we might attribute to this public/private heuristic has to do with the kinds of questions we ask in our assessment. Because of the dominance of process pedagogy, private processes have become tempting assessment "outcomes." The portfolio grading movement has focused on an effort to assess private processes with its cover letter and draft-oriented portrait of the writer. With our version of group grading, we have asked a different kind of question, a question about a public, not a private matter: "How adequate are the essays our students write according to a clearly articulated local public standard?" This Jamesian clarification of first questions and practical consequences has also been an issue close to White's (1996b) own principal beliefs about assessment.

> An assessment is a means of gathering information to answer questions. So, we should be clear about what questions we are asking, what information we need to answer them, and how we will use that information before we decide about the assessment. This way of thinking about assessment seems obvious enough, but very few assessment programs of any kind actually follow it. (p. 106)

Once we had our grading groups in place, we had to ask ourselves what we actually needed to see in the final portfolios. Drafts? Cover letters? Personal histories? Notes from the teachers? We finally settled on just one thing: the writing itself. This was our third adjustment, although in a way it was no adjustment at all, because the "proficiency-checking" essays and portfolios used by others tended also to be final products only. Our adjustment was to the then-developing expectations of the final course portfolio, as articulated by Elbow, Belanoff, and others. Our assessment question was not, "What kinds of processes have our students developed?" (although this remained an important *teaching* question for us all). Our question, again, was, "How adequate are the essays our students write according to a clearly articulated local public standard?"

By the summer of 1996, then, as we began talking with entering students about our first-year composition curriculum, we had a 2- or 3-year history of this highly articulated collaborative group grading system. Now, rather than devote our presemester workshops to slapdash norming sessions, we were able to engage all 30 or 35 of our composition faculty in a large-group discussion of the smaller grading groups—which, by the way, we changed every semester so that individual teachers normed themselves with different faculty every term. Our workshop discussions helped us, as public representatives of the composition program, understand what our faculty really valued—what kinds of assignments worked best for them, how they handled various writing genres, what they expected in terms of research and documentation, and what really caused students to get a C or a D in the required course. This collected knowledge became the material of our presentations to entering students, and thus three crucial circuits were complete: Individual faculty articulated and negotiated their expectations to others; the composition faculty as a whole articulated their expectations to the program directors; and the program directors articulated the program's expectations to the entering students. It should be noted as well here that Das Bender documents in Chapter 21 the ways that DSP helps to usher the private language and literacy experiences of ESL students into the public sphere of the university. In each case, there was both explanation and reaction: Composition faculty responded to one another by sharing and debating their values and expectations; the program directors responded to the composition faculty by mediating faculty values and university-wide expectations of the first-year writing requirement; and the entering students responded to the program directors by choosing the course that seemed the best fit for them.

Perhaps the overriding dynamic we have observed in our work as program directors is that what is tested and proven in the privacy of our own writing lives and classroom practices needs expression in the public realm of assessment. White (1996a) points out, if writing teachers had full control over writing assessment, "the ideal assessment would likely be an expanded version of classroom assessment—such as we now see in portfolios" (p. 14). Our first-year program, from directed self placement to portfolio-based collaborative grading, is, in our minds, an "expanded"—that is, programwide—"version of classroom assessment." We have taken the private practices of good teachers—offering choice to students, offering models for success, emphasizing outcomes, articulating what we value in good writing, and so on—and developed public practices that support the same principles.

REFERENCES

James, W. (1983). *Talks to teachers on psychology: And to students on some of life's ideals*. Cambridge, MA: Harvard University Press. (Original work published 1899)

Peirce, C. S. (1878, January). How to make our ideas clear. *Popular Science Monthly, 12*, 286-302.

Smit, D., Kolonosky, P., & Seltzer, K. (1991). Implementing a portfolio system. In P. Belanoff & M. Dickson (Eds.), *Portfolios: Process and product* (pp. 46-56). Portsmouth, NH: Heinemann-Boynton/Cook.

White, E. M. (1985). *Teaching and assessing writing: Recent advances in understanding, evaluating, and improving student performance*. San Francisco, CA: Jossey-Bass.

White, E. M. (1996a). Power and agenda setting in writing assessment. In E. M. White, W. D. Lutz, & S. Kamusikiri (Eds.), *Assessment of writing: Politics, policies, practices* (pp. 9-24). New York, NY: Modern Language Association.

White, E. M. (1996b). Writing assessment beyond the classroom: Will writing teachers play a role? In L. Z. Bloom, D. A. Daiker, & E. M. White (Eds.), *Composition in the twenty-first century: Crisis and change* (pp. 101-111). Carbondale, IL: Southern Illinois University Press.

White, E. M. (2001). The opening of the modern era of writing assessment: A narrative. *College English, 63*(3), 306-320.

21

ASSESSING GENERATION 1.5 LEARNERS
THE REVELATIONS OF DIRECTED SELF-PLACEMENT

Gita DasBender
Seton Hall University

In 1984, Edward M. White described holistic scoring of student writing as inherently opposed to analytic methods of assessment and multiple-choice testing. White was arguing against "analytic reductionism," the tendency to scrutinize elements of writing to prove that the whole is no more than the sum of its parts, but more importantly, he was drawing attention to what he called the "rediscovery of the functioning human being behind the text" (p. 400). It was clear then that White's advocacy was not merely the result of a new movement in developing economical, efficient, and reliable assessment tools, but of his unwavering faith in the human element that was involved in the writing process. Reading and writing are deeply individual acts that require complex cognitive skills and engage the entire self, and in acknowledging that the writer and writing arise from the same spirit of imagination, White poignantly called for "even the meanest bit of halting prose, even the most down-trodden of our fellow creatures ... to be taken as a living and vital unit of meaning, an artistic and human whole" (p. 409). White's contribution to the philosophy and practice of assessment has shaped the field of composition studies for two-and-a-half decades and provided a basis for understanding the writing student as a whole, complex entity.

The rapid growth of a culturally and linguistically diverse and hence more complex student body in U.S. higher education makes White's vision of assessment timelier than ever. Along with visa-bearing international students, resident ESL and multilingual students continue to fill our classrooms and assessment of these groups remains complicated. Getting a better sense of individual students' abilities may help us understand the larger issues of how this group negotiates its way through academic settings, but to make their experience in the college classroom meaningful, examination of effective placement instruments such as Directed Self-Placement allow us to better understand their self-perception and literacy histories. In this chapter I address the issue of placement of multilingual students by examining the use of Directed Self-Placement at Seton Hall University, where I am the Coordinator of Second Language Writing.

BACKGROUND

Yancey (1999), framing and historically situating writing assessment, examined three waves of the assessment movement: The first governed by objective, multiple-choice testing; the second defined by White's holistic essay scoring; and the third dominated by portfolio scoring with an emphasis on reflection. Yancey also revealed the emergent self that takes shape with the advent of the scored essay and gathers agency through self-reflection in the portfolio. Although this self is "constructed quite explicitly through reflection" (p. 500), it is also constructed through other types of writing activities—both public and private—which ultimately makes the representation of this self a rather complex matter. Nonetheless, Yancey perhaps imagined that the reflection accompanying self-assessment would shape the fourth overlapping wave of assessment that focused on "individual assessment as an interpretive act" (p. 501). Acknowledging the social, rhetorical, and hermeneutic nature of assessment, Yancey noted that, as indicated by the rise of Directed Self Placement, reflection is a growing part of nonportfolio placement processes (p. 501).

In Chapter 17 Elbow refers to new workable alternatives to placement testing and calls Directed Self Placement (DSP) "an elegant and easy one [which is] no longer a new and odd experiment." That DSP is no longer viewed as an experimental practice but as one that has gained professional legitimacy lends credibility to its continued use in university programs such as the one at Seton Hall University. Around the time Yancey was writing, DSP was still in its incipient stages but has now grown into a full-fledged placement and assessment tool. Concomitant with White's view of assessment as a humane exercise, Royer and Gilles (1998) developed self-placement as a mechanism for students' "self-determined advance and ... restoration of interpersonal agency" (p. 61). Well aware of the disenfranchising effect of traditional placement practices that deny students a voice in course selection, they explained that students' awareness of their goals, attitudes, educational history, and writing ability all played a crucial role in guiding them toward proper placement. They also weighed the risks of leaving the choice of placement up to students and concluded that students' success or failure in a course *they* determined best suited them would either confirm the students' belief in their own abilities to succeed, or indicate that they had seriously overestimated their capacities. In either case, the responsibility for judging the most appropriate learning environment—in essence, for self-determination—lay with the students who were guided through the process and not solely with placement administrators.

It is clear that in helping students create a composite image of themselves as readers, writers, and learners that generally corresponds to a mainstream, remedial, or ESL profile, DSP gives them an opportunity to evaluate their abilities and decide placement accordingly. Testing of writing ability is not a neutral act; the assumption that the writing reflects the cognitive capacities of the writer is often inescapable. In this sense, DSP begins to look like a type of "holistic" placement that addresses some of the problems associated with testing and assessment of language minority students noted by Hamp-Lyons (1996).

GENERATION 1.5 AND PLACEMENT

The issue of providing fair and appropriate college-level education for non-English language background American high school graduates is mired in all sorts of complexities. In 1988, Rumbaut and Ima, in their study of Southeast Asian refugee youth, who were born abroad but were educated and came of age in the United States, coined the term "1.5 generation" to highlight how the population formed a distinct group that fell in between first- and second-generation immigrants and belonged wholly to neither. Harklau, Losey, and Siegal (1999) adopted the term while noting that despite its broad application, the term best characterized multilingual students who immigrate to the United States as school-age children and graduate from American high schools. The writers acknowledged that the use of varied titles for U.S.-educated English-language learners in their collection reflects the difficulty of categorizing and situating this group in the current conversation about linguistically diverse college writers. However, since the publication of Harklau, Siegal, and Losey (1999), the term generation 1.5 has been used extensively for such a diverse body of students that scholars have questioned its efficacy, expressing concern over its broad application, and have called for an examination of the assumptions that underlie its continued use (Benesch, 2009; Matsuda & Matsuda, 2009; Schwartz, 2004). Matsuda and Matsuda (2009) warned that if the term were to be used as descriptor, it needed to be revelatory and not one that obscured the diversity of the students it represents. Yet unease over and arguments about nomenclature do not help in addressing the very real needs of a population that appears distinct from ESL, international, or native-speaking students and yet displays characteristic features from each of these groups. In this chapter I use the terms generation 1.5 and multilingual students interchangeably both to acknowledge the broad category of language learners to which they belong and to underscore their shifting, unstable identities.

Of all academic concerns related to generation 1.5 students, placement into writing courses is critical given that placement tests determine entrance into appropriate courses which then have an impact on students' success with college writing. Because generation 1.5 students (whether or not they have taken ESL or other language courses in elementary and middle school) have received a large portion of their formal education in English and are products of American secondary education, they often tend to identify themselves more with monolingual native speakers of English and, for lack of precise placement tools, get placed into mainstream writing courses. But as language-minority students who speak their native languages at home just as often as English (Reynolds, Bae, & Wilson, 2009), some generation 1.5 students may well be suited for, and benefit from, ESL or second language writing courses. Although they may be quite fluent in spoken English, multilingual students may struggle with rhetorical conventions, grammar, and the demands of academic writing in general (Blumenthal, 2002; Crosby, 2009).

Yet not very much has been written about placement practices for generation 1.5 students. Schwartz (2004) reminds us that because determining the complex cultural and educational experiences of these students is a difficult matter, no easy placement solution exists for this group. One experiment with online placement practices for second-language writers at Wright State University is "not entirely self-placement [but] it does afford students some agency" (Crusan, 2006, p. 214). However, a closer look at this population's literacy background and language skills and abilities may allow us to better address their academic needs. Di Gennaro (2008) echoes this idea and notes that research that compares writing performance with personal and academic profiles of generation 1.5 students will not only provide deeper insight into whether specific writing performance patterns exist for this group but also help in determining placement procedures. Given this complex scenario, a better understanding of the academic literacy and linguistic history of generation 1.5 students (Crosby, 2009; Di Gennaro, 2008; Ortermeier-Hooper, 2008) is crucial to proper placement and assessment practices.

DIRECTED SELF-PLACEMENT AS A LEARNING TOOL

Because Directed Self Placement has the potential for providing an in-depth view into students' learning behaviors, academic experiences, and self-perceptions, it has been employed as a tool both for assessing and placing generation 1.5 students in Seton Hall University's writing program. At Seton Hall, DSP has been administered since 2005, when it was first piloted as an online survey for incoming freshman with SAT Reading and Writing scores of 550 or below. Since then approximately 600 to 700 students have taken the placement survey every year. The survey is available online in the form of a questionnaire and includes an essay assignment that provides a writing sample for students and DSP administrators to review in the process of making placement choices.

Three full-time writing faculty are normed in late spring, before the placement process begins, and each continues to score and review approximately one-third of the total placements. The essays are scored holistically on a scale of 1 to 6, with the scores of 1 and 2 indicating low writing proficiency, 3 and 4 acceptable proficiency, and 5 and 6 advanced proficiency. The essay scores are designed for internal use, that is, the scores are taken into account as one among several factors for individual placement advisement. For instance, a student with a score of either 1 or 2 is understood to have low preparedness for college composition, and if the student selects the program's freestanding writing course, Core English 1201, the faculty is likely to contact the student and advise him or her to consider placing into the program's linked course—Core English 1201 with Reading and Writing Workshop—Core English 0160, designed for Basic Skills students. A score of 3 may indicate acceptable proficiency for placement into the mainstream course, but student responses to the survey questions guide placement advisement. In the majority of cases, essay scores of 3 or below alert the scorer to a potentially underprepared student who may need guidance with placement options, whereas scores of 4 and above are understood to reflect adequate proficiency. The survey review website allows the scorers not only to record the essay scores but also to include brief impressionistic notes that justify the score.

After students identify themselves and write the sample essay, they are required to respond to questions that help them reflect on their reading and writing experiences and provide an in-depth reading, writing, and language inventory. This is followed by a list of the various types of writing courses offered by the department and a set of course profiles for students who are native speakers of English or for whom English is a second or nonprimary language. After students determine which profile fits them the best, they select the course they believe they will benefit from the most.

When the DSP program was instituted, the survey instrument was created mainly to help native speakers of English determine whether or not they fit the profile of the Basic Writer so they could place themselves in the Reading and Writing Workshop for developmental writers that was linked to Core English 1201—the first-year writing course that all incoming freshmen are required to take. Only a single question about students' language experience—which determined whether or not they spoke a home language other than English and with what frequency—helped in placing L2 students. Program administrators quickly realized that the survey instrument not only failed to include questions about multilingual students' experiences but that the group was subsumed within the Basic Writer category. And even as this instrument worked for the purpose for which it was designed, and most international and recent immigrant language learners rightfully placed themselves into second language writing courses in the program, we continued to learn about students in free-standing sections of Core English who struggled with literacy issues and demonstrated problems with language development, students who fit the generation 1.5 profile. The question we faced was: If Directed Self Placement was successful in guiding students to the courses they perceived to be appropriate, how could we address the needs of this specific population who opted to be in mainstream writing courses but struggled to succeed in them? It gradually became clear that the questionnaire had to include questions that would not only help to identify language minority students but also provide more details about the language and education history of this group. As a result, three new questions (numbers 2 to 4) were added to the survey that assisted us in identifying and guiding the placement of L2 students. Overall, the four questions directed to multilingual students were:

1. Which of the following best describes your experience with English? (You may choose more than one.)
    - My first language is English, and English is the only language spoken at home.
    - My first language is English, but another language is also spoken at home._My first language is not English, but English is usually/always spoken at home.
    - My first language is not English, and I am not entirely comfortable speaking and writing in English.
2. If you are an immigrant student, at what grade did you enter the U.S education system?
3. Were you ever required to take ESL classes in school?
4. If you were identified as ESL, at what grade did you take your last ESL course?

Survey questions such as these have the potential of serving a dual purpose and give students and administrators a glimpse into those complex experiences that make placement seem so problematic. By answering these questions students get a better sense of several aspects of their language history: how extensively they engaged with English and other languages, for how long they have been part of an environment in which English is the medium of instruction, and for how long they received English language instruction if they were identified as second-language learners. In developing these questions our hope was that the answers would not only assist students in their self-placement decisions but allow the program to understand the linguistic history of our multilingual students even as we reviewed other aspects of the survey.

Since 2005 two writing program directors and I have been faculty reviewers of DSP (and scorers of the writing sample), and we have had access to the survey database during the summer months when we review the surveys and communicate with students who we think need guidance about their placement choices. However, as a researcher, according to the policies of the Institutional Review Board, I had to receive student permission in order to review the surveys of the specific population—immigrant students—that I was studying. To gain access to the placement surveys I conducted a follow-up survey for multilingual students at the end of the Fall semester. Although my main intention was to learn about this population's experience with DSP, to understand how well the writing course served their needs, and to elicit feedback on which needs remained unmet, I included a question that asked students if they were willing to give the researcher permission to access data from their DSP survey. Of the 38 students who took the Fall follow-up survey, 24 gave me permission to review their DSP answers. I turn here to the results of this descriptive, base-line study.

WHAT DSP REVEALS

If we are to assume that there is no such thing as a "typical" generation 1.5 student—the construct itself has been established as problematic—but only individuals who are U.S. residents, born to immigrant parents and very likely exposed to languages other than English, it is worthwhile to examine their language and literacy profile. Of all the students (n = 24) who gave me permission to review their DSP survey, half had primary schooling—specifically grades 1 through 5—in the United States and half entered American schools between grades 8 and 12. However, the majority of the students—20 out of 24 —admitted to speaking another language at home most of the time. Eleven students—almost half—had taken ESL courses in school and, of these, seven graduated out of ESL in elementary school and four in middle school. Thus according to this data, the majority of students identified as ESL did not need language assistance beyond elementary school.

The academic literacy profile of the group also yielded interesting results. Exactly half the students had read more than four books that were not part of assignments in school the previous year. The other half read one to two books on average on their own. Whereas eight had written between one and four essays of three or more pages with at least two drafts in high school, 16 had written between five and eight essays demonstrating a decent amount of writing practice. The majority of students agreed (Table 21.1) that they often wrote and revised for themselves, were comfortable writing for themselves, were comfortable reading nonfiction books and articles, considered themselves strong readers and writers, and were experienced in conducting research using a wide range of sources including databases. The pattern that emerges is that of a population that is not only engaged in reading and writing activities in high school but also confident with academic tasks such as reading and writing about nonfiction, revision, and research activities.

Interestingly, the population also demonstrates control over learning behaviors and attitudes. The majority agreed that they were not easily distracted from studying, were confident that they could overcome problems when doing poorly in English, and persevered in completing unpleasant or difficult writing tasks. This is a glowing picture indeed, and reflects a language minority group's positive attitude and deep sense of confidence toward academic experiences. The postessay questions (Table 21.2) also reflect high confidence in students' perception of their abilities as readers and writers.

More than half of the respondents demonstrated moderate to high confidence with regard to reading comprehension, textual support and idea development, focus and organization, and grammatical correctness. This portrait also correlates with the placement data (Table 21.3).

Of the 24 students who permitted me to access their DSP survey responses, only three placed themselves in College English for ESL students, and two placed themselves in the program's second-language writing course linked to a Reading and Writing workshop. Clearly, if self-placement is any indication of perceptions of linguistic proficiency and confidence in one's ability to succeed, the majority of generation 1.5 students identified with native-English speakers and placed themselves in mainstream writing courses, whether they were free-standing or linked to a Reading and Writing workshop.

Table 21.1. Academic Literacy Profile (n = 24)

	Strongly Agree	Agree	Mildly Agree	Mildly Disagree	Disagree	Strongly Disagree
I often write and revise for myself	10	6	5	2	1	0
For many of the essays I wrote in high school English classes, I turned in at least two drafts.	3	6	9	4	1	1
I am always comfortable writing for school.	5	12	3	4	0	0
I am comfortable reading nonfiction books and articles.	10	9	3	1	1	0
I consider myself a strong reader and writer.	4	7	6	4	2	1
I am very experienced conducting research using a wide range of sources (e.g., print materials, online databases, NOT just Googling).	5	14	1	3	1	0
I generally complete work on time.	13	8	2	1	0	0
It's usually hard to talk me out of studying.	5	9	7	3	0	0
If I am doing poorly in English, I know how to overcome the problems I have and succeed.	11	7	4	1	1	0
When I have unpleasant or difficult written work to do, I generally stick to it until I finish it.	9	9	5	1	0	0
Almost everyone in my high school goes on to a four-year college immediately after graduating.	8	5	6	2	2	1

Table 21.2. Post-essay Questions on Reading and Writing (n = 24)

	Very confident	Moderately confident	Somewhat confident	Not very Confident	Not at all confident
How confident are you that you identified the main idea of the passage you read?	10	8	4	2	0
How confident are you that you wrote an essay that has a clear focus throughout and that is well organized?	7	9	6	2	0
How confident are you that you provided evidence from the text to effectively support and explain your position?	9	9	6	0	0
How confident are you that you wrote sentences that are clear and mostly free of errors?	4	10	8	2	0

Table 21.3. Placement (n = 24)

College English 1201	14
College English 1201 for ESL	3
College English 1201 and Reading/ Writing Workshop (0160)	5
College English 1201 and Reading/Writing Workshop for ESL students (0180)	2

BEYOND DSP—FOLLOW-UP SURVEY RESULTS

The follow-up survey, an online questionnaire intended only for multilingual students who had graduated from American high schools, was conducted in the last week of classes of the Fall semester of 2009. The survey was designed to mainly elicit feedback on the language background and first-semester writing experience of generation 1.5 students, but it also gave me the opportunity to request access to the respondents' DSP survey. Additionally, the survey revealed that DSP as a method of placement found high approval among the respondents. Twenty-eight students agreed that their overall opinion about being able to place themselves in English courses ranged from positive to very positive, whereas two disagreed with a positive experience.

Despite the academically prepared and confident image that multilingual students present in the DSP survey, their response to a question in the follow-up survey (n = 38) about the level of difficulty they had with reading and writing (Table 21.4) shows that when pressed for a more in-depth evaluation of skills, students tend to admit that certain academic tasks are indeed a challenge for them.

Table 21.4. In-depth Evaluation of Skills, Difficulty with Reading and Writing (n = 38)

	Not Difficult	Somewhat Difficult	Difficult	Very Difficult
Reading Comprehension	24	11	3	0
Critical thinking	22	13	2	1
Textual analysis	23	11	3	1
Structure and organization	20	12	6	0
Grammar	18	11	7	2

About one-third of the population found reading comprehension, critical thinking, textual analysis, and structure and organization—all crucial learning tasks according to the WPA Outcomes Statement—to be difficult or somewhat difficult. This finding seems consistent with the discussion in generation 1.5 literature that multilingual students often struggle with critical literacy issues (Crosby, 2009; Murie & Fitzpatrick, 2009; Thonus, 2003). Most interestingly, 21 students—more than half—admitted that they struggled with grammar whereas the majority—35 students—agreed that the course had helped improve their language skills (Table 21.5).

Table 21.5. In-depth Evaluation of Skills, General English Language Skills (n = 38)

My English language skills improved in this class	
Strongly Agree	14
Agree	21
Disagree	2
Strongly Disagree	1

When asked about what types of resources they currently relied on for additional help in their writing courses, the majority indicated that they relied extensively or to a reasonable degree on a combination of resources: writing faculty, Writing Center tutors, and peers in the course. A majority of students also noted that they would benefit greatly from conferences with writing faculty, Writing Center tutoring, and individual grammar tutorials (Table 21.6).

Table 21.6. Services (n = 38)

	Significantly Benefit	Somewhat Benefit	Not Benefit At All
Conferences with writing faculty	17	9	12
Writing Center tutoring	15	17	6
Individual Grammar Tutorial in Writing Center	15	13	10
Professional tutoring outside the university	8	17	13
Other	5	9	24

Finally, in response to an open-ended question about what they found most difficult when composing a piece of writing in English, students voiced their concerns mainly about grammar, organization, sentence structure, and vocabulary.

IMPLICATIONS

There is no doubt that the generation 1.5 student population remains somewhat elusive because of its very diverse nature, and much is unknown about the effect of academic and linguistic background on success or failure at the university level. However this study shows that placement and assessment tools that are designed to elicit information about language and literacy history can provide insight into their self-perceptions, assist with placement choices, and ultimately help address their academic needs. This study suggests that if the practice of Directed Self Placement is meant to function as its creators had imagined—as an instrument that provides agency and control over placement options—then generation 1.5 students tend to exert control over their academic future by selecting mainstream writing courses rather than developmental or ESL versions. Even as they admit to being multilingual, they represent themselves as highly literate, comfortable with academic tasks, and generally confident about their success in a college setting.

However, as the data from the follow-up survey suggests, despite initial positive beliefs about language proficiency, students express concern about their lack of critical, analytical skills and difficulty with structural elements of language use—specifically grammar and organization—at the end of the first semester of writing. It is indeed striking that although this population finds self-placement procedures and the benefits of the selected course to be very satisfactory, and they report having made progress with grammar and organization, language instruction seems to be a need that is not sufficiently met. The study suggests that generation 1.5 students' self-perceptions as reflected in their DSP literacy profile—and just as importantly, their identification with native English speakers—is at odds with their self-professed linguistic abilities. This does not simply reflect eagerness to assert a monolingual academic identity and to assimilate into mainstream courses; it is a revelation of the complex set of assumptions that underlie multilingual students' beliefs, attitudes, and judgments about critical literacy and language proficiency. If we are to serve this population better, we need to have a broader and deeper understanding of their language and literacy experiences and be keenly aware of language learning as a long, complicated process for which additional resources need to be in place regardless of the type of course in which the student places. At the same time, studies that examine generation 1.5 students' unique position as language learners could help program administrators and faculty better understand the precise nature of their linguistic concerns and address them directly.

REFERENCES

Benesch, S. (2009). Interrogating in-between-ness: A postmodern perspective on immigrant students. In M. Roberge, M. Siegel, & L. Harklau (Eds.), *Generation 1.5 in college composition* (pp. 65-72). New York, NY: Routledge.

Blumenthal, A. J. (2002). English as a second language at the community college: An exploration of context and concerns. *New Directions for Community Colleges, 117*, 45–53.

Crosby, C. (2009). Academic reading and writing difficulties and strategic knowledge of generation 1.5 learners. In M. Roberge, M. Siegel, & L. Harklau (Eds.), *Generation 1.5 in college composition* (pp. 105-119). New York, NY: Routledge.

Crusan, D. (2006). The politics of implementing directed self-placement for second language writers. In P. K. Matsuda, C. Ortmeier-Hooper, & X. Yu (Eds.), *The politics of second language writing* (pp. 205-217). West Lafayette, IN: Parlor Press.

Di Gennaro, K. (2008). Assessment of generation 1.5 learners for placement into college writing courses. *Journal of Basic Writing, 27*(1), 61-79.

Hamp-Lyons, L. (1996). Applying ethical standards to portfolio assessment of writing in English as second language. In M. Milanovich & N. Saville (Eds.), *Performing testing and assessment: Selected papers from the 15th Language Testing Research Colloquium* (pp. 151-164). Cambridge, UK: Cambridge University Press.

Harklau, L., Losey, K.M, & Siegal, M. (Eds.). (1999). *Generation 1.5 meets college composition: Issues in the teaching of writing to U.S.-educated learners of ESL.* Mahwah, NJ: Lawrence Erlbaum Associates.

Harklau, L., Siegal, M., & Losey, K. M. (1999). Linguistically diverse students and college writing: What is equitable and appropriate? In L. Harklau, K.M. Losey, & M. Siegal (Eds.), *Generation 1.5 meets college composition* (pp. 1-14). Mahwah, NJ: Lawrence Erlbaum Associates.

Matsuda, P., & Matsuda, A. (2009). The erasure of resident ESL students. In M. Roberge, M. Siegal, & L. Harklau (Eds.), *Generation 1.5 in college composition* (pp. 50-64). New York, NY: Routledge.

Murie, R., & Fitzpatrick, R. (2009). Situation generation 1.5 in the academy. In M. Roberge, M. Siegal, & L. Harklau (Eds.), *Generation 1.5 in college composition* (pp. 153-169). New York, NY: Routledge.

Ortmeier-Hopper, C. (2008). English may be my second language but I'm not "ESL." *College Composition and Communication, 59*(3), 389-419.

Reynolds, D. W., Bae, K., & Wilson, J. S. (2009). Individualizing pedagogy: Responding to diverse needs in freshman composition for non-native speakers. In M. Roberge, M. Siegal, & L. Harklau (Eds.), *Generation 1.5 in college composition* (pp. 185-202). New York, NY: Routledge.

Royer, D. J., & Gilles, R. (1998). Directed self-placement: An attitude of orientation. *College Composition and Communication, 50*(1), 54-70.

Rumbaut, R. G., & Ima, K. (1988). *The adaption of Southeast Asian refugee youth: A comparative study. Final report to the Office of Resettlement* (ERIC ED 299372). San Diego, CA: San Diego State University.

Schwartz, G.G. (2004). Coming to terms: Generation 1.5 students in mainstream composition. *The Reading Matrix, 4*(3), 40-57.

Thonus, T. (2003). Serving generation 1.5 learners in the university writing center. *TESOL Journal, 12*(1), 17-24.

White, E. M. (1984). Holisticism. *College Composition and Communication, 35*(4), 400-409.

Yancey, K.B. (1999). Looking back as we look forward: Historicizing writing assessment. *College Composition and Communication, 50*(3), 483-503.

22

LINKING WRITING AND SPEAKING IN ASSESSING ENGLISH AS A SECOND LANGUAGE PROFICIENCY

Liz Hamp-Lyons
University of Bedfordshire

When Edward White wrote the first edition of his seminal book, *Teaching and Assessing Writing* (1985), he spent the first chapter simply arguing why real writing should be assessed at all. Of course, to the very few of us outside the United States who read his book in its first years, that chapter was one to be skipped, because we had little idea what he railing against: The so-called "objective" assessment of writing by multiple-choice items had not taken over in Europe or the rest of the inner circle English-speaking world as it had in the United States. I admired the professionalism of his work and his skills as a writer (although it was odd to read in Kenneth Eble's Foreword that Ed "writes with a skill uncommon among teachers of writing"!) , but it was only after I had moved to the United States and joined the English Composition Board at the University of Michigan and read work by English Department colleagues Richard Bailey (1983), Dan Fader (1986), and Jay Robinson that I began to understand why teachers and education researchers in the country were so anxious that "Johnny couldn't write" (Palmer, 1977), and why White's arguments in favor of direct writing assessment were so important. Bailey (personal communication, 2009) reflects back and says:

"We went to schools to show:

- Michigan cared about writing.
- All teachers could judge and teach writing.
- Writing was not just the province of English.

We didn't do tests to see if writing assessments were better than tests involving knowledge of grammar, identification of errors, etc. We simply asserted that writing was the best evidence."

The work of Bailey (1983), Fader (1986), Robinson (1985), and others, described in Stock (1983), and of many of their doctoral graduates in English and Education since, displays a consistent concern for teachers and schools in keeping with the arguments for the "western," "organic" approach to English teaching expressed by Newton Scott almost a century earlier:

> The teaching of English, more than the teaching of any other subject, is a matter of sympathy, of personal appeal, of mind catching fire from mind. Spontaneity and enthusiasm are the very breath in its lungs. Without these, drill and recitation and correction count for little. (1901, p. 371)

Newton Scott argued that schools and universities should be in partnership to achieve the same ultimate ends, and that schools should not be focusing on preparing students for university by preparing them to pass entrance examinations, but both schools and universities should be considering "the normal course of development of young persons of high school age," thus making the teacher "responsible to the university not for the completion of some set of formal requirements, but for developing to the utmost the minds and characters of the pupils in his charge" (p. 370). In this he opposed himself to what he saw as the "eastern" model of universities such as Harvard and Yale with their emphasis on test scores. Newton Scott lost that battle at the time and for the next 80 years or more exam-oriented schooling and narrowly prescriptive curricula were the consequence.

But while the University of Michigan was courageously (re)introducing direct writing assessment, and when White was arguing (as he has consistently argued ever since) for high-caliber essay assessments and professional scoring of essay exams, in the United Kingdom and much of the world (primarily that not dominated by U.S. principles of education) direct assessment of student writing and the assessment of most school subjects by writing about content had remained the norm (Baird, 2010). England had experimented with multiple-choice tests of English subjects in the early 1970s, but the liberal spirit of the times and the activism of English teachers resisted, and these quickly fell out of favor except in large-scale English as a Foreign

Language (EFL) tests such as the University of Cambridge Local Examinations Syndicate exams. The development of the English Language Testing Service by the British Council's team of applied linguists in the late 1970s was part of the liberal spirit of the time: the ELTS was intended to ease the path for able adults, non-native speakers/writers of English, from the far-flung former Empire into higher/further education in Britain, by offering candidates a test of English that would probe their "true ability" in communicating in English (Carroll, 1981). The ELTS's speaking and writing components were broadly discipline-related and in approach were a generation ahead of "speaking" and "writing" tests in the American TOEFL (ETS).

EXPERIMENTING IN WRITING ASSESSMENT

The background I took to the University of Michigan with me was a complicated but useful one. I had taught English in further education (similar to community college in the United States) to native speakers who had left full-time education at 16 and returned as underqualified adults. I had taught EFL to young adults in Greece, and English to university students in Iran and Malaysia. For my PhD I had researched the writing component of the previously mentioned English Language Testing Service (ELTS had empirically and inductively developed a multiple-trait rating scale from the original rudimentary holistic scale [Hamp-Lyons, 1991b]). I found that mixed background useful both for my main role in the English Composition Board with the MWA (Michigan Writing Assessment—the university-wide postacceptance placement writing), and in consulting with Michigan's English Language Institute's Testing Division on the MELAB (Michigan English Language Assessment Battery) writing component. In all these projects I have been convinced that analytic scoring (or rather, what I prefer to refer to as "multiple-trait" scoring, a more psychologically and linguistically informed view of writing behavior) has provided the best way both to score validly and reliably, and to provide some degree of diagnostic information for those who will be receiving the students.

In this I, of course, parted company with White, whose essay "Holisticism" (1984) eloquently argued that "[a]nalytic reductionism assumes that knowledge of the parts will lead to understanding of the whole, a theory which works very well with machinery or other objects, but less well with art forms or life forms" (p. 400). In many ways I sympathized with the underlying values White was espousing, and I certainly understood very well his need to overtly oppose the extreme analyticism of multiple-choice testing. I celebrated, as he did, the rapid shift in the minds of English teachers to embrace the (holistic) scoring of real writing. But I was also quite sure that, in fact, we will not understand the whole of anything fully if we do not understand how its parts work.

This view, that of an applied linguist rather than a compositionist, led me to look for a third way, a thoughtful, empirically derived way to look closely at what a writer was doing with a text, and put words to the characteristics and quality of that "doing." The other powerful influence on my thinking about designing rating scales for the assessment of writing had come from Jacobs, Zinkgraf, Wormuth, Hartfiel, and Hughey (1981), themselves practitioners in English as a Second Language (ESL), who wrote a very practical and detailed book with a title that might well have made White's hair curl: *Testing ESL Composition: A Practical Approach*. Jacobs et al. describe their approach as "holistic," following the definition proposed by Cooper (1977). The practice they sought to oppose was "frequency count marking," a method of extreme simplicity and lack of subtlety that nevertheless was popular at that time (and remains so in some of the world's education systems). But curiously from my point of view, what Jacobs et al. described as "holistic" was in fact anything but: They had taken to heart Cooper's definition of "holistic" as "any procedures which stop short of enumerating linguistic, rhetorical, or informational features of a piece of writing" (1977, p. 4). Under the umbrella of holisticism, then, they provided a highly detailed scale with five "component scales" (content, organization, vocabulary, language use, and mechanics), each scored in one of four score clusters, and each characterized by a string of words or phrases (e.g., "adequate range," "demonstrates mastery of conventions," "frequent errors of word/idiom form"). These "component scales" are not unlike what I have come to call "traits," or identifiable and characterizable "domains" of performance, except that they are more accuracy-dominated than the British communicative "revolution" (Morrow 1981), with its rejection of narrow language correctness as a value, would have been comfortable with.

The work was impressive, and the attention to supporting information and the provision of training stages to help teachers put it into practice even more so for me; but the level of detail was, I felt, intimidating for ordinary teachers and likely to be too time consuming for application in large-scale assessments.

APPLYING WRITING TOOLS TO SPEAKING ASSESSMENT

Since my time at the University of Michigan, I have worked in many situations where I have found the "multiple-trait" approach[1] to discovering, designing, and validating salient traits for effectively assessing writing. In several recent projects my research and development work has shifted focus, and I have worked on speaking assessment, particularly large-scale assessment of school-level English as a second language learners' English-speaking proficiency. In a series of funded research studies and development projects commissioned by the Hong Kong Examinations and Education Authority, colleagues and I have argued and illustrated (Davison, 2007; Davison & Hamp-Lyons, 2009; Hamp-Lyons, 2009; Hamp-Lyons & Tavares, 2011) that a person will get better at speaking by speaking; that assessing how well they can speak in English is best done by having them do so; and that advising them on how to improve their speaking skills can be facilitated by paying close attention to the way they are speaking now. Although this work has been done with second-language learners of English, I believe it is equally applicable in first-language contexts too.

It is curious to me that although applied linguists and language assessment researchers lack the sense American compositionists have of *writing as performance*, they have a much stronger sense of *speaking as performance*. There is substantial research into how speaking works and what "good" speaking "sounds like" (Hughes, 2011; Lazaraton, 2002; Szecpek Reed, 2010). Yet, despite this knowledge, the related field of language-assessment research into speaking assessment in "real-like" situations such as job interviews or academic seminars is far less developed than research. Compared to what we in writing assessment know, there is very little guidance on how such speaking performances could/should be rated. Before discussing and illustrating how multiple-trait assessment can be and has been applied in the speaking-assessment context, I briefly explain the school-based assessment (SBA) innovation that we have developed for Hong Kong secondary education.

ASSESSING SECOND LANGUAGE SPEAKING PROFICIENCY: THE SBA

In 2005, a team at the University of Hong Kong[2] was asked to bring the principles of *assessment for learning* into assessing student speaking in contexts as authentic as possible, within the classroom, and to provide an explicit and principled approach to teacher professional development in school-based assessment that might be transportable into other school subjects. Although school-based assessment is in principle an "alternative" form of assessment, a key requirement of this project was that in this case it needed to also serve a high-stakes purpose. Judgments made by class teachers about their students' English-speaking proficiency would be included as marks within the reporting of traditional test scores. How could we create an assessment that would be welcomed by teachers as beneficial to their teaching, and yet would meet reliability requirements for the examination authority's reporting requirements?

OVERVIEW OF ENGLISH LANGUAGE SBA

The solution to the assessment of English-speaking proficiency we came up with has two key dimensions: first, it is school- and classroom-based. This means that judgments of students' speaking are made by the students' own teachers, and the assessment takes place in the classroom during normal lesson time. Second, the scores form part of a high-stakes English exam, originally one of the subjects in the Hong Kong Certificate of Education, now extended and applied within the English subject in the Hong Kong Diploma of Secondary Education. The Hong Kong-wide assessment we have developed and implemented is unavoidably complex and can only be sketched briefly here: Those interested can find out a good deal more at http://www.hkeaa.edu.hk/en/sba/sba_hkdse_core/dse_subject.html?24 and within this URL will find a series of open-access files that provide details of many aspects of the SBA, including the full sets of criteria

Format of the SBA[3]

The speaking assessment itself is based on topics and texts drawn from a program of independent reading/viewing ("texts" encompass books and video/film, fiction, and nonfiction material). In preparation for the classroom-based speaking assessment, students complete the following key activities:

- select and read/view at least four texts over the course of 3 years; and
- keep a log book or brief notes of comments/personal reflections on their reading/viewing.

Based around their reading/viewing, students will:

- take part in a number of discussions in small groups with classmates on what they have read/viewed, of which two will be selected for formal score reporting; and
- make individual presentations to a small group or their whole class on the books/videos/films that they have read/viewed, of which one or two will be selected for formal score reporting.

These classroom activities are formalized as two assessable task types, group interaction and oral presentation: these two task activity types have been found to be frequent and important for non-native speakers when in English-language-use situations. Through their integration into regular classroom work, the aim is that these assessable activities will embody principles of *assessment for learning* (Black, Harrison, Lee, Marshall, & Wiliam 2003), but as we shall see later, this is difficult to achieve at the same time as conducting what is ultimately a high-stakes test.

Task Type 1: Individual Presentation

- Individual speaker presents ideas or information over a sustained period (2-3 minutes).
- May be quite informal, depending on task and audience.
- Being based in reading or viewing, some substantive content is expected.
- Requires comparatively long turns, hence requires a fairly explicit structure to help the audience.

Task Type 2: Group Interaction

- An exchange of short turns or dialogue between two or more speakers.
- Usually quite informal.
- Because of short turns, there is less explicit structuring.
- Needs attention to turn-taking skills and planning of how to initiate, maintain, and control the interaction through suggestions, questions, and expansion of ideas.

Both text types also require:

- The capacity to speak intelligibly and reasonably fluently with suitable intonation, volume, and stress, using pauses and body language such as eye contact appropriately and effectively.
- Vocabulary and language patterns that are accurate, appropriate, and varied.
- Language that is natural and interactive, not memorized or read aloud, although a few notes[4] are allowed.

Examples of both types of presentations can be viewed on the website.

These task descriptions make it easy to elicit the assessment traits (in this program these are referred to as *domains* because this is the more familiar word in Hong Kong education circles), illustrating the close synergy between tasks and traits also emphasized in trait-based writing assessment. The domains are broadly the same for the two task types: Pronunciation and Delivery; Communication Strategies, Vocabulary and Language Patterns; and Ideas and Organisation. However, as a result of the empirical derivation of the expectations of performance for the two tasks, the detailed specifications of some domains vary a little in some of their features between task types (e.g,, in Individual Presentation, the "volume" feature of the Pronunciation and Delivery domain is more important than it is in Group Presentation).

This assessment may not seem especially groundbreaking, until we realize that in every secondary school (approx. 600) in Hong Kong, every English teacher (about 3,000 in any one year) who teaches Years 4 and 5 has to be able to implement it *in the classroom*, and to do so *in a way that leads to reliable as well as valid speaking scores for her/his own students.* In 2010 approximately 113,000 students completed school-based speaking assessment for English: Clearly, implementing a wholly teacher-delivered assessment on such a huge scale has necessitated a tremendous amount of professional development (PD) for teachers. Because it was simply impossible to deliver PD this quickly to such a large number of teachers, in addition to "live" versions of the materials to be delivered in face-to-face PD courses, we developed a series of CD and DVD presented materials and trained 42 "group coordinators" to work with the materials in school groups and put the processes into practice in their own schools.

A significant portion of the training material is dedicated to the learning aspects of the SBA—as it should be: We have never lost sight of the purpose, that *assessment for learning* takes *learning* as its focus and not *assessment.* In classroom contexts, assessment is the necessary process that tells us whether and how, and how much, students have learned. Teachers have to learn how to do this. The commitment to professional development and to expanding teacher-led forms of assessment and feedback throughout the secondary school years can be seen in the project *Aligning assessment with curriculum reform in junior secondary English Language Teaching* (Davison & Mok, 2009; available on the Web).

THE KEY COMPONENTS OF SBA ASSESSMENT TRAINING

Obviously, given the above, the SBA uses criterion-referenced assessment, as do all *assessment for learning* initiatives (Black, Harrison, Lee, Marshall, & Wiliam, 2003). As Sadler (1989, 2005), Moss (2004), and others have argued, assessment that supports learning must begin with a clearly defined construct. As Hundleby in Chapter 6 and Peckham in Chapter 9 have also argued, if we do not know what we want to measure, we will never know if we have measured it. Criteria and their features and exponents are the key elements of domains (i.e., traits) in this speaking assessment as they are in almost all modern writing assessment.

Criteria and descriptors. Criterion-referenced scoring demands specified and elaborated criteria that are comprehensible to those who use them, at each stage of the process. The scoring instrument we have developed, for use by the teachers in their classrooms, is a matrix that has six levels of proficiency (necessary to be in line with previous assessment perceptions held throughout Hong Kong, but also broadly in line with common assessment practice), each of which is characterized across the four domains. As an example, Appendix A shows the full specification of the second domain, *Communication Strategies*, which has three important aspects or features.

If we think of any rating scale as a grid or matrix, obviously we expect to achieve clarity in two directions—vertically and horizontally. The *domains* are the horizontal specifications, as exemplified in Appendix A: We also need level descriptors as the realizations of the vertical specifications 1 through 6. Appendix B shows a slice of the rating scale: The level descriptors of all four domains on the horizontal axes for the level four vertical (i.e., proficiency) axis of the rating scale. Looking closely at Appendix B, we can see that the four "domains" represent four "traits" that teachers have seen and that we as researchers have identified and articulated in more detail in a language of *speaking-as-performance*. What we have, then, is a "multiple-trait" rating scale. Through working directly with a group of 40+ Hong Kong classroom teachers, over a summer in a series of six development and validation sessions, to talk about what real students were doing with the language, it was possible to approximate and successively refine this scale and the core teacher group members' understanding of it sufficiently that they were able to reliably score a wide range of student performances for inclusion into training materials. In the first year of full implementation, the system was used by all teachers with all students in all schools. A full statistical analysis of score data and subsequent moderation of score patterns by the Hong Kong Examinations and Assessment Authority resulted in less than 2% changes to scores, and the speaking assessment was found to be more reliable than the other, more traditional, elements of the English exam.

The team has now worked with the English language SBA for speaking over a 5-year period, and we have just completed an extension of the structure into a third year of senior secondary schooling (due to the change in the educational system in Hong Kong from the British 3+2+2+3 into 3+3+4). We have also conducted a series of funded research projects into various aspects of school-based assessment. The domains—that is, the criteria and descriptors within each of the domain/trait specifications in this multiple-trait scale—have become the key to reliable assessment because they have been developed to clarify and articulate the *construct* that is being judged. But the criteria have also become key in the teaching and learning process, of which the few minutes of assessment are just a small part—and for the same reason: because they enable teachers to put words to the expectations of speaking performance and proficiency they expect students to display. The criteria are, then, also key to valid assessment. This is important because as mentioned earlier, and as found in a number of empirical studies into attempts to combine assessment for learning with formal assessment (Black & William, 1998), it has been found that they sit as uneasy bedfellows at best. In the fifth year of use of the SBA speaking assessment, it is becoming clear that a fully specified multiple-trait (domain) instrument not only strongly supports reliable assessment, but also a sense of ownership and competence in teachers, and a sense of accountability in both the teachers within their schools, and the authority to the schools, teachers, and students.

The increasing use and adaptation of the criteria by and for teachers, for focused-teaching sequences, for helping students learn to self-assess and to give feedback to their peers (Hamp-Lyons, 2009; Hamp-Lyons & Tavares, 2011), and for use in earlier school years (Davison & Mok, 2009), suggests that these key domains of language proficiency are becoming understood and accepted throughout the school system.

Tasks. But I have brought more than an understanding of rating scales from writing assessment into my work with speaking assessment. Writing assessment has had a continuing concern with tasks, and this too is of significance in SBA as can be seen in the specification of two task types above. Our teachers needed, and many still need, help in designing tasks that are suitable for use as part of the normal curriculum to structure teaching and learning around reading and speaking in English, but that can *also* be used as a capstone activity to assess students on their speaking proficiency in a more integrated way. Tasks that are used for both learning, and assessment for learning, need to elicit the desired type(s) of performance, to offer every student, whatever their proficiency level, the chance to demonstrate what they do in English, and to be authentic and credible in the classroom, and they also need to provide viable and reasonable assessment moments that the teacher can concentrate on for a short period, and score on the criteria. Appendix C is an example of an SBA/assessment for learning task. All the sample tasks are available online and in the DVD materials for the teachers' use. The proforma it is shown in is used for all sample tasks, and available in blank form for teachers to use when they create their own classroom tasks.

Samples of performance: Teachers as raters. For performance assessment to succeed, whether writing or speaking performance is being assessed, teachers must have practice in looking at samples and scoring them. Each teacher will usually only see student performances from her/his own class, and occasionally from a few other classes in the same school. But in this context the SBA must be effective as an assessment across the whole of Hong Kong (about 113,000 students in 2010), and reliability of scoring is important because teachers across all of Hong Kong must benchmark their judgments to the same rating scale. A wide selection of examples of students at different levels doing different task types and different tasks is therefore necessary to ensure that teachers really do grasp the construct of speaking proficiency that underlies all the teaching and learning materials for speaking as well as the rating criteria and descriptors: This is a validity requirement. The training materials therefore include one DVD that focuses on taking teachers through the entire process of understanding what is assessed, why and how, scoring practice with a lead teacher, scoring an "anchor set," and learning the consensus scores the samples had been given. An additional DVD provides further validated examples of a range of performances for use by trainers and lead teachers who need to refresh teachers on the standards.

In developing all the above, I have drawn directly on what I have learned from my work in writing assessment and have aligned that understanding with the curriculum components of the overall system developed by my project colleague Chris Davison. In this work I have affirmed again the value of seeing language performance as complex, as built of many strands and influences, as mutable yet explicable. Certainly, a speaking or writing performance may be described as "good," or "adequate," or even "extraordinary," but holisticism will never enable us to explain why it is so extraordinary, or merely adequate. It will never help us to talk to a student about persistent articulation errors in final consonant clusters (a perennial Chinese learner problem) while also complimenting her/him for listening attentively and effectively building on a point made by a classmate. Holisticism is not generative, it is egocentric. Holisticism looks inward, at the reader, not outward, at the speaker or writer. Holisticism is not teacherly.

Therefore, with great respect and appreciation for the contributions made by Ed White to writing assessment—contributions without which we may not have arrived at the better place we are now in—I have to say: You cannot build a sturdy house with only one brick.

APPENDIX A

Domain II: Communication Strategies
It is made up of three important areas: ***Body Language*, *Timing*, *Asking/ Responding to Questions***

Body Language is very important to successful oral communication—speaking and listening—whether taking part in a group interaction or in giving a presentation to classmates, parents, teachers, etc. The kinds of body language we use in the two kinds of situations are slightly different. First, what is body language? The key aspects of body language are:

- Gaze (eye contact with individuals; looking around a group to show awareness of the audience and to create a feeling of inclusion; NOT looking at others when speaking gives the impression of inattentiveness);
- Facial expression (positive feeling / negative feeling [smile / frown]; taut facial muscles instead of lax ones [taut suggests interest and lax suggests detachment]; strength of facial expression [the larger the audience, the more "dramatic" or obvious expressions needs to be]);
- Head movement (nodding indicates interest and encouragement; absence of head movement suggests lack of attention) and
- Body direction (leaning forward suggests participation, leaning back suggests detachment, lack of interest, lack of confidence, etc.).

A high score for body language comes from the way the student puts all these aspects together and maintains good body language all the way through the task. Students need to learn that the more they rely on notes or memorised material, the weaker their body language is likely to be (see also **Domain III**).

Timing
It is important to get any task done well; but when the task is being assessed, it's even more important. In the HKDSE English oral language SBA tasks, each student has a limited amount of time to do the task (somewhere around 3-5 minutes) for an individual presentation, and a fair share of 3 minutes multiplied by the number of students taking part in a group interaction. If one student takes too long for an individual presentation, the audience may get bored; if the student is too brief, s/he won't be able to give enough ideas or support. If a student takes too long for his/her turn in a group interac-

tion, groupmates will feel that they haven't had their own proper share of time; if a student contributes too little s/he makes the other group members work harder, and doesn't show enough evidence that s/he can participate in a group discussion.

Asking/Responding to Questions

Teachers should refer to the Framework of Guiding Questions (see Appendix IV on the 2012 HKDSE SBA Introductory DVD) to see the kinds of questions that can be asked, and how these may be adapted to students of different language levels. Students scoring 4 or higher are expected to be able to show some degree of ability to ask useful questions in a group discussion and to answer questions their groupmates ask about what they say in their own turns. Students scoring 3 or 4 may ask simple questions that are appropriate to their level.

Students scoring 5 or 6 on an individual presentation should show that they can elicit responses from the audience, that they can answer them if they are clearly-formulated, or that they can make a suitable comment on a point made.

APPENDIX B

Criterial Descriptors for the Features of LEVEL 4 on all four Domains

Pronunciation and Delivery	Communication Strategies	Vocabulary and Language Patterns	Ideas and Organization
Can project the voice mostly satisfactorily without artificial aids.	**Can** use some features of appropriate body language to display and encourage interest.	**Can** use mostly appropriate vocabulary.	**Can** present relevant literal ideas clearly in a well-organised structure, perhaps with occasional reference to a notecard.
Can pronounce most sounds/sound clusters and all common words clearly and accurately; less common words can be understood although there may be articulation errors (e.g. dropping final consonants).	**Can** use a range of appropriate turn-taking strategies to participate in interaction (e.g. by making suggestions in a group discussion), and can sometimes help draw others in (e.g., by asking for their views),	**Can** use language patterns that are usually accurate, and without errors that impede communication.	**Can** often respond appropriately to others; can sustain and may extend some conversational exchanges
Can speak at a deliberate pace, with some hesitation but using sufficient intonation conventions to convey meaning	**Can** interact using a mixture of mainly natural language and formulaic expressions.	**Can** self-correct when concentrating carefully, or when asked to do so.	**However: Can do these things less well when attempting to respond to interpretive or critical questions**, or when trying to interpret information and present elaborated ideas.
		May refer to a note card but is not dependent on notes.	

APPENDIX C

Sample Assessment Task 22

Name of Task: Two stars and a wish (for higher ability S5 students.)
Oral Text-type: ☐ individual presentation ☑ interaction

Communication Functions:
☑ describing ☑ reporting ☑ explaining ☑ discussing
☐ classifying ☐ comparing ☐ persuading ☐ others: ______

Audience–teacher plus:	Targeted audience:	Role(s) of audience:
☐ a student partner ☐ small groups ☐ class ☐ more than one class	☐ fellow students ☐ students from other classes ☐ teacher(s) ☐ other: ______	☐ giving non-verbal responses only ☐ questioning/commenting ☐ interacting with no limitations

Where on this continuum would you place the task?

☑ spontaneous, informal dialogue, e.g. small group interaction	☐ interactive, planned yet dialogic, e.g. semi-formal group report, interactive factual report	☐ individual long term of planned, spoken text, e.g. news reporting, story telling	☐ individual long term that is planned, cohesive, organized, formal, e.g. spoken report, a speech

This task is suitable for use with the following genre(s):
☐ print/non-print fiction
☐ print/non-print biography/autobiography
☑ factual books/documentaries on common topics, e.g. sports, hobbies, travel
☐ books/films on real life issues, e.g. environmental, social, economic

Preparation:
Ask students to be prepared to talk for one minute about a book/documentary they have recently read/viewed. They may use the questions in Appendix 2 as reference and write down some notes in point-form on a 4 x 6 card. Prepare a copy of the "guiding Questions for Students" in Appendix 14.

Description of pre-assessment activities:
1. Distribute and discuss the "Guiding Questions for Students. Explain to students that they can ask questions at different levels.
2. Tell students something about a factual book/documentary you have read.
3. Divide the students into small groups.
4. Ask them to come up with some questions to ask you, so they can find out more about the book/documentary you read/viewed.
5. Ask students to work out at least one question for each level of the Guiding Questions.
6. Invite students to ask you some first level questions for the first minute, second level questions

APPENDIX C (CON'T)
Sample Assessment Task 22

for the second minute and all the way up to the fifth level questions. (Tell them that you will only provide an answer if they ask the right level of questions.)

7. Compliment your students on the good questions they asked you.
8. After students are familiar with the various types of questions they could ask, ask students to take turns talking about their book/documentary to their group members (one minute for each turn.) Students may use their 4 x 6 note card for reference, but they should try to look up and speak as naturally as possible.
9. After each 1-minute talk, the group members will ask the presenter some guiding questions at level up questions.
10. When time is over, and (or two) of the group members is/are nominated to "give a star" - to say something they he/she would like to know more about, or that they wish had been explained.

Planned SBA Task:

Ask students to talk about another factual book/documentary they have read/viewed in a group, following the procedure in step 9. The teacher-assessor can also ask questions along the questioning continuum from the "framework of guiding question" in the SBA guidelines. When the teacher has completed his/her probing, group members will be invited to "give two stars" and "make a wish" similar to the procedure in step 10 or the pre-assessment activity.

Tips/comments:

- The pre-assessment activities can help students think about the types of questions that they might be asked during the SBA and in turn they will be more prepared to answer high level questions during the actual assessment.
- Concluding the discussion with "two stars and a wish" is a nice way to round up the discussion. It also encourages students to pay attention to the information they hear during the student presentation and helps students practise expressing praise, and using appropriate language to make a gentle critical comment.
- Remember the focus of this task should be on students' interaction. The one-minute talk at the beginning is only a warm-up activity which allows the students to provide some background information to his/her group members to generate the interaction.
- Alternatively, teachers could use this task for individual presentations by increasing the 1-minute talk to 2-3 minutes. The discussion which comes afterward should not be counted as part of the SBA task, but an extension of the assessment for learning.

Name of Task ***Choosing a gift for a character 1**

Oral Text-type: ☐ **individual presentation** ☑ **interaction**

☑ **describing**	☐ **reporting**	☑ **explaining**	☑ **discussing**
☐ **classifying**	☐ **comparing**	☑ **persuading**	☐ **others:** ________

APPENDIX C (CON'T)

Sample Assessment Task 22

Audience—teacher plus:

- ☐ a student partner
- ☑ small groups
- ☐ class
- ☐ school
- ☑ fellow students
- ☐ students from other classes
- ☑ teacher(s)
- ☐ others: ______________

Role(s) of audience:

- ☐ giving non-verbal responses only
- ☑ questioning/commenting
- ☑ interacting with no limitations

Where on this continuum would you place the task?

- ☑ spontaneous, informal dialogue, e.g. small group interaction
- ☐ interactive, planned yet dialogic, e.g. semi-formal group report, interactive factual report
- ☐ individual long term of planned, spoken text, e.g. news reporting, story telling
- ☐ individual long term that is planned, cohesive, organized, formal, e.g. spoken report, a speech

This task is suitable for use with the following genre(s):

- ☑ print/non-print fiction
- ☐ print/non-print biography/autobiography
- ☐ factual books/documentaries on common topics, e.g. sports, hobbies, travel
- ☐ books/films on real life issues e.g. environmental, social, economic

Preparation: Think of a character from a book or a film which students are familiar with. Prepare a short segment of the film or a short passage about the character.

Description of pre-assessment activities:

Give a quick summary of the story and highlight the character you have in mind.

Tell students that they need to think of a gift for the character to help solve his/her problems, change his/her attitudes, improve his/her life conditions, etc. Show students a short segment of the film* or read a short passage about the character.

Divide the students into groups of 3-4. Ask each of them to think of a gift for the character and explain their choices with reference to the information they just read or viewed. Encourage students to ask for clarification, show agreement and disagreement during their discussion. Then select the best gift for the character as a group.

Invite students from each group to describe their gift and explain their choice.

On the day of the performance, students can conduct peer evaluations using the guidelines and evaluation forms in Appendix 3 for reference..

APPENDIX C (CON'T)
Sample Assessment Task 22

Planned SBA Task:

Divide the class into groups of three. Ask each group of students to find and read a book/view a film of their choice. After reading/viewing, each student in the group should adopt a different character and familiarize themselves with the story/events involved with that particular character. On the day of the assessment, the teacher-assessor will ask each student some questions randomly to get some background information about the book/film they have read/viewed. Some of the basic questions may include the following:

a) What is the title of your book/film?
b) What level of difficulty is it?
c) What type of genre/story is it? (science, fiction, biography, romance, adventure, detective, horror, true, etc.
d) When and where is the story set if it is a story?
e) What is the book/film about?

The teacher-assessor will randomly call on a student and ask him/her to describe the characteristics/personalities of his/her chosen character and highlight one of the events that character took part in. As a group, the students have to discuss and select a gift for the character based on the information provided by the student. Then another student will be called on the describe another character and then the group will select another gift for that character.

Variation:

Ask students to read/view another book/film and familiarize themselves with the story/events involved with a particular character. On the day of the assessment, students will be assigned to work with another 2 or 3 students who have read/viewed a different book/film. Each of them will take turns providing some general information about the book/film they read/viewed. Then as a group, they will discuss and select a gift for each of the characters.

Tips/comments:

- Giving students opportunities to hold discussions in class in the pre-assessment activities can help them gather more experience to interact with other.
- This task is relatively easy. It encourages students to think creatively and attentively to the needs of others. This task is suitable for students from different levels.

ENDNOTES

1. The term I coined for the PhD (1986) and have used in my published work on assessing writing since.
2. Led by Dr. Chris Davison and myself; Chris Davison heads up the work in teacher/professional development, and I head up the work in assessment.
3. This overview is substantially based on the materials developed by the SBA team, led by Chris Davison and myself, for the 2006-11 HKCEE version of SBA-English. These materials can be accessed online at www.hku.hk/~sbapro and go to *Resources*. The version we have more recently developed for the HKDSE, to be first assessed in 2012, contains a second component, not described here, but available at the url above (http://www.hkeaa.edu.hk./en/sba/sba_hkdse_core/dse_subject.html?2&4).
4. Due to the emphasis on preparation and memorization in the Hong Kong culture, "a few notes" has become formalized as no more than one 6x4 notecard.

REFERENCES

Bailey, R. W. (1983). Writing across the curriculum: The British approach. In P. L. Stock (Ed.), *Forum—essays on theory and practice in the teaching of writing* (pp. 24-32). Montclair, NJ: Boynton/Cook Publishers.

Baird, J. A. (2010). Editorial. *Assessment in Education: Principles, Policy and Practice, 17*(1), 1-5.

Black, P., Harrison, C., Lee, C., Marshall, B., & Wiliam, D. (2003). *Assessment for learning: Putting it into practice*. Maidenhead, UK: Open University Press.

Black, P., & William, D. (1998). Assessment and classroom learning. *Assessment in Education, 5*(3), 7-74.

Carroll, B. (1981). Specifications for an English Language Testing Service. In J.C. Alderson (Ed.), *Issues in language testing* (pp. 66-80). London, UK: The British Council.

Cooper, C. (1977). Holistic evaluation of writing. In C. Cooper & L. Odell (Eds.), *Evaluating writing: Describing, measuring, judging* (pp. 3-32). Urbana, IL: National Council of Teachers of English.

Davison, C. (2007). Views from the chalkface: English language school-based assessment in Hong Kong. *Language Assessment Quarterly, 4*(1), 37-68.

Davison, C., & Hamp-Lyons, L. (2009). The Hong Kong Certificate of Education: Hong Kong Certificate of School-based assessment reform in Hong Kong English Language Education. In L. Cheng & A. Curtis (Eds.), *English language assessment and the Chinese Learner* (pp. 216 –251). London, UK: Routledge.

Davison, C., & Mok J. (Eds.). (2009). *Aligning assessment with curriculum reform in junior secondary English language teaching*. Hong Kong: Quality Education Fund/Faculty of Education, The University of Hong Kong.

Fader, D. (1986). Writing samples and virtues. In K. L. Greenberg, H. S. Weiner, & R.A. Donovan (Eds.), *Writing assessment: Issues and strategies* (pp. 79-92). White Plains, NY: Longman.

Hamp-Lyons. L. (1991). Reconstructing "academic writing proficiency". In L. Hamp-Lyons (Ed.), *Assessing second language writing in academic contexts* (pp. 127-153). Norwood, NJ: Ablex.

Hamp-Lyons, L. (2009). Assessment for learning through peer feedback and self assessment. In C. Davison & J. Mok (Eds.), *Aligning assessment with curriculum reform in junior secondary English language teaching*. Hong Kong: Quality Education Fund/Faculty of Education, The University of Hong Kong. Web.

Hamp-Lyons, L., & N. Tavares. (2011). Interactive assessment—a dialogic and collaborative approach to assessing learners' oral language. In D. Tsagari & I. Csepes (Eds.), *Classroom-based language assessment* (pp 29-46.). Frankfurt, Germany: Peter Lang.

Hughes, R. (2011). *Teaching and researching speaking* (2nd ed.). London, UK: Pearson Education.

Jacobs, H., Zinkgraf, S., Wormuth, D., Hartfiel, V., & Hughey, J. (1981). Testing ESL composition: A practical approach. Rowley, MA: Newbury House.

Lazaraton, A. (2002). *A qualitative approach to the validation of oral language tests.* Studies in Language Testing. Cambridge, UK: Cambridge University Press.

Morrow, K. (1981). Communicative language testing—evolution or revolution? In J.C. Alderson (Ed.), *Issues in language testing* (pp. 9-25). London, UK: The British Council.

Moss, P. A. (2004). Reconceptualizing validity for classroom assessment. *Educational Measurement: Issues and Practice, 22*(4), 13-25.

Palmer, R.E. (1977). Why Johnny can't write and what to DO about it. *Southern Medical Journal, 77(*8), 899-901.

Robinson, J. (1985). Literacy in the Department of English. *College English, 47*, 282-298.

Sadler, D. R. (2005). Interpretations of criteria-based assessment and grading in higher education. *Assessment & Evaluation in Higher Education, 30*(2), 175-194.

Sadler, D. R. (1989). Formative assessment and the design of instructional systems. *Instructional Science, 18(*2), 119-144.

Scott, F.N. (1901). College entrance requirements in English. *School Review, 9*, 365-378.

Stock, P. L. (Ed.). (1983). *Forum—essays on theory and practice in the teaching of writing*. Montclair, NJ: Boynton/Cook Publishers.

Szecpek Reed, B. (2010). *Analyzing conversation: An introduction to prosody.* London: Palgrave MacMillan.

White, E. (1984). Holisticism. *College Composition and Communication, 35*(4), 400-409.

White, E. M. (1985). *Teaching and assessing writing: Recent advances in understanding, evaluating, and improving student performance.* San Francisco, CA: Jossey-Bass.

White, E. (1994). Issues and problems in writing assessment. *Assessing Writing, 1*(1), 11-27.

IV

TOWARD A VALID FUTURE

EMW Reflection: I retired for the first time from Cal State, San Bernardino, in 1997, though I continued teaching there part-time for three more years before I retired for the second time. In 2000, my wife Volney and I moved to Flagstaff, Arizona, since I had become a visiting professor at the University of Arizona, only 250 miles away. I taught on and off, mostly on, until I retired for the third time in 2009. Flagstaff is a lovely mountain town, where it is easy to stay in good physical condition (as this picture from October 2011 shows) and good health. I keep writing books, book chapters, articles, and maybe someday I'll finish the memoir I've been working on since my first retirement.

IV

TOWARD A VALID FUTURE

THE USES AND MISUSES OF WRITING ASSESSMENT

Tension between the composition community and the educational measurement community is a theme that runs through this volume. The history of those tensions is presented by Yancey (1999) in her important essay, "Looking Back as We Look Forward: Historicizing Writing Assessment." The history of writing assessment from 1950 is depicted in a metaphor of three waves. The first, from approximately 1950 to 1970, was focused on objective tests constructed, administered, and validated by educational measurement professionals with little or no input from classroom teachers or awareness of classroom pedagogy (Palmer, 1961). The primary claim for validity in the first wave was reliability—that measurement must be consistent, constant, and efficient among raters and across test administrations.

The second wave largely began with the work of Edward M. White in the California State University system in the early 1970s. During this wave, writing teachers who became familiar with the language of educational measurement and the principles embodied in that language were led by hybrid practitioners, typified by White (2001) himself. These writing teachers worked closely with educational measurement professionals. Because teachers of writing were now at the table when decisions were made, the focus of assessment shifted emphasis from reliability to validity: To be a valid measure of writing ability, writing itself must be understood as a complex form of communication. The consequence was a movement away from sole use of highly reliable indirect measures (such as multiple-choice questions that addressed knowledge of conventions) to direct measures of writing (such as holistically scored essays that measured analytic thought).

The third wave began in the mid 1980s with criticisms of both the artificiality of the timed impromptu essay as a vehicle for direct measures of writing (Albertson & Marwitz, 2001; Biola, 1982; Caudery, 1990) and holistic scoring of those essays (Charney, 1984; Williamson & Huot, 1993). Concurrent with such critique was the simultaneous development of the student portfolio as a vehicle for writing assessment. The reliability and validity of a single essay had been challenged even by such high priests of educational measurement as Paul Diederich, who wrote in 1974 that for a valid and reliable writing assessment, there should be at least two pieces of writing evaluated. Moreover, the two essays should differ in rhetorical form and be written at different times. Responsive to strategies designed to improve assessment, writing instructors such as Peter Elbow and Pat Belanoff (1986) asked a common sense question: If two essays written to different rhetorical forms were better than one, and if a separation in time yields longitudinal performance information, then why not evaluate the varied writing that students perform in their writing class? Thus, the defining assessment instrument of the third wave—portfolio assessment—was born.

Yancey notes that another feature of the third wave was the recognition of writing assessment as an area of expertise within the field of composition. Emerging was a large explosion of amateurs such as Elbow and Belanoff (1997) who were proud of their insistence that writing pedagogy must become increasingly interrelated with valid assessment. This formulation of the dichotomy of the amateur versus the professional tester, however, goes back much farther. Carl Campbell Brigham (1937), the principal inventor of the SAT—who later fought against the creation of the Education Testing Service—felt that the opposition between what he called "testers" and teachers was largely because "testers having chosen their own weapons and set up their own target then told educators that this was the right one to shoot at" (p. 758). Although Brigham thought that testers and teachers could work together, his vision of a new testing organization was one that favored the trained teacher over the educational measurement specialist.

> Since the testers of today are for the most part insensitive to the nature of the things they are trying to measure, a major function of the new organization must be the training and recruitment of better personnel. As it is probably simpler to teach cultured men [sic] testing than to give testers culture, the research wing should act as a training school for promising young men [sic] drafted from the major fields of learning. (p. 758)

Elbow and Belanoff leveraged their status as nonassessment specialists to stress the very point made by Brigham more than a half-century earlier: If writing assessment is to have valid use, the role of classroom practice must inform the assessment design.

This fourth section of this volume takes its cue from Brigham: All the chapters are by university academics who teach in the field of Rhetoric and Composition/Writing Studies. The stories they tell vary considerably. Some recount victories, defeats, or both. One tries to expose the absurdity of those in the mass-market testing industry who, under White's Law, "would have testing done unto thee." All follow Yancey's (1999) observation that contemporary writing assessment is reflective about its practice and the practices to which it connects. Each is aligned with Gallagher's (2011) belief that the writing assessment scene will benefit by preserving and enhancing the educational prerogatives of instructors and their students.

The final section begins with Richard Haswell extolling the power of numbers in arguments about writing policy. In a chapter that combines classical rhetoric and modern politics in the analysis of five case studies, Haswell demonstrates the rhetorical power of quantification. Humpty Dumpty tells *Alice in Through the Looking Glass* (Carroll, 1871/1980) that a word means "just what I choose it to mean—neither more nor less." When Alice objects, Humpty Dumpty states, "The question is ... which is to be master — that's all." Haswell makes a similar case for numbers: The first to use numbers is often the one who wins the argument. Beginning with a perceptive analysis of an paragraph that, at first glance, looks like narrative devoid of enumeration, Haswell demonstrates that the writer employs numbers in anticipation of possible objections. Defining this strategy as a "a rhetoric of anticipatory enumeration," Haswell demonstrates that this tactic is a subspecies of the classical rhetorical strategy of *procatalepsis*: a rhetorical move to anticipate an audience's possible objections to a claim and to refute those objections before they are made. Haswell's case studies demonstrate the power of numbers as a preemptive strategy in the service of scholarship that is replicable, agreeable, and data supported (Haswell, 2005).

Yet *procatalepsis* works another way, as Les Perelman demonstrates, when mass-market writing assessment is examined as its own self-contained system. In "Mass Market Writing Assessment as Bullshit," Perelman adapts Haswell's advice to argue with numbers to expose absurdities that result from the conflicting demands for representation and efficiency. When robust representation of writing ability is viewed as achievable solely through efficient test design, the result is bullshit. As a twenty-first-century term nearly synonymous with that useful nineteenth-century term, humbug, Perelman deals with the theme of misrepresentation, applying what P. T. Barnum called a "Humbugometer" to the timed impromptu essay, the distortion of holistic scoring, and writing research itself. Drawing on applications by Frankfurt (2005) of insincere actions and untruthful behaviors, Perelman takes to task mass-market writing assessment that has its origins in the College Board's early-twentieth-century effort to standardize college admissions, its impetus in federal, regional, and local demands for accountability rising after World War II, and its current manifestation in the 2008 reauthorization of the Higher Education Act (H. R. 4137). Such assessments are contemporary artifacts of a consumer culture that craves mass sales, Perelman argues, thus giving customers products that attend more to gloss than horsepower. The ironies from this postmodern manufacturing nightmare are disarming: students writing to con pressured readers, evaluative standards lacking discriminative power, and reports more forceful than true.

Just as demands for accountability frame large-scale assessment, such demands also frame locally based assessment. Peggy O'Neill addresses the relationship between assessment in instruction to determine how writing assessment practices frame the construct of writing and the programs promoting those constructs. She analyzes assessment practices at two different institutions. Both were locally situated and developed, and both had an essential writing-across-the-curriculum/writing-in-the-disciplines (WAC/WID) component. Yet despite these apparent strengths, the assessments favored a view of writing—timed, impromptu, first-draft essays—from the second wave of assessment. These signaling effects, defined by president emeritus of the University of California Richard Atkinson (2004) as the powerful messages that testing sends, complicate the WAC/WID view of writing as a complex cognitive act. Assessment, O'Neill argues, thus requires a careful and always evolving balancing act between roles as researcher and politician. A program of writing assessment is not, she concludes, a concrete structure but a conceptual framework. As she demonstrates, the ecology of the conceptual framework itself may be the subject of important analysis.

Cindy Moore is equally ambitious in trying to reframe assessment. First, she adopts the position of Patricia Lynn that rather than just redefining terms such as *reliability* and *validity*, the field of Rhetoric and Composition/Writing Studies needs to establish a language of its own, substituting *meaningfulness* for *validity* and *ethics* for *reliability*. Moore then explores how the history of the feminist, sociolinguistic program of language (Pauwels, 2003) provides models for successful change as well much evidence for its difficulty. She predicts that opposing such changes with the major stakeholders in writing assessment, including theorists who have spent considerable time and effort in working to redefine and reshape conventional terminology and large testing organizations whose hegemonic control is partially based on their control of the language of educational measurement. Moore sees a grassroots movement of Rhetoric and Composition/Writing Studies professionals to change the forms of the language of assessment as an empowering project much in the way that the feminist language project empowered feminism.

The final chapter in this section is by Kathleen Blake Yancey. Her analysis of the rhetorical situation of writing assessment serves as the bookend to her 1999 article, as well as to John Brereton's chapter on the origins of the Harvard Placement Examination that begins this volume. Using and extending Lloyd Bitzer's (1966) concept of *local exigence*, an occasion requiring response, Yancey describes the development of first and second waves of writing assessment. She then extends *local exigence* to the concept of *self-created exigence*, a means of developing innovative practice independent of any specific local need. *Self-created exigence,* Yancey argues, propelled both the third wave of writing assessment and is now creating the fourth wave. This newest wave, characterized by increased participation of the federal government in postsecondary assessment and by research conducted by members of the Rhetoric and Composition/Writing Studies community, has been accompanied by a new model of inquiry. This new model, independent of any specific local need, is located in multiple, diverse communities. As such, it holds the potential to yield innovative questions, frame new inquiry methods, produce important knowledge, and communicate that knowledge in creative ways. In the relatively short span of 27 years from the 1985 publication of *Teaching and Assessing Writing* to the present writing, writing assessment has progressed in theory, design, and application. As this edited collection demonstrates, the evolution of writing assessment continues. Just beyond the horizon, the future is bright and exciting.

REFERENCES

Albertson, K., & Marwitz, M. (2001). The silent scream: Students negotiating timed writing assessments. *Teaching English in the Two-Year College, 29*(2), 144-153

Atkinson, R. C. (2004, April). *AERA public service award address.* Address presented at the American Education Research Association, San Diego, CA.

Barnum, P. T. (1866). *The humbugs of the world: An account of humbugs, delusions, impositions, quackeries, deceits and deceivers generally, in all ages.* New York, NY: Carleton.

Biola, H. R. (1982). Time limits and topic assignments for essay tests. *Research in the Teaching of English, 16*(1), 97-98.

Bitzer, L. (1968). The rhetorical situation. *Philosophy and Rhetoric, 1*(1), 1-14.

Brigham, C. C. (1937, December.). The place of research in a testing organization. *School and Society, 11*, 756-759.

Carroll, L. (1871/1980). *Through the looking-glass and what Alice found there.* London, UK: Macmillan.

Caudery, T. (1990). The validity of timed essay tests in the assessment of writing skills. *English Language Teaching Journal, 44*(2), 122-131.

Charney, D. (1984). The validity of using holistic scoring to evaluate writing: A critical overview. *Research in the Teaching of English, 18*(1), 65-83.

Diederich, P. B. (1974). *Measuring growth in English.* Urbana, IL: National Council of Teachers of English.

Elbow, P., & Belanoff, P. (1986). Portfolios as a substitute for proficiency examinations. *College Composition and Communication, 37*(3), 336-339.

Elbow, P., & Belanoff, P. (1997). Reflections on an explosion: Portfolios in the 90s and beyond. In K. Yancey & I. Weiser (Eds.), *Situating portfolios: Four perspectives* (pp. 21-34). Logan, UT: Utah State University Press.

Frankfurt, H. G. (2005). *On bullshit.* Princeton, NJ and Oxford, UK: Princeton University Press.

Gallagher, C. W. (2011). Being there: (Re)making the assessment scene. *College Composition and Communication, 32*(3), 450-476.

Haswell, R. (2005). NCTE/CCCC's recent war on scholarship. *Written Communication, 22*(2), 198-223.

H. R. 4137. (2008). *Extension of Higher Education Act of 1965.* 110th Cong. Web.

Palmer, O. (1961). Sense or nonsense? The objective testing of English composition. *The English Journal, 50*(5), 314-320.

Pauwels, A. (2003). Linguistic sexism and feminist linguistic activism. In J. Holmes & M. Meyerhoff (Eds.), *The handbook of language and gender* (pp. 550-570). Malden, MA: Blackwell.

White, E. M. (2001). The opening of the modern era of writing assessment: A narrative. *College English, 63*(3), 306-320.

White, E. M. (1985). *Teaching and assessing writing: Recent advances in understanding, evaluating, and improving student performance.* San Francisco, CA: Jossey-Bass.

Williamson, M., &. Huot, B. (1993). *Validating holistic scoring for writing assessment: Theoretical and empirical foundations.* Cresskill, NJ: Hampton Press.

Yancey, K. B. (1999). Looking back as we look forward: Historicizing writing assessment. *College Composition and Communication, 50*(3), 483-503.

23

FIGHTING NUMBER WITH NUMBER

Richard H. Haswell
Texas A&M University, Corpus Christi

"Numbers lie." "Lies, damned lies, and statistics." "Manipulation of the figures." "Doctoring the books." So the chorus runs.

Fear of numbering is widespread and chronic. In composition studies, for instance, the case against number-based scholarship has been made and remade. Only trivial things can be measured. The relationship between rhetorical values is not mathematical. Data analysis breaks language effect into pieces and does not reassemble it back into a whole. Numbers themselves are abstract, not real, and research findings in the form of unbodied averages and correlations cannot be transferred to the living bodies of students in classrooms. In testing, numbers only simplify complex abilities and performances, falsely rationalize the intuitive, and encourage comparison of academic and demographic contexts that are singular, not comparable. The professional chorus has lasted decades. We embraced Huff's *How to Lie with Statistics* (1954) and rarely opened Siegel's *Nonparametric Statistics for the Behavioral Sciences* (1956).

Both books are still in print, suggesting a tenacious cultural contradiction. Algorithms and arithmophobia go hand in hand. Numbers are like microbes and fires—people both need and fear them. But in composition studies, the contradiction takes on an added irony. As Huff's title makes explicit, numbering is not just a method of analysis but also an argument with generic handles. You would think that long ago compositionists would have fancied, or at least investigated, the rhetorical properties of numbering. As Sontag (1978) said about photographers, of whom people also have both a need and a fear, the work that numberers do "is no generic exception to the usually shady commerce between art and truth" (p. 6). Why shouldn't our profession, which studies and teaches the way language does dubious business with art and truth, buy into numbering as a profitable trade in persuasion and argumentation?

In this chapter, I set aside that question as self-evident. Instead, I point out one simple way compositionists can analyze numbering as a rhetorical commerce, and then add a way, perhaps not so simple, they can adapt this commerce as an argument for one of their own causes, the championing of local over outside assessment of writing. This rhetorical argument, technically a counterargument, I call *anticipatory* or *procataleptic numbering*. I hasten to add, before I lose 95% of my readers, that my focus is not on statistics per se. I am not instructing the world of composition in the latest fashion in Rausch modeling. The commerce of rhetorical numbering, as will be shown, can employ the full range of number use, starting with numeration so fundamental readers hardly recognize it as such.

Edward White has never feared numbers. From his annual validation studies of the California State University system's Freshman English Equivalency Examination during the 1970s (beginning with White, 1973), through his retention study of basic writers in the system two decades later (White, 1995), he has applied statistical methods with understanding, circumspection, and persuasive effect. He also has long warned—so long it is sometimes called "White's law"—that if local composition programs do not create their own large-scale assessment, outsiders usually accompanied by a national commercial testing firm will do it for them. Currently White's warning is more relevant than ever, with the Department of Education, blue-ribbon panels, state higher-education boards, boards of regents, and politicians on the make continuing to push mandatory proficiency level testing of student writing from the schools into state universities (see O'Neill, Chapter 25).

In this chapter I want to show how anticipatory numbering, the report of data from local testing, as much as the testing itself, forms a powerful argument to stave off outside assessment. Just as fire can be fought with fire, we can fight numbers with numbers. When the evaluators arrive to burn our courses down to the bare number, they will find that there is nothing left to consume. Will the strategy work?

THE UNIVERSAL RHETORICAL APPEAL OF NUMBERS

As I have suggested, among many of my colleagues a first reaction to any proposal to fight numbers with numbers would not be "Will it work?" but "How could we stoop so low?" But when we consider numbering as a rhetorical as well as a methodological tool, then the issue is no longer whether composition studies should be using it. They already are. This simple point could be demonstrated with any piece ever written by a compositionist. I use an essay by Powell (2000) as an example of classroom research whose effectiveness of argument I admire.

Powell calls his essay a "blunder narrative." It recounts a writing class he taught using techniques of "radical critique," during which things went radically wrong. The following paragraph, of which the underscoring is mine, sets the stage for the coming disaster.

> I had come a long way, in more ways than one, to the classroom I found myself in—but perhaps not as far as I should have, in terms of experience, anyway. I had been teaching for just two and a half years when I walked into that room, having come from a semester of TAing and another year of adjuncting in upper East Tennessee. Though I had taught only one section of basic (still called "developmental") writing at that time, I had taught basic writers, to be sure. At both the community college and the regional university where I cut my teeth, many students were the first of their family to attend college, many were nontraditional and working class, many were underprepared by poorly funded rural school systems. But like most TAs and adjuncts I had almost no training in teaching writing—and none specifically in teaching basic writing. During my year of adjuncting I learned mostly how to drive very quickly between four different teachings sites. (p. 13)

Numbers figure heavily. He has been teaching "for just two and a half years," he had taught "only one" section of basic writing, he teaches at "four different" teaching sites. Even where precise numbers are not given, facts offered may have a numerical base. For instance, he says "many students were underprepared by poorly funded rural school systems," and the "many," the "poorly," and the "under-" of "underprepared" all presuppose countable information: percentages, dollar amounts, and educational measures such as grades or test scores.

The rhetorical strategy is double. In the first place, countable information, such as the reference to the "four different teaching sites," persuades because it is exact and factual, adding weight to the paragraph's specificity. I find it ironic that anti-numbers compositionists resist a rhetorical means that writing teachers have ranked among the top three most important qualities of writing that they teach. Indeed, if a composition student had submitted Powell's paragraph, how many writing teachers would have circled the *manys* in the fourth sentence and asked in the margin, "Can you be more specific?"

The second strategy of countable information is much less discussed. It is usually tacit and always powerful, and lies at the heart of my advice on doing battle with outside assessors. I am going to give the strategy its proper name, "counterargument," but I need to define what I mean by the term because it has been used in a number of different ways. A writer counter-argues by writing into a claim an argument countering the reader's anticipated argument against the claim. The rhetorical strategy of anticipating objections or counterclaims is very old. Classical rhetoricians called it *procatalepsis*.

At its most explicit, counterargument uses phrases such as "it is true that" and "of course:" For instance: *We need to revise the plan* [the claim]. *It's true that it will mean one more committee meeting than I had scheduled* [the anticipated objection], *but without a revision our proposal will not be approved by the dean* [the counterargument].

But more often counterargument is implicit, and one of its favorite tacit forms is countable information. Powell wants to claim that the blunders of his course were partly due to his inexperience. But he anticipates the objection that they may instead have been due to his laziness or lack of concern. So he writes, "During my year of adjuncting I learned mostly how to drive very quickly between four different teaching sites." The word "four" makes a hefty counterargument for it is not only specific but also verifiable.

Note that I do not say verified. One of the clever features of countable information as a rhetorical tactic is that it not only anticipates arguments against the writer's claim but it does so by offering information that technically can be verified but for any number of reasons probably will not be. So when Powell writes that at the institution where he taught "many students were the first of their family to attend college," he is anticipating and forestalling the argument that as a teacher he has not been on the front lines, but he is also supporting this counterargument with a verifiable fact that may be difficult or even impossible to verify. Even on the unlikely chance that the college kept records of first-generation status, what reader is going to go to the trouble to look up the fact, especially because it seems the author has already done so? Powell's "many" is a simple instance of numbers fighting numbers. Note also that the looseness of his numbering ("many" means somewhere between precisely X and precisely Y students, with X and Y undefined) may add a strategic twist to his counterargument. If it turns out that only 10% of the entering class were first-generation students, he can still claim that number as "many." Numbers can serve to countermand numbers even when they are ill-defined.

By the way, despite his adroit rhetorical use of numbers, Powell adds his voice to the anti-numbers chorus of his profession. He offers his piece, he says, as "teacher lore" that will not be validated through "data's claims to empiricism." A few pages before the paragraph in which he relies on data-based school records ("underprepared"), he writes,

> I'm not going to go any farther down the data road. I believe we need to pause at this crossroads, though, to think for a minute about data and the students that I am going to talk about. As basic writing students, they have not only been data-ed by way of being placed in this class, they have, many of them, been in some ways the victims of data for a while before arriving here. GPAs and test scores have limited their opportunities for participation in various facets of their public lives—employment, extracurriculars, advanced placement classes, to say nothing of university admissions. (p. 10, emphasis added)

Powell is arguing that writing teachers have their own unique experience of student writers and student writing, and they do not need numbers to express that experience, and certainly they do not want "a rational analysis to test it against" (p. 10).

So the very people in our field who attack the methodology of numbers use numbers rhetorically to defend their position, arguing against an argumentative strategy that d serves them well against others who would attack that position. I understand that Powell is opposed to a particular kind of numbering, namely, the *methodology* of enumeration, "a rational analysis," administered by standardized, nonteacher forms of accountability. The question is whether a *rhetoric* of anticipatory enumeration, a kind of "rational analysis" that Powell and everybody else uses, can serve to fend off that attack.

RHETORICAL NUMBERING IN LOCAL ASSESSMENT OF WRITING: FIVE CASES

Here is my argument. In writing assessment battles it seems as if the only game is one number against another number, better against worse. Has the SAT verbal proficiency score that in 2005 included a 25-minute essay been a more powerful predictor of first-year college grades than the old SAT verbal without the essay; that is, which of two predictability coefficients is better? I am saying, however, that often it is not what number beats what other number but who numbers first. In assessment possession, numeration is nine-tenths of the law. As I say, anticipatory numbering works like a back fire, using up the fuel that later assessment needs in order to proceed. It operates as do all counterarguments by occupying the high ground first and thereby seizing the advantage (*procatalepsis* literally meant to secure and hold down first; the Roman rhetoricians translated the Greek term as *occupatio*, literally the seizing of property through legal means). In writing assessment such a tactic works out in a number of psychological and pragmatic ways that may have little connection with the traditional testing issues of validity, reliability, fairness, and statistical significance.

Here are five exemplary cases, of which I have first-hand knowledge, where this strategy, conscious or not, served writing administrators in defense of their property.

1. Duke University

In Spring 2003, Duke's University Writing Program studied its first-year, one-semester writing course (Writing 20). The program was under some pressure to show that the course, required of all Duke's high-caliber students, was teaching them more than what they already could do by way of academic essay writing. The program ran a pre/post study with 244 students, using common topics and looking for improvement over the 15 weeks. The results showed only a qualified success. The number of student essays written below "course goals" dropped from 29% (pre) to 20% (post). The number of "very strong" papers rose from 10% (pre) to 19% (post). As for showing individual gain in writing performance over the semester, fewer than half (44%) raised their rating by one or more categories (University Writing Program, 2003).

The outcomes may have been problematic, but notice how the bad-news numbers anticipate any objection that Duke's in-house validation might well have lacked objectivity. Also the care and complexity of the study (the analysis is much more detailed than I indicate) forestall objections that it could have been run more cheaply, because anything cheaper, such as a computerized analysis, would only produce simplistic findings with little insight into the course. In short, the figures have been run, undermining any reason for someone else to run them again. Writing 20 at Duke is still in the curriculum.

2. University of California Santa Barbara

UC Santa Barbara ran a similar pre/post study of their Writing 2 course, "Introduction to Academic Writing." They were interested in seeing whether the 6-week version of the course taught during the summer was as effective as the 10-week version, offered also during the summer and during the regular academic year. They tested three sections of the course, all taught by the same teacher, during the summer and fall of 2002, comparing the second essay with the third and last essay. Among other criteria, they applied a measurement of elaboration of ideas. Students in the 6-week summer course dropped from 9.3 to 7.7 on the scale; the 10-week summer course students gained from 8.6 to 8.8; and the 10-week fall students dropped from 9.3 to 8.6. Personal information collected from the students helped explain these counter-intuitive findings. Students who had postponed Writing 2 until the summer knew themselves as less-proficient writers and wanted a reduced schedule so they could concentrate on the course, yet some felt that the accelerated 6-week summer course did not give them the time needed to produce a full-bodied final paper (McLeod, Horn, & Haswell, 2005).

Note that of the pre/post figures reported above only the drop from 9.3 to 7.7 proved statistically significant (t-test -3.58, $p < .005$). Of course, confidence testing (which sets many a compositionist's teeth on edge, with numbers seemingly just begetting more numbers) does not alter the original data, just suggests how the data should be interpreted. It leaves the original numbers, and the kind of textual and contextual analysis they report, to anticipate the argument, common with college administrators and boards, that standardized assessment can do a better job of evaluating writing than can local assessment. The counterargument here is elementary and decisive. Does any standardized test measure development of ideas? Does it integrate student motivation with student performance? Ours did.

3. University X

Annually a university (preferring not to be named) validates its junior-level essay examination that allows some 1,400 students to challenge the required upper-division writing requirement. Over the years Engineering students have done more poorly on this challenge exam than students from two other large academic divisions (see Table 23.1).

Table 23.1. Pass Rate on a Junior-level Writing Examination for Three Academic Divisions Over Four Academic Years

Year	Arts & Sciences	Agriculture & Environ. Sci.	Engineering
Year One	63%	51%	31%
Year Two	53%	56%	44%
Year Three	56%	50%	41%
Year Four	61%	62%	49%

Notice how these numbers, easily obtained from the databank kept by the administrators of the test, anticipate another common objection of national assessment to local assessment efforts: Local outcomes are less useful than national, which are standardized, adjusted annually, and comparable across institutions. The counterargument of these numbers from University X is simple. Next year any national test would be able to provide only one year's worth of data. We already have 4 years worth (outcomes we have adjusted ourselves) and next year we will have 5. It will take a national test 4 years to give us similar data, and it is replicated findings that are needed to warrant an investigation into possible test bias against the Engineering students, an investigation we are undertaking now and one that should not be delayed 4 more years. The rhetorical force of these numbers is almost brutal: Here is years of work we have done. Why scrap them? As for cross-institutional comparisons, although the local test is more valid for local purposes than any standardized test, its outcomes can be compared when other universities adopt it.

4. Texas A&M University, Corpus Christi

A common argument for outside assessment is that local efforts will be designed to protect the teacherly status quo. To its credit, the Southern Association of Colleges accreditation policy prefers local evaluation of instructional programs, but only so long as the evaluation pinpoints areas amenable to instructional improvement. Implied is a variant of Ed White's law, that if the local evaluation effort fails to locate instructional shortcomings, evaluation will be imposed from without. Again numbers provide the counterargument. Indeed, in this situation, they may be the only counterargument. For their 2000 SAC review, the English Department at Texas A&M University, Corpus Christi evaluated the second semester of their first-year writing course (English 1302), which focuses on the academic research paper. The department hypothesized that English 1302 students may be learning documentation techniques that they subsequently forget, and that the error-prone documentation style of juniors and seniors is not attributable to English 1302. They compared research papers written by students in English 1302 with research papers written by upper-division students in courses outside of the English department. Part of the study simply measured the documentation system used by the writer and judged whether it was used consistently or "unconventionally" (see Table 23.2).

The count did not support the department's hypothesis, an irritating vagary endemic to numbers and perhaps one reason they are feared. It seems upper-division students have problems in documentation not because they have forgotten their first-year composition teacher's teachings but because their courses were asking them to use a system their first-year teacher had

Table 23.2. Frequency of Documentation System Used in a First-year English Composition Course and in Upper-division Non-English Courses

Documentation System	First-year English	Upper-division Non-English
APA	04%	25%
CBE	—	02%
Chicago	—	15%
MLA	79%	13%
Unconventional	16%	45%

not taught. The rise in "unconventional" systems with upper-division students is as easily attributable to stumbling self-learning as it is to forgotten learning. But the numbers also anticipate any objection that the TAMU-CC English Department had designed this evaluation to protect the way their course is taught. The numbers say without equivocation that English teachers should stop teaching a documentation style (MLA) that few of their students will later use. Rhetorically, what better way to persuade SAC accreditors that the TAMU-CC English Department had followed SAC guidelines?

5. Washington State University

In 1993 WSU began a junior-level writing portfolio examination that placed students into an upper-division writing course should they need it (for more on WSU's junior-level exam, see Kelly-Riley's and Condon's chapters, this volume). The test required students to submit three pieces of extended discourse that they had written for three different courses, as well as spend 2 hours composing impromptu. Soon objections to the exam arose from department chairs who felt that the portfolio requirement might delay graduation of some of their students. For this reason there was talk of replacing the portfolio assessment with a standardized sit down machine-scored exam. As it happened, academic hours earned at the time each student sat for the test formed part of the exam database, so at the end of the fourth year of implementation, exam administrators ran the numbers. The results supported the chairs (See Table 23.3).

For whatever reasons, more and more students were postponing the examination. During the first 2 years, only 15% of exam-takers were seniors, but in the third and fourth year, fully half were (Haswell, 1997). The findings did not lead to a replacement of the portfolio exam but to restrictions when students could take it, and 18 years later the exam is still in place.

Table 23.3. Academic Hours Earned When Students Sat for a Junior-level Writing Examination, Compared Biennially

Hours Earned	1993-1995 (N = 2,186)	1995-1997 (N = 4,140)
60 or less	19%	05%
61-75	41%	15%
76-90	25%	30%
91-105	11%	24%
106 or more	04%	26%

Factually the numbers supported the criticism of the testing, but rhetorically they anticipated and defused the criticism by arguing that the exam administrators were responsibly monitoring the exam with exactness and objectivity. It is crucial to see that had anyone other than the people running the assessment come up with these very same numbers first, then the program would have been in much more jeopardy.

THE PROCATALEPSIS OF ENUMERATION

In sum, all these numbers anticipate the main charge that outsider advocates for accountability level against those inside: Your students, your curriculum, your teachers all need to be evaluated in a rigorous and objective way. The counter-charge written into the kind of data I have presented is hard to answer: We have already evaluated them that way. To the call for accountability, these numbers respond that we have already counted. As I say, and as White's law says, so much of the assessment war is decided simply by who numbers first. But the procatalepsis of enumeration secures an advantage in more than just being one step ahead of the outside evaluators. It sets the agenda for evaluation. These data say, care about students. They say, investigate problems that can be fixed. They say, have an insider's knowledge of the territory. And to the objection (incidentally, the highly unlikely objection) that these data suffer from methodological problems such as rater reliability, internal validity, or sampling error, the *pre-existence* of the numbers say, tell us what is wrong and we will fix it. Procatalepsis is proactivity.

I am aware of the hazards of my argument. It sounds as if I am more interested in rhetoric than method. It so happens that I am not. Rhetoric and rigor are not mutually exclusive. (The research design of my examples, by the way, are more defensible than that of any national standardized examination you can name.) Of course, one should be as hardnosed in research method as time, money, and wits allow. And of course one should be aware of the ways to lie and bullshit with statistics (see Perelman, Chapter 24). But one can still appreciate the rhetorical impact of numbers, use good numbers to fight bad numbers, light the good fire to undercut the bad fire. When the currency is numbers, it is not a good time to be numerophobic.

REFERENCES

Haswell, R. H. (1997). *Washington State University portfolio examination: Second findings*. Pullman, WA: University Assessment Office.

Huff, D. (1954). *How to lie with statistics*. New York, NY: Norton.

McLeod, S., Horn, H., & Haswell, R. H. (2005). Accelerated classes and the writers at the bottom: A local assessment story. *College Composition and Communication, 56*(4), 556-80.

Powell, D. R. (2000). The story of the story is the story: Placing the blunder narrative. In J. P. Tassoni & W. H. Thelin (Eds.), *Blundering for a change: Errors and expectations in critical pedagogy* (pp. 9-23). Portsmouth, NH: Boynton/Cook Heinemann.

Siegel, S. (1956). *Nonparametric statistics for the behavioral sciences*. New York, NY McGraw-Hill.

Sontag, S. (1978). *On photography*. New York:, NY Farrar, Straus, and Giroux.

University Writing Program. (2003). *Assessment project report*. Durham, NC: Thompson Writing Program, Duke University.

White, E. M. (1973). *Comparison and contrast: The 1973 California State University and Colleges Freshman English Equivalency Examination* (ERIC Document Reproduction Service, ED 114 825). Los Angeles, CA: Office of the Chancellor, the California State University and Colleges

White, E. M. (1995). The importance of placement and basic studies: Helping students succeed under the new elitism. *Journal of Basic Writing, 14*(2), 75-84.

24

MASS-MARKET WRITING ASSESSMENTS AS BULLSHIT

Les Perelman
Massachusetts Institute of Technology

In Summer 2007, one of the almost 1,000 scorers of the English Language and Composition Advanced Placement, Edward M. White (2008), wrote on the airplane home a 5-paragraph essay that reflected and responded to the hundreds of 5-paragraph essays he read while participating in the grading of 280,000 tests written by high school students. The fourth and "clincher" paragraph of this essay reads:

> The last reason to write this way is the most important. Once you have it down, you can use it for practically anything. Does God exist? Well you can say yes and give three reasons, or no and give three different reasons. It doesn't really matter. You're sure to get a good grade whatever you pick to put into the formula. And that's the real reason for education, to get those good grades without thinking too much and using up too much time. (p. 525)

Such an approach to truth goes back at least to the Sophists, and the attitude expressed by White's student's direct ancestor, Polus, who in Plato's *Gorgias* states that a rhetorician need have no special knowledge of a specific subject when persuading people about that subject (460b-460c) (Plato, 2004).

Socrates, of course, attacks this position, and much more recently, the contemporary philosopher Harry G. Frankfurt (2004) has attempted to develop a fairly rigorous philosophical definition of what these students are doing in his seminal monograph *On Bullshit* and his response (Frankfurt, 2002) to Cohen's (2002) essay "Deeper into Bullshit." As Frankfurt (2004) begins his monograph, "One of the most salient features of our culture is that there is so much bullshit." (p. 1). As Frankfurt argues, bullshit is actually is more dangerous than outright lying because while the liar knows the truth, although he wants to lead his audience away from it, the bullshitter is unconcerned with the truth, "but that the motive guiding and controlling it is unconcerned with how the things of which he speaks truly are" (p. 55).

Bullshit is dangerous. Eubanks and Schaeffer (2008), however, claim in their essay that some forms of unprototypical academic bullshit may "be both unavoidable and beneficial" (p. 372) (but they never fully support that assertion in their essay nor do they refer to Cohen's extension of Frankfurt's definition [which bears some similarity to their own analysis] nor of Frankfurt's reply to Cohen). Similarly, Smagorinsky, Daigle, O'Donnell Allen, and Bynum (2010) argue based on the protocol analysis of one essay by one student that "bullshitting can serve as a key developmental tool in its promotion of exploratory thinking and speech through which learners may approach tasks at new levels of complexity" (p. 401). Both Tietge (2006) and Fredal (2011) present thoughtful analyses of the relationship of rhetoric to bullshit .

The examples of harmful bullshit, however, are everywhere. One only has to look at the historical examples in Tuchman's (1984) book, *The March of Folly*. A more contemporary example can be found in the rationales for the American Invasion of Iraq in 2002-03. Significantly for this essay, the George W. Bush Administration had exactly three supporting arguments to justify the Invasion of Iraq: (a) Saddam Hussein had Weapons of Mass Destruction; (b) Saddam Hussein supported Osama bin Laden and Al Qaida; and (c) Saddam Hussein brutally repressed his own people. (Someone in the White House must have done well on the SAT Writing Test.) The first assertion has been proven false by postwar inspections (S. Rep. No. 108-301, 2004). There is no real evidence to support the second assertion and some evidence to refute it (S. Rep. No. 109-331, 2006). The third assertion is clearly true, but it is equally true for many other countries that the United States did not invade. Thus we can classify two of the three reasons for the United States invading Iraq as bullshit. It is just not that these statements are false. Truth or falsity does not determine bullshit, but rather the bullshiter's intention to be unconcerned with truth or falsehood. There may have been some people in the White House who knew that Saddam Hussein did not possess nuclear arms capability, but for most of them, they just accepted the statement and did not want to hear any evidence to the contrary (Wilson, 2004).

Bullshit does not only harm public affairs; it is bad for business and manufacturing. Elsewhere, I have documented how the explosion of Space Shuttle *Challenger* was caused by the management of Morton-Thiokol ignoring the categories of truth or falsehood, opting instead to "put on their management hats," which meant essentially that they were supposed to be unconcerned with the probability of the O-rings failing in the extremely cold weather and be concerned with the economic profits of the company (Perelman, 1994).

Education should be the enemy of bullshit. Although there may, in some disciplines, be multiple truths, the intention of educated discourse, be it for academic or nonacademic purposes, is to represent at least one truth. Yet mass-market testing practices and organizations, especially when assessing writing, have whole-heartedly embraced bullshit.[1] In the remainder of this chapter, I demonstrate how testing organizations within the area of writing assessment both encourage and practice bullshitting in three distinct ways. First, the timed impromptu essay not only invites students to bullshit, it encourages the practice. Second, the distortion of holistic scoring practiced by most mass-market organizations, with its reliance on conformity and reliability at the cost of ignoring intellectual content is, itself, a form of bullshit. Finally, the research conducted by these testing organizations often produces reports containing substantial amounts of bullshit.

In 2005, I discovered that several of the top sample student essays in the booklet handed out by the College Board at the 2005 meeting of the Conference on College Composition and Communication, *ScoreWrite™: A Guide to Preparing for the New SAT® Essay* (The College Board, 2005), contained facts that were wildly untrue or completely irrelevant. I contacted the College Board and discovered in a phone conversation with Wayne Camara, the Vice President for Research and Development, that the official scoring guide for readers explicitly instructed readers not to penalize students for presenting incorrect information. A few weeks later, Michael Winerip, an education reporter for the *New York Times*, shared with me the "Official Guide for Scorers of the SAT Writing Essay," which explains: "Writers may make errors in facts or information that do not affect the quality of their essays. For example, a writer may state 'The American Revolution began in 1842' or 'Anna Karenina,' a play by the French author Joseph Conrad, was a very upbeat literary work. ... You are scoring the writing, and not the correctness of facts" (Winerip, 2005). Clearly, individuals who knew the truth about the historical event or the novel did not intentionally lie. Simply, there was no reason to do so. In most cases, except in the bizarre universe of mass-market testing, giving correct information is always safer than presenting information that may be easily identified as false. We may assume then that the SAT Writing Test, like the test taken by White's 5-paragraph essay student, rewards putative facts, regardless if they are true or false. In terms of this discussion, they reward bullshit.

Test preparation companies and authors of test preparation guides also advise students to make up information. Indeed, one subheading in the chapter on the SAT Writing Section in a popular SAT prep book is "Making Stuff Up" (Berger, Colton, Mistry, & Rossi, 2008). The section explicitly advises students not to lie. It instructs them to state as supporting facts information that could possibly be true; that is bullshit.

There are other strong indications that the SAT, and most probably similar tests, reward bullshit. At the end of the College Board booklet, there is an advertisement for "The Official SAT Online Course," which in addition to its other features "offers auto essay scoring for practice SAT essays including the *ScoreWrite*™ essay." A new version of the *ScoreWrite*™ Manual exists and is available online (The College Board, 2010).

"Auto essay scoring" means machine scoring, and although I have learned from my colleagues at MIT that machine scoring can do very well in scoring short written responses in very circumscribed knowledge domains, it is extremely invalid in scoring arguments or longer technical responses. What machine scoring can do is what is implicitly or explicitly asked of human graders in mass-market assessments to ensure interrater reliability: count. Scorers look for support and development in such features as length, the number of proper nouns, and the number of direct quotations. They look for infrequently used words such as *plethora*, *myriad*, and *egregious*. Moreover, they are explicitly instructed to not notice errors of fact. In sum, they are taught to grade like machines. The result is that the testing companies can show a close correlation between these graders and Automated Essay scoring (AES). What machines cannot do, especially in analyzing essays that are not constrained by a very narrow content domain, and human graders are forbidden to do while grading the SAT, is to differentiate false statements from true ones. That is, both humans and machines happily accept bullshit.

I have been testing this hypothesis for several years by coaching now a total of 15 students retaking the SAT and 11 students taking the GRE, the GMAT (both graded by a machine and human grader), and the MCAT. [Full disclosure: I do not ask for any compensation for my coaching but ask the students (all of them are over 18) to send me their score along with a copy of the essay if the particular test makes it available to them. If they feel that my coaching has monetary value to them, I ask them to make a contribution of any amount to FairTest.org.] I coach them to include lots of detail and proper nouns and quotations regardless of whether they make sense. "Don't worry about the truth," I tell them. In sum, I tell them to bullshit and, frighteningly, it works very well. In all 15 cases in which I coached students retaking the SAT, I have raised their essay scores in the writing section, even though all of their original scores were already above the mean. The following is a transcript of part of an essay written by one of my early participants:

> A major reason why cooperation is a preference to competition is because competition induces civil struggle at a time of crisis while cooperation reduces tension. In the 1930's, American businesses were locked in a fierce economic competition with Russian merchants for fear that their communist philosophies would dominate American markets. As a result, American competition drove the country into an economic depression and the only way to pull them out of it was through civil cooperation. American president Franklin Delenor [sic] Roosevelt advocated for civil unity despite the communist threat of success by quoting "the only thing we need to fear is itself," which desdained [sic] competition as an alternative to cooperation for success. In the end, the American economy pulled out of the depression and succeeded communism.
>
> Because of the spirit of unity it induces, cooperation is the key to success. People unified work as a larger and stronger than those separated by competition, allowing utmost success to transpire.

The student who wrote this essay received two independent scores of "5" (the 92nd percentile) compared to the two "4s" the student received the first time he/she took the SAT. I interviewed the student after the return of the score and paper online, and the student responded that he/she was unsure of the details about the Great Depression so some hastily and partially thought out details from the Cold War were added. The student was amazed my strategy worked so well.

When I recounted this incident to my students at MIT, they were not nearly so amazed. Their almost unanimous response was, "Didn't you know that you always make up supporting evidence when taking standardized writing tests?" "Of course you make up personal stories," one of my students told me, "it takes less time than trying to remember one and you can always make it fit your thesis." My students at MIT, of course, are the students who excelled on the SAT, making me realize the paradox that students need to disregard the truth to get into an institution like MIT that venerates it. Mass-market testing makes them into bullshiters in order to get into a place that has little tolerance for bullshit.

THE FORMAT OF THE TIMED-IMPROMPTU AND BULLSHIT

The timed impromptu is often justified as being very similar to the essay tests that students will take as part of many college courses. But such a comparison is inherently flawed. The prompts for college essay tests are based on having students display and use knowledge, modes of analysis, or both particular to the field of study as the content and engine driving the writing of the essay. The prompts used in mass-market writing assessments are not based on the extensive readings, lectures, and class discussions that provide the content for the college essay test. The mass-market writing prompt is designed to be accessible to anyone taking the test without any additional input such as readings longer than a paragraph. In essence, the topics invite students to write about subjects for which they have little if any real information and about which they may never have given much consideration. As Frankfurt (2004) notes in his essay, "Bullshit is unavoidable whenever circumstances require someone to talk without knowing what he is talking about." (p. 63). It was precisely this extreme construct underrepresentation that led me and others to develop iMOAT (see Peckham, Chapter 9).

White (1995) places the timed impromptu between two other assessment instruments, indirect multiple-choice tests and portfolio assessments. He then argues that in certain venues, such as freshman placement tests, the timed impromptu is an appropriate assessment tool because for many schools, "Most of us would be happy if our entering freshmen really knew how to predicate and read" (p. 33). White's analysis, however, is illuminating but incomplete. He essentially positions writing assessment upon two axes. The first is indirect (e.g., multiple choice) versus direct (i.e., writing). The second axis differentiates first-draft writing (the timed impromptu) from collections of revised writing (the writing portfolio). There is a third and very important axis, writing with knowledge of the topic and writing without knowledge of the topic, that is, writing bullshit. In real life, there are many instances in which an individual has to write on demand. In most of the cases, such as a student taking an exam in a specific subject, it is assumed that the writer has some familiarity with the content. I may get an email from a Dean, for example, asking for a quick response on strategies for reducing plagiarism or on the possible use of a specific writing test in the admission process. Because these are issues I have knowledge of, I can send a rapid reply that is based on my knowledge of the subject. I am not writing bullshit. No Dean, Provost, or President has, however, emailed me asking "Is failure necessary for success? Please reply in 25 minutes." If I received such a request, my reply would certainly be bullshit.

DISTORTED ESSAY SCORING AS BULLSHIT

How did the essay on "Franklin Delenor Roosevelt" receive two scores of 5? According to the current rubric on the College Board web site:

> An essay in this category demonstrates reasonably consistent mastery, although it has occasional errors or lapses in quality. A typical essay:

- Effectively develops a point of view on the issue and demonstrates strong critical thinking, generally using appropriate examples, reasons and other evidence to support its position
- Is well organized and focused, demonstrating coherence and progression of ideas
- Exhibits facility in the use of language, using appropriate vocabulary. (The College Board, 2010)

The essay in question clearly has more than "occasional errors or lapses in quality." Indeed, it would be difficult to argue that this essay's claim that the Great Depression was caused by competition between American business and Russian merchants with communist philosophies "demonstrates strong critical thinking, generally using appropriate examples ... to support its position."

In both his landmark essay "Holisticism (1984) and the subsequent two editions of *Teaching and Assessing Writing* (1994), which incorporate much of the original essay, White warns of many of the pitfalls that can occur during a holistic scoring session, especially the problems produced when readers "feel intimidated or coerced by insensitive leaders, or harassed by an uncomfortable or autocratic working environment." (p. 408). The grading environments for most mass-market writing assessments are what Robert Schaeffer of Fair Test calls "cyber sweatshops" (Owen, 2006, p. 26). Graders are not part of an interpretative community as envisioned by White, but moonlighting teachers and graduate students. Often they are not even grading together, but are grading alone on their home computer in minimum segments of 4 hours and are expected to grade 20 essays each hour, or one essay every 3 minutes. The all too human reactions to these more than uncomfortable work environments is chronicled by Farley (2009) in his memoir of 15 years in the standardized testing industry. Describing his first experience in a holistic reading for National Computer Systems (now part of Pearson Education) he recounts how he and other readers started just skimming the first paragraph of essays and then scored mainly on length and spelling. Readers and table leaders stopped caring about insightful rank ordering; they just wanted to get the job done the easiest way possible. Thus, their scores did not reflect a thoughtful evaluation of student writing, but successful attempts to quickly give an essay a score that would not appear to be deviant. In short, the scoring itself was bullshit.

Not all holistic scoring sessions are bullshit. I have been running sessions for 30 years, and agree with White (1996) that when done well, with sensitivity and respect for the readers and a primary concern about the quality of the reading rather than its economic cost, holistic scoring is a reliable method for assessing writing. As White (1996) notes, however, when testing firms are in control they desire procedures that will produce scores quickly and cheaply.

RESEARCH ON WRITING ASSESSMENT AS BULLSHIT

In March 2006, newspapers began reporting that a mechanical error had caused the misscoring of thousands of SAT tests from October 2005. Within a 2-week period, the College Board announced three times that their earlier assessments of the scale of the problem were low, and, in the end reported that approximately 4,400 students received official scores lower than what they actually earned, and 613 students received scores that overreported their performance. Some critics, such as one Dean of Admissions, implied that the College Board staff was lying (Arenson, 2006). I believe a better explanation was that they were bullshitting—they had no real estimation of the extent of the problem and kept trying to minimize it because they wanted it to be so, not that they knew it was untrue.

This same mindset infects the institutional research of mass-market testing organizations. Elliot (2005) chronicles many excellent researchers in the field of writing research. Some of the greatest, including Paul Diederich, Fred Godshalk, and Hunter Breland worked for the Educational Testing Service. Even before ETS was created, however, giants in the field such as Carl Brigham (1937) had warned of the tendency in a large new testing organization to replace solid research with propaganda. Propaganda is not necessarily bullshit, but bullshit often serves as Propaganda.

Confirming some of Brigham's fears, few recent College Board Research, ETS Research, or Pearson Educational Research Reports discuss failings or problems in any of the standardized tests owned, developed, or administered by these companies. Like Lake Woebegone, these are communities where all the children are above average. Moreover, it has become commonplace for the abstracts of many of these research reports to include assertions that are not supported by data in the actual report. Because of space limitations, I focus on only one report, which is representative of the bullshit contained in many of them.

In 2005, the College Board modified the SAT by adding what had been "The SAT II Writing Test" as "the Writing Section" of the SAT itself. The first College Board research report that year was *A Survey to Evaluate the Alignment of the New SAT® Writing and Critical Reading Sections to Curricula and Instructional Practices* (Milewski, Johnson, Glazer, & Kubota, 2005). Although the report begins by stating that "researchers are encouraged to freely express their professional judgment," several of the key conclusions do not reflect the common standards of judgment in social science based on the data presented. Instead, the report asserts a strong alignment between the new SAT Writing and Critical Reading sections, high school and college curricula, and instruction because the authors wish it so. These assertions are, of course, bullshit.

The report also contains some outright factual errors, but, because the most glaring of these errors in the Abstract is contradicted on the same page, I attribute it more to a lack of concern for accuracy than to an active intention to lie. The abstract reports that a total of 2,351 high school students and college teachers were surveyed about student reading and writing skills. Yet on the same page, it is later stated that the survey was sent out to approximately 38,000 teachers. (At the end of the report, the exact number, 38,848, is given.) We also learn in the introduction that not all of the 2,351 respondents came from the original survey, which was conducted on the web. Because the return rate was low, over a quarter of these respondents were readers for the Advanced Placement (AP) English Examinations, who used a paper form rather than the web-based instrument. Of course, these readers, who are being trained and paid by the College Board may not be a representative sample of the over 37,000 surveyed teachers who chose not to respond to the survey.

Although the descriptive information on all the participants is given on page four of the report, the statistics do not segregate the AP readers from the ordinary responders. Moreover, although this section reports that the high school teachers had more education than national samples and that the college professors overrepresented public institutions, it asserts, "Despite the over and underrepresentation, the current sample can still be considered representative of high school and college faculty" (p. 4).

No mention of the low response rate or the possible bias in the addition of the AP readers is made until the end of the report in a section entitled "Limitations and Next Steps." The actual response rate to the online survey was 4.45%, well below the median return rate of 30% for online surveys and less than half of the minimum acceptable return rate of 10% even for extremely large surveys like this one (Armstrong & Overton, 1977; Punch, 2003; Sheehan, 2001). The authors of the report acknowledge at least part of the problem at the end by stating, "The low response rate limits the generalizability of the survey results and suggests that volunteer bias might be at play" (p. 23). Moreover, it is only in this section, at the end of the report, that the authors give the exact number of respondents who were AP graders, 622 or 26.5% of the total sample. Although they admit that these teachers might not be representative of the general population of teachers, the authors neglect to mention that the table training they received as graders that same week might increase their bias.

There is a question, however, whether we can consider these kinds of deceptions as bullshit. The authors do admit that their study has limitations; they just do not mention that these limitations make the data highly limited if not worthless, and they hide the extent of the problem until the end of the report. But the primary assertion of the study, that the reading and writing abilities the SAT claims to measure align with high school and college curricula, is, in the terminology of Scottish Law, Not Proven. The assertion could be true, or it could be false. The methodology of the study, however, is largely unconcerned with that central issue, leading to the conclusion that as a whole, the report falls under Frankfurt's definition of bullshit.

This conclusion is reinforced by other assertions in the report. Of the college instructors participating in the study, 814, who taught writing, language arts, or English, were classified as *English professors*. Another 230 college faculty, who taught history, political science, psychology, or biology were classified as *Humanities professors*. A graph in the report exhibits that slightly more than 20% of English professors employed multiple-choice tests, whereas slightly fewer than 60% of the Humanities professors gave multiple-choice exams. Then, even though the English professors constituted 78% of the college professors, the report states that both high school teachers and college professors give multiple-choice tests. The report also asserts that the test emphasizes Writing Across the Curriculum because prompts such as "Are people motivated to achieve by personal satisfaction rather than by money or fame?" are "relevant to a wide range of fields and interests rather than narrowly related to specific topics or disciplines" (p. 23). In addition, the report asserts that essay prompts, which contain passages of four or five sentences totaling approximately 75-80 words for an essay to be written in 25 minutes measures students' abilities to use "writing and reading as tools for critical thinking." Such claims are clearly bullshit. It is not that the authors know that the claims are false; they, like the high achieving students writing the SAT essays, just do not really care about the truth.

Carl C. Brigham, the originator of the SAT and a eugenist who renounced eugenics and the entire concept of aptitude testing when confronted with convincing and contradictory data, saw the dangers of mass market testing over 70 years ago. Discussing the possible creation of ETS, he wrote (1937):

> It is easy for a powerful organization to set up false ideals. The new organization must be so contrived that it will always remain the servant of education and never become its master. It should inquire into the nature of values but it should not determine those values.
>
> At the present time there are men of learning who sense these values intuitively yet are unable to put them on canvas with pigments which stand reproduction. Testing situations, when properly formulated, and with responses fully analyzed, constitute the most searching system of lenses yet contrived for photographing the canvas and making it generally available to mankind. The artist must work with the technician to get the results for which he is striving.
>
> To-day most testers are content to buy a cheap, ready-made camera with a poor lens, fixed focus and no range finder, and to do a develop

> while-you-wait business with stragglers on the sidewalk in front of the studio. Furthermore, they claim that the present camera can reproduce every detail of the completed masterpiece within—although they have merely peeked in the door and have never seen the canvas.
>
> The new organization must plan to discard most of its present apparatus within five to ten years and approach its larger problem in a spirit of humility. The ideals of research are lofty, but its spirit is meek. An organization with major purpose research—and not propaganda—will be of great service to education. Education can not to-day afford to let the sidewalk vendor dictate its objectives, but it can properly help him adapt his apparatus to its own purposes. (p. 758)

Brigham's metaphor of the sidewalk photographer who claims that his little box camera can capture every detail of a masterpiece he has never seen is a clear description of a master bullshitter (although Brigham would have never used that term). I prefer a more contemporary metaphor. Mass market testing organizations want mass sales, giving their customers not nutritious food that will make them wise and healthy, but quickly produced products that may look attractive but actually hurt the mind and body rather than improve it. They do not foster education; they promote McLearning, high in sugar, salt, and fat, with low, if any, real nutritive value. But like the hamburger chain, the aim of mass-market testers is not education; it is an obese bottom line on the balance sheet.

ENDNOTE

1. Two books that discuss the inherent lack of concern with truth among large-scale testing companies are Farley (2009) and Lemann (1999).

REFERENCES

Arenson, K. W. (2006, March 23). SAT problems even larger than reported. *The New York Times*, p. 1.

Armstrong, J. S., & Overton, T. S. (1977). Estimating nonresponse bias in mail surveys. *Journal of Marketing Research, 14*(3), 396-402.

Berger, L., Colton, M., Mistry, M., & Rossi, P. (2008). *Up your score: The underground guide to the SAT 2009-2010 edition.* New York, NY: Workman Publishing Company.

Brigham, C. C. (1937, December). The place of research in a testing organization. *School and Society*, 756-759.

Cohen, G. A. (2002). Deeper into bullshit. In S. Buss & L. Overton (Eds.), *Contours of agency: Themes from the philosophy of Harry Frankfurt* (pp. 321-336). Cambridge, MA: MIT Press.

The College Board. (2010). *SAT essay scoring—How essays are scored*. Web.

The College Board. (2005). *ScoreWrite: A guide for preparing for the new SAT essay*. New York, NY: The College Board.

Elliot, N. (2005). *On a scale: A social history of writing assessment in America*. New York, NY: Peter Lang.

Eubanks, P., & Schaeffer, J. D. (2008). A kind word for bullshit: The problem of academic writing. *College Composition and Communication, 59*(3), 372-88.

Farley, T. (2009). *Making the grade: My misadventures in the standardized testing industry*. Sausalito, CA: PoliPoint Press.

Frankfurt, H. G. (2002). Response to G.A. Cohen. In S. Buss & L. Overton (Eds.), *Contours of agency: Themes from the philosophy of Harry Frankfurt* (pp. 337-339). Cambridge, MA: MIT Press.

Frankfurt, H. G. (2004). *On bullshit*. Princeton, NJ and Oxford, UK: Princeton University Press.

Fredal J. (2011). Rhetoric and bullshit. *College English, 73*(3), 243-259.

Lemann, N. (1999). *The big test: The secret history of the American meritocracy*. New York, NY: Farrar, Straus, and Giroux.

Milewski, G. B., Johnson, D., Glazer, N., & Kubota, M. (2005). *A survey to evaluate the alignment of the New SAT Writing and Critical Reading sections to curricula and instructional practices* (College Board Research Report 2005-1). New York, NY: College Board. Web.

Owen, D. (2006, April 3). The S.A.T.'s watchdog. *The New Yorker*, 26.

Perelman, L. (1994). The rhetoric of a major malfunction: The institutional and rhetorical dimensions of the explosion of the space shuttle Challenger. In C. Sides (Ed.), *Technical communication frontiers: Essays in theory* (pp. 43-59). St. Paul, MN: Association of Teachers of Technical Writing.

Plato. (2004). *Gorgias* (C. Emlyn-Jones, Ed.) (W. Hamilton & C. Emlyn-Jones, Trans.). London, UK and New York, NY: Penguin.

Punch, K. F. (2003). *Survey research: The basics*. London, UK: Sage.

S. Rep. No. 108-301. (2004).

S. Rep. No. 109-331. (2006).

Sheehan, K. (2001, January). E-mail survey response rates: A review. *Journal of Computer Mediated Communication, 6*(2). Web.

Smagorinsky, P., Daigle, E. A., O'Donnell-Allen, C., & Bynum, S. (2010). Bullshit in academic writing: A protocol analysis of a senior's process of interpreting *Much Ado about Nothing*. *Research in the Teaching of English, 44*(4), 368-405.

Tietge, D. J. (2006). Rhetoric is not bullshit. In G. L. Hardcastle & G. A. Reisch (Eds.), *Bullshit and philosophy*. Chicago, IL and LaSalle, IL: Open Court.

Tuchman, B. (1984). *The march of folly: From Troy to Vietnam*. New York, NY: Knopf.

White, E. M. (1984). Holisticism. *College Composition and Communication, 35*(4), 400-409.

White, E. M. (1994). *Teaching and assessing writing* (2nd ed.). San Francisco, CA: Jossey-Bass.

White, E. M. (1995). An apologia for the timed impromptu essay test. *College Composition and Communication, 46*(1), 30-45.

White, E. M. (1996). Power and agenda setting in writing assessment. In E. M. White, W. Lutz, & S. Kamusikiri (Eds.), *Assessment of writing: Politics, policies, practices* (pp. 9-24). New York, NY: Modern Language Association.

White, E. M. (2008). My five-paragraph-theme. *College Composition and Communication, 59*(3), 524-524.

Wilson, J. (2004). *The politics of truth: A diplomat's memoir: Inside the lies that led to war and betrayed my wife's CIA identity*. New York, NY: Caroll & Graf Publishers.

Winerip, M. (2005, May 4). SAT essay test rewards length and ignores errors of fact. *The New York Times*. Web.

25

HOW DOES WRITING ASSESSMENT FRAME COLLEGE WRITING PROGRAMS?

Peggy O'Neill
Loyola University Maryland

> I give you White's law, the truth of which I have noted for over twenty years: Assess thyself or assessment will be done unto thee.
> —Edward White (posted to Writing Program Administrators LISTSERVE, December 7, 1996)

In general, White's law is a smart one to follow, especially these days with discussions about national assessments for higher education percolating up through the K-12 educational system and flowing into conversations about higher education. Reports such as *A Test of Leadership* called for more accountability by institutions to demonstrate student learning (U.S. Department of Education, 2006). Initiatives such as the Voluntary System of Accountability, a national project that aimed to measure the "value-added" by postsecondary education, reinforced the focus on assessment (McPherson & Schulenberger, 2006). Accrediting agencies (both regional, such as the Northwest Commission on Colleges and Universities, and disciplinary-based, such as ABET and NCATE) have increased demands for outcomes-based approaches to assessment of student learning. More recently, the Common Core State Standards Initiative (CCSSI, 2010), which identified what it called College and Career Readiness Standards, has moved to use assessments as the bridge between high school and college credit-bearing courses, according to the Frequently Asked Questions section of its webpage. These general discussions about assessment often target, or even include, writing and writing assessment because writing is identified as "an essential skill" for success in the twenty-first century workplace. For example, in the reports released by the National Commission on Writing (2004, 2005), research with employers identified the critical role writing plays for entry into professional jobs and advancement once employed. In the CCSSI (2010), writing is a critical component of the English Language Arts as well as the sciences and social sciences. Writing also has played a critical role in the disciplines as it is used for learning, demonstrating that learning, making knowledge, and communicating that knowledge (e.g., Arum & Roksa, 2010; Bazerman, 2004; Bean, 2001; Carter, 2003; Emig, 1977; Jolliffe, 1988; Yancey & Huot, 1997). Because of the critical functions writing plays within the university and beyond, it is—and has been—an important area in higher education assessments, used, for example, as part of admissions, placement, proficiency, graduation, and program evaluation (Murphy Carlson, Rooney, & CCCC Committee on Assessment, 1993).

Composition and rhetoric professionals have long been involved in writing assessment. Writing assessment has influenced the hiring and staffing practices as well as the institutional status of composition since the late 1800s (Connors, 1997; Elliot, 2005; Huot, O'Neill, & Moore, 2010). In fact, assessment is linked to how writing was introduced into the college curriculum and to the beginning of contemporary composition and rhetoric as a discipline (e.g., Brereton, 1995; Connors, 1997; Kitzhaber, 1990; O'Neill, 1998; Traschel, 1992). Edward White's writings have demonstrated that the linkage of assessment with composition has remained strong throughout the twentieth century; and given the current climate, it promises to remain an important factor in postsecondary writing programs. With initiatives like CCSSI and the ongoing demand for more accountability for higher education, writing programs—and the instructors and administrators who work in them—may experience even more pressure to conduct assessments at the local level, to participate in less localized efforts, and to respond to the results of writing assessments (Adler-Kassner & O'Neill, 2010; Gallagher, 2010). Participation by composition scholars and teachers in writing assessments, no doubt, has influenced writing assessment as a field, leading to the development of both theory and practice as illustrated through the work of many compositionists (e.g., Broad, 2003; Elbow & Belanoff, 1986; Haswell, 2001; Huot, 2002; Smith, 1993; White, 1994; Williamson & Huot, 1993). This volume itself attests to the many ways that compositionists and educators from a wide range of fields continue to influence writing assessment through the work of large-scale projects such as the National Writing Project's Analytical Writing Continuum (Swain and

LeMahieu) and the National Assessment of Educational Progress (Persky), or debate about issues such as standardized exams (Perelman), assessment of non-native speakers of English (Hamp-Lyons), and race (Inoue and Poe).

However, the influence has worked the other way as well—the assessments have shaped the writing programs and the field. For example, Elbow and Belanoff (1986), who introduced the use of program-wide writing portfolios as a means for replacing the timed impromptu exit exam that was in place at their institution, explained that the portfolio improved the teaching of writing with instructors meeting to discuss writing and the evaluation of it. Elbow and Belanoff's work also inspired many compositionists to develop portfolio programs not only to replace exit exams or serve as proficiency exams but also for other purposes such as placement and program evaluation (e.g., Belanoff & Dickson, 1991; Black, Daiker, Sommers, & Stygall, 1994; Borrowman, 1999; Smit, 1994; Thais & Zawacki, 1997; Willard-Traub, Decker, Reed, & Johnston, 1999; Yancey & Weiser, 1997). The spread of portfolios created opportunities for researchers such as Broad (2003), who developed studies and published results much as earlier scholars had in conjunction with essay exams and holistic scoring (e.g, Cooper & Odell, 1977; White 1994; Williamson & Huot, 1993). Many scholars explained the benefits of writing assessment programs that had teachers read student writing, whether essays or portfolios. For example, White (1994) argued, drawing on a large research study he did with Linda Polin, that "bringing members of a writing faculty together to develop and score an assessment is the single most effective way to organize a faculty development program" (p. 168). Broad et al. (2009) summarized the benefits of five different writing assessment programs that used dynamic criteria mapping as a means of "discovering and negotiating the rhetorical values at play in a particular writing program" (p. 156).

Although there are surely positive effects of locally designed writing assessments that are aligned with local contexts and assessment theory, there may also be unintended consequences that are less positive, even detrimental, or more likely, not clearly positive or negative. The very act of assessment changes the nature of the phenomenon being assessed whether it is the individual students' performances, the teacher's instruction, or the program itself. This change, of course, may be part of the assessment program's goals. However, some of the changes or consequences may not be intended. Sewell (1996) reported that the graduate student teachers in the program she studied were concerned with how their students' cover letters represented them as instructors so they "tried to exert more control over the way their students crafted the cover letter" (p. 6). She found that because the instructors felt exposed by the cover letters, they devoted more classroom time to the cover letters than they did other writing assignments. The portfolio program, she concluded, contributed to the new instructors' "diminished sense of authority" even though the portfolio was low stakes for the instructors (the readings were not closely monitored and the instructors assigned the students' course grades). Sewell (1996) made clear that these consequences were unintended but also very real. Broad (1994) explained that in his experience as a researcher and reader at several different institutions, instructors "complain of a contradiction between the experiences in the 'calibration' or 'norming' sessions and the way administrators represent them" (p. 270). He concluded that often instructors' "sense of professionalism, dignity, intellectual activity, and community" was undermined through their participation in locally designed and administered writing assessment programs (p. 270).

Assessment has continued to develop as a scholarly field in rhetoric and composition, and the demand for assessments has intensified since these earlier works. To explore how assessment functioned more recently in writing programs, I studied a variety of writing programs that had established writing assessments. I examined both the theoretical and practical aspects of the writing programs and the writing assessments to determine how writing assessments framed writing, writing programs, and writing instructors and professionals. In this chapter, I focus on two writing across the curriculum/writing in the disciplines (WAC/WID)[1] programs, one housed in an English department and one a stand-alone program, both of which developed and administered institutional-wide writing assessments. Data, collected over several years, included site visits, interviews, examination of institutional documents, and published accounts when available.[2] In this chapter, I describe how writing is framed within these institutions and programs and how the assessments have constructed, or contributed, to this frame.

Framing, although often used as a metaphor in everyday communication, is also a more technical term used by communication, media, and linguistic scholars. Frames influence our understanding or perspective of a situation, issue, or phenomenon. Bolman and Deal (2003) explain that frames, which they liken to "windows, maps, tools, lenses, orientations [or] perspectives" shape our understanding of what is or is not plausible or visible (p. 12). Like a skeleton or a frame of a house, a conceptual frame is often unseen or unarticulated, yet it supports and gives shape to what is clearly visible. "The process of framing, then, results in the construction of ideological structures that shape understandings of how things work, why things are as they are, and what should happen based on that status" (Adler-Kassner & O'Neill, 2010, p. 19). In other words, frames, according to cognitive linguists, influence how we make sense of the world around us and what we value (Lakoff, 2004). White (1990) made a similar point about how our discourse communities influence the assumptions and values we bring to a writing assessment although he was drawing from a different set of theorists. Writing assessment functions as a frame (a structure) and a framing process (an activity) because it shapes our understanding of writing and writing programs. It frequently functions to give shape to writing programs, the work that happens in them, and what is valued. After exploring the framing of writing through the writing assessments in these two programs, I conclude by considering potential implications for composition and rhetoric from this type of framing.

FARMVILLE STATE UNIVERSITY

At this large land-grant institution, the state, like many, required institutions to implement assessments in core competencies, including written literacy. However, institutions were not required to use a specific assessment or procedure. The writing program director opted to be pro-active and worked to design a comprehensive writing assessment that would serve the writing program, including both the instructors and students, and fulfill the state mandates. The director and her staff educated themselves on assessment, designed a program that included both placement and proficiency, and drew on the best practices of the field. They also saw the assessment as a site for research and faculty education.

At the beginning of the process, the writing program was housed in the English department and directed by English faculty, with first-year courses taught primarily by English graduate students and adjunct faculty. The new writing assessment system was designed and administered by the writing director. By all accounts, there was a symbiotic relationship between the writing assessments and the writing program. Writing instructors, both first year and in the disciplines, participated in norming sessions, in reading and evaluating the work. The feedback loop—that is, how the results and experiences of the assessment influenced the instruction and instructors—seemed implicit because the program was so closely tied to the writing program—both the first year and then later the WAC/WID program and writing center. With the director and her staff responsible for preparing instructors, providing support, as well as administering the assessment, the results informed the decisions and actions of the program administration. Over time, however, the writing program was separated from the English department, forming a stand-alone program responsible for the placement and proficiency exams, the WAC/WID program, and the writing center. The first-year writing program, however, remained in the English department. An English faculty member administered the first-year curriculum and the instructors, most of whom were English graduate students. A director of the writing program was hired, with tenure and a nominal teaching load in English, and served on the English department's composition committee. The composition director served on the university-wide writing program committee. Informants agreed, however, that the director of the writing program functioned independently of the English department. The WAC and writing center coordinator had a joint appointment in English and the writing program, although as a nontenure, full-time faculty member. The coordinator of the assessments was a full-time staff position. Writing instructors from the English department—mostly graduate student teaching assistants and part-time lecturers—were still hired as readers for the writing exams and as staff for the writing center.

Eventually, there was little if any formal articulation between the composition program, directed by a tenured English department faculty member, and the writing program director outside of the shared committees. Funding of the writing program was independent of the English department, and the reporting structure was also outside the English department. A university-wide committee oversaw the writing program, and eventually the writing program became part of the general education college, which oversees a variety of undergraduate programs. In effect, although the composition program and the writing program were expected to cooperate with each other, they functioned independently of each other. Over time, as personnel in various key positions changed, the close relationship between the composition program and the writing program deteriorated. Recently, the faculty director of the writing program was replaced by a staff position.

At this institution, the teaching of writing was formally separated from the assessment of writing. In fact, the writing program is primarily associated with assessment—the placement and proficiency exams and the support for students who did not pass their proficiency exam. The WAC/WID coordinator, along with others from the writing program and/or university writing committee members, reviewed syllabi to certify WID courses and offered tutorial sessions for those students who had not passed the rising junior writing exam. Faculty development included two workshops a year, which served a small percentage of the faculty teaching writing intensive courses. All personnel in the writing program held staff positions, graduate student assistantships, or nontenure line faculty positions.

Participants in both the composition program and the writing program expressed concern over the relationship between the two programs and what they articulated as competing philosophies. These differences were characterized in different ways by different informants (e.g., instrumental vs. theoretical; practical vs. impractical; white, middle class vs. global, cultural, or racial; and simplistic vs. complex). Graduate students reported feeling a disconnect between what they did in the writing program and what they were learning about composition theory and practice through the composition program. For example, several students explained that the composition teaching practicum they had to take seemed at odds with the evaluation of writing they did in the writing program. All the graduate students interviewed valued the writing program work as well as work done in their graduate courses, but they felt, at times, caught between the composition program and the writing program. The writing program provided many opportunities for graduate students, beyond serving as readers, to learn about writing program administration, to conduct research, and to develop expertise in assessment or other areas relevant to composition studies. Likewise, the composition program and the English department provided students with opportunities for professional development beyond teaching first-year composition. The uneasy relationship between the two programs highlighted the graduate students' sense of vulnerability as they negotiated the tension between the two programs. The graduate student instructors acknowledged the benefit to their teaching from the experience reading placement exams and proficiency exams—both of which included timed impromptus based on a brief reading and a self-reflection essay. This feedback loop, however, was informal and specific to the instructors and did not occur at a more formal, programmatic level. For instance, during the time of the study, the composition program administered a portfolio assessment program, yet the writing assessment coordinator—an expert in assessment through experience, graduate study, and institutional position—was not involved in the development or maintenance of it. In fact, she administered the composition placement assessment as part of her writing program responsibilities. The two programs, as the graduate students explained and the program directors confirmed, operated independently from each other with two distinct philosophies that were, in many ways, at odds.

In the wider university community, the writing program enjoyed lots of visibility and a positive ethos. The WID component of the program, and the writing proficiency assessment, a junior level rising exam—which included the impromptu essay exam and a collection of student writing produced in classes from across the campus—were viewed as strong, positive programs. The program enjoyed many accolades, including national recognition, and faculty and administrators across campus supported it. Although individual faculty acknowledged the expertise of several of the writing program personnel, they also understood that the program operated outside the departmental structure and this limited the program's voice in terms of faculty governance and debates. Faculty and program personnel also acknowledged that because the directors were not faculty, they did not have the rights and responsibilities of faculty, which meant the program and its personnel were vulnerable in ways departments and faculty members were not. Writing program administrators did not have a seat—or a vote—in academic affairs as tenure-line faculty members did. They had to work through faculty who served on the university writing committee. Although the committee members did position themselves as strong advocates, their commitment to the program had to be balanced with other commitments, such as to their discipline or other university-wide initiatives that could at times be in conflict or competition with the writing program for resources or recognition. Although university administration supported the program, it could be gutted or restructured more easily than a department if administration or university priorities changed. During the time of the study, in fact, there were several moments when critical decisions about the writing program's staffing, reporting lines, and independence were made, highlighting the program's position and vulnerability.

In many ways, this writing program was considered successful, established, and theoretically grounded in best practice. It highlighted the need for all students, regardless of major, to develop competency in writing as part of their undergraduate education. It provided support to students who did not meet that competency, it made a substantial contribution to the English graduate students' education, and it contributed to the scholarship of the field by supporting empirical research. However, there were some troubling aspects in how writing—as a discipline and a course of study—was framed by this program.

Writing assessment was important, but it belonged outside the regular departmental structure and separate from the teaching of writing, which was still controlled by the departments and faculty. Unlike in other curricular areas or outcomes, passing a writing course or courses was not enough to certify that a student had achieved adequate expertise; outside verification was needed through an exam. Most of the labor involved in the writing program—from the administration to the exam readers and the writing tutors—were either staff or contingent faculty. Whereas tenured faculty read the proficiency exams, most of the readers for both placement and proficiency were contingent instructors. The writing assessment coordinator—and later the new director—did not teach as part of her responsibilities although she occasionally did as an adjunct instructor. The director was also not required to publish and remain an active scholar, yet she did. Although both the teaching and scholarship were supported by the university administration, they were considered "extra" and not part of the position's job description. None of the writing program personnel were tenure-line faculty so they had no voice in university governance and relied on others—such as faculty on its governing committee or administrators—to speak for it in many venues across campus. The program also did not offer courses in writing except for one-credit tutorial sections, linked to WID courses offered through departments, for students who had failed (or did not take) the proficiency exam.

UNIVERSITY OF THE LIBERAL ARTS

This religiously affiliated midsize university served a diverse population of more than 4,000 undergraduates, spread across five colleges and 61 majors. Located in a large city, it drew both commuter and residential students. The general education program was firmly grounded in the liberal arts, yet it had many professional programs such as nursing and business.

Writing was housed in the English department, with a tenured professor serving as a WAC coordinator. Although a writing course was required for all first-year students, it was administered through the English department, and there was no separate composition program or composition director. Tenure-line English faculty members taught composition; however, there were also many contingent instructors but no graduate student teaching assistants. Many of the contingent instructors were experienced and long-term adjuncts. A full-time, nontenure line English faculty member administered the university-wide writing center. English Language Learners participated in a specially designed program distinct from the English department. The WAC program at this institution had been in place since the mid 1980s. A diffused model, there were no designated writing intensive courses in the majors. The first-year writing course, offered through English, was considered an introduction to general academic writing (not literary analysis). Students were expected to have writing intensive courses in almost all core courses, and departments were responsible for the writing of their majors. Students did do a lot of writing due to small class sizes (average class size of 19), the liberal arts general education curriculum, and the faculty's emphasis on teaching, and so the WAC program had been considered successful. The WAC expert, an English faculty member who taught literature and writing courses, served as a consulting professor to support faculty in terms of effective writing pedagogy across the campus.

Over a decade ago, the university was critiqued by its accrediting agency for lack of assessment that demonstrated student learning. In response to this critique, the university devoted resources to developing a more robust assessment system. The WAC coordinator was tapped for this work and has since become a campus expert on direct assessment. Drawing on the work of Barbara Walvoord, he used his work with WAC as a springboard for collecting evidence of student learning across the disciplines. The assessment model used writing as means for gathering evidence that students across the majors were meeting the university learning outcomes. Effective written communication abilities were considered critical learning outcomes, as is the case at most colleges and universities. Much as the WAC program did, the assessment functions in a more diffused way with faculty participation as its foundation. Although there had been some sense of a mandate for departments to assess student learning, the program worked on an ad hoc basis with the WAC expert serving as a consultant to individual departments to help them develop ideas.

During the study, the writing assessment program went from the first year to the senior year and was very much a work-in-progress. The writing assessment program assumed that students start as novice academic writers in their first year with the goal that they become expert insiders able to produce effective disciplinary texts in their major by the time they graduate. A general writing assessment that all students took was being piloted. It involved two parts: First, the first-year seminar instructor completed a questionnaire about each student's writing performance at the end of the course. Then, in the sophomore year, each student took a timed essay exam based on a reading in a discipline-specific course that all students typically took in their second year as part of the general education curriculum. Students were given a discipline-specific reading ahead of time and had 50 minutes to write in response to a prompt. The test was administered during a regular class period in the common general education course. Faculty from across the disciplines read and scored the exams based on a common rubric developed by the faculty through the WAC coordinator's leadership. The results of the essay exam and the rubric were used to identify weak writers who received a letter encouraging them to take an additional writing course, which counted as elective credit. There was no other consequence for the students nor any follow up with students in terms of their writing as they completed their education.

At the senior level, students participated in a writing assignment embedded in a course—ideally a required senior seminar. These assignments were aimed at one or two specific learning outcomes for the major and were low or no stakes for individual students, serving instead as a means of program evaluation. Although the WAC coordinator worked with the departments throughout the process, the assignment was developed by the disciplinary faculty and evaluated by them. The results of the embedded assessment were shared with the department faculty who discussed the strengths and weaknesses of their majors, making adjustments to their curriculum if needed. A short report was written by a department member and submitted to the university assessment committee. Some departments included all faculty in this process regardless of status and rank, whereas others only had tenured faculty participate even if many courses were taught by contingent faculty. Faculty members from several different departments considered this approach to assessment useful for them as teachers, for the curriculum, and ultimately for students. Some of these faculty members presented at conferences or published articles about the assessments and the process.

Although this program was beneficial in many ways and met writing assessment guidelines as articulated by writing assessment scholars (e.g., Huot, 2002; O'Neill, Moore, & Huot, 2009; White, 1994), there were also some consequences that may not be universally praised. As the WAC coordinator explained, one loss was the lack of attention to writing to learn activities, which had been a hallmark of WAC/WID programs. He explained that his interactions with discipline faculty over the last decade had been so focused on the assessments that other aspects of WAC—such as writing to learn and more general faculty development—were ignored unless they directly related to the assessment. In other words, writing across the curriculum had been re-envisioned as writing assessment across the curriculum. The focus on the local, discipline-specific approach was very labor intensive so that the WAC coordinator worked with one or two departments at a time. Likewise, the specific assessment activities were not transferable from department to department. In the earlier WAC program, faculty workshops included faculty from multiple departments across campus. Although there was cross-discipline work with the core writing exam, that work was without stable support by the administration. Faculty members who participated reported that they saw the work with colleagues from across campus as an important benefit of the program. Yet, only a small percentage of faculty had participated. In addition, the focus was only on one type of writing, and it privileged one discipline because the prompt was directly linked to a specific course in the humanities. In scoring sessions and interviews, faculty members from other disciplines explained that their lack of knowledge related to the specific reading and its disciplinary context created tension for them as readers and sometimes among readers. Students with more content knowledge associated with the specific reading or discipline were perceived to have an advantage. Although the WAC coordinator had a clear theory of how students developed as writers from their first year through to their senior year, most faculty in the disciplines did not seem to share an understanding of this. In fact, there seemed to be a gap between the general education writing assessment and the senior discipline-specific assessments.

In this program, WAC became closely aligned with assessment. And although the coordinator did an extraordinary amount of work to ensure that the assessments included faculty, focused on teaching and learning, produced meaningful results for the local participants, and were theoretically informed, it was still associated with external mandates and top-down approaches. The beginning of the assessment program, as well as more recent efforts, was directly linked to accreditation. This is a reality in higher education, but it still creates resistance, animosity, or indifference in faculty who may minimally comply because they must but who are more concerned about how they will meet other demands, especially those associated with research and publication. Some faculty members were excited by the writing assessment work tied to their major but, by all accounts, that was not universal. One chair, for example, reported that the assessment report he submitted did not accurately represent the indifference and resistance of his faculty. Another group of faculty realized the potential of assessment for their teaching and student learning but expressed serious concern about the time to design and carry out embedded writing assessments. Many faculty members on campus were unaware of both the proficiency writing assessment all students participated in as sophomores and the disciplinary-specific senior assessments. The general education assessment system also lacked stable institutional funding and support. Although the coordinator secured outside grants to use in development, those were not subsidized by ongoing, consistent resources beyond course release time and small, contingent budgets. For example, the contract of a nontenure line coordinator of the sophomore assessment was not renewed by his disciplinary department. Although he had been a successful instructor and served an important role in the development of the general education writing assessment, the upper administration would not retain him. In another example, resources were not allocated for validation inquiry even after many years of "piloting" the mid-career proficiency exam. The embedded assessments were carried out with relatively little funding beyond the course release the WAC coordinator received, small stipends to departments, and the external grants he garnered.

IMPLICATIONS OF THE FRAMING OF WRITING THROUGH ASSESSMENTS

As composition and rhetoric faculty follow White's law to "assess thyself," they need to consider the implications—both intended and unintended—of how writing is framed through the assessment system whether that system is locally designed or not. This framing ultimately will influence how others understand writing and writing assessment as well as the role of composition and rhetoric in the academy. It will also determine, in many ways, the work and activities that composition and rhetoric instructors, administrators, and scholars do—and are supported in doing by their administrators. Or as "Smith's Law" states, which William L. Smith recently expressed in an email to me: "All is lost if the administration doesn't pony up. Assessment is expensive. Therefore, you gotta understand what makes the administration pay attention—and that means showing 'em what's gotta be changed" (personal communication, January 31, 2011).

Although the two writing programs described here are very different, they both are framed in large part by the assessment programs that were closely linked to the WAC/WID programs. This framing provided structure and support and helped to shape how participants—from students to teachers of writing to the administration—understood writing and writing assessment. This frame also identified values and created ways of organizing activities related to WAC/WID. The writing assessments clearly indicated that writing and writing competency were important. Because the assessment programs were not tied to only one specific course, and not limited to English courses, they clearly signaled that writing was not discipline specific, not something "mastered" in first-year composition. Both assessment programs reinforced this position by involving faculty from across the disciplines in the assessments. Both also envisioned the assessment as part of a larger approach to the teaching and assessing of writing. Individual students, in both programs, who "failed" the mid-career writing assessments, were offered support by the institutions in getting additional help, which emphasized learning and development rather than punishment. And both writing programs and assessments were designed to fit the needs of the particular institutions and their curriculum, resources, and personnel.

Clearly, there were many positive components of these writing programs and the assessment programs they developed and propagated. Both were locally situated but informed by current theories and best practices. Both highlighted writing as an essential component of success in the academy and in being prepared for experiences beyond the institution. Both were considered valuable to the local institutions, writing programs, and instructors. Both also depended, in large part, on not only formal structures but informal, personal connections to maintain their effectiveness. These benefits framed writing and writing instruction as something not tied to one specific discipline, as a developmental process, as valuable horizontally as well as vertically across disciplines. Both programs also valued the input of classroom instructors to evaluate student writing as part of the work of a particular course—one through the freshman seminar rubric and the senior embedded assessments and one through a collection of papers students submitted as part of the mid-career portfolio. Having an institution-wide assessment at mid-career also signaled to students, faculty, policymakers, and others that writing was taken seriously by the institutions. Both writing assessments also provided a shape or structure that faculty and administrators used for professional development of instructors and for student learning. And because both programs were administered by professionals who were writing scholars and teachers, both institutions valued, to some extent, the expertise associated with composition as a discipline.

A closer look at this positive framing, however, leads to a more complicated situation, specifically in how the assessments have perpetuated some of the issues and challenges that compositionists have been arguing about for over a century, such as the disciplinary status of writing and writing professionals and how writing is defined and valued (e.g., Brereton, 1995; Connors, 1997; Crowley, 1998; Stewart & Stewart, 1997). In other words, writing—and specifically writing assessment—was a way of disciplining both writing as a field and the people involved in it. There was clearly a sense of some types of writing—in both cases relatively brief, timed, one draft essays—over others. Although Farmville University does include longer papers from classes in the junior-level writing assessment, those papers were only examined if students did not pass the timed essays. In other words, the timed, one draft essays determined whether the longer, more developed, texts were examined by the faculty evaluators. At University of the Liberal Arts, the mid-career writing assessment, drafted during one 50-minute class session, was the only writing the faculty evaluators read. The rubric, which the freshman seminar instructors completed, relied on the writing done in the course, but there was no other examination of student writing. The embedded assessments were done in departments and procedures varied. The instructor of the course with the embedded assignment evaluated the student writing, and how much other faculty examined student work varied. Because the definition of writing was disciplinary dependent, the type of writing varied considerably across departments. Some may even have had little writing in a traditional, text-based understanding of writing. For example, one department focused on interpreting and constructing graphs for the embedded assessment, which was appropriate for the discipline but did not focus on discursive texts.

At both of these institutions, writing professionals were included in tenure-line faculty positions although this was complicated, especially for those charged with the assessment. At Farmville, the link between the writing program and faculty members and departments degenerated to the point where the writing program was no longer administered by a faculty member, and it did not offer courses (the tutorials were not full-fledged courses and were linked to WID courses offered by departments). At the University of the Liberal Arts, the writing program coordinator, a tenured faculty member, had no institutional authority beyond consulting with colleagues and departments who invited him. The administration of the mid-career assessment was ad hoc and contingent at best even after several years of pilots. The administration did not acknowledge the time and expertise needed for writing assessment—the WAC coordinator, by his own admission, had little if any expertise in the area when he began. He folded the assessment into his other work, which cut into those activities. A contingent instructor eventually received some compensation to help administer the proficiency exam, but the university administration refused to make that position permanent, so when he was not renewed, the position was eliminated.

Both of these writing assessment programs grew out of the vision of a particular rhetoric and composition scholar and administrator who had chosen to see the external demand for assessment as an opportunity to design assessment programs that supported WAC/WID. In other words, they enacted White's law and managed to actively frame the assessments in ways that supported their vision of WAC/WID. At Farmville University, that framing had shifted somewhat so that institution-wide assessment was separated from the instruction at the first year and only marginally connected to it in WAC. Separating the teaching and assessment of writing can undermine some of the very benefits associated with assessment and disrupt its link to teaching and learning. Although the University of the Liberal Arts managed to maintain the connections with teaching, learning and assessment, that position seemed tenuous, dependent as it was on the commitment, enthusiasm, and ethos of the particular WAC coordinator. The institution's long-term commitment to his vision of writing and assessment remained unclear.

These programs offer some insight to other faculty whose institutions or programs are facing external mandates to assess. Securing a long-term commitment, resources, and support across the institution is critical. Likewise, approaching the work with the perspective of a researcher can help not only the faculty administrator's career but can also garner recognition and confer value through grants received, presentations, and publications. They also illustrate how difficult it can be to meet the demands of both disciplinary standards and institutional realities—a balance that both programs had initially achieved to some extent but that was difficult to maintain. Examining them over time also demonstrated that the demands and contexts of assessments are ever changing so that the assessment frameworks need to be flexible, allowing for additions or renovations. An assessment program is not, after all, a concrete structure but rather a conceptual framework that needs to take into account the status quo—current theory, practice, resources, and personnel—while accommodating new knowledge, shifting contexts, and future needs.

ENDNOTES

1. For information about WAC/WID see Fulwiler and Young (1990), Gere (1985), and McLeod and Soven (2006).
2. I also reviewed published literature about this programs; however, I do not quote from these documents nor cite them because my IRB approval specified anonymity to the participants and institutions. Pseudonyms are used for the institutions and all personnel and some identifying information had to be modified or deleted.

REFERENCES

Adler-Kassner, L., & O'Neill, P. (2010). *Reframing writing assessment to improve teaching and learning*. Logan, UT: Utah State University Press.

Arum, R., & Roksa, J. (2010). *Academically adrift: Limited learning on college campuses*. Chicago, IL: University of Chicago Press.

Bazerman, C. (2004). Speech acts, genres, and activity systems: How texts organize activity and people. In C. Bazerman & P. A. Prior (Eds.), *What writing does and how it does it: An introduction to analyzing texts and textual practices* (pp. 309-339). Mahwah, NJ: Erlbaum.

Bean, J. C. (2001). *Engaging ideas: A professor's guide to integrating writing, critical thinking, and active learning in the classroom*. San Francisco, CA: Jossey-Bass.

Belanoff, P., & Dickson, M. (Eds.). (1991). *Portfolios: Process and product*. Portsmouth, NH: Boynton/Cook.

Black, L., Daiker, D.A., Sommers, J., & Stygall, G. (Eds.). (1994). *New directions in portfolio assessment: Reflective practice, critical theory, and large-scale scoring*. Portsmouth, NH: Boynton/Cook Heinemann.

Bolman, L., & Deal, T. (2003). *Reframing organizations: Artistry, choice, and leadership*. San Francisco. CA: Jossey-Bass.

Borrowman, S. (1999). The trinity of portfolio placement: Validity, reliability, and curriculum reform. *WPA: Writing Program Administration, 23*(1/2), 7–28.

Brereton, J. C. (Ed.). (1995). *Origins of composition studies in the American college 1875–1925: A documentary history*. Pittsburgh, PA: University of Pittsburgh Press.

Broad, R. L., (1994). "Portfolio scoring": A contradiction in terms. In L. Black, D.A. Daiker, J. Sommers, & G. Stygall (Eds.), *New directions in portfolio assessment: Reflective practice, critical theory, and large-scale scoring* (pp. 263-77). Portsmouth, NH: Boynton/Cook Heinemann.

Broad, B. (2003). *What we really value: Beyond rubrics in teaching and assessing writing*. Logan, UT: Utah State University Press.

Broad, B., Adler-Kassner, L., Alford, B., Detweiler, J., Estrem, H., Harrington, S., & Weeden, S. (2009). *Organic writing assessment: Dynamic criteria mapping in action*. Logan, UT: Utah State University Press.

Carter, M. (2003). A process for establishing outcomes-based assessment plans for writing and speaking in the disciplines. *Language and Learning Across the Disciplines, 6*(1). Web.

Common Core State Standards Initiative. (2010). *National Governors Association and Council of Chief State School Officers*. Web.

Connors, R. J. (1997). *Composition-rhetoric: Backgrounds, theory, and pedagogy*. Pittsburgh, PA: University of Pittsburgh Press.

Cooper, C.R., & Odell, L. (Eds.). (1977). *Evaluating writing: Describing, measuring, judging*. Urbana, IL: National Council of Teachers of English.

Crowley, S. (1998). *Composition in the university: Historical and polemical essays*. Pittsburgh, PA: University of Pittsburgh Press.

Elbow, P., & Belanoff, P. (1986). Staffroom interchange: Portfolios as a substitute for proficiency examinations. *College Composition and Communication, 37*(3), 336–339.

Elliot, N. (2005). *On a scale: A social history of writing assessment in America*. New York, NY: Peter Lang.

Emig, J. (1977). Writing as a mode of learning. *College Composition and Communication, 28*(2), 122-128.

Fulwiler, T., & Young, A. (Eds.). (1990). *Programs that work: Models and methods for writing across the curriculum*. Portsmouth, NH: Boynton-Cook.

Gallagher, C. W. (2010). Opinion: At the precipice of speech: English studies, science, and policy (or) relevancy. *College English, 73*(1), 73-90.

Gere, A. R. (Ed.). (1985). *Roots in the sawdust: Writing to learn across the disciplines*. Urbana, IL: National Council of Teachers of English.

Haswell, R. H. (Ed.). (2001). *Beyond outcomes: Assessment and instruction within a university writing program*. Westport, CT: Ablex.

Huot, B. (2002). *(Re)Articulating writing assessment for teaching and learning*. Logan, UT: Utah State University Press.

Huot, B., O'Neill, P., & Moore, C. (2010). A usable past for writing assessment. *College English, 72*(5), 495-517.

Jolliffe, D. A. (Ed.). (1988). *Writing in academic disciplines*. Norwood, NJ: Ablex Publishing

Kitzhaber, A. R. (1990). *Rhetoric in American colleges, 1850–1900*. Dallas, TX: Southern Methodist University Press.

Lakoff, G. (2004). *Don't think of an elephant! Know your values and frame the debate*. White River Junction, VT: Chelsea Green.

McLeod, S.H., & Soven, M. I. (Eds.). (2006). *Composing a community: A history of writing across the curriculum*. Anderson, SC: Parlor Press.

McPherson, P., & Shulenberger, D. (2006). *Toward a Voluntary System of Accountability program (VSA) for public universities and colleges*. Washington, DC: National Association of State Universities and Land-Grant Colleges. Web.

Murphy, S., Carlson, S., & Rooney, P. with the CCCC Committee on Assessment. (1993). *Report to the CCCC Executive Committee: Survey of Postsecondary Writing Assessment Practices*. Unpublished manuscript.

National Commission on Writing. (2004). *Writing: A ticket to work . . . or a ticket out*. New York, NY: College Entrance Examination Board. Web.

National Commission on Writing. (2005). *Writing: A powerful message from state governments*. New York, NY: College Entrance Examination Board. Web.

O'Neill, P. A. (1998). *Writing assessment and the disciplinarity of composition*. Unpublished dissertation, University of Louisville, Louisville, KY.

O'Neill, P. A., Moore, C., & Huot, B. (2009). *A guide to college writing assessment*. Logan, UT: Utah State University Press.

Sewell, L. (1996). *Cover(t) letters: How new graduate instructors experience portfolio evaluation*. Paper presented at the Conference on College Composition and Communication. Milwaukee, WI.

Smit, D. W. (1994). A WPA's nightmare: Reflections on using portfolios as a course exit exam. In L. Black, D. A. Daiker, J. Sommers, & G. Stygall (Eds.), *New directions in portfolio assessment: Reflective practice, critical theory, and large-scale scoring* (pp. 303-313). Portsmouth, NH: Boynton/Cook Heinemann.

Smith, W. L. (1993). Assessing the reliability and adequacy of using holistic scoring of essays as a college composition placement technique. In M.M. Williamson &

B.A. Huot (Eds.), *Validating holistic scoring: Theoretical and empirical foundations* (pp. 142-205). Cresskill, NJ: Hampton Press.

Smith, W. L. (2011). [E-mail to P. O'Neill]. Baltimore, MD: Loyola University of Maryland.

Stewart, D. C., & Stewart, P. L. (1997). *The life and legacy of Fred Newton Scott.* Pittsburgh, PA: University of Pittsburgh Press.

Thais, C., & Zawacki, T. M. (1997). How portfolios for proficiency help shape a WAC program. In K.B. Yancey & B. Huot (Eds.), *Assessing writing across the curriculum: Diverse approaches and practices* (pp. 29-96). Greenwich, CT: Ablex.

Trachsel, M. (1992). *Institutionalizing literacy: The historical role of college entrance exams in English.* Carbondale, IL: Southern Illinois University Press.

U.S. Department of Education. (2006). *A test of leadership: Charting the future of U.S. higher education.* Washington, DC: Author.

White, E. M. (1990). Language and reality in writing assessment. *College Composition and Communication, 41*(2), 187-200.

White, E. M. (1994). *Teaching and assessing writing* (2nd ed.). Portland, ME: Calendar Islands.

Willard-Traub, M., Decker, E., Reed, R., & Johnston, J. (1999). The development of large-scale portfolio placement at the University of Michigan 1992–1998. *Assessing Writing, 6*(1), 41–84.

Williamson, M. M., & Huot, B. A. (Eds.). (1993). *Validating holistic scoring: Theoretical and empirical foundations.* Cresskill, NJ: Hampton Press.

Yancey, K. B., & Huot, B., (Eds.). (1997). *Assessing writing across the curriculum: Diverse approaches and practices.* Greenwich, CT: Ablex.

Yancey, K. B., & Weiser, I. (Eds.). (1997). *Situating portfolios: Four perspectives.* Logan, UT: Utah State University Press.

26

CHANGING THE LANGUAGE OF ASSESSMENT
LESSONS FROM FEMINISM

Cindy Moore
Loyola University Maryland

Though most composition specialists have been engaged for years in assessing student learning outside the classroom—for placement, proficiency, or program review—we have yet to feel confident about our role in large-scale university assessment efforts. We are encouraged to design and facilitate various types of writing assessments but know that, despite our expertise or experience, we likely will be questioned about the efficacy of our approaches, especially if they appear at odds with approaches more familiar to upper level administrators or institutional assessment personnel. Our collective lack of confidence is too often compounded by frantic professional listserv postings with subject lines like "Help!! Good Assessment??" and conference panel stories about carefully conceived portfolio initiatives being rejected in favor of multiple choice exams.

To be sure, many large-scale writing assessment initiatives have been compromised by a mismatch between the question being asked (e.g., Is this student ready for English 100?) and the method proposed to answer it, which is why so much of our assessment scholarship has been focused on describing and rationalizing methods for evaluating writing that are in line with what we know about teaching and learning. Over the years, such scholarship has helped us justify approaches that make sense to us while, at the same time, satisfying institutional demands for evidence of student achievement. However, it is also the case that much of the anxiety surrounding large-scale assessment has less to do with the potential methods *themselves* and more to do with how those methods are described and debated—as, for example, being less or more "valid" or "reliable," relative to a presumed, but often unarticulated, standard. I have attended more than a few university-sponsored assessment meetings whose published agenda was sidetracked by requests from well-meaning faculty, within and beyond English departments, for explanations of how, for instance, *objective* differs from *outcome*, or why it is necessary to "measure" the student learning that they routinely evaluate, in various ways, against their own course goals. For many assessment practitioners (i.e., those of us who actually *do* assessment), the barrier between good intentions and truly informed, useful institutional assessment is not necessarily a lack of knowledge about how to determine whether students can demonstrate a certain skill or ability, but unfamiliarity with, misconceptions about, or, in some cases, negative gut reactions to the language used to discuss potentially useful methods.

As if to acknowledge the potential linguistic barriers to good assessment, some writing assessment scholars have started to spend more time in their work defining (and redefining) commonly used assessment terms for the broader composition community. Following the lead of educational measurement specialists like Pamela Moss (1994), writing assessment experts such as Huot (2002), Broad (2003), and O'Neill (2011) affirm the long-acknowledged linguistic tenet that language matters, as they take pains to explain and illustrate how traditional assessment terms (most notably *validity* and *reliability*) can be used both to promote meaningful assessments and to highlight the usefulness of results. In their view, because conceptions of such terms within the wider educational assessment community have been evolving over the years to accommodate new, context-sensitive perspectives on knowledge and meaning, they work well for a field like Composition and Rhetoric whose own theories have been changing, yet whose members must use a common language to communicate with faculty, staff, administrators, and legislators representing a broad spectrum of disciplinary and professional experiences. For these scholars, it is not the words themselves that are problematic, but the unspecified, oversimplified, or old-fashioned ways they are sometimes used.

Other scholars, however, are skeptical about the benefits of sticking with traditional assessment language, whether it is redefined for contemporary purposes or not. Most notable among skeptics within Composition and Rhetoric is Lynne (2004), whose book outlines a case for adopting new terminology for writing assessment. The central premise of the book, developed through what Lynne describes as Foucauldian "archeological" analysis of current assessment discourse (p. 10), is that the use of traditional assessment language necessarily implies a traditional theoretical framework; that is, our perspective on assessment is, in essence, restricted by the language we use to discuss it. Examining Huot's many efforts to revisit and reread traditional assessment theory, including the language used to describe that theory, Lynne argues that although they may be "safe," they are "not necessarily best or most productive" (p. 115). Instead of what she perceives as a problematic move on the part of Huot and others to "co-opt" traditional assessment terminology for contemporary uses, Lynne calls for a whole new assessment language—a language that is more obviously aligned with the discipline's humanistic history and evolving theoretical beliefs, a language that is, in a word, "ours."

Specifically, Lynne calls for a temporary "separation" from or "suspension of" an inherently objectivist assessment paradigm, signaled by a new "vocabulary of writing assessment that is grounded in and responsible to [social constructionist] theoretical principles already at work within composition studies" (pp. 111-114, 116). The key terms in this new vocabulary, intended to replace *validity* and *reliability*, respectively, are *meaningfulness* (which, for Lynne, highlights purpose and "significance" within a particular assessment context) and *ethics* (which foregrounds the political dynamics that may affect the perceived fairness of an assessment and use of results) (p. 118). These terms, Lynne explains,

> provide a broader view and would, at least potentially, address the primary assessment concerns of compositionists: that, for example, assessment be substantive, purposeful, responsive, and fair. These terms, I believe, provide a lexicon for theorizing writing assessment dependent not on inappropriate objectivist epistemologies, but on principles accepted within the composition community. (p. 117)

According to Lynne, these new assessment terms, rather than implying an *a priori* set of criteria that must be met in every assessment circumstance, "suggest a relational or collective value structure." They "suggest neither objectivity nor subjectivity, but social reality constructed by persons in concert and in specific settings" (p. 121).

Lynne's proposal, reminiscent of other, similar proposals to substitute new words for troublesome terms familiar to compositionists, in an effort to challenge or change dominant theoretical perspectives (e.g., Bowden's [1999] *dance* for *voice*), is appealing at first glance. If we see language and perception as inextricably linked, a new set of assessment terms promises to not only mitigate resistance to large-scale assessment initiatives from those unfamiliar with the traditional language, but to expand our thinking about assessment. However, what decades of feminist theory, particularly feminist linguistic theory, demonstrate is that real language change—the kind of change that both reflects and shapes thinking—is not automatic, never easy, and, depending upon the particular social context, may not even be possible. This is not to suggest that change should not be pursued, but rather that it should be pursued with an appreciation of the specific conditions required to inspire and sustain it.

FEMINIST CHALLENGES TO LANGUAGE AND THE PROSPECTS FOR LANGUAGE CHANGE

Though writing specialists have used feminist theory for decades to help us understand the potential influence of gender on our work as teachers and researchers, we have not applied it very fully to what has become one of our field's most pressing concerns: large-scale assessment. Holdstein's (1996) observation that, as a discipline, we "have been remiss in leaving [institutional] assessment all but untouched" by critical theories that specifically highlight gender issues (and, by extension, "facts" of "culture, race, class [and] sexual orientation") (pp. 205, 206) retains its resonance today, despite many attempts to theorize assessment in ways that are consistent with contemporary thinking about language, learning, and teaching. Among the many aspects of large-scale assessment that remain ripe for feminist analysis, one that seems particularly salient in the current accountability climate is the language used to prompt, design, facilitate, and even assess assessments.

Although Lynne does not position herself as a feminist, her argument for language change echoes feminist cross-disciplinary challenges to language associated with patriarchal culture, including the culture of the Academy, during the 1970s and early 1980s. In "Linguistic Sexism and Feminist Linguistic Activism," linguist Anne Pauwels (2003) identifies three approaches to language change pursued by feminists during this period: "linguistic disruption," proposals for "a new woman-centered language," and calls to "amend" "existing forms, rules, and uses of language" (pp. 555-556). Linguistic disruption, according to Pauwels, involved "revaluing" or "reclaiming" commonly used terms to call attention to the ways that language supports gender-based discrimination. Disruption includes "breaking morphological rules" (Pauwels' example is substituting *herstory* for *history*); violating traditional grammatical and spelling conventions (e.g., replacing *he* with *she* to indicate a generic subject; using *wimmin* for *women*); or "inverting gender stereotypes" by, for instance, describing a prominent male politician in terms of his hair and clothing styles instead of focusing on his ideas (p. 555). "Experiments" with women-centered words and discursive forms include Laadan, the language conceived by science fiction writer/linguist

Suzette Haden Elgin, and *ecriture feminine*, a fluid essayistic form used and promoted by French feminist theorists such as Helene Cixous and Luce Irigaray (pp. 555-556). Although not mentioned specifically by Pauwels, Mary Daly's *Wickedary* (1987), in which she proposes a new woman-centered lexicon (including some of the examples mentioned by Pauwels), would also serve as a good illustration of this type of language change initiative. The language amendment strategy, also known as "form replacement," involved two primary "mechanisms": gender neutralization, whereby sexism is "neutralized" or "minimized" at the word level by, for example, dropping suffixes that marked for gender (e.g., -ess [actress], -ette [usherette], -trix [aviatrix]) (p. 556-557), and gender specification, which involved deliberately substituting one gender specific term for another (e.g., *she* for *he*) (p. 556). Given Lynne's attempt to cast her proposed assessment terms as "new" and reflective of the field's "own" perspectives on teaching and learning, her call for language change appears most similar to the linguistic experiments of feminists like Elgin and Daly. Indeed, Lynne appears to align herself with these "more radical" efforts, intended to result in discourse more "capable of expressing a woman's point of view" (Pauwels, 2003 p. 555), when she writes that her proposed terms "demonstrate possibilities for composition scholars to theorize assessment according to *our own understanding* of what it means to write and to learn to write" (p. 168, emphasis added).

Although identifying connections between current challenges to assessment language and feminist challenges to patriarchal language is interesting in its own right, what seems most useful for us is to consider which attempts at change actually succeeded—and why. For Pauwels (2003), the success of feminist "language activism" should be "judged ultimately against the goals it set out to achieve. Such goals included raising awareness of the gender bias in language and prompting adoption within the speech community of proposed changes, in a manner that promoted gender equality" (p. 561). Within this framework, she identifies form replacement strategy, specifically attempts at gender neutralization, as particularly successful in changing both habits of speech and habits of mind regarding gender. In fact, she highlights the strategy as the indisputable favorite among activists for "promoting linguistic equality" in predominantly English speaking countries (p. 559), contrasting it with "experiments in women-centered languages and discourses," which, according to her, "have remained largely the domain of creative writers" (p. 556). That said, in light of the goals for language change specified by Pauwels, it also seems clear that the favored "more familiar" strategy of "amending" forms, rules, and uses (p. 556) may not have succeeded without the consciousness-raising effect that other strategies (i.e., linguistic disruption, proposals for a new lexicon and grammar) had among feminist activists—a point worth remembering, with respect to Lynne's recent challenges to assessment language.

Ultimately, what sociolinguists like Pauwels advocate is consideration of language-change proposals within a broad linguistic and sociopolitical context. If they are to succeed at changing perceptions (the unequivocal desired result), attempts at language change must not only be considered locally (i.e., as important to the agenda of a specific group or movement), but more globally (i.e., as important to the larger community of language users). Even a seemingly insignificant linguistic move like dropping a suffix must be evaluated within the broader social context to determine the likelihood of a broad spectrum of speakers recognizing the need for change and then actually adopting the proposed alternative. The move to, for example, drop the gender marking suffix in *poetess* can only be effective within a larger social context where there is a real shift in the number of women recognized not only as "real" writers, but writers of "real" poetry. Second, and along the same lines, the proposed change must make sense to language users; they must be able to recognize gender bias in a word like *poetess* and be willing to use *poet* as a gender-neutral term. Calls for change must be considered within a linguistic context, too, that is, in terms of the "typological features and structural properties of a language" as well as any "deeply ingrained prescriptive rules or norms" (p. 556). Depending upon how closely aligned particular grammatical systems are with cultural realities (e.g., gender hierarchies), a language may be more or less able to accommodate form replacement or other language-change strategies (p. 556-559). Pauwels (2003) suggests, for example, that efforts during the 1980s to "neutralize" feminine forms in the Dutch language were "linguistically more viable" than similar efforts to change other languages because Dutch was already "moving away from the use of gender-marking suffixes" (p. 558).

Pauwels' emphasis on the importance of looking at language change within the broadest possible context is supported by the work of other feminist sociolinguists, most notably Deborah Cameron, who has dedicated her career to highlighting the relationship between sociopolitical power and language. In "Non-sexist Language: Lost in Translation?," a controversial essay that was originally published in 1995 but whose continuing relevance is underscored by its reappearance in a 2006 collection of her most important work, Cameron discusses some of the limitations of calls for change at the word level—especially those that are depoliticized in an effort to make them seem more commonsensical or "reasonable." Analyzing entries in contemporary feminist guides to nonsexist language use, Cameron details the drawbacks of simply calling for substitutions of one (seemingly sexist) word for another (presumably nonsexist) word (e.g., *himmicane* for *hurricane*). As she argues, the challenges are often very ethnocentric (i.e., the substitutions may make sense for an American speaker, but not to a British speaker, whose pronunciation of terms may be different); they often ignore the connections between sexism and other forms of discrimination (e.g., racial, sexual); and, especially important for our purposes, their proponents "[fail] to see sexism as a systemic relation to power, as opposed to a set of misguided beliefs and stereotypes about men and women" (pp. 21-24). Simply substituting one word or phrase for another, without taking into account the larger cultural values reflected and shaped by both new terms and old, she suggests, will not necessarily lead to either meaningful linguistic change or the larger political change that the proposed alternatives are meant to effect. Though people might agree to use the new terms or phrases, "there is no chance that they will do it with any commitment or skill" if they don't understand why the change is necessary or beneficial in the first place (p. 26). As Cameron (2006) writes,

> If you do not explain to people what the political rationale is for identifying certain ways of using language as "sexist," they may stick to the letter of your prescriptions, but they will disregard the spirit. They will think, or pretend to think, that the problem is not to do with meaning or content, but simply consists of a few isolated forms like "man", [sic.] and the solution is to mechanically change every occurrence of these forms irrespective of the context (this is the source of all those side-splitting examples like "personagement"). (p. 26)

In a subsequent essay, Cameron discusses the theoretical work that led linguists writing in the 1970s and early 1980s to themselves suggest an easy relationship between change at the word level and change at the conceptual level, without considering social context. According to Cameron (1998), many linguists during that time were especially influenced by what she terms an "extremely 'strong' version" of the Sapir-Whorf hypothesis, based on the work of linguists Edward Sapir and Benjamin Whorf, who posited that 'our worldview is determined by the structures of the particular native language we happen to speak'" (p. 150). Their now-classic example is that Eskimos have many words for snow, which allows them to think about snow differently than people who live in other climates. Influenced by this work, which, according to Cameron, was probably "overstated" in the first place, linguists like Dale Spender and Suzette Haden Elgin suggested that oppression of women was largely due to a "man made language" that restricted the ability of women and men to think about themselves and their situations in new ways. Though Cameron affirms a connection between language and perception, she questions the strength of the relationship, pointing out, for example, that the fact that "'printers have a lot of terms for type fonts" or "surfers have words for many different kinds of waves'" does not mean printers and surfers think differently than the rest of us. Suggesting that perceptions and understandings are "mediated" by, or negotiated through, language rather than determined by it, Cameron (1998) asserts that it is just as likely that people perceive a phenomenon first and then begin a process of discovering terms that will represent the new perceptions (p. 151). Where Cameron (1998) sees a potentially stronger connection between language and perception (and, thus, possibility of social change), is at the level of grammar, of syntactical rules, for example. Even at this level, however, research results are mixed as to whether challenges to traditional grammatical norms and structures lead to alterations in thinking. It is unclear, for example, whether *he* is always, in all contexts, perceived as a generic pronoun and, thus, truly constrains the ability of language users to think about men and women differently (pp. 151-52). For Cameron, use of *he* to represent all people is "symbolically insulting," rather than intellectually limiting, and is best challenged on that front (p. 152).

What complicates matters related to language change even further, then, is that proposals for change must account for *actual language use*. Moreover, we cannot count on people to act in predictable ways when using language—even within groups that appear highly homogeneous. Actual usage depends, to an often great degree, on how a particular person is identifying at a particular moment in time, within a particular communicative context. Myerhoff (1996) shows how decades of scholarship on language and identity make it difficult to know for certain how any one person will use language. Drawing on sociolinguistic research as well as theoretical work in sociology, intercultural communication, and social psychology, Myerhoff challenges the notion that people use language in consistent ways based on unitary, fixed identity—in this case gender. As Myerhoff (1996) puts it, "The nature of a single encounter, and the types of group or personal identity that shape communication within it, will depend on which social or personal identity is most salient to the interactants at that time" (p. 203). Although people often do "identify" as women or men in speaking situations, gendered identity intersects with other identities (e.g., ethnicity, age, class), which makes it hard to distinguish between utterances made "as a woman," for example, versus utterances made because of age or class identification. Even more importantly, gender is not always the most dominant or "salient" identification in any given interaction. As Myerhoff (1996) explains, "There are some clear examples of linguistic variation in the literature that indicate speakers do not consistently identify with the same social grouping" (p. 205). That is, a person's age or class—or more important for our purposes, expertise, professional status, and/or education—may influence language use to a lesser or greater degree, depending on the communicative context. Further, even when a group of people identify in a similar way (e.g., as women, as middle-aged, as upper-class), they may not necessarily share a common way of conceiving or enacting their identities. In fact, they might not even define identity categories like gender, race, and sexuality in the same way. Myerhoff (1996) cites a study involving interviews with women who identified themselves as either more or less "traditional" with respect to roles for women and men. Interestingly, the interviews revealed that although both groups typically viewed "male characteristics" negatively and "favour[ed] basic levels of equal rights/equal opportunities for women," they did not share a common definition of what it means to be a woman: "Traditional women saw their feminine or womanly identity as complementary to men's masculine identity, whereas non-traditional women saw the comparison in more competitive terms" (p. 214).

Because, from a sociolinguistic point of view, meaningful language change requires both linguistic viability and social-political feasibility, the most effective efforts involve what is known in the linguistic community as "language planning." Typically, according to Pauwels (2003), such planning happens when authoritative bodies (educational institutions, the media, politicians, prominent linguists, etc.) recognize that a change is needed and attempt to implement that change from above. (A recent example would be the effort to rename "swine flu" as H1N1 to minimize damage to the pork industry.) Sometimes, however, change is implemented from the bottom up. For second-wave feminists, language change was "principally a grassroots-driven phenomenon" because the usual authoritative bodies were uncooperative (p. 560). The grassroots linguistic activism that resulted in many of the changes we see today took place on many fronts: Well-known feminist authors wrote about the importance of language change and used proposed terms in their work; feminist activists within and outside the academy developed guidelines and policies on nonsexist language use and proposed amendments to important civil rights acts that included attention to language change. As Pauwels (2003) writes,

> Terminology commissions, education ministries, employment councils, language academies, and other public agencies charged with making amendments to official (occupational) nomenclature and terminology called upon feminist language planners to assist them in this task. This in turn triggered requests for non-sexist language guidelines and policies to be developed for other public and private agencies covered under EEO and anti-discrimination legislation. (p. 561)

IMPLICATIONS FOR WRITING ASSESSMENT

Given the difficulties associated with changing language in a way that alters perception, it is important for writing specialists to understand the conditions that appear necessary for sustainable change and how to shape such conditions or take advantage of them. Linguists like those whose work I discussed above underscore the importance of examining words within both a larger linguistic context and broader social context. Though social constructionist theory problematizes easy distinctions between the two types of contexts, an attempt at separation can help us determine whether individuals will see the need for alternatives; whether they will use the alternatives (assuming they see a need); and how they will use the alternatives toward productive ends.

It is worth emphasizing again that although language, especially at a grammatical level, both reflects and, to varying degrees, affects perception, it does not necessarily *determine* perception. If it did, then critiques of the language and reflections on the way we think, given the language we have, would be exceedingly difficult, if not impossible. With respect to the language of assessment, then, terms like *validity* and *reliability* might, in some cases, restrict how some people think about assessment. Yet the terms themselves do not necessarily make it impossible—or even that difficult—to imagine alternatives to traditional assessment methods; nor will new terms necessarily inspire new ways of thinking about assessment. After all, much of the most groundbreaking work in writing assessment practice (e.g., holistic essay scoring, portfolio assessment, directed self-placement) has, in fact, been done within the context of a traditional assessment paradigm with traditional assessment language. In fact, it was a perceived tension between the new methods and the older assessment frameworks that inspired the questioning of traditional terminology that led to better, deeper, more-nuanced understandings of those terms for particular assessment tasks and contexts. As just one example of such questioning, Moss (1994) wondered in the early 1990s how the necessity of "some degree" of standardization for demonstrating validity and reliability within the educational measurement community could be reconciled with "emerging views of literacy" that "suggest[ed] the need for less standardized forms of assessment," such as writing portfolios (p. 110).

It is also worth reiterating that many respected scholars within the broader educational assessment community see validity as a multifaceted, context-bound concept that is not at odds with current writing theory and pedagogy. As Huot (2002) explains, for example, prominent "validity theorists" began, in the 1980s, to articulate a view of validity as a complex, context-sensitive evidence-gathering process that accounts for far more than the "empirical or technical aspects of the way we assess" (e.g., design of tests, scoring rubrics, etc.) (p. 93). To many assessment experts outside composition and rhetoric, validity is seen as a product of a careful, theory-grounded "argument" that addresses "technical documentation" (i.e., the content of an assessment, key constructs) as well as "political considerations important to administrative and governmental agencies," "the impact on the educational environment," and "the consequences for individual students and teachers"

(p. 55). A similar case can be made for reliability. Influenced by the groundbreaking work of educational assessment scholars such as Moss, William Smith, and Jay Parkes (among others), O'Neill (2011) considers reliability as an argument whose evidence must extend beyond simple statistical statements regarding the relative precision of test scores to articulation of the values and beliefs informing assessment design (including, e.g., the purpose of the assessment, the audience, the intended use of results) as well as an explanation of how various kinds of evidence support decisions about students and programs. If, as Lynne's work suggests, writing faculty charged with assessing student-composed texts for placement, proficiency, or program review continue to associate terms like *validity* and *reliability* with an older, objectivist paradigm that reduces highly dynamic, contingent processes to oversimplified mathematical statements, that is not necessarily a problem of *terminology*, but a problem of *definition*.

If we apply tenets of language planning outlined by Pauwels (2003) to a hypothetical effort to change the language of large-scale writing assessment, then, several important issues become apparent. Most obviously, the people who would be the most evident agents of language change will not necessarily see a need for such change. These potential change agents would include recognized writing assessment scholars (who, on the whole, are more committed to clarifying unfamiliar or misunderstood terminology than they are to changing it) as well as the testing companies (who profit from widespread misperceptions of what the terms and their underlying concepts really mean). If most people (including writing faculty charged with doing assessment) do not understand that validity is, from the perspective of many notable educational measurement theorists, best seen as an argument whose evidence must include data about consequences (for students, teachers, and curriculum), then there will be little call to question the use of standardized test scores to gauge students' ability to write an analytical essay for a particular purpose or audience. If there *is* an impulse to question (because, e.g., the test just "feels" inappropriate), there will not be enough knowledge or understanding to make a persuasive case for alternatives. Similarly, if school administrators, faculty, and staff do not know that establishing the reliability of an assessment involves much more than providing rates of agreement between scores or among scorers, they will continue to buy prepackaged standardized placement exams (whose marketers ensure that a student's score will not vary between Monday and Friday of the same week) or to support yearly "norming" sessions to improve the likelihood that diverse faculty who read university-required exit essays will interpret success in the same way. Given that the testing industry has become a formidable lobby in Washington, it seems reasonable to assume that legislators will not be inclined to question reductive notions of achievement or the oversimplified concepts they are based on, either. If we consider the process, described by

Pauwels, surrounding nonsexist language initiatives in the 1970s and early 1980s, then we must wonder how significant changes are possible, when key stakeholders likely would either ignore or resist calls for language change.

Of course, lack of interest in change at the top of the perceived power hierarchy often inspires a grassroots movement, as was the case for second-wave feminists. Yet, although those identifying as feminists during this important era were united enough in spirit and philosophy to work together to effect change at many levels, it is unclear whether that would or could happen among the broader "community of practice" known as "composition and rhetoric," for whom disciplinary identity is just one identity among many and may not be the most salient identity at any given time. If we assume, for the moment, the possibility of a strong sense of common cause based on similar identification or positioning (an assumption I challenge later), a grassroots effort would require assessment practitioners—actual users of the language in the field—to perceive, as a collective, a need for new terms, which, in turn, would require an understanding of why the old terms do not work—not just on an emotional level, but on an intellectual level. New terms adopted by people who are ambivalent about or do not fully appreciate the need for change will not have the desired impact on perception. Referring specifically to attempts to eradicate sexist terminology from a language, Cameron once asserted that "'in the mouths of sexists, language can always be sexist'" (Pauwels, 2003, p. 567). What this means for us, as assessment practitioners, is that new words alone (i.e., without a widespread willingness among practitioners to both see a need for change and, more importantly, to identify as agents of change) will have very little impact on practice.

It is true that many writing specialists feel uncomfortable with traditional assessment terminology. Lynne is not the first to question the relevance and/or applicability of *validity*, *reliability*, and closely related terms. Twenty years ago, for instance, White (1990) questioned the usefulness of "positivist" words commonly used to establish the overall reliability of an assessment, for example, *true score*, *measurement error*, *pre-/post-test* (p. 193). However, as feminist attempts at language change indicate, challenging old words is one thing; replacing them with new words in an effort to inspire real shifts in perception is another thing altogether. Whereas a term like *meaningfulness* might very well draw the attention of some writing specialists to the "purpose" and "substance" (or "significance") of an assessment, as Lynne (2004) suggests (pp. 115-141), it may resonate differently with others. Indeed, in the postmodern theoretical world that Lynne invokes, a term like *meaning* has been deconstructed to the point of utter relativism for many in English Studies. Substituting a term like *ethical* for *reliable* is perhaps more problematic in a postmodern world where conversations about appropriate behavior often begin with a question like, "Well, what do you exactly mean by *right*?" For feminists whose early or mid-career reading included Gilligan's *In a Different Voice* (1982), the term *ethical* typically calls up at least two visions of what Lynne calls "accountability": responsibility to legal or moral doctrine and responsibility to the well-being of other people, namely friends and family. As Gilligan took pains to point out, these often conflicting responsibilities—conjured by a single term—are not always easily reconciled. One reflects a more individualistic, positivist paradigm; one a more social, communal, context-based paradigm. It is a mistake to suggest that the word itself, without careful definition, will naturally inspire a social constructionist mindset toward assessment.

Further, even if we, as a community, could agree on alternative terms and their meanings, we, as *individuals*, may opt not to use them because of the particular discursive contexts in which we find ourselves, as we design, propose, and facilitate large-scale writing assessments. If sociological and sociolinguistic theories hold, in a discussion concerning assessment, people may identify in a variety of different ways—not always in terms of their most obvious group membership (e.g., women, men, African Americans, etc.) or, for our purposes, academic discipline. This makes it harder for us to assume that just because we are all writing specialists, we will always position ourselves in that way and use the particular language sanctioned by the group. We might, instead, identify with our subdiscipline (composition studies, rhetorical history, professional writing, etc.) or in terms of our position within our institution or the Academy, more generally. Relevant here is Myerhoff 's explanation of "ethnolinguistic vitality," which she attributes to Giles et al. and defines as "a measure of the perceived institutional, linguistic and social support of a particular group's language variety" (1996, p. 219). Within this framework, if identifying with one group's language will not further our communicative interests, then we are very likely to identify with a group that has higher vitality or institutional support (p. 219). In other words, if I am discussing assessment with a dean, provost, institutional assessment personnel, or science faculty member at a school that highlights a commitment to the sciences, I may identify less as a humanities faculty member, less as a compositionist, and more as an experience-certified assessment expert, choosing the traditional language of assessment over any recently proposed alternatives—even if I believe that the alternatives are better. As White (1990) understood, dissatisfaction with current terminology does not necessarily translate into a predictable use of alternative terms because we (composition/rhetoric specialists) cannot isolate ourselves or our work from other important stakeholders whose values and ways of talking about assessment differ from ours. In fact, White (1990) argues that our ultimate success in helping others to understand our values and terms may depend on our willingness to become "bilingual in measurement and writing," able to understand the views and languages of others as we help them to appreciate ours (p. 199).

From a feminist standpoint, my identification with discipline or department may be destabilized further if I am the only woman in the room and the only faculty member who is a member of a traditionally feminine or feminized discipline (like Composition). As several female writing program administrators have convincingly argued, once I step my female body out of my program, out of my department, and into another context, with its own set of histories and expectations, I cannot assume that my expertise or my language will be interpreted in the same way (see, e.g., Barr-Ebest, 1995; Miller, 1996; Schell, 1998). In fact, from a sociolinguistic perspective, any attempts to speak differently without careful consideration of the particular context might actually work to concretize perceived marginal status. As Cameron suggests throughout her work, language reflects not just conceptual frames but very real sociopolitical power structures that, when ignored, are often reinforced (rather than reshaped or replaced). If I then use terminology that may be seen as feminine (e.g., any word associated with maintaining human relationships through, say, collaboration), then I risk losing even more status. In her discussion of the efficacy of various approaches to language change, Pauwels illustrates how using feminine forms in a traditionally masculine context may work to "marginalize" both the language user and the forms themselves. According to her, it was the recognition of this downside to introducing new feminine occupational forms to the Dutch language that led many Dutch language change advocates to propose gender-neutral forms rather than "new female nouns" to describe members of professions that were still male dominated (pp. 556-557). Though this strategy was opposed by some who felt it was "better to be named and to be visible in language" through new feminine forms, Pauwels makes the point that the "gender neutralization strategy" seemed to make the most sense to the most people and, thus, promised more, in terms of meaningful, sustainable change (pp. 557-558).

CONCLUSION

Beyond suggesting potential obstacles to substituting new assessment terminology for old, critical theories and historical accounts of broader language-change efforts can help us see the best paths toward reconciling the ways we talk about assessment with the ways we think about assessment. Like other contemporary critical theories, feminist theory demands an awareness of the complex connections between language and thought, language and sociopolitical tradition, and language and current power dynamics. Where it becomes especially relevant to us is in its historical illustrations of these connections—illustrations that effectively highlight the struggle of a disempowered group to achieve recognition of its experiences, ways of knowing, and achievements in language. Where it becomes especially *helpful* is in its explicit and implicit comparisons of various routes toward productive—and lasting—language change. Linguists like Pauwels and Cameron make it clear—and feminist advocacy efforts of the 1970s and 1980s confirm—that, although attempts to substitute brand new terms for older objectionable ones may help to raise awareness about the relationship between language and thought, they may not actually succeed in altering how people talk or think. That said, such efforts *can* inspire excitement among people who feel similarly alienated from traditional discourse forms and may pave the way for other, less "radical" proposals to be adopted. In fact, one could argue that proposals like Lynne's, reminiscent of the work of Mary Daley and Suzette Haden Elgin, prompt other scholars to be more careful, more deliberate, in what Huot (2002) calls "re-articulations" of key assessment terminology.

Ultimately, the strategy that has worked best for feminists and, I would argue, will work best for us, is a carefully conceived, theory-based "form replacement" process that involves "proposing amendments to existing forms, rules, and uses of language" (Pauwels, 2003, p. 556) so that they serve our purposes better. As suggested earlier, such a strategy is already being used within composition and rhetoric. Scholars like Huot and O'Neill have been working to reframe terms like *validity* and *reliability* so that their applicability and appropriateness for writing assessment are more apparent.[1] Others have taken a slightly different tact by proposing the adoption of "new" terms that are embedded in—or closely associated with—the older traditional terms, but are less seemingly scientific, and can be theorized in ways that make sense for a wide range of assessment scholars and practitioners.

Swain and LeMahieu in Chapter 2, for example, discuss attempts to ensure that a National Writing Project assessment initiative was more text-based and less writer/reader-based by replacing key terms like *voice* and *word choice* with the closely related, but conceptually different, *stance* and *diction*, respectively. Within the college assessment arena, Shale (1996) has argued that *generalizability* might be a useful alternative to *reliability* because it requires systematic inquiry and attention to score correlation and consistency without, at the same time, demanding adherence to rigid statistical formulas that result in "true scores," or absolute statements about an activity as complex and context bound as writing. Drawing on the work of educational assessment theorists like Cronbach, Shale (1996) observes that, within the theoretical framework of generalizability, student writing is not "measured" against a static set of expectations for writer, evaluator, and/or writing/reading test "conditions," but rather is seen as one piece of information about learning that, when combined with other "samples," helps to determine the most reasonable, most "useful" set of expectations. Those expectations are then regularly reexamined based on subsequent samples (pp. 85-89). That is, *generalizability* can do the traditional "work" of reliability in a way that is consistent with contemporary literacy theories.

Of course, the negotiation between new and old (and beyond either/or) that this language change strategy represents is, in itself, consistent with the social constructionist theories that critics of traditional assessment approaches, like Lynne, espouse. In fact, in its focus on a both/and way of thinking, the strategy is not only feminist but decidedly postmodernist. Though it holds much promise for moving our discussion of assessment language forward, its success will finally depend on our collective willingness to educate ourselves about the familiar frameworks we seek to change, so we can truly understand whether—and, if so, what—new terms are required to change them. This, of course, will demand a singularity of purpose which has become rare—not just within our field and throughout the Academy, but throughout the country. It will also demand time (to read, think, discuss, and implement what we discover). Yet because large-scale assessments, if done well, promise to help us sustain the best we have to offer as teachers and scholars, I remain optimistic that we will do what is necessary to find the right words—the words that best help us carry out our work.

ENDNOTE

1. For a recent published discussion of validity and reliability, see Chapter 3, "Considering Theory," in O'Neill, Moore, and Huot (2009).

REFERENCES

Barr-Ebest, S. (1995). Gender differences in writing program administration. *WPA: Writing Program Administration, 18*(3), 53-73.

Bowden, D. (1999). *The mythology of voice*. Portsmouth, NH: Boynton/Cook, Heinemann.

Broad, B. (2003). *What we really value: Beyond rubrics in teaching and assessing writing*. Logan, UT: Utah State University Press.

Cameron, D. (1998). Feminist linguistic theories. In S. Jackson & J. Jones (Eds.), *Contemporary feminist theories* (pp. 147-161). New York, NY: New York University Press.

Cameron, D. (2006). *On language and sexual politics*. London, UK and New York, NY: Routledge.

Daly, M. (1987). *Webster's first new intergalactic wickedary of the English language.* Boston, MA: Beacon.

Gilligan, C. (1982). *In a different voice: Psychological theory and women's development.* Cambridge, MA: Harvard University Press.

Holdstein, D. (1996). Gender, feminism, and institution-wide assessment programs. In E. White, W.D. Lutz, & S. Kamusikiri (Eds.), *Assessment of writing: Politics, policies, practices* (pp. 204-225). New York, NY: Modern Language Association.

Huot, B. (2002). *(Re)articulating writing assessment for teaching and learning.* Logan, UT: Utah State University Press.

Lynne, P. (2004). *Coming to terms: A theory of writing assessment.* Logan, UT: Utah State University Press.

Miller, H. (1996). Postmasculinist directions in writing program administration. *WPA: Writing Program Administration, 20*(1-2), 49-61.

Moss, P. (1994). Validity in high stakes writing assessment: Problems and possibilities. *Assessing Writing, 1*(1), 109-128.

Myerhoff, M. (1996). Dealing with gender identity as a sociolinguistic variable. In V.L. Bergvall, J.M. Bing, & A. F. Freed (Eds.), *Rethinking language and gender research: Theory and practice* (pp. 202-227). London, UK and New York, NY: Longman.

O'Neill, P. (2011). Reframing reliability for writing assessment. *Journal of Writing Assessment, 4*(1). Web.

O'Neill, P., Moore, C., & Huot, B. (2009). *A guide to college writing assessment.* Logan, UT: Utah State University Press.

Pauwels, A. (2003). Linguistic sexism and feminist linguistic activism. In J. Holmes & M. Meyerhoff (Eds.), *The handbook of language and gender.* Malden, MA: Blackwell.

Shale, D. (1996). Essay reliability: Form and meaning. In E.M. White, W.D. Lutz, & S. Kamusikiri (Eds.), *Assessment of writing: Politics, policies, practices* (pp. 76-96). New York, NY: Modern Language Association.

Schell, E. (1998). Who's the boss? The possibilities and pitfalls of collaborative administration for untenured WPAs. *WPA: Writing Program Administration, 21*(2-3), 65-80.

White, E. M. (1990). Language and reality in writing assessment. *College Composition and Communication, 41*(2), 187-200.

27

THE RHETORICAL SITUATION OF WRITING ASSESSMENT
EXIGENCE, LOCATION, AND THE MAKING OF KNOWLEDGE

Kathleen Blake Yancey
Florida State University

Over the last 50 years, the field of writing assessment has exploded. Focusing initially on individual assessment in the first and second waves of writing assessment, scholars of this new practice helped steer a (partial) shift from first-wave multiple-choice tests of writing to second-wave essay tests (Yancey, 1999). A key practice across fields permitting this shift was an *alignment* of two kinds: between classroom practice and assessment; and between the technologies of assessment in wave-one-multiple choice and wave-two-essay. In the first case and as has been well-documented, most (if not all) teachers and some assessment experts argued that we should align both emerging research about composing processes and classroom practices with a new assessment practice, specifically with a new practice focused on student work. Such an alignment meant that the sample of *someone else's work* provided by an anonymous testing agency critiqued and edited by the student would be replaced by an essay test *composed* by the *student*. In the second case, such a shift from measure of editing to measure of composing was possible in large part because a means of quantifying a review of student writing—through the now familiar technology of holistic scoring—aligned this new practice with earlier technologies of assessment.[1] The third wave of writing assessment, focusing on portfolio assessment (which also entailed a new portfolio pedagogy), developed much differently, of course, but also through a kind of alignment. Led by teachers in both K-12 and higher education, the third wave moved again to align practice and assessment, in this case to put into a productive dialogue the new pedagogies engaging students in elaborated composing processes and nascent reflective practice with a portfolio providing a new kind of space for a plural representation of student work.

In retrospect, one might make another argument as well: that the kinds of changes identified above were made possible because of at least two other factors. The first of these is *local exigence*, what Bitzer (1968) describes as an occasion or imperfection requiring response. In developing holistically scored essays as a writing technology, for instance, Edward White, a faculty member who became an administrator, understood *the* problem of writing assessment as the problem at *his* institution. The exigence for his consideration was available to White chiefly from his vantage point as the first director of the California State University (CSU) Freshman English Equivalency Examination Program. Put another way, White sought to address the specific need of a specific program, and as important, in that context, he understood the three variables that had to be accounted for in order to make essay testing feasible in the CSU system:

> While some ... chancellors, regents, and the like are impervious to argument, most are not; many of those who employ multiple-choice tests as the only measure of writing ability are properly defensive of their stance but will include actual writing samples if they can be shown that writing tests can be properly constructed, reliably scored, and economically handled. (White, 1994b, p. xiv)

Now history, this three-part template for using student writing as the sample—tests that are *properly constructed*, *reliably scored*, and *economically handled*—provided the mechanism for migrating to holistically scored essays. Likewise, in other assessment practices, we see a similar process of local exigence providing a motive for raising new questions and developing new approaches. Directed Self Placement (DSP), for example, has taken various forms depending on the nature of the exigence: The pilot version at Colgate (Howard, 2001) was very different than the placement device created at Southern Illinois University (Blakesley, Harvey, & Reynolds, 2003) and a bit different still at Grand Valley State University—all, however, bound by local exigence.

The second wave of writing assessment was more than an exercise in meeting local needs, however, regardless of how important those might be; a second factor accounting for the success of the second wave is that the local needs were identified as *prototypical*, and information about ways to address them was widely disseminated. In the case of essay testing, for example, we see through White's account a glimpse of how the prototype developed and how the dissemination proceeded:

> As our committees entered into essay test development, we found ourselves dealing with basic questions about the goals of writing instruction; as we included more and more faculty in our holistic scoring sessions, we noticed that changes in the teaching of writing were beginning to occur on many of the CSU campuses. The workshops I conducted at the Bay Area Writing Project in Berkeley (and then at many of its satellite projects as it grew to become the National Writing Project) proved that teachers in the grade and high schools also found the connection between measurement and teaching interesting and important. Increasingly in recent years, faculty have come to me after attending my workshops at schools and universities, asking where the materials and ideas of the workshop could be found in print. This book is my attempt to meet that need in the larger context of general concern about student writing performance. (White, 1994b, pp. xv-xvi)

Such dissemination, of course—through *workshops*, *materials*, and *this book*, among others—helped determine the efficacy of the local "solution" and its potential for adaptation to other like situations. In similar fashion, information about DSP has appeared in various journals, including *Assessing Writing*, *College Composition and Communication*, and *WPA: Writing Program Administration*; at conferences like WPA; in at least one volume devoted exclusively to the topic (Royer & Gilles, 2003), and not surprisingly in the 21st century, a website for DSP.

A SELF-DESIGNED EXIGENCE

During the third wave of writing assessment (focused on portfolios and other authentic assessment practices), however, and into what is now taking form as the fourth wave—characterized in part by the increased participation of the federal government in postsecondary assessment and by our own work in outcomes development and assessment (Yancey, forthcoming)—another means of developing and disseminating new practices was initiated. Rather than the new practice being created in response to a single local exigence, this second means of developing innovative assessment practice relied on a *self-created exigence* independent of any specific local need. In some ways and as I explain, this model has accounted for much of what we know about portfolios today, in both print and electronic versions. Here, I outline two such efforts, articulating how they developed and were practiced and what they have contributed to the field.

The first, Portnet, founded by Michael Allen (1995) in concert with nine other colleagues around the country, functioned as something of a prototype for the second. Existing as a working group for about 4 years, it targeted three goals: raising new questions about portfolio assessment, helping to refine portfolio practice in a wide range of settings, and designing a new means of collaborating on and researching portfolio assessment questions. Created 10 years later, the second effort, the Inter/National Coalition for Electronic Portfolio Research (INCEPR), has cast a much wider and more systematic net. In its 6 years of existence and through a cohort model, the INCEPR has brought together assessment practitioners and other campus stakeholders from multiple disciplines in over 50 institutions in six countries to document the learning that takes place in electronic portfolios. And as I detail here, a good deal of what we know about eportfolio assessment has been developed through this model, and its current efforts are taking up the most interesting, challenging, and promising work in electronic portfolio assessment today, that is, work on the vocabulary and practices keyed to the unique affordances of eportfolios.

PORTNET BEGINS

At the Miami University conference on portfolio assessment in 1992, Michael Allen invited nine colleagues from across the nation, literally from Florida to Alaska, to work with him on a portfolio project. More specifically, he wanted us, first, to contribute portfolios from our campuses and, second, to read portfolios from other campuses so that we could learn something about what he called "outside reading." Each of us, he explained, would select from 5 to 10 portfolios from our classes or programs—from basic writing program portfolios to a WAC-inflected class portfolio, they represented a wide range of writing situations—and share them with someone else in the group so that we could all read, review, score, and discuss that process. Or, explore how we read portfolios of student writing.

> As Allen explains, the initial process was a bit cumbersome. To prepare, we were asked to write up a program description, and send those materials along with scores, rubrics, scoring guides, anchor portfolios—anything used in scoring their local portfolios—to me [Allen]; I would take out the scores and send the rest of the package on to an "outside" reader, who would send scores and comments about the portfolios and the program back to me, when I would return them to the local readers.

> This process would be completed twice, to ensure that each portfolio set was read by two outside readers. In so doing, I wanted to construct an "outside reading" procedure that would mirror the way most programmatic portfolios seemed to be evaluated locally: by having two readers read, and then having a third read in case of a conflict between the two readers' scores. (1995, p. 69)

As he notes, the scoring procedure was adopted from holistic assessment, and in this sense it was the kind of alignment characterizing the earlier waves of writing assessment: the technology used in one means of assessment, in this case the holistic assessment of wave two, being used for another, the portfolio assessment of wave three. But more importantly, Allen's more specific question about reading focused on what he saw as a *misalignment*: the role of calibration or norming in holistic assessment and whether it was even needed for portfolios:

> I wondered if outside readings would be useful (or even interesting) without the standardizing procedures of inter-rater reliability and other elements of psychometrics. Moreover, I wanted to keep the experiment to two outside readers; the simple weight of logistics—photocopying portfolios and accompanying materials (program descriptions, etc.), sending them out, and waiting for people to have the time to read—suggested that asking unpaid readers to read a third set of "conflict" portfolios might be too much to ask. After all the scores were in, I would send out a comparison of scores, and we would see what kind of agreement or disagreement we had among local and outside readers, and also what kinds of reader problems and portfolio issues might have arisen as outside readers commented on local portfolios and programs. As I explained this project to others, some of the people I first talked to were suspicious of my focus on agreement among scores but saw the project as a way of exploring related issues: How do we read portfolios? Do different people read different parts of portfolios differently? How many different types of portfolios are there? What, ultimately, is a portfolio? All these questions seemed a logical extension of the project; even before it started, the project had started to change and grow. (1995, pp. 69-70)

From that project came many presentations, several publications, and at least some of what we know about print portfolios. Interestingly, as suggested above, we began by mailing student portfolios to each other, and we seemed more like a collection of individuals than a group. But that changed once we created our own listserv: Portnet as group *and* site *and* research project was born. Because the electronic environment was new, we had to learn new ways of behaving, and because we did not know everyone in the group initially, we had to be particularly sensitive to that which we could *not* see. When the project concluded—and like many collaborative and virtual projects, it had a lifespan—we had learned a good deal, especially in two areas: about portfolio assessment issues, especially about the role of shared evaluation; and about structures that foster such collaborative work.

PROCESSES, LEARNING, AND COLLABORATION

To talk about our process, we used the language of the old technology, but largely as a fulcrum for consideration of how the new reading process related to the old. Some members of Portnet likened our reading to the kind of "training" or "norming" session that precedes a scoring session. Others, like Allen himself, saw the process differently.

> There wasn't the same drive to "calibrate" our readings so that we all read the same way, as there often is in a more formal "training" session; moreover, our scoring was as much a discussion of meta-issues (how should we read a reflective letter?) as it was about scoring the portfolio, and certainly the "talk" was far more varied (informal, formal, analytical) than most training or scoring sessions we had been involved with. (1995, pp. 82-83)

As important from my perspective, it was in the midst of and through this "meta" process that a good deal of what I learned took place. In looking at others' portfolios, for instance, I saw for myself how important it is to have an organizational schema for the portfolio: Without it, a reader is simultaneously trying to discern organization while trying to read, a case of multitasking or cognitive overload. A more theoretical issue for me, however, was reflection: In our reading process, the question of the genre of reflection inside the portfolio loomed large. We were very divided about the preferred genre, for example, as well as about what it is we really were interested in having students contribute. We vacillated between wanting students to "prove" to us what they had learned and wanting them to have the freedom to *explore* what they *might* have learned, a conflict that continues to vex the role of reflection in portfolio assessment even today (Hesse, personal communication, 2010).

This kind of thinking, growing out of our collaborative review of portfolios and portfolio reflections and discussions, informed the theory of reflection that I later articulated in *Reflection in the Writing Classroom* (1998). There, among other kinds of reflection and reflective practices, I defined a specific kind of *portfolio reflection*—reflection-in-presentation—that benefited from the kinds of insights my colleagues made. George Meece's sense of the potential capaciousness of the reflective text, for instance, helped me see that our need for assessment ought not to trump a student's opportunity to learn and that such an opportunity to learn is social, in dialogue, and *transacting with a reader.*

> Portnet . . . [has] read . . . [portfolios] together and . . . thought together—most of this online—about programmatic portfolios, about the role of reflection-in-presentation in an assessment context. . . . In response to what it is that we expect of reflection, George Meese, for instance, seems to place reflection within the genre of the capacious essay identified earlier: as a text that both satisfies a writer's need to make sense of something while at the same time *transacting* with a reader. (quoted in Yancey, 1998, p. 163)

What each of us gained individually from Portnet varied: I was more interested in reflection, others in the influence of specific assignments on portfolio reading and on how representations of process contributed to our constructions of student development. Our learning was also collaborative. Allen's interest in the reading process was one we all shared, and it was the beginning point of our work together, both as a research group and as our shared activity: It always began with reading. On the basis of this work, Allen began to theorize what he called "shared evaluation":

> As a term, "shared evaluation" implies social construction even as "validity" and "reliability" imply the ideal text against which individual student texts are evaluated. As we have practiced it (and if we have indeed practiced it), a shared evaluation rests upon the following features:
> 1. A tentative score based on an evaluator's reading of a student text.
> 2. An openness of evaluators to other evaluators' perspectives.
> 3. An exchange of discursive analysis of the student text.
> 4. An examination of assessment issues that may arise from the exchange of evaluators' perspectives. (Allen, 1995, p. 84)

Put in these terms, the theory sounds dry, but the language we created put a vernacular face on an intellectually rich finding:

> Pat [Belanoff] and Mary Kay [Crouch] were able to do what participants soon called "putting on another hat." Familiar with their own portfolio programs, and highly critical of the other program, the outside readers could nonetheless assume some of Keats' "negative capability" and momentarily change their roles, put aside their local criteria and standards in order to be fair, and evaluate the portfolios according to the outside program's criteria and standards. (Allen, 1995, p. 76)

Allen's (1995) argument is not that this "shared evaluation" can replace current methods of large-scale scoring, but rather that it can lead to increased fairness:

> an outside reading, response, or check (the choice probably depending on one's philosophical orientation) can lead a local assessment procedure to increased fairness. The cooperative, social construction implied by "shared evaluation" seems connected to a fundamental aspect of hermeneutics—not so much as Moss defined it, but as Richard Rorty (1979) expressed it in *Philosophy and the Mirror of Nature*. He saw hermeneutics as opposed to epistemology (read: "empiricism" or "psychometrics") and saw the differences in terms of conversation, whether such conversation is united by a common goal or a common "civility." (p. 84)

Interestingly, it is this kind of process that provides, some 15 years later, the basic model for the Association of American Colleges and Universities (AACU) VALUE project. Funded by State Farm Insurance and the Fund for the Improvement of Postsecondary Education (FIPSE), the AACU VALUE project brought together faculty in different disciplines, including writing, from across the country to engage in designing scoring guides that can be used in an Allen-like shared evaluation process:

> It builds on a philosophy of learning assessment that privileges multiple expert judgments of the quality of student work over reliance on standardized tests administered to samples of students outside of their required courses. The assessment approaches that VALUE advances are based on the shared understanding of faculty and academic professionals on campuses from across the country. (VALUE website)

In a second phase of the project, faculty also applied the guides to eportfolios. In the process of creating guides, faculty from various institutional types gathered together electronically, much as in Portnet, and in designing guides, they thought of them much like the *WPA Outcomes Statement for First-Year Composition* (Council of Writing Program Administrators, 2000, 2008), that is, as boundary objects that speak to national outcomes but that can be adapted at each local campus. And as in Portnet, both VALUE processes engaged faculty in learning—about their own values, about outcomes, and about guides—in "meta" conversational spaces.[2]

But there was a third kind of learning as well: We also learned something about how to make such collaborative, self-initiated work "work"—through creating structures that supported it; tapping and designing rhythms that worked in concert with the structures; and deliberately flagging verbal signals we sent each other. Allen was the leader of the group: He organized our efforts, set our schedules, convened our online conversations. But as a leader, he was facilitative, toggling back and forth between leading us and following our lead. Over time, especially once the online environment *became* our research space, we found that a monthly review provided enough material and activity for us to think with and not so much as to overwhelm us. The most productive schedule, in terms of activity and "findings," involved each of us taking a month for a set of "our" portfolios; the institutional host could then pose specific questions, learn from our colleagues how they read our students' work, and take that back to our own campuses while at the same time continue to pursue our shared questions, whether they be on reading practices, reflection, or signs of student development.

In sum, functioning through both alignment and misalignment, Portnet was a learning experience in *many* ways.

THE INTER/NATIONAL COALITION FOR ELECTRONIC PORTFOLIO RESEARCH BEGINS

About 10 years later, motivated by questions about whether or not electronic portfolios were contributing to the learning of students and interested in providing an empirical answer to that question, Barbara Cambridge and I founded the National Coalition for Electronic Portfolio Research (NCEPR). As was the case with Portnet, NCEPR was located in a self-designed exigence, and in this case our intent was twofold: to respond to the individual needs of campuses but also, and more importantly, to address the concerns and questions that we in an emerging field shared. Our model was at once simple but innovative: invite institutions to apply; select 10 applications from which we would form a cohort that would collaborate for 3 years; and require the institutions to fund the individual team's efforts. Given that practice often anticipates theory, the motivations of institutions to join such a group were similar, as Cambridge (2009) explains:

> Coalition organizers, experienced with print and digital portfolios, recognized that research needed to catch up with practice. They realized that as the power of electronic portfolios became more and more apparent, practitioners would want to go to scale, a move requiring agreements about learning outcomes being supported through portfolios and infusion of resources justified by evidence. They realized also that although many faculty members were asking excellent questions about their practices, designed inquiries into those practices were few and far between. The Coalition was established to bring together practitioners ready to ask penetrating questions about their practices and ready to apply findings to improve their practices and those of others (pp. xi-xii).

Our first two cohorts, of the six who have thus far constituted the Coalition, pursued their own questions—IUPUI, for instance, pursuing ways of connecting a new general education program with an outcomes-based electronic portfolio, and Virginia Tech examining the influence of a systematic and continuing eportfolio on the development of preservice teachers—as we together studied reflection in theory and in practice, the latter through analysis of student artifacts. The third cohort, cosponsored by NASPA (Student Affairs Administrators in Higher Education), included teams from the United States, Canada, and the United Kingdom and focused on eportfolios as a site for integrative learning in three contexts: learning in school contexts, cocurricular learning, and learning outside of school. The fourth cohort, based in the United Kingdom and including teams from the United Kingdom, Europe, and one from the United States, focused on eportfolios and Professional Development Planning (PDP), an initiative introduced by the government as part of "widening participation," which is the phrase used to describe efforts to include students who historically have not attended college. The fifth cohort, which concludes in the spring of 2011, began exploring issues directly related to assessment: The University of Cincinnati, for instance, studied the efficacy of the Collegiate Learning Assessment (CLA) relative to the eportfolio, and the University of Denver has researched the role of the reflective text in their writing eportfolio.

21ST CENTURY COLLABORATION AND EARLY FINDINGS

Given that we are now in the 21st century, we have built into the Coalition model multiple forms of communication and dissemination. We meet twice a year, we host live web chats, and we have both a website and a NING site, the former to share meeting information and reports of research with the wider world, the latter a space for our library of materials and own discussion. In addition, we have presented at many conferences—discipline-specific conferences like CCCC, higher education conferences like AACU, and assessment conferences like the IUPUI Assessment Institute. Our work has been published in multiple venues, from AACU's *Peer Review* to the web journal *Academic Commons*, from the *Journal of General Education* to our own volume published by Stylus (Cambridge, Cambridge, & Yancey, 2009).

In assembling such a diverse group of eportfolio researchers and in moving outside our familiar and comfortable "enclave," we have done exactly what White advised 16 years ago. As he noted, "[a]n assessment program with wide concerns can be successful only if it makes use of the contributions varied perspectives can make" (1994a, p. 25). In our case, the *assessment program* is an inter-institutional one with widely divergent institutional interests, but with a shared commitment to student learning. Likewise, because we are diverse—in addition to participants from multiple countries, we have every institutional type but one represented (an absence we are seeking to remedy)—we include the multiple perspectives White recommends, and because of our invitational design—where schools literally have to sign on to a shared agenda in advance, and schools need to support it materially—and our "open source" sharing of results on our website, we make visible our directions and aims. In White's (1994a) recommendations, he forecasts the features that we have designed into this collaborative model:

> In the same way, scholarship in writing assessment needs to set agendas through negotiation by interested parties. We should state overtly where we are coming from and why we select the issues we do, we should make our invisible agendas visible, and we should consider how those in different places might view our data, theories, or findings. (p. 25)

Two examples of specific institutional findings illustrate the efficacy of our model and the role it has played in what we can now claim about eportfolio assessment and its role in fostering learning and its role in making knowledge. A first example is the set of research projects that institutions have taken up. LaGuardia Community College and Kapiliani Community College, for example, were very interested in the effect on students of creating eportfolios, especially in three terms: student engagement, course completion, and retention. In other words, they wanted to know what Cambridge and I had wanted to know when we began: Do eportfolios work? Through mapping student participation in eportfolio projects to larger data sets, both schools began to find an answer:

> [w]hen the eportfolio is designed by the student as much as by the institution, implementation efforts are more likely to succeed. As important, where programs are successful in so motivating students, they see higher rates on key educational metrics when comparing students creating eportfolios with students who haven't. Such metrics include higher rates of student engagement on a local measure of engagement (Kirkpatrick et al. [at Kapiliani, 2009]) as well as on the nationally normed Community College Survey of Student Engagement; higher rates of course completion; and higher rates of retention (Eynon [at LaGuardia, 2009]). In these terms, eportfolios work. (Yancey, 2009a, p. 28)

In a very different project (but in the same cohort as Kapiliani), the University of Georgia was interested in writing and the ability of the eportfolio to support revision. More specifically, the team investigated three questions. "First, *does* revision improve the quality of written products in FYC ePortfolios? Second, *how* does what very successful and unsuccessful revisers say about their own revision processes help us understand revision as a practice? Finally, what role is played by the "e" in ePortfolios?" (Desmet, Griffin, Miller, Balthazor, & Cummings, 2009, p. 156). Of course, what one hopes for is that what we in composition have preached for years—that revision enhances writing—is an accurate claim. In one case study deriving from their research, what Desmet et al. found, however, was much more nuanced:

> [t]he writer fails to achieve the sense of an overarching structure that characterizes expert writers; she describes revision as a set of steps or perhaps epiphanies, drawing systematically on a series of tropes from her rhetorical inventory rather than constructing a new metaphor that could encompass her whole experience. Her sense of the writing process is more segmented than recursive. So while this writer's reflective rhetoric does not place her clearly as either a novice or an experienced reviser, as defined by past studies and theories, what seems significant in her case is the strong disparity between the persuasiveness of her Reflective Introduction in the ePortfolio and the ratings of her revised essay by anonymous raters. This student communicates a better understanding of revision than she is yet able to put into practice. As a writer, she may still be "in process," but the evidence of her ePortfolio gives a more complex, and encouraging picture of her achievement in FYC than can the revised, polished essays the portfolio frames and contextualizes. (p. 161)

This finding is interesting on three levels. On the first level, it connects nicely to the issue of "fictionalizing" that both Charles Schuster and I have raised. Schuster's (1994) view is that the reflective letter invites a fictionalizing that is at odds with the value of the portfolio text writ large, mine (a) that the value of such fictionalizing depends on context; in a classroom it can be valuable as a kind of rehearsal for students to fictionalize themselves into a rhetorical situation, and indeed it may be a developmental phase; (b) that the ability to fictionalize may exceed the ability to implement the fictions imagined, as we see in the University of Georgia study; and (c) that in an assessment context it can be tricky.[3] On the second level, this finding is different from the LaGuardia/Kapiliani finding in that it does not map to larger data sets, but instead to the theories of novice and expert writers that have informed our field (see, e.g., Beaufort, 2007), indicating that these twin concepts may be too dichotomous to provide a sufficiently sophisticated map of writing development. On the third level, this assessment activity is, in Condon's terms described in Chapter 13, doubly generative: It contributes both to what we understand how about portfolio assessment works *and* to our understanding of development in writing.

Beyond individual findings such as those detailed above, we also articulated new findings generated from the collaborative exploration. For example, as indicated previously, we studied reflection exclusively in cohorts one and two, and to a lesser extent in other cohorts as well. Based on this research (an account of which is provided in Cambridge et al., 2009), we began articulating what we might call propositions. Two of them, for instance, focus on the relationship between reflection and arrangement: We understand that

- the structures we provide will shape reflection. Where the structure provides scaffolding, where it invites connections, it invites the meaning-making characteristic of deep learning.
- asking students to create their own structures may be a critical move, allowing them to articulate both curricular understandings and personal connections, and in the process demonstrating the mapping development we associate with expertise. (Yancey, 2009b, p. 14)

Taken together, of course, these propositions create a new exigence for portfolio assessment.

COHORT SIX: EXPLORING THE E IN EPORTFOLIOS AND ITS ROLE IN ASSESSMENT

In 2009, as we—and since early on Darren Cambridge was a coleader as well—considered what a sixth cohort might look like, we decided that the eportfolio community was prepared to address questions focused on assessment. In other words, practice had developed to a point where the need for assessment keyed to three dimensions of eportfolios—the multimedia artifacts in portfolios, the networking capability of eportfolios, and eportfolios as a composition (Yancey, 2004)—required a cohort-like focused inquiry. The sixth cohort, including teams from the United States and Australia, has been assembled to take up this work specifically; and several of the institutions have linked our project to institutional accreditation and/or Quality Enhancement Plans (QEPs, the mid-cycle assessment and resource-building process used by the South Atlantic/SACS accrediting body).

In establishing this cohort, like Allen before us, we operated on a principle of alignment and one of misalignment. In carrying forward the collaborative research, we were aligned with earlier practice; in studying the specific affordances of eportfolios, we capitalized on what we saw as a *misalignment* between the kinds of work we see in eportfolios and the language and values used to describe that work. The perception of misalignment draws from several sources. A first is the 2011 NAEP, which is requiring students to compose at the keyboard, and thus assumes a digital technology informed construct of writing (Murphy & Yancey, 2007). A second is the previously mentioned AACU VALUE project. As worthy as it is—and to engage faculty in coming together to express their values is worthy, much as we see in the WPA Outcomes effort—the results are, as I have written elsewhere, technology invisible:

> This model of eportfolio assessment thus presents a strong design, with the student as knowledge-maker at the center. At the same time, it's fair to note that nothing in the AACU outcomes stipulates technological expertise or understands composing in a specifically digital way. It doesn't preclude such composing, either, of course. But in this sense, this eportfolio is technology invisible. (Yancey, 2010, p. 193)

Relative to an eportfolio, such invisibility means that one cannot assess the work itself. For example, in such a model, one cannot acknowledge the links that may be at the heart of a digital portfolio, nor the interface design. This of course more generally means that the measure is not valid—if we take one component of validity to be consonance between work assigned and work assessed—the affordances and values of work itself needs to be built into the assessment model.

Although the cohort is just beginning, it is useful to note the four themes organizing our research. Each, as indicated below, is stated as a proposition that we will reiteratively test over our 3 years together.

- Interaction of Pieces of Evidence
  - For meaningful assessment, interaction of pieces of evidence within an eportfolio is more important than single pieces of evidence.
- Relationship between Evidence and Reflection
  - Reflection on pieces of evidence within an eportfolio and on the eportfolio as a whole provides information for assessment that is not available by other means.
- Meaningful Comparison without Standardization
  - Eportfolios enable meaningful comparison of student learning across institutions (and other contexts) without standardization.
- Material Practices
  - The material practice of eportfolio composition generates distinctive knowledge about learning.

The first two of these, we believe, are well grounded in the research. The third, given the push-back on portfolios of the kind we see evidence of in the higher education community (see, e.g., Shavelson, Klein, & Benjamin, 2009), will be more difficult to evidence. The fourth is an area directly related to the issue of construct but conceptualized very differently. We are hopeful that at the end of our process, we will have much to contribute to the field.

CONCLUSION

In closing Chapter 13, Condon states what he sees as the potential of portfolios:

> Portfolios can, of course, accommodate the need for regimentation, for placements, rankings, and judgments. But even the most casual user of a portfolio sees the potential for more. My students readily see the material differences in the learning experience that engages them in constructing a portfolio, as opposed to the learning experience that culminates in a test. Faculty portfolio raters testify that exposure to actual student performances on actual classroom assignments leads raters to change their own expectations and their own assignments for the better when they move back into their teaching roles. Portfolio based writing assessment is materially and operationally different from previous kinds of assessment, and while we have so far established that portfolio ratings can operate within accepted assessment parameters, we have also established that portfolios help us answer questions that former methods cannot. (p. 241)

As is no doubt obvious, I concur. And as important, we can make such an observation based on the research, of course, of those who have come before. It is still common for scholars to focus on the institutional exigence, and such focus will continue to help us refine current practices and develop new ones. But alongside this model is now another, the collaborative model, located in a self-designed exigence. As represented in the two groups profiled here—Portnet and the I/NCEPR—this kind of collaborative effort looks backward and forward. In the first instance, looking backward, these efforts have aligned some of their practices with those which came before; looking forward, Portnet and I/NCEPR located their work in a misalignment, a point of dissonance that provided a site for invention.

Stated simply: located in multiple diversities, Portnet and I/NCEPR point the way toward new ways of identifying critical questions, of organizing methods to inquire into them, of producing new knowledge, and of designing new ways of sharing both their knowledge and progress.

ENDNOTES

1. As Bill Condon in Chapter 13 makes clear, such alignment comes at a cost.
2. As was the case with Portnet, a good deal of what was learned in the AACU VALUE effort occurred in the meta-conversations.
3. This view of reflection is, of course, very different from the view put forward by White. As I have stated elsewhere:

   > Our *understanding* of reflection, and of its role in portfolios and in learning, has likewise changed. Early on in the portfolio movement, Chris Anson categorized reflection as a secondary text in dialogue with—but mostly in support of—the primary texts of a portfolio, a view that many portfolio scholars shared. In my *Reflection in the Writing Classroom*, I suggested reflective texts weren't secondary but were primary even if they were different that primary texts, that the relationship between the kinds of texts was more dialogic. More recently, Ed White has suggested that the reflective text can function as a surrogate for the full portfolio in an assessment context; he thus sees it as a pseudo- and global primary text. (Yancey, 2011, p. 734, italics added)

   Given these two divergent views, what role does reflection play in assessment and curricula? Current thinking is informed by two important theories. One is that reflective texts and portfolio texts serve different functions, are equally valuable, and work together.

REFERENCES

AACU VALUE Project. (2007-2010). *Valid assessment of learning in undergraduate education*. Washington, DC: Association of American Colleges and Universities. Web.

Allen, M. (1995). Valuing differences: Portnet's first year. *Assessing Writing, 2*(1), 67-91.

Beaufort, A. (2007). *Writing in college and beyond*. Logan, UT: Utah State University Press.

Bitzer, L. (1968). The rhetorical situation. *Philosophy and Rhetoric, 1*(1), 1-14.

Blakesley, D., Harvey, E., & Reynolds, E. (2003). Southern Illinois Carbondale as an institutional model: The English 100/101 stretch and directed self placement program. In D. Royer & R. Gilles (Eds.), *Directed self placement: Principles and practices* (pp. 207-243). Cresskill, NJ: Hampton Press.

Cambridge, B. (2009). Introduction. In D. Cambridge, B. Cambridge, & K. B. Yancey (Eds.), *Electronic portfolios 2.0: Emergent research on implementation and impact* (pp. xi-xvi). Washington, DC: Stylus.

Cambridge, D., Cambridge, B., & Yancey, K. B. (Eds.). (2009). *Electronic portfolios 2.0: Emergent research on implementation and impact*. Washington, DC: Stylus.

Council of Writing Program Administrators (2000, 2008). *WPA Outcomes Statement for First-Year Composition.* Web.

Desmet, C., Griffin, J., Miller, D., Balthazor, R., & Cummings, R. (2009). Re-visioning revision with ePortfolios in the University of Georgia first-year composition program. In D. Cambridge, B. Cambridge, & K. B. Yancey (Eds.), *Electronic portfolios 2.0: Emergent research on implementation and impact* (pp. 155-165). Washington, DC: Stylus.

Howard, R. (2001). Assumptions and applications of student self-assessment. In J. Smith & K. B. Yancey (Eds.), *Student self-assessment and development in writing* (pp. 35-58). Cresskill, NJ: Hampton Press.

Inter/National coalition for electronic portfolio research. (2003-present). Web.

Murphy, S., & Yancey, K. B. (2007). Construct and consequence: Validity in writing assessment. In C. Bazerman (Ed.), *A handbook of research on writing: History, Society, school, individual, text* (pp. 365-387). New York, NY: Routledge.

Royer, D. J., & Gilles, R. (Eds.). (2003) *Directed self placement: Principles and practices*. Cresskill, NJ: Hampton Press.

Schuster, C. (1994). Climbing the slippery slope of writing assessment; The programmatic use of writing portfolios. In L. Black, D. Daiker, J. Sommers, & G. Stygall (Eds.), *New directions in portfolio assessment: Reflective practice, critical theory, and large-scale scoring* (pp. 314-325). Portsmouth, NH: Boynton/Cook.

Shavelson, R., Klein, S., & Benjamin, R. (2009). The limitations of portfolios. *Inside higher ed*. Web.

White, E. M. (1994a). Issues and problems in writing assessment. *Assessing Writing, 1*(1), 11-28.

White, E. M. (1994b). *Teaching and assessing writing: Recent advances in understanding, evaluating, and improving student performance*. San Francisco, CA: Jossey-Bass.

Yancey, K. B. (1998). *Reflection in the writing classroom*. Logan, UT: Utah State University Press.

Yancey, K. B. (1999). Looking back as we look forward: Historicizing writing assessment. *College Composition and Communication, 50*(3), 483-503.

Yancey, K. B. (2004). Postmodernism, palimpsest, and portfolios: Theoretical issues in the representation of student work. *College Composition and Communication, 55*(4), 738-762.

Yancey, K. B. (2009a). Electronic portfolios a decade into the twenty-first century: What we know, what we need to know. *Peer Review, 11*(1), 28-33.

Yancey, K. B. (2009b) Reflection and electronic portfolios: Inventing the self and reinventing the university. In D. Cambridge, B. Cambridge, & K. B. Yancey (Eds.), *Electronic portfolios 2.0: Emergent research on implementation and impact* (pp. 5-17). Washington, DC: Stylus.

Yancey, K. B. (2010). Electronic portfolios and writing assessment: A work in progress. In M. C. Paretti & K. Powell (Eds.), *Assessment in writing. Assessment in the disciplines* (pp. 183-205). Tallahassee, FL: Association of Institutional Research.

Yancey, K. B. (2011). Portfolios, learning, and agency: Promises, perceptions, possibilities. *JAC, 31*(3-4), 717-736.

Yancey, K. B. (forthcoming). Writing assessment in the early 21st century: A primer. In K. Ritter (Ed.), *Defining composition studies: Research, scholarship, and inquiry for the twenty-first century*. Logan, UT: Utah State University Press.

AFTERWORD

EMW Reflection: Talk about peak experiences! In May and June 2011, we toured Peru, an exhilarating trip. Much of the time, we were close to 15,000 feet high in the Andes, where the air is thin and the climbing strenuous. When I compare this fellow on the top of the world with the boy in Brooklyn, the first photo in this book, both the similarities and differences are striking. It has been quite a trip.

Photo by Frank Sposito

AFTERWORD
LOOKING BACKWARD AND FORWARD

Edward M. White

When I began working in the area of writing assessment in 1971, a collection of essays like this one would have been beyond imagining. Charged as I was that year by the other English chairs in the (then) California State College system with finding out what was known among English faculty about the subject, I sought out scholars, advisers, consultants, even anyone mildly curious about it. I drew almost a total blank. There were a few college professors who had participated in an ETS Advanced Placement scoring, as I had, and a few officers in professional organizations such as MLA and NCTE who had vague memories of someone somewhere who might know something; I diligently pursued all leads but they led to what I later called a "lateral passing movement": No one confessed to first-hand knowledge about such matters, but they could name others who might, although when I reached them they all denied the charge. I was left with two books from 1963, both of which tangentially dealt with writing assessment: Kitzhaber's (1963) analysis of the writing program at Dartmouth College, based on an elaborate error count of student writing, and a national study of writing research by Braddock, Lloyd Jones, and Schoer (1963) proclaiming that our field was like chemistry as it was emerging from alchemy. It would be 6 years before the first collection of essays on the subject emerged, *Evaluating Writing: Describing, Measuring,*

Judging (Cooper & Odell, 1977). Meanwhile, I was on my own, standing alone, almost wholly ignorant of a field whose complexity I hardly knew about, with my research skill tested only by my dissertation on theory of comedy as manifest in Jane Austen's fiction.

Those who taught writing courses in American colleges and universities 40 years ago were usually literature professors with little or no interest in or understanding of rhetoric or writing pedagogy. Freshman English, as the required course was called, was generally an introduction to the study of literature and the assumption behind the curriculum was that students would become acceptable college writers by reading and writing about literature. Classroom instruction focused on the reading of literature and served as a kind of introduction to the English major. The same assumptions were made in the high schools, and there was just enough evidence that such a curriculum worked pretty well for the most talented and privileged students that few questioned it. Although an increasing number of college students demonstrated little or no ability to write college papers, it was easy and customary to blame the previous teachers for low standards and to drop such students as not ready for college work. Assessment rested wholly in the teacher's hands.

Meanwhile, as the testing industry grew in size and importance, led by the College Board and the Educational Testing Service, new standards for assessment began to emerge from the social sciences and statistics, and new pressures for opening college education to new kinds of students began to appear throughout American society. Furthermore, these outside assessments had begun to affect college admissions, through the College Board examinations, and high school college curricula and standards, through the Advanced Placement Program and, later, through the College Level Examination Program. The book-length study by Elliot (2005) of these often unwelcome outside assessments on colleges and universities illuminates this interaction. The discipline of educational measurement sought to bring statistical authority and accountability into the individualistic and wide-ranging academic world of English teachers, who reacted with suspicion and hostility to a view of its work that appeared to be, and often was, reductionist. That collision is still continuing and appears throughout this book in a variety of ways. But what is most remarkable about this book is the assumption by most of the contributors that educational measurement and writing instruction have become partners rather than opponents, that this shotgun marriage will last and perhaps even bear valuable progeny.

I had been made an "expert" in the field by appointment 40 years ago, though I was a fairly typical English professor, trained in literary history and theory. Now I had to earn some credentials in assessment, and fast. The only way to do this, I realized quickly, was to try to bridge the large gap between the two worlds I have been describing: that of literature-oriented writing teachers and that of statistically oriented measurement specialists. I do not repeat here the detailed story I told in "The Origins of the Modern Era of Writing Assessment" (2001), but I see now that I did have two accidental attributes working in my favor: As a writer and teacher, I knew how complicated writing was and so I had a deep suspicion of oversimplification; as an experienced English department chair, I knew how important genuine consultation with my peers and considered political responses would be. I also had enjoyed mathematics in school and did not share the deep suspicion of numbers that most of my English department colleagues felt. In addition, now, in semiretirement, as I read through the essays in the collection you have in your hands, I have come to realize that almost everything I did emerged from a set of principles that seemed just common sense to me at the time and that many of these same threads still occupy the many scholars who have contributed to this volume:

1. Writing is a complex and crucial ability, developed over an extended period of time, and essential for thought, learning, and (see Aristotle and Thomas Jefferson) citizenship.
2. Writing assessment is much more than testing; it involves understanding writing pedagogy, curriculum, outcomes, and data management. It necessarily involves more than one discipline.

THE COMPLEXITY AND IMPORTANCE OF WRITING

Writing is such a complex endeavor that it should be no surprise that conflicting definitions of college writing are common. (See, e.g., the two volumes published by the National Council of Teachers of English entitled *What Is College-Level Writing?* [2006, 2010] and Peter Elbow's review essay). The long history of rhetoric is replete with connections of writing to thinking itself and to the public function of political speech. Different definitions of writing in college lead to different pedagogies, which in turn give birth to different ways of assessing the effectiveness of writing instruction. As long as these differences were neither discussed nor seen as important, everyone involved could go about their work in relative isolation, comfortable with their own practices. But the collision of measurement specialists and their claims to represent the outcomes of instruction, driven by accountability demands that led two thirds of the states to mandate postsecondary assessment by 1989 (Cohen & Kisher, 2010), brought the vague and sometimes contradictory claims and goals of college writing programs into the open. A steady stream of federal reports such as *Straight Talk about College Costs and Prices* (National Commission on the Cost of Higher Education,

1998) and *A Test of Leadership: Charting the Future of U. S. Higher Education* (U.S. Department of Education, 2006), led to accountability demands that required all involved to define with some clarity just what they envisioned the goals of writing instruction to be. At the same time, on-campus competition for funding, in the face of regular and increasing budget cuts, led to faculty and administrative questions about the efficacy of composition requirements. Those defending those requirements were being asked to define their goals with new clarity and also to provide some kind of evidence that those goals were being met. These demands often led to healthy, if frustrating discussion about just what college writing instruction was designed to accomplish.

For instance, whereas statements from administrators and the public about the importance of writing in college are more or less routine, in practice many administrators and faculty outside those teaching composition and rhetoric see writing in reductive ways—as spelling, say, or fine points of usage. Thus it is common to find writing assessments ignoring such matters as organization of ideas, use of evidence to support arguments, clarity of thought, creativity, and other sophisticated matters that have concerned teachers since the age of Pericles. On the California campus where I spent most of my career, I maintained a continuous and frustrating battle with the counseling center about the demeaning way it advised students about their undergraduate writing requirements. Our writing courses, including the advanced ones, were called "remedialwriting," a single word, which needed to be gotten "out of the way," so more important matters could be attended to. The reductionist assessments such attitudes generate are as present now as they were 40 years ago, and the continuing efforts of writing faculty to demonstrate the importance of writing (as thinking made visible) for education and society as a whole are no less strenuous. Those of us most dedicated to the discipline of rhetoric and composition (as it is now called, complete with its own code series from the Classification of Instructional Programs implemented by the National Center for Educational Statistics), are ever ready to remind our colleagues that Thomas Jefferson was most proud of founding the University of Virginia and argued that—because democracy derived its legitimacy from the consent of the governed—an uninformed consent was no consent at all. Yet we continue to confront writing assessments that fail to tell us anything about the complex sociocognitive processes that students will need to master if they are to become truly educated and be able to participate effectively in shared governance.

It was painfully obvious 40 years ago that much of the substance of college writing instruction had been omitted from the writing assessments then in use beyond the individual classroom. At the same time, it was clear that teacher assessment of student writing was way too idiosyncratic to be useful for the many assessments that were taking place outside the classroom. If the goal of attaining meaningful and responsive writing assessments was to be reached, and if writing was to maintain its position as the central and most important foundation for advanced education, some kind of meeting of the minds would have to occur.

I wish I could say that these goals had been achieved during the 40 years I and some others have been pursuing them. Certainly some progress has been made, and much evidence of that progress appears in this book. But the problem of achieving enough consensus on assessment to reinforce the importance of writing remains acute today, indeed, as many chapters in this book make clear, much more so than it was two generations ago. The advent of computer scoring of writing, the appearance of wealthy business moguls as education testing advocates, and the large-scale governmental assessments of students to determine the value of their teachers have brought a new urgency to writing assessment as this book goes to press. These well-intentioned efforts have led to further reductions in the understanding of writing and new simplifications to what is being measured and what it means. As Barry Maid and Barbara D'Angelo put it, with remarkable understatement, "The reality is that teaching writing is not as simple as it used to appear to be" (p. 112). But this volume offers some hope for the future: It demonstrates conclusively that we now have a community of scholars and a body of scholarship focused on the assessment of writing and writing programs that bring together deep understanding of the importance and value of writing and a commitment to responsible writing assessment.

BRINGING TOGETHER THE WORLDS OF WRITING TEACHERS AND OF WRITING ASSESSMENT

The gulf between the worlds those who administer and teach writing in American colleges and universities and of those in the educational measurement community is vast and deep, beyond even what C. P. Snow described as "the two cultures" in 1961 and Hunter Breland recalled in this context in 1996. It illustrates what the linguist Benjamin Whorf (1956) asserted, speaking of different language cultures: Those speaking different languages do not merely see things differently, he argued; they inhabit different worlds. Yet, unless the inhabitants of these worlds can understand enough of each other's perspectives to respect and listen to each other, there is no hope that we will achieve more responsible and more useful writing assessments. Before I speak to some of the ways in which the contributors to this volume have moved us towards this goal, let me define the nature of the gulf.

Those of us steeped in the traditions of the humanities tend to see the world in the light of those traditions, along with a certain self-righteousness about our specialized knowledge. Our discipline goes back thousands of years, to the classical rhetoricians and the ancient poets and bards, and however the realities of a particular classroom in a particular school may overshadow that vision, some glimmer of it remains, at least with some teachers and some students.

Unless those in the educational measurement community have some understanding of this context, they remain forever mystified by certain attitudes writing teachers bring to assessment. Take the concept of *reliability*, for instance. In the measurement community, reliability is a basic requirement for the generation of data; it means your scores show consistency and accuracy. Unless you have meaningful data, you cannot use your results. An unreliable measure is a waste of time and money. It seems so reasonable as to be beyond question. So why does the Americanist on the assessment committee quote Ralph Waldo Emerson, "A foolish consistency is the hobgoblin of little minds"? and act as if reliability is a problem rather than a virtue? Foreign as the concept may be to statistical values, reliability is not a basic good in the humanities. In the arts, differences of opinion are not only to be expected but are to be valued. Which is the best painting by Titian? The best symphony by Beethoven? The strongest argument for the existence of God? What ignoramus would expect agreement of 0.90 or higher on such questions as these? So why should we desire a high rate of agreement on which is the best essay or portfolio in the sample group?

A wise measurement specialist will readily agree that in many matters, particularly in art, disagreement is more valuable than agreement. But then he or she will argue on grounds of fairness to the students taking a test that a rating or a ranking, when necessary, should not depend on the whims of individual raters but rather on a group agreement on particular standards. And, perhaps, even attempt to make the case that if the raters cannot agree on common standards, they need to seek an assessment device which will be demonstrably more fair to the students. The point is not that reliability is a universal value, but that in a testing situation all the values appropriate to art do not necessarily apply; consistency of grading is, in that case, a higher value than individual expression. Some humanists will not be convinced, but the conversation can go forward toward a compromise resolution.

For the same kinds of reasons, most humanists will never be comfortable with computer scoring of student writing, however much the data show similarities with human scoring. Evaluating writing, for writing specialists, has to do with reading for meaning, not counting such surface matters as grammar and usage, all a computer can do. Writing is intended to convey meaning from one human being to another, and its generation of a score for sorting purposes is a secondary and artificial use. Students who know they are writing only for scoring by computer will use their ingenuity to impress the computer (by, for instance, omitting verbs and using many semicolons, as one computer algorithm has it) instead of accomplishing the intended assignment. Indeed, why not purchase a paper from one of the "essay generator" programs available on the web because all that matters is generation of a grade?

It is important to realize that nobody is "wrong" in this diversity of world views. The measurement specialist is most concerned with the generation of accurate and valid information on student performance, consistent with limited budgets and modern technology, matters frequently neglected in the writing research. I am delighted to see that this collection has a generous sampling of work from that community, although it continues to reflect some of the features of that world that maintain the gulf, such as heavy citations from College Board studies and very few from the composition journals that feature scholarship in writing assessment. (But the writing specialists rarely cite work in the measurement journals, a similar narrowness.) I learned to respect the work of these measurement specialists early on, and I am sometimes embarrassed by my disciplinary colleagues who feel that only they have the right to assess student writing or writing programs. Writing is too important to be closely held by those in the field of rhetoric and composition, and we need to welcome others to the enterprise.

LOOKING FORWARD

I have refrained from citing chapters in this book to illustrate the ways in which they have developed the many threads that now make up the area of writing assessment. In part, this has been because, from John Brereton's opening chapter onward, I have wanted to applaud the originality and creativity of each of the contributors. If I speak in detail about some, I risk ignoring others equally valuable. But I do want to mention in closing the way in which this volume as a whole ends one period of our study and opens up another. Kathi Yancey touches on this prospect for the future in her closing essay about eportfolios, but in one way or another every essay implies new directions for the next 40 years.

It is particularly exciting to me to see some of the contributors using this opportunity to think again about matters that early research, some of it mine, some not, presumably settled. Modern scholarship in composition has not yet learned how to build systematically on the findings of the past. Writing assessment, as a new field within rhetoric and composition, seems to suggest that every project should begin afresh, rather than with a literature review. I applaud John Brereton and Chris Anson, who review and revise early work of their own for this volume, and the team of Mya Poe and Asao Inoue for revisiting and renewing the study I did with Leon Thomas on the racial implications of the Cal State English Placement Test some 30 years ago. Indeed, I cannot think of another replication study in rhetoric and composition, though I can come up with many now classic studies ripe for replication under new conditions. I take this to be another sign of the maturing of the field, with openings to the future, just as significant as the bridging of the gulf between writing and measurement specialists. Indeed, the appearance of this volume itself, unimaginable, as I said at the start, 40 years ago, demonstrates both the maturity of the field and its creative opportunities in the future.

And finally I must express my gratitude to Norbert Elliot and Les Perelman for having the vision for this book, for having the stamina to put it all together, and for encouraging the contributors to do original and creative work. This book may have started with me as a focus but it has grown beyond me in all kinds of ways. I think it marks the beginning of a new phase in writing assessment studies and will remain a landmark for many years. I salute the contributors for their important and original work and the editors for making it all happen. It is surely the best gift a scholar can receive and one I am pleased and proud to share with all those interested in the past and future of writing in American colleges and universities.

REFERENCES

Breland, H. (1996). Computer-assisted writing assessment: The politics of science versus the humanities. In E. M. White, W. D. Lutz, & S. Kamusikiri (Eds.), *Assessment of writing: Politics, policies, practices* (pp. 249-256). New York, NY: Modern Language Association.

Braddock, R., Lloyd-Jones, R., & Schoer, L. (1963). *Research in written composition*. Champaign, IL: National Council of Teachers of English.

Cohen, A. M, & Kisher, C. B. (2010). *The shaping of American higher education: Emergence and growth of the contemporary system* (2nd ed.). San Francisco, CA: Jossey-Bass.

Cooper, C. R., & Odell, L. (Eds.). (1977). *Evaluating writing: Describing, measuring, judging*. Urbana, IL: National Council of Teachers of English.

Elliot, N. (2005). *On a scale: A social history of writing assessment in America*. New York, NY: Peter Lang.

Elbow, P. (2011). What is real college writing? Let the disagreement never end [Review of the books *What is "college level" writing?* By P. Sullivan & H. Tinberg (Eds.), and *What is "college level" writing? Volume 2: Assignments, readings, and student writing samples*, by P. Sullivan, H. Tinberg, & S. Blau (Eds.)]. *Writing Program Administration, 34*(2), 153-161.

Kitzhaber, A. R. (1963). *Themes, theory, and therapy: The teaching of writing in college*. New York, NY: McGraw-Hill.
National Commission on the Cost of Higher Education (1998). *Straight talk about college costs and prices: Report of the National Commission on the Cost of* Higher Education. Phoenix, AZ: Oryx Press.
U.S. Department of Education (2006). *A test of leadership: Charting the future of U.S. higher education*. Washington, DC: U.S. Department of Education.
White, E. M. (1960). *Jane Austen and the art of parody* (Unpublished doctoral dissertation). Harvard University, Cambridge, MA.
White, E. M. (2001). Opening the modern era of writing assessment: A narrative. *College English, 63*(3), 306-320.
Whorf, B. L. (1956). Science and linguistics. In J. B. Carol (Ed.), *Language, thought, and reality: Selected writings* (pp. 207-219). Cambridge, MA: Massachusetts Institute of Technology.

AUTHOR PROFILES

Chris M. Anson is University Distinguished Professor, Professor of English, and Director of the Campus Writing and Speaking Program at North Carolina State University

Doug Baldwin, Executive Director and Strategic Program Advisor for Higher Education Assessment at Educational Testing Service, has worked on writing assessments since 1996. A former high school English teacher and college composition and ESL instructor, Baldwin has worked on numerous performance assessments, both national and international; advised college faculty on writing across the curriculum and rising-junior writing assessments; and published and delivered papers on many facets of constructed-response assessments.

John Brereton is Professor Emeritus, University of Massachusetts, Boston. He also served as Executive Director of the Calderwood Writing Initiative at the Boston Athenaeum.

Bob Broad is Professor of English at Illinois State University. He studies writing assessment, communal assessment, and portfolio assessment. He authored *What We Really Value: Beyond Rubrics in Teaching and Assessing Writing* (2003) and co-authored *Organic Writing Assessment: Dynamic Criteria Mapping in Action* (2009). His scholarship has appeared in the journals *College English*, *Research in the Teaching of English*, *Assessing Writing*, and the *Journal of Writing Assessment*, as well as in several book collections.

Jill Burstein is a Principal Research Scientist in ETS Research & Development. Her expertise and research interests focus on computational linguistics, specifically for the development of educational technology. Her inventions include automated essay scoring systems and tools to support teachers of English learners. She received her BA in Linguistics and Spanish from New York University and her MA and PhD in Linguistics from the City University of New York, Graduate Center.

William Condon is Professor of English at Washington State University. He was Principal Investigator of a 3-year FIPSE grant devoted to faculty development and statewide accountability assessment around teaching critical thinking. Co-author of *Writing the Information Superhighway* and *Assessing the Portfolio: Principles for Theory, Practice, and Research*, he has published articles about writing assessment, program evaluation, and writing across the curriculum.

Barbara J. D'Angelo is Clinical Assistant Professor of Technical Communication at Arizona State University. Her current interests are curriculum development, program assessment, and information literacy.

Gita DasBender is a Senior Faculty Associate in the Department of English at Seton Hall University where she is the Coordinator for Second Language Writing. Her research areas include second language writing assessment, knowledge transfer for multilingual students, critical literacy and generation 1.5 learners, directed self-placement, creative nonfiction, and the essay.

Paul Deane is Principal Research Scientist at ETS in Princeton, New Jersey. He coordinates ETS' research on writing within the CBAL Initiative (Cognitively-Based Assessment of, for, and as Learning) and is a member of the ETS Automated Scoring and Natural Language Processing group. He is a graduate of the University of Chicago, where he received his doctorate in linguistics, and has published extensively on a variety of topics including natural language semantics, grammar and cognition, natural language processing techniques, and writing assessment.

Norbert Elliot is Professor of English at New Jersey Institute of Technology.

Peter Elbow is Professor of English Emeritus at the University of Massachusetts at Amherst. He directed the writing program there and at SUNY Stony Brook—and has taught also at MIT, Franconia College, and

Evergreen State College. At Stony Brook, he and Pat Belanoff inaugurated program-wide portfolio evaluation. His new book, *Vernacular Eloquence: What Speech Can Learn from Writing*, was published in 2012.

Mary Fowles is a Principal Assessment Designer in the Assessment Division of (ETS). During her long career at ETS, she has coordinated the development of a wide range of assessment programs and projects involving essay tests, portfolios, individual presentations, group interactions, and other kinds of performance assessments. These range from high-stakes testing programs for graduate admissions to writing-to-learn and other classroom-based research projects in the United States to evaluation workshops and scoring sessions with teachers around the world. She has authored numerous research reports on writing assessment issues and is currently developing new models for classroom-based formative assessment of students' critical thinking and writing skills.

Roger Gilles is Professor of Writing at Grand Valley State University. He has collaborated with Dan Royer on a number of works related to placement, assessment, and program development. He teaches courses in business communication and writing in the disciplines.

Liz Hamp-Lyons received her PhD at the University of Edinburgh, Scotland, and has worked in writing assessment for both English as a first language and (primarily) English as a second/foreign language students since. Her edited collection, *Assessing Second Language Writing in Academic Contexts,* was the first book to bring together work on L2 writing assessment. She is currently Honorary Professor at the Centre for Research in English Language Learning and Assessment (CRELLA), University of Bedfordshire, and at the University of Hong Kong.

Richard H. Haswell is Hass Professor Emeritus at Texas A&M University-Corpus Christi. Retired in 2006 from a teaching career of 45 years, he remains active in scholarly ways. In 2010, with Janis Haswell he published *Authoring: An Essay for the English Profession on Potentiality and Singularity*. A sequel, on hospitality and English studies, is forthcoming. CompPile, an online bibliography of writing-studies scholarship, 1939-current, has reached over 100,000 records.

Anne Herrington is Distinguished Professor of English, the University of Massachusetts at Amherst, where she is also Site Director of the Western Massachusetts Writing Project. Her primary research areas include assessment, writing and learning in the disciplines, and qualitative research methodologies.

Margaret Hundleby is Science Writing Consultant in the Learning Commons at the University of Guelph, Ontario.

Asao B. Inoue is an Associate Professor and Co-Director of First Year Writing at California State University, Fresno, where he conducts writing assessment research with a focus on racial formations. He is also the Book Review Editor for *Composition Studies*. His work has appeared in *Assessing Writing*, *Journal of Writing Assessment*, and *WPA: Writing Program Administration*. Currently, he is finishing a monograph on the technology of writing assessment and race, and is co-editing a collection on writing assessment and race with Mya Poe.

Diane Kelly-Riley has been the director of the Writing Assessment Program at Washington State University since 1996. She also directs the WSU Writing Program, recipient of the 2008-09 CCCC Writing Program Certificate of Excellence. Her research areas include race and writing assessment, validity issues for college writing assessment, critical thinking, writing across the curriculum, and writing program administration. She is co-editor of the *Journal of Writing Assessment*.

Paul LeMahieu is Senior Managing Partner, Design, Development and Improvement Research at the Carnegie Foundation for the Advancement of Teaching. Previously, he was Director of Research and Evaluation at the National Writing Project (NWP) in Berkeley. He has also served as Superintendent of Education for the state of Hawaii. He has also held the top educational research position for the state of Delaware and the Pittsburgh Public Schools.

Jon A. Leydens is Associate Professor in the Division of Liberal Arts and International Studies at the Colorado School of Mines, where he has been since 1997. From 1997 to 2011, he served as Writing Program Administrator and as Chair of the WAC Program. His research is in rhetoric and communication within diverse engineering contexts. Currently he is researching the status of engineering communication as an emerging field and intersections between engineering and social justice.

Barry M. Maid is Professor of Technical Communication at Arizona State University. His current interests are in program assessment, information literacy, and social media.

Cindy Moore is Associate Professor of Writing and Department Chair, Loyola University, Maryland.

Charles Moran is Emeritus Professor of English at the University of Massachusetts at Amherst. With Anne Herrington and Kevin Hodgson, he has most recently co-edited *Teaching the New Writing: Technology, Change, and Assessment* and, with Anne Herrington, *Genre Across the Curriculum.* His research interests have included computers and writing, genre theory, and eighteenth-century English literature.

Lee Odell is Professor of Composition Theory and Research and Associate Dean of the School of Humanities and Social Science at Rensselaer Polytechnic Institute.

Barbara M. Olds is Acting Deputy Assistant Director and Senior Advisor to the Directorate for Education and Human Resources (EHR) of the U. S. National Science Foundation, where she focuses on issues related to international science and engineering education, program and project evaluation, and education and education research policy. She is Professor Emerita of Liberal Arts and International Studies at the Colorado School of Mines, where she helped to establish a WAC program.

Peggy O'Neill is Professor of Writing, directs the composition program, and teaches in the Writing Department at Loyola University Maryland. Her scholarship focuses on writing pedagogy, assessment, and program administration. Her scholarship appears in several journals as well as edited collections. She has co-authored two books, *A Guide to College Writing Assessment* (with Cindy Moore and Brian Huot) and *Reframing Writing Assessment to Improve Teaching and Learning* (with Linda Adler-Kassner), and has edited or co-edited four books.

Irvin Peckham is Professor of English at Louisiana State University. He is the author of *Going North, Thinking West: The Intersections of Social Class, Critical Thinking, and Politicized Writing Instruction*, and numerous articles on assessment and the relationship of writing to social class.

Hilary Persky is the Writing Assessment Coordinator at ETS for the National Assessment of Educational Progress.

Les Perelman is Director of Writing Across the Curriculum in the Program in Writing and Humanistic Studies at the Massachusetts Institute of Technology, where he has also served as an Associate Dean in the Office of the Dean of Undergraduate Education. He was Project Director and co-Principal Investigator for a grant to MIT from the National Science Foundation to develop a model Communication-Intensive Undergraduate Program in Science and Engineering. He also served as Principal Investigator for the development of the iCampus/MIT Online Assessment Tool (iMOAT).

Mya Poe is an Assistant Professor of English at Penn State University, where her research focuses on issues of race, internationalization, and professional identity in the development of writing abilities. Her co-authored book, *Learning to Communicate in Science and Engineering*, was published in 2010, and her work has appeared in journals such as *College Composition and Communication*. She is currently working on an edited collection and a single-authored book about race and writing assessment.

Dan Royer is Professor of Writing at Grand Valley State University. He has collaborated with Roger Gilles on a number of works related to placement, assessment, and program development. He teaches courses in professional writing, document production and design, and writing for the web.

Sherry Swain in chair of the National Writing Project State Networks.

Kathleen Blake Yancey, Kellogg W. Hunt Professor of English and Distinguished Research Professor, directs the Graduate Program in Rhetoric and Composition at Florida State University. A past leader of several scholarly organizations—NCTE, CCCC, and WPA—she has edited two journals—*Journal of Writing Assessment* and *College Composition and Communication*—and co-directs the Inter/National Coalition for Electronic Portfolio Research. Author, editor, or co-editor of 11 books and over 75 articles and chapters, she researches literacy, technologies, culture, and assessment.

Edward M. White taught his first college class as a teaching assistant at Harvard in 1958 and served as an instructor at Wellesley College. After retiring as Emeritus Professor of English from California State University, San Bernardino, in 1997, he joined the English faculty at the University of Arizona, where he is a visiting scholar in both the writing program and the graduate program in Rhetoric, Composition, and the Teaching of English. He has published over 100 articles and book chapters and has written or edited 13 books. He is at work on a new book on assessing writing programs.

INDEX

CPSIA information can be obtained at www.ICGtesting.com
Printed in the USA
LVOW06s1511301113

363333LV00001B/26/P

9 781612 890876